# Body and Flesh
## A Philosophical Reader

Edited by Donn Welton

Copyright © Blackwell Publishers Ltd, 1998

First published 1998

Reprinted 1998, 2001

Blackwell Publishers Inc.
350 Main Street
Malden, Massachusetts 02148
USA

Blackwell Publishers Ltd
108 Cowley Road
Oxford OX4 1JF
UK

*Library of Congress Cataloging-in-Publication Data*

Body and flesh: a philosophical reader / edited by Donn Welton.
    p.   cm.
  Includes index.
   ISBN 1–57718–125–5 (alk. paper). – ISBN 1–57718–126–3 (pbk.: alk. paper)
   1. Body, Human (Philosophy) I. Welton, Donn.
B105.B64B63    1998
128′. 6–dc21                                    97–16963
                                            CIP

*British Library Cataloguing in Publication Data*

A CIP catalogue record for this book is available from the British Library.

Typeset in 10 on 11½ pt Ehrhardt
by Pure Tech India Ltd, Pondicherry
Printed and bound in Great Britain by MPG Books Ltd, Bodmin, Cornwall

This book is printed on acid-free paper

# Contents

# Acknowledgments

I would especially like to thank Elisa Leibowitz for her assistance with the early stage of this project, Lanei Rodemegen for long hours spent proofing the text, and Nathalie Manners and Hilary Scannell for shepherding this collection through Blackwell Publishers.

# Introduction: Situating the Body

## Donn Welton

This collection of essays, which combines exceptional pieces that have been published already with new and original work that appears here for the first time, does more than present essays that cluster around philosophical questions concerning the body. It attempts to add some systematicity to the field by exploring various "constitutional matrices" essential to bodily life (part II) as one suggestive way of cutting through differences in theoretical approaches (part I), and then by enriching this preliminary and partial characterization of the body through various studies of yet other matrices that focus on the body as it is deployed and configured in a variety of experiential, social, and technological contexts (part III). It hopes to track a certain line of continuity, if not unity, through an otherwise bewildering field of study. At the same time, these analyses are suggestive and not exhaustive of each of the three parts of our study. While this anthology does hope to add order, it has no illusions of being complete.

If we begin by stepping back from the special concerns of the philosophy of mind and look at the issue of the body from a very general interdisciplinary perspective, we can say that this collection begins to chart a course beyond two warring theories of human existence by looking at and then challenging an underlying characterization of the body that they share.

For several decades psychology and, more broadly, philosophical anthropology have been caught between two antagonistic and irreconcilable approaches to our understanding of persons, between biology and sociology. At least this is what the textbooks tell us. In fact, the opposition is really between any theory of the structure and development of human experience and interaction that looks exclusively to bio-physical reality as its sole source, and those that reduce it to structures and "mechanisms" of formation that belong to a social or symbolic order and are largely independent of the physical world. The contrast, then, is not between these disciplines as sciences but between these disciplines taken as foundations, between biologism and sociologism.

In the first case, the truth about human beings is restricted to an experimental scientific approach that views the physical, chemical, and biological features of the organism as basic, and all larger psychological as well as all sociological phenomena as derived from them. What is "really real" is the underlying level of bio-physical nature. Behind this theory is the belief that any rigorous understanding of human phenomena would necessarily employ material explanations that refer to underlying physio–biological causal mechanisms (as we find in biology, neurophysiology, physical anthropology, and the older materialistic psychology).

In the second approach, used especially by those social scientists who attempt to model explanations in their discipline after the natural sciences, basic reality is not restricted to physical phenomena but is placed, as it were, one step above this, and is understood as a natural complex (consisting of sets of behaviors or pieces of rule-governed action) that can be submitted to functional causal explanations that correlate observable independent and dependent variables (as in behaviorism, empirical anthropology, and many forms of current experimental, cognitive psychology and empirical sociology). Everything from acts of charity to acts of aggression, from sexual preferences to patterns of parenting, from learning language to writing poetry is explained by reference to mathematizable correlations between observable variables.

There is an important variation on the second sociological approach in which human phenomena are taken as qualitatively different from mathematizable data and then explained by recourse to the social context in which they are constructed. In this variation it is generally recognized that what sets one phenomenon in contrast to another is the configuration of its significance (or meaning, *Bedeutsamkeit*). Correspondingly, various types of symbolic or communicative interaction and of internalization are used to explain both the uniqueness of human social reality and then the production of everything from human actions to preferences to underlying dispositional tendencies. The body, in turn, becomes "a social structure composed of many souls." If the first relies upon controlled observation, the second looks to rigorous interpretation as its primary research tool.

All these approaches focus is on the psychological life or the "soul" of persons and its ties to the body. But the way the body is placed *in relation to* psycho-social life is radically different. Biologism thinks of the bio-physical composition and causal chains of the body as sufficient to explain everything that we might attribute to conscious life. Sociologism takes the body as consisting of bio-physical materials that either are then shaped into units of behavior that correlate to variables (first variation), or are organized by acts of interpretation that employ socially stable, semantic oppositions that reflect the socio-political codes of a given society, which are then internalized by its members through processes of symbolic interaction (second variation). Not only thinking, not only perception, but even the configuration of the body itself is a product of interpretation, of an "apprehension" that takes the body according to the conceptual schemes mediated by language. What is surprising, however, is that both approaches, different as they are, characterize the body *itself* as *Körper*, as "physical body" or, better, as an item having the status of a thing: the first understands it as a physical organism whose causal interactions are sufficient to explain the mental; the second treats it as an ensemble of materials (content) given significance and thereby organization (form) by the community. In neither case have we moved beyond our understanding of the body as an "object." Behind the differences between biologism and sociologism is a shared *objectivism*.

The approaches to the body taken in this collection, different as they are, all directly challenge the underlying assumption of objectivism. They do so either by directly employing or, even when they reject it, harking back to the phenomenological distinction between *Körper* and *Leib*, between "physical body" and "lived-body," between an "objective" characterization of the body, such as we find in natural scientific inquiry (anatomy, physiology, neurology, biology, and chemistry), and an experiential characterization that describes certain structures of our body in terms appropriate to the way we *are* and *have* a body, which is to say, to the way it is involved with human environments. This is not the body as "object" but as "subject," which is really to say that we have a form of constitution that cannot be contained by the dyad of subject and object. Perhaps we could say that it is situated *beneath* that difference as it serves as the silent background to focused intentional acts, different forms of action, and even our most intimate kinds of interaction. While concrete studies of how *Körper* and *Leib* are related are few and far between, Maurice Merleau-Ponty being the great exception, it is relatively easy to see the connection in principle: the first gets at complex neurophysiological processes that serve as the causal basis for the second, certain global or structural features that characterize the way the body is "lived" and the way it is engaged with things of significance and its surroundings. The first is a micro, the second a macro description of the same natural complex. For example, studies have shown that there are three basic spatial contrasts that organize experienced space (at least in simplified or reduced environments): over and under, left and right, and near and far. These coordinates, shaping our spatial fields, are themselves rooted in certain features of the body as lived – such as our erect posture, the sense of gravity, standing upright, and schemes of motility. These features, for their part, are caused by extremely complex bio-physical processes. We get at them by submitting the body to bio-physical analysis (in a very broad sense). To put it in conceptual terms, such underlying bio-physical processes are the necessary condition for having the body as lived. At the same time, these macro-features form a higher order complex of their own, capable of interacting with other features not derived from the neurophysiology of the body but also belonging to that higher system. In our example the features of the body as lived, such as erect posture, are themselves constitutive of the coordinates of bodily involvement, such as over and under. Unlike the first, the latter are not caused by the body (under a physical description), nor are they features of that body. While physical causal explanations provide necessary conditions they do not supply sufficient conditions for the coordinates, which are themselves aspects of a relational structure that undergirds the structure of intentionality.

This difference between physical and lived body actually accounts for the division historically between the pre-understanding of the body operative in most analytic philosophy, which took a bio-physical characterization as canonical and then attempted to place or displace the mind's relation to it, and the approach taken by continental theorists, who argued that the organization of the body involves at least these two levels, that the lived-body and its features can be rigorously described, and that this is what gives us our most fruitful insights into the relationship between body and mind. But within continental thought in this century, not surprisingly, the concept of the lived-body, introduced by Edmund Husserl and then rigorously analyzed by Merleau-Ponty and others, underwent a significant development. This development has been tracked in a second collection, *Continental Theories of the Body* (also published by Blackwell), which, properly speaking, might serve as an historical preface to this book. Several of the essays in the present collection work with the contrast between physical and lived body but then extend it in significant ways. Others challenge it and attempt to use post-phenomenological methods to place and then develop a different theory of the configuration of the body. While there are clear differences between them, what is being contested is precisely how we understand the *constitution* of the lived-body, if I can be allowed to capture this in a slogan; we are thus clearly beyond the alternative of biologism or sociologism in any standard sense.

Viewed theoretically, there are several pressing issues that situate the problem of the body for us today, giving it a distinct configuration and setting it in contrast to the way the body was treated in earlier studies:

- the place of biologically based patterns of action in an account of the body;
- the issue of whether sensibility (*Sinnlichkeit*) and then the materiality of the body is itself constituted;
- the question of whether bodily structures have an organization that allows us to treat them as "inscriptions";
- the issue of how to place different types of bodily experience in relation to each other;
- the differences in male and female bodily comportment;
- the question of gender identity.

We will find these issues woven throughout many of the essays in this collection. The conjunction of these issues have pressed thinkers into new theoretical approaches. We open this collection by turning to them.

# I

Hermeneutics was basically a discipline concerned with the production of literary texts. When it raised the question of the body, or any "nonliterary" object, for that matter, it did so only by speaking about the various signifiers, strings, and narratives used to represent the body. In short, it dealt with the body as symbolized, as sign with multiple meanings, some literal, more metaphorical. In some of its more aggressive moments it would argue that all we can know of the body is mediated by such symbols and thus we can never get beyond our representations of it. But when settled and at peace with other disciplines, it recognized that its accounts of the production of literary texts were largely accounts of how various genres or disciplines represented their domains, and did not directly provide an analysis of the constitution of those regions (outside of literary objects) to which the texts referred.

The crucial transformation effected by Jacques Derrida and deconstruction was to extend the notion of production into that of constitution at the same time that it radically changed the concept of a text. Meaning, for example, is no longer understood as an ideal, mental entity, given expression by signs, that is itself the content of a speaker's intentions to refer to an object in a determinate way. Rather, meaning is literally no-thing, mental or physical, and is found only in the differential relationship between signs in semantic fields. With this, deconstruction cut loose the two standard anchors of a speech-act theory of intentionality, be it Husserl's or Searle's. It argued, first, not only that *referents* exist only under a description, a point that we clearly find in Frege and Husserl, but also that the referent just is a certain crossing of differences and contrasts found in a semantic field. The referent becomes the intersection of a family of such determinations, which is to say that its being is understood relationally only as its difference. Secondly, the dyads used to demarcate the *subject* (inner vs. outer, subject vs. object, ego vs. mental event, and, in particular, mind vs. body) are not understood as terms that pick out positive entities or regions that exist outside systems of signification and that, as transcendental, are construed as constituting or controlling signification. In fact, we can say what the mind or the body is only if we see it as a node whose being is determined by the configuration of the ties it has to yet other nodes in a web of signifiers. As such it is a "trace." It is what it is not.

This analysis, occupying what Husserl would have called a transcendental domain, would have been little more than a theory about how philosophy and then literature are to be understood were it not for the work of Michel Foucault. Foucault was able to bridge this new metatheoretical conception with the way in which certain applied scientific fields of inquiry are historically constructed. He did so by introducing the notion of epistemic practices, which themselves have a certain history, and by understanding the relationship between those practices and the deployment of systems of power. As a consequence the transformations constitutive of the subject are understood as socially generated practices that, in the deployment of social and political powers across the body, inscribe their relations into the very structure of its being and thereby constitute its presence or, more accurately, the shift in the way it is present from one epoch to the next.

This is the context in which we should understand the essays by Judith Butler, Susan Bordo, and Susan Hekman. Whatever their differences might be, Butler's and Bordo's theories clearly go beyond older sociological theories, as they accept neither that picture of social reality nor those theories' account of the mechanisms of symbolic interaction and internalization. At the same time, both authors argue for a form of social constructionism.

This section opens, however, not with their essays but with a piece by Rom Harré, one of the best accounts available of the distinction between sex, which is a biological category, and gender, which has different structures. He amasses strong arguments for the difference between them and for the thesis that gender is not biologically determined but socially constructed. Some might be convinced that the distinction is so well defined that it can withstand the challenges that follow.

This contrast between sex and gender is directly attacked by Butler, who argues that the difference is not tenable because we can never discover a body, even in its materiality, that is prior to cultural inscription, signification and form. She understands it as a signifier or nexus of signification whose meaning is not only discovered but constituted by its relation to yet other signifiers in a system of epistemic production. Bordo initially believed that Butler underplayed some of the seminal insights of Foucault in her theory and did not anchor the theory in praxis. She then offered a suggestive account of the production of materiality. Hekman's comparison suggests, however, that the difference between them may be more in emphasis than substance. At the same time Hekman raises issues of her own. A second book by Butler anticipated some of them and so I reproduce the introduction to it as a way of indicating the line she would take in response. Bordo has written a reply to Hekman's essay and in so doing given us interesting insights into the question of materiality, as well as further reflections on her overall approach to the question of the body.

Both Bordo and Butler, in the final analysis, argue for forms of social constructionism. It is only when we turn to what Carol Bigwood calls "renaturalization theory" that we find an alternative to their approaches. Bigwood's essay is a programmatic call for a return to the approach of Merleau-Ponty, while Maxine Sheets-Johnstone, whose essay is found in the second part, attempts to destabilize the terms of Butler's and Bordo's accounts by calling for an "evolutionary genealogy" of the body.

The question of which theoretical approach is correct may not be decidable at the level of a reflection upon a theory as theory. Rather than attempting this, this collection takes an alternative approach in two steps. Part II looks to studies of specific clusters of bodily constitution, while part III extends this study as it traces the deployment of the body in specific social and cultural contexts. It would be an interesting exercise to return to part I after reading them and then ask if we are not in a better position to see how they should be assessed.

## II

There are various types of bodily constitution, as we will see, but they are not related to each other hierarchically. In place of the classical phenomenological trope of "levels" or "layers" or "strata" of constitution, images that are constantly employed in Husserl's account and most later phenomenological studies, I would suggest that each type forms a *matrix* in which a certain type of constitution originates, and that the relation of one to yet others is itself a function of how the body is involved in situations. The difficulty, in short, with Husserl's image of strata is that a matrix "higher" or "founded" on one style of interactions or set of interests can be understood as "founding" or "lower" from the perspective of another style or set. The concept of matrices, by contrast, suggests that bodily constitution involves the confluence of various schemes of constitution, that the body can be characterized as a *nexus* of various matrices. This is the notion, I would suggest, that is required by the studies we find in this volume. Part III continues the study of matrices by attending to specific actions, states, and disciplines of the body.

What keeps continental theories of the body within the same family is that they all are concerned with the question of the *constitution* of the body. An analysis of constitution is quite different from a natural scientific account of the *composition* of the body, of its physio-biological structures and processes. To put it in its broadest terms, terms that do not restrict the notion of the lived-body to the body as experienced, constitutional accounts of the body attend to the internal connection between meaning or significance and the way the body is involved in situations. The various terms used to characterize the body here (such as body image, body schemata, spatiality, affective body, habitudes, and sensibilities) understand its structure and deployment as internally linked to the significance of the situation in which we find ourselves, and to the sense of any number of things which we take to hand. The body, even as it is reflexively shaped by its own involvements, is understood as a primary source of this significance.

Drew Leder's essay clarifies the phenomenological distinction between the physical and the lived-body by setting its analysis in contrast to the whole mechanistic model of the body we inherited from René Descartes. Being a medical doctor, he is especially interested in the implications of the concept of the lived-body for medical practice. This distinction is then extended in a study of deafferented subjects by Shaun Gallagher and Jonathan Cole as they employ a contrast between body image and body scheme to characterize the way in which a person who has lost normal feeling of his body gains mastery over it. An account of spatiality naturally belongs here, but I am publishing a translation of Elmar Holenstein's essay "The zero-point of orientation" in the collection *Continental Theories of the Body*, as it also discusses Husserl at length. This deals with the question of the constitution of lived space and attempts to describe its structure as rooted not in the body alone, as Husserl thought, but in the relationship between the body and the environment. The interested reader might turn to that piece before continuing with the next essay.

Each of the essays thus far treats the body synchronically. Sheets-Johnstone argues for the importance of a diachronic evolutionary analysis, which looks at the way in which certain corporeal archetypes are woven into specific forms of "intercorporeal life." While each of the essays in this volume is but an invitation to read the work of their authors, this is especially true of her piece. My paper attempts to place the notion of the body in relation to Nancy Chodorow's account of the development of affects, arguing that a proper understanding of the role of the body might enable us to distinguish between eros and affection. At the same time, this requires us to deepen the concept of the lived-body through the notion of the *flesh*. Edward Casey's essay, which is a bridge to those in the next part, incorporates action into his account of the body and uses certain insights of Bourdieu as a way of understanding bodily habits and gestures. As is typical of his work, it is rich in description and insight.

## III

The final part of this collection concentrates on a number of areas where we find deep interconnections between the specificity of Western culture and the body. But it opens with an essay that attempts to describe a configuration of the body that has deeply influenced the way it is understood in Western culture but which is not specifically indebted to Greek philosophical thought for its formulation. My essay on the body as found in the Hebrew and then early Christian Scriptures allows us to glimpse a concept of the body that is significantly different from what we find in Plato and Aristotle, and that directly bears on our efforts to understand the body in a postmodern context. From this we turn to two of Iris Young's ground-breaking essays, on the difference between the way boys and girls throw a ball, and then on the experience of the body in pregnancy. They are followed by an insightful new afterword in which she reflects upon the value and the limits of these pieces. The disease of anorexia, which until recently was special to women, has been studied by Bordo in other essays; the one reproduced here concentrates on the way our culture can be reflected in the demands for slenderness placed on women today. By contrast, we look to Klaus Theweleit to describe the disciplining of male bodies in German army life. The way in which we treat our bodies as objects to be sculpted is studied in Kathryn Pauly Morgan's penetrating account of cosmetic surgery. She shows that the "plastic" body described by Bordo is one that we shape not just by regimens of discipline but also by the violence of the knife. A final essay by Don Ihde, one of the founding fathers of the new discipline of philosophy of technology, treats the body in the context of our most recent electronic construction. He studies the experience of bodies in virtual reality, concentrating on the transforming or "morphing" of the body that comes by extending our sensibilities in computer generated reality.

This collection, in attempting to deal with these diverse issues, breaks new ground in several areas:

- It reframes a concept of the body that places it outside the parameters established by Cartesian philosophy and modern science.
- It gives an account of the lived-body that connects it without reducing it to the biological body.
- It is a study of how the body brings elements of its own to the configuration of psychological life.
- It extends the initial concept of the lived-body, organized by the issue of its role in cognition, into the areas of affection and desire, into the concept of the flesh.
- It analyzes the roots of eros and its differences from affection.
- It studies the exchange between social structures, bodily constitution, and bodily "styles" of action.

- It looks at the reconfiguration of the body through its instrumentalization in the hands of various technologies.

It is my hope that each of the essays collected here will contribute to our understanding of the altogether enigmatic nature of human embodiment. For it, the most obvious of things, is one of the most perplexing.

# PART I
## Contested Constructions

# 1
# Sex and Gender

## Man and Woman*
### Rom Harré

### Are "man" and "woman" natural kinds?

Is the distinction "man"/"woman" anything like the chemical distinction "acid"/
"alkali?" Acids and alkalis are distinguishable not only by reference to their observable behavior, but also in chemical theory. They differ in atomic architecture or
real essence – the outermost shell of electrons having only one member in acids and
seven in alkalis. Is there a real essence to manhood and womanhood that grounds the
use of genital or primary sexual characteristics as signifiers for dividing people into
fundamental kinds for general purposes? The discovery of the genetic mechanism by
which the sexual characteristics of human beings are determined might lead one to
suppose that in the distinction between XX and XY chromosomes there is a perfect
analog of the distinction between the one outer electron and seven outer electrons
that grounds the acid/alkali distinction in a well-defined real essence.

A way of telling how far a distinction is natural, and the criteria for it organized
around something like the difference between nominal and real essence, is to see
what considerations are advanced to resolve anomalous cases, beings which, on the
face of it, fit neatly into neither category. Does sex-reassignment surgery bring about
a change in body-kind? Ronald Richards became Renée Richards and James Morris
is now Jan Morris. Were these cases of change of body-kind? The two are instructively different. Richards used "her" body (with its pre-given musculature, acquired
when "she" was a man) for competitive tennis. Women players protested against
"her" appearance in tournaments in the women's division. According to the pro-
testers, Richards had a man's body, despite the surgical mimicry of female genitals.
Male muscles confer an advantage in tennis. This was a categorization by something
like nominal essence. I have been unable to find any evidence that women journalists
or travel writers protested against Jan Morris working in their professions. A male
brain, if there is such a thing, does not confer any advantage in intellectual pursuits.
In both cases the social location of anomalous individuals is determined by nominal
essence alone.

However, there are human beings who are genitally female, but with the musculature of human males. Are they to count as women? If the Richards case is to serve
as a precedent, the matter is disputable. Should the brawny Russian contestants in
the women's field events be barred from the Olympic Games? The solution that has

* Rom Harré, ["Man and woman,"] *Physical Being: A Theory for a Corporeal Psychology* (Oxford:
Blackwell, 1991), pp. 42–60.

been universally adopted in athletics is philosophically instructive. Contestants are classified into genders by real essence of sex. Chromosomes are what count, no matter what are the secondary sexual characteristics. Chromosomal endowment works for athletes much as atomic architecture works for acids and alkalis.

But there are further complications. People presenting themselves for sex-reas-signment surgery often claim to have really been a man or a woman all along, despite being embodied as a member of the opposite sex. In some sex-reassignment clinics an attempt of sorts has been made to fill out this idea biologically (Garfinkel, 1967). Between chromosomal endowment and somatic constitution lies a world of endo-crine chemistry, the hormones. These are characteristically distributed according to sex. Are they responsible for gender? Do they make males into men and females into women? In the case reported by Garfinkel Agnes's claim to be really a girl was supported by proof (faked in his/her case) of a hormone profile typical of a human female. Since these chemical messengers are largely responsible for secondary sexual characteristics, such as mammary development, distribution of body hair and so on, their implication in the nominal essences of the sexes is obvious. If female hormones in a male body can make room for doubt as to which gender a person really is, then biological determinism has overtaken social construction as the dominant process in the differentiation of people by gender. To restore the hegemony of the construc-tionist thesis much more analysis is required. First, however, I need to develop the power of the nominal/real essence distinction to include tertiary sex differences.

Male and female bodies differ in two ways. Sexual dimorphism of the genital organs is sharply defined. In popular conceptions of maleness and femaleness the secondary sexual characteristics, such as skeletal form, distribution of body fat, and so on are equally "dimporhic." Since the genitals are usually hidden, secondary characteristics take on an emblematic or symbolic role by which a person's sex is displayed. The emblematic role for category assignment played by overall body shape, for instance, is possible only if central cases of a very variable characteristic are taken as typical. A certain size and shape of bosom and of the orientation of the limbs defines the womanly figure. Since "rightness" of bodily being is defined with respect to central cases, they are subject to deliberate manipulation and control by those on the "wrong" side of the inevitable variations. Both breast-reduction and breast-enhancement surgery are on offer for women, while men can have the loose skin of an aging belly nicely tucked up. I shall return to a closer study of the process by which such norms are created in the next section.

In true human fashion Ossa is piled on Pelion, and in all societies of which we have any knowledge tertiary sexual markers have been added to those distinguishing characteristics that, with a little help, nature has provided. Men and women adopt different hair styles and dress in different garments. The differences may be extreme, as in the Victorian distinctions between the wearers of trousers and the wearers of skirts. Or it may be subtle, as in the differences in cut and colour of the ubiquitous *shalwa* and *kemis* of Islamic tradition. Many people have succeeded in living as a member of the "opposite" sex merely by cross dressing. Since the real sex of a human being is defined on the basis of hidden differences in body form and equipment, an illusion of sexual category is easily created by the use of emblematic clothing and the appropriate hair style.

Conceptual clarity in these matters can be assisted by thinking in terms of a double application of the overt-nominal/covert-real essence distinction. Chromoso-mal difference serves as the real essence of the distinction in sex, the overt manifestation of which in complementary, and in principle visible, genitals is thus nominal. But since the genitals are usually hidden, their differences serve as the real essence of the public manifestation of sex differences, whether in tidied-up secondary characteristics or in manufactured tertiary. The possession of male organs is so uniformly correlated with the wearing of coat and trousers, short haircuts, an interest in guns and the ability to mend fuses, but a hopeless incapacity for changing babies' nappies, that these tertiary characteristics denote one's sexual category for all practical purposes. The irony is intentional. An equally diverse catalog could be provided for the female of the species. Why are the socially contrived tertiary characteristics apparently so well correlated with biologically determined primary ones? Is it because, in subtle ways, the tertiary are also biologically determined?

But there are further complications in linking body-kind as nominal essence to a biological real essence through primary – that is, genital – differences between embodied persons. There are the recently discovered envelope-and-core anomalies, as I shall call them, which must be accommodated in any scheme. It turns out that the primary sex-distinguishing attributes are controlled by two sets of genes, whose activity is normally nicely synchronized. It can happen that while the "core" of a human body is one sex, the "envelope" has not developed the sex characteristics to match it. The commonest pattern is a male core within a female envelope. Some cases have been reported in which only the accident of exploratory surgery has revealed a male interior anatomy mismatched to female external genitalia. Most surprising of all is a genetic anomaly discovered in a small Caribbean island. All the members of a certain lineage are born as girls, insofar as external signs of sex are concerned. Half of these children develop external male organs at puberty, turning into functionally perfect males, as they would have done at a very early stage in the course of a normal maturation. All the children are brought up as girls, since the parents have no way of telling which ones will undergo metamorphosis at the critical age. This lineage offers us a living laboratory for testing certain feminist theories about the cultural sources of feminine stereotypes in style of living. As far as I know, no detailed social-psychological studies of these people have been undertaken to explore such matters. However, from the point of view of the analysis, introducing concepts of potentiality into the kinds story has some disturbing consequences. "Body-kind" begins to look rather less well defined than the usual ways of commonsense thinking would have it.

To sum up: the model of nominal (overt) and real (covert) essence taken from the philosophy of chemical kinds can be applied to sex differences, provided that we are ready to deal *ad hoc* with the complexity of the double application of the overt/covert (displayed/hidden) distinction. "Male" and "female" do seem to be body-kinds. But does the same hold true for "masculine" and "feminine."

## Mappings: the case for interpreting gender as a social construction

To take the discussion far enough to try to answer the question with which I ended the last section, a new distinction is needed. Let us use the words "male" and "female" for strict biologically defined difference in sex, and the words "masculine" and "feminine" for the psychological and social distinction of gender. The question above can now be rephrased. Is gender determined by sex? It has been argued that not only are the differences in gender socially defined, but they are also socially determined. Gender is a social construction. People embodied as females are expected to be sweet and neat, kind and good at nursing – that is, to be feminine, while those embodied as males are expected to be rough and tough and good at fighting – that is, to be masculine. I shall call the realization of such a set of expectations a "mapping" between sex and gender. The matter is complicated because of the role that secondary and tertiary sexual characteristics play in the gender distinction. Husky, bearded hulks are "obviously" rough and tough, while dainty, peach-complexioned beauties are "obviously" sweet and neat. We shall encounter more than one mapping. The tidy fit of masculine-and feminine-people categories to male and female body-kinds is the traditional mapping. Most people at most epochs and in most cultures have taken something like the traditional mapping to be natural, and even divinely ordered.

At birth human infants are only rarely of ambiguous sex. Only about one in 54,000 children is of indeterminate sex. Male and female are therefore clearly bipolar categories. A person is either one or the other, and almost no one is in between. In the traditional mapping the social and cultural norms of gender take on a matching bipolar and exclusive dichotomy.

The first point to notice is that between gender, which is largely tertiary, and sex, which is primary, lies the important range of secondary sexual characteristics. Most secondary characteristics such as body form (womanly hour glass or manly inverted triangle), distribution of body hair, height, distribution of body fat and so on are not bipolar. They are bimodal. That is, while the majority of female human beings are less hirsute than the majority of males, there are some females who are hairier than some men and some males are more glabrous than some females. Graphically these distributions appear as in figure 1. In a bipolar distribution assignment to sex/ gender on any secondary variable is sharp and dichotomous (see figure 2). Unmodified by cultural norms, it is true to say that all secondary characteristics are

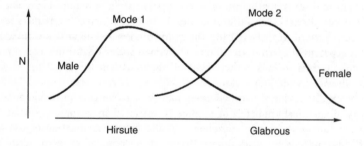

Figure 1

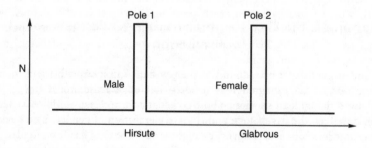

Figure 2

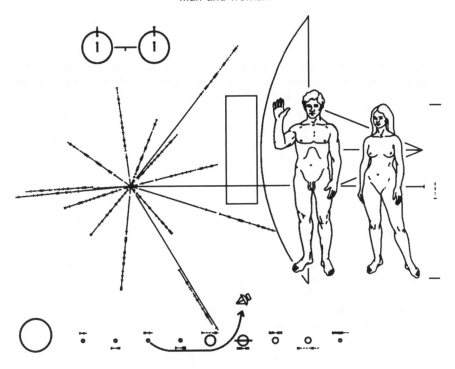

*Figure 3*   Cosmic messenger body images (Reproduced by kind permission of NASA)

bimodal. Since secondary sexual characteristics are serving as emblematic nominal essences (Perper, 1985) for the primary, it is easy to see how a mapping of secondary on the primary is necessary. Ambiguities in secondary characteristics should be remedied to conform to the strict bipolarity of primary sex. The bodies of men and women should be polarized in all their characteristics. They should appear as such even in messages to extra-galactic civilizations (figure 3). A socially enforced technology of stays, padded brassières, hair pieces, padded shoulders, built-up heels, lady shavers, depilatories and so on is made available to remedy the biologically given bimodality of secondary sexual characteristics. Tertiary characteristics, prime candidates for an iconography of bipolar primary sexuality, such as styles of clothing, can be made bipolar from their moment of introduction, since they are artifacts.

But what of character, personality, intellectual and practical capacity and talent? Should they too be polarized to fit neatly onto the polarity of sexually defined body-kinds? The mappings between primary and secondary have in fact been repeated in almost all aspects of life. People are assigned to polarized ways of being, to the masculine or the feminine gender. Embodiment is socially fateful.

Men and women have been found to judge other people's actions and to assess their own conduct according to very different styles of reasoning. Carol Gilligan (1982) showed that at least some men tend to adopt a form of self-definition that lays "out across the coordinates of time and space a hierarchical order in which to define [their] place, describing [themselves] as distinct by locating [their] particular position in the world" (p. 35). But a woman "counterposes an ideal of care, against which she measures the worth of her activity" (ibid.). Feminine actions are made determinate within a framework of obligations and duties that serve to nourish and sustain a network of concrete social relationships, which often tend to take precedence over abstract moral principles.

The obviously pejorative implications of terms for those who have made various cross-mappings illustrate the social force with which conformity to traditional patterns of behaviour is exacted. If a person embodied as a female adopts some of the characterological attributes as tertiary markers of manood, she is a "tomboy," "mannish" or "butch." If anyone embodied as a male takes on any of the characteristics of femininity, he is "effeminate" or a "pansy." However contingent the traditional mapping may appear in thought and in the political prospectus of feminism, it tends to be sharply defined and firmly maintained in everyday life.

Challenges to the seeming inevitability and apparent "naturalness" of the traditional mappings have come from two quarters. Feminists have argued that when women are released from social bondage, whether they have abandoned the traditional feminine virtues or no, they can do anything that had previously been reserved for men on grounds of their masculinity. Therefore distinctively feminine behavior, capacities and achievements are nothing but the results of a socially driven imposition of conventions on an essentially common humanity.

The assumption that the traditional mapping from polarized bodies to polarized social and intellectual characteristics is natural has also been queried by developmental psychologists (Lloyd and Duveen, 1990). They have suggested that infants are taught to be boys and girls, to be masculine and feminine, albeit in subtle and little-attended to ways. Not surprisingly, feminists have found this suggestion congenial, since it seems that what man has made woman can unmake.

Arguments about the causality of the mappings have mainly assumed that biological and cultural explanations are mutually exclusive. However, there are other possibilities. Convincing evidence has been found (e.g. Trebarthen, 1979) of pre-programmed infant behavior that seems to trigger off certain mothering routines, perhaps pre-programmed in women. It has also been suggested that a baby's body shape, particularly that of the head, can also have such an effect. These mothering routines elicit, in their turn, reactions from the infant. It may be that in some such interaction of fixed action patterns the basic differentia that we see as differences in gender are brought about; the traditional mappings would be both "natural" and also socially constructed in that an essential interaction pattern is required to complete the cycle.

One could also argue that even if gender differences owe nothing to genetic programming, the bipolarities of masculine and feminine ways of being are conducive to the survival of the tribe and the general biological welfare of human beings. Those cultures that imposed the "traditional" mappings on their members would develop ways of life through which more infants grew to maturity. Such tribes and their cultures would survive. Those with social practices more vulnerable to biological hazard would disappear and take their cultures with them. A similar line of argument has been proposed by Reynolds and Tanner (1983), linking religious practices to long-term biological advantage. If there is anything in this argument, it would call for a different style of feminism.

Ajudicating between these positions is impossible in the present state of our knowledge. Objective discussion of the nature of the "traditional" mappings has been made more difficult by the politicization of body-kinds in some contemporary feminist writing. It is worth remarking that feminist reform of social restrictions on the activities of women could be based on the bimodality of actual distributions of powers and skills between the sexes: the distribution of all those characteristics that I have comprehended under gender overlap.

One way of establishing the mere contingency of a correlation is to build up a repertoire of thought experiments in which other correlations among the relevant variables are shown to be possible. Suggestions for mappings other than the traditional one-to-one correlation between sex and gender have come from several feminist authors.

1   The androgynous mapping aims for one universal human social-behavioral type, on to which both male and female embodiments are to be mapped. The masculine/feminine distinction would necessarily disappear in the new social order.

2   The radical-feminist mapping is formally identical with the traditional way of socially stereotyping embodiment, but calls for a reversal of the social evaluation of the masculine and feminine as person kinds. It is argued that the feminine stereotype ought to be celebrated as morally superior and psychologically "healthier" than the masculine.

3   Post-feminists, like radical feminists, do not argue for the abolition of the masculine/feminine distinction, but for a dismantling of the social processes by which that distinction is rigidly mapped onto the biological dichotomy of persons embodied as males and females. Thus, it is argued, any human being can, and should, be enabled to adopt a masculine or feminine mode of life regardless of natural genital endowment. This is the position of authors like Davies (1990).

4   Finally, a fourth position has emerged, most notably as advocated by J. Kristeva (1981), if I have understood her somewhat delphic pronouncements aright. The radical and post-feminist positions remain in her scheme as necessary stages in personal/social development, to be transcended at a third stage when there comes to be a social order in which there are no dichotomous distinctions isomorphic with biological gender.

Could these alternative mappings serve as the foundations for possible ways of life? We must bear in mind that the Western tribe is no longer in danger of biological extinction – rather the contrary. No woman need devote more than a small part of her total life-span to reproducing the human race, biologically and culturally. She can be confident that nearly all her offspring will survive to maturity.

Objections to androgyny have been assembled by Morawski (1982) in the context of a general critique of what one might call "classical" feminist sex-role psychology. Citing a variety of sources (it must be admitted of variable quality), she points out that at least five major assumptions of the tradition should be questioned. These challenges are almost a roll-call of the high points of the third-level feminist standpoint. Thus the traditional treatment assumed that in the world they were investigating there actually was (1) evaluative opposition of sex roles; (2) evaluative preferences for the masculine; (3) covert prescription of sex-roles as developmental ends; (4) no role flexibility nor role change; (5) context independence. These challenges lead to a theory of a kind of base-level androgyny against which historically situated and context-sensitive sex-role acquisition and display could be studied. But as Morawski points out, "androgyny" has itself taken on a pro-evaluation for some of these investigators and the fact of its historical location is ignored. Furthermore, the concept of androgyny has been used in a context-insensitive way. This critique can be taken further. Post-feminists of a certain variety (Paglia, 1990) would now argue that in fact the reproduction of a society of well-adjusted people requires the nuclear, or better the extended, family, with complementary styles of parenting, caring, etc. Hence the historical survival of these styles as gender roles, and of course the desirability of somehow preserving them, even if the rigid mappings of the traditional system are relaxed.

A philosophical basis for radical feminism could be devised by taking account of what one might call "obligations to humanity." In giving absolute priority to the feminine ways of life, not only do women take on the obligation to maintain the human species, but they could also claim to act as repositories of a morally superior form of life. Thus women are endowed not only with obligations, but with the right to claim a certain moral hegemony. In this way radical feminism differs sharply from androgyny. In taking up the masculine way of life, which is what political androgyny amounts to in practice, women also take on the masculine moral order. It has also been suggested that the feminist ways of being are spreading in Western societies through a subtle and non-political development. There has been a remarkable rise in the number of small-scale service industries, managed predominantly by women. Success in such businesses demands just those qualities of character and styles of action that are immanent in Gilligan fashion in the "woman's voice." In the end the shift from the production of goods to the provision of services may change the social order quite radically. But it will be in the direction of the "traditional" mapping. What will change will be the tendency to give political and moral priority to the "man's voice."

In considering the viability of the world conjured up in the Davies–Kristeva thought experiment, we are driven back to technical questions of socio-biology. Accepting that the complementary forms of life, traditionally polarized between the male and female sexes, are both desirable and of equal value, the viability of their proposal turns on the explanation of the evident bimodal distribution of Gilligan's "voices." This distribution has been confirmed in a very interesting way by a study of men's and women's conversational patterns (Tannen, 1990). A movement to revive "traditional values" in a modified form seems to be gaining ground among middle-class women. For instance, there seems to be growing support for events like Christine Vollmer's 16th International Congress for the Family (1990) (cf. the report in *The Times* [London], 4 July 1990, p. 20).

Discussion of this matter has been clouded by feminist political rhetoric and outbursts of moral indignation. The only works, among the many I have skimmed, that address the issue reasonably dispassionately are Tiger and Shepher's (1975) *Women in the Kibbutz* and Mary Midgeley's (1978) *Beast and Man*. Tiger and Shepher's results were at best equivocal. While there can be no doubt that many Israeli women have returned to traditional gender roles from the egalitarian beginnings of the kibbutz movement, there are other possible explanations than the "gentle pressure of the genes." For instance, throughout the period they describe, large numbers of immigrants have arrived bringing with them traditional social assumptions and gendered ways of life. Moral right or wrong and social or biological origin are two independent disjunctions.

## The mechanisms of assignment of biologically categorized human beings to socially defined kinds of people

Having arrived at a fairly well-specified conceptual system for discussing body-kind judgments based ultimately on sex, as the doubly hidden real essence of body-kind, the question of the mechanisms of the formation of gender identity out of sex can be raised. How do the mappings of social–cultural identities (man/woman) onto biological sex (male/female) come about? Feminists sometimes talk of a "cultural process" and sometimes, particularly in French writing, they call upon Freudian psychodynamic accounts. Freud's theory of the formation of sexual identity can be summarized in short compass. It depends on the assumption that there are quite specific attitudes that very young children are supposed to take up to their own genitals, and to those of the other sex. Freud presupposes that small children both know that there is another sex, and in some detail what the alternative equipment is actually like. Boys become masculine by the resolution of castration anxiety, while girls become feminine through the resolution of penis envy. These resolutions are accomplished, it is supposed, through complex psychological processes in which the child's relations to each parent as not only a gendered, but also a sexed, being are the salient matters.

Infantile sexuality is the same, he asserts, in boys and girls, and is active in both, realized in masturbation. This mode of realization is a simple consequence of the biological arrangement of the genitals in both sexes. Transition to a more mature sense of differential embodiments, which Freud saw as masculine and feminine – that is, the embodiment of people as men and women – requires a psychological repression of the active aspect of genital sexuality by girls alone. Boys remain active in relation to their sexuality throughout their development. The repression required of girls is tied in with the alleged physiological change in the "leading genital zone," which occurs only for women. According to Freud, in the course of this alleged transformation the sexual salience of the vagina (passive sexuality) is substituted for that of the clitoris (active sexuality) as the focus of sexual feeling. The former awaits the active male while the latter is actively stimulated by the female herself. Thus the psychological stereotype of feminine passivity is grounded, so says Freud, in the physiological imperative (Freud, 1953 [1905]: 219–24, 235). Thus men, as embodied in the masculine mode, are the direct heirs of boys, and retain their active sense of sexuality.

That this is the most arrant nonsense is easily seen from historical studies, for instance that of Gillis (in Stearns and Stearns, 1988). The idea that a feminine mode of embodiment entails a necessarily passive role in the relation between the sexes is a late-historical transformation, whose etiology can be traced step by step. According to Gillis (p. 93), "men as well as women [before the Napoleonic era] were taught from childhood to think of themselves as connected interdependent parts of a larger whole, whether it be the family or community. Boundaries between persons [considered as essentially embodied] were viewed as porous." As Gillis says, *soma* and *psyche* were not separated in early-modern people. It is of the greatest importance to realize that in these fundamental respects there were no important differences between the modes of embodiment of men and of women. Each sex was embodied in the same way. "The body was simultaneously the symbol of their [that is young people's] connectedness and the means through which men as well as women managed to secure and repair cooperative achievements" (p. 96).

The appearance of the grounding ideas of the passive feminine embodiment idea assumed universal by many feminists can be traced to the early years of the nineteenth century. Commenting on the new emotionology of the period, Gillis says (p. 107): "Because men were supposedly driven by stronger inner impulse, they were expected to take the initiative in love as well as in sex. The older forms of courtship, in which women often acted forcefully both physically and symbolically, gave way to a new etiquette in which the male was invariably the suitor." This transformation had come about through a systematic series of redefinitions in which, to quote Gillis again, "heterosexual love was redefined as pure feeling... the old ways of symboliz-ing love, using the body, became taboo. The body itself underwent a radical sexualization, ceasing to be the vehicle for public performance" and becoming the location of private feeling. *Soma* and *psyche* had been torn apart, never to be reunited in the next one and a half centuries.

Other aspects of Freud's treatment of the psychology of people differentiated by sex and gender need not detain us, since my interest is exclusively in the sources of ideas of body-kinds and their characteristics.

Freud's account of the conceptualization of male and female bodies as kinds, the origin of the masculine/feminine distinction, is based on the assumption of the absolute salience of genitalia. It is the kind of account that a physically idle (non-sporting), urban (no garden), middle-class (no manual labour) intellectual would be inclined to give. But with the breaking out of that cocoon into the world where most people live and have always lived, quite different saliences appear. It seems to me that Connell (1983, 1989) proposes an account of the genesis of the concept of "male body as being of the masculine body kind" (itself a generic concept with species) that is much nearer the mark, even though his material is drawn from the last bastion of male supremacy, Australia.

Masculinity, in exemplary cults of male physicality, is not sex oriented, but to do with the manifestation of the appearances of power... "To be an adult male is distinctly to occupy space, to have a physical presence in the world," says Connell (1983: 19). The male sense of masculine embodiment is a combination of force and skill. "Force, meaning the irresistible occupation of space; skill, meaning the ability to operate on space or the objects in it (including other bodies). The combination of the two is power" (Connell, 1983: 18). Connell's analysis of the genesis of these conceptualizations through which men define their own masculinity shows how thoroughly the process is one of social construction. His own research focus has been on sport as the locus of the formative development of masculinity as a self-definition, but one could equally have focused on the institutions of manual labor, either as a way of earning a living or as a middle-class pastime. The embedding of the body in specific sporting or laboring activities has a profound effect on "ideal definitions of how the male body should look and work." These definitions (and they will be multiple because they are tied to specific activities such as football, surfing, basketball, boxing, driving heavy machinery, digging trenches, and so on) are radically distinct from maleness simply defined sexually, either absolutely with respect to genital endowment or relatively with respect to what it is to be bodily female. The non-sexual mode of definition has further profound con-sequences, says Connell (1983: 27). "It is important that [male-defining properties] are attributes of the body as a whole; they are not focused, even symbolically, on particular parts of it." Since, according to Connell (1983: 27), "there is a whole range of ways in which the body can be defined, perceived, etc. as masculine; and a whole range of ways in which, and ages at which, that bodily masculinity can be called in question," research into origins must be particularistic and its results can only be exemplary, neither universal nor normative. In a recent paper (Connell, 1989) the "Iron Man" surfing cult provides the setting for an idiographic, but exemplary, study of the details of the social construction of that mode of bodily masculinity. The body-kind, as a species of the masculine genus, is defined not only through the exigencies of the sport itself, but also through the uses the media of television, newspapers, and magazines make of an "Iron Man" as exemplary of just that mode of masculinity. So much for the account of the genesis of the sense of masculine embodiment.

Connell also goes on to comment on the consequences of this for the relations between men and women. Here one is forced reluctantly to part company with him. His material seems to show the separateness of masculinity from femininity, and the marginalization of women within the social order of sport (or heavy labor, for that matter). But – and perhaps the Australian context is exerting a distorting effect – he links this to the cult of "hegemonic masculinity" in the book of 1983. However, in the later piece of 1989 he observes that "oddly childish turns of phrase, etc." are used by an exemplary Iron Man. This form of bodily realized masculinity does not engender hegemony, even in Australia. My impression is of women tolerating, and even babying, this great infant. The power of small women over huge men is legendary. But further pursuit of this issue is outside my remit. As an account of how one form of masculine embodiment comes about, "Iron Man" is surely definitive.

In general a social psychology of the female body as a kind is not likely to find a source of most women's sense of their bodies as feminine in sport. It hardly needs emphasizing that the ontology of sports of whatever kind rests on a primary male embodiment of the participants. This is simply a historical fact about the origins of what we now call "sports." Insofar as women share musculature, cardiovascular capacity and manipulative skills with men, "sport" is, of course, open to them, insofar as the local culture allows. The distinctive moral orders that, as Gilligan has amply demonstrated, typify men's and women's styles of involvement with one another, must present competitive sport as a dilemma for women. A careful study of the spontaneous rhetoric surrounding the Mary Decker–Zola Budd collision in the Olympics of 1984 might be illuminating. But to pursue this byway is also not germane to my purposes.

There may be all sorts of ways in which women's bodies are classified as feminine. Clearly, in the eyes of men, the female body-kind is generic, and its species is defined in relation to local conventions of sexual attractiveness. More interesting are the kind concepts adopted and put to use by women of themselves. In Connell's treatment of the origin of one kind of masculinity as a body-kind we have seen functional or action aspects come to the fore, for which the bodily form is only an enabling condition. These action aspects become salient, or even indeed possible, only within certain socially defined frames of activity, for instance football. A similar suggestion has been made for feminine body-kinds in general.

We have good reason to reject Freud's account of the biological origins of a feminine body-kind characterized by passivity. However, it is not the only theory of the origin of body-kinds to make essential use of biology. I shall set this approach out in such a way as to introduce both ideas about the content of the concept of feminine body-kind and ideas about the process by which a person embodied as a biological female comes to regard herself as embodied in a feminine body and what the body-kind is taken to be. While Freud built his theory around the idea of modes of sexual excitation and the anatomy of the genitals, our second theory adverts only to the maternal function, which could of course be fulfilled without sexual inter-course, given the technical possibilities of embryo implantation and AID. It is built up on quite a different aspect of the sexual biology of gender from that which so obsessed Freud.

According to Grosz (1987), the feminine mode of embodiment is derived from the biological function of maternity – thus to experience oneself as embodied in a feminine body-kind is to experience oneself as a mother or a potential mother. Again, as in Freud's genital account, the feminine or womanly way of life is a mere repetition of an aspect of the biological body-kind, female.

Arguing that this concept of the feminine is just a cultural artifact, Grosz proposes a number of novel possibilities, all of which depend on a specific account of the processes by which the feminine mode of embodiment *concept*, which she takes to be already in place, has been created. This is the metaphor of "inscription": "the corporeal may be approached, as it were, from the outside [in contrast to an approach she calls 'embodied subjectivity' culled from Freud and Lacan]: it can be seen as a surface, an externality that presents itself to others and to culture as a *writing* or inscriptive surface" (Grosz, 1987: 10).

The metaphor is partially couched in talk of techniques by which a body of some person is "coordinated, structured and experienced," which include such diverse matters as diet and pleasures, supplemented by reference to techniques that "constitute, maintain or modify" that body, such as surgery. Grosz goes on to claim, though without citing empirical evidence, that

> the inscription of its [i.e. the body's] "external" surface is directed towards the acquisition of appropriate cultural attitudes, beliefs and values. In other words, the metaphor of the body as a writing surface explains the ways in which the body's interiority is produced through its external inscription.                    (p. 20)

Presented in the abstract, the theory is hard to assess, but it might be filled out as follows: women's clothes, which are cut so as to emphasize breasts and hips, "inscribe" maternity on the bodies of those who wear them. These clothes are presented as the dictates of fashion. However, by wearing them women come to think of themselves as primarily maternal. The fashion is actually, though unintentionally, "directed towards the acquisition" of the proper female attitude, namely maternal. But one might equally well argue that there already exists an imperative in any society to highlight maternal functions and the fashion will hardly be needed to set it in motion, nor is it likely to stem it. There were very unmaternal fashions in vogue in the 1920s, with little discernible effect on the contemporary emphasis on feminine bodies as mother-worthy. Grosz's idea is interesting, but it is seriously under-researched.

More plausible is the idea of "inhibited intentionality" (Young, 1980) as the message that is inscribed on the female body and leads to the development of a cluster of beliefs and attitudes towards it, thus defining the concept of feminine embodiment. This theory is offered as an explanation for the seemingly ubiquitous fact that girls, from infancy, are less physically aggressive than boys, readier to step back from bodily confrontations, less willing, apparently, to follow through a physical intention with full-blooded action. It is argued that girls are systematically *trained* to "inhibit their intentionality." Battered wives are common, but battered husbands are rare. This commonplace observation derives from early childhood, when girls are expected to be sweet and neat and boys to be rough and tough. Of course this distinction is never better than bimodal, so we need concepts like "tomboy" and "sissy" to mark imperfectly differentiated individuals. Drawing on the brilliant analyses of Gillis and Carol Stearns, it becomes possible to see that the term "inhibited intentionality" does refer to something. But it is the historically contingent separation of *soma* and *psyche*, and the feminization of feeling that went along with it.

So far as I can see, there is no evidence whatever for the thesis of universal inhibited intentionality as the feminine mode of embodiment. Gillis's study, to which I have already referred, shows that restrictions on the frequency and robustness of bodily contact between persons of different sex are very recent, while Carol Stearns has given us good grounds for thinking that in seventeenth-century Britain and North America violent physical interaction was the norm among excited adults. So much for any suggestion of universality for the phenomenon of inhibited intentionality. One can also query its contemporary application. There is nothing of inhibited intentionality about a woman beating an egg (or a carpet), spitting on a hankie and scrubbing a grubby child, playing a musical instrument, driving a VW GTI down the M40, milking a cow and so on. I, for one, am surrounded by vigorous and physically decisive women. If inhibited intentionality exists, it must be somewhere over the hill.

The Connell–Grosz accounts favor the kind of half-way social-constructionist analysis of the mappings of social and physical characteristics onto the bipolarity of sex to create gender that has been appearing and reappearing throughout this chapter. The mapping brings about a social arrangement conducive to human biological survival. With the threat of extinction gone, new social arrangements, such as those sketched by Kristeva and Davies become biologically possible. We are currently seeing a bimodal distribution of "masculine" and "feminine" forms of domestic life appearing. Whether the final transition to a completely free permutation of forms of life among the sexes is possible is a matter of the facts of genetic programming. The evidence is not yet in.

## Voluptuous consanguinity

The duality of body types so far described is created by the creation of a polarized distribution of secondary and tertiary sexual characteristics on a spectrum of continuously varying body attributes. In the "Romantic" age in the late eighteenth and early nineteenth centuries another ideal-body typology appeared, expressed in sculpture and poetry (Hagstrum, 1989). In this scheme there was only one gender, though there were, of course, two sexes. The Romantic movement anticipated certain trends in contemporary thought such as the transcendence of bimodality of gender which gives a privileged and foundational role to sexual dimorphism. But it also serves as a correction to the coarse-grained anachronism of those feminist writers who project an undifferentiated and oppressive "paternalism" into past centuries.[1]

The Platonic ideal of androgyny is not realizable, according to its author, in the everyday world of appearances. Hagstrum (1989: 78) points out how far the Romantic idea of androgynous beings differed. The new ideal puts its expression in sculpture and in poetry, and is presented as a way in which embodied human beings can *actually* be conceptualized. The legend of Cupid and Psyche captured the interest of both poets and sculptors. In the sculptured rendering of the time the bodies of the lovers are presented as identical in general form, in stature and in the delicate molding of flesh. Their sexual dimorphism is, one might say, almost incidental.

This change of mapping (which may or may not have supplanted a "modern" bimodalism) was accompanied by a transformation of the conceptual repertoire with which sexuality was expressed. The new conceptions are everywhere, but they are eminently visible in the poetry of Shelley. To quote Hagstrum again, the Romantic ideal of sexuality is "compounded of the incestuous, the homoerotic and the narcissistic" – but above all the incestuous. Coleridge treats conjugal love as a mere step from the love of siblings. The apotheosis of love is that which develops between beings as similar to one another as nature will allow. If not between brother and sister, at least it proposes a sexual love between beings of one body form. The corporeal androgyny towards which one might strive in real life could even be idealized further into an imaginary world of doubly sexed "sexless" beings, hermaphrodites. Politically the Shelleys, Percy and Mary, were not unaware that these ideals of the erotic life had profound implications for the political organization of society around a system of male hegemony and female dependence. In the Romantic period, and indeed one might say, throughout the subsequent century, the forms of private sensibility and of public life have never been so far apart, nor at such odds. Hagstrum remarks on the fact that both Comte and Jung, at the beginning and at the end of the Victorian era, idealized a race of beings whose bodily forms were not diversified into the masculine and feminine.

## Notes

1   As Estelle Cohen (1989) has argued, the rise of a new form of economic organization in the later eighteenth century led to a situation in which "women's public status declined at the same time as their sphere of activity contracted to the household. One form of power and influence was traded in for another."

## References

Cohen, E. (1989) "Medical debates on woman's 'nature' in England and Holland in 1700." Paper read at History of Medicine Seminar, Oxford University.

Connell, R. W. (1983) *Which Way is Up? Essays on Class, Sex and Culture* (ch. 2). London: Allen and Unwin.

Connell, R. W. (1989) "An Iron Man: the body and some contradictions of hegemonic masculinity." In M. Messner and D. F. Sabo (eds), *Critical Perspectives on Sport, Patriarchy and Man*. New York: Sage.

Davies, B. (1990) *Frogs and Snails and Feminist Tales*. London: Allen and Unwin.

Della Porta, B. (1560/1658) *Natural Magick*. London: Young and Speed.

Freud, S. (1905/1953) "Three essays on sexuality." In E. Jones (ed.), *The Complete Psychological Works of Sigmund Freud*, vol. VII. London: Hogarth.

Garfinkel, H. (1967) *Studies in Ethnomethodology*. Princeton: Princeton University Press.

Gilligan, C. (1982) *In a Different Voice*. Cambridge, Mass.: Harvard University Press.

Gillis, J. R. (1988) "From ritual to romance." In C. Z. Stearns and P. W. Stearns, *Emotions and Social Change: Towards a New Psychohistory*. New York and London: Holmes and Meier.

Grosz, E. (1987) "Corporeal feminism." *Australian Feminist Studies*, 5, 1–15.

Hagstrum, J. (1989) *Eros and Vision*. Evanston, Ill.: Northwestern University Press.

Kristeva, J. (1981) "Women's time." *Signs*, 7, 13–35.

Lloyd, B. and Duveen, G. (1990) "A semiotic analysis of the development of social representations of gender." In G. Duveen and B. Lloyd (eds), *Social Representations and the Development of Knowledge*. Cambridge: Cambridge University Press.

Midgeley, M. (1978) *Beast and Man*. Ithaca: Cornell University Press.

Morawski, J. G. (1982) "On thinking about history as social psychology." *Personality and Social Psychology Bulletin*, 8, 393–401.

Paglia, C. (1990) *Sexual Personae*. New Haven, Conn.: Yale University Press.

Perper, T. (1985) *Sex Signals: The Biology of Love* (pp. 184–6). Philadelphia: ISI Press.

Reynolds, V. and Tanner, R. F. E. (1983) *The Biology of Religion*. Harlow: Longmans.

Schwartz, D. (1986) *Never Satisfied: A Cultural History of Diet, Fantasies and Fat*. New York: Free Press.

Stearns, C. Z. and Stearns, P. N. (1988) *Emotion and Social Changes: Towards a New Psychohistory*. New York and London: Holmes and Meier.

Tannen, D. (1990) *You Just Don't Understand*. New York: Morrow.

Tiger, L. and Shepher, S. (1975) *Women in the Kibbutz* (chs. 1 and 2). New York: Harcourt, Brace, Jovanovich.

Trebarthen, C. (1979) "Competition and cooperation in early childhood: a description of primary intersubjectivity." In M. Bullowa (ed.), *Before Speech*. Cambridge: Cambridge University Press.

Young, I. (1980) "Throwing like a girl." *Human Studies*, 3, 137–56.

# 2
# Gender and Performance

## Selections from *Gender Trouble**
### *Judith Butler*

*One is not born a woman, but rather becomes one.*

> Simone de Beauvoir

*Strictly speaking, "women" cannot be said to exist.*

> Julia Kristeva

*Woman does not have a sex.*

> Luce Irigaray

*The deployment of sexuality . . . established this notion of sex.*

> Michel Foucault

*The category of sex is the political category that founds society as heterosexual.*

> Monique Wittig

## "Women" as the subject of feminism

For the most part, feminist theory has assumed that there is some existing identity, understood through the category of women, who not only initiates feminist interests and goals within discourse, but constitutes the subject for whom political representation is pursued. But *politics* and *representation* are controversial terms. On the one hand, *representation* serves as the operative term within a political process that seeks to extend visibility and legitimacy to women as political subjects; on the other hand, representation is the normative function of a language which is said either to reveal or to distort what is assumed to be true about the category of women. For feminist theory, the development of a language that fully or adequately represents women has seemed necessary to foster the political visibility of women. This has seemed obviously important considering the pervasive cultural condition in which women's lives were either misrepresented or not represented at all.

Recently, this prevailing conception of the relation between feminist theory and politics has come under challenge from within feminist discourse. The very subject

* Judith Butler, *Gender Trouble: Feminism and the Subversion of Identity* (New York: Routledge, 1990), pp. 1–3, 6–16, 32–3, 128–32, 134–8.

of women is no longer understood in stable or abiding terms. There is a great deal of material that not only questions the viability of "the subject" as the ultimate candidate for representation or, indeed, liberation, but there is very little agreement after all on what it is that constitutes, or ought to constitute, the category of women. The domains of political and linguistic "representation" set out in advance the criterion by which subjects themselves are formed, with the result that representation is extended only to what can be acknowledged as a subject. In other words, the qualification for being a subject must first be met before representation can be extended.

Foucault points out that juridical systems of power *produce* the subjects they subsequently come to represent.[1] Juridical notions of power appear to regulate political life in purely negative terms – that is, through the limitation, prohibition, regulation, control, and even "protection" of individuals related to that political structure through the contingent and retractable operation of choice. But the subjects regulated by such structures are, by virtue of being subjected to them, formed, defined, and reproduced in accordance with the requirements of those structures. If this analysis is right, then the juridical formation of language and politics that represents women as "the subject" of feminism is itself a discursive formation and effect of a given version of representational politics. And the feminist subject turns out to be discursively constituted by the very political system that is supposed to facilitate its emancipation. This becomes politically problematic if that system can be shown to produce gendered subjects along a differential axis of domination or to produce subjects who are presumed to be masculine. In such cases, an uncritical appeal to such a system for the emancipation of "women" will be clearly self-defeating.

The question of "the subject" is crucial for politics, and for feminist politics in particular, because juridical subjects are invariably produced through certain exclusionary practices that do not "show" once the juridical structure of politics has been established. In other words, the political construction of the subject proceeds with certain legitimating and exclusionary aims, and these political operations are effectively concealed and naturalized by a political analysis that takes juridical structures as their foundation. Juridical power inevitably "produces" what it claims merely to represent; hence, politics must be concerned with this dual function of power: the juridical and the productive. In effect, the law produces and then conceals the notion of "a subject before the law"[2] in order to invoke that discursive formation as a naturalized foundational premiss that subsequently legitimates that law's own regulatory hegemony. It is not enough to inquire into how women might become more fully represented in language and politics. Feminist critique ought also to understand how the category of "women," the subject of feminism, is produced and restrained by the very structures of power through which emancipation is sought.

Indeed, the question of women as the subject of feminism raises the possibility that there may not be a subject who stands "before" the law, awaiting representation in or by the law. Perhaps the subject, as well as the invocation of a temporal "before," is constituted by the law as the fictive foundation of its own claim to legitimacy. The prevailing assumption of the ontological integrity of the subject before the law might be understood as the contemporary trace of the state of nature hypothesis, that foundationalist fable constitutive of the juridical structures of classical liberalism. The performative invocation of a nonhistorical "before" becomes the foundational premise that guarantees a presocial ontology of persons who freely consent to be governed and, thereby, constitute the legitimacy of the social contract.

Apart from the foundationalist fictions that support the notion of the subject, however, there is the political problem that feminism encounters in the assumption that the term *women* denotes a common identity. Rather than a stable signifier that commands the assent of those whom it purports to describe and represent, *women*, even in the plural, has become a troublesome term, a site of contest, a cause for anxiety. As Denise Riley's title suggests, *Am I That Name?* is a question produced by the very possibility of the name's multiple significations.[3] If one "is" a woman, that is surely not all one is; the term fails to be exhaustive, not because a pregendered "person" transcends the specific paraphernalia of its gender, but because gender is not always constituted coherently or consistently in different historical contexts, and because gender intersects with racial, class, ethnic, sexual, and regional modalities of discursively constituted identities. As a result, it becomes impossible to separate out "gender" from the political and cultural intersections in which it is invariably produced and maintained . . .

## The compulsory order of sex/gender/desire

Although the unproblematic unity of "women" is often invoked to construct a solidarity of identity, a split is introduced in the feminist subject by the distinction between sex and gender. Originally intended to dispute the biology-is-destiny formulation, the distinction between sex and gender serves the argument that whatever biological intractability sex appears to have, gender is culturally constructed; hence, gender is neither the causal result of sex nor as seemingly fixed as sex. The unity of the subject is thus already potentially contested by the distinction that permits of gender as a multiple interpretation of sex.

If gender is the cultural meanings that the sexed body assumes, then a gender cannot be said to follow from a sex in any one way. Taken to its logical limit, the sex/gender distinction suggests a radical discontinuity between sexed bodies and culturally constructed genders. Assuming for the moment the stability of binary sex, it does not follow that the construction of "men" will accrue exclusively to the bodies of males or that "women" will interpret only female bodies. Further, even if the sexes appear to be unproblematically binary in their morphology and constitution (which will become a question), there is no reason to assume that genders ought also to remain as two.[4] The presumption of a binary gender system implicitly retains the belief in a mimetic relation of gender to sex whereby gender mirrors sex or is otherwise restricted by it. When the constructed status of gender is theorized as radically independent of sex, gender itself becomes a free-floating artifice, with the consequence that *man* and *masculine* might just as easily signify a female body as a male one, and *woman* and *feminine* a male body as easily as a female one.

This radical splitting of the gendered subject poses yet another set of problems. Can we refer to a "given" sex or a "given" gender without first inquiring into how sex and/or gender is given, through what means? And what is "sex" anyway? Is it natural, anatomical, chromosomal, or hormonal, and how is a feminist critic to assess the scientific discourses which purport to establish such "facts" for us?[5] Does sex have a history?[6] Does each sex have a different history, or histories? Is there a history of how the duality of sex was established, a genealogy that might expose the binary options as a variable construction? Are the ostensibly natural facts of sex discursively produced by various scientific discourses in the service of other political and social interests? If the immutable character of sex is contested, perhaps this construct called "sex" is as culturally constructed as gender; indeed, perhaps it was always already gender, with the consequence that the distinction between sex and gender turns out to be no distinction at all.[7]

It would make no sense, then, to define gender as the cultural interpretation of sex, if sex itself is a gendered category. Gender ought not to be conceived merely as the cultural inscription of meaning on a pregiven sex (a juridical conception); gender must also designate the very apparatus of production whereby the sexes themselves are established. As a result, gender is not to culture as sex is to nature; gender is also the discursive/cultural means by which "sexed nature" or "a natural sex" is produced and established as "prediscursive," prior to culture, a politically neutral surface *on which* culture acts . . . At this juncture it is already clear that one way the internal stability and binary frame for sex is effectively secured is by casting the duality of sex in a prediscursive domain. This production of sex *as* the prediscursive ought to be understood as the effect of the apparatus of cultural construction designated by *gender*. How, then, does gender need to be reformulated to encompass the power relations that produce the effect of a prediscursive sex and so conceal that very operation of discursive production?

## Gender: the circular ruins of contemporary debate

Is there "a" gender which persons are said *to have*, or is it an essential attribute that a person is said *to be*, as implied in the question "What gender are you?" When feminist theorists claim that gender is the cultural interpretation of sex or that gender is culturally constructed, what is the manner or mechanism of this construction? If gender is constructed, could it be constructed differently, or does its constructedness imply some form of social determinism, foreclosing the possibility of agency and transformation? Does "construction" suggest that certain laws generate gender differences along universal axes of sexual difference? How and where does the construction of gender take place? What sense can we make of a construction that cannot assume a human constructor prior to that construction? On some accounts, the notion that gender is constructed suggests a certain determinism of gender meanings inscribed on anatomically differentiated bodies, where those bodies are understood as passive recipients of an inexorable cultural law. When the relevant "culture" that "constructs" gender is understood in terms of such a law or set of laws, then it seems that gender is as determined and fixed as it was under the biology-is-destiny formulation. In such a case, not biology, but culture, becomes destiny.

On the other hand, Simone de Beauvoir suggests in *The Second Sex* that "one is not born a woman, but, rather, becomes one."[8] For Beauvoir, gender is "constructed," but implied in her formulation is an agent, a *cogito*, who somehow takes on or appropriates that gender and could, in principle, take on some other gender. Is gender as variable and volitional as Beauvoir's account seems to suggest? Can "construction" in such a case be reduced to a form of choice? Beauvoir is clear that one "becomes" a woman, but always under a cultural compulsion to become one. And clearly, the compulsion does not come from "sex." There is nothing in her account that guarantees that the "one" who becomes a woman is necessarily female. If "the body is a situation,"[9] as she claims, there is no recourse to a body that has not always already been interpreted by cultural meanings; hence, sex could not qualify as a prediscursive anatomical facticity. Indeed, sex, by definition, will be shown to have been gender all along.[10]

The controversy over the meaning of *construction* appears to founder on the conventional philosophical polarity between free will and determinism. As a consequence, one might reasonably suspect that some common linguistic restriction on thought both forms and limits the terms of the debate. Within those terms, "the body" appears as a passive medium on which cultural meanings are inscribed or as the instrument through which an appropriative and interpretive will determines a cultural meaning for itself. In either case, the body is figured as a mere *instrument* or *medium* for which a set of cultural meanings are only externally related. But "the body" is itself a construction, as are the myriad "bodies" that constitute the domain of gendered subjects. Bodies cannot be said to have a signifiable existence prior to the mark of their gender; the question then emerges: to what extent does the body *come into being* in and through the mark(s) of gender? How do we reconceive the body no longer as a passive medium or instrument awaiting the enlivening capacity of a distinctly immaterial will?[11]

Whether gender or sex is fixed or free is a function of a discourse which, it will be suggested, seeks to set certain limits to analysis or to safeguard certain tenets of humanism as presuppositional to any analysis of gender. The locus of intractability, whether in "sex" or "gender" or in the very meaning of "construction," provides a clue to what cultural possibilities can and cannot become mobilized through any further analysis. The limits of the discursive analysis of gender presuppose and preempt the possibilities of imaginable and realizable gender configurations within culture. This is not to say that any and all gendered possibilities are open, but that the boundaries of analysis suggest the limits of a discursively conditioned experience. These limits are always set within the terms of a hegemonic cultural discourse predicated on binary structures that appear as the language of universal rationality. Constraint is thus built into what that language constitutes as the imaginable domain of gender.

Although social scientists refer to gender as a "factor" or a "dimension" of an analysis, it is also applied to embodied persons as "a mark" of biological, linguistic, and/or cultural difference. In these latter cases, gender can be understood as a signification that an (already) sexually differentiated body assumes, but even then that signification exists only *in relation* to another, opposing signification. Some feminist theorists claim that gender is "a relation," indeed, a set of relations, and not an individual attribute. Others, following Beauvoir, would argue that only the feminine gender is marked, that the universal person and the masculine gender are conflated, thereby defining women in terms of their sex and extolling men as the bearers of a body-transcendent universal personhood.

In a move that complicates the discussion further, Luce Irigaray argues that women constitute a paradox, if not a contradiction, within the discourse of identity itself. Women are the "sex" which is not "one." Within a language pervasively masculinist, a phallogocentric language, women constitute the *unrepresentable*. In other words, women represent the sex that cannot be thought, a linguistic absence and opacity. Within a language that rests on univocal signification, the female sex constitutes the unconstrainable and undesignatable. In this sense, women are the sex which is not "one," but multiple.[12] In opposition to Beauvoir, for whom women are designated as the Other, Irigaray argues that both the subject and the Other are masculine mainstays of a closed phallogocentric signifying economy that achieves its totalizing goal through the exclusion of the feminine altogether. For Beauvoir, women are the negative of men, the lack against which masculine identity differentiates itself; for Irigaray, that particular dialectic constitutes a system that excludes an entirely different economy of signification. Women are not only represented falsely within the Sartrian frame of signifying-subject and signified-Other, but the falsity of the signification points out the entire structure of representation as inadequate. The sex which is not one, then, provides a point of departure for a criticism of hegemonic Western representation and of the metaphysics of substance that structures the very notion of the subject.

What is the metaphysics of substance, and how does it inform thinking about the categories of sex? In the first instance, humanist conceptions of the subject tend to assume a substantive person who is the bearer of various essential and nonessential attributes. A humanist feminist position might understand gender as an *attribute* of a person who is characterized essentially as a pregendered substance or "core," called the person, denoting a universal capacity for reason, moral deliberation, or language. The universal conception of the person, however, is displaced as a point of departure for a social theory of gender by those historical and anthropological positions that understand gender as a *relation* among socially constituted subjects in specifiable contexts. This relational or contextual point of view suggests that what the person "is," and, indeed, what gender "is," is always relative to the constructed relations in which it is determined.[13] As a shifting and contextual phenomenon, gender does not denote a substantive being, but a relative point of convergence among culturally and historically specific sets of relations.

Irigaray would maintain, however, that the feminine "sex" is a point of linguistic *absence*, the impossibility of a grammatically denoted substance, and, hence, the point of view that exposes that substance as an abiding and foundational illusion of a masculinist discourse. This absence is not marked as such within the masculine signifying economy – a contention that reverses Beauvoir's argument (and Wittig's) that the female sex *is* marked, while the male sex is not. For Irigaray, the female sex is not a "lack" or an "Other" that immanently and negatively defines the subject in its masculinity. On the contrary, the female sex eludes the very requirements of representation, for she is neither "Other" nor the "lack," those categories remaining relative to the Sartrian subject, immanent to that phallogocentric scheme. Hence, for Irigaray, the feminine could never be the *mark of a subject*, as Beauvoir would suggest. Further, the feminine could not be theorized in terms of a determinate *relation* between the masculine and the feminine within any given discourse, for discourse is not a relevant notion here. Even in their variety, discourses constitute so many modalities of phallogocentric language. The female sex is thus also *the subject* that is not one. The relation between masculine and feminine cannot be represented in a signifying economy in which the masculine constitutes the closed circle of signifier and signified. Paradoxically enough, Beauvoir prefigured this impossibility in *The Second Sex* when she argued that men could not settle the question of women because they would then be acting as both judge and party to the case.[14]

The distinctions among the above positions are far from discrete; each of them can be understood to problematize the locality and meaning of both the "subject" and "gender" within the context of socially instituted gender asymmetry. The interpretive possibilities of gender are in no sense exhausted by the alternatives suggested above. The problematic circularity of a feminist inquiry into gender is underscored by the presence of positions which, on the one hand, presume that gender is a secondary characteristic of persons and those which, on the other hand, argue that the very notion of the person, positioned within language as a "subject," is a masculinist construction and prerogative which effectively excludes the structural and semantic possibility of a feminine gender. The consequence of such sharp disagreements about the meaning of gender (indeed, whether *gender* is the term to be argued about at all, or whether the discursive construction of *sex* is, indeed, more fundamental, or perhaps *women* or *woman* and/or *men* and *man*) establishes the need for a radical rethinking of the categories of identity within the context of relations of radical gender asymmetry.

For Beauvoir, the "subject" within the existential analytic of misogyny is always already masculine, conflated with the universal, differentiating itself from a feminine "Other" outside the universalizing norms of personhood, hopelessly "particular," embodied, condemned to immanence. Although Beauvoir is often understood to be calling for the right of women, in effect, to become existential subjects and, hence, for inclusion within the terms of an abstract universality, her position also implies a fundamental critique of the very disembodiment of the abstract masculine epistemological subject.[15] That subject is abstract to the extent that it disavows its socially marked embodiment and, further, projects that disavowed and disparaged embodiment on to the feminine sphere, effectively renaming the body as female. This association of the body with the female works along magical relations of reciprocity whereby the female sex becomes restricted to its body, and the male body, fully disavowed, becomes, paradoxically, the incorporeal instrument of an ostensibly radical freedom. Beauvoir's analysis implicitly poses the question: through what act of negation and disavowal does the masculine pose as a disembodied universality and the feminine get constructed as a disavowed corporeality? The dialectic of master–slave, here fully reformulated within the nonreciprocal terms of gender asymmetry, prefigures what Irigaray will later describe as the masculine signifying economy that includes both the existential subject and its Other.

Beauvoir proposes that the female body ought to be the situation and instrumentality of women's freedom, not a defining and limiting essence.[16] The theory of embodiment informing Beauvoir's analysis is clearly limited by the uncritical reproduction of the Cartesian distinction between freedom and the body. Despite my own previous efforts to argue the contrary, it appears that Beauvoir maintains the mind/body dualism, even as she proposes a synthesis of those terms.[17] The preservation of that very distinction can be read as symptomatic of the very phallogocentrism that Beauvoir underestimates. In the philosophical tradition that begins with Plato and continues through Descartes, Husserl, and Sartre, the ontological distinction between soul (consciousness, mind) and body invariably supports relations of political and psychic subordination and hierarchy. The mind not only subjugates the body, but occasionally entertains the fantasy of fleeing its embodiment altogether. The cultural associations of mind with masculinity and body with femininity are well documented within the field of philosophy and feminism.[18] As a result, any uncritical reproduction of the mind/body distinction ought to be rethought for the implicit gender hierarchy that the distinction has conventionally produced, maintained, and rationalized.

The discursive construction of "the body" and its separation from "freedom" in Beauvoir fails to mark along the axis of gender the very mind–body distinction that is supposed to illuminate the persistence of gender asymmetry. Officially, Beauvoir contends that the female body is marked within masculinist discourse, whereby the masculine body, in its conflation with the universal, remains unmarked. Irigaray clearly suggests that both marker and marked are maintained within a masculinist mode of signification in which the female body is "marked off," as it were, from the domain of the signifiable. In post-Hegelian terms, she is "canceled," but not preserved. On Irigaray's reading, Beauvoir's claim that woman "is sex" is reversed to mean that she is not the sex she is designated to be, but, rather, the masculine sex *encore* (and *en corps*) parading in the mode of otherness. For Irigaray, that phallogocentric mode of signifying the female sex perpetually reproduces phantasms of its own self-amplifying desire. Instead of a self-limiting linguistic gesture that grants alterity or difference to women, phallogocentrism offers a name to eclipse the feminine and take its place.

## Theorizing the binary, the unitary, and beyond

Beauvoir and Irigaray clearly differ over the fundamental structures by which gender asymmetry is reproduced; Beauvoir turns to the failed reciprocity of an asymmetrical dialectic, while Irigaray suggests that the dialectic itself is the mono-logic elaboration of a masculinist signifying economy. Although Irigaray clearly broadens the scope of feminist critique by exposing the epistemological, ontological, and logical structures of a masculinist signifying economy, the power of her analysis is undercut precisely by its globalizing reach. Is it possible to identify a monolithic as well as a monologic masculinist economy that traverses the array of cultural and historical contexts in which sexual difference takes place? Is the failure to acknowledge the specific cultural operations of gender oppression itself a kind of episte-mological imperialism, one which is not ameliorated by the simple elaboration of cultural differences as "examples" of the selfsame phallogocentrism? The effort to *include* "Other" cultures as variegated amplifications of a global phallogocentrism constitutes an appropriative act that risks a repetition of the self-aggrandizing gesture of phallogocentrism, colonizing under the sign of the same those differences that might otherwise call that totalizing concept into question.[19]

Feminist critique ought to explore the totalizing claims of a masculinist signifying economy, but also remain self-critical with respect to the totalizing gestures of feminism. The effort to identify the enemy as singular in form is a reverse-discourse that uncritically mimics the strategy of the oppressor instead of offering a different set of terms. That the tactic can operate in feminist and antifeminist contexts alike suggests that the colonizing gesture is not primarily or irreducibly masculinist. It can operate to effect other relations of racial, class, and heterosexist subordination, to name but a few. And clearly, listing the varieties of oppression, as I began to do, assumes their discrete, sequential coexistence along a horizontal axis that does not describe their convergences within the social field. A vertical model is similarly insufficient; oppressions cannot be summarily ranked, causally related, distributed among planes of "originality" and "derivativeness."[20] Indeed, the field of power structured in part by the imperializing gesture of dialectical appropriation exceeds and encompasses the axis of sexual difference, offering a mapping of intersecting differentials which cannot be summarily hierarchized either within the terms of phallogocentrism or any other candidate for the position of "primary condition of oppression." Rather than an exclusive tactic of masculinist signifying economies, dialectical appropriation and suppression of the Other is one tactic among many, deployed centrally but not exclusively in the service of expanding and rationalizing the masculinist domain.

The contemporary feminist debates over essentialism raise the question of the universality of female identity and masculinist oppression in other ways. Universalistic claims are based on a common or shared epistemological standpoint, understood as the articulated consciousness or shared structures of oppression or in the ostensibly transcultural structures of femininity, maternity, sexuality, and/or *écriture feminine*. The opening discussion in this chapter argued that this globalizing gesture has spawned a number of criticisms from women who claim that the category of "women" is normative and exclusionary and is invoked with the unmarked dimensions of class and racial privilege intact. In other words, the insistence upon the coherence and unity of the category of women has effectively refused the multiplicity of cultural, social, and political intersections in which the concrete array of "women" are constructed.

Some efforts have been made to formulate coalitional politics which do not assume in advance what the content of "women" will be. They propose instead a set of dialogic encounters by which variously positioned women articulate separate identities within the framework of an emergent coalition. Clearly, the value of coalitional politics is not to be underestimated, but the very form of coalition, of an emerging and unpredictable assemblage of positions, cannot be figured in advance. Despite the clearly democratizing impulse that motivates coalition building, the coalitional theorist can inadvertently reinsert herself as sovereign of the process by trying to assert an ideal form for coalitional structures *in advance*, one that will effectively guarantee unity as the outcome. Related efforts to determine what is and is not the true shape of a dialogue, what constitutes a subject-position, and, most importantly, when "unity" has been reached, can impede the self-shaping and self-limiting dynamics of coalition.

The insistence in advance on coalitional "unity" as a goal assumes that solidarity, whatever its price, is a prerequisite for political action. But what sort of politics demands that kind of advance purchase on unity? Perhaps a coalition needs to acknowledge its contradictions and take action with those contradictions intact. Perhaps also part of what dialogic understanding entails is the acceptance of divergence, breakage, splinter, and fragmentation as part of the often tortuous process of democratization. The very notion of "dialogue" is culturally specific and historically bound, and while one speaker may feel secure that a conversation is happening, another may be sure it·is not. The power relations that condition and limit dialogic possibilities need first to be interrogated. Otherwise, the model of dialogue risks relapsing into a liberal model that assumes that speaking agents occupy equal positions of power and speak with the same presuppositions about what constitutes "agreement" and "unity" and, indeed, that those are the goals to be sought. It would be wrong to assume in advance that there is a category of "women" that simply needs to be filled in with various components of race, class, age, ethnicity, and sexuality in order to become complete. The assumption of its essential incompleteness permits that category to serve as a permanently available site of contested meanings. The definitional incompleteness of the category might then serve as a normative ideal relieved of coercive force.

Is "unity" necessary for effective political action? Is the premature insistence on the goal of unity precisely the cause of an ever more bitter fragmentation among the ranks? Certain forms of acknowledged fragmentation might facilate coalitional action precisely because the "unity" of the category of women is neither presupposed nor desired. Does "unity" set up an exclusionary norm of solidarity at the level of identity that rules out the possibility of a set of actions which disrupt the very borders of identity concepts, or which seek to accomplish precisely that disruption as an explicit political aim? Without the presupposition or goal of "unity," which is, in either case, always instituted at a conceptual level, provisional unities might emerge in the context of concrete actions that have purposes other than the articulation of identity. Without the compulsory expectation that feminist actions must be instituted from some stable, unified, and agreed upon identity, those actions might well get a quicker start and seem more congenial to a number of "women" for whom the meaning of the category is permanently moot.

This antifoundationalist approach to coalitional politics assumes neither that "identity" is a premise nor that the shape or meaning of a coalitional assemblage can be known prior to its achievement. Because the articulation of an identity within available cultural terms instates a definition that forecloses in advance the emergence of new identity concepts in and through politically engaged actions, the foundation-alist tactic cannot take the transformation or expansion of existing identity concepts as a normative goal. Moreover, when agreed-upon identities or agreed-upon dialogic structures, through which already established identities are communicated, no longer constitute the theme or subject of politics, then identities can come into being and dissolve depending on the concrete practices that constitute them. Certain political practices institute identities on a contingent basis in order to accomplish whatever aims are in view. Coalitional politics requires neither an expanded category of "women" nor an internally multiplicitous self that offers its complexity at once.

Gender is a complexity whose totality is permanently deferred, never fully what it is at any given juncture in time. An open coalition, then, will affirm identities that are alternately instituted and relinquished according to the purposes at hand; it will be an open assemblage that permits of multiple convergences and divergences without obedience to a normative *telos* of definitional closure...

Clearly this project does not propose to lay out within traditional philosophical terms an *ontology* of gender whereby the meaning of *being* a woman or a man is elucidated within the terms of phenomenology. The presumption here is that the "being" of gender is *an effect*, an object of a genealogical investigation that maps out the political parameters of its construction in the mode of ontology. To claim that gender is constructed is not to assert its illusoriness or artificiality, where those terms are understood to reside within a binary that counterposes the "real" and the "authentic" as oppositional. As a genealogy of gender ontology, this inquiry seeks to understand the discursive production of the plausibility of that binary relation and to suggest that certain cultural configurations of gender take the place of "the real" and consolidate and augment their hegemony through that felicitous self-naturalization.

If there is something right in Beauvoir's claim that one is not born, but rather *becomes* a woman, it follows that *woman* itself is a term in process, a becoming, a constructing that cannot rightfully be said to originate or to end. As an ongoing discursive practice, it is open to intervention and resignification. Even when gender seems to congeal into the most reified forms, the "congealing" is itself an insistent and insidious practice, sustained and regulated by various social means. It is, for Beauvoir, never possible finally to become a woman, as if there were a *telos* that governs the process of acculturation and construction. Gender is the repeated stylization of the body, a set of repeated acts within a highly rigid regulatory frame that congeal over time to produce the appearance of substance, of a natural sort of being. A political genealogy of gender ontologies, if it is successful, will deconstruct the substantive appearance of gender into its constitutive acts and locate and account for those acts within the compulsory frames set by the various forces that police the social appearance of gender. To expose the contingent acts that create the appearance of a naturalistic necessity, a move which has been a part of cultural critique at least since Marx, is a task that now takes on the added burden of showing how the very notion of the subject, intelligible only through its appearance as gendered, admits of possibilities that have been forcibly foreclosed by the various reifications of gender that have constituted its contingent ontologies...

## Bodily inscriptions, performative subversions

Garbo "got in drag" whenever she took some heavy glamour part, whenever she melted in or out of a man's arms, whenever she simply let that heavenly-flexed neck...bear the weight of her thrown-back head...How resplendent seems the art of acting! It is all *impersonation*, whether the sex underneath is true or not.
    (Parker Tyler, "The Garbo image," quoted in Esther Newton, *Mother Camp*)

Categories of true sex, discrete gender, and specific sexuality have constituted the stable point of reference for a great deal of feminist theory and politics. These constructs of identity serve as the points of epistemic departure from which theory emerges and politics itself is shaped. In the case of feminism, politics is ostensibly shaped to express the interests, the perspectives, of "women." But is there a political shape to "women," as it were, that precedes and prefigures the political elaboration of their interests and epistemic point of view? How is that identity shaped, and is it a political shaping that takes the very morphology and boundary of the sexed body as the ground, surface, or site of cultural inscription? What circumscribes that site as "the female body?" Is "the body" or "the sexed body" the firm foundation on which gender and systems of compulsory sexuality operate? Or is "the body" itself shaped by political forces with strategic interests in keeping that body bounded and constituted by the markers of sex?

The sex/gender distinction and the category of sex itself appear to presuppose a generalization of "the body" that preexists the acquisition of its sexed significance. This "body" often appears to be a passive medium that is signified by an inscription from a cultural source figured as "external" to that body. Any theory of the culturally constructed body, however, ought to question "the body" as a construct of suspect generality when it is figured as passive and prior to discourse. There are Christian and Cartesian precedents to such views which, prior to the emergence of vitalistic biologies in the nineteenth century, understand "the body" as so much inert matter, signifying nothing or, more specifically, signifying a profane void, the fallen state: deception, sin, the premonitional metaphorics of hell and the eternal feminine. There are many occasions in both Sartre's and Beauvoir's work where "the body" is figured as a mute facticity, anticipating some meaning that can be attributed only by a transcendent consciousness, understood in Cartesian terms as radically immaterial. But what establishes this dualism for us? What separates off "the body" as indifferent to signification, and signification itself as the act of a radically disembodied consciousness or, rather, the act that radically disembodies that consciousness? To what extent is that Cartesian dualism presupposed in phenomenology adapted to the structuralist frame in which mind/body is redescribed as culture/nature? With respect to gender discourse, to what extent do these problematic dualisms still operate within the very descriptions that are supposed to lead us out of that binarism and its implicit hierarchy? How are the contours of the body clearly marked as the taken-for-granted ground or surface upon which gender significations are inscribed, a mere facticity devoid of value, prior to significance?

Wittig suggests that a culturally specific epistemic *a priori* establishes the natural-ness of "sex." But by what enigmatic means has "the body" been accepted as a *prima facie* given that admits of no genealogy? Even within Foucault's essay on the very theme of genealogy, the body is figured as a surface and the scene of a cultural inscription: "the body is the inscribed surface of events."[21]

The task of genealogy, he claims, is "to expose a body totally imprinted by history." His sentence continues, however, by referring to the goal of "history" – here clearly understood on the model of Freud's "civilization" – as the "destruction of the body" (p. 148). Forces and impulses with multiple directionalities are precisely that which history both destroys and preserves through the *entstehung* (historical event) of inscription. As "a volume in perpetual disintegration" (p. 148), the body is always under siege, suffering destruction by the very terms of history. And history is the creation of values and meanings by a signifying practice that requires the subjection of the body. This corporeal destruction is necessary to produce the speaking subject and its significations. This is a body, described through the language of surface and force, weakened through a "single drama" of domination, inscription, and creation (p. 150). This is not the *modus vivendi* of one kind of history rather than another, but is, for Foucault, "history" (p. 148) in its essential and repressive gesture.

Although Foucault writes, "Nothing in man [*sic*] – not even his body – is sufficiently stable to serve as the basis for self-recognition or for understanding other men [*sic*]" (p. 53), he nevertheless points to the constancy of cultural inscrip-tion as a "single drama" that acts on the body. If the creation of values, that historical mode of signification, requires the destruction of the body, much as the instrument of torture in Kafka's *In the Penal Colony* destroys the body on which it writes, then there must be a body prior to that inscription, stable and self-identical, subject to that sacrificial destruction. In a sense, for Foucault, as for Nietzsche, cultural values emerge as the result of an inscription on the body, understood as a medium, indeed, a blank page; in order for this inscription to signify, however, that medium must itself be destroyed – that is, fully transvaluated into a sublimated domain of values. Within the metaphorics of this notion of cultural values is the figure of history as a relentless writing instrument, and the body as the medium which must be destroyed and transfigured in order for "culture" to emerge.

By maintaining a body prior to its cultural inscription, Foucault appears to assume a materiality prior to signification and form. Because this distinction oper-ates as essential to the task of genealogy as he defines it, the distinction itself is precluded as an object of genealogical investigation. Occasionally in his analysis of Herculine, Foucault subscribes to a prediscursive multiplicity of bodily forces that break through the surface of the body to disrupt the regulating practices of cultural coherence imposed upon that body by a power regime, understood as a vicissitude of "history." If the presumption of some kind of precategorial source of disruption is refused, is it still possible to give a genealogical account of the demarcation of the body as such as a signifying practice? This demarcation is not initiated by a reified history or by a subject. This marking is the result of a diffuse and active structuring of the social field. This signifying practice effects a social space for and of the body within certain regulatory grids of intelligibility.

Mary Douglas' *Purity and Danger* suggests that the very contours of "the body" are established through markings that seek to establish specific codes of cultural coherence. Any discourse that establishes the boundaries of the body serves the purpose of instating and naturalizing certain taboos regarding the appropriate limits, postures, and modes of exchange that define what it is that constitutes bodies:

ideas about separating, purifying, demarcating and punishing transgressions have as their main function to impose system on an inherently untidy experience. It is only by exaggerating the difference between within and without, above and below, male and female, with and against, that a semblance of order is created.[22]

Although Douglas clearly subscribes to a structuralist distinction between an inherently unruly nature and an order imposed by cultural means, the "untidiness" to which she refers can be redescribed as a region of *cultural* unruliness and disorder. Assuming the inevitably binary structure of the nature/culture distinction, Douglas cannot point toward an alternative configuration of culture in which such distinctions become malleable or proliferate beyond the binary frame. Her analysis, however, provides a possible point of departure for understanding the relationship by which social taboos institute and maintain the boundaries of the body as such. Her analysis suggests that what constitutes the limit of the body is never merely material, but that the surface, the skin, is systematically signified by taboos and anticipated transgressions; indeed, the boundaries of the body become, within her analysis, the limits of the social *per se*. A poststructuralist appropriation of her view might well understand the boundaries of the body as the limits of the socially *hegemonic*. In a variety of cultures, she maintains, there are

> pollution powers which inhere in the structure of ideas itself and which punish a symbolic breaking of that which should be joined or joining of that which should be separate. It follows from this that pollution is a type of danger which is not likely to occur except where the lines of structure, cosmic or social, are clearly defined.
>
> A polluting person is always in the wrong. He [*sic*] has developed some wrong condition or simply crossed over some line which should not have been crossed and this displacement unleashes danger for someone...[23]

Regardless of the compelling metaphors of the spatial distinctions of inner and outer, they remain linguistic terms that facilitate and articulate a set of fantasies, feared and desired. "Inner" and "outer" make sense only with reference to a mediating boundary that strives for stability. And this stability, this coherence, is determined in large part by cultural orders that sanction the subject and compel its differentiation from the abject. Hence, "inner" and "outer" constitute a binary distinction that stabilizes and consolidates the coherent subject. When that subject is challenged, the meaning and necessity of the terms are subject to displacement. If the "inner world" no longer designates a *topos*, then the internal fixity of the self and, indeed, the internal locale of gender identity, become similarly suspect. The critical question is not *how* did that identity become *internalized?* as if internalization were a process or a mechanism that might be descriptively reconstructed. Rather, the question is: from what strategic position in public discourse and for what reasons has the trope of interiority and the disjunctive binary of inner/outer taken hold? In what language is "inner space" figured? What kind of figuration is it, and through what figure of the body is it signified? How does a body figure on its surface the very invisibility of its hidden depth?

## From interiority to gender performatives

In *Discipline and Punish* Foucault challenges the language of internalization as it operates in the service of the disciplinary regime of the subjection and subjectivation of criminals.[24] Although Foucault objected to what he understood to be the psycho-analytic belief in the "inner" truth of sex in *The History of Sexuality*, he turns to a criticism of the doctrine of internalization for separate purposes in the context of his history of criminology. In a sense, *Discipline and Punish* can be read as Foucault's effort to rewrite Nietzsche's doctrine of internalization in *On the Genealogy of Morals* on the model of *inscription*. In the context of prisoners, Foucault writes, the strategy has been not to enforce a repression of their desires, but to compel their bodies to signify the prohibitive law as their very essence, style, and necessity. That law is not literally internalized, but incorporated, with the consequence that bodies are pro-duced which signify that law on and through the body; there the law is manifest as the essence of their selves, the meaning of their soul, their conscience, the law of their desire. In effect, the law is at once fully manifest and fully latent, for it never appears as external to the bodies it subjects and subjectivates. Foucault writes:

> It would be wrong to say that the soul is an illusion, or an ideological effect. On the contrary, it exists, it has a reality, it is produced permanently *around, on, within*, the body by the functioning of a power that is exercised on those that are punished [my emphasis].[25]

The figure of the interior soul understood as "within" the body is signified through its inscription *on* the body, even though its primary mode of signification is through its very absence, its potent invisibility. The effect of a structuring inner space is produced through the signification of a body as a vital and sacred enclosure. The soul is precisely what the body lacks; hence, the body presents itself as a signifying lack. That lack which *is* the body signifies the soul as that which cannot show. In this sense, then, the soul is a surface signification that contests and displaces the inner/outer distinction itself, a figure of interior psychic space inscribed *on* the body as a social signification that perpetually renounces itself as such. In Foucault's terms, the soul is not imprisoned by or within the body, as some Christian imagery would suggest, but "the soul is the prison of the body."[26]

The redescription of intrapsychic processes in terms of the surface politics of the body implies a corollary redescription of gender as the disciplinary production of the figures of fantasy through the play of presence and absence on the body's surface, the construction of the gendered body through a series of exclusions and denials, signifying absences. But what determines the manifest and latent text of the body politic? What is the prohibitive law that generates the corporeal stylization of gender, the fantasied and fantastic figuration of the body? We have already con-sidered the incest taboo and the prior taboo against homosexuality as the generative moments of gender identity, the prohibitions that produce identity along the culturally intelligible grids of an idealized and compulsory heterosexuality. That disciplinary production of gender effects a false stabilization of gender in the interests of the heterosexual construction and regulation of sexuality within the reproductive domain. The construction of coherence conceals the gender discon-tinuities that run rampant within heterosexual, bisexual, and gay and lesbian contexts in which gender does not necessarily follow from sex, and desire, or sexuality generally, does not seem to follow from gender – indeed, where none of these dimensions of significant corporeality express or reflect one another. When the disorganization and disaggregation of the field of bodies disrupt the regulatory fiction of heterosexual coherence, it seems that the expressive model loses its descriptive force. That regulatory ideal is then exposed as a norm and a fiction that disguises itself as a developmental law regulating the sexual field that it purports to describe.

According to the understanding of identification as an enacted fantasy or incorporation, however, it is clear that coherence is desired, wished for, idealized, and that this idealization is an effect of a corporeal signification. In other words, acts, gestures, and desire produce the effect of an internal core or substance, but produce this *on the surface* of the body, through the play of signifying absences that suggest, but never reveal, the organizing principle of identity as a cause. Such acts, gestures, enactments, generally construed, are *performative* in the sense that the essence or identity that they otherwise purport to express are *fabrications* manufactured and sustained through corporeal signs and other discursive means. That the gendered body is performative suggests that it has no ontological status apart from the various acts which constitute its reality. This also suggests that if that reality is fabricated as an interior essence, that very interiority is an effect and function of a decidedly public and social discourse, the public regulation of fantasy through the surface politics of the body, the gender border control that differentiates inner from outer, and so institutes the "integrity" of the subject. In other words, acts and gestures, articulated and enacted desires create the illusion of an interior and organizing gender core, an illusion discursively maintained for the purposes of the regulation of sexuality within the obligatory frame of reproductive heterosexuality. If the "cause" of desire, gesture, and act can be localized within the "self" of the actor, then the political regulations and disciplinary practices which produce that ostensibly coherent gender are effectively displaced from view. The displacement of a political and discursive origin of gender identity onto a psychological "core" precludes an analysis of the political constitution of the gendered subject and its fabricated notions about the ineffable interiority of its sex or of its true identity.

If the inner truth of gender is a fabrication and if a true gender is a fantasy instituted and inscribed on the surface of bodies, then it seems that genders can be neither true nor false, but are only produced as the truth effects of a discourse of primary and stable identity. In *Mother Camp: Female Impersonators in America*, anthropologist Esther Newton suggests that the structure of impersonation reveals one of the key fabricating mechanisms through which the social construction of gender takes place.[27] I would suggest as well that drag fully subverts the distinction between inner and outer psychic space and effectively mocks both the expressive model of gender and the notion of a true gender identity. Newton writes:

> At its most complex, [drag] is a double inversion that says, "appearance is an illusion." Drag says [Newton's curious personification] "my 'outside' appearance is feminine, but my essence 'inside' [the body] is masculine." At the same time it symbolizes the opposite inversion; "my appearance 'outside' [my body, my gender] is masculine but my essence 'inside' [myself] is feminine."[28]

Both claims to truth contradict one another and so displace the entire enactment of gender significations from the discourse of truth and falsity.

The notion of an original or primary gender identity is often parodied within the cultural practices of drag, cross-dressing, and the sexual stylization of butch/femme identities. Within feminist theory, such parodic identities have been understood to be either degrading to women, in the case of drag and cross-dressing, or an uncritical appropriation of sex-role stereotyping from within the practice of heterosexuality, especially in the case of butch/femme lesbian identities. But the relation between the "imitation" and the "original" is, I think, more complicated than that critique generally allows. Moreover, it gives us a clue to the way in which the relationship between primary identification – that is, the original meanings accorded to gender – and subsequent gender experience might be reframed. The performance of drag plays upon the distinction between the anatomy of the performer and the gender that is being performed. But we are actually in the presence of three contingent dimensions of significant corporeality: anatomical sex, gender identity, and gender performance. If the anatomy of the performer is already distinct from the gender of the performer, and both of those are distinct from the gender of the performance, then the performance suggests a dissonance not only between sex and performance, but sex and gender, and gender and performance. As much as drag creates a unified picture of "woman" (what its critics often oppose), it also reveals the distinctness of those aspects of gendered experience which are falsely naturalized as a unity through the regulatory fiction of heterosexual coherence. *In imitating gender, drag implicitly reveals the imitative structure of gender itself – as well as its contingency*. Indeed, part of the pleasure, the giddiness of the performance is in the recognition of a radical contingency in the relation between sex and gender in the face of cultural configurations of causal unities that are regularly assumed to be natural and necessary. In the place of the law of heterosexual coherence, we see sex and gender denaturalized by means of a performance which avows their distinctness and dramatizes the cultural mechanism of their fabricated unity.

The notion of gender parody defended here does not assume that there is an original which such parodic identities imitate. Indeed, the parody is *of* the very notion of an original; just as the psychoanalytic notion of gender identification is constituted by a fantasy of a fantasy, the transfiguration of an Other who is always already a "figure" in that double sense, so gender parody reveals that the original identity after which gender fashions itself is an imitation without an origin. To be more precise, it is a production which, in effect – that is, in its effect – postures as an imitation. This perpetual displacement constitutes a fluidity of identities that suggests an openness to resignification and recontextualization; parodic proliferation deprives hegemonic culture and its critics of the claim to naturalized or essentialist gender identities. Although the gender meanings taken up in these parodic styles are clearly part of hegemonic, misogynist culture, they are nevertheless denaturalized and mobilized through their parodic recontextualization. As imitations which effectively displace the meaning of the original, they imitate the myth of originality itself. In the place of an original identification which serves as a determining cause, gender identity might be reconceived as a personal/cultural history of received meanings subject to a set of imitative practices which refer laterally to other imitations and which, jointly, construct the illusion of a primary and interior gendered self or parody the mechanism of that construction . . .

## Notes

1   See Michel Foucault, "Right of death and power over life," in *The History of Sexuality*, vol. 1: *An Introduction*, trans. Robert Hurley (New York: Vintage, 1980), originally published as *Histoire de la sexualité*. I *La volonté de savoir* (Paris: Gallimard, 1978). In that final chapter, Foucault discusses the relation between the juridical and productive law. His notion of the productivity of the law is clearly derived from Nietzsche, although not identical with Nietzsche's will-to-power. The use of Foucault's notion of productive power is not meant as a simple minded "application" of Foucault to gender issues.

2    References throughout this work to a subject before the law are extrapolations of Derrida's reading of Kafka's parable "Before the law," in *Kafka and the Contemporary Critical Perform-ance: Centenary Readings*, ed. Alan Udoff (Bloomington: Indiana University Press, 1987).

3    See Denise Riley, *Am I That Name? Feminism and the Category of "Women" in History* (New York: Macmillan, 1988).

4    For an interesting study of the *berdache* and multiple-gender arrangements in Native American cultures, see Walter L. Williams, *The Spirit and the Flesh: Sexual Diversity in American Indian Culture* (Boston: Beacon Press, 1988). See also Sherry B. Ortner and Harriet Whitehead, eds., *Sexual Meanings: The Cultural Construction of Sexuality* (New York: Cambridge University Press, 1981). For a politically sensitive and provocative analysis of the *berdache*, transsexuals, and the contingency of gender dichotomies, see Suzanne J. Kessler and Wendy McKenna, *Gender: An Ethnomethodological Approach* (Chicago: University of Chicago Press, 1978).

5    A great deal of feminist research has been conducted within the fields of biology and the history of science that assesses the political interests inherent in the various discriminatory procedures that establish the scientific basis for sex. See Ruth Hubbard and Marian Lowe (eds.) *Genes and Gender*, vols. 1 and 2 (New York: Gordian Press, 1978, 1979); the two issues on feminism and science of *Hypatia: A Journal of Feminist Philosophy*, vol. 2, no. 3, 1987, and vol. 3, no. 1, 1988, and especially The Biology and Gender Study Group, "The importance of feminist critique for contemporary cell biology" in this last issue; Sandra Harding, *The Science Question in Feminism* (Ithaca: Cornell University Press, 1986); Evelyn Fox-Keller, *Reflections on Gender and Science* (New Haven: Yale University Press, 1984); Donna Haraway, "In the beginning was the word: the genesis of biological theory," *Signs: Journal of Women in Culture and Society*, vol. 6, no. 3, 1981; Donna Haraway, *Primate Visions* (New York: Routledge, 1989); Sandra Harding and Jean F. O'Barr, *Sex and Scientific Inquiry* (Chicago: University of Chicago Press, 1987); Anne Fausto-Sterling, *Myths of Gender: Biological Theories About Women and Men* (New York: Norton, 1979).

6    Clearly Foucault's *History of Sexuality* offers one way to rethink the history of "sex" within a given modern Eurocentric context. For a more detailed consideration see Thomas Lacquer and Catherine Gallagher, eds., *The Making of the Modern Body: Sexuality and Society in the 19th Century* (Berkeley: University of California Press, 1987), originally published as an issue of *Representations*, no. 14, Spring 1986.

7    See my "Variations on sex and gender: Beauvoir, Wittig, Foucault," in *Feminism as Critique*, eds., Seyla Benhabib and Drucilla Cornell (Basil Blackwell, dist. by University of Minnesota Press, 1987).

8    Simone de Beauvoir, *The Second Sex*, trans. E. M. Parshley (New York: Vintage, 1973), p. 301.

9    Ibid., p. 38.

10    See my "Sex and gender in Beauvoir's *Second Sex*," *Yale French Studies, Simone de Beauvoir: Witness to a Century*, no. 72, Winter, 1986.

11    Note the extent to which phenomenological theories such as Sartre's, Merleau-Ponty's, and Beauvoir's tend to use the term *embodiment*. Drawn as it is from theological contexts, the term tends to figure "the" body as a mode of incarnation and, hence, to preserve the external and dualistic relationship between a signifying immateriality and the materiality of the body itself.

12    See Luce Irigaray, *The Sex Which Is Not One*, trans. Catherine Porter with Carolyn Burke (Ithaca: Cornell University Press, 1985), originally published as *Ce sexe qui n'en est pas un* (Paris: Éditions de Minuit, 1977).

13    See Joan Scott, "Gender as a useful category of historical analysis," in *Gender and the Politics of History* (New York: Columbia University Press, 1988), pp. 28–52, repr. from *American Historical Review*, vol. 91, no. 5, 1986.

14    Beauvoir, *The Second Sex*, p. xxvi.

15    See my "Sex and gender in Beauvoir's *Second Sex*."

16    The normative ideal of the body as both a "situation" and an "instrumentality" is embraced by both Beauvoir with respect to gender and Frantz Fanon with respect to race. Fanon concludes his analysis of colonization through recourse to the body as an instrument of freedom, where freedom is, in Cartesian fashion, equated with a consciousness capable of doubt: "O my body, make of me always a man who questions!" (Frantz Fanon, *Black Skin,*

*White Masks* [New York: Grove Press, 1967], p. 323, originally published as *Peau noire, masques blancs* [Paris: Éditions de Seuil, 1952]).

17  The radical ontological disjunction in Sartre between consciousness and the body is part of the Cartesian inheritance of his philosophy. Significantly, it is Descartes' distinction that Hegel implicitly interrogates at the outset of the "Master – slave" section of *The Phenomenology of Spirit*. Beauvoir's analysis of the masculine Subject and the feminine Other is clearly situated in Hegel's dialectic and in the Sartrian reformulation of that dialectic in the section on sadism and masochism in *Being and Nothingness*. Critical of the very possibility of a "synthesis" of consciousness and the body, Sartre effectively returns to the Cartesian problematic that Hegel sought to overcome. Beauvoir insists that the body can be the instrument and situation of freedom and that sex can be the occasion for a gender that is not a reification, but a modality of freedom. At first this appears to be a synthesis of body and consciousness, where consciousness is understood as the condition of freedom. The question that remains, however, is whether this synthesis requires and maintains the ontological distinction between body and mind of which it is composed and, by association, the hierarchy of mind over body and of masculine over feminine.

18  See Elizabeth V. Spelman, "Woman as body: ancient and contemporary views," *Feminist Studies*, vol. 8, no. 1, Spring, 1982.

19  Gayatri Spivak most pointedly elaborates this particular kind of binary explanation as a colonizing act of marginalization. In a critique of the "self-presence of the cognizing supra-historical self," which is characteristic of the epistemic imperialism of the philosophical *cogito*, she locates politics in the production of knowledge that creates and censors the margins that constitute, through exclusion, the contingent intelligibility of that subject's given knowledge-regime: "I call 'politics as such' the prohibition of marginality that is implicit in the production of any explanation. From that point of view, the choice of particular binary oppositions ... is no mere intellectual strategy. It is, in each case, the condition of the possibility for centralization (with appropriate apologies) and, correspondingly, marginalization" (Gayatri Chakravorty Spivak, "Explanation and culture: marginalia," in *In Other Worlds: Essays in Cultural Politics* [New York: Routledge, 1987], p. 113).

20  See the argument against "ranking oppressions" in Cherríe Moraga, "La Güera," in *This Bridge Called My Back: Writings of Radical Women of Color*, eds. Gloria Anzaldua and Cherríe Moraga (New York: Kitchen Table, Women of Color Press, 1982).

21  Michel Foucault, "Nietzsche, genealogy, history," in *Language, Counter-Memory, Practice: Selected Essays and Interviews by Michel Foucault*, trans. Donald F. Bouchard and Sherry Simon, ed. Donald F. Bouchard (Ithaca: Cornell University Press, 1977), p. 148. References in the text are to this essay.

22  Mary Douglas, *Purity and Danger* (London, Boston, and Henley: Routledge and Kegan Paul, 1969), p. 4.

23  Ibid., p. 113.

24  Parts of the following discussion were published in two different contexts, in my "Gender trouble, feminist theory, and psychoanalytic discourse," in *Feminism/Postmodernism*, ed. Linda J. Nicholson (New York: Routledge, 1989) and "Performative acts and gender constitution: an essay in phenomenology and feminist theory," *Theatre Journal*, vol. 20, no. 3, Winter 1988.

25  Michel Foucault, *Discipline and Punish: the Birth of the Prison*, trans. Alan Sheridan (New York: Vintage, 1979), p. 29.

26  Ibid., p. 30.

27  See the chapter "Role models" in Esther Newton, *Mother Camp: Female Impersonators in America* (Chicago: University of Chicago Press, 1972).

28  Ibid., p. 103.

# 3
# Power, Practice, and the Body

## "Material Girl":
## The Effacements of Postmodern Culture*

*Susan Bordo*

### Plasticity as postmodern paradigm

In a culture in which organ transplants, life-extension machinery, microsurgery, and artificial organs have entered everyday medicine, we seem on the verge of practical realization of the seventeenth-century imagination of body as machine. But if we have technically and technologically realized that conception, it can also be argued that metaphysically we have deconstructed it. In the early modern era, machine imagery helped to articulate a totally determined human body whose basic functionings the human being was helpless to alter. The then-dominant metaphors for this body – clocks, watches, collections of springs – imagined a system that is set, wound up, whether by nature or by God the watchmaker, ticking away in a predictable, orderly manner, regulated by laws over which the human being has no control. Understanding the system, we can help it to perform efficiently, and we can intervene when it malfunctions. But we cannot radically alter its configuration.

Pursuing this modern, determinist fantasy to its limits, fed by the currents of consumer capitalism, modern ideologies of the self, and their crystallization in the dominance of United States mass culture, Western science and technology have now arrived, paradoxically but predictably (for it was an element, though submerged and illicit, in the mechanist conception all along), at a new, postmodern imagination of human freedom from bodily determination. Gradually and surely, a technology that was first aimed at the replacement of malfunctioning parts has generated an industry and an ideology fueled by fantasies of rearranging, transforming, and correcting, an ideology of limitless improvement and change, defying the historicity, the mortality, and, indeed, the very materiality of the body. In place of that materiality, we now have what I will call cultural plastic. In place of God the watchmaker, we now have ourselves, the master sculptors of that plastic. This disdain for material limits and the concomitant intoxication with freedom, change, and self-determination are enacted not only on the level of the contemporary technology of the body but in a wide range of contexts, including much of contemporary discourse on the body, both popular and academic. In this essay, looking at a variety of these discursive contexts, I attempt to describe key elements of this paradigm of plasticity and expose

* Susan Bordo, "Material girl," *Unbearable Weight* (Berkeley: University of California Press, 1993), pp. 245–75.

some of its effacements – the material and social realities it denies or renders invisible.

## Plastic bodies

"Create a masterpiece, sculpt your body into a work of art," urges *Fit* magazine. "You visualize what you want to look like, and then you create that form." "The challenge presents itself: to rearrange things."[1] The precision technology of body-sculpting, once the secret of the Arnold Schwarzeneggers and Rachel McLishes of the professional body-building world, has now become available to anyone who can afford the price of membership in a gym. "I now look at bodies," says John Travolta, after training for the movie *Staying Alive*, "almost like pieces of clay that can be molded."[2] On the medical front, plastic surgery, whose repeated and purely cosmetic employment has been legitimated by Michael Jackson, Cher, and others, has become a fabulously expanding industry, extending its domain from nose jobs, face lifts, tummy tucks, and breast augmentations to collagen-plumped lips and liposuction-shaped ankles, calves, and buttocks. In 1989, 681,000 procedures were done, up 80 percent over 1981; over half of these were performed on patients between the ages of eighteen and thirty-five.[3] The trendy *Details* magazine describes "surgical stretching, tucking and sucking" as "another fabulous [fashion] accessory" and invites readers to share their cosmetic-surgery experiences in their monthly column "Knife-styles of the Rich and Famous." In that column, the transportation of fat from one part of the body to another is described as breezily as changing hats might be:

> Dr Brown is an artist. He doesn't just pull and tuck and forget about you...He did liposuction on my neck, did the nose job and tightened up my forehead to give it a better line. Then he took some fat from the side of my waist and injected it into my hands. It goes in as a lump, and then he smooths it out with his hands to where it looks good. I'll tell you something, the nose and neck made a big change, but nothing in comparison to how fabulous my hands look. The fat just smoothed out all the lines, the veins don't stick up anymore, the skin actually looks soft and great. [But] you have to be careful not to bang your hands.[4]

Popular culture does not apply any brakes to these fantasies of rearrangement and self-transformation. Rather, we are constantly told that we can "choose" our own bodies. "The proper diet, the right amount of exercise and you can have, pretty much, any body you desire," claims Evian. Of course, the rhetoric of choice and self-determination and the breezy analogies comparing cosmetic surgery to fashion accessorizing are deeply mystifying. They efface, not only the inequalities of privilege, money, and time that prohibit most people from indulging in these practices, but the desperation that characterizes the lives of those who do. "I will do anything, *anything*, to make myself look and feel better," says Tina Lizardi (whose "Knife-styles" experience I quoted from above). Medical science has now designated a new category of "polysurgical addicts" (or, in more casual references, "scalpel slaves") who return for operation after operation, in perpetual quest of the elusive yet ruthlessly normalizing goal, the "perfect" body.[5] The dark underside of the practices of body transformation and rearrangement reveals botched and sometimes fatal operations, exercise addictions, eating disorders. And of course, despite the claims of the Evian ad, one cannot have *any* body that one wants – for not every body will *do*. The very advertisements whose copy speaks of choice and self-determination visually legislate the effacement of individual and cultural difference and circumscribe our choices.

That we are surrounded by homogenizing and normalizing images – images whose content is far from arbitrary, but is instead suffused with the dominance of gendered, racial, class, and other cultural iconography – seems so obvious as to be almost embarrassing to be arguing here. Yet contemporary understandings of the behaviors I have been describing not only construct the situation very differently but do so in terms that preempt precisely such a critique of cultural imagery. Moreover, they reproduce, on the level of discourse and interpretation, the same conditions that postmodern bodies enact on the level of cultural practice: a construction of life as plastic possibility and weightless choice, undetermined by history, social location, or even individual biography. A 1988 *Donahue* show offers my first illustration.

The show's focus was a series of television commercials for DuraSoft colored contact lenses. In these commercials as they were originally aired, a woman was shown in a dreamlike, romantic fantasy – for example, parachuting slowly and gracefully from the heavens. The male voiceover then described the woman in soft, lush terms: "If I believed in angels, I'd say that's what she was – an angel, dropped from the sky like an answer to a prayer, with eyes as brown as bark." [Significant pause] "No...I *don't think so*." [At this point, the tape would be rewound to return us to:] "With eyes as violet as the colors of a child's imagination." The commercial concludes: "DuraSoft colored contact lenses. Get brown eyes a second look."

The question posed by Phil Donahue: is this ad racist? Donahue clearly thought there was controversy to be stirred up here, for he stocked his audience full of women of color and white women to discuss the implications of the ad. But Donahue was apparently living in a different decade from most of his audience, who repeatedly declared that there was nothing "wrong" with the ad, and everything "wrong" with any inclinations to "make it a political question." Here are some comments taken from the transcript of the show:

"Why does it have to be a political question? I mean, people perm their hair. It's just because they like the way it looks. It's not something sociological. Maybe black women like the way they look with green contacts. It's to be more attractive. It's not something that makes them – I mean, why do punk rockers have purple hair? Because they feel it makes them feel better." [white woman]

"What's the fuss? When I put on my blue lenses, it makes me feel good. It makes me feel sexy, different, the other woman, so to speak, which is like fun." [black woman]

"I perm my hair, you're wearing make-up, what's the difference?" [white woman]

"I want to be versatile...having different looks, being able to change from one look to the other." [black female model]

"We all do the same thing, when we're feeling good we wear new makeup, hairstyles, we buy new clothes. So now it's contact lenses. What difference does it make?" [white woman]

"It goes both ways...Bo Derek puts her hair in cornstalks, or corn...or whatever that thing is called. White women try to get tan." [white woman]

"She's not trying to be white, she's trying to be different." [about a black woman with blue contact lenses]

"It's fashion, women are never happy with themselves."

"I put them in as toys, just for fun, change. Nothing too serious, and I really enjoy them." [black woman][6]

Some points to note here: first, putting on makeup, styling hair, and so forth are conceived of only as free play, fun, a matter of creative expression. This they surely are. But they are also experienced by many women as necessary before they will show themselves to the world, even on a quick trip to the corner mailbox. The one comment that hints at women's (by now depressingly well documented) dissatisfaction with their appearance trivializes that dissatisfaction and puts it beyond the pale of cultural critique: "It's fashion." What she means is, "It's *only* fashion," whose whimsical and politically neutral vicissitudes supply endless amusement for women's eternally superficial values. ("Women are never happy with themselves.") If we are never happy with ourselves, it is implied, that is due to our female nature, not to be taken too seriously or made into a political question. Second, the content of fashion, the specific ideals that women are drawn to embody (ideals that vary historically, racially, and along class and other lines) are seen as arbitrary, without meaning; interpretation is neither required nor even appropriate. Rather, all motivation and value come from the interest and allure – the "sexiness" – of change and difference itself. Blue contact lenses for a black woman, it is admitted, make her "other" ("the other woman"). But that "other" is not a racial or cultural "other"; she is sexy because of the piquancy, the novelty, the erotics of putting on a different self. *Any* different self would do, it is implied.

Closely connected to this is the construction of *all* cosmetic changes as the same: perms for the white women, corn rows on Bo Derek, tanning, makeup, changing hairstyles, blue contacts for black women – all are seen as having equal political valence (which is to say, *no* political valence) and the same cultural meaning (which is to say, *no* political meaning) in the heterogeneous yet undifferentiated context of the things "all" women do "to be more attractive." The one woman in the audience who offered a different construction of this behavior, who insisted that the styles we aspire to do not simply reflect the free play of fashion or female nature – who went so far, indeed, as to claim that we "are brainwashed to think blond hair and blue eyes is the most beautiful of all," was regarded with hostile silence. Then, a few moments later, someone challenged: "Is there anything *wrong* with blue eyes and blond hair?" The audience enthusiastically applauded this defender of democratic values.

This "conversation" – a paradigmatically postmodern conversation, as I will argue shortly – effaces the same general elements as the rhetoric of body transformation discussed earlier. First, it effaces the inequalities of social position and the historical origins which, for example, render Bo Derek's corn rows and black women's hair-straightening utterly noncommensurate. On the one hand, we have Bo Derek's privilege, not only as so unimpeachably white as to permit an exotic touch of "otherness" with no danger of racial contamination, but her trend-setting position as a famous movie star. Contrasting to this, and mediating a black woman's "choice" to straighten her hair, is a cultural history of racist body-discriminations such as the nineteenth-century comb-test, which allowed admission to churches and clubs only to those blacks who could pass through their hair without snagging a fine-tooth comb hanging outside the door. (A variety of comparable tests – the pine-slab test, the brown bag test – determined whether one's skin was adequately light to pass muster.)[7]

Second, and following from these historical practices, there is a disciplinary reality that is effaced in the construction of all self-transformation as equally arbitrary, all variants of the same trivial game, without differing cultural valence. I use the term *disciplinary* here in the Foucauldian sense, as pointing to practices that do not merely transform but *normalize* the subject. That is, to repeat a point made earlier, not every body will do. A 1989 poll of *Essence* magazine readers revealed that 68 percent of those who responded wear their hair straightened chemically or by hot comb.[8] "Just for fun"? For the kick of being "different"? When we look at the pursuit of beauty as a normalizing discipline, it becomes clear that not all body transformations are the same. The general tyranny of fashion – perpetual, elusive, and instructing the female body in a pedagogy of personal inadequacy and lack – is a powerful discipline for the normalization of *all* women in this culture. But even as we are all normalized to the requirements of appropriate feminine insecurity and preoccupation with appearance, more specific requirements emerge in different cultural and historical contexts, and for different groups. When Bo Derek put her hair in corn rows, she was engaging in normalizing feminine practice. But when Oprah Winfrey admitted on her show that all her life she has desperately longed to have "hair that swings from side to side" when she shakes her head, she revealed the power of racial as well as gender normalization, normalization not only to "femininity," but to the Caucasian standards of beauty that still dominate on television, in movies, in popular magazines. (When I was a child, I felt the same way about my thick, then curly, "Jewish" hair as Oprah did about hers.) Neither Oprah nor the *Essence* readers nor the many Jewish women (myself included) who ironed their hair in the 1960s have creatively or playfully invented themselves here.

DuraSoft knows this, even if Donahue's audience does not. Since the campaign first began, the company has replaced the original, upfront magazine advertisement with a more euphemistic variant, from which the word *brown* has been tastefully effaced. (In case it has become too subtle for the average reader, the model now is black – although it should be noted that DuraSoft's failure to appreciate brown eyes also renders the eyes of most of the world not worth "a second look".) In the television commercial, a comparable "brownwash" was effected; here "eyes as brown as..." was retained, but the derogatory nouns – "brown as boots," "brown as bark" – were eliminated. The announcer simply was left speechless: "eyes as brown as... brown as..." and then, presumably having been unable to come up with an enticing simile, shifted to "violet." As in the expurgated magazine ad, the television commercial ended: "Get *your* eyes a second look."

When I showed my students these ads, many of them were as dismissive as the *Donahue* audience, convinced that I was once again turning innocent images and practices into political issues. I persisted: if racial standards of beauty are not at work here, then why no brown contacts for blue-eyed people? A month later, two of my students triumphantly produced a DuraSoft ad for brown contacts, appearing in *Essence* magazine, and with an advertising campaign directed solely at *already* brown-eyed consumers, offering the promise *not* of "getting blue eyes a second look" by becoming excitingly darker, but of "subtly enhancing" dark eyes, by making them *lighter* brown. The creators of the DuraSoft campaign clearly know that not all differences are the same in our culture, and they continue, albeit in ever more mystified form, to exploit and perpetuate that fact.[9]

## Plastic discourse

The *Donahue* DuraSoft show (indeed, any talk show) provides a perfect example of what we might call a postmodern conversation. All sense of history and all ability (or inclination) to sustain cultural criticism, to make the distinctions and discriminations that would permit such criticism, have disappeared. Rather, in this conversation, "anything goes" – and any positioned social critique (for example, the woman who, speaking clearly from consciousness of racial oppression, insisted that the attraction of blond hair and blue eyes has a cultural meaning significantly different from that of purple hair) is immediately destabilized. Instead of distinctions, endless *differences* reign – an undifferentiated pastiche of differences, a grab bag in which no items are assigned any more importance or centrality than any others. Television is, of course, the great teacher here, our prime modeler of plastic pluralism: if one *Donahue* show features a feminist talking about battered wives, the next show will feature mistreated husbands. Women who love too much, the sex habits of priests, disturbed children of psychiatrists, daughters who have no manners, male strippers, relatives who haven't spoken in ten years all have their day alongside incest, rape, and US foreign policy. All are given equal weight by the great leveler – the frame of the television screen.

This spectacle of difference defeats the ability to sustain coherent political critique. Everything is the same in its unvalenced difference. ("I perm my hair, you're wearing makeup, what's the difference?") Particulars reign, and generality – which collects, organizes, and prioritizes, suspending attention to particularity in the interests of connection, emphasis, and criticism – is suspect. So, whenever some critically charged generalization was suggested on Donahue's DuraSoft show, someone else would invariably offer a counterexample – I have blue eyes, and I'm a black woman; Bo Derek wears corn rows – to fragment the critique. What is remarkable is that people accept these examples as *refutations* of social critique. They almost invariably back down, utterly confused as to how to maintain their critical generalization in the face of the destabilizing example. Sometimes they qualify, claiming they meant some people, not all. But of course they meant neither all nor some. They meant *most* – that is, they were trying to make a claim about social or cultural *patterns* – and that is a stance that is increasingly difficult to sustain in a postmodern context, where we are surrounded by endlessly displaced images and are given no orienting context in which to make discriminations.

Those who insist on an orienting context (and who therefore do not permit particulars to reign in all their absolute "difference") are seen as "totalizing," that is, as constructing a falsely coherent and morally coercive universe that marginalizes and effaces the experiences and values of others. ("Is there anything *wrong* with blue eyes and blond hair?") As someone who is frequently interviewed by local television and newspaper reporters, I have often found my feminist arguments framed in this way, as they were in an article on breast-augmentation surgery. After several pages of "expert" recommendations from plastic surgeons, my cautions about the politics of female body transformation (none of them critical of individuals contemplating plastic surgery, all of them of a cultural nature) were briefly quoted by the reporter, who then went on to end the piece with a comment on *my* critique – from the director of communications for the American Society of Plastic and Reconstructive Surgery:

> Those not considering plastic surgery shouldn't be too critical of those who do. It's the hardest thing for people to understand. What's important is if it's a problem to that person. We're all different, but we all want to look better. We're just different in what extent we'll go to. But none of us can say we don't want to look the best we can.[10]

With this tolerant, egalitarian stroke, the media liaison of the most powerful plastic surgery lobby in the country presents herself as the protector of "difference" against the homogenizing and stifling regime of the feminist dictator.

Academics do not usually like to think of themselves as embodying the values and preoccupations of popular culture on the plane of high theory or intellectual discourse. We prefer to see ourselves as the demystifyers of popular discourse, bringers-to-consciousness-and-clarity rather than unconscious reproducers of culture. Despite what we would *like* to believe of ourselves, however, we are always within the society that we criticize, and never so strikingly as at the present postmodern moment. All the elements of what I have here called postmodern conversation – intoxication with individual choice and creative *jouissance*, delight with the piquancy of particularity and mistrust of pattern and seeming coherence, celebration of "difference" along with an absence of critical perspective differentiating and weighing "differences," suspicion of the totalitarian nature of generalization along with a rush to protect difference from its homogenizing abuses – have become recognizable and familiar in much of contemporary intellectual discourse. Within this theoretically self-conscious universe, moreover, these elements are not merely embodied (as in the *Donahue* show's DuraSoft conversation) but explicitly thematized and *celebrated*, as inaugurating new constructions of the self, no longer caught in the mythology of the unified subject, embracing of multiplicity, challenging the dreary and moralizing generalizations about gender, race, and so forth that have so preoccupied liberal and left humanism.

For this celebratory, academic postmodernism, it has become highly unfashionable – and "totalizing" – to talk about the grip of culture on the body. Such a perspective, it is argued, casts active and creative subjects as passive dupes of ideology; it gives too much to dominant ideology, imagining it as seamless and univocal, overlooking both the gaps which are continually allowing for the eruption of "difference" and the polysemous, unstable, open nature of all cultural texts. To talk about the grip of culture on the body (as, for example, in "old" feminist discourse about the objectification and sexualization of the female body) is to fail to acknowledge, as one theorist put it, "the cultural work by which nomadic, fragmented, active subjects confound dominant discourse."[11]

So, for example, contemporary culture critic John Fiske is harshly critical of what he describes as the view of television as a "dominating monster" with "homogenizing power" over the perceptions of viewers. Such a view, he argues, imagines the audience as "powerless and undiscriminating" and overlooks the fact that:

> Pleasure results from a particular relationship between meanings and power . . . There is no pleasure in being a "cultural dope." . . . Pleasure results from the production of meanings of the world and of self that are felt to serve the interests of the reader rather than those of the dominant. The subordinate may be disempowered, but they are not powerless. There is a power in resisting power, there is a power in maintaining one's social identity in opposition to that proposed by the dominant ideology, there is a power in asserting one's own subcultural values against the dominant ones. There is, in short, a power in being different.[12]

Fiske then goes on to produce numerous examples of how *Dallas*, *Hart to Hart*, and so forth have been read (or so he argues) by various subcultures to make their own "socially pertinent" and empowering meanings out of "the semiotic resources provided by television."

Note, in Fiske's insistent, repetitive invocation of the category of power, a characteristically postmodern flattening of the terrain of power relations, a lack of differentiation between, for example, the power involved in creative *reading* in the isolation of one's own home and the power held by those who control the material production of television shows, or the power involved in public protest and action against the conditions of that production and the power of the dominant meanings – for instance, racist and sexist images and messages – therein produced. For Fiske, of course, there *are* no such dominant meanings, that is, no element whose ability to grip the imagination of the viewer is greater than the viewer's ability to "just say no" through resistant reading of the text. That ethnic and subcultural meaning *may* be wrested from *Dallas* and *Hart to Hart* becomes for Fiske proof that dominating images and messages are only in the minds of those totalitarian critics who would condescendingly "rescue" the disempowered from those forces that are in fact the very medium of their creative freedom and resistance ("the semiotic resources of television").

Fiske's conception of power – a terrain without hills and valleys, where all forces have become "resources" – reflects a very common postmodern misappropriation of Foucault. Fiske conceives of power as in the *possession* of individuals or groups, something they "have" – a conception Foucault takes great pains to criticize – rather than (as in Foucault's reconstruction) a dynamic of noncentralized forces, its dominant historical forms attaining their hegemony, not from magisterial design or decree, but through multiple "processes, of different origin and scattered location," regulating and normalizing the most intimate and minute elements of the construction of time, space, desire, embodiment.[13] This conception of power does *not* entail that there are no dominant positions, social structures, or ideologies emerging from the play of forces; the fact that power is not held by any *one* does not mean that it is equally held by *all*. It is in fact not "held" at all; rather, people and groups are positioned differentially within it. This model is particularly useful for the analysis of male dominance and female subordination, so much of which is reproduced "voluntarily," through our self-normalization to everyday habits of masculinity and femininity. Within such a model, one can acknowledge that women may indeed contribute to the perpetuation of female subordination (for example, by embracing, taking pleasure in, and even feeling empowered by the cultural objectification and sexualization of the female body) without this entailing that they have power in the production and reproduction of sexist culture.

Foucault does insist on the *instability* of modern power relations – that is, he emphasizes that resistance is perpetual and unpredictable, and hegemony precarious. This notion is transformed by Fiske (perhaps under the influence of a more deconstructionist brand of postmodernism) into a notion of resistance as *jouissance*, a creative and pleasurable eruption of cultural "difference" through the "seams" of the text. What this celebration of creative reading as resistance effaces is the arduous and frequently frustrated historical struggle that is required for the subordinated to articulate and assert the value of their "difference" in the face of dominant meanings – meanings which often offer a pedagogy directed at the reinforcement of feelings of inferiority, marginality, ugliness. During the early fifties, when *Brown v. the Board of Education* was wending its way through the courts, as a demonstration of the destructive psychological effects of segregation black children were asked to look at *two baby dolls*, identical in all respects except color. The children were asked a series of questions: which is the nice doll? Which is the bad doll? Which doll would you like to play with? The majority of black children, Kenneth Clark reports, attributed the positive characteristics to the white doll, the negative characteristics to the black. When Clark asked one final question, "Which doll is like you?" they looked at him, he says, "as though he were the devil himself" for putting them in that predicament, for forcing them to face the inexorable and hideous logical implications of their situation. Northern children often ran out of the room; southern children tended to answer the question in shamed embarrassment. Clark recalls one little boy who laughed, "Who am I like? That doll! It's a nigger and I'm a nigger!"[14]

Failing to acknowledge the psychological and cultural potency of normalizing imagery can be just as effective in effacing people's experiences of racial oppression as lack of attentiveness to cultural and ethnic differences – a fact postmodern critics sometimes seem to forget. This is not to deny what Fiske calls "the power of being different"; it is, rather, to insist that it is won through ongoing political *struggle* rather than through an act of creative interpretation. Here, once again, although many postmodern academics may claim Foucault as their guiding light, they differ from him in significant and revealing ways. For Foucault, the metaphorical terrain of resistance is explicitly that of the "battle"; the "points of confrontation" may be "innumerable" and "instable," but they involve a serious, often deadly struggle of embodied (that is, historically situated and shaped) forces.[15] Barbara Kruger exemplifies this conception of resistance in a poster that represents the contemporary contest over reproductive control through the metaphor of the body as battleground. Some progressive developers of children's toys have self-consciously entered into struggle with racial and other forms of normalization. The Kenya Doll comes in three different skin tones ("so your girl is bound to feel pretty and proud") and attempts to create a future in which hair-straightening *will* be merely one decorative option among others. Such products, to my mind, are potentially effective "sites of resistance" precisely because they recognize that the body is a battleground whose self-determination has to be fought for.

The metaphor of the body as battleground, rather than postmodern playground, captures, as well, the *practical* difficulties involved in the political struggle to empower "difference." *Essence* magazine has consciously and strenuously tried to promote diverse images of black strength, beauty, and self-acceptance. Beauty features celebrate the glory of black skin and lush lips; other departments feature interviews with accomplished black women writers, activists, teachers, many of whom display styles of body and dress that challenge the hegemony of white Anglo-Saxon standards. The magazine's advertisers, however, continually play upon and perpetuate consumers' feelings of inadequacy and insecurity over the racial characteristics of their bodies. They insist that, in order to be beautiful, hair must be straightened and eyes lightened; they almost always employ models with fair skin, Anglo-Saxon features, and "hair that moves," insuring association of their products with fantasies of becoming what the white culture most prizes and rewards.

This ongoing battle over the black woman's body and the power of its "differences" ("differences" which actual black women embody to widely varying degrees, of course) is made manifest in the twentieth-anniversary issue, where a feature celebrating "The beauty of black" faced an advertisement visually legislating virtually the opposite (and offering, significantly, "escape"). This invitation to cognitive dissonance reveals what *Essence* must grapple with, in every issue, as it tries to keep its message of African American self-acceptance clear and dominant, while submitting to economic necessities on which its survival depends. Let me make it clear here that such self-acceptance, not the reverse tyranny that constructs light-skinned and Anglo-featured African Americans as "not black enough," is the message *Essence* is trying to convey, against a culture that *denies* "the beauty of black" at every turn. This terrain, clearly, is not a playground but a mine-field that constantly threatens to deconstruct "difference" *literally* and not merely literarily.

## "Material girl": Madonna as postmodern heroine

John Fiske's conception of "difference," in the section quoted above, at least imagines resistance as challenging specifiable historical forms of dominance. Women, he argues, connect with subversive "feminine" values leaking through the patriarchal plot of soap operas; blacks laugh to themselves at the glossy, materialist-cowboy culture of *Dallas*. Such examples suggest a resistance directed against *particular* historical forms of power and subjectivity. For some postmodern theorists, however, resistance is imagined as the refusal to embody *any* positioned subjectivity at all; what is celebrated is continual creative escape from location, containment, and definition. So, as Susan Rubin Suleiman advises, we must move beyond the valorization of historically suppressed values (for example, those values that have been culturally constructed as belonging to an inferior, female domain and generally expunged from Western science, philosophy, and religion) and toward "endless complication" and a "dizzying accumulation of narratives."[16] She appreciatively (and perhaps misleadingly) invokes Derrida's metaphor of "incalculable choreographies"[17] to capture the dancing, elusive, continually changing subjectivity that she envisions, a subjectivity without gender, without history, without location. From this perspective, the truly resistant female body is, not the body that wages war on feminine sexualization and objectification, but the body that, as Cathy Schwichtenberg has put it, "uses simulation strategically in ways that challenge the stable notion of gender as the edifice of sexual difference . . . [in] an erotic politics in which the female body can be refashioned in the flux of identities that speak in plural styles."[18] For this erotic politics, the new postmodern heroine is Madonna.

This celebration of Madonna as postmodern heroine does not mark the first time Madonna has been portrayed as a subversive culture-figure. Until the early 1990s, however, Madonna's resistance has been interpreted along "body as battleground" lines, as deriving from her refusal to allow herself to be constructed as a passive object of patriarchal desire. John Fiske, for example, argues that this was a large part of Madonna's original appeal to her "wanna-bes" – those hordes of middle-class pre-teeners who mimicked Madonna's moves and costumes. For the "wanna-bes," Madonna demonstrated the possibility of a female heterosexuality that was independent of patriarchal control, a sexuality that defied rather than rejected the male gaze, teasing it with her own gaze, deliberately trashy and vulgar, challenging anyone to call her a whore, and ultimately not giving a damn how she might be judged. Madonna's rebellious sexuality, in this reading, offered itself, not as coming into being through the look of the "other," but as self-defining and in love with, happy with itself – an attitude that is rather difficult for women to achieve in this culture and that helps to explain, as Fiske argues, her enormous appeal for pre-teen girls.[19] "I like the way she handles herself, sort of take it or leave it; she's sexy but she doesn't need men . . . she's kind of there all by herself," says one. "She gives us ideas. It's really women's lib, not being afraid of what guys think," says another.[20]

Madonna herself, significantly and unlike most sex symbols, has never advertised herself as disdainful of feminism or constructed feminists as man-haters. Rather, in a 1985 *Time* interview, she suggests that her lack of inhibition in "being herself" and her "luxuriant" expression of "strong" sexuality constitute her brand of feminist celebration.[21] Some feminist theorists would agree. Molly Hite, for example, argues that "asserting female desire in a culture in which female sexuality is viewed as so inextricably conjoined with passivity" is "transgressive":

Implied in this strategy is the old paradox of the speaking statue, the created thing that magically begins to create, for when a woman writes – self-consciously from her muted position as a woman and not as an honorary man – about female desire, female sexuality, female sensuous experience generally, her performance has the effect of giving voice to pure corporeality, of turning a product of the dominant meaning-system into a producer of meanings. A woman, conventionally identified with her body, writes about that identification, and as a consequence, feminity – silent and inert by definition – erupts into patriarchy as an impossible discourse.[22]

Not all feminists would agree with this, of course. For the sake of the contrast I want to draw here, however, let us grant it, and note, as well, that an argument similar to Fiske's can be made concerning Madonna's refusal to be obedient to dominant and normalizing standards of female *beauty*. I am now talking, of course, about Madonna in her more fleshy days. In those days, Madonna saw herself as willfully out of step with the times. "Back in the fifties," she says in the *Time* interview, "women weren't ashamed of their bodies." (The fact that she is dead wrong is not relevant here.) Identifying herself with her construction of that time and what she calls its lack of "suppression" of femininity, she looks down her nose at the "androgynous" clothes of our own time and speaks warmly of her own stomach, "not really flat" but "round and the skin is smooth and I like it." Contrasting herself to anorectics, whom she sees as self-denying and self-hating, completely in the thrall of externally imposed standards of worthiness, Madonna (as she saw herself) stood for self-definition through the assertion of her own (traditionally "female" and now anachronistic) body-type.

Of course, this is no longer Madonna's body type. Shortly after her 1987 marriage to Sean Penn she began a strenuous reducing and exercise program, now runs several miles a day, lifts weights, and has developed, in obedience to dominant contemporary norms, a tight, slender, muscular body. Why did she decide to shape up? "I didn't have a flat stomach anymore," she has said. "I had become well-rounded." Please note the sharp about-face here, from pride to embarrassment. My goal here, however, is not to suggest that Madonna's formerly voluptuous body was a non-alienated, freely expressive body, a "natural" body. While the slender body is the current cultural ideal, the voluptuous female body is a cultural form, too (as are all bodies), and was a coercive ideal in the fifties. My point is that in terms of Madonna's own former lexicon of meanings – in which feminine voluptuousness and the choice to be round in a culture of the lean were clearly connected to spontaneity, self-definition, and defiance of the cultural gaze – the terms set by that gaze have now triumphed. Madonna has been normalized; more precisely, she has self-normalized. Her "wanna-bes" are following suit. Studies suggest that as many as 80 percent of nine-year-old suburban girls (the majority of whom are far from overweight) are making rigorous dieting and exercise the organizing discipline of their lives.[23] They do not require Madonna's example, of course, to believe that they must be thin to be acceptable. But Madonna clearly no longer provides a model of resistance or "difference" for them.

None of this "materiality" – that is, the obsessive body-praxis that regulates and disciplines Madonna's life and the lives of the young (and not so young) women who emulate her – makes its way into the representation of Madonna as postmodern heroine. In the terms of this representation (in both its popular and scholarly instantiations) Madonna is "in control of her image, not trapped by it"; the proof lies in her ironic and chameleon-like approach to the construction of her identity, her ability to "slip in and out of character at will," to defy definition, to keep them guessing.[24] In this coding of things, as in the fantasies of the polysurgical addict (and, as I argue elsewhere in this volume, the eating-disordered woman), *control and power*, words that are invoked over and over in discussions of Madonna, have become equivalent to *self-creating*. Madonna's new body has no material history; it conceals its continual struggle to maintain itself, it does not reveal its pain. (Significantly, Madonna's "self-exposé," the documentary *Truth or Dare*, does not include any scenes of Madonna's daily workouts.) It is merely another creative transformation of an ever-elusive subjectivity. "More dazzling and determined not to stop changing," as *Cosmopolitan* describes Madonna: "whether in looks or career, this multitalented dazzler will never be trapped in *any* mold!"[25] The plasticity of Madonna's subjectivity is emphasized again and again in the popular press, particularly by Madonna herself. It is how she tells the story of her "power" in the industry: "In pop music, generally, people have one image. You get pigeonholed. I'm lucky enough to be able to change and still be accepted...play a part, change characters, looks, attitudes."[26]

Madonna claims that her creative work, too, is meant to escape definition. "Everything I do is meant to have several meanings, to be ambiguous," she says. She resists, however (in true postmodern fashion), the attribution of serious artistic intent; rather (as she told *Cosmo*), she favors irony and ambiguity, "to entertain myself" and (as she told *Vanity Fair*) out of "rebelliousness and a desire to fuck with people."[27] It is the postmodern nature of her music and videos that has most entranced academic critics, whose accolades reproduce in highly theoretical language the notions emphasized in the popular press. Susan McClary writes:

> Madonna's art itself repeatedly deconstructs the traditional notion of the unified subject with finite ego boundaries. Her pieces explore...various ways of constituting identities that refuse stability, that remain fluid, that resist definition. This tendency in her work has become increasingly pronounced; for instance, in her recent controversial video "Express yourself"...she slips in and out of every subject position offered within the video's narrative context...refusing more than ever to deliver the security of a clear, unambiguous message or an "authentic" self.[28]

Later in the same piece, McClary describes "Open your heart to me," which features Madonna as a porn star in a peep show, as creating "an image of open-ended *jouissance* – an erotic energy that continually escapes containment."[29] Now, many feminist viewers may find this particular video quite disturbing, for a number of reasons. First, unlike many of Madonna's older videos, "Open your heart to me" does not visually emphasize Madonna's subjectivity or desire – as "Lucky star," for example, did through frequent shots of Madonna's face and eyes, flirting with and controlling the reactions of the viewer. Rather, "Open your heart to me" places the viewer in the position of the voyeur by presenting Madonna's body as object, now perfectly taut and tightly managed for display. To be sure, we do not identify with the slimy men, drooling over Madonna's performance, who are depicted in the video; but, as E. Ann Kaplan has pointed out, the way men view women *in* the filmic world is only one species of objectifying gaze. There is also the viewer's gaze, which may be encouraged by the director to be either more or less objectifying.[30] In "Open your heart to me," as in virtually all rock videos, the female body is offered to the viewer purely as a spectacle, an object of sight, a visual commodity to be consumed. Madonna's weight loss and dazzling shaping-up job make the spectacle of her body all the more compelling; we are riveted to her body, fascinated by it. Many men and women may experience the primary reality of the video as the elicitation of desire *for* that perfect body; women, however, may also be gripped by the desire (very likely impossible to achieve) to *become* that perfect body.

These elements can be effaced, of course, by a deliberate abstraction of the video from the cultural context in which it is historically embedded – the continuing containment, sexualization, and objectification of the female body – and in which the viewer is implicated as well and instead treating the video as a purely formal text. Taken as such, "Open your heart to me" presents itself as what E. Ann Kaplan calls a "postmodern video": it refuses to "take a clear position vis-à-vis its images" and similarly refuses a "clear position for the spectator within the filmic world . . . leaving him/her decentered, confused."[31] McClary's reading of "Open your heart to me" emphasizes precisely these postmodern elements, insisting on the ambiguous and unstable nature of the relationships depicted in the narrative of the video, and the frequent elements of parody and play. "The usual power relationship between the voyeuristic male gaze and object" is "destabilized," she claims, by the portrayal of the male patrons of the porno house as leering and pathetic. At the same time, the portrayal of Madonna as porno queen-object is deconstructed, McClary argues, by the end of the video, which has Madonna changing her clothes to those of a little boy and tripping off playfully, leaving the manager of the house sputtering behind her. McClary reads this as "escape to androgyny," which "refuses essentialist gender categories and turns sexual identity into a kind of play." As for the gaze of the viewer, she admits that it is "risky" to "invoke the image of porn queen in order to perform its deconstruction," but concludes that the deconstruction is successful: "In this video, Madonna confronts the most pernicious of her stereotypes and attempts to channel it into a very different realm: a realm where the feminine object need not be the object of the patriarchal gaze, where its energy can motivate play and nonsexual pleasure."[32]

I would argue, however, that despite the video's evasions of clear or fixed meaning there is a dominant position in this video: it is that of the objectifying gaze. One is not really decentered and confused by this video, despite the "ambiguities" it formally contains. Indeed, the video's postmodern conceits, I would suggest, facilitate rather than deconstruct the presentation of Madonna's body as an object on display. For in the absence of a coherent critical position telling us how to read the images, the individual images themselves become preeminent, hypnotic, fixating. Indeed, I would say that ultimately this video is entirely about Madonna's body, the narrative context virtually irrelevant, an excuse to showcase the physical achievements of the star, a video centerfold. On this level, any parodic or destabilizing element appears as cynically, mechanically tacked on, in bad faith, a way of claiming trendy status for what is really just cheesecake – or, perhaps, soft-core pornography.

Indeed, it may be worse than that. If the playful "tag" ending of "Open your heart to me" is successful in deconstructing the notion that the objectification, the sexualization of women's bodies is a serious business, then Madonna's *jouissance* may be "fucking with" her youthful viewer's perceptions in a dangerous way. Judging from the proliferation of rock and rap lyrics celebrating the rape, abuse, and humiliation of women, the message – not Madonna's responsibility alone, of course, but hers among others, surely – is getting through. The artists who perform these misogynist songs also claim to be speaking playfully, tongue-in-cheek, and to be daring and resistant transgressors of cultural structures that contain and define. Ice T, whose rap lyrics gleefully describe the gang rape of a woman – with a flashlight, to "make her tits light up" – claims that he is only "telling it like it is" among black street youth (he compares himself to Richard Wright), and he scoffs at feminist humorlessness, implying, as well, that it is racist and repressive for white feminists to try to deny him his indigenous "style." The fact that Richard Wright embedded his depiction of Bigger Thomas within a critique of the racist culture that shaped him, and that *Native Son* is meant to be a *tragedy*, was not, apparently, noticed in Ice T's postmodern reading of the book, whose critical point of view he utterly ignores. Nor does he seem concerned about what appears to be a growing fad – not only among street gangs, but in fraternity houses as well – for gang rape, often with an unconscious woman, and surrounded by male spectators. (Some of the terms popularly used to describe these rapes include "beaching" – the woman being likened to a "beached whale" – and "spectoring," to emphasize how integral a role the onlookers play.)

My argument here is a plea, not for censorship, but for recognition of the social contexts and consequences of images from popular culture, consequences that are frequently effaced in postmodern and other celebrations of "resistant" elements in these images. To turn back to Madonna and the liberating postmodern subjectivity that McClary and others claim she is offering: the notion that one can play a porno house by night and regain one's androgynous innocence by day does not seem to me to be a refusal of essentialist categories about gender, but rather a new inscription of mind/body dualism. What the body does is immaterial, so long as the imagination is free. This abstract, unsituated, disembodied freedom, I have argued in this essay, glorifies itself only through the effacement of the material praxis of people's lives, the normalizing power of cultural images, and the continuing social realities of dominance and subordination.

## Notes

Earlier versions of this essay were delivered at the 1988 meetings of the Society for Phenomenology and Existentialist Philosophy, Duke University, Syracuse University, the 1990 meetings of the Popular Culture Association, the State University of New York at Binghamton's 1990 Conference on Feminism and Cultural Studies: Theory, History, Experience, and Sienna College. I thank all those who offered comments on those occasions, and Cynthia Willett and Cathy Schwichtenberg for reading an earlier written draft and making suggestions on it. This version was originally published in *Michigan Quarterly Review* (Fall 1990), and is here reprinted with some revisions and several new illustrations.

1   Quoted in Trix Rosen, *Strong and Sexy* (New York: Putnam, 1983), pp. 72, 61.
2   "Travolta: 'You really can make yourself over,'" *Syracuse Herald-American*, January 13, 1985.
3   "Popular plastic surgery," *Cosmopolitan* (May 1990): 96.
4   Tina Lizardi and Martha Frankel, "Hand job," *Details* (February 1990): 38.
5   Jennet Conant, Jeanne Gordon, and Jennifer Donovan, "Scalpel slaves just can't quit," *Newsweek* (January 11, 1988): 58–9.
6   *Donahue* transcript 05257, n.d., Multimedia Entertainment, Cincinnati, Ohio.
7   Dahleen Glanton, "Racism within a race," *Syracuse Herald-American*, September 19, 1989.
8   *Essence* reader opinion poll (June 1989): 71.
9   Since this essay first appeared, DuraSoft has altered its campaign once more, renaming the lenses "Complements" and emphasizing how "natural" and subtle they are. "No one will know you're wearing them," they assure. One ad for "Complements" features identical black twins, one with brown eyes and one wearing blue lenses, as if to show that DuraSoft finds nothing "wrong" with brown eyes. The issue, rather, is self-determination: "Choosing your very own eye color is now the most natural thing in the world."
10  Linda Bien, "Building a better bust," *Syracuse Herald-American*, March 4, 1990.
11  This was said by Janice Radway in an oral presentation of her work, Duke University, Spring, 1989.

12  John Fiske, *Television Culture* (New York: Methuen, 1987), p. 19.

13  Michel Foucault, *Discipline and Punish* (New York: Vintage, 1979), p. 138.

14  Related in Bill Moyers, "A walk through the twentieth century: the second American Revolution," PBS Boston.

15  Foucault, *Discipline and Punish*, pp. 26–7.

16  Susan Rubin Suleiman, "(Re)writing the body: the politics and poetics of female eroticism," in Susan Rubin Suleiman (ed.), *The Female Body in Western Culture* (Cambridge: Harvard University Press, 1986), p. 24.

17  Jacques Derrida and Christie V. McDonald, "Choreographies," *Diacritics*, vol. 12, no. 2 (1982): 76.

18  Cathy Schwichtenberg, "Postmodern feminism and Madonna: toward an erotic politics of the female body," paper presented at the University of Utah Humanities Center, National Conference on Rewriting the (Post)Modern: (Post) Colonialism/Feminism/Late Capitalism, March 30–31, 1990.

19  John Fiske, "British cultural studies and television," in Robert C. Allen (ed.), *Channels of Discourse* (Chapel Hill: University of North Carolina Press, 1987), pp. 254–90.

20  Quoted in John Skow, "Madonna rocks the land," *Time* (May 27, 1985): 77.

21  Ibid., p. 81.

22  Molly Hite, "Writing – and reading – the body: female sexuality and recent feminist fiction," in *Feminist Studies* vol. 14, no. 1 Spring (1988): 121–2.

23  "Fat or not, 4th grade girls diet lest they be teased or unloved," *Wall Street Journal*, February 11, 1986.

24  Catherine Texier, "Have women surrendered in MTV's battle of the sexes?" *New York Times*, April 22, 1990, p. 31.

25  *Cosmopolitan* (July 1987): cover.

26  David Ansen, "Magnificent maverick," *Cosmopolitan* (May 1990): 311.

27  Ansen, "Magnificent maverick," p. 311; Kevin Sessums, "White heat," *Vanity Fair* (April 1990): 208.

28  Susan McClary, "Living to tell: Madonna's resurrection of the fleshy," *Genders*, no. 7 (1990): 2.

29  McClary, "Living to tell," p. 12.

30  E. Ann Kaplan, "Is the gaze male?" in Ann Snitow, Christine Stansell, and Sharon Thompson (eds), *Powers of Desire: The Politics of Sexuality* (New York: Monthly Review Press, 1983), pp. 309–27.

31  E. Ann Kaplan, *Rocking Around the Clock: Music Television, Postmodernism and Consumer Culture* (New York: Methuen, 1987), p. 63.

32  McClary, "Living to tell," p. 13.

# 4
# The Question of Materiality

## Material Bodies

### Susan Hekman

The theories of the body found in the works of Susan Bordo and Judith Butler almost cry out for comparison. Bordo and Butler are two of the most insightful and influential feminist theorists writing today. Both are centrally concerned with the body and its place in feminist theory. Both are concerned to fashion a feminist politics around the concept of the resistant body. And, most strikingly, both define their theoretical foundation as Foucault's concept of the body as a cultural text. What makes a comparison between the two so compelling, however, is that in their most recent work, Bordo and Butler have defined opposing positions on the body, and, most particularly, its materiality. Bordo claims that the materiality of the body must be at the center of feminist theory, while Butler counters that feminism must reject the metaphysical assumptions implicit in this claim. The purpose of this essay is to trace the evolution of these two theories of the body with the aim not of resolving their differences, but of identifying their significance for feminist theory.

Looking at the earliest definitions of the body in feminist theory offered by Bordo and Butler, it is difficult to imagine how their theories have diverged so significantly. Listen to Bordo in a passage first published in 1985:

> Throughout my discussion, it will be assumed that the body, far from being some fundamentally stable, acultural constant to which we must *contrast* all culturally relative and institutional forms, is constantly "in the grip," as Foucault puts it, of cultural practices...Rather, there *is* no "natural body"...Our bodies, no less than anything else that is human, are constituted by culture.                (1988: 90)

This Foucauldian rejection of any definition of the "natural body" or "natural sex" characterizes Bordo's analysis of the body throughout her work. But Bordo also adopts another significant aspect of Foucault's theorization of the body: its role as a "direct locus of social control" (1989: 13). Like Foucault, Bordo argues that the cultural representations of the body can be seen as a set of practical rules through which the body is trained, shaped, and responds. But, she cautions, this "practical body" is no brutely biological or material entity. Rather, it is a culturally mediated form subject to interpretation and description (1989: 25).

It is difficult to identify a difference between this position and that which Butler articulates in her early work. In her first book, *Subjects of Desire* (1987), Butler identifies Foucault as the origin of a "major conceptual reorientation" of Western thought, a shift that she strongly endorses. She defines Foucault's critique of the desiring subject and his proposal to write a "history of bodies" as the focus of this conceptual shift (1987: 235). Concurring with Foucault's rejection of the meta-physics of a "natural" sex, body, and desire, she concludes that "the 'truth' of desire may well lie in a history of bodies as yet unwritten" (1987: 238). In an article that pre-dates *Gender Trouble*, furthermore, she praises Simone de Beauvoir for defining the body as an historical idea, not a natural fact. For the body to have meaning for us, she claims, it must be signified within an historically specific discourse of meaning (1989: 254).

Within a few years, however, these two theorists of the body as cultural text have not only developed opposing theories of the body but have come to represent two distinct camps in feminist theory. Bordo's influential article, "Feminism, postmo-dernism, and gender-skepticism" (1990) has been interpreted as a direct attack on postmodern feminism and its alleged rejection of the materiality of the body. In what may be a critique specifically of Butler's work, Bordo argues, "If the body is a metaphor for our locatedness in space and time and thus for the finitude of human perception and knowledge, then the postmodern body is no body at all" (1990: 145). The result, she argues, is a "stylish nihilism" that precludes feminist politics. Butler, on the other hand, published a book devoted almost exclusively to defending her rejection of a simple understanding of the materiality of the body. In *Bodies That Matter* (1993a) she argues that grounding feminist theory in materiality will not work because matter itself has a history, it is already sedimented in discourse (1993a: 29). Materiality, she argues, should be the *object* of feminist inquiry, not its ground (1993a: 49).

It is necessary to go back to the first works of each theorist to understand how this split occurred. Susan Bordo first made her mark in feminist theory with her book, *The Flight to Objectivity* (1987). This book, a psychological and psychocultural analysis of the thought of Descartes, seems on the face of it to have little to do with Bordo's theorization of the body. But a reading of this book from the perspect-ive of her later work reveals its theoretical connection. If, as Bordo argues, the body is a cultural text, then the first task of the theorist must be to establish what culture writes on the body, what text is inscribed. Bordo's argument in *The Flight to Objectivity* is that the origin of our culture's text for the body, and particularly the female body, is the work of Descartes.

Bordo develops this thesis through a careful and complex argument. She asserts that although Western thought had, since Plato, associated the body with the female and nature, a realm inferior to that of culture and the male, it was only in the work of Descartes that knowledge itself became masculinized. Descartes defined the body as the chief, if not the sole impediment to knowledge, resulting, Bordo argues, in an "acute historical flight from the feminine," the material world (1987: 9). In her effort to explain Descartes' approach, Bordo turns to a psychoanalytic perspective. Descartes' quest for certainty, she asserts, is rooted in his desperate need for reassurance that some knowledge could be stable in an unstable world. To achieve this reassurance, she argues, he turns to God the father and away from the maternal earth, nature, and body. She concludes that the work of Descartes defines the attitude toward the body that characterizes all subsequent modern philosophy: body and mind are mutually exclusive and the body is the "prison" that the mind must escape to achieve knowledge.

Bordo's analysis of the thought of Descartes provides the template for her subsequent analysis of the materiality of the female body in Western culture. She argues that it is Descartes' definition of the body as a prison that explains our culture's attitudes toward the body and the quintessential representation of the body, woman. It is this definition that guides her analysis of diseases such as anorexia and bulimia, diseases that primarily affect female bodies. In one of her first articles on anorexia nervosa (1988), Bordo argues that we must do more than merely identify a connection between these diseases and prevailing cultural conceptions of femininity – we must offer a detailed analysis of that relationship. In the case of anorexia this means that we must do more than connect this disease to the cult of slenderness currently dominant in our culture; we must explain why that cult exists and where it originated. Her principal thesis, here and in subsequent articles, is that these diseases expose a kind of fault line in culture: by exaggerating particular cultural tendencies they reveal their pathological character more clearly. She argues that a variety of cultural currents or streams converge in anorexia, what she calls "axes of continuity." The anorexic's body is the point of convergence of these cultural streams; it is a kind of protest written on the bodies of women.

In a study of hysteria, agoraphobia, and anorexia Bordo expands on these themes to argue that there is a continuum between these primarily female disorders and "normal" feminine practice (1989). Looking at these diseases, we find the body of the sufferer deeply inscribed with an ideological construction emblematic of the definition of femininity prevalent in the period. Because those constructions are written in hyperbolic terms, the bodies of the disordered women become graphic cultural texts (1989: 16). In another context she puts her point even more forcefully. Diseases such as anorexia and bulimia, she argues, cannot be explained either medically or psychologically: they are "cultural diseases." Anorexia, she asserts, is an overdetermined symptom of some of the multifaceted distresses of our age (1993: 141). Specifically, "the anorexic's metaphysics makes explicit various elements, historically grounded in Plato and Augustine, that run deep in our culture" (1993: 147). The bulimic, on the other hand, graphically illustrates the contradictory construction of self in our society: instant gratification of desire coupled with the demand for control, slenderness, and a taut body (1993: 199). Far from being an aberration, the bulimic emerges as a "characteristic modern personality construction" (1993: 200).

Bordo begins her collection of essays, *Unbearable Weight* (1993) with Delmore Schwartz's poem, "The heavy bear." The image of the body as bear epitomizes the cultural coding of the female body in Western society; Bordo uses it to summarize her theories about the body in the collected articles. Several of the essays address an issue that has recently come to the forefront of Bordo's work: the place of postmodernism in feminist theories of the body. Her discussion of this issue is framed by two claims. First, she asserts that it was feminists, not Foucault, who inaugurated the "new scholarship on the body"; long before feminism entered into its "marriage" with poststructuralist thought feminist theorists were exploring bodies as cultural codes (1993: 17). Second, she claims that her own interest in Foucault stems from his insights into the workings of power in our society. I draw two conclusions from these claims: first, that, for Bordo, in the marriage of feminism and poststructuralism/Foucault, feminism is and must be the dominant partner; second, that it is the political implications of Foucault's perspective that are and must be the focus of its application in feminist theory.

This second point is particularly important in explaining Bordo's attitude toward postmodernism. In the introduction to the volume Bordo employs a Foucauldian analysis to develop an understanding of the "practical metaphysics" of the mind/body dualism (1993: 13). Central to Bordo's approach is her goal of developing an effective *political* discourse about the female body. Throughout her work Bordo distinguishes between what Foucault calls the "intelligible body," scientific, philo-sophical, and esthetic representations of the body, and the "useful" or practical body, a set of practical rules by which the body is shaped, trained, and responds (1989: 25). These two concepts of Foucault explain the connection between the two aspects of Bordo's work. Her analysis of Descartes is an exploration of the intelligible body; her analysis of "female diseases" that of the practical/useful body. But in both analyses, the practical, political consequences are paramount; politics drives theory.

It is in Bordo's well-known article (also reprinted in *Unbearable Weight*), "Femin-ism, postmodernism and gender-skepticism" (1990) that her attitude toward post-modern approaches to the body is most fully developed. Bordo identifies what she calls "gender-skepticism" as an "important cultural foundation," but then goes on to defend the continued use of gender analysis in feminist theory. "Gender theor-ists" such as Dinnerstein, Chodorow, and Gilligan, she claims, discovered patterns that "resonate experientially and illuminate culturally. They cleared a space, described a new territory, which radically altered the male-dominated normative terms of discourse about reality and experience" (1990: 137). The same cannot be said for what Bordo calls gender-skepticism, an approach, she asserts, that incurs serious problems for feminist theory. First, although the critics of gender analysis have accurately revealed that gender is only one axis of identity-formation, what they overlook is that if we try to include too many axes of analysis at once, the analytic focus of our arguments will be lost (1990: 139). Second, the gender skeptics, by questioning everything at once, putting everything into play, risk trying to be everywhere at once. The "postmodern dream" of being everywhere, she asserts, will lead to being nowhere, losing the very locatedness that they sought in the first place. The result of these analyses, she claims, is "endless play," the "fantasy of escape from human locatedness" (1990: 142). Finally, by overemphasizing gender as a fantasy and a choice, the gender skeptics forget that our world is, in fact, structured by gender dualities and if we want to change the politics of that world we must come to grips with those dualities. Today, she concludes, feminists are less in danger of totalizing theories than increasing paralysis at the fear of being essentialists (1990: 142).

The last two articles reprinted in *Unbearable Weight* further clarify the nature of Bordo's opposition to postmodernism. In "Material girl" Bordo contrasts the analysis of the materiality of the body with what she calls "cultural plastic." She identifies a "common postmodern misappropriation of Foucault" as the assumption that power is everywhere and undifferentiated, lacking "hills and valleys." Against this Bordo argues for an interpretation of Foucault as revealing the normalizing practices of cultural discourses. She implies that the postmodern's emphasis on fiction, fantasy, and pastiche makes it impossible for them to understand the hegemonic power of the normalizing discourses of gender. In "Postmodern subjects, postmodern bodies, postmodern resistance," this criticism becomes even more explicit. In a critique of Butler's *Gender Trouble*, Bordo argues: "Butler's world is one in which language swallows everything up, voraciously, a theoretical pasta-machine through which the categories of competing frameworks are pressed and reprocessed as 'tropes.'" Characterizing Butler's position as "celebratory postmo-dernism," Bordo rejects it on the grounds that it lacks a cultural context. This is, in one sense, an odd argument: the postmodern critique is nothing if not cultural; for postmodernism everything is a cultural text, even the body and its materiality. But Bordo's point is that all cultural texts are not equal. The hegemonic cultural texts, those that are manifest in Foucault's analysis of normalizing practices, define "reality" for gendered bodies. And that reality, Bordo argues, is no cause for celebration. She concludes: "My own resistance to being swept up in a celebratory postmodernism is due in part to the fact that the particular power-terrain I have been examining in this book does not offer much cause for celebration" (1993: 295).

At this point in the development of her theory, it is easier to define what Bordo's conception of the materiality of the body is *not* rather than what it *is*. It is neither biological nor physical, although it impinges on both of these realms. It is a cultural construction but, importantly, a construction that structures what counts as "material" and "real" within a culture. As such it must be the focus of feminist analysis and, significantly, feminist resistance. Central to Bordo's approach is her insistence that we must resist the cultural definitions of the body and its materiality as they are given to us and particularly as they are exaggerated in diseases such as anorexia and bulimia. Bordo's formulation is insightful and powerful. It enables us to understand bodies and their diseases in revolutionary new ways. But it also raises a difficult question that Bordo does not adequately address: if our resistance to the cultural construction of the body cannot appeal to a "real" or "natural" body, and, thus, that resistance is also a cultural construction, then how can it be effective as resistance?

This is precisely the question that sets the stage for Judith Butler's analysis of the body in feminist theory. Like Bordo, her first book appears to have little to do with her feminist concern with the body, but in retrospect supplies the theoretical underpinning for that concern. Taken as a whole, Butler's work is remarkably linear. Beginning with *Subjects of Desire* (1987) she defines a change in Western thought away from the metaphysical foundations that have grounded it since its inception. She then systematically examines a progression of twentieth-century thinkers who profess to embrace this conceptual shift and finds each to be insufficiently radical: each retains a remnant of the metaphysical baggage that defines the tradition. Finally, in *Bodies That Matter* (1993) she is forced by the logic of this progression to articulate her own anti-metaphysical view.

In *Subjects of Desire* Butler traces the concept of desire in Western philosophical thought from its position as one of the defining aspects of the autonomous human subject to the refutation of Hegel's metaphysically supported subject in twentieth-century French philosophy. It is not difficult to show, as Butler does, that, through the work of Hegel, the concept of desire is rooted in a metaphysical belief in a pre-linguistic human identity. Butler analyzes how this belief breaks down in the work of the twentieth-century French critics of Hegel's desiring subject. In the cases of Sartre, Deleuze, and Lacan, Butler finds that despite their claims to abandon the metaphysical subject, each theorist retains a concept of something "beyond" culturally instituted desire. This line of argument takes an interesting turn when Butler moves to an analysis of Foucault. Foucault, Butler claims, gives us a dialectic without a subject and without teleology; he undermines the hegemony of the binary opposition itself (1987: 225). She concludes: "[Foucault's] critique of 'the desiring subject,' and his proposal to write a history of bodies in its place constitutes a major conceptual re-orientation which, if successful, would signal the definitive closure of Hegel's narrative of desire" (1987: 235).

On the last page of *Subjects of Desire* Butler writes: "the 'truth' of desire may well lie in a history of bodies as yet unwritten" (1987: 238). This statement provides an apt summary of Butler's goal in her subsequent work. In the book that has made her (in)famous, *Gender Trouble* (1990), Butler starts this history. But she discovers that, from a feminist perspective, before she can talk about bodies and their history, she must first confront an array of concepts: sex, gender, and woman. These concepts, she finds, bring the metaphysical assumptions of the philosophical tradition into feminist theory. Her first task, thus, is to expose and dispose of these metaphysical remains.

Butler begins *Gender Trouble* by asserting that in order to oppose the epistemic/ ontological regime that governs Western thought, we must expose the foundational categories of sex, gender, and the body as effects of a specific formation of power/ discourse (1990: x). Central to her argument is the assertion that these foundational categories structure not only patriarchal thought, but feminist thought as well. Guiding feminist theory since its inception has been the foundational category, "woman," and the assumption that this concept is its necessary foundation. Butler questions this assumption on two levels. First, she claims that we do not, in fact, need a unitary concept of "woman" to ground feminist politics but, rather, that we should make the construction of a variable notion of identity our political goal. Second, she argues that such a unitary concept actually reifies regulating gender relations; it is, in effect, conservative rather than revolutionary (1990: 5).

The centerpiece of Butler's argument is a radically new concept of gender. She rejects the widely held feminist assumption that gender is the cultural inscription of meaning on a pregiven biological sex. Instead, she claims that gender is the apparatus of production whereby the sexes themselves are established. It follows that gender is the discursive/cultural means by which "natural sex" is produced (1990: 7). It is "a complexity whose totality is permanently deferred" (1990: 16), "a free-floating artifice" (1990: 6). Another way of putting Butler's point is that it only makes sense to define gender as a cultural construct if "natural sex" can also be defined; sex and gender are the two poles of a binary. Implicit in this binary, furthermore, is the definition of "natural sex" in terms of heterosexual desire. Butler's goal is to deconstruct this binary.

She does so by advancing her well-known definition of gender as a performance: "There is no gender identity behind the expressions of gender; that identity is performativity constituted by the very 'expressions' that are said to be its results" (1990: 25). Further, for Butler, just as there is no gender identity behind the expressions of gender, there is no emancipatory sexuality before or after the law. This has important political and strategic consequences. To create "gender trouble," to disrupt the performance of gender that is culturally expected, we cannot appeal to natural sex, but, instead, must fashion performances that can effect this disruption. Since there is no radical repudiation of a culturally constructed sexuality, we must construct our resistance by asking what forms of representation do not constitute a simple imitation, reproduction and hence consolidation of law. As Butler puts it: "What kind of subversive repetition might call into question the regulatory practice of identity itself?" (1990: 32).

The main body of *Gender Trouble* consists of an analysis of the work of contemporary theorists who might help her answer this question. Butler discovers useful insights in the work of Kristeva, Foucault, and Wittig, but she ultimately finds all of them wanting for the same reason: they appeal to some version of a founding sex, sexuality, or body. Butler's analysis of Foucault in particular reveals the principal elements of her approach to the body. Foucault seems to provide precisely the approach to sex, sexuality, and the body that Butler is seeking. He interprets all aspects of sex as the product of the historically specific organization of sexuality; he treats sex as an effect rather than an origin. Yet Butler faults Foucault for what she calls a contradiction in his work: invoking a trope of prediscursive libidinal multiplicity that presupposes a sex before the law (1990: 97). Against this Butler wants to argue for a conception of the body not as the ground of desire, but its occasion and object. "Always already a cultural sign, the body sets limits to the imaginary meanings that it occasions, but it is never free of imaginary construction" (1990: 71). Thus the fantasized body cannot be contrasted to the "real" body, or, as in Foucault, pre-discursive sex. It can only be contrasted to another cultural fantasy.

Butler's political strategy flows directly from this critique. She argues that grounding feminist theory in a "natural" body or sex is not only incoherent, it is counterproductive; it takes "the focus of feminist theory away from the concrete terms of cultural struggle" (1990: 38). If gender is a disciplinary production, a "fantasy" even, then we can make gender trouble only by deploying other practices, creating other fantasies. In her discussion of gay and lesbian practice she makes this very clear: "In my view, the normative forces for gay and lesbian practice ought to be on the parodic redeployment of power rather than on the impossible fantasy of full transcendence" (1990: 124). Gender cannot be declared either true or false, she argues, but it can be "rendered thoroughly and radically incredible" (1990: 141). The subversion of identity can only occur within the practices that constitute identity. Our critical task, she concludes, is to locate strategies of subversive repetition within cultural constructions of gender (1990: 145–7).

*Gender Trouble* had a revolutionary impact on feminist theory. Its defenders hailed it as brilliant, a theoretical breakthrough, an epistemic shift in feminist thought. Its detractors identified it as the epitome of the "stylish nihilism" that characterizes the allegedly subversive approach of postmodern feminism. By defining gender as a fantasy and a performance, they argued, Butler's position obviates the possibility of a viable feminist politics. Butler's next book, *Bodies That Matter* (1993a) is largely an answer to these criticisms. In it she attempts to clarify what she means by gender as a performance and to defend the feminist body politics that follow from that definition.

In the introduction to the book Butler examines the claim that informs the position of her critics (including Bordo): feminism as a critical practice must be grounded in the sexed specificity of the female body (1993a: 28). Reflecting on this claim Butler confesses: "I began writing this book by trying to consider the materiality of the body only to find that the thought of materiality invariably moved me into other domains . . . I could not fix bodies as simple objects of thought" (1993a: ix). These sentences set the tone for the dense, complicated, and sometimes impenetrable analyses that follow. Butler begins her argument by attacking the presuppositions of her critics and defending her deconstructive method. The essentialism implicit in her critics' position, she argues, errs in positing a prelinguistic site of "sex" and endowing it with ontological status. Against this Butler argues that "this sex posited as prior to construction will, by virtue of being posited, become the effect of that very positing, the construction of construction", a site or surface on which theory acts (1993a: 5–6). The point of deconstruction, she asserts, is not that everything is discursively constituted, because this refuses the "constitutive force of exclusion" (1993a: 8).

Butler claims that her goal in the book is a radical resignification of the symbolic domain in order to expand what counts as a valued and valuable body in the world (1993a: 22). She starts with an analysis of materiality, assessing the claim that recourse to matter and the materiality of sex is necessary to ground feminist practice. Her counter is that matter itself has a history: it cannot ground feminist claims because it is already sedimented within discourses on sex and sexuality (1993a: 29). The materiality of the body, thus, is not prior to discourse, but is its effect (1993a: 30). It follows that to invoke matter is to invoke a sedimented history of materiality. This definition leads her to the conclusion that materiality should be the *object* of feminist inquiry, not its ground (1993a: 49).

Making materiality the object of feminist inquiry involves, for Butler, understanding the feminine and matter as the excluded, the abject. The nature and possibilities of this exclusion concern Butler throughout the book. Her central argument is twofold: first, she asserts that the excluded, the abject, is a discursive product, not an alternative origin possessing independent ontological status; second, she argues that the task of feminist theory must be to "refigure this necessary 'outside' as a future horizon, one in which the violence of exclusion is perpetually in the process of being overcome" (1993a: 53). In other words, we must preserve this discursively constituted outside as the site of disruption.

With this analysis behind her, Butler is now ready to clarify her position on gender as performance. Many of the readers of *Gender Trouble* took Butler to be arguing that we choose our gender much as we choose our clothes, a position dangerously close to the humanist notion of autonomous choice. In *Bodies That Matter* Butler rejects this interpretation by appealing to speech act theory. She now defines a performative as "that discursive practice that enacts or produces that which it names" (1993a: 13). The "law of sex," she argues, is "repeatedly fortified and idealized as the law only to the extent that it is reiterated as the law" (1993a: 14). It follows that the materiality of sex is constructed through a ritualized repetition of norms; performativity is not an act of "choice," but a reiteration of norms, in this case the "law of sex" (1993a: 12).

What this comes to is that, for Butler, there is no "choice" of gender, because even, or especially, "deviant" gender roles are discursively constituted by the symbolic. By "choosing" one of these "deviant" roles, the subject reinforces and reinscribes the "law of sex" that she claims to reject. Butler's prescriptions for a feminist politics, then, come to something like this: feminists can deploy the categories of abjection which, although constituted by the hegemonic law of sex, can be used to destabilize that law. Although categories such as "queer" are not inherently destabilizing, they can and should be used as a site of resignification and refiguration of the symbolic that produces them. In other words, it is not enough to be "queer," one must be "critically queer." This is quite persuasive, but it also creates a problem for formulating this politics. If the excluded, the abject, is as much a discursive product of the law of sex as the hegemonic heterosexual norm, then how can the abject be defined as a realm of resignification that destabilizes the hegemonic? How can it become the site where disruption will occur? Butler herself acknowledges that this is a problem. At the end of her book she asks, "How will we know the difference between the power we promote and the power we oppose?" (1993a: 241).

The disagreement between Bordo and Butler on the materiality of the body is representative of a growing split between postmodern feminists and their critics that is of crucial importance to feminist theory. Examining the evolution of the theories of Bordo and Butler suggests that while both have followed the discursive path defined by Foucault, they have defined discursivity and, hence, materiality in different ways. Bordo has objected to what she calls the radical discursivity of theorists such as Butler for two reasons. First, like a growing number of critics of postmodern feminism, she claims that a strictly discursive/linguistic approach precludes the possibility of a feminist politics. Specifically, she claims that it lacks concrete material analyses of the inscription of phallocentric dualistic culture on gendered bodies (1989: 27). If gender is defined as a fiction, a fantasy, how, she asks, can we fashion a politics to combat the effects of the hegemony of dualistic gender?

Second, she argues that we must retain a notion of the "reality" of gendered bodies. In a particularly revealing passage, she argues: "I view our bodies as a site of struggle where we must *work* to keep our daily practices in the service of resistance to gender domination ... [This] demands an awareness of the often contradictory relations between image and practice between rhetoric and reality" (1989: 28). But this is also a very puzzling passage. What can the distinction between "rhetoric and reality" mean to a self-declared Foucauldian who argues that discourses structure bodies? At the risk of putting words in Bordo's mouth, I would argue that for Bordo the hegemonic gender discourse of our society creates a very real reality for gendered bodies, a reality in which bodies suffer and die. Her claim is that theorists such as Butler, by treating gender as a fiction, cannot fashion a feminist politics that can adequately deal with this reality.

Butler is well aware of this criticism; in a sense, *Bodies That Matter* is an extended attempt to answer it. But it is in another context that Butler addresses this criticism most directly. In an article significantly entitled "Contingent foundations" (1992), Butler argues that the charge that a postmodern position cannot assess the material violence that women suffer misconstrues the point at issue. She asserts that deconstructing the concept of matter or bodies does not negate or refuse either term, but displaces them from the context in which they have been deployed with the aim of repeating them subversively. She then goes on to examine one of the principal examples of material violence against women – rape. She argues persuasively that "rape" is discursively constituted, that the legal definition of what counts as "rape" has changed over time. Most significantly, rape in certain situations, e.g. within marriage, is not constructed as "rape" at all. Her point is that even something as basic as the violence of rape is not "simply" material, but that the "politics of violence operates through regulating what will and will not be able to appear as the effect of violence" (1992: 18).[1]

I would like to suggest that if we compare this passage to one of Bordo's analyses of how culture sculpts the body through the incidence of disease we find more commonalities than differences. This leads me to conclude that the feminist political strategies that Bordo and Butler advocate are not as dissimilar as their theoretical differences suggest. Butler argues that we must embrace the abject, the excluded, as a site of the possibility of refiguring the hegemonic symbolic, imagining a future horizon that values bodies differently. Bordo's work can be read as an example of how such a reinscription might work in practice. Bordo takes the excluded identities of the anorexic and the bulimic as sites of resistance, as places where a critique of hegemonic subjectivity is enacted. The anorexic and the bulimic exaggerate the contradictions and exclusions of the hegemonic construction of subjectivity that feminists seek to displace. They do so not by appealing to the real or material, but by magnifying key aspects of that construction, turning them into grotesques. In both Bordo and Butler's theories the critical construction of exclusion is deployed to resignify the symbolic that constructs that exclusion.

I am not trying to suggest that these commonalities obscure the differences between the two theorists. But I think that we should emphasize and build on these commonalities rather than allow feminist politics to stagnate in a fruitless debate over their differences. Although bodies are cultural texts, some texts are more important than others and the hegemonic texts that sculpt female bodies cause pain and suffering for "real," "material" women. Bordo's objection to postmodernist feminism is, I think, irrefutable: this is not a fiction or a fantasy because hegemonic gendered discourses create "reality" for gendered bodies. Despite their differences, I think that both Bordo and Butler want to devise a feminist politics that can relieve the pain of those bodies.

## Notes

1   In a related context, Butler even argues that death is not a simple existential possibility but is articulated through the discourse of medical decisions – something that would happen if certain actions were not taken (1993b: 5).

## References

Bordo, Susan (1987) *The Flight to Objectivity*. Albany: SUNY Press.

Bordo, Susan (1988) "Anorexia nervosa: psychopathology as the crystalization of culture." In Irene Diamond and Lee Quinby (eds), *Feminism and Foucault*. Boston: Northeastern University Press, pp. 87–117.

Bordo, Susan (1989) "The body and the reproduction of femininity: a feminist appropriation of Foucault." In Alison Jaggar and Susan Bordo (eds), *Gender/Body/Knowledge*. New York: Routledge, pp. 13–33.

Bordo, Susan (1990) "Feminism, postmodernism and gender-skepticism." In Linda Nicholson (ed.), *Feminism/Postmodernism*. New York: Routledge, pp. 133–56.

Bordo, Susan (1993) *Unbearable Weight: Feminism, Western Culture, and the Body*. Berkeley: University of California Press.

Butler, Judith (1987) *Subjects of Desire: Hegelian reflections in twentieth century France*. New York: Columbia University Press.

Butler, Judith (1989) "Gendering the body: Beauvoir's philosophical contribution." In Ann Garry and Marilyn Pearsal (eds), *Women, Knowledge, and Reality*. Boston: Unwin Hyman, pp. 253–62.

Butler, Judith (1990). *Gender Trouble: Feminism and the Subversion of Identity*. New York: Routledge.

Butler, Judith (1992) "Contingent foundations: feminism and the question of postmodernism." In Judith Butler and Joan Scott (eds), *Feminists Theorize the Political*. New York: Routledge, pp. 3–21.

Butler, Judith (1993a) *Bodies That Matter*. New York: Routledge.

Butler, Judith (1993b) Editor's introduction. In *Erotic Welfare* by Linda Singer, ed. Judith Butler. New York: Routledge, pp. 1–15.

# Selection from *Bodies that Matter**

## *Judith Butler*

*Why should our bodies end at the skin, or include at best other beings encapsulated by skin?*

> Donna Haraway, *A Manifesto for Cyborgs*

*If one really thinks about the body as such, there is no possible outline of the body as such. There are thinkings of the systematicity of the body, there are value codings of the body. The body, as such, cannot be thought, and I certainly cannot approach it.*

> Gayatri Chakravorty Spivak, "In a word,"
> interview with Ellen Rooney

*There is no nature, only the effects of nature: denaturalization or naturalization.*

> Jacques Derrida, *Donner le Temps*

Is there a way to link the question of the materiality of the body to the performativity of gender? And how does the category of "sex" figure within such a relationship? Consider first that sexual difference is often invoked as an issue of material differences. Sexual difference, however, is never simply a function of material differences which are not in some way both marked and formed by discursive practices. Further, to claim that sexual differences are indissociable from discursive demarcations is not the same as claiming that discourse causes sexual difference. The category of "sex" is, from the start, normative; it is what Foucault has called a "regulatory ideal." In this sense, then, "sex" not only functions as a norm, but is part of a regulatory practice that produces the bodies it governs, that is, whose regulatory force is made clear as a kind of productive power, the power to produce – demarcate, circulate, differentiate – the bodies it controls. Thus, "sex" is a regulatory ideal whose materialization is compelled, and this materialization takes place (or fails to take place) through certain highly regulated practices. In other words, "sex" is an ideal construct which is forcibly materialized through time. It is not a simple fact or static condition of a body, but a process whereby regulatory norms materialize "sex" and achieve this materialization through a forcible reiteration of those norms. That this reiteration is necessary is a sign that materialization is never quite complete, that bodies never quite comply with the norms by which their materialization is impelled. Indeed, it is the instabilities, the possibilities for rematerialization, opened up by this process that mark one domain in which the force of the regulatory law can be turned against itself to spawn rearticulations that call into question the hegemonic force of that very regulatory law.

But how, then, does the notion of gender performativity relate to this conception of materialization? In the first instance, performativity must be understood not as a singular or deliberate "act," but, rather, as the reiterative and citational practice by which discourse produces the effects that it names. What will, I hope, become clear in what follows is that the regulatory norms of "sex" work in a performative fashion to constitute the materiality of bodies and, more specifically, to materialize the body's sex, to materialize sexual difference in the service of the consolidation of the heterosexual imperative.

* Judith Butler, "Introduction," *Bodies that Matter* (New York: Routledge, 1993), pp. 1–16.

In this sense, what constitutes the fixity of the body, its contours, its movements, will be fully material, but materiality will be rethought as the effect of power, as power's most productive effect. And there will be no way to understand "gender" as a cultural construct which is imposed upon the surface of matter, understood either as "the body" or its given sex. Rather, once "sex" itself is understood in its normativity, the materiality of the body will not be thinkable apart from the materialization of that regulatory norm. "Sex" is, thus, not simply what one has, or a static description of what one is: it will be one of the norms by which the "one" becomes viable at all, that which qualifies a body for life within the domain of cultural intelligibility.[1]

At stake in such a reformulation of the materiality of bodies will be the following: (1) the recasting of the matter of bodies as the effect of a dynamic of power, such that the matter of bodies will be indissociable from the regulatory norms that govern their materialization and the signification of those material effects; (2) the understanding of performativity not as the act by which a subject brings into being what she/he names, but, rather, as that reiterative power of discourse to produce the phenomena that it regulates and constrains; (3) the construal of "sex" no longer as a bodily given on which the construct of gender is artificially imposed, but as a cultural norm which governs the materialization of bodies; (4) a rethinking of the process by which a bodily norm is assumed, appropriated, taken on as not, strictly speaking, undergone *by a subject*, but rather that the subject, the speaking "I," is formed by virtue of having gone through such a process of assuming a sex; and (5) a linking of this process of "assuming" a sex with the question of *identification*, and with the discursive means by which the heterosexual imperative enables certain sexed identifications and fore-closes and/or disavows other identifications. This exclusionary matrix by which subjects are formed thus requires the simultaneous production of a domain of abject beings, those who are not yet "subjects," but who form the constitutive outside to the domain of the subject. The abject[2] designates here precisely those "unlivable" and "uninhabitable" zones of social life which are nevertheless densely populated by those who do not enjoy the status of the subject, but whose living under the sign of the "unlivable" is required to circumscribe the domain of the subject. This zone of uninhabitability will constitute the defining limit of the subject's domain; it will constitute that site of dreaded identification against which – and by virtue of which – the domain of the subject will circumscribe its own claim to autonomy and to life. In this sense, then, the subject is constituted through the force of exclusion and abjec-tion, one which produces a constitutive outside to the subject, an abjected outside, which is, after all, "inside" the subject as its own founding repudiation.

The forming of a subject requires an identification with the normative phantasm of "sex," and this identification takes place through a repudiation which produces a domain of abjection, a repudiation without which the subject cannot emerge. This is a repudiation which creates the valence of "abjection" and its status for the subject as a threatening specter. Further, the materialization of a given sex will centrally concern *the regulation of identificatory practices* such that the identification with the abjection of sex will be persistently disavowed. And yet, this disavowed abjection will threaten to expose the self-grounding presumptions of the sexed subject, grounded as that subject is in a repudiation whose consequences it cannot fully control. The task will be to consider this threat and disruption not as a permanent contestation of social norms condemned to the pathos of perpetual failure, but rather as a critical resource in the struggle to rearticulate the very terms of symbolic legitimacy and intelligibility.

Lastly, the mobilization of the categories of sex within political discourse will be haunted in some ways by the very instabilities that the categories effectively produce and foreclose. Although the political discourses that mobilize identity categories tend to cultivate identifications in the service of a political goal, it may be that the persistence of *dis*identification is equally crucial to the rearticulation of democratic contestation. Indeed, it may be precisely through practices which underscore disidentification with those regulatory norms by which sexual difference is materialized that both feminist and queer politics are mobilized. Such collective disidentifications can facilitate a reconceptualization of which bodies matter, and which bodies are yet to emerge as critical matters of concern.

## From construction to materialization

The relation between culture and nature presupposed by some models of gender "construction" implies a culture or an agency of the social which acts upon a nature, which is itself presupposed as a passive surface, outside the social and yet its necessary counterpart. One question that feminists have raised, then, is whether the discourse which figures the action of construction as a kind of imprinting or imposition is not tacitly masculinist, whereas the figure of the passive surface, awaiting that penetrating act whereby meaning is endowed, is not tacitly or – perhaps – quite obviously feminine. Is sex to gender as feminine is to masculine?[3]

Other feminist scholars have argued that the very concept of nature needs to be rethought, for the concept of nature has a history, and the figuring of nature as the blank and lifeless page, as that which is, as it were, always already dead, is decidedly modern, linked perhaps to the emergence of technological means of domination. Indeed, some have argued that a rethinking of "nature" as a set of dynamic interrelations suits both feminist and ecological aims (and has for some produced an otherwise unlikely alliance with the work of Gilles Deleuze). This rethinking also calls into question the model of construction whereby the social unilaterally acts on the natural and invests it with its parameters and its meanings. Indeed, as much as the radical distinction between sex and gender has been crucial to the de Beauvoirian version of feminism, it has come under criticism in more recent years for degrading the natural as that which is "before" intelligibility, in need of the mark, if not the mar, of the social to signify, to be known, to acquire value. This misses the point that nature has a history, and not merely a social one, but, also, that sex is positioned ambiguously in relation to that concept and its history. The concept of "sex" is itself troubled terrain, formed through a series of contestations over what ought to be decisive criterion for distinguishing between the two sexes; the concept of sex has a history that is covered over by the figure of the site or surface of inscription. Figured as such a site or surface, however, the natural is construed as that which is also without value; moreover, it assumes its value at the same time that it assumes its social character, that is, at the same time that nature relinquishes itself as the natural. According to this view, then, the social construction of the natural presupposes the cancelation of the natural by the social. Insofar as it relies on this construal, the sex/gender distinction founders along parallel lines; if gender is the social significance that sex assumes within a given culture – and for the sake of argument we will let "social" and "cultural" stand in an uneasy interchangeability – then what, if anything, is left of "sex" once it has assumed its social character as gender? At issue is the meaning of "assumption," where to be "assumed" is to be taken up into a more elevated sphere, as in "the Assumption of the Virgin." If gender consists of the social meanings that sex assumes, then sex does not *accrue* social meanings as additive properties but, rather, *is replaced by* the social meanings it takes on; sex is relinquished in the course of that assumption, and gender emerges, not as a term in a continued relationship of opposition to sex, but as the term which absorbs and displaces "sex," the mark of its full substantiation into gender or what, from a materialist point of view, might constitute a full *de*substantiation.

When the sex/gender distinction is joined with a notion of radical linguistic constructivism, the problem becomes even worse, for the "sex" which is referred to as prior to gender will itself be a postulation, a construction, offered within language, as that which is prior to language, prior to construction. But this sex posited as prior to construction will, by virtue of being posited, become the effect of that very positing, the construction of construction. If gender is the social construction of sex, and if there is no access to this "sex" except by means of its construction, then it appears not only that sex is absorbed by gender, but that "sex" becomes something like a fiction, perhaps a fantasy, retroactively installed at a prelinguistic site to which there is no direct access.

But is it right to claim that "sex" vanishes altogether, that it is a fiction over and against what is true, that it is a fantasy over and against what is reality? Or do these very oppositions need to be rethought such that if "sex" is a fiction, it is one within whose necessities we live, without which life itself would be unthinkable? And if "sex" is a fantasy, is it perhaps a phantasmatic field that constitutes the very terrain of cultural intelligibility? Would such a rethinking of such conventional oppositions entail a rethinking of "constructivism" in its usual sense?

The radical constructivist position has tended to produce the premise that both refutes and confirms its own enterprise. If such a theory cannot take account of sex as the site or surface on which it acts, then it ends up presuming sex as the unconstructed, and so concedes the limits of linguistic constructivism, inadvertently circumscribing that which remains unaccountable within the terms of construction. If, on the other hand, sex is a contrived premiss, a fiction, then gender does not presume a sex which it acts upon, but rather, gender produces the misnomer of a prediscursive "sex," and the meaning of construction becomes that of linguistic monism, whereby everything is only and always language. Then, what ensues is an exasperated debate which many of us have tired of hearing: either (1) constructivism is reduced to a position of linguistic monism, whereby linguistic construction is understood to be generative and deterministic. Critics making that presumption can be heard to say, "If everything is discourse, what about the body?" or (2) when construction is figuratively reduced to a verbal action which appears to presuppose a subject, critics working within such a presumption can be heard to say, "If gender is constructed, then who is doing the constructing?" Though, of course, (3) the most pertinent formulation of this question is the following: "If the subject is constructed, then who is constructing the subject?" In the first case, construction has taken the place of a godlike agency which not only causes but composes everything which is its object; it is the divine performative, bringing into being and exhaustively constituting that which it names, or, rather, it is that kind of transitive referring which names and inaugurates at once. For something to be constructed, according to this view of construction, is for it to be created and determined through that process.

In the second and third cases, the seductions of grammar appear to hold sway; the critic asks, Must there not be a human agent, a subject, if you will, who guides the course of construction? If the first version of constructivism presumes that construction operates deterministically, making a mockery of human agency, the second understands constructivism as presupposing a voluntarist subject who makes its gender through an instrumental action. A construction is understood in this latter case to be a kind of manipulable artifice, a conception that not only presupposes a subject, but rehabilitates precisely the voluntarist subject of humanism that constructivism has, on occasion, sought to put into question.

If gender is a construction, must there be an "I" or a "we" who enacts or performs that construction? How can there be an activity, a constructing, without presupposing an agent who precedes and performs that activity? How would we account for the motivation and direction of construction without such a subject? As a rejoinder, I would suggest that it takes a certain suspicion toward grammar to reconceive the matter in a different light. For if gender is constructed, it is not necessarily constructed by an "I" or a "we" who stands before that construction in any spatial or temporal sense of "before." Indeed, it is unclear that there can be an "I" or a "we" who has not been submitted, subjected to gender, where gendering is, among other things, the differentiating relations by which speaking subjects come into being. Subjected to gender, but subjectivated by gender, the "I" neither precedes nor follows the process of this gendering, but emerges only within and as the matrix of gender relations themselves.

This then returns us to the second objection, the one which claims that constructivism forecloses agency, preempts the agency of the subject, and finds itself presupposing the subject that it calls into question. To claim that the subject is itself produced in and as a gendered matrix of relations is not to do away with the subject, but only to ask after the conditions of its emergence and operation. The "activity" of this gendering cannot, strictly speaking, be a human act or expression, a willful appropriation, and it is certainly *not* a question of taking on a mask; it is the matrix through which all willing first becomes possible, its enabling cultural condition. In this sense, the matrix of gender relations is prior to the emergence of the "human". Consider the medical interpellation which (the recent emergence of the sonogram notwithstanding) shifts an infant from an "it" to a "she" or a "he," and in that naming, the girl is "girled," brought into the domain of language and kinship through the interpellation of gender. But that "girling" of the girl does not end there; on the contrary, that founding interpellation is reiterated by various authorities and throughout various intervals of time to reenforce or contest this naturalized effect. The naming is at once the setting of a boundary, and also the repeated inculcation of a norm.

Such attributions or interpellations contribute to that field of discourse and power that orchestrates, delimits, and sustains that which qualifies as "the human." We see this most clearly in the examples of those abjected beings who do not appear properly gendered; it is their very humanness that comes into question. Indeed, the construction of gender operates through *exclusionary* means, such that the human is not only produced over and against the inhuman, but through a set of foreclosures, radical erasures, that are, strictly speaking, refused the possibility of cultural articulation. Hence, it is not enough to claim that human subjects are constructed, for the construction of the human is a differential operation that produces the more and the less "human," the inhuman, the humanly unthinkable. These excluded sites come to bound the "human" as its constitutive outside, and to haunt those boundaries as the persistent possibility of their disruption and rearticulation.[4]

Paradoxically, the inquiry into the kinds of erasures and exclusions by which the construction of the subject operates is no longer constructivism, but neither is it essentialism. For there is an "outside" to what is constructed by discourse, but this is not an absolute "outside," an ontological thereness that exceeds or counters the boundaries of discourse;[5] as a constitutive "outside," it is that which can only be thought – when it can – in relation to that discourse, at and as its most tenuous borders. The debate between constructivism and essentialism thus misses the point of deconstruction altogether, for the point has never been that "everything is discursively constructed"; that point, when and where it is made, belongs to a kind of discursive monism or linguisticism that refuses the constitutive force of exclusion, erasure, violent foreclosure, abjection and its disruptive return within the very terms of discursive legitimacy.

And to say that there is a matrix of gender relations that institutes and sustains the subject is not to claim that there is a singular matrix that acts in a singular and deterministic way to produce a subject as its effect. That is to install the "matrix" in the subject-position within a grammatical formulation which itself needs to be rethought. Indeed, the propositional form "Discourse constructs the subject" retains the subject-position of the grammatical formulation even as it reverses the place of subject and discourse. Construction must mean more than such a simple reversal of terms.

There are defenders and critics of construction, who construe that position along structuralist lines. They often claim that there are structures that construct the subject, impersonal forces, such as culture or discourse or power, where these terms occupy the grammatical site of the subject after the "human" has been dislodged from its place. In such a view, the grammatical and metaphysical place of the subject is retained even as the candidate that occupies that place appears to rotate. As a result, construction is still understood as a unilateral process initiated by a prior subject, fortifying that presumption of the metaphysics of the subject that where there is activity, there lurks behind it an initiating and willful subject. On such a view, discourse or language or the social becomes personified, and in the person-ification the metaphysics of the subject is reconsolidated.

In this second view, construction is not an activity, but an act, one which happens once and whose effects are firmly fixed. Thus, constructivism is reduced to deter-minism and implies the evacuation or displacement of human agency.

This view informs the misreading by which Foucault is criticized for "personify-ing" power: if power is misconstrued as a grammatical and metaphysical subject, and if that metaphysical site within humanist discourse has been the privileged site of the human, then power appears to have displaced the human as the origin of activity. But if Foucault's view of power is understood as the disruption and subversion of this grammar and metaphysics of the subject, if power orchestrates the formation and sustenance of subjects, then it cannot be accounted for in terms of the "subject" which is its effect. And here it would be no more right to claim that the term "construction" belongs at the grammatical site of subject, for construction is neither a subject nor its act, but a process of reiteration by which both "subjects" and "acts" come to appear at all. There is no power that acts, but only a reiterated acting that is power in its persistence and instability.

What I would propose in place of these conceptions of construction is a return to the notion of matter, not as site or surface, but as *a process of materialization that stabilizes over time to produce the effect of boundary, fixity, and surface we call matter.* That matter is always materialized has, I think, to be thought in relation to the productive and, indeed, materializing effects of regulatory power in the Foucauldian sense.[6] Thus, the question is no longer, how is gender constituted as and through a certain interpretation of sex (a question that leaves the "matter" of sex untheorized), but rather, through what regulatory norms is sex itself materialized? And how is it that treating the materiality of sex as a given presupposes and consolidates the normative conditions of its own emergence?

Crucially, then, construction is neither a single act nor a causal process initiated by a subject and culminating in a set of fixed effects. Construction not only takes place *in* time, but is itself a temporal process which operates through the reiteration of norms; sex is both produced and destabilized in the course of this reiteration.[7] As a sedimented effect of a reiterative or ritual practice, sex acquires its naturalized effect, and, yet, it is also by virtue of this reiteration that gaps and fissures are opened up as the constitutive instabilities in such constructions, as that which escapes or exceeds the norm, as that which cannot be wholly defined or fixed by the repetitive labor of that norm. This instability is the *de*constituting possibility in the very process of repetition, the power that undoes the very effects by which "sex" is stabilized, the possibility to put the consolidation of the norms of "sex" into a potentially productive crisis.[8]

Certain formulations of the radical constructivist position appear almost compulsively to produce a moment of recurrent exasperation, for it seems that when the constructivist is construed as a linguistic idealist, the constructivist refutes the reality of bodies, the relevance of science, the alleged facts of birth, aging, illness, and death. The critic might also suspect the constructivist of a certain somatophobia and seek assurances that this abstracted theorist will admit that there are, minimally, sexually differentiated parts, activities, capacities, hormonal and chromosomal differences that can be conceded without reference to "construction." Although at this moment I want to offer an absolute reassurance to my interlocutor, some anxiety prevails. To "concede" the undeniability of "sex" or its "materiality" is always to concede some version of "sex," some formation of "materiality." Is the discourse in and through which that concession occurs – and, yes, that concession invariably does occur – not itself formative of the very phenomenon that it concedes? To claim that discourse is formative is not to claim that it originates, causes, or exhaustively composes that which it concedes; rather, it is to claim that there is no reference to a pure body which is not at the same time a further formation of that body. In this sense, the linguistic capacity to refer to sexed bodies is not denied, but the very meaning of "referentiality" is altered. In philosophical terms, the constative claim is always to some degree performative.

In relation to sex, then, if one concedes the materiality of sex or of the body, does that very conceding operate – performatively – to materialize that sex? And further, how is it that the reiterated concession of that sex – one which need not take place in speech or writing but might be "signaled" in a much more inchoate way – constitutes the sedimentation and production of that material effect?

The moderate critic might concede that *some part* of "sex" is constructed, but some other is certainly not, and then, of course, find him or herself not only under some obligation to draw the line between what is and is not constructed, but to explain how it is that "sex" comes in parts whose differentiation is not a matter of construction. But as that line of demarcation between such ostensible parts gets drawn, the "unconstructed" becomes bounded once again through a signifying practice, and the very boundary which is meant to protect some part of sex from the taint of constructivism is now defined by the anti-constructivist's own construction. Is construction something which happens to a ready-made object, a pregiven thing, and does it happen *in degrees?* Or are we perhaps referring on both sides of the debate to an inevitable practice of signification, of demarcating and delimiting that to which we then "refer," such that our "references" always presuppose – and often conceal – this prior delimitation? Indeed, to "refer" naively or directly to such an extra-discursive object will always require the prior delimitation of the extra-discursive. And insofar as the extra-discursive is delimited, it is formed by the very discourse from which it seeks to free itself. This delimitation, which often is enacted as an untheorized presupposition in any act of description, marks a boundary that includes and excludes, that decides, as it were, what will and will not be the stuff of the object to which we then refer. This marking off will have some normative force and, indeed, some violence, for it can construct only through erasing; it can bound a thing only through enforcing a certain criterion, a principle of selectivity.

What will and will not be included within the boundaries of "sex" will be set by a more or less tacit operation of exclusion. If we call into question the fixity of the structuralist law that divides and bounds the "sexes" by virtue of their dyadic differentiation within the heterosexual matrix, it will be from the exterior regions of that boundary (not from a "position," but from the discursive possibilities opened up by the constitutive outside of hegemonic positions), and it will constitute the disruptive return of the excluded from within the very logic of the heterosexual symbolic.

The trajectory of this text, then, will pursue the possibility of such disruption, but proceed indirectly by responding to two interrelated questions that have been posed to constructivist accounts of gender, not to defend constructivism per se, but to interrogate the erasures and exclusions that constitute its limits. These criticisms presuppose a set of metaphysical oppositions between materialism and idealism embedded in received grammar which, I will argue, are critically redefined by a poststructuralist rewriting of discursive performativity as it operates in the materialization of sex.

## Performativity as citationality

When, in Lacanian parlance, one is said to assume a "sex," the grammar of the phrase creates the expectation that there is a "one" who, upon waking, looks up and deliberates on which "sex" it will assume today, a grammar in which "assumption" is quickly assimilated to the notion of a highly reflective choice. But if this "assumption" is *compelled* by a regulatory apparatus of heterosexuality, one which reiterates itself through the forcible production of "sex," then the "assumption" of sex is constrained from the start. And if there is *agency*, it is to be found, paradoxically, in the possibilities opened up in and by that constrained appropriation of the regulatory law, by the materialization of that law, the compulsory appropriation and identification with those normative demands. The forming, crafting, bearing, circulation, signification of that sexed body will not be a set of actions performed in compliance with the law; on the contrary, they will be a set of actions mobilized by the law, the citational accumulation and dissimulation of the law that produces material effects, the lived necessity of those effects as well as the lived contestation of that necessity.

Performativity is thus not a singular "act," for it is always a reiteration of a norm or set of norms, and to the extent that it acquires an act-like status in the present, it conceals or dissimulates the conventions of which it is a repetition. Moreover, this act is not primarily theatrical; indeed, its apparent theatricality is produced to the extent that its historicity remains dissimulated (and, conversely, its theatricality gains a certain inevitability given the impossibility of a full disclosure of its historicity). Within speech act theory, a performative is that discursive practice that enacts or produces that which it names.[9] According to the biblical rendition of the performative, i.e. "Let there be light!," it appears that it is by virtue of *the power of a subject or its will* that a phenomenon is named into being. In a critical reformulation of the performative, Derrida makes clear that this power is not the function of an originating will, but is always derivative:

> Could a performative utterance succeed if its formulation did not repeat a "coded" or iterable utterance, or in other words, if the formula I pronounce in order to open a meeting, launch a ship or a marriage were not identifiable as conforming with an iterable model, if it were not then identifiable in some way as a "citation"? . . . in such a typology, the category of intention will not disappear; it will have its place, but from that place it will no longer be able to govern the entire scene and system of utterance [*l'énonciation*].[10]

To what extent does discourse gain the authority to bring about what it names through citing the conventions of authority? And does a subject appear as the author of its discursive effects to the extent that the citational practice by which he/she is conditioned and mobilized remains unmarked? Indeed, could it be that the production of the subject as originator of his/her effects is precisely a consequence of this dissimulated citationality? Further, if a subject comes to be through a subjection to the norms of sex, a subjection which requires an assumption of the norms of sex, can we read that "assumption" as precisely a modality of this kind of citationality? In other words, the norm of sex takes hold to the extent that it is "cited" as such a norm, but it also derives its power through the citations that it compels. And how is it that we might read the "citing" of the norms of sex as the process of approximating or "identifying with" such norms?

Further, to what extent within psychoanalysis is the sexed body secured through identificatory practices governed by regulatory schemas? Identification is used here not as an imitative activity by which a conscious being models itself after another; on the contrary, identification is the assimilating passion by which an ego first emerges.[11] Freud argues that "the ego is first and foremost a bodily ego," that this ego is, further, "a projection of a surface,"[12] what we might redescribe as an imaginary morphology. Moreover, I would argue, this imaginary morphology is not a presocial or presymbolic operation, but is itself orchestrated through regulatory schemas that produce intelligible morphological possibilities. These regulatory schemas are not timeless structures, but historically revisable criteria of intelligibility which produce and vanquish bodies that matter.

If the formulation of a bodily ego, a sense of stable contour, and the fixing of spatial boundary is achieved through identificatory practices, and if psychoanalysis documents the hegemonic workings of those identifications, can we then read psychoanalysis for the inculcation of the heterosexual matrix at the level of bodily morphogenesis? What Lacan calls the "assumption" or "accession" to the symbolic law can be read as a kind of *citing* of the law, and so offers an opportunity to link the question of the materialization of "sex" with the reworking of performativity as citationality. Although Lacan claims that the symbolic law has a semi-autonomous status prior to the assumption of sexed positions by a subject, these normative positions, i.e. the "sexes," are only known through the approximations that they occasion. The force and necessity of these norms ("sex" as a symbolic function is to be understood as a kind of commandment or injunction) is thus functionally *dependent on* the approximation and citation of the law; the law without its approximation is no law or, rather, it remains a governing law only for those who would affirm it on the basis of religious faith. If "sex" is assumed in the same way that a law is cited – an analogy which will be supported later in this text – then "the law of sex" is repeatedly fortified and idealized as the law only to the extent that it is reiterated as the law, produced as the law, the anterior and inapproximable ideal, by the very citations it is said to command. Reading the meaning of "assumption" in Lacan as citation, the law is no longer given in a fixed form *prior* to its citation, but is produced through citation as that which precedes and exceeds the mortal approximations enacted by the subject.

In this way, the symbolic law in Lacan can be subject to the same kind of critique that Nietzsche formulated of the notion of God: the power attributed to this prior and ideal power is derived and deflected from the attribution itself.[13] It is this insight into the illegitimacy of the symbolic law of sex that is dramatized to a certain degree in the contemporary film *Paris is Burning*: the ideal that is mirrored depends on that very mirroring to be sustained as an ideal. And though the symbolic appears to be a force that cannot be contravened without psychosis, the symbolic ought to be rethought as a series of normativizing injunctions that secure the borders of sex through the threat of psychosis, abjection, psychic unlivability. And further, that this "law" can only remain a law to the extent that it compels the differentiated citations and approximations called "feminine" and "masculine." The presumption that the symbolic law of sex enjoys a separable ontology prior and autonomous to its assumption is contravened by the notion that the citation of the law is the very mechanism of its production and articulation. What is "forced" by the symbolic, then, is a citation of its law that reiterates and consolidates the ruse of its own force. What would it mean to "cite" the law to produce it differently, to "cite" the law in order to reiterate and coopt its power, to expose the heterosexual matrix and to displace the effect of its necessity?

The process of that sedimentation or what we might call *materialization* will be a kind of citationality, the acquisition of being through the citing of power, a citing that establishes an originary complicity with power in the formation of the "I."

In this sense, the agency denoted by the performativity of "sex" will be directly counter to any notion of a voluntarist subject who exists quite apart from the regulatory norms which she/he opposes. The paradox of subjectivation (*assujetisse-ment*) is precisely that the subject who would resist such norms is itself enabled, if not produced, by such norms. Although this constitutive constraint does not fore-close the possibility of agency, it does locate agency as a reiterative or rearticulatory practice, immanent to power, and not a relation of external opposition to power.

As a result of this reformulation of performativity, (a) gender performativity cannot be theorized apart from the forcible and reiterative practice of regulatory sexual regimes; (b) the account of agency conditioned by those very regimes of discourse/power cannot be conflated with voluntarism or individualism, much less with consumerism, and in no way presupposes a choosing subject; (c) the regime of heterosexuality operates to circumscribe and contour the "materiality" of sex, and that "materiality" is formed and sustained through and as a materialization of regulatory norms that are in part those of heterosexual hegemony; (d) the mater-ialization of norms requires those identificatory processes by which norms are assumed or appropriated, and these identifications precede and enable the formation of a subject, but are not, strictly speaking, performed by a subject; and (e) the limits of constructivism are exposed at those boundaries of bodily life where abjected or delegitimated bodies fail to count as "bodies." If the materiality of sex is demarcated in discourse, then this demarcation will produce a domain of excluded and delegitimated "sex." Hence, it will be as important to think about how and to what end bodies are constructed as is it will be to think about how and to what end bodies are *not* constructed and, further, to ask after how bodies which fail to materialize provide the necessary "outside," if not the necessary support, for the bodies which, in materializing the norm, qualify as bodies that matter.

How, then, can one think through the matter of bodies as a kind of materialization governed by regulatory norms in order to ascertain the workings of heterosexual hegemony in the formation of what qualifies as a viable body? How does that materialization of the norm in bodily formation produce a domain of abjected bodies, a field of deformation, which, in failing to qualify as the fully human, fortifies those regulatory norms? What challenge does that excluded and abjected realm produce to a symbolic hegemony that might force a radical rearticulation of what qualifies as bodies that matter, ways of living that count as "life," lives worth protecting, lives worth saving, lives worth grieving?

## Notes

1   Clearly, sex is not the only such norm by which bodies become materialized, and it is unclear whether "sex" can operate as a norm apart from other normative requirements on bodies. This will become clear in later sections of this text.

2   Abjection (in latin, *ab-jicere*) literally means to cast off, away, or out and, hence, presupposes and produces a domain of agency from which it is differentiated. Here the casting away resonates with the psychoanalytic notion of *Verwerfung*, implying a foreclosure which founds the subject and which, accordingly, establishes that foundation as tenuous. Whereas the psychoanalytic notion of *Verwerfung*, translated as "foreclosure," produces sociality through a repudiation of a primary signifier which produces an unconscious or, in Lacan's theory, the register of the real, the notion of *abjection* designates a degraded or cast out status within the terms of sociality. Indeed, what is foreclosed or repudiated *within* psychoanalytic terms is precisely what may not reenter the field of the social without threatening psychosis, that is, the dissolution of the subject itself. I want to propose that certain abject zones within sociality also deliver this threat, constituting zones of uninhabitability which a subject fantasizes as threatening its own integrity with the prospect of a psychotic dissolution ("I would rather die than do or be that!"). See the entry under "Forclusion" in Jean Laplanche and J.-B. Pontalis, *Vocabulaire de la psychanalyse* (Paris: Presses Universitaires de France, 1967), pp. 163–7.

3   See Sherry Ortner, "Is female to male as nature is to culture?", in *Woman, Culture, and Society*, Michele Rosaldo and Louise Lamphere (Stanford: Stanford University Press, 1974), pp. 67–88.

4   For different but related approaches to this problematic of exclusion, abjection, and the creation of "the human," see Julia Kristeva, *Powers of Horror: An Essay on Abjection*, tr. Leon Roudiez (New York: Columbia University Press, 1982); John Fletcher and Andrew Benjamin (eds), *Abjection, Melancholia and Love: The Work of Julia Kristeva* (New York and London: Routledge, 1990); Jean-François Lyotard, *The Inhuman: Reflections on Time*, tr. Geoffrey Bennington and Rachel Bowlby (Stanford: Stanford University Press, 1991).

5   For a very provocative reading which shows how the problem of linguistic referentiality is linked with the specific problem of referring to bodies, and what might be meant by "reference" in such a case, see Cathy Caruth, "The claims of reference," *The Yale Journal of Criticism*, vol. 4, no. 1 (1990), pp. 193–206.

6   Although Foucault distinguishes between juridical and productive models of power in *The History of Sexuality*, vol. I, tr. Robert Hurley (New York: Vintage, 1978), I have argued that the

two models presuppose each other. The production of a subject – its subjection (*assujetissement*) – is one means of its regulation. See my "Sexual inversions," in Domna Stanton (ed.), *Discourses of Sexuality* (Ann Arbor: University of Michigan Press, 1992), pp. 344–61.

7  It is not simply a matter of construing performativity as a repetition of acts, as if "acts" remain intact and self-identical as they are repeated in time, and where "time" is understood as external to the "acts" themselves. On the contrary, an act is itself a repetition, a sedimentation, and congealment of the past which is precisely foreclosed in its act-like status. In this sense an "act" is always a provisional failure of memory. In what follows, I make use of the Lacanian notion that every act is to be construed as a repetition, the repetition of what cannot be recollected, of the irrecoverable, and is thus the haunting spectre of the subject's deconstitution. The Derridean notion of iterability, formulated in response to the theorization of speech acts by John Searle and J. L. Austin, also implies that every act is itself a recitation, the citing of a prior chain of acts which are implied in a present act and which perpetually drain any "present" act of its presentness. See note 9 below for the difference between a repetition in the service of the fantasy of mastery (i.e. a repetition of acts which build the subject, and which are said to be the constructive or constituting acts of a subject) and a notion of repetition-compulsion, taken from Freud, which breaks apart that fantasy of mastery and sets its limits.

8  The notion of temporality ought not to be construed as a simple succession of distinct "moments," all of which are equally distant from one another. Such a spatialized mapping of time substitutes a certain mathematical model for the kind of duration which resists such spatializing metaphors. Efforts to describe or name this temporal span tend to engage spatial mapping, as philosophers from Bergson through Heidegger have argued. Hence, it is important to underscore the effect of *sedimentation* that the temporality of construction implies. Here what are called "moments" are not distinct and equivalent units of time, for the "past" will be the accumulation and congealing of such "moments" to the point of their indistinguishability. But it will also consist of that which is refused from construction, the domains of the repressed, forgotten, and the irrecoverably foreclosed. That which is not included – exteriorized by boundary – as a phenomenal constituent of the sedimented effect called "construction" will be as crucial to its definition as that which is included; this exteriority is not distinguishable as a "moment." Indeed, the notion of the "moment" may well be nothing other than a retrospective fantasy of mathematical mastery imposed upon the interrupted durations of the past.

To argue that construction is fundamentally a matter of iteration is to make the temporal modality of "construction" into a priority. To the extent that such a theory requires a spatialization of time through the postulation of discrete and bounded moments, this temporal account of construction presupposes a spatialization of temporality itself, what one might, following Heidegger, understand as the reduction of temporality to time.

The Foucauldian emphasis on *convergent* relations of power (which might in a tentative way be contrasted with the Derridean emphasis on iterability) implies a mapping of power relations that in the course of a genealogical process form a constructed effect. The notion of convergence presupposes both motion and space; as a result, it appears to elude the paradox noted above in which the very account of temporality requires the spatialization of the "moment." On the other hand, Foucault's account of convergence does not fully theorize what is at work in the "movement" by which power and discourse are said to converge. In a sense, the "mapping" of power does not fully theorize temporality.

Significantly, the Derridean analysis of iterability is to be distinguished from simple repetition in which the distances between temporal "moments" are treated as uniform in their spatial extension. The "betweenness" that differentiates "moments" of time is not one that can, within Derridean terms, be spatialized or bounded as an identifiable object. It is the non-thematizable *différance* which erodes and contests any and all claims to discrete identity, including the discrete identity of the "moment." What differentiates moments is not a spatially extended duration, for if it were, it would also count as a "moment," and so fail to account for what falls between moments. This "*entre*," that which is at once "between" and "outside," is something like non-thematizable space and non-thematizable time as they converge.

Foucault's language of construction includes terms like "augmentation," "proliferation," and "convergence," all of which presume a temporal domain not explicitly theorized. Part of the problem here is that whereas Foucault appears to want his account of genealogical effects to be historically specific, he would favor an account of genealogy over a philosophical account of temporality. In "The subject and power" (Hubert Dreyfus and Paul Rabinow (eds), *Michel Foucault: Beyond Structuralism and Hermeneutics* [Chicago: Northwestern University Press, 1983]), Foucault refers to "the diversity of...logical sequence" that characterizes power relations. He would doubtless reject the apparent linearity implied by models of iterability which link them with the linearity of older models of historical sequence. And yet, we do not receive a specification of "sequence"; is it the very notion of "sequence" that varies historically, or are there configurations of sequence that vary, with sequence itself remaining invariant? The specific social formation and figuration of temporality is in some ways unattended by both positions. Here one might consult the work of Pierre Bourdieu to understand the temporality of social construction.

9 See J. L. Austin, *How to Do Things With Words*, J. O. Urmson and Marina Sbisà (eds) (Cambridge, Mass.: Harvard University Press, 1955), and *Philosophical Papers* (Oxford: Oxford University Press, 1961), especially pp. 233–52; Shoshana Felman, *The Literary Speech-Act: Don Juan with J. L. Austin, or Seduction in Two Languages*, tr. Catherine Porter (Ithaca: Cornell University Press, 1983); Barbara Johnson, "Poetry and performative language: Mallarmé and Austin," in *The Critical Difference: Essays in the Contemporary Rhetoric of Reading* (Baltimore: Johns Hopkins University Press, 1980), pp. 52–66; Mary Louise Pratt, *A Speech Act Theory of Literary Discourse* (Bloomington: Indiana University Press, 1977); and Ludwig Wittgenstein, *Philosophical Investigations*, tr. G. E. M. Anscombe (New York: Macmillan, 1958), part 1.

10 Jacques Derrida, "Signature, event, context," in *Limited, Inc.*, Gerald Graff (ed.), tr. Samuel Weber and Jeffrey Mehlman (Evanston: Northwestern University Press, 1988), p. 18.

11 See Michel Borch-Jacobsen, *The Freudian Subject*, tr. Catherine Porter (Stanford: Stanford University Press, 1988). Whereas Borch-Jacobsen offers an interesting theory of how identification precedes and forms the ego, he tends to assert the priority of identification to any libidinal experience, where I would insist that identification is itself a passionate or libidinal assimilation. See also the useful distinction between an imitative model and a mimetic model of identification in Ruth Leys, "The real Miss Beauchamp: gender and the subject of imitation" in Judith Butler and Joan Scott (eds), *Feminists Theorize the Political* (New York: Routledge, 1992), pp. 167–214; Kaja Silverman, *Male Subjectivity at the Margins* (New York: Routledge, 1992), pp. 262–70; Mary Ann Doane, "Misrecognition and identity," in Ron Burnett (ed.), *Explorations in Film Theory: Selected Essays from Ciné-Tracts* (Bloomington: Indiana University Press, 1991), pp. 15–25; and Diana Fuss, "Freud's fallen women: identification, desire, and 'A case of homosexuality in a woman,'" in *The Yale Journal of Criticism*, vol. 6, no. 1 (1993), pp. 1–23.

12 Sigmund Freud, *The Ego and the Id*, James Strachey, ed., tr. Joan Riviere (New York: Norton, 1960), p. 16.

13 Nietzsche argues that the ideal of God was produced "[i]n the same measure" as a human sense of failure and wretchedness, and that the production of God was, indeed, the idealization which instituted and reenforced that wretchedness; see Friedrich Nietzsche, *On the Genealogy of Morals*, tr. Walter Kaufmann (New York: Vintage, 1969), section 20. That the symbolic law in Lacan produces "failure" to approximate the sexed ideals embodied and enforced by the law, is usually understood as a promising sign that the law is not fully efficacious, that it does not exhaustively constitute the psyche of any given subject. And yet, to what extent does this conception of the law produce the very failure that it seeks to order, and maintain an ontological distance between the law and its failed approximations such that the deviant approximations have no power to alter the workings of the law itself?

# Bringing Body to Theory

## *Susan Bordo*

## I

There's nothing like reading interpretation and criticism of one's own work to confirm the more mundane, living reality to the postmodern pronouncement that the author is dead. The work itself, moreover, often feels all-too-alive, slippery and wiggly as it is handled and given shape by other people's psyches and concerns, other political and intellectual agendas than one's own. It's an unnerving and challenging experience – I imagine not too different from a parent's recognition that her children have minds of their own – in which one has to learn to accept with grace exactly what all one's efforts have been aiming at: a once-intimate part of you is out there, going its own way, able to exist quite well without you.

Sometimes, though, there *is* the pleasure and relief of feeling understood (which does not necessarily mean receiving praise; some of the most admiring readings of my work discuss a text that I barely recognize). "Yes, that's it, you've got it, that's what I was trying to say, that's the thing that's most important to me." The author may be "privileging" her reading of the text in feeling that these are moments of truth, recognition, clarity. But that's an author's privilege, and irresistible in any case. Susan Hekman's intelligent, non-ideological, perceptive, and integrative reading of my work and Judith Butler's not only takes extraordinary care to read the texts with a view to discovering our projects as *we* have conceived and pursued them (perhaps, at times, as they have pursued us), but also places them in a broad perspective that allows them to speak to each other in a way that they haven't before. I felt understood by her reading, and I also learned about my work from it. I believe it is one of the most useful, difference-respecting but polarity-busting discussions of feminist theory I have read.

Hekman's piece enabled me to see with greater clarity something that has been playing at the edges of my thinking for some time. Although Butler and I may have strong theoretical differences (with shared Foucauldian premises, as Hekman points out), there is an important way in which each of us may have performed – if not in the letter of our texts, then in the social and intellectual uses, the cultural life of our texts – exactly the kind of work the other calls for. Hekman points to my analysis of eating disorders as a concrete, "practical" illustration (and confirmation) of Butler's notion that the body of the abject, as an exaggeration of contradictions and exclusions within the dominant order – making explicit what is latently "grotesque" about it – can function (as Hekman puts it) as a "site of the possibility of refiguring the hegemonic symbolic, imagining a future horizon that values bodies differently." Without making exaggerated claims for my own work, I hope that this has been the case. I am immensely gratified when I receive information which leads me to believe that it has contributed to changing therapeutic theory and practice concerning what I argue are "cultural pathologies" of the body, to helping women with eating problems reinterpret and revalue their bodies, and to encouraging other philosophers to bring the concreteness of the body (as opposed to an abstract "theory of" the body) into their own work. These are "sites" of culture whose practices I address in my work, and whose future I care very much about.

I would add to Hekman's wonderful insight about my "practical" relation to Butler's theory of resistance a corresponding point about Butler's work-as-cultural-praxis in relation to my ideas about the social responsibilities of philosophers. Frequently, I have taken issue with the baroque obscurity of postmodern prose, including Butler's. One aspect of my frustration is that illuminating and potentially liberating insights remain the property of a privileged few. I love Foucault's image of ideas as intellectual "hand grenades," and I personally value culturally lobbed disturbance over hothouse scholarly conversation. But the fact is that Butler's work has inspired and generated such a massive intellectual and artistic "deployment" of energy and creativity that it *has* an incredibly vibrant and important life beyond the confines of the academy. And it has touched people in personal ways too, as they have reinterpreted and revalued their sexuality, their "marginality," and their role as culture-makers. In cultural *practice* – always my central emphasis – Butler's work has proven to *be* accessible, *has* been an intellectual "hand grenade."

In addition to tracing differences and points of connection between Butler's work and my own, Hekman raises some questions for each of us. The challenges she poses to me – to make explicit both my conception of the "materiality" of the body and my theory of "resistance" – have frequently been posed to me by philosophers and theorists. My reaction to them has been ambivalent. On the one hand, I want to say (and sometimes have said, when pressed too hard): "Leave me alone! I don't do that kind of thing and don't want to!" I have always considered myself a phenomenologist and diagnostician of culture, who uses diverse theoretical tools to excavate and expose hidden or unquestioned aspects of concrete forms, occurrences, texts, practices. Although my work is highly theoretical in that it is always analyzing and interpreting (always "reading into things," as my students sometimes complain), it is not aimed at articulating or defending an over-arching theory of body, resistance, or anything else. I don't consider that I "do theory" or "have" a theory, but rather that I *use* theory, fairly promiscuously, but with a decided preference for certain types.

On the other hand, I have sometimes felt – precisely because I have such preferences, and have invoked them in order to criticize other approaches – that it is disingenuous of me to disown my theory in this way. Also, silence on these issues would allow certain common misinterpretations (from my point of view) of my arguments and ideas to flourish unchecked. But there are more important issues at stake, too, which go beyond the interpretation of my work. My critique of theory, like all my work, is cultural criticism, that is, is directed at particular styles of theorizing not at "theory" in general. Theorizing, like all human activities, has taken many different historical forms and served many different purposes. My criticism of postmodern theory is that despite its alliance with "the body" it often seems to be scaling the heights with pure mind. I am not "anti-theory." But my criticisms of *certain kinds* of theorizing – as excessively estheticized, or pretentious, or unhinged from social context – have sometimes been mistaken as indicating that I am. This, in turn, has led to characterizations of my work as "practical" rather than "theoretical," perpetuating one of the (gender and race-coded) dualities I most abhor and contributing to the notion that the only "real" theory is what I would describe as "meta-theory."

Nowadays, few academics engage in general theory-building – an enterprise that has been criticized as universalizing and "totalizing."[1] But many academics do engage in meta-theory, and regard it as the most rigorous form of scholarship. Meta-theory is talk *about* theory: about the presuppositions, implications, complexities of various theoretical formulations, conflicts among theories, internal contradictions, unintended alliances (e.g. with essentialism, foundationalism, relativism), and so forth. Meta-theory is important and interesting, and has a privileged place among philosophers and social theorists. But theory needn't be the object of analysis in order for a discussion to qualify as theoretical; it can be an animating force "behind" an analysis. What it animates can vary widely; it may be social, political or historical analysis, a piece of cultural criticism, or even an exploration of personal experience. However, among those who see themselves as "theoreticians" (especially philosophers) there has been a tendency to view these analyses hierarchically; the more particular one gets – and certainly, the more personal one gets – the less "theoretical" one's work is regarded as being. Work that theorizes about the body through the situation of women, particularly if it makes use of personal experience, has rarely been accorded the privileged status of "theory." This has been the fate of much early feminist writing (before we learned to gussy our discussions up with sophisticated jargon drawn from male theorists).

In "Feminism, Foucault, and the politics of the body" (1993a), I recall my own inadvertent collusion with such tendencies, remembering how in a 1980 review of Foucault's *History of Sexuality*, I had noted many similarities between Foucault's notion of the "deployment of sexuality" and Marcuse's earlier conception of "the mobilization and administration of libido," while never for a moment considering the relevance to my discussion of the extensive feminist literature, from the sixties and seventies on the social construction and deployment of female sexuality, beauty, and femininity. I was thoroughly familiar with that literature. Yet I hadn't credited it with having a *theoretical* perspective on the body. Why not? Although acknowledging that the works themselves were not particularly theoretically self-conscious, I also had to admit that:

> In 1980, despite the fact that I was writing a dissertation historically critiquing the duality male mind/female body, I still expected "theory" only from men. Moreover – and here my inability to "transcend" these dualisms reveals itself more subtly – I was unable to recognize *embodied* theory when it was staring me in the face. For it is hardly the case that these early feminist works were not theoretical, but rather that their theory never drew attention to *itself*, never made an appearance except as it shaped the "matter" of their argument. That is, theory was rarely abstracted, objectified and elaborated as of interest in itself. Works that perform such abstraction and elaboration get taken much more seriously than works which do not. This is as true or truer in 1992 [when I wrote these words] as it was in 1980.

In "The feminist as other" (1996), I discuss how feminist writing, even when acknowledged as theoretical, is often read as being "only" about gender (read: women), without more general cultural implications, and so remains marginalized in the "women's issues" section of our bookstores, anthologies, conferences, courses, and narratives of intellectual history. So, Foucault becomes the "father" of "the politics of the body," while the work of feminists is constructed as in "daughterly" (at best, little-sisterly) relation to the very paradigm shift that they helped bring, through significant social and intellectual struggle, into being. At the same time, the fact that *Foucault's* "body" is gendered – a bias discussed by feminists, of course, but largely ignored by the "real" Foucault scholars – remains obscured:

> When feminists talk about the discipline of the body involved in the construction of femininity, it is read as having implications only for women and the "peculiarities"

[a reference to Beauvoir] of their bodies. When Foucault, on the other hand, talks about the discipline of the body involved in the construction of the soldier, it is read as gender-neutral and broadly applicable. The soldier-body is no less gendered a norm, of course, than the body-as-decorative-object. But this is obscured because we view the woman's body under the sign of her Otherness while regarding the male body – as Beauvoir puts it – as in "direct and normal relation to the world." The ironies engendered by this are dizzying. The male body becomes "The Body" proper (as in: "Foucault altered our understanding of the body") while the female body remains marked by its difference (as in: "Feminism showed us the oppressiveness of femininity.") At the same time, however, the male body *as* male body disappears completely, *its* concrete specificity submerged in its collapse into the universal. Thus, while men are the cultural theorists *of* the body, only women *have* bodies. Meanwhile, of course, the absent male body continues to operate illicitly as the (scientific, philosophical, medical) norm for all.

So: I have come to realize that by not taking responsibility for the theoretical commitments of my *own* work, I may be contributing to some of the intellectual assumptions and biases I complain about most bitterly. Perhaps it's time for me to embrace the theory in my work, not as a temporary partner providing solace or excitement for the night, but as a quite serious and committed relationship which deserves acknowledgment and legitimization.

## II

In direct contrast to German philosophy, which descends from heaven to earth, here we ascend from earth to heaven. That is to say, we do not set out from what men say, imagine, conceive, nor from men as narrated, thought of, imagined, conceived, in order to arrive at men in the flesh. We set out from real, active men, and on the basis of their real life process we demonstrate the development of the ideological reflexes and echoes of this life process. The phantoms formed in the human brain are also, necessarily sublimates of their material life process, which is empirically verifiable and bound to material premises. Morality, religion, metaphysics, all the rest of ideology and their corresponding forms of consciousness, thus no longer have the semblance of independence. They have no history, no development; but men, developing their material production and their material intercourse, alter, along with this, their real existence, their thinking, and the products of their thinking. Life is not determined by consciousness, but consciousness by life.

(From Karl Marx, *The German Ideology*)

Some readers may be surprised that I have opened this discussion with a quote from Marx. But Marx was my first intellectual hero, and while I do not consider myself a Marxist, my own "materialism" has roots in his. Despite Marx's own pronouncements that he is standing idealism on its head, I have never understood him to be "reversing" Hegel by elevating some *other* realm of human activity (call it the "material realm") to a position of priority over the realm of "consciousness." What drew me to Marx was what I took to be his insistence on the *concreteness* of human existence – consciousness included – against abstract conceptions of "Man," "Reason," "Freedom," and so forth. Consciousness, while it may fancy itself in league with platonic forms or transcendental subjectivity, does not fly with the angels but walks the earth. Its biography is as concrete and historical as any other feature of human life.

In "Feminism, Foucault, and the politics of the body," I discuss the important role that historical thinking – which developed out of my participation in feminism, and later also drew me to Foucault – played in my intellectual development: "As a philosopher and a feminist," I wrote, "historicism was for me the great liberator of thought, challenging both the most stubborn pretensions of my discipline (to the possession of eternal truths, atemporal foundations, universal reason) and enduring social myths about human nature and gender by showing them to be, in Nietzsche's words, 'human, all too human.'" But claims to privileged foundations or absolute truth can take other forms than that of the Platonic or Cartesian (or Hegelian) overseer of reality. My earliest critiques were aimed at these "masculine" forms of philosophical hubris (*cultural* forms, not to be simply equated with the work of Plato, Descartes, or Hegel, but representing dominant traditions of philosophizing grounded in particular interpretations of their work). I later found cultural overseers exercising their muscles in areas closer to home.

I vividly recall the first time I insisted on the "materiality" of the body at a continental philosophy conference. It was not a pleasant experience. It was ten years ago, "textuality" was still the rage, "essentialism" was the horror of horrors, and the word "material" – since become so fashionable – was decidedly not *comme il faut*. The paper I was presenting was an early version of "Material girl: the effacements of postmodern culture" (1990), and when the word "material" came out of my mouth it was as though I had farted in public. This is no exaggeration. I felt the atmosphere in the room shift palpably, as those who had been comfortable in the assurance that I was a right-minded person (after all, I was working out of Foucault, wasn't I?) all at once felt something unexpected and foul enter the room. In the discussion period, some feminist scholars generously gave me the opportunity to clarify and save myself, with questions like "You aren't *really* positing, *are you*, a body that is unmediated, 'natural,' outside of language and discourse, which is not open to a multiplicity of interpretive readings, *are you?*" I tried to explain what I was doing, but it was no use. None of my explanations were able to sufficiently cleanse me of the taint of the retrograde notion of a "material body." I was not invited to dinner after the talk with the rest of the feminist theorists, and when I came upon one of the conference organizers speaking to a keynote speaker outside the hotel, they fell into awkward silence.

The incident was a watershed for me, and nearly drove me out of academia. Instead, I decided that I had my work cut out for me. "Material" and "matter" are no longer dirty words, and I like to think that I have played a role in bringing about that change, and in encouraging open criticism of some of the dogmas that once reigned in feminist theory. In attaching itself to certain intellectual fashions, feminist theory has been, of course, no different than any other scholarly culture; what's different, perhaps, is feminism's responsiveness to challenge, and its willingness to change. That has been enormously gratifying to witness. I now see graduate students insisting that theory be held responsible to their experiences as embodied beings, I see them incorporating cultural criticism and personal experience within theoretical dissertations, I see them wanting to write in accessible styles – and I see feminist faculty encouraging them, and trying to break through some old habits and dogmas of our own.

Ten years ago, I had absolutely no use for biological or evolutionary paradigms of the body, and was just as phobic about "genes" as any other self-respecting social constructionist. The word "natural" elicited lectures from me on ideology and mystification. Today, I am more agnostic and humble – and less politically trigger-happy – about the role of biology and evolution. I still believe that the body, as Butler has trenchantly put it, is "never free of imaginary construction" (1990: 71). I therefore continue to insist, along with other social critics of scientism, that what constitutes our knowledge of biology is always mediated by the conceptual frameworks – cultural as well as scientific paradigms – that we bring into the laboratory. But for me, this does not distinguish science from any other human enterprise, and thus should occasion no more prima facie suspicion of science than anything else. For me, there is a big leap from acknowledging that the science of biology is mediated by historically located, conceptual frameworks (an acknowledgment which adds a cultural dimension to what Kant argued) to reducing the concept of "biology" to the status of "fiction" or "fantasy." If biology is a "fantasy," so too is every other framework for understanding the body, social constructionism and performative theories included.

I think that Butler would agree with my last statement – in theory. In practice, though, she is what I would call a "discourse foundationalist." For the discourse foundationalist, insights into our embeddedness in discourse function as a "bottom line," a privileged framework which is used to deconstruct other frameworks of understanding to its own preferred elements (that's why I offer the image of a "theoretical pasta-machine" which converts everything that passes through it into a "trope") and, having done this, dispense with them as so much detritus. Certainly, we are embedded in language. We are also creatures with a physiology that limits us, even in the kinds of languages we have developed. Humanists are appalled when evolutionary biologists reduce our "privileged shrine" (as Maxine Sheets-Johnstone jibes) of language to merely one variant of primate "vocal and facial display." Is it any less reductive when *we* evaporate concepts like "genes" (or "matter") into "tropes" of scientific fiction?

These reductions (with guilt equally distributed on both sides, as far as I can see) have played a large role in fomenting the hostile polarization of the sciences and the humanities at universities today, and in perpetuating the fragmenting Cartesian division that has structured the disciplines. The humanities (with literature and philosophy at the forefront) have perfected an identification with disembodied pure mind (read, for much contemporary literary theory and philosophy: "language"), while the sciences have reduced experimental rigor to the study of *res extensa* – mindless bodies. (Anyone who doubts the latter should try to find entries for "consciousness," "mind," "experience," or even "thinking" in the indexes of most texts on biology and evolution.) These "academically propagated creatures," as Sheets-Johnstone states, "mindless bodies on the one hand and disembodied minds on the other . . . are profoundly unnatural species" (1990: 8–9).

Let's agree we cannot "get outside" the (historically sedimented) discourses and representations that shape our reality. Does this mean that all we are legitimately permitted to talk about is our reality *as* discourse and representation? And what makes "matter" an "effect of discourse" and the "trope" a foundational explanatory concept? The "trope" has a history, too, is no more "prior to discourse" than "matter." And in any case, whatever we believe on a "meta" level, we all still go on talking and arguing (and it is to be hoped evaluating, and discriminating, and thoughtfully considering) as if there were more than just competing fictions at stake, and this is how it must (and should) be for embodied beings. For myself, today I am less inclined than I used to be to dismiss the claims of geneticists. As I grow older and fall prey to the same disorders as everyone else in my family, I feel my own genetic inheritance more acutely than I did when I was younger and naively convinced of my power to "resist" becoming anything like my father and mother.

This doesn't mean that I'm not still suspicious of arguments about the biological basis of homosexuality, or race, or differences between men and women. But historical vigilance is not a metaphysical position, it's a critical attitude. And it's one that needs to be taken towards all our intellectual attachments, not just science. All disciplines, all scholars, all scientists, all social policy makers need to be critically aware and self-scrutinizing of the cultural assumptions we bring to our work, and the cultural uses being made of our work. The problem with many scientists who have recently inveighed against "cultural studies" is not that they insist on the "reality" of the world or scientific objectivity as a regulative ideal – both of which I and many other cultural theorists "believe in," too – but that they take their *own* objectivity as an accomplished and unquestionable premise, and refuse to look at their own beliefs and practices through culturally and historically informed eyes. But then, so too do many postmodernists.

These issues are intimately related to my conception of "materiality" – which for better or worse has not changed much over the last ten years. First, the obvious (or I hope obvious): in speaking of "materiality," I am neither invoking some "matter" of the body to oppose to its "form," nor am I insisting on the primacy of the brute "matter" of things, or the "natural" or the instinctual against the culturally overlaid or linguistic. "Materiality," for me, is not *stuff*, not substance, not nature. (It is not even exclusively about "the body" – except insofar as "the body" has been imagined as the cultural repository for the features of human existence on which I am insisting, shortly to be described.) So much for what "materiality" is *not* for me. What it *is*, as Susan Hekman rightly says, is less clear. This doesn't surprise me, because I invoke the concept as a kind of umbrella metaphor, or governing image, that embraces a cluster of values – epistemological, dialogical or conversational, political, existential, perhaps even ethical – that I am advocating for.

"Materiality," in the broadest terms, signifies for me our finitude. It refers to our inescapable physical locatedness in time and space, in history and culture, both of which not only shape us (the social constructionist premise, which I share with other postmoderns) but also *limit* us (which some postmoderns appear to me to deny). As Nietzsche rightly insisted, we are always standing *someplace* and seeing from *some* where, and thus are always partial and selective thinkers. But the desire, the anxiety, to get "above and beyond" our finite selves (as Dewey, mincing no words, put it) is intense. Intellectuals have different ways of enacting such a fantasy. The presumption that one has attained a "view from nowhere" is the classic philosophical one, and the subject of *The Flight to Objectivity* (1987) and my early writing on the hubris and self-deception of philosophical fantasies of escape from the body (e.g. "The cultural overseer and the tragic hero" [1982]). The "dream of being everywhere" is the postmodern version, discussed in my critiques of contemporary theory ("Feminism, postmodernism and gender skepticism" [1990] "Feminist skepticism and the 'maleness' of philosophy" [1988; 1992]). Neither image of transcendence owns the finiteness of our condition as knowers or the historical nature of its own "existence." When I was studying philosophy, in a discipline of which the Cartesian overseer was still king, his gender, race, and class biases yet to be challenged, the "view from nowhere" ruled the roost. But today I sometimes wish, dazed and confused by some slithery, postmodern conversation, that the Cartesian overseer would make a return appearance and "clear" the air. (Of course, he hasn't actually gone away, he's just in another room.)

Our materiality (which includes history, race, gender, and so forth, but also the biology and evolutionary history of our bodies, and our dependence on the natural environment) impinges on us – shapes, constrains, and empowers us – both as thinkers and knowers, and also as "practical," fleshly bodies. The latter has been an important focus of my work on eating disorders, contemporary technologies of reshaping the self, and now my current work on masculinity. But my conception of the "socially constructed body" tends to be more "materially" inclined than many other contemporary academic writers'. This is not because (as some critics have charged) I invoke some "essential female subject" or "gender core" as a ground. I don't even believe, as Hekman says – one of the few places where I believe she has misinterpreted me – that feminism as critical practice "must be grounded in the sexed specificity of the female body." In my view, that has been *one* of feminism's key critical projects, but (like everything else) its vitality and efficacy are dependent upon historical, cultural context.

Drawing on Ann Snitow's satirical but telling distinction between "red bloomer" feminists (who emphasize, even revel in, sexed specificity) and "transcenders" (who want to deconstruct gender, even sex), I argue that each of these poles is "necessary to feminist struggle and change." My criticism of the postmodern feminist infatuation with "transcendence" concerns the discrepancy that I see between the currently dominant theory (deconstructing gender) and the bodily, institutional, practical realities of our culture. These are very much gendered and, as Hekman correctly points out in explicating my conception of "material," their inscriptions cannot be simply evaporated, for they "cause pain and suffering for 'real,' 'material' women..." Here, Hekman understands what those critics who have charged me with "essentialism" have missed: in insisting on the materiality of gender I am not invoking "nature" or importing covert essences. Our materiality includes our biology – but that is for scientists to explore. As a cultural critic and philosopher of the body, I explore – and urge that we not lose sight of – the concrete consequences – for "our bodies, ourselves" – of living in a gendered and racially ordered world.

My work on the body is more "material" than many because I believe that the study of representations and cultural "discourse" – while an important part of the cultural study of the body – cannot by itself stand as a history of the body. Those discourses impinge on us as fleshly bodies, and often in ways that cannot be determined from a study of representations alone. To make such determinations, we need to get down and dirty with the body on the level of its practices – to look at what we are eating (or not eating), the lengths we will go to keep ourselves perpetually young, the practices that we engage in, emulating TV and pop icons, and so forth. Our assessments of gender and race inequities must consider not only the most avant-garde images from *Details* or *Interview* magazine, but what people are doing to their bodies in the more mundane service of the "normal" – the kinds of cosmetic surgeries they are having, the hours they spend on the stairmaster, what they feel about themselves when they look in the mirror. In studying masculinity, we must not only study "the phallus," symbol of masculine power and authority and capable of being assumed by women as well as men, but also *men's* bodies in their historical diversity and concrete, fleshly vulnerability.

Such talk makes many philosophers queasy. The first time I said the word "thigh" in a talk to (mostly male) philosophers, the gulps were audible; now that I'm working on male bodies, I expect them to be even louder. But it's not just prudishness that makes philosophers blanch at mention of body parts. Many philosophers have been drawn to philosophy or "theory" because of the promise of a high, heady, and "untouchable" (as Dewey puts it) realm of ideas where they can imagine themselves as masters rather than creatures of the universe. As bodies, as Dewey points out, we are most definitely not masters of our own lives, let alone the universe.

Keeping track of the practical life of our bodies is important to keeping us intellectually honest. Intellectuals tend to grossly conflate the articulation of an idea or argument to their *own* satisfaction or excitement (or the excitement and satisfaction of their academic cohorts) with the "reality" of things outside the domain of their own activity. It's a kind of idealism, and image-makers do it, too. Ingrid Sischy, editor of *Interview* magazine, proclaims in a recent editorial that we are living in an age in which beauty has had "its chains taken off." Pardon me? Sischy may view the difference between a skinny model in a Dior suit and a skinny model with a nose-ring as bold and innovative; but teenagers are still starving themselves, all the same.

Our ideas, of course, are a part of reality, and they can change it. Imaginative interpretations (and images) excite and inspire, they start important cultural conversations going; if we were limited to mirroring reality (as if that were possible), things would be pretty dreary. But just because an idea or image – of the body, say – is thrillingly "transgressive" to a bunch of artists or academics does not mean we should start trumpeting the dawn of a new age. We can, of course, argue anything we want "in theory." But, as I write in *Unbearable Weight* (1993b):

> The actuality and effectiveness of social resistance can be determined only by examining historical situations . . . Failure to recognize this can result in theorizing potentially transformative but still highly contained forms of subjectivity as though they were on equal footing with historically dominant forms and romanticizing the degree of cultural challenge that is occurring.

Only an examination of concrete, historical situations can determine whether resistance is taking place or the body being "rewritten" or dualisms being "transcended." This is why *Unbearable Weight* insists that assessing where we stand *vis-à-vis* the dualisms of mind/body, male/female, black/white and so on requires concrete exploration and critique of the many practical, institutional, and cultural arenas (including the esthetics and ethics of the body) which have been and continue to be shaped by those dualisms. We cannot make the mistake of imagining that they have been "transcended" or "resisted" just because we can "destabilize" them in theory. I believe that many postmodern readings of the body become lost in the fascinating, ingenious (and often, prematurely celebratory) routes that imagination, intellect and political fervor can take when looking at bodily "texts" without attention to the concrete contexts – social, political, cultural, practical – in which they are embedded. And so they need to be reminded of the materiality of the body.

This, in a nutshell, was my problem with Butler's original reading of drag-as-parody, and the reason why I question (in "Postmodern subjects, postmodern bodies" [1992]) whether "there is a body" in *Gender Trouble*. The body's materiality, for me (as I hope has become clear in the course of this piece), is first and foremost about concreteness, and concrete (and limiting) *location*. In *Gender Trouble*, Butler claims a great deal for the destabilizing power of parodic bodies, a power which for her derives from highly general and abstract features of parody – one might say, from its grammar. She does not concretize and specify the "body-in-drag" itself, or locate it in the concrete contexts which, from my point of view, will determine just where and how "destabilizing" the parody is. Yet she concludes that "drag 'effectively mocks... the notion of true gender identity' and 'displaces the entire enactment of gender significations from the discourse of truth and falsity.'"

Queer theorists are now doing exciting work complicating Butler's position by looking at diverse forms of drag in concrete, social contexts. And Butler has since modified her own position. I mention my critique of *Gender Trouble* here in order to clarify a common misunderstanding about the nature of my criticisms of that book. I do *not* see Butler as arguing that "we choose our gender much as we choose our clothes." This would be a crude and silly reading of Butler (although accurate with respect to some other postmodern authors), and it is not mine. (For me, the act of choosing clothes is hardly the best metaphor for an act of autonomy, anyway!) What I charge Butler with is a philosophical abstractness that – combined with a post-modern taste for the "instability" of texts – leads to what is perhaps an over-estimation of the degree of subversion of norms that is taking place at any time. As I argue against *Gender Trouble's* abstract theory of parody:

> Subversion is contextual, historical, and above all, social. No matter how exciting the destabilizing potential of texts, bodily or otherwise, whether those texts are subversive or recuperative or both or neither cannot be determined in abstraction from actual social practice.

Butler has since acknowledged (in *Bodies That Matter*) the importance of such considerations.

Perhaps another point of confusion about my position has been that for me – although not, apparently, for many other theorists – questions of "autonomy" and questions of "resistance" are separate ones. That is, whether or not our actions can be said to be autonomous or "free" is distinct from the question of which of those actions can be said to "resist" a social norm. Questions concerning free will, determinism, and autonomy are either metaphysical questions I couldn't begin to imagine *how* to answer or they are so dependent on definition that they can be answered in any number of equally arbitrary ways. In neither case do they provide information about the sort of cultural diagnoses I am interested in.

Am I behaving autonomously when I choose my clothes? If I imagine autonomy as having to do with interpretation and creative negotiation of cultural forms, I would say that I have "autonomy" in choosing my clothes. But if this is my definition of autonomy, then it applies as well to just about every conceivable human activity beyond the purely instinctual, including many of those performed in conditions of outright servitude. If, on the other hand, I define "autonomy" as requiring that I act without the mediation of culture, then no, I certainly don't have "autonomy" in picking my clothes. But what actions *would* qualify as autonomous in this way? However I define autonomy, the cultural world is impinging on me in the same *concrete* ways, and these are what I am interested in assessing.

Nowadays, academics may be more likely to speak of "agency" rather than "autonomy" or "freedom." But usually, they are after the same prize. "God made man but not the sin in him," Augustine said, trying to salvage "free will" for Christians. Academic attempts to prove that human beings have "agency," I believe, are no less motivated by extra-intellectual investments. We want to believe that our choices are "ours," we don't like to feel that we are being pushed around. For some reason, although I am quite rebellious when it comes to concrete cultural interactions, I have never felt the need to assert my metaphysical autonomy. I resent many of the norms of our culture, and resist obedience to them. (The more normative cosmetic surgery to "correct" aging becomes, the less likely I am to have it.) But I am quite willing to grant that my defiance is as "determined" in me (by my genes, upbringing, moment in history) as another person's conformity. The fraught issue, for me, is figuring out the meaning and consequences – both personal and political – of my actions. In having a facelift, or my "Jewish" nose bobbed, what norms would I be servicing? What effect will these actions have on my sense of who I am? On my acceptance of my finitude, my mortality? On the values I am communicating to those who look up to me for guidance? On shaping – in my own small way – the culture of the future?

In assessing resistance – as I understand that activity – I am not asking questions about whether or not an action is "free" or "determined," chosen or culturally coerced, performed by agents or automatons. I am looking at the concrete consequences of actions, trying to assess in what direction(s) they are moving (or reproducing) the institutions and practices of society. This will always be an enormously complex cultural determination, which can only yield a provisional and perhaps ambiguous conclusion, and it *will* require theory. Examining what's going on in the material realm, Marx's comment in *German Ideology* to the contrary, is never a matter of purely "empirical" verification. For we need to learn to "see" what is around us, as Marx was well aware, and for that we need tools which will bring what is obscured (and sometimes deliberately mystified) into clear relief. Even so, the map is seldom clearly marked.

As Hekman insightfully points out, both Butler and I (following Foucault) view resistance as produced from "within" rather than outside a dominant order. This is an important commonality in our work. We share a view of power that recognizes that precisely when an order seems at its most definitive peak, it is releasing the lava that may bury it (or, at least, heat things up for it.) The seeds of transformation are indeed everywhere, always. But how can we determine the status of our own activity within these (historical) processes? This is a question that is frequently posed to Foucauldians, and Butler asks it of herself in *Bodies That Matter*: "How will we know the difference between the power we promote and the power we oppose?" Susan Hekman poses a similar challenge to me: "If our resistance to the cultural construction of the body cannot appeal to a 'real' or 'natural' body, and thus, that resistance is also a cultural construction, then how can it be effective as resistance?" And she poses a variant of this to Butler, as well: "If the excluded, the abject, is as much a discursive product of the law of sex as the hegemonic heterosexual norm, then how can the abject be defined as a realm of resignification that destabilizes the hegemonic? How can it be the site where disruption will occur?"

It's interesting (and makes a great deal of sense) that for all our differences, in the final analysis Butler and I are presented with the same sort of challenge. Perhaps more strenuously than most, Butler and I have each insisted – although focusing on different arenas, hers the discursive/linguistic, mine the practical/ material – on the impossibility of "getting outside" history. I believe that this is a core conviction that goes to the heart of what drives both of us as philosophers, and – paradoxically but predictably – it may be where we have each seen the other lacking, slipping in the rigor and consistency of her dedication. But in this particular challenge to both of us our core similarity emerges in clear relief. I would like to end this piece by responding, perhaps in a way that applies to both of us.

Sometimes, I have heard variants of this challenge posed in terms such as: "How is resistance possible in a Foucauldian world?" Posing it in this way gets at the heart of what is wrong with a whole set of questions that academics have been asking recently. In "Rehabilitating the 'I'" (1993), Mario Moussa and I describe such questions as a postmodern return of Zeno's paradox:

> For Zeno, the problem was how to account for movement; for many postmoderns, it is how to account for political action. Of course, movement occurred no matter how much it puzzled the philosophers, and the same goes for action. Yet academics continue to write as though action is impossible without the adequate theory.

Foucault himself never asked how resistance is possible. Instead, he asked other, more concrete questions, concerning how to interrupt various entrenched discourses, how to excavate their human origins so their "necessity" will be exposed as a lie, what cultural edifices need to have an intellectual "hand grenade" tossed their way. He also took part in political movements, as do many academics (even as they ask these questions about the "possibility" of resistance).

"Theories" of resistance can indeed function, at certain historical junctures, as intellectual "hand grenades." But theories of resistance are not *required* for social or cultural change. It's always amazed me when critics comment that *Unbearable Weight* underestimates or "does not account for" resistance. Sometimes, that criticism will be accompanied by the complaint that the picture I paint is too grim or depressing. I wonder when making people feel good became a criterion for the adequacy of social criticism? My point in the book is precisely to *encourage* "resistance" to certain discourses and practices, by breaking up some of the illusions which permit them to function smoothly. I do indeed find certain aspects of our situation grim; if I didn't, why would I want to resist them? If I put a more cheerful face on it all, would that make resistance to them more "possible?" Postmoderns like to see resistance "acknowledged" in texts, and "accounted for" by theories. But texts and theories can also function as *practices* of resistance, which work in a variety of ways to help instigate change.

I don't overestimate the power of my books to do this, though. Here, Susan Hekman's question to me is relevant. How resistance is produced, whether it is imagined as a cultural construction or an act of pure freedom, whether it appeals to a "natural" body or a cyborg or no body at all – these, to me, have no bearing on the issue of effectiveness. The fact that resistance is produced out of a hegemonic order does not preclude it from transforming that order, any more than the fact that we are our parents' children precludes us from living lives very different from theirs. But clearly, so long as we think our parents' lives were swell, we will do little to break away. So I think of the development of an oppositional or critical attitude as more important than the question of where resistance originates or what it appeals to.

There are lots of wells from which to draw an oppositional spirit and project – the experience of abjection and exclusion being an extremely powerful one, as Butler and I agree. Sometimes that experience can result in a conscious politics, sometimes not. Those of us who do philosophy in an oppositional or critical mode could be described as trying to make explicit the elements which would enable this (and many of us, coming to philosophy out of our own history of exclusion, may be an example of it as well). But often, there are no clear diagrams for the excluded to appeal to, yet they become agents of social transformation. Sometimes our bodies resist even without our conscious participation.

Certain and conclusive knowledge of the effectiveness of any of this, however, is not available to us. That would only come at the end of the line – and we are not standing there. We are standing in concrete bodies, in a particular time and place, in the "middle" of things, *always*. The most sophisticated theory cannot alter this limitation on our knowledge, while too-rigid adherence to theory can make us too inflexible, too attached to a set of ideas, to freshly assess what is going on around us, to stay alert in what Foucault called an attitude of "hyper and pessimistic activism." Thus, my answer to Butler's question: we *cannot* know with certainty whether we are opposing the power we oppose, or promoting it. But all this means is that we are fallible, our assessments provisional, our actions subject to revision. It should not be taken as cause for fatalism, or passivity. (Actually, I believe it is mostly philosophers who respond with despair to the impossibility of certainty; most people become fatalistic and passive when they despair of *changing* things, and do not require certainty in order to try to do so.) To act responsibly and with hope, it's not necessary that we know the final outcome of our actions. We assess what we take to be the chief dangers or needs of a situation – the practices that require demystification, criticism, transformation – and *act*, both individually and collectively, ready to change course if we discover something we didn't notice at the outset, or something that has emerged since we began. "The essence of being radical is physical," as Foucault said in a late interview, "the essence of being radical is the radicalness of existence itself."

## Notes

I would like to thank Virginia Blum, Binnie Klein, Edward Lee, Dana Nelson, Suzanne Pucci, Ted Schatzki, and Paul Taylor for reading and commenting on drafts of this piece. Their criticisms and insights have been invaluable. Thanks also to Donn Welton, for inviting me to contribute a theoretical overview of my work to this collection.

1  I take issue with some of those critiques in "Feminism, postmodernism, and gender-skepticism." I think general theories can play a crucial role in breaking apart sedimented ways of thinking and helping people to see things in radically new ways. Where would feminist theory, for example, be without the bold strokes of those who first looked around and saw *gender* where it had previously been invisible? The fact that those theories needed to be complicated (by race, for example) should not be seen as their "fatal flaw," but part of the necessary elaboration of the theory.

## References

Bordo, Susan (1982) "The cultural overseer and the tragic hero," *Soundings*, vol. 55, no. 2, 181–205.

Bordo, Susan (1987) *The Flight to Objectivity*. New York: SUNY Press, 1987.

Bordo, Susan (1988) "Feminist skepticism and the 'maleness' of philosophy," abridged version in *The Journal of Philosophy*, vol. 75 no. 11 full version in E. Harvey and K. O'Kruhlik (ed), *Women and Reason*, University of Michigan Press.

Bordo, Susan (1989) "Feminism, postmodernism and gender-skepticism," in Linda Nicholson (ed.), *Feminism/Postmodernism*. New York: Routledge. Later reprinted in *Unbearable Weight*.

Bordo, Susan (1990) "Material girl: the effacements of postmodern culture," in *Michigan Quarterly Review*, Fall, later reprinted in *Unbearable Weight*.

Bordo, Susan (1992) "Postmodern subjects, postmodern bodies," *Feminist Studies*, vol. 18, no. 1, 159–76. Later reprinted in *Unbearable Weight*.

Bordo, Susan (1993a) "Feminism, Foucault, and the politics of the body," in Carolyn Romanza-noglu (ed.), *Up Against Foucault*, Routledge.

Bordo, Susan (1993b) *Unbearable Weight*, Berkeley: University of California Press.

Bordo, Susan (1996) "The feminist as other," in Janet Kourani, (ed.) *Philosophy in a Different Voice*. Princeton: Princeton U. Press (also in *Metaphilosophy*, January/April. vol. 27, 1995).

Bordo, Susan and Mousa, Mario (1993) "Rehabilitating the 'I'", in Hugh Silverman (ed.), *Questioning Foundations*. New York: Routledge.

Butler, Judith (1990) *Gender Trouble*. New York: Routledge.

Butler, Judith (1993) *Bodies That Matter*. New York: Routledge.

Foucault, Michel (1983) "On the genealogy of ethics," interview with H. Dreyfus and P. Rabinow, in *Michel Foucault: Beyond Structuralism and Hermeneutics*, pp. 251–2.

Foucault, Michel (1989) "Clarifications on the question of power" an interview with Pasquale Pasquino, in *Foucault Live*, New York: Semiotext(e), p. 191.

Hekman, Susan, "Material bodies," in this volume.

Sheets-Johnstone, Maxine (1990) *The Roots of Thinking*. Philadelphia: Temple University Press.

# 5

# Renaturalization Theory

## Renaturalizing the Body
## (with the Help of Merleau-Ponty)*

### Carol Bigwood

I am writing seven months pregnant, bending over my large round belly to write at
the desk, thinking about the connection between body and gender. He kicks and
squirms, there amidst my thoughts. "He" because I saw on the ultrasound a protrud-
ance between its legs, and that has certainly made a difference in the way I experience
this pregnancy. Male stereotypes arise, alienating me from this alive and kicking
creature carried deep inside. I combat them with resolutions about how this boy
will be brought up differently. No throwing stones, no hockey, no... silly rules.
Not even born and already fighting with the bind of gender division. Either pink
or blue. I console myself: at least at first he will be a baby and I'll dress him in all
colors.

### Is "woman" dead?

"Could it be possible?" thought Sarathustra, "This old witch in the forest has not yet
heard that woman is dead!"

(freely adapted from Nietzsche [1976: 12])

An important task of feminism, especially in the 1970s, has been one of, on the one
hand, exposing the phallocentric nature of Western history, culture, institutional,
and political power structures, and so-called human ideals and, on the other hand,
discovering and reclaiming suppressed "women's" history, values, and experience.
There are many feminists in different disciplines who continue this project today.
Of increasing concern to many contemporary feminist theorists, however, is the very
use of gender as a category for criticizing Western culture and for valorizing specific
female values. To assume that the term "woman" denotes a stable, coherent,
common identity and to criticize a universal oppressive structure called the "patriarchy" has recently come to be viewed as a theoretically disastrous move because it
is said to be essentialist (i.e. it pays insufficient attention to historical and cultural
diversity) and to enforce a hierarchical and heterosexual gender division that
marginalizes bisexuals and homosexuals.

Susan Bordo aptly calls this contemporary current in feminism, which has
emerged in different forms and across different disciplines, "gender skepticism."

* Carol Bigwood, "Renaturalizing the body (with the help of Merleau-Ponty)," *Hypatia*, vol. 6, no.
3 (Fall 1991), 54–73.

Gender skepticism holds that "any attempt to 'cut' reality and perspective along gender lines is methodologically flawed and essentializing" (Bordo, 1990: 134). Bordo sees this view as dangerous to feminism mainly because it threatens feminism as a movement of cultural resistance and transformation. Like Bordo, I am sympathetic to the concerns of this new trend in feminism and see this new shift in focus as dangerous to the culturally transformative possibilities that feminism has to offer. In order that the wind not be knocked out of feminism's sails, we need to retain genderized notions like "female," "woman," and "feminine" and thereby continue to develop a feminist ontology, epistemology, and politics that challenge the current social order. Moreover, when one looks at the long list of feminists accused of different kinds of essentialism one fears that the recent move to purge the last vestiges of essentialism from feminism may be unwittingly in danger of turning into a kind of gender theory inquisition where certain strands of feminism are silenced as theoretically heretical. Finding ways of reconciling the established feminist project to reclaim female perspectives with the renewed attempt to purge feminism of essentialism would seem, then, to be an important feminist task. Ways need to be found, for example, to historically contextualize broad categories like "female experience" and "woman," and to use these concepts so that they are neither exclusionary, nor fleshless abstractions.[1]

"Woman" is not dead or a fiction but rather is under close consideration. As I see it, such questioning and criticism of well-worn concepts can be most healthy and strengthening. It gives feminists who advocate the revolutionary potential of feminine ways of being, such as nurturance, holism, and gentleness, puzzles that are difficult to work out but can nonetheless only help to clarify their project.[2] Many have recognized that a key piece in this puzzle is *the body*. As a result of the renewed effort to question gender, it has become clear that in advocating female specificity, we need, first, to affirm to some extent a loose and noncausal linkage between the female body and women's ways of being, between the body and gender, and second, to show that the category "woman" need not be determined by a fixed biological body.

> Since I decided to get pregnant, there is a growing awareness of the domestic institution that is waiting to envelop me. It was really my project from the start. I was the one who wanted to experience having another child. I planned it carefully. I will have it just after my Ph.D. No, I had better take this one year, full-time position. Now's the time, interrupt your career now, before a tenure track comes up for grabs. Have it at the beginning of April, breastfeed for five months, and then teach again in September. Calculations and more calculations. Counting the days: OK, let's try today. Waiting. Yes, I think I'm pregnant. I feel full. There's new life. No, I'm not pregnant at all.
>
> It didn't happen as planned. The baby will be born in September. I gave up an extension of my contract. I couldn't see breastfeeding, teaching, and commuting two hundred miles, or uprooting my family just for a year. So, I'll stay at home with the baby for this year – and write.

If we do not admit somewhere along the line of our argument that there is a certain continuity between the body and gender (and, moreover, begin to describe this continuity as I will attempt to do in this paper), then we will tend to ignore the specific needs for social change in women's lives due precisely to their being embodied as women. Given the *phallocentrism* of our present way of being, women still need to find and develop ways of living in the world that are appropriate to their unique *bodily* being and no longer be forced to live within specifically male-oriented institutions that favor male modes of embodiment. Any deep changes in the social order, for example, must take into account the fact that it is women who bear babies. But whether one has children or not, the fact that one has a female body often makes important differences in the constitution of a woman's social experience. Moreover, unless we recognize and investigate a link between gender and the body, the theoretical position of gender specificity is left, as it were, without a leg to stand on. One could always comfortably refer to past and present examples of "women's" values and experience, since one could claim that they are purely relative to historical cultures. But it would be unproductive to bring forward the concept of "woman," even as a provisional term, when envisioning a future society, since the concept prejudices the new ground with a fixed gender. We need, then, to go even further than retaining the concept of "woman" as a temporary politically expedient move and affirm a certain indeterminate but lasting continuity between styles of gender and the body.

In affirming a link between gender and the body, however, we need not resort to fixed, biological differences that dictate innate ahistorical differences and inflexible cross-cultural categories. We need a new model of the body that leads neither to biological determinism nor to gender skepticism and cultural relativism.[3] The body must be understood as culturally and historically contextualized, on the one hand, and yet as part of our embodied givenness, on the other. In the following pages, I will argue that our human bodily being takes place within a natural-cultural situation and thus is neither the result of biological determinants nor purely culturally constructed. With the help of Merleau-Ponty's phenomenology of the body, I will present a paradigm of the body as an *indeterminate constancy*, focusing in particular on his attempt to recover a noncultural, nonlinguistic body that accompanies and is intertwined with our cultural existence, and thereby arguing for what I call the body's fleshy presencing in the world-earth-home.

I use the term "world-earth-home" as a feminist adaptation of Heidegger's notion of "world" used in his *Being and Time*. The notion of "world" would seem to be biased in favor of a male perspective on our being, for our being here is not merely a being in the *world*. "World" connotes a man's world and his public institutions, thereby tending to neglect the private realm, and, moreover, connotes a human world in opposition to the earth. My term "world-earth," by contrast, reminds us that we are here with other animals and on an earth that gives rise to a myriad of life that, unfortunately, has become marginal to our human world (or, worse yet, thoughtlessly used up by it). The term "home," moreover, reminds us that we are here as human beings not primarily to participate within the public political socio-economic world but to dwell humanly, in other words, to be "at home," whether we are in our offices, in the woods, or in our ownmost dwellings.

## Is any body home?

The deeper feminists dig into the notion of gender, the more it seems to be a product of early childhood socialization, psychological development, gender identity formation, and cultural ideology. Gender identities and roles have been found to vary in different cultures and historical periods. Moreover, as feminists convincingly argue, biological accounts of the sexual difference are not objective and gender neutral but often invested with gender, class, cultural, and racial biases. Given all of this, it would seem that women and men are not innately endowed with feminine and masculine qualities through their biological sex but rather that gender is culturally constructed. Gender thus freed from, rather than grounded in, the body has the advantage of being open to radical change.[4]

That gender is culturally constructed has received new support from a major strand of poststructuralist feminists who have worked to redefine the body itself as a product of cultural meaning. To discuss and criticize such a poststructuralist "denaturalization" of gender and the body, I will focus on Judith Butler's recent book *Gender Trouble* (1990) as a strong example of a developed poststructuralist, gender-skeptical position.[5]

Butler critically takes up Foucault's analysis of the body (with the occasional use of Merleau-Pontian terminology) to help purge gender from its connections with the body and any "natural" determinations. That gender has been "naturalized" means that it has been understood to rest on the firm foundation of the "natural" body, where "natural" means ahistorical and cross-cultural and thereby "fixed." She maintains, to the contrary, that both gender and the body are merely the products of conventional cultural forms of meaning, practice, and discourse and are wrongly used to found various epistemological and ontological claims. Gender, she says, is a corporeal style, a play of signifying practices inscribed on the surface of bodies and within a cultural field of gender hierarchy and compulsory heterosexuality. Gender identities are created through a stylized repetition of acts, bodily gestures, and desires that produce the illusory effect of an internal stable core and give the appearance of a naturalistic configuration of sexual bodies (Butler, 1990: 136). Our present gender distinctions, then, are cultural constructions that conceal their artificial origins and masquerade as natural configurations of sexual bodies (Butler, 1990: 139–41). Butler's goal is to proliferate gender configurations, destabilize coherent gender identities, and thereby deprive the "naturalizing narratives of compulsory heterosexuality of their central protagonists: man and woman" (Butler, 1990: 146).

Now Butler does not make the mistake of claiming that the body is a "natural" surface or a passive medium for "cultural" inscription, thereby falling into a nature/ culture dichotomy.[6] She is critical of the hierarchical binary relation between culture and nature in which culture freely imposes meaning on nature, rendering it Other (Butler, 1990: 37). Using Foucault's analysis of the body, Butler maintains that the body is not an abiding *natural* ground, an "immediate given," but is always already a *cultural* sign (Butler, 1990: 71). It is not a ready surface awaiting signification, but a set of boundaries, a "surface whose permeability is politically regulated and established," for instance through prohibitions (Butler, 1990: 33 and 139). The "natural-ness" of the body is illusory and thoroughly culturally produced, and thus gender is not to culture as the sexed body is to nature (Butler, 1990: 37).[7]

What body can this be that is but a cultural surface, inscribed by cultural significations, and masquerading as natural?[8] What meaning is left to "gender" (from the Greek *genos* meaning "origin") once separated from living fleshy bodies and set adrift in a sea of cultural significations, discursive practices, and power configurations? It seems to me that in her zeal to advocate a gender fluidity, Butler goes too far in her denaturalization of the body. Her Foucauldian attempt to avoid metaphysical foundationalism leaves us with a disembodied body and a free-floating gender artifice in a sea of cultural meaning production.

What is most disturbing and dangerous in her poststructuralist analysis is its complete abandonment of nature and support of purely cultural determinants in the construction of gender. It is true that, for Butler, nature is thankfully no longer the opposite of culture, but it has lost any independent, non-anthropocentric presence to become merely the product of human action. A body and nature formed solely by social and political significations, discourses, and inscriptions are cultural products, disemboweled of their full existential content. The poststructuralist body, it is true, is historically and culturally contextualized and thereby achieves some of our experienced significances. However, the poststructuralist body is contextualized only as a place marker in quasi-linguistic systems of signifiers. It is so fluid it can take on almost limitless embodiments.[9] It has no real terrestrial *weight*.

> Going into my ninth month now: feeling heavy, out of breath, emptying my bladder every hour, bleeding hemorrhoids, sweating under my pendulous breasts. This weight. It is not a weight that I willfully bear with muscular strength like a pack on my back. It is a weight that I live with, that has slowly entered into every aspect of my bodily being. Heavy like stone. If this were a permanent female state...! To unwillingly bear a pregnancy like this in the center of one's being would be one of the worst forms of torture. Far better to push a boulder uphill like Sisyphus.

If we reduce the body as a whole to a purely cultural phenomenon and gender to a free-floating artifice, then we are unwittingly perpetuating the deep modern alienation of our human being from nature.[10] We are also reinforcing the anthropocentric, and the androcentric, worldview that sees everything only in the light of "human" cultural use.[11] Such alienation and anthropocentrism cripple our sentience to the extent that we are able to contact only ourselves and our own products. It is indeed difficult for us in this age in which the subjectivism of the human being has reached its height, and in which we have assumed the technological command of the earth and all beings, not to presume that our given situation (including that of gender) is fully within our control. Given that we order and constitute everything from the perspective of our self-certain subjectivity and with our progressively more powerful technology, it is difficult to allow for the presencing of anything but ourselves and our own products.

> As I write a cicada calls from a pine tree behind me, numerous crickets creak in the grass, a bee buzzes over a white clover, flies whining here and there, a car in the distance goes down the highway. There is a slight breeze. The leaves of a birch and some low bushes beside me rustle, waver, tremble. Patches of sunlight on the solid, grey granite boulders. Flecks of mica. A crow caws suddenly, clear and distinct. Another car down the highway. The sky, simply a pale blue.

We cannot take the broad lines of existence fully into our cultural hands and bend them as we will. This is not because history is predetermined or, in the case of gender, that our biology is our destiny, but that the way life articulates itself has as much to do with the response of other nonhuman beings, with the currents of the earthly and skyly environment, and with temporal contingencies, as it does with our subjectivist cultural wills.

The crux of the matter, then, as I see it, is to "renaturalize" the body, truly releasing it from a dichotomized nature and culture. We need to work out a new "natural-cultural" model of the body that goes beyond both the fixed, biological body and the poststructuralist culturally inscribed body. Butler is right to argue that there is no "pure" body or untouched nature prior to culture, but her solution to the myth of a purely natural state prior to culture is merely to posit a "pure" culture that is always already there. This pure cultural state prior to nature, it seems to me, is also a myth. As deep ecologists have pointed out, our human being takes place within a *natural*-cultural relational field: it is not only involved in cultural fields of forces but is a part of an interconnected web of relations with the nonhuman.[12] While we should applaud poststructuralism's criticism of metaphysical foundationalism, as well as its attempt to free gender from our modern conceptions of a biologically fixed body, the postmodernist disembodied body, which privileges culture over nature and the body, reinforces the same phallocentric metaphysical structures that have contributed to the domination of women and nature.[13] The underlying metaphysical presuppositions that have guided Western thought on the body and nature must be uprooted as must its reliance on secure and certain rational foundations for they are intimately connected and mutually reinforce each other.[14]

## Our incarnate yet indeterminate bodies

Is this really my belly? I am so fat, enormous. Constant adjustment to my body image. They look at me in my bikini with my protruding bare belly. I can't carry myself with my usual athleticism. I become self-conscious by the surprised gaze of others. No longer nice to look at. Knocked-up, taken, unappealing. In the eyes of others, before being a person, I am first and foremost pregnant. I refuse to be embarrassed; I am still my own body – but I try to be discreet so as not to appear too bold. Well, this is what I wanted: to experience pregnancy.

Merleau-Ponty's philosophy of the body, which owes much to Husserl's phenomenological work, offers a fresh paradigm of the body that goes beyond the biological account. A serious problem with the scientific account of the body is that science distances the body, admitting only phenomena that can be mathematized and objectified, and thereby ignores the body as it is *lived* by each of us. In response to the limitations of the scientific method, the phenomenological method entails describing phenomena as they *appear* to us and are lived by us in our experiences. It attempts to describe the world-earth-home, which is already there before theoretical reflection, in order to reachieve for philosophy a direct and primitive contact that goes on behind our everyday attitudes. If we look at the body from a phenomenological point of view rather than as a merely biologically functioning entity, we can find a way of affirming sexual difference while allowing for its inevitable indeterminacy and open possibilities for historical and cultural variation.

Since feminism needs a model of the body that is not biologically fixed, I believe Merleau-Ponty's work can lead us to some methodological and philosophical "grounding" for the feminist task of describing an incarnate genderized body.[15] Merleau-Ponty's phenomenology of the body is far more developed than any other and thus provides a solid beginning from which to develop a feminist philosophy of the body. This feminist reappropriation of his work, however, must rework many of his notions since the "neutral" human body he attempts to describe is often prejudiced in favor of the male body.[16] Although I cannot undertake a feminist phenomenology in the space provided, let me outline a few of his main positions in order to demonstrate how helpful his phenomenology of the body can be for clarifying some of the difficulties involved in the present feminist debate on gender and the body.

Working within a dialectical framework, Merleau-Ponty hopes to expose the limitations of both the empiricists' denigration of the body as a passive receptor, and then active calculator, of sense-data and the idealists' disregard of the body in favor of consciousness (which the idealists claim is the truly active performer in the constitution of phenomena). As he describes it, the body is a *sentience* that is born *together* with a certain existential environment. It does not just passively receive sense-data but has a unique sensitivity to its environs. It genuinely experiences rather than merely records phenomena as empiricists claim, and it does this through an *openness* that is fundamental to its sentience. The body is actively and continually in *touch* with its surroundings. It is directed outside itself, inextricably entangled in existence. In order to understand the active participation of our bodies in the constitution of our world-earth-home, let us take up his example of sensuous contact, that of deeply looking up at the sky.

If I fully attend to the sky, gazing up into its blue, my body gradually adopts a certain bodily attitude in response to the spacious blue. My eyes and my whole body slowly yield, relax, enter into a sensuous rhythm of existence that is already there and that is peculiar to the sky in its blue depths. In its contact, my body adopts a "certain living pulsation" that is not its own, but that it lives through and that also lives through it, and becomes my body's being of the moment (Merleau-Ponty, 1962: 214–15). My living situation becomes one of blue. I can feel the blue's profundity and become immersed in it because of a bodily *openness* that lets the sky pulse through me and, in the same trembling stroke, lets my bodily sensing breathe life into the blue sky. Existence realizes itself in the body because of this incarnate communion with the world. I am not a passive spectator of the sky, but I commune with it, or rather a "coition" takes place in which the sky and myself are only abstract moments of a single incarnate communication. This bodily-skyly sensibility that tremulously runs through me and that is neither passively received nor actively willed makes me realize an "anonymous self" that has "already" sided with, and is already open to, nature and my surroundings (Merleau-Ponty, 1962: 216).

This body that is sensitive and in deep communion with its environment is not the biological object-body that science describes but is the "living body" or the "phenomenological body."[17] It is not a separate physical entity in a world external to it but rather is of the same stuff as its environs. Nor is it in the world like an object in a container but is with the world-earth-home, oriented toward it and directed toward certain tasks as part of it. The phenomenological body is not fixed but continually emerges anew out of an ever changing weave of relations to earth and sky, things, tasks, and other bodies. The living world, moreover, is not understood as a collection of fully determinate objects or as a material objective reality merely external to the body. Rather, the world-earth-home is an ever-present horizon latent in all our experiences. It is a unified contingent field of relations present to the body as its familiar situation (Merleau-Ponty, 1962: 92).

Keeping in mind the *participation* of the body in the incarnate constitution of sensory experience, and this communion of body and its environs, will help us ward off our inclinations to give empiricist interpretations of the body. However, we have yet to deal more directly with idealist objections. An idealist would object that the intellect not the body is the active subject of sensation here, that sensation takes place in the mind. For Merleau-Ponty, by contrast, living bodily sensation has to be *experienced* and not merely thought about. It takes place within a particular situation of tasks and relations, of which the lived-body is the locus. The sympathetic relation of our sentient body with the sensible world-earth-home, then, is primarily a *precognitive* one.[18] Experience shows that as living bodies we are sensibly attuned to, and harmonized with, our surroundings through a "latent knowledge" that is present before any effort of our cognition (Merleau-Ponty, 1962: 20). It is not our intellectual judging that makes sentience possible but rather this silent, noncognitive, intimate bonding of our body with the world–earth–home. As living bodies, we are not in full cognitive possession of determinate, sensed objects but are irretrievably immersed in an ever-changing and indeterminate context of relations. We find ourselves in a field constantly filled with fleeting plays of colors, noises, and tactile feelings that nonetheless usually emerge as meaningful, but by means of a communication with our surroundings that is more ancient than thought (Merleau-Ponty, 1962: 254).

Given this description of the body's sympathetic relation to its surroundings, bodily "sentience" emerges as a third term and resolves the metaphysical dualism of passive matter and active spirit and of conscious subject and object-world. Though the body is primarily nonrational and nonlinguistic in its communications, it nevertheless is full of a significance and has a way of ordering of its own. As I have already argued, it is important to maintain this nonlinguistic, noncognitive *sens* or bodily meaning that poststructuralist feminist theory neglects in its affirmation of only cultural meanings. The poststructuralist's culturally inscribed body is disembodied and lacks terrestrial weight and locatedness because, like both empiricist and idealist accounts of the body, it has left out this aspect of the body's incarnate situation.

In order to understand in more detail what Merleau-Ponty means by the noncognitive or nonlinguistic order of the body that the quasi-rationalist poststructuralist account of the body has overlooked, let us discuss an important perceptual capacity of our bodies, namely, our ability to see things as unified. Merleau-Ponty describes how the parts of a thing are not bound together by a merely external association acquired through experience (Merleau-Ponty, 1962: 15). To see is not to experience a host of impressions accompanied, for example, by memories capable of clenching them (Merleau-Ponty, 1962: 22). Nor does a thing appear as unified because we judge it to be so according to adequate signs in the visual field (Merleau-Ponty, 1962: 35). The unity of a thing is not arrived at by a cognitive operation of association or judgment but by a noncognitive apprehension of immanent meanings in the sensible field.

Let us take another of his examples (Merleau-Ponty, 1962: 17). I am walking toward a ship that had long ago run aground on a beach and is now merging into the sand. For a moment I do not perceive the resemblances or proximities that finally come together to form a unified upper part of the ship. How is it that the figure emerges as unified from the background of sand and trees? Merleau-Ponty helpfully describes the experience by noting that at that moment when the landscape was on the point of altering, there was something immanent in the tension of the visual field. An order was about to spring upon me as a reply to questions merely latent in the landscape. Tensions run like lines of force across our visual field and breathe a secret and magic life in it for perception by exerting here and there forces of distortion, contraction, and expansion (Merleau-Ponty, 1962: 48–9). Relationships that I first perceived start breaking apart and new ones form, motivated by an immanent significance in the perceptual field.

Our sentient body is attuned to this life "which steals across the visual field and binds its parts together" (Merleau-Ponty, 1962: 35). It gathers at a stroke the meanings that unite clusters of relations. Or rather, it both discovers the "meanings" that they have, and sees to it that they have meaning (Merleau-Ponty, 1962: 36). In other words, perception actively apprehends meanings, but meanings that are inherent in sensible signs of the visual field and cannot be said to belong to the intellect. It does not cognitively constitute cognitive meanings but takes up perceptual meanings that are already there, latent to varying extents in the background. It does this through a silent communication and a uniquely bodily questioning that can only find its echo in the perceptual horizon.

Our perceptual body is guided in its syntheses by "motives" in the environment, not causes or categories. Motives are not objective causes of perception because motives are far from articulate and determinate, and thus leave so much room for variation in the way the body can take them up and combine them. Motives present only a practical significance that asks for bodily recognition. They are a part of an open situation that asks for a certain kind of resolution (Merleau-Ponty, 1962: 71). It is always indeterminate whether the phenomenal meanings that motives hold out are released and find their echo in the body. Our phenomenological bodies, then, are not biological fixed entities geared into and determined by a purely physical world but are fluid movements toward a situation wherein it must find its indeterminate supports.

Moreover, the "signs" offered to perception are not separable from their living significance, even theoretically (Merleau-Ponty, 1962: 38). The incarnate sign does not refer to its signified but is filled with its significance (Merleau-Ponty, 1962: 161). The immanent meanings or significances inherent in the signs of the visual field are not cognitive or linguistic. We must, Merleau-Ponty points out, give "meaning" a new meaning if we are to understand these non-cognitive capacities of a body that has already sided with its perceptual surroundings (Merleau-Ponty, 1962: 146–7). We can go a long way in understanding this new meaning simply by noting that in French "meaning" is *sens*, which means "sense," "significance," and "direction," for the meaning of "meaning" is thereby broadened to include nonlinguistic and noncognitive meanings. Latent sensory meanings are open and indeterminate tensions that guide our perception, and yet to be phenomenally meaning-ful they must be taken up by perception.

Perception, for its part, is not in possession of fully determinate objects but rather is a logic lived through that cannot account for itself (Merleau-Ponty, 1962: 49). Its syntheses are always partial and of limited power, dependent on their being blended with things. When I suddenly see that there is a ship in the sand, my eyes anchor themselves on the boat and the surroundings recede into the background. My eyes "inhabit" the boat, synthesizing it as a unified thing. However, the boat does not thereby become a completed object, translucent to consciousness (Merleau-Ponty, 1962: 71). An object purports to be the same for everybody, valid in all times and places, and to be there in itself arrayed before consciousness. A perceived thing, for living experience, however, remains indeterminate and incomplete. Such significances remain somewhat confused; such meanings somewhat opaque.

A thing can "appear," display itself, only because of other "hidden" aspects of itself. A necessary aspect of our incarnate bodily situation, then, is that there is always a horizon of other things and sides of the thing that are not sensed, a background that nonetheless *persists* as a nonsensory presence. I "sense" this hidden spatial side of things, even though this sensing is not physiological. Bodily perception, moreover, is incomplete, not only because it is spatially spread beyond its present focus, but also because it is temporal and must be untiringly reiterated in us. Our living present is torn between a past that it takes up and a future that it projects. There is more being beyond what I sense at this moment because my incarnate existence takes place within the indeterminate horizons of space and time.

This indeterminacy and "ambiguity" of our incarnate natural-cultural situation are crucial for understanding and reconceptualizing the nature of our body. If our existence is always indeterminate to varying degrees insofar as it is the unending process whereby the hitherto meaningless takes on meaning and, moreover, is ambiguous because the primary sensory meanings that are reached through our coexistence with others and things always have several meanings, then there can be no inflexible bodily structures that could once and for all determine our sexuality. We can never posit a single completed and explicit totality such as a binary gender division because the world-earth-home is an open and indefinite multiplicity of relationships that are of reciprocal implication and that our bodies ambiguously join (Merleau-Ponty, 1962: 71).[19] However, even though our bodies are not fixed foundations, this does not mean that our bodies are merely cultural constructions or that gender can be entirely purged from the body. Our body is our medium for having a cultural world, indeed, for having any world at all (Merleau-Ponty, 1962: 146). It is not a "fixed given" untouched by the dominant representational system, yet its anchorage in the world nonetheless consists of an interconnected web of relations with the human and nonhuman, the cultural and natural.

> I try to adjust to active matter. All around, a thankless task. I have been infiltrated. My walk has changed, the way I sit, stand, eat, sleep, the way I breathe, the way I make love. I can't sit up straight at my desk for long anymore. I have to lean back on the chair to write over my belly, legs apart, giving my belly as much room as possible. All of a sudden it seems my belly has become too big too fast for me to adjust to it as mine.

The poststructuralist account of the body leaves out this "anonymous" noncognitive cleaving of our bodies to others and things, to the general incarnate structure of the world. This "nonpersonal" perceptual existence that underlies and intertwines with our personal cultural and intellectual lives Merleau-Ponty indeed calls a "natural" body. It runs through us, independently of us, providing the possibility of phenomenal presence (Merleau-Ponty, 1962: 165). Every perception takes place in this atmosphere of generality and is presented to us anonymously. Just as we are thrown into our mortal situation where we find ourselves "already born" and "still alive," so are we thrown open into incarnate situations, modalities of existence already destined for a fleshy world. Just as birth and death are nonpersonal horizons, so is there a nonpersonal body, systems of anonymous functions, blind adherences to beings that I am not the cause of and for which I am not responsible (Merleau-Ponty, 1962: 216). I am "connatural" with the world through no effort on my part (Merleau-Ponty, 1962: 217). This "connatural" body that continually finds its way into the core of our most personal lives untiringly enunciates our communications to others and things. It is not, however, a "firm foundation" or "origin" in the sense of a fixed metaphysical ground that certifies but is a ground in the sense of an *indeterminate* constancy and one that can be easily repressed, ignored, or forgotten.

The "connatural" body is neither empirically nor logically prior to the "cultural" body but is existentially a codeterminant of the body and thus can be at least distinguished abstractly from cultural determinants. There can be no doubt that we are in communication with an inexhaustible sensory world that we do not possess and that takes place anterior to ourselves. However, this nonpersonal self cannot be actually separated from its intermingling existence in things and in our personal life. It is an implication of a certain manner we all have of existing in our incarnate situation and of being involved with a field of presence that has indeterminate spatiotemporal horizons. Our "connatural" body is an indeterminate constancy, not an a priori closed to historical change and cultural variation but a kind of a priori that continually opens us to them.

This fresh model of the body helps us realize, then, that we exist simultaneously in cultural and natural ways that are inextricably tangled.[20] We are always already situated in an intersubjective (and thereby already cultural), spatiotemporal, fleshy (and thereby already natural) world before we creatively adopt a personal position in it. Moreover, nothing determines us from the outside or inside, precisely because we are from the start outside ourselves, thrown open to our surroundings in a semi-determinate but constant coition with things (Merleau-Ponty, 1962: 456). There is, in the final analysis, only this incarnate communication, this natural-cultural momentum of existence, this "unmotivated upsurge of being" of which the body and the environment are only abstract moments (Merleau-Ponty, 1962: xiv).

We are never just a factual thing and never a bare transcendent consciousness. Moreover, the world-earth-home is both already constituted and yet never completely constituted (Merleau-Ponty; 1962: 453). There are no immediate "givens" in perception because phenomena can be phenomenal only to the extent that they are internally, if mysteriously, taken up by us, melded with the body and lived. Our human body with its habits weave things into a human environment and into an infinite number of possible environments, eluding the simplicity of a merely physical bodily life. Yet, on the other hand, there is not a single human cultural configuration or form of behaviour that does not owe something to "natural" existence, that is not bound up with the rest of the intersensory environs (Merleau-Ponty, 1962: 189).

We do not need to denaturalize gender if we understand nature as an indeterminate yet intimate characteristic of our incarnate situation. Gender is not "caused" by a fixed anatomical and biological functionalist structure of our sexual bodies. Yet it is "motivated" by ambiguous, natural-cultural structures of the body, and thus we must affirm a certain continuity in the connection of gender to the body. Our human manners of existing maintain a fidelity to a certain enduring bodiliness that coheres from culture to culture without ever being identical, and yet our human existence is not an innate human essence or structure guaranteed at birth but must be historically constantly reforged.

It is important to realize, for example, that the body's organization, though not fixed, is far from being completely contingent and arbitrary. It is not that the body's phenomenological structure depends only on what we decide to make significant or that we can manipulate and construct it as we want. The sexual body's phenomenal organization is seen as arbitrary only if we take an abstract biological view of the body, regarding its parts as isolatable fragments of matter and ignoring their living function. On the contrary, the "parts" of the body, understood phenomenologically, are repeatedly integrated into functional totalities, into distinctive ways of patterning our surroundings (Merleau-Ponty, 1962: 170). Human functions are integrated into intersensory and motor syntheses in such a way that our bodily composition maintains an indeterminate and fluid constancy. Thus, for Merleau-Ponty everything in the human body is both a "necessity" and a "contingency" because human existence is the perpetual transformation of contingency into necessity and the dissolution of the latter into the former (Merleau-Ponty, 1962: 170).

In this paper I have shown through the work of Merleau-Ponty that "nature" is a codetermining force in the constitution of our bodies. A specific phenomenology of the female body must recognize and begin with this earthy significance of the body that is so quickly repressed in our ecodestructive world. The female body has its own indeterminate natural structures that noncausally motivate womanly ways of being in the world-earth-home. An obvious example of the noncognitive "connatural" body that is often part of the female incarnate situation is that which I call the "mothering body."

The female experience of pregnancy, childbirth, and breast-feeding perspicaciously shows up a female bodily wisdom and fleshy openness that intertwines with a mother's personal and cultural life. In pregnancy, a woman actively and continually responds to the fresh "phusical" (from the Greek *phusis*, commonly translated as "nature") upsurge that independently runs through her body with a life of its own. She creatively takes up the profound changes of her body, constantly readjusting her body image and weaving subtle relations to a phusical pulse that has emerged from elsewhere. Motivated by her new mothering body, she makes dramatic changes in her cultural, social, and personal life. For example, a modern Western middle-class woman may educate herself on the details of pregnancy, childcare, and breast-feeding, make adjustments in her career and home to accommodate the newborn, change her eating and sleeping habits, wear different clothes, and make new friends with other mothers. Although a woman has much flexibility in taking up the pressing but indeterminate directives given by her mothering body, she is not like a subject in control of a growing object inside her. It becomes especially clear in the case of pregnancy that, as Merleau-Ponty argues, the metaphysical dichotomous categories of subject and object, and self and other, fail to describe our incarnate situation, for the "subject" is blurred and diffused in pregnancy. A woman is inhabited by a growing sentience that is not truly "other" to herself.[21]

Repressing her mothering body (which is encouraged in our culture) and attempting to revert back to her familiar "self," she may experience the lack of control over her rapidly changing body and the ever more demanding growth within as frightening. At such times, however, there is a need to recall the wisdom of the mothering body that has already sided with, and is already sensitively attuned to, a phusical current entwining her flesh with that of the unborn before any of her efforts.[22] It is especially in labor that a mother needs to trust the "intelligence" of her "connatural" body. It would be difficult to find another experience where the body is so dramatically gripped by what Merleau-Ponty calls a "certain living pulsation" not the body's own but that it lives through and that also lives through it. The laboring mother is advised to relax as fully as possible into the natural rhythms of the contractions, thereby allowing her body to do its own profound work in preparation for the birth. It is not, however, that the laboring mother merely "lets nature take its course," for her manner of giving birth is codetermined, for example, by her individual strength and attitude, the medical institution and/or midwife, and her labor coaches.

> I went into labour about 3 a.m. The contractions came on immediately hard and strong. On all fours, I breathed through each one, determined to ride out the waves of pain. Unfortunately, his head was stuck in the wrong position for birth. Timeless, dark, fleshy pain. I was no longer giving birth but losing life. The epidural saved me, after which I fiercely pushed him wrong way out, his heart stopping with every contraction.
>     My heart goes out to all those unknown women who died giving birth.

Breastfeeding is a more visible continuation of the connatural existence of the mothering body that takes place anterior to herself. Mother and newborn together learn how to adjust to this new phusical expression. The gush of sweet milk from soft warm flesh undifferentiated from its own is always on the horizon of the newborn's ever-expanding world-earth-home. Mother's body is the constant pleasurable flesh that helps cushion and establish the new little being in a social and cultural environment.[23]

We are living in a historical period in which, through technological advances in our information, transportation, and production systems, the cultural world has become small and accessible, and nature has shrunk to a mere standing reserve of energy, resources awaiting human disposal.[24] In our modern everyday lives, our sentience is attuned to things only sufficiently attentively to discover in them their familiar cultural presence but not to disclose the nonhuman element that is an essential part of the thing's presencing (Merleau-Ponty, 1962: 322). Sometimes, such as when we linger in a forest or over a work of art, we glimpse this bare "that it is" of a thing, this aspect of the thing that holds itself aloof from us, transcending our experience of it (Heidegger, 1971: 65). At such times we may be struck by wonder at this upsurge of existence beyond our control. It seems to me that in our feminist attempts to change the prevailing social system by reconceptualizing sexual difference, we would do well to keep trying to reflect on the wonder of our female bodily situation.

Born September 6, 1990, in unbearable pain. Inside-out-flesh lying on my stomach, its arms and legs moving as though swimming. Months later and still, in a peaceful moment, I look in wonder at the bright, open being blissfully suckling my breast.

## Notes

1   We do not need to deny, for instance, a commonality of experience in principle but to become sensitive to marginalized women and to contextualize our generalizations by making them as historically and culturally specific as is appropriate to the claims we are making. The point of feminist theory should never be, in any case, to abstract a few universal unchanging propositions concerning women that are emptied of all concrete particulars but rather to form the woof that allows for a rich, multicolored weave of female experience.

I believe it is possible, for example, to explore and describe the broad lived lines of the female body, which most women share to some extent regardless of their class, race, or sexual orientation, while allowing for one's descriptions to be enriched by the great range in the way women experience their bodies. What is important is to avoid setting up one's general description as the fixed norm from which other descriptions can only appear as deviations. In working out a new model of the body, for example, one's generalizations must be *indeterminate* enough so as to adapt to concrete diversity and temporality.

2   For example, what is left of a characteristic such as nurturance to affirm as specifically "female" given the extent to which it has been culturally informed? Indeed, why advocate it as specifically "female" if it is to be so thoroughly reworked in a new nonsexist society as to bear little resemblance to its past culturally genderized form?

3   The well-known problem of advocating that gender is rooted in the body is that it predetermines on biological grounds the nature and roles of the sexes. It is claimed that women, because of their biological reproductive function, "naturally" belong in the home having babies and taking care of children. According to such accounts the circumstances of female oppression are biological and thus unalterable. Biology has been used to perpetuate hierarchical power relations between the sexes that keep women dependent, suppressed, and excluded from culture. Aristotle and Freud, for example, argued that women by nature are inferior to men.

4   Earlier feminists, for instance, who understood gender as separate from the body envisioned an androgynous society in which gender would be up to individual conscious choice and

tendencies, in which being human would be stressed, and sexual difference would be of comparatively little significance; see, for example, Trebilcot (1981) and Ferguson (1981). The new poststructuralist feminists do not advocate androgyny but a proliferation of gender identities; see, for example, Scott (1988: 45) and Butler (1990: 127).

5 I am not including here the French feminist poststructuralists (Kristeva, Irigaray, and Cixous) since they lead us in quite a different direction from "gender-skepticism." The strand of poststructuralist feminism I am thinking of can be seen, for example, in Poovey (1988), Scott (1988), and in many of the articles in Nicholson (1990). There are, of course, variations within this strand of poststructuralism on the formation of gender and its relation to the body. I use Butler's Foucauldian-Merleau-Pontian analysis in *Gender Trouble* because it is the most thorough and convincing account I have come across. For other arguments that attempt to separate gender from the body, see Flax (1990), and Scott (1988). For criticisms of post-structuralism in feminism see Teresa De Lauretis (1988), Bordo (1990), DiStefano (1990), Harding (1990), Benhabib (1990), and Hartsock (1990).

6 Beavoir, for example, endorsing Sartre's dialectic between the for-itself and the in-itself, made the mistake of seeing nature as a resistant materiality, medium, surface, or object, and the female body as such a passivity that should be transcended by cultural projects (see Butler, 1990: 8).

7 Butler is critical of what she sees as vestiges of foundationalism and the nature/culture dichotomy in Foucault's own theory. Foucault, she claims, appears to maintain a "natural" body prior to signification, inscription, and form. The body is a medium, or a blank page upon which history writes. Since in the historical process of signification the body is destroyed and transvalued into a sublimated domain of values, then "there must be a body prior to that inscription, stable, and self-identical, subject to that sacrificial destruction" (Butler, 1990: 130). Foucault, moreover, subscribes to a prediscursive multiplicity of bodily forces that can break through the surface of the body to disrupt the regulatory practices of culture imposed on the body. It seems to me, however, the fact that Foucault maintains some kind of "natural" body is valuable since he directs us back to Merleau-Ponty. Other phenomenologists like Levin and Dreyfus have begun to develop these connections.

8 For another criticism of the postmodern body, see Bordo (1990: 143–5).

9 Cultural construction is "limited" only internally by its own cultural discursive practices (Butler, 1990: 8, 139, and 145).

10 We also thereby open up possibilities for new cultural and technological manipulations of our sexual bodies. Although technological advances such as handing over our reproductive func-tion to machines are perhaps unlikely and would be difficult to implement practically, by disconnecting gender from the body and ignoring its noncultural significance, we are theoret-ically granting approval to any technological manipulations of our bodies that would serve gender fluidity.

11 Ecofeminists claim that the domination of nature amounts to a masculine domination and that the domination of nonhuman nature and the domination of women are intimately connected and mutually reinforcing (see, for example, King, 1983: 16).

12 This main claim of the deep ecology movement that the nature/culture dichotomy should be replaced with a relational total-field image was introduced by Naess (1973).

13 The body and nature in Western metaphysics have traditionally been put in opposition to mind, spirit, and reason and, moreover, the feminine has been identified with the body, and the masculine with mind, spirit, and reason. See, for example, Lloyd (1984).

14 A "sign" of the poststructuralist disregard of nature is the very language poststructuralists use. Their semiotic terminology and textual metaphors are alienated from embodied existence. Feminist discourse, it has been argued, should, on the contrary, attempt to disrupt such fleshless terminology and ground language in experience. When poststructuralists make epistemological and ontological claims about our being, they generally place too much weight on language as a constituting force and on cognitive meaning.

15 For some excellent beginning articles in this area see Young (1990: 141–209).

16 See, for example, the criticisms in Butler (1989: 85–100). I certainly agree with some of her analysis of Merleau-Ponty's masculine biases (and believe there are similar masculine biases as well as anthropocentric biases in his broader ontology). However, as will become clear in the following pages, I do not agree with Butler's claim that Merleau-Ponty relies on a "natural"

body of biological subsistence that is removed from the domain of the historical and cultural. See, for example, his statement quoted in note 20.

17 Merleau-Ponty called it the "body-subject," meaning that the body, rather than cognition, is the main subject of human activity and relationship. However, he dropped this term in his later writing because it was too easily misinterpreted as a kind of subjectivism.

18 This precognitive relation that Merleau-Ponty describes is better understood as a *non*cognitive relation, for the term "precognitive" is already prejudiced in favour of the cognitive since it implies that the relation in question is already destined for a cognitive articulation. In contrast, the term "noncognitive" does not suggest a fulfillment in the cognitive but more of an independent existence or at least coexistence. For similar reasons, I will use the terms "nonlinguistic," "noncultural," and "nonpersonal."

19 Thus, our present binary gender structure is a result of the way we have taken up the indeterminate significances latent in our fleshy being. It is perhaps conceivable that we could take up the ambiguous confluences of meanings latent in our sexual bodies in such a way that a gender proliferation resulted. However, such a radical reconceptualization is unlikely since it seems to me that certain general and broad ways of our sexual reproductive bodily being would have to be suppressed.

20 "It is impossible," Merleau-Ponty concludes, "to superimpose on man a lower level of behaviour which one chooses to call natural, followed by a manufactured cultural or spiritual world. Everything is both manufactured and natural in man..." (Merleau-Ponty, 1962: 189).

21 Young (1990: 160–76) develops Kristeva's point that the subject is not experienced as unified in pregnancy, thereby offering a challenge to the subject/object dualism. I think, however, that even a split subject reifies the subject-object dichotomy. Young's chapter on pregnancy provides excellent phenomenological descriptions of pregnancy and birth from a woman's perspective.

22 As Young (1990: 167) notes, "Though she [the pregnant subject] does not plan and direct it [pregnancy], neither does it merely wash over her; rather, she *is* this process, this change."

23 Because breast-feeding is a social and, in a broad sense, a sexual activity and, moreover, demands a relative proximity to one's baby, it is perhaps the most culturally repressed aspect of the mothering body. Our Western patriarchal culture replaced breast-feeding with bottle-feeding in the late nineteenth and early twentieth centuries and later pushed substitute baby milk on the Third World with disastrous results. Most Western women today do not receive the social support and knowledge needed to confidently take up this remarkable communication of the mothering body and, indeed, are prevented from involving themselves in it because the public workplace is geared to the male body.

24 That the modern world reduces nature to a "standing-reserve" of energy resources, standing by to be further ordered is discussed extensively in Heidegger (1977).

# References

Benhabib, Seyla (1990) "Epistemologies of postmodernism: a rejoinder to Jean-Francois Lyotard". In *Feminism/Postmodernism*. Linda J. Nicholson, ed. London and New York: Routledge.

Bordo, Susan (1990). "Feminism, postmodernism, and gender-skepticism." In *Feminism/Postmodernism*. Linda J. Nicholson, ed. London and New York: Routledge.

Butler, Judith (1989). "Sexual ideology and phenomenological description: a feminist critique of Merleau-Ponty's *Phenomenology of Perception*." In *The Thinking Muse: Feminism and Modern French Philosophy*. Jeffner Allen and Iris Marion Young, eds. Indianapolis: Indiana University Press.

Butler Judith (1990) *Gender Trouble: Feminism and the Subversion of Identity*. New York: Routledge, Chapman and Hall, Inc.

De Lauretis, Teresa (1988). "The essence of the triangle or, taking the risk of essentialism seriously: feminist theory in Italy, the US and Britain." *Differences: A Journal of Feminist Cultural Studies* 1(2): 3–37.

DiStefano, Christine (1990). "Dilemmas of difference: feminism, modernity and postmodernism." In *Feminism/Postmodernism*. Linda J. Nicholson, ed. New York: Routledge.

Ferguson, Ann (1981) "Androgyny as an ideal for human development." In *Feminism and Philosophy*. Mary Vetterling-Braggin, Frederick A. Elliston and Jane English, eds. Totowa, NJ: Littlefield, Adams and Co.

Flax, Jane (1990) "Postmodernism and gender relations in feminist theory" In *Feminism/Postmodernism*. Linda J. Nicholson, ed. New York: Routledge.

Harding, Sandra (1990). "Feminism, science, and the anti-Enlightenment critiques." In *Feminism/Postmodernism*. Linda J. Nicholson, ed. New York: Routledge.

Hartsock, Nancy (1990) "Foucault on power: a theory for women?" In *Feminism/Postmodernism*. Linda J. Nicholson, ed. London and New York: Routledge.

Heidegger, Martin (1962) *Being and Time*. John Macquarrie and Edward Robinson, trans. New York: Harper and Row.

Heidegger, Martin (1971) "The origin of the work of art." In *Poetry, Language, Thought*. Albert Hofstadter, trans. New York: Harper Colophon Books.

Heidegger, Martin (1977) "The question concerning technology." In *The Question Concerning Technology and other Essays*. William Lovitt, trans. New York: Garland Publishing.

Heidegger, Martin (1982) *Nietzsche*. Vol. 4: *Nihilism*. David Farrell Krell, ed. and Frank A. Capuzzi, trans. San Francisco: Harper and Row.

Kahn, Robbie Pfeufer (1989) "Mother's milk: the 'moment of nurture' revisited." *Resources for Feminist Research* 18(3): 29–36.

King, Ynestra (1983) "The ecology of feminism and the feminism of ecology." *Harbinger: The Journal of Social Ecology* 1.

Lloyd, Genevieve (1984) *The Man of Reason: "Male" and "Female" in Western Philosophy*. Minneapolis: University of Minnesota Press.

Merleau-Ponty, Maurice (1962). *The Phenomenology of Perception*. Colin Smith, trans. New Jersey: Routledge and Kegan Paul.

Naess, Arne (1973) "The shallow and the deep, long-range ecology movement: a summary." *Inquiry* 16: 95–100.

Nicholson, Linda J., ed. (1990) *Feminism/Postmodernism*. New York: Routledge.

Nietzsche, Friedrich (1976). *Thus spake Zarathustra*. R. J. Hollindale, trans. New York: Penguin.

Palmer, Gabrielle. (1988). *The Politics of Breastfeeding*. London: Pandora Press.

Poovey, Mary. (1988) "Feminism and deconstruction." *Feminist Studies* 14(1): 51–66.

Scott, Joan W. (1988). "Deconstructing equality versus difference: or, the uses of poststructuralist theory for feminism." *Feminist Studies* 14(1): 33–50.

Trebilcot, Joyce (1981) "Two forms of androgynism." In *Feminism and Philosophy*. Mary Vetterling-Braggin, Frederick A. Elliston, and Jane English, eds. Totowa, NJ: Littlefield, Adams and Co.

Young, Iris, Marion (1990) *Throwing like a Girl and other Essays in Feminist Philosophy and Social Theory*. Indianapolis: Indiana University Press.

# PART II
## Constitutional Matrices

# 6
# Lived Body

# A Tale of Two Bodies: the Cartesian Corpse and the Lived Body*

## Drew Leder

Open a medical textbook; lie down upon a physician's examining table; attend grand rounds at a teaching hospital; and you find yourself immersed in a complex web of discourses and practices which together constitute the paradigm of modern medicine. This paradigm involves certain governing assumptions which are often overlooked because they are simply taken for granted. These include assumptions concerning the nature of disease entities, the canons of acceptable explanation, the modes of proper treatment. Moreover, such assumptions can ultimately be traced back to an implicit metaphysics. Ours is not a medicine of evil spirits or angry Gods, but of material causes and manifestations. If we are to understand the strengths and limits of our medicine and envision its alternatives, we must come to grips with the world-view it assumes. In what follows I shall address a key aspect of this world-view – the notion of "body" operative in modern medicine. After doing so, I will suggest a relevant alternative developed in twentieth-century phenomenology: that is, the model of the "lived body."

I consider modern medicine to be based, first and foremost, not upon the lived body, but upon the dead, or inanimate, body. This seems to present a paradox. After all, the dead body is frequently the symbol of the failure and termination of the therapeutic project. The business of the doctor is to attend the living, not the dead, and to preserve life in all but extreme circumstances. In what sense then does the dead body serve to guide and regulate modern medicine? To explain this point I will turn to the work of René Descartes, the philosophical father of modern scientific medicine. I will suggest that the figure of the dead body played a threefold role within Descartes's project, serving to *motivate* his scientific explorations, crucial to his investigative *methodology*, and lying at the heart of his *metaphysics*.[1]

## Descartes and the dead body

In examining the concerns which motivate Descartes's work, one finds time and time again a preoccupation with immortality. One of his two stated goals for the *Meditations* is that this treatise provide grounds for the belief "that the human soul

* Drew Leder, "A tale of two bodies: the Cartesian corpse and the lived body," *The Body in Medical Thought and Practice*, ed. by Drew Leder (Dordrecht: Kluwer Academic Publishers, 1992), pp. 17–35.

does not perish with the human body" (1911: 133). His proof of mind–body dualism serves such an end. As he writes in the earlier *Discourse on Method*:

> As a matter of fact, when one comes to know how greatly they differ, we understand much better the reasons which go to prove that our soul is in its nature entirely independent of body, and in consequence that it is not liable to die with it. (1911: 118)

That this interest in immortality is not simply a pretense designed to satisfy the church, but a profound existential concern of Descartes, is suggested by abundant biographical material. For example, in a letter to Huygens he confesses that religious teachings on the afterlife fail to convince; he, as most men, needs the testimony of "evident natural reasons" to support the notion that our souls "last longer than our bodies, and are destined by nature for pleasures and felicities much greater than those we enjoy in this world" (1970: 134–5).

   The threat posed by the perishable body helped provoke not only Descartes's metaphysical, but his scientific, work. He himself regarded as the chief end of his studies the development of a new medicine that would overcome disease, free the human race from the infirmities of old age, and vastly increase the life span. The preservation of health, he argues, is "without doubt the chief blessing and the foundation of all other blessings in this life" (1911: 119–20). Again, such goals were rooted in a personal concern with mortality. As he writes in two letters to Huygens:

> I have never taken such pains to protect my health as now, and whereas I used to think that death might rob me of thirty or forty years at most, it could not now surprise me unless it threatened my hope of living for more than a hundred years.
> (Vrooman, 1970: 142)

> The fact that my hair is turning gray warns me that I should spend all my time trying to set back the process. That is what I am working on now, and I hope all my efforts will succeed even though I lack sufficient experimentation.          (Vrooman, 1970: 142)

When such efforts failed to prevent a fatal bout of pneumonia, a Belgian newspaper reported, "In Sweden a fool has just died who used to say that he could live as long as he wanted" (Vrooman, 1970: 249).

   The dead body not only represents a threat which helps motivate Descartes's work; it is also incorporated into this work, playing a central *methodological* role. In order to advance medical knowledge, Descartes engaged for years in the dissection of dead animals and animal parts. At certain periods of his life he paid almost daily visits to butcher shops, collecting material for this purpose. As he writes to Mersenne in 1639, "I have spent much time on dissection during the last eleven years, and I doubt whether there is any doctor who has made such detailed observations as I" (1970: 64).

   One's methodology of investigation is inevitably tied to one's model of the real. Descartes's extensive use of dissection implies that the dead body also plays a key role within his *metaphysics* of embodiment. I will suggest that this is, indeed, the case; dissection of dead bodies can become a primary instrument of knowledge because Descartes models the living body first and foremost upon the inanimate. At first glance this seems paradoxical; Descartes defied tradition by arguing that the principle of animation is to be found in the body itself, not simply the soul. Whereas Augustine and many other medieval thinkers understood the body as something corpse-like unless infused with soul, Descartes argues that vitality arises from the body's own mechanical processes. As he writes to Henry More, "I do not deny life to animals, since I regard it as consisting simply in the heat of the heart" (1970: 245). Nor is death the result of the soul's departure:

> death never comes to pass by reason of the soul, but only because some one of the principal parts of the body decays: and we may judge that the body of a living man differs from that of a dead man just as does a watch or other automaton (i.e. a machine that moves of itself), when it is wound up and contains in itself the corporeal principle of those movements for which it is designed along with all that is requisite for its action, from the same watch or other machine when it is broken and when the principle of its movement ceases to act.                                          (1911: 333)

While Descartes thus locates life within the body itself, this is made possible only by a deeper concession to death. As the above quotation suggests, the body's "life" is modeled first and foremost upon the workings of *inanimate* machines. Descartes was fascinated by the automatons of his day which, while able to perform a variety of functions, even to imitate the behavior of living creatures, were in fact driven by mechanical forces. He reconceives the human body as just such a machine. As Descartes concludes the *Treatise of Man*, "the fire which burns continually in its heart ... is of no other nature than all those fires that occur in inanimate bodies" (1972: 113). The living body is not fundamentally different from the lifeless; it is a kind of animated corpse, a functioning mechanism.

This image of human embodiment is part and parcel of a larger ontology. To use Carolyn Merchant's phrase, mechanist philosophy effects something like "the death of nature" (1980). Within the world-views of Aristotelianism and natural magic, nature was understood as seeking to realize certain aims, or as exhibiting occult sympathies and antipathies. Descartes replaced this vision of an animate, ensouled nature with that of nature as *res extensa* – a plenum of passive matter driven by mechanical forces. This is a *dead* universe, devoid of subjectivity and intention. The human body is then regarded as a part of *res extensa*, and thereby modeled upon the lifeless machine. Whether engaged in metaphysical or scientific investigations, Descartes remained ever attuned to the practical import of his work. As he writes in the *Discourse on Method*:

> it is possible to attain knowledge which is very useful in life, and that, instead of that speculative philosophy which is taught in the Schools, we may find a practical philosophy by means of which, knowing the force and the action of fire, water, air, the stars, heavens and all other bodies that environ us, as distinctly as we know the different crafts of our artisans, we can in the same way employ them in all those uses to which they are adapted, and thus render ourselves the masters and possessors of nature.                                          (1911: 119)

Descartes's ontology is thus intertwined with a project of mastery. Thinkers such as Merchant (1980), Heidegger (1977), and Jonas (1966: 188–210) have explored this intimate connection between mechanist science and modern technology. Prior to the advent of mechanism, certain prohibitions remained against human tampering with nature. Insofar as natural bodies were seen by pre-modern thinkers as alive and exhibiting intrinsic ends, there were limits placed upon their use. For example, as Merchant discusses, the mining of ores was long regarded as a violation of the earth's womb and thus subject to normative constraints (1980: 29–41).

However, when nature was reconceived as lifeless mechanism, such constraints were lifted. *Res extensa*, devoid of intrinsic subjectivity, could be reshaped in a limitless fashion.

Moreover, the mechanist world-view facilitates the development of the tools needed for this reshaping. To understand an object in mechanist terms is to break it down into its constituent elements and analyze their interaction. But the knowledge so gained is precisely the sort needed if we wish to commandeer events. As Jonas writes of modern science, "To know a thing means to know how it is or can be made and therefore means being able to repeat or vary or anticipate the process of making" (1966: 203–4). Once we understand the mechanical elements and forces involved in a natural process, we can in principle alter or artificially duplicate it. This sort of knowledge thus grants us power over nature. Such was not the case with the final causes and substantial forms studied by the medievals. These were basically immutable, indivisible, God-given essences, to be contemplated, not altered at will. The mechanist world-view allows the crucial shift from passive contemplation to the active manipulation which characterizes the modern age.

## The dead body and modern medicine

I have suggested that Cartesian thought is profoundly shaped by the figure of the dead body. This body poses a threat which helps provoke Descartes's metaphysical and scientific explorations; it provides a tool for securing knowledge; and finally, it rests at the heart of the mechanist world-view and its associated projects of mastery.

Modern medicine is profoundly Cartesian in spirit (Capra, 1983). As such, this notion of embodiment, one in which the non-living takes primacy over the living, has extensively shaped medical theory and practice. I will seek only to briefly illustrate this point in relation to the disease categories, diagnostic techniques, and therapeutic procedures of modern medicine.

The influence of mechanism and its "ontology of death" is revealed through attending to medical history. As Foucault (1975: 124–48) and Engelhardt (1986: 176–84) describe, in the eighteenth century, classifications of disease shifted from a basis in the symptoms experienced by the living patient to a basis in the organic lesions found in the corpse. The lived experience of illness came to be seen as epiphenomenal; the real disease unfolded in the material world of *res extensa* and could best be exposed by the pathologist's knife. As Foucault writes of this view:

> That which hides and envelops, the curtain of night over truth, is, paradoxically, life; and death, on the contrary, opens up to the light of day the black coffer of the body.
>
> (1975: 166)

This focus upon the corpse as the scene of revelation helped stimulate the dramatic growth of medical technology. As Reiser discusses, seventeenth-century diagnosis was based largely upon the patient's own account of the illness. It was not unusual to arrive at a diagnosis through the mail, utilizing the patient's self-description (1978: 16). However, as the organic lesions exposed at death came to be seen as primary, doctors sought instruments that would allow a comparable perception of the living. A nineteenth-century physician thus characterizes the stethoscope: "We anatomize by auscultation (if I may say so), while the patient is yet alive" (Reiser, 1978: 30). Such technologies as the stethoscope, the blood test, the X-ray, allow a kind of dissection of the living body, analyzing it into its component parts, exposing what life ordinarily conceals.

The epistemological primacy of the corpse has shaped not only medical techno-logy, but diverse aspects of training and practice. Medical education still begins with the dissection of a cadaver, just as the clinical case ends in the pathologist's lab. In between, the living patient is often treated in a cadaverous or machine-like fashion. We see this, for example, in the traditional physical examination. The patient is asked to assume a corpse-like pose, flat, passive, naked, mute. The entire ritual and context serves to reduce the living body to something almost dead. Personal identity is stripped away as the patient is removed from his or her habitual surroundings, activities, even clothes. Then too, the patient's voice is, for long stretches, silenced. After all, a heartbeat cannot be heard above a patient's query – hence, the irony in the title of Richard Baron's article: "I can't hear you while I'm listening" (1985). While the doctor performing a physical examination is an active and engaged explorer, the patient is placed in a position of corpse-like passivity. Even when called upon to act or respond, it is largely in the machine-mode; the knee is tapped to provoke reflexes; the abdomen is poked to see if pain ensues; the patient is asked to take a deep breath to hear whether the lungs produce audible rattles.

Given the vision of embodiment which underlies our disease categories and diagnostic methods, it is not surprising that the process often culminates in mechan-istic forms of treatment. Faced, for example, with a patient suffering from heart disease, the doctor may prescribe a drug which will bring about multiple physiolo-gical changes. Exercise may be recommended to strengthen the heart muscle, along with a diet to regulate blood pressure and atherosclerotic progression. If a surgical procedure is needed, the body is opened up and certain vessels may then be replaced. In each case, the doctor uses means which will alter the body as one would a mechanical thing, substituting parts, altering inputs and outputs, and regulating processes. At the core of modern medical practice is the Cartesian revelation: *the living body can be treated as essentially no different from a machine.* Though any good clinician also engages the patient-*as-person*, the predominant thrust of modern medical therapeutics has been upon such mechanistic inter-ventions.

I earlier discussed how the mechanist model of nature subserves a project of control. Once we analyze a natural object into its component parts and their interactions – that is, see how it is made – we can make it ourselves, or alter it in desired directions. Herein lies the enormous power of modern medicine. We have learned to understand, remake or transform, components of the body-machine. When disease intervenes, we can intervene too. We know enough about the mechanics of bodily processes to assert over them a degree of intentional control. Few of us would want to abandon this therapeutic power. If faced with heart disease, most will gladly reach for the medical armamentarium – drugs, diet, surgery, and the like – and its promise, often delivered, of a prolonged or improved life.

Yet the machine-model of the body has given rise not only to therapeutic triumphs but to limitations and distortions in medical practice. For example, it is by now a cliché that modern medicine often neglects the import of psychosocial factors in the etiology and treatment of disease. Not as widely recognized are the metaphysical roots of this neglect. Insofar as the body is modeled upon a lifeless machine, the role of subjective experience in determining one's health history will tend to be overlooked. After all, a machine does not experience, does not inhabit an "existential world." When it misperforms, this can be explained with exclusive reference to mechanical forces. Not so with human disease and the response to treatment. Here, experiential factors seem to play a huge part – emotions, desires, perceptions, interpretations. There is mounting evidence that emotional stress, intersubjective losses, and personality styles can play a crucial role in bringing about illness. Similarly, one's response to treatment may depend upon such "subjective" factors, as one's affective state, one's "will to live," or the quality of the treater–patient relation. Such humanistic variables continually peek through the cracks in the façade of mechanistic medicine. Even the medical researcher must constantly control for the "placebo effect" based on the patient's beliefs and interpretations. While clinicians will often acknowledge the importance of such subjective phenomena, medicine's ability to address them has been systematically hampered by the Cartesian model of embodiment.[2]

This model has also served to distort the quality of provider–patient relations. Patients often complain that they have been dealt with by their health-care providers or institutions in a dehumanized fashion: as if they were but a disease entity, or a piece of meat to be prodded, punctured, and otherwise ignored. This practice is rooted not simply in personal insensitivities but, again, in a metaphysical model. Insofar as the patient to be examined is modeled on the automaton, he or she as *living person* with wishes, questions, pains and fears, can all too easily be overlooked. When fixing a machine such things need not be considered. Within this framework, human sensitivity to the suffering of a fellow human being remains possible, but is hardly encouraged. In fact, it demands an almost schizophrenic shift between, at one moment, examining the machine-body, and at the next, acknowledging the person to whom it belongs.

# The lived body

Given the problems inherent in the Cartesian model of embodiment, it is important to explore relevant alternatives. If we wish to reform medical practice in fundamental ways it is not sufficient to propose piecemeal changes in medical education, financing, and the like, while leaving unchallenged the conceptual structure upon which modern medicine rests. It is, however, no easy matter to challenge Cartesianism; this position is by now so firmly entrenched in our culture that it is difficult to think outside of its paramaters. Even those who seek "holistic" alternatives often find themselves caught in dualistic terms, asserting the importance of mind, soul, or spirit vis-à-vis bodily events. Such a framework fails to rethink the body itself and develop a systematic alternative to the machine-model which for so long has governed our thinking.

However, such an alternative has been developed by a variety of twentieth-century philosophers and physicians, including Merleau-Ponty (1962, 1968), Marcel (1952, 1956), Plügge (1962, 1967), Buytendijk (1974), van den Berg (1952), Zaner (1964, 1981, 1988), and several others. This model has been termed that of the "lived body." The term "lived body" derives from the German *Leib*. In German, the term *Leib* is employed when one is referring to living bodies, while the term *Körper* is used to designate inanimate or dead bodies: the body of a rock, for example, or of a human corpse. The Cartesian paradigm can be said to eradicate the essential difference between the *Leib* and the *Körper*. The former becomes but a special case of the latter, one instance of the general class of physical things. The notion of "lived body" rejects this conflation. It holds that the body of a living being has an essential structure of its own which cannot be captured by the language and concepts used to explain inanimate nature.

If one notion can be said to lie at the heart of this paradigm, it is that the lived body is an "intending" entity. The notion of intentionality is a complex one in the history of philosophy, having its roots in medieval thought, revived for the modern era by the psychologist Brentano (1973), and playing a central role within twentieth-century phenomenological thought. In the hands of each user, the term takes on a somewhat different meaning. In saying that the lived body is an "intending" entity, I mean simply that it is bound up with, and directed toward, an experienced world. It is a being in relationship to that which is other: other people, other things, an environment. Moreover, in a significant sense, the lived body helps to constitute this world-as-experienced. We cannot understand the meaning and form of objects without reference to the bodily powers through which we engage them – our senses, motility, language, desires. The lived body is not just one thing *in* the world, but a way in which the world comes to be.

For example, in the midst of my writing, I leave my chair and computer screen behind, seeking a glass of orange juice. The action can be described in terms of a series of mechanistic events involving neuronal firings, muscular contractions, and the like. However, if this becomes our exclusive, or even dominant, mode of understanding embodiment, it renders obscure the *bodily intentionality* through which we constitute and respond to our world. It was, after all, my body that first summoned me to rise, my thirst, my exhaustion, leading me to the refrigerator. The juice stands out from the perceptual and conative background as just what is called for and my arm reaches for it as the result of a complex coordination of sensorimotor powers. The world of thirst, tiredness, orange juice, refrigerators, as well as computer screens, written language, readers and the like, always stands in relation to a subject-body which experiences and constructs this world. Just as this bodily intentionality is obscured by the notion of the mechanistic body, so too is it obscured by recourse to an "immaterial mind" as the locus of all this intending. I was not led to the juice by a series of mental calculations concerning descending blood sugar levels, the need for osmotic adjustments, and the like. Rather, my action unfolded through a series of pre-thematic motives and responses welling up from within my embodiment itself, with its own wisdom and sensorimotor wizardry.

The philosophers and physicians mentioned above have clarified the intending nature of the lived body through a series of detailed regional studies. To take but one example, Erwin Straus discusses the forms of spatiality opened up through the different senses (1963, 1966). Sight discloses a world of stable entities, simultaneously arrayed in definite positions. Conversely, through sound we apprehend becoming, not being, that is, pulses, activities, effects. Sound can fill up and homogenize experienced space, whereas vision separates and delineates spatial regions. Moreover, sight and hearing establish different subject–object relations. Vision generally involves the subject in an active stance, a turning toward the object, which maintains a clear distance between the perceiver and perceived. But we are at the mercy of sounds; they press upon us even without our consent, abolishing distance in sometimes discomforting, sometimes ecstatic, ways.

The distinction between such sense experiences gives rise to important ramifications, both clinical and philosophical. For example, Straus argues that the prevalence of *auditory* hallucinations in schizophrenics can be traced to this experiential quality of sound, its capacity to overcome distance, take over space, and dissolve boundaries (1966: 277–89). Jonas, reflecting upon the Western philosophical corpus, notes its strong reliance on metaphors of sight, from the Platonic "eye of the soul" to the Cartesian "light of reason"; he suggests the very notion of *theoria*, that is, of a distanced, objectified knowledge, is drawn from our experience of vision (1966: 135–56).

While our different sense organs thus open onto genuinely distinct phenomenal realms, our lived body, in ordinary life, weaves these together into one world. When, for example, I notice a singing bird, I do not experience it as two objects, one visual, one auditory; I perceive one bird through the different perspectives of my senses. As Merleau-Ponty points out, this unity of experienced objects is not accomplished through the application of mental rules and categories, but through a pre-conscious power of bodily synthesis (1962: 232). Moreover, this synthesis extends beyond the boundaries of the senses to interweave perception with movement. We see things arrayed about us as "here" or "there", "near" or "far", because we are able to move through space and take up different vantage points. The perceived *meaning* of objects is similarly dependent upon our motility and the projects it makes possible. A chair invites my weary bones to rest. A hammer, shaped to my grip, allows me to build. The things amidst which I dwell are charged with a practical significance based upon my lived body's needs and capacities.

I shall not here explore in detail the rich phenomenology of the lived body. Authors have addressed such diverse topics as the body's upright posture, sexuality, powers of expression, visceral functioning, etc., and the ways in which these serve both to construct and respond to our experienced world. However, the overall effect of such work is to displace our notion of the body from that formulated within the Cartesian tradition. The body is not simply a thing in the world, but an intentional entity which gives rise to a world. Yet to be the latter is not to negate the former. While the body has a subjective role, it is also a body-object, a material thing. The eye is both the seat of an existential power, and an apparatus involving cornea, lens, and optic nerve. As that which opens up the visible world, the eye also takes its place within this world as a visible object of determinate color and shape.

The lived body is thus an "intertwining" to use Merleau-Ponty's term (1968: 130–55), both perceiver and perceived, intentional and material. This intertwining is torn asunder by the Cartesian framework. For Cartesianism, at least in its crude form, rigidly separates thinking (*res cogitans*) from materiality (*res extensa*). But the "lived body" is a concept designed to carry us beyond ontological dualism, while acknowledging the divergence of perspectives and languages through which the self can be approached. To be human is to be the site of an intentionality which is materially determined and enacted. This existential situation, inherently ambiguous and double-sided, is never captured by Cartesian dualism, or its reductive idealist and materialist offshoots.

## Medicine and the lived body

I have suggested above, and elsewhere, that many of the flaws of modern medicine – depersonalization, overspecialization, the neglect of psychosocial factors in the etiology and treatment of disease – can be traced to medicine's reliance on the Cartesian model of embodiment (1984). Here the dead body, the machine-body, are made paradigmatic. But what if we were to ground medical theory and practice on a notion of the lived body? Just as the lived body is an intertwining of intentionality and materiality, subject and object, so we would arrive at a medicine of the *intertwining*. That is, our notions of disease and treatment would always involve a chiasmatic blending of biological and existential terms, wherein these terms are not seen as ultimately opposed, but mutually implicatory and involved in intricate "logics" of exchange.

This point can perhaps best be clarified through a prosaic example rather than theoretical formulations. For this purpose, consider the case of a person who approaches her health-care provider with a chief complaint of headaches and dizziness.

On examination, the patient is found to be hypertensive. Ordinarily the hypertension might be understood and treated primarily in mechanistic terms: for example, through a low-salt diet and medications to facilitate diuresis and lower peripheral resistance. The body's circulatory dynamics are thus mechanically readjusted. To begin from the perspective of the lived body need not imply that such interventions are prohibited. The lived body, after all, does exhibit the aspect of a thing-in-the-world, a complex of physiological mechanisms. However, to begin with the lived body is to understand the physiological as always intertwined with, and an expression of, the body's intentionality. As such, hypertension should be understood in the context of the person's existential grasp of the world.

Let us imagine this person as involved in a difficult marriage and stressful job situation. The sense of limitation and frustration which are a daily reality lead not only to a clenched fist, a sore neck, but to a constricting of the arteries. The patient inhabits, we might say, a *constricted world*, and this constriction expresses itself through both surface and visceral musculature. So, too, the temporality of her life-world. Perhaps she is the impatient sort always rushing to finish projects and make her next appointment. In her struggle to compress time, even her visceral functions – breathing, heartbeat – become compressed and accelerated in ways that can lead to dysfunction. Even when there is nothing she can do to bring about a desired outcome, her body engages in a symphony of virtual action. Trapped in a room with a slow conversationalist, she leans forward, taps her foot, clenches the side of her chair. The internal clenching of blood vessels, the hypertension (so aptly named) that may result, is but one more expression of this style of being-in-the-world. So too, the grab for a cigarette with its paradoxical calming and stimulating effect, the wolfing down of a high-calorie and high-cholesterol fast-food lunch, each of which may contribute in their own way to the development of her illness.

Admittedly, what is discussed above in intentional terms can be reformulated in mechanical terms concerning neurohormonal effects, preload and afterload, peripheral resistance, etc. Moreover, one ought not to deny the importance of genetic factors in the etiology of disease processes such as hypertension. The existential account does not replace the biological account, but rather places it within a broader perspective. The anatomy and physiology of the lived body are always intertwined with the body's intentionality in ways that undermine facile claims of priority. Just as our physical structure lays the groundwork for our mode of being-in-the-world, so our interactions with this world fold back to reshape our body in ways conducive to health or illness. A medicine of the lived body dwells in this intertwining.

When disease is understood to have an existential dimension no less important than its physiology, the methods and meanings of clinical diagnosis shift. The traditional physical examination, the use of the sphygmomanometer, blood tests, and other relevant technologies, would hardly be excluded. These allow the lived body to speak forth its illness in terms of biological mechanisms and disruptions. However, the history takes on a heightened importance in a medicine of the lived body. Through hearing the patient's *story*, one comes to know in detail of her world as she embodies it: her habits of exercise, diet and substance use, the state of her job or marriage, her emotional proclivities, her modes of dealing with stress. Only in this broader context will the full significance and etiology of her illness emerge. From this perspective, a diagnosis of "essential hypertension" is woefully inadequate, telling us little about the *dis-ease* that has arisen in the patient's life and body. Diagnosis too must dwell in the intertwining, illuminating the intentional/physiological dimensions of illness.

Similarly, treatment takes on a fuller profile when it is understood not as "fixing the machine" but as addressing the lived body and its world-relations. The healthcare provider may indeed employ relevant medications, but this by itself does little to counter the existential preconditions of disease. Other more complex options are opened up by a medicine of the intertwining. The patient might consider marriage counseling or changing her job. It may be more appropriate to seek an alteration in her world, rather than to focus initially on visceral processes. The lived body always reaches beyond itself, and medical interventions need not be bounded by the flesh. Insofar as the body is directly addressed, attempts may be made to alter its intentional style, not simply its mechanics. For example, the patient might employ meditation or relaxation training to transform her sense of embodied temporality: to "slow down," to "ease up," to "let go," in ways that will find expression in her vasculature. The use of visual imagery or cognitive therapy may diminish her sense of the world-as-threat; an exercise program may provide a way of releasing tension. As the lived body is a multi-leveled structure of conscious and autonomic functions, a place where psychological history is sedimented, interpersonal relations enacted, biological mechanisms homeostatically maintained, a medicine of the intertwining recognizes multiple points of possible intervention.

There are advantages and disadvantages to approaching the lived body from different therapeutic perspectives. Clearly some of the forms of treatment mentioned above – for example, counseling or therapy – may seem time consuming, expensive, and uncertain in their results when compared with simply prescribing a medication. It is no easy matter to alter the body–world relation, the long-standing features of personality and life-style that lie at the origin of so many diseases. On the other hand, the recourse to medication, while relatively cheap and quick, fails to address this existential etiology of the disease. While one machine malfunction is kept in check, the "dis-ease" in its broader sense, involving modes of constriction, acceleration, and dissatisfaction, is apt to progress and surface elsewhere in the lived body. As in the case of many illnesses, the ideal solution would not simply be an either/or, but a both/and: a therapeutic program that lives comfortably in the intertwining of physiological and existential perspectives.

Whatever point at which one chooses to intervene, such a medicine of the lived body would be sensitive to effects and alterations elsewhere in the intertwining. For example, even in the simplest case where essential hypertension is diagnosed and medication(s) prescribed, there will be multiple ripples in the existential domain. The very pronouncement of the diagnosis may provoke fear, confusion, and stress, mimicking, to a degree, existential features of the illness. On the other hand, if sensitively presented in the context of a positive provider–patient relation, the diagnosis may become part of the healing. Moreover, the medications, by changing the body's physiology, will have existential effects of their own. Depending upon the drug(s) used, they may bring about diarrhea, depression, etc., or more positively, the relief of highly disturbing symptoms. To biologically intervene is almost invariably to intervene on the existential plane. The use of medicines and surgeries, no less than the originating illness, can give rise to transformations in self-image, social relations, patterns of desire, experience of space and time, etc. Within the Cartesian paradigm of "fixing the machine" it is all too easy to forget such effects of treatment, focusing instead on the "hard numbers" that indicate physiological healing or regression.

Just as a medicine of the lived body would attend to the existential effects of biological intervention, so, too, to the reverse; that is, when treatment is enacted on the existential plane, it is important to monitor the physiological outcomes. If, for example, the patient undergoes a stress reduction program, or switches jobs, blood pressure must be monitored to see if it responds. *To attend to the lived body is not to forsake the tools and learning that Cartesian medicine has provided. It is merely to refuse to grant this mechanical wisdom the status of ruling paradigm.* Instead, this wisdom takes on the humbler role of a regional method, elucidating the lived body from one possible perspective, but incapable of capturing its multifaceted richness. The full significance of human disease and health necessarily eludes the model of body-as-machine.

Certain objections can be raised to this (admittedly introductory) presentation of a medicine of the lived body. First, it might be claimed that this analysis is only relevant to particular diseases that involve a strong emotional, psychosomatic, or "life-style" component. In choosing to discuss essential hypertension I might be said to have "stacked the deck" in this direction, while ignoring other diseases with unambiguous mechanistic causes. Are there not, after all, modes of hypertension arising from pheochromocytomas, renal abnormalities, primary aldosteronism, and the like, where the patient's intentionality may have little to do with etiology? Are there not a multitude of other diseases and injuries, where the mechanistic model proves quite sufficient for our needs?

My answer must be twofold. First, epidemiological studies suggest that the percentage of medical problems that can be so classified is surprisingly small. To take the example we have been using, in less than 10 percent of patients presenting with hypertension can a specific organic etiology be identified. This may well change in the future, but it suggests the limitations of the Cartesian model of disease. The lethal diseases of the modern industrial age, most prominently cardio-vascular disease and cancer, have been shown to be intimately bound up with sociocultural and personal intentionalities; that is, life-style, emotions, environmen-tal agents, habits of diet, drug use and exercise. It is becoming increasingly clear that our diseases are not just mechanical affairs, but a matter of how we live our lives and inhabit our world.

However, even in the case of unambiguous organic etiologies – for example, fractured bones sustained through no fault of the victim – a medicine of the intertwining is equally *à-propos*. Though intentional factors may not be implicated in *causing* this dysfunction, it surely is involved in constructing a *response*. To operate most effectively the clinician or clinical team must do more than set the fractures properly; they must address the pain, the restricted motility, the con-stricted possibilities that reconfigure the patient's world. This is an injury to the body-as-lived, not just the body-as-machine, and so should be regarded. It is against this broader background that key clinical questions can most fully be addressed: whether or not to hospitalize, what regimen of rehabilitation to choose, how to best help the patient cope with his/her disability, how to mobilize a social support system. While not all illnesses have intentional causalities, they all have existential effects, and unfold no less in the intertwining.

A second objection may be raised to the model I am here advancing: not that it is wrong *per se*, but rather that it is trivial. After all, is not the notion of "treating the whole person" a gratuitous platitude, a banner carried by "holistic practitioners," advocates of the "biopsychosocial" approach, and a half-dozen other theoretical schools? And even if not theoretically articulated, isn't this the kind of thing that any good practitioner will intuitively do – that is, take a good social history, relate to the person-as-person, address the life-disruptions of illness, seek a broad variety of clinical responses?

While there is some truth to such rejoinders, they are incomplete. On the theoretical level, it is true that a variety of perspectives have emerged both from mainstream medicine and its radical alternatives that seek to break the hold of Cartesianism. However, this turns out to be no easy task. Because Cartesianism has fractured the language of the self, many theories remain caught in the dilemma of hyphenated disjunctions. We are told we must remember the importance of the "mind" and the "mind–body" interaction in disease, but this leaves our Cartesian description of self essentially intact, and our notion of "body" unreformed. Or we are told to attend to the biological, psychological, and sociological dimensions of illness, but provided with no theoretical terms capable of unifying these domains; the very term "biopsychosocial" represents an uneasy recourse to concepts strung side-by-side. The notion of the lived body, on the other hand, has the advantage of providing a genuinely integrative framework. From this perspective, intentionality is viewed as necessarily embodied, enacted and determined in the material domain. It is the very nature of the lived body to be both perceiver and perceived, subject and object. The notion of this intertwining guides this paradigm from the start and provides a way to think beyond Cartesianism.

On the practical level, while it is true that many practitioners intuitively treat the lived body, it is undeniable that Cartesianism has had profound effects. The sense of the patient as a living, experiencing, suffering person has been systematically truncated by the model of the body-as-machine, a model that has shaped our understanding of disease, our modes of professional training, diagnosis, and treatment, even the offices and hospitals in which medicine is practiced. The approach of any practitioner to any patient is necessarily predetermined by this vast complex of factors, and in ways that tend to lead down reductionist paths. The truly "humanistic" practitioner often finds his or her interests frustrated by "the system," frequently non-reimbursable on insurance forms, at best regarded as of secondary importance. From the standpoint of the lived body, humanistic concerns are no longer secondary, a matter of mere "bedside manner" – rather, they become core to every aspect of medical thought and practice.

To conceptualize the physiology of the body without recourse to intentional terms; to understand that this body can be analyzed mechanistically: such was the great triumph of Cartesian medicine. The successes of Cartesianism are arrayed before us, but so too its profound limitations. There is a need for a re-transformation of thought concerning embodiment, the emergence of a new paradigm. This need not involve discarding the knowledge and techniques that Cartesian medicine has yielded. Rather, Cartesian medicine should be relativized as one option, one perspective, subsumed within a broader framework. The notion of the lived body, I would suggest, provides such a framework worthy of further reflection.

## Notes

1 This discussion of Descartes, Cartesian medicine, and the corpse, draws closely upon a previous work of mine (Leder 1990: 138–48).
2 Ironically, while Cartesian metaphysics may be at the root of our mechanistic medicine, Descartes himself was something of a "holistic practitioner": in his correspondence with Princess Elizabeth, he emphasizes the importance of diet, exercise, but most of all, cultivating positive thinking, as treatment for her maladies (1970: 153, 161–3).

## Bibliography

Baron, R. J. (1985) "An introduction to medical phenomenology: I can't hear you while I'm listening," *Annals of Internal Medicine* 103, 606–11.
Brentano, F. (1973) *Psychology from an Empirical Standpoint* (ed. Oskar Kraus, transl. by Antos C. Rancurello, D. B. Terrell, and Linda L. McAlister), Routledge and Kegan Paul, London.
Buytendijk, F. J. J. (1974) *Prolegomena to an Anthropological Physiology*, Duquesne University Press, Pittsburgh, PA.
Capra, F. (1983) *The Turning Point*, Bantam Books, New York, NY.
Descartes, R. (1911) *The Philosophical Works of Descartes*, vol. 1 (transl. by Elizabeth S. Haldane and G. R. T. Ross). Cambridge University Press, Cambridge.
Descartes, R. (1970) *Philosophical Letters* (transl. and ed. by Anthony Kenny), University of Minnesota Press, Minneapolis, MN.
Descartes, R. (1972) *Treatise of Man* (transl. and ed. by Thomas Steele Hall), Harvard University Press, Cambridge, MA.
Engelhardt, H. T., Jr. (1986) *The Foundations of Bioethics*, Oxford University Press, New York, NY.
Foucault, M. (1975) *The Birth of the Clinic* (transl. by A. M. Sheridan Smith), Vintage Books, New York, NY.
Heidegger, M. (1977) *The Question Concerning Technology and Other Essays* (transl. by William Lovitt), Harper and Row, New York, NY.
Jonas, H. (1966) *The Phenomenon of Life*, University of Chicago Press, IL.
Leder, D. (1984) "Medicine and paradigms of embodiment," *The Journal of Medicine and Philosophy* 9, 29–43.
Leder, D. (1990) *The Absent Body*, University of Chicago Press, Chicago, IL.
Marcel, G. (1952) *Metaphysical Journal* (transl. Bernard Wall), Henry Regnery Co., Chicago, IL.
Marcel, G. (1956) *Being and Having: An Existentialist Diary* (transl. by K. Farrer), Harper and Row, New York, NY.
Merchant, C. (1980) *The Death of Nature*, Harper and Row, San Francisco, CA.
Merleau-Ponty, M. (1962) *Phenomenology of Perception* (transl. by Colin Smith), Routledge and Kegan Paul, London.
Merleau-Ponty, M. (1968) *The Visible and the Invisible* (transl. by Alphonso Lingus), Northwestern University Press, Evanston, IL.
Plügge, H. (1962) *Wohlbefinden und Missbefinden*, Max Niemeyer Verlag, Tübingen, Germany.
Plügge, H. (1967), *Der Mensch und sein Leib*, Max Niemeyer Verlag, Tübingen, Germany.
Reiser, S. (1978) *Medicine and the Reign of Technology*, Cambridge University Press, Cambridge.
Straus, E. (1963) *The Primary World of Senses* (transl. by Jacob Needleman), The Free Press of Glencoe, Glencoe, NY.
Straus, E. (1966) *Phenomenological Psychology* (transl. by Erling Eng), Basic Books, New York, NY.
van den Berg, J. H. (1952) "The human body and the significance of human movement," *Philosophy and Phenomenological Research* 13, 159–83.
Vrooman, J. R. (1970) *René Descartes: A Biography*, G. P. Putnam's Sons, New York, NY.
Zaner, R. (1964) *The Problem of Embodiment*, Martinus Nijhoff, The Hague, Netherlands.
Zaner, R. (1981) *The Context of Self: A Phenomenological Inquiry Using Medicine as a Clue*, Ohio University Press, Athens, OH.
Zaner, R. (1988), *Ethics and the Clinical Encounter*, Prentice Hall, Englewood Cliffs, NJ.

# 7

# Body Image and Body Schema

## Body Image and Body Schema in a Deafferented Subject*

### *Shaun Gallagher and Jonathan Cole*

In a majority of situations the normal adult maintains posture or moves without consciously monitoring motor activity. Posture and movement are usually close to automatic; they tend to take care of themselves, outside of attentive regard. One's body, in such cases, effaces itself as one is geared into a particular intentional goal. This effacement is possible because of the normal functioning of a body schema. Body schema can be defined as a system of preconscious, subpersonal processes that play a dynamic role in governing posture and movement (Head, 1920). There is an important and often overlooked conceptual difference between the subpersonal body schema and what is usually called *body image*. The latter is most often defined as a conscious idea or mental representation that one has of one's own body (see for example, Adame et al. 1991; Gardner and Moncrieff, 1988; Schilder, 1935). Despite the conceptual difference many researchers use the terms interchangeably, leading to both a terminological and conceptual confusion.[1]

Gallagher (1986) has argued that a clear conceptual distinction between body image and body schema would be helpful in working out their functional differences. But the conceptual distinction should not imply that on the behavioral level the image and schema are unconnected or that they do not sometimes affect one another. To develop the distinction further and to clarify the functional interrelations of body image and schema, this paper examines the unusual case of a subject with a severely impaired body schema. IW suffers from the effects of a large fiber peripheral neuropathy that involves the loss of proprioception and the sense of touch from the neck down (Cole, 1995). Despite the dramatic effects of the disabling neuropathy IW regained a controlled posture and locomotion by consciously monitoring his position and movement. We suggest that, in this case, control over posture and movement were achieved by a partial and imperfect functional substitution of body image for body schema.

## Body schema and body image: a conceptual distinction

In a recent review, Parsons (1990) defines the concept of *body image* in a complex and ambiguous way. On the one hand, he considers the body image to be nonconscious:

* Shaun Gallagher and Jonathan Cole, "Body image and body schema in a deafferented subject," *The Journal of Mind and Behavior*, vol. 16 (Autumn 1995), 369–90.

a set of "processes underlying the mental simulation of one's action and ... not directly accessible to consciousness" (p. 46). In this sense it operates as a subpersonal representation that depends on information provided by "proprioceptive, kinesthetic, muscular, articular, postural, tactile, cutaneous, vestibular, equilibrium, visual, and auditory senses, as well as [information] from our sense of physical effort and from contact with objects and among our body parts" (p. 46). On the other hand, Parsons, citing Lackner (1988), indicates that some of this information contributes to a conscious, perceptual representation of the body, the "mental simulation" itself, in which "the apparent position of some parts affects the represented shape of others" (p. 46). He also cites Head (1920) and uses the term *body schema* interchangeably with *body image*.

This recent definition expresses an ambiguity that has characterized studies of body perception since Schilder (1935) used the terms *body image* and *body schema* interchangeably to signify the image or conscious representation of one's own body. Poeck and Orgass (1971) and Gallagher (1986) summarize a long tradition of ambiguous terminological usage and conceptual misusage in clinical studies of body perception and movement. In light of the fact that the terms *schema* and *image* have frequently been used interchangeably to mean processes that range from reflective cognition, to physiological functions, to unconscious representation, a clear conceptual distinction may be helpful for understanding both the production and the perception of movement. Among the various issues involved in the problem of defining the distinction between schema and image the following one is most relevant to our considerations here.

The *body image* consists of a complex set of intentional states – perceptions, mental representations, beliefs, and attitudes – in which the intentional object of such states is one's own body. Thus the body image involves a reflective intentionality. Three modalities of this reflective intentionality are often distinguished in studies involving body image (e.g. Cash and Brown, 1987; Gardner and Moncrieff, 1988; Powers et al., 1987):

1   the subject's *perceptual* experience of his/her own body;
2   the subject's *conceptual* understanding (including mythical and/or scientific knowledge) of the body in general; and
3   the subject's *emotional* attitude toward his/her own body.

The latter two aspects, (2) and (3), do not always involve conscious awareness, but are maintained as a set of beliefs or attitudes and in that sense form part of an intentional system.

In contrast to the reflective intentionality of the body image, a *body schema* involves a system of motor capacities, abilities, and habits that enable movement and the maintenance of posture. The body schema is not a perception, a belief, or an attitude. Rather, it is a system of motor and postural functions that operate below the level of self-referential intentionality, although such functions can enter into and support intentional activity. The preconscious, subpersonal processes carried out by the body-schema system are tacitly keyed into the environment and play a dynamic role in governing posture and movement. Although the body-schema system can have specific effects on cognitive experience (Gallagher, 1995), it does not have the status of a conscious representation or belief.

In most instances, movement and maintenance of posture are accomplished automatically by the body, and for this reason the normal adult neither needs nor has a constant body awareness. Indeed, in most activities that are oriented toward an intentional goal the body tends to efface itself with respect to conscious awareness. This functional effacement of the body is possible because in normal circumstances a body schema continues to perform its motor and postural functions without need of conscious control. It continues to operate, and in many cases operates best, when the intentional object of perception is something other than one's own body. Crook makes this point clear: "We all know that in normal conscious states our awareness of bodily sensation is limited – pushed aside by the fact that our attention is locked upon some social or situational issue. It is almost as if (as in the learning of a task) the functions of the body are on automatic pilot and do not usually have to be attended to consciously" (1987: 390–1).[2]

Although the control and coordination of movements are normally accomplished by a body schema without the help of conscious attention, and in some cases even without conscious awareness of what our body is doing, there are instances in which the perception of one's own movements can be complexly interrelated to their accomplishment. Conscious perception of my own body can be used to monitor and control my posture and movements. The visual, tactile, and proprioceptive awareness that I have of my body may help me to learn a new dance step, improve my tennis game, or imitate the movements of others. Ordinarily, however, in walking I do not have to think about putting one foot in front of another; I do not have to think through the action of reaching for something. I may be marginally aware that I am moving in certain ways, but it is not usually the center of my attention. And marginal awareness may not capture the whole movement. If I am marginally aware that I am reaching for something, I may not be aware at all of the fact that for balance my left leg has stretched in a certain way, or that my toes have curled against the floor. Posture and the majority of bodily movements usually operate without the help of a body image.

To the extent that one does become aware of one's own body in terms of becoming conscious of limb position, movement, or posture, then such an awareness helps to constitute the perceptual aspect of the body image. When the body does appear in consciousness, it often appears as clearly differentiated from its environment. Body image boundaries tend to be relatively clearly defined (see Fisher, 1964; Fisher and Cleveland, 1958). The body schema, in contrast, can be functionally integrated with its environment, even to the extent that it frequently incorporates certain objects into its operations – the hammer in the carpenter's hand, the feather in the woman's hat, and so forth. Under these circumstances one's perception of body boundary may end at one's finger tips even when a particular schema projects itself to include the hammer that one is using. This distinction is not absolute, however, and may involve a temporal component. More permanent attachments to the body – such as prosthetic devices – can become incorporated into both the image and the schema of the body affecting our bearing and approach to the world in both conscious projection and movement. Similarly some prostheses and even clothes greatly affect the way in which we view ourselves and our personal image (Saadah and Melzack, 1994).

It is also important to note that social and cultural factors affect perceptual, conceptual, and emotional aspects of body image. For example, I may be emotionally dissatisfied with the way my body looks because it does not match up to the cultural ideal of beauty or strength. Or I may be emotionally dissatisfied because of an altered and abnormal sense of body image, for example, in anorexia.

Two other issues are worth mentioning here. First, the body image, as a reflective intentional system, ordinarily represents the body as *my own* body, as a personal body that belongs to me. It contributes to a sense of an overall personal self. In some pathological cases (e.g. body neglect, anosognosia) a subject is sometimes alienated from a specific part or side of the body, and that part or side is experienced as "unowned" or owned by someone else. Clearly this can be described as a distortion of body image.

In contrast to both normal and abnormal experiences of body image, the body schema consists of a system of prepersonal, anonymous processes. Even in cases of intentional movement, most bodily adjustments that subtend balance and posture are not subject to my personal decision. Rather, various neural motor programs command muscle groups to make automatic schematic adjustments that remain below the threshold of my awareness and outside of my personal control. In some cases of body neglect it is possible for the body schema to function normally in spite of extreme problems with body image. Thus, in a subject who suffers from body neglect, the neglected side of the body may still function in processes like walking, dressing, and eating (Denny-Brown et al., 1952; Melzack, 1989).

Second, body image involves a partial, abstract, and articulated perception of the body insofar as thought, attention, and emotional evaluation attend to only one part or area or aspect of the body at a time. It is also possible that as a set of beliefs or attitudes about the body, the body image can involve inconsistency or contradictions. The body schema, on the other hand, functions in a more integrated and holistic way. A slight change in posture, for example, involves a global adjustment across a large number of muscle systems. Proprioceptive information, originating in different parts of the body, does not function in an isolated or disintegrated manner but adds together to modulate postural control (Roll and Roll, 1988).

The conceptual distinctions that we have outlined are based more on phenomenology than on a study of empirical function, and they do not tell us in precise terms what the body schema is or how it functions. Furthermore, sensory and motor aspects of experience are difficult to separate because they alter each other in a reciprocal fashion. A number of questions can be raised in this context. To what extent may the body schema be separated into sensory and motor components and what might the interrelationship between these two aspects be? To what extent does the body schema play a role in the production of the body image? How do proprioceptive information and the performance of movement structure body perception? Also, what role does the perception of movement (the body image) play in the performance of movement?[3] In other words, although we have argued for a conceptual distinction between body image and body schema, it also seems reasonable to believe that body image and body schema are interrelated on the level of motor behavior and proprioceptive processes. To clarify these issues we examine an extremely unusual case of a subject, IW, who has lost proprioception and the sense of touch from the neck down. As a result his movement is accomplished under the control of a highly developed body image, and without the full contribution of a body schema.

## A case of impaired body schema

IW suffers from an acute sensory neuropathy in which large fibers below the neck have been destroyed by illness.[4] As a result IW has no proprioceptive function and no sense of touch below the neck. He is still capable of movement and he experiences hot, cold, pain, and muscle fatigue, but he has no proprioceptive sense of posture or limb location. Prior to the neuropathy he had normal posture and was capable of normal movement. At the onset of the neuropathy IW's initial experience was of complete loss of control of posture and movement. He could not sit up or move his limbs in any controllable way. For the first three months, even with a visual perception of the location of his limbs, he could not control his movement. In the course of the following two years, while in a rehabilitation hospital, he gained sufficient motor control to feed himself, write, and walk. He went on to master everyday motor tasks of personal care, housekeeping, and those movements required to work in an office setting.

To maintain his posture and to control his movement IW must not only keep parts of his body in his visual field, but also conceptualize postures and movements. Without proprioceptive and tactile information he neither knows where his limbs are nor controls his posture unless he looks at and thinks about his body. Maintaining posture is, for him, an activity rather than an automatic process. His movement requires constant visual and mental concentration. In darkness he is unable to control movement; when he walks he cannot daydream, but must concentrate constantly on his movement. When he writes he has to concentrate on holding the pen and on his body posture. IW learned through trial and error the amount of force needed to pick up and hold an egg without breaking it. If his attention is directed toward a different task while holding an egg, his hand crushes the egg.

In terms of the distinction between body image and schema, IW has lost the major functional aspects of his body schema, and thereby the possibility of normally unattended movement. He is forced to compensate for that loss by depending on his body image (itself modified in important aspects) in a way that normal subjects do not.

To what extent does IW have a body schema? At the earliest stage of his illness IW had no control over his movements and was unable to put intention into action. There was, one might say, a disconnection of will from the specifics of movement. If IW decided to move his arm in an upward direction, and then tried to carry out the intended motion, the arm and other parts of his body would move in relatively unpredictable ways. Without support, IW was unable to maintain anything other than a prone posture. He had no proprioceptive awareness of the position of his limbs, so he could not locate them unless he saw them. But even with vision, in this earliest stage, he had no control over his movement. Because of the absence of proprioceptive and tactile feedback his entire body-schema system failed.

That proprioception is a major source of information for the maintenance of posture and the governance of movement – that is, for the normal functioning of the body schema – is clear from IW's experience. But proprioception is not the only source. IW, as a result of extreme effort and hard work, recovered control over his movement and regained a close-to-normal life. He did not do this by recovering proprioceptive sense, but by rebuilding a partial body schema and by using body image to help control movement. This case, then, promises to throw light on the distinction between body image and schema, and to resolve a number of issues concerning relations between the perception and the performance of movement.

## Movement with and without proprioception

The body schema consists of certain functions that operate across various parts of a complex system responsible for maintaining posture and governing movement. This system might best be conceived as consisting of three sets of functions. The first set involves the input and processing of new information about posture and movement that is constantly provided by a number of sources, including proprioception. A second set involves motor habits, learned movement patterns ("motor schemas" or programs). The final set of functions consists of certain intermodal abilities that allow for communication between proprioceptive information and perceptual awareness, and an integration of sensory information and movement. In all three of its functional aspects, the body-schema system is interrelated with perceptual aspects of the body image.

### Proprioception and other inputs

The body works to maintain posture or govern movement on the basis of information received from numerous sources. Besides proprioceptive information from kinetic, muscular, articular, and cutaneous sources, contributions also originate in vestibular and equilibrial functions. Parsons (1990) mentions visual sense as a source of information vital to posture and movement. Visual sense, in this regard, can be distinguished into (a) exteroceptive sense, that is, direct visual observation of the movements of limbs (see e.g. Crook, 1987) and (b) "visual proprioception" (Gibson, 1979; Jouen, 1988; Neisser, 1976). Exteroceptive sense (e.g. the visual perception of one's own body) helps to constitute the perceptual aspect of the body image, and in some instances contributes to a conscious control of posture and movement (Gurfinkel and Levick, 1991). Visual proprioception is more directly related to the body schema and involves the subpersonal processing of visual information about environmental motion in the visual field. Outside of conscious awareness, adjustments in posture are made in order to compensate for changes in the "optical flow" or movement in the visual environment (Assaiante et al., 1988; Brandt, 1988; Lee and Lishman, 1975). Extraocular muscles also provide proprioceptive information that contributes to head stabilization and whole-body posture (Roll and Roll, 1988; Roll et al. 1991).

Proprioception, in the ordinary sense of being mechanical or non-visual, is obviously a major source of information concerning present bodily position and posture. Proprioception, however, serves a twofold function, and for our purposes it is important to maintain a clear conceptual distinction between proprioceptive *information*, which informs the body schema and the automatic performance of movement, and proprioceptive *awareness*, which is a conscious perception of movement and position.

Proprioceptive information consists of subpersonal, physiological information – the result of physical stimuli at certain proprioceptors. As such, proprioceptive information updates the body with respect to its posture and movement and thus plays an essential role in the body-schema system. It contributes to the automatic control of posture and movement even when my consciousness is totally taken up with action or cognition that does not involve the explicit self-referential intentionality of a body percept. Proprioceptive information in this purely physiological aspect is neither an attentive perceptual activity nor an activity that we are usually aware of. Proprioceptive information, however, can serve as the physiological basis of a body-awareness. The same proprioceptors, and in some cases the same neural structures, supply the information necessary for both the automatic governing of movement and the perceptual sensation of one's own movements (Phillips, 1986).

Thus, the term *proprioception* is often equated with joint and movement sense and defined as a form of awareness that directly provides a knowledge, representation, or image of our body (e.g. O'Shaughnessy, 1995). Because of proprioceptive awareness, for example, I can tell you where my legs are even with my eyes closed. Proprioceptive awareness is a felt experience of bodily position that helps to constitute the perceptual aspect of the body image. Although, in the normal adult, in some circumstances, proprioceptive experience may be used to monitor and assist motor activity, the majority of normal adult movements do not require anything like the explicit proprioceptive awareness involved in a body percept. Rather, posture and movement are normally governed by the more automatic processes of the body schema (Gurfinkel and Levick, 1991).

In IW there is no proprioception from the neck down, and this affects both his body image and body schema, but in different ways. Normally, information from proprioceptive and other sources constantly updates the body-schema system regarding posture and movement. Of these various sources, IW still has input from vestibular and equilibrial sources, and visual proprioception. He has a grossly impoverished sense of physical effort, but it is of no use in movement control (Cole and Sedgwick, 1992). He has lost tactile and proprioceptive information, so there is no kinesthetic, cutaneous, muscular, or articular input. In effect, following the onset of the neuropathy, the major contributors of body schematic information were disrupted.

IW depends heavily on visual perception of limb movement along with visual proprioception in order to control his movement. To maintain balanced posture, for example, he has learned to designate a stationary object in the environment as a reference point which he keeps in his visual field. Deprived of vision, in a darkened room, IW will not be able to maintain posture, for then he will have lost both visual inspection of his body and visual fixation on an external point. This indicates that he makes up for his loss of proprioception with a high reliance on visual perception and visual proprioception to supply a running account of limb position. Since his muscles still work and he has a "crude" sense of effort in this connection, he is able to tense his muscles and freeze in position.[5] He can do this in an articulated manner, so, for example, he is able to maintain posture in legs and trunk while working with his hands.

All of this – visual perception of limb position, visual proprioception, freezing of position, and movement of limbs – takes an effort of concentration. Whereas in normal subjects the control of posture and movement takes place without conscious attention and without thinking about it, in IW, conscious attention – a conscious processing of information about body and environment – is what informs, updates, and coordinates his postural and motor processes.

## Motor habits

Motor habits, a repertoire of motor programs or "motor schemas," are flexible and corrigible patterns of movements. Some are entirely learned; others, which may be innate, are elaborated through experience and practice. Examples of motor habits include swallowing, walking, and writing. We normally learn to ride a bicycle or to swim, for instance, by attending to the task; but subsequently we ride or swim without any thought of motor action. Such programs may not persist indefinitely and in order to maintain them they need to be refreshed by use and resultant feedback. IW had built up a set of motor schemas over the course of nineteen years prior to his illness. Although it is likely that these were not destroyed by the loss of proprioception and touch, they were no longer accessible when he lost proprioceptive feedback.

There are at least two ways to explain the effects of IW's lack of proprioceptive information on motor habits. The first involves the problem of updating and access to programs that continue to exist. When, for example, one buttons one's shirt, one accesses a motor habit that carries through the action without the need of attention to how exactly one moves one's fingers. Normally this is possible because proprioceptive information updates the motor process with regard to finger location and movement. If the process is not kept updated in this manner, if proprioception fails to register the present motor state, or fails to provide the proper cues, then either the motor program cannot be accessed, even if it remains theoretically intact, or it must be accessed in an alternative way.[6] The loss of proprioceptive information, which would, in normal circumstances, keep the system updated with regard to present posture and limb position, puts IW in this type of situation – his motor system doesn't know where it is in the movement process.

A second possible explanation involves the retention or lack of retention of motor schemas. Like non-motor habits, when motor schemas are not used, they fade and cease to exist (Head, 1920). Because of the lack of proprioceptive updating, IW has been unable to put most of his motor patterns to use, and it remains unclear to what extent such patterns continue to exist, or to what extent IW can establish new motor schemas.

Observation of IW's movements, and his own phenomenological report indicate that very little of his motor activity is governed by automatic motor schemas. Although it is probable that he was able to recover as well as he has because he had already learned normal patterns of movement prior to his illness, this does not mean that the movements are the same as they were before. The differences between IW's movement and normal movement are large enough to suggest that his movements are reinvented, not reaccessed. Still, not all aspects of his movements in walking are under his volitional control the whole time. His recoveries in writing and walking, for instance, have probably depended on his ability to delegate some aspects of the motor act to a rudimentary, close to automatic, schematic level. On the first explanation, this may indicate some minimal access to intact motor schemas (Bernett, et al., 1989). It would be consistent with the second explanation to say, not that his movements are completely relearned motor skills or motor programs, but that the conscious control of movement becomes less exacting with practice. For example, when he relearnt to walk it required all his concentration. Now he estimates that walking over a flat, well-lit surface takes about 50–70 percent of his attention, though walking over an uneven surface still requires 100 percent. Thus, IW's success in recovering useful movement function has depended primarily on his finite mental concentration, and, to a much lessor degree on reaccessing or relearning motor programs which are, so far, poorly understood.

To what extent might the kind of updating provided by the visual perception of one's own limbs supply information that would allow access to or engagement of motor schemas? This remains unclear. Normally vision, understood as exteroceptive perception, is not designed to serve this function except in a very limited way. Control of volitional movement does not normally travel from the body image to the body schema except in very abstract, self-conscious movement. Outside of practical situations, for example when one is thinking philosophically about the nature of the will, one might abstractly command one's arm to raise itself. But in most everyday circumstances, volitional movement means reaching to grasp something, or pointing to something, and the focus is on the something, not on the motor act of reaching or grasping or pointing. These movements tend to follow automatically from the intention. In IW, however, focused, visual attention had to be realigned toward the actual motor accomplishment.

## Intermodal communication

Just as the loss of proprioceptive information impairs the body schema and disrupts the control of posture and movement, so the loss of proprioceptive awareness results in an impoverishment of the perceptual aspect of the body image. Although IW still had a visual perception of his body, this was not enough at first to gain control over his posture or movement. Because of the absence of proprioception, another important part of the body-schema system, a capacity for intermodal communication, failed. The normal intermodal communication between proprioception and vision had been disrupted. For example, I am able to imitate the bodily movement of another person without drawing up a theory of how to do it, because what I see is automatically translated into a proprioceptive sense of how to move.[7] The possibility of intermodal translation between vision and proprioception, an innate feature of our sensory-motor system, allows visual perception to inform and coordinate movement. In IW, the language of proprioception was missing, and he had to learn to use vision (constantly updating information on present posture and movement), as a partial substitute for proprioception, to drive motor processes directly.

IW's sense of his body as under his control had disappeared. He lost not only the kind of automatic motions that allow normal subjects to walk without seeing or thinking of their legs; he lost controlled voluntary movement. Even with vision and thought he could not at first control motility. The perceptual aspect of the body image does not normally fulfill this function without the co-operation of proprioception and the body schema. In the early stage of IW's illness his body image was not adequate to compensate for the missing proprioception.

Although it is unclear how vision might control movement without proprioceptive feedback, the realignment toward visual and cognitive control of movement appears to result in some differences from normal motor control. Such differences can be ascertained through the technique of transcranial magnetic stimulation of the brain which now makes it possible to stimulate the motor system in humans at both cortical and subcortical levels. This involves a painless procedure in which a magnetic flux, discharged through a coil placed over the scalp, produces a magnetic field within the brain. This, in turn, produces a small electrical field which discharges those neurons that are close to their threshold for activation and leads to a muscle twitch (see, for example, Rothwell et al., 1987). At low intensities of stimulation only neurons close to their discharge potential are activated. Magnetic stimulation can be used, therefore, to investigate those cells being kept close to that level. In the motor system it allows study of those neurons related to the neural basis of attention to movement. In the normal subject magnetic stimulation of a small movement area of the brain will produce a small twitch movement in an arm or leg. If a magnetic pulse is superimposed at the time the subject is in the process of making a movement, then a much larger twitch is produced. In addition, the threshold to produce the twitch falls dramatically when the person is beginning a movement of his or her own.

Cole et al. (1995) studied IW using the magnetic stimulation technique. They demonstrated that he has a more focused command of movement. IW was asked to move his thumb while an appropriately directed magnetic pulse was superimposed. His focusing of command onto movement of the thumb was far more accurately limited to the thumb than in control subjects. Whereas in control subjects thumb movement facilitated other movements when magnetic pulse was superimposed, this was not the case with IW. Clearly his need to attend to his movement alters the way in which he produces a movement.

In these types of experiments, imagined movement also lowers threshold and promotes a larger twitch. IW was asked to imagine moving his thumb while a magnetic stimulation was superimposed. Under these conditions IW is still able to reduce the threshold for producing a movement in the thumb muscle alone, in contrast to control subjects who are unable to limit the effect to the thumb muscle (Cole et al., 1995). Thus, in IW's progression from will to motor control, his voluntary control is more focused, and, compared to control subjects, there is less difference between a real movement and an imagined movement.

## Image-controlled movement

In place of missing body schema processes, IW has substituted cognitively driven processes that function only within the framework of a body image that is consciously and continually maintained. If he is denied access to a visual awareness of his body's position in the perceptual field, or denied the ability to think about his body, then his motor control ceases to function. What is the exact nature of the body image that IW uses to control his posture and movement? To what extent is his conscious effort a matter of visual attention, or simply keeping certain body parts within the visual field? To what extent does it consist of a set of judgments – i.e. thoughtful judgments about what his body is doing?

According to IW's own phenomenological reports, when he is moving he does not think about specific muscle groups, but simply that he will move an arm or finger. Normally when he is making a coordinated movement he will think of the coordinated moving part, e.g. reaching out his arm, and of the necessary postural adjustments required to avoid falling over once his balance is shifted by the outstretched arm. It appears that he does not think about muscle operations themselves. This was the case even when he was relearning to move. His conscious effort in moving essentially consists of a set of judgments or internal motor commands; he then monitors the movement with vision and uses the visual feedback to maintain movement.

There is evidence that IW has automated parts of this process. There is some phasic activation and relaxation of calf muscles in relation to gait cycle which are not under visual control and which may be nonconscious (Bernett et al., 1989). IW himself reports that walking on flat surfaces takes approximately half of the concentration required when he first relearned the process. One may hypothesize that in learning to stand and then walk part of the process involved the development of such automated or semi-automated programs for it seems inconceivable that he could attend to all aspects of walking in terms of each muscle, and simultaneously coordinate balance and forward motion. One way to conceive of this is to say that he has re-established access to motor programs learned prior to his illness; but access to motor programs is minimal or unlikely for reasons indicated above. Alternatively, he may have established some set of learned motor strategies monitored at the level of the body image – a set of sequential motor steps that he can follow without an inordinate (debilitating) amount of attention.

Some evidence for the latter alternative can be found in IW's performance in mirror drawing. When asked to trace the edges of the star of David with a finger while viewing it inverted through a mirror, normal subjects find it difficult to turn the corners because of the conflict between proprioceptive information, not affected by the mirror, and visual information which is affected. One would expect IW to have no trouble tracing the edges, because in his case there could be no proprioceptive interference with visual guidance. Another deafferented subject, GL, who suffers from a similar loss of proprioception was able to do the task effortlessly the first time.[8] IW, however, was much more like control subjects in that when he came to a point on the star there was a conflict. This conflict, however, cannot be due to proprioceptive interference, since he has no proprioception. The hypothesis is that the interference comes from learned motor strategies or internal sequential motor images that IW generates cognitively without proprioceptive feedback. This aspect of IW's recovery, the construction of image-based motor sequences, is being investigated at present.[9]

On the basis of such motor strategies IW is able to maintain simple repetitive movement for up to a minute, for example, repetitive touching of thumb and fingers. Similar to control subjects, when required to concentrate on a simple subtraction problem (serially subtracting 4s or 7s from 100) IW's performance of repetitive movement deteriorated within seconds. In contrast to control subjects, however, to alter a repetitive movement IW requires visual feedback (Cole and Sedgwick, 1992).

There is also evidence for the retention over a period of twenty years of certain coordinated "reflex" motor actions, although they are of no use to IW in controlling movement. If one takes a drink off a tray the arm of the subject carrying the tray will move upward as the drink is taken off. The upward movement does not happen, however, if it is the holder of the tray who removes the drink. This "waiter's illusion" depends on a reflex motor program, and still occurs in deafferented subjects (Forget and Lamarre, 1995). A few other coordinated actions have been found, though interestingly none is of any use to deafferented subjects. If IW falls, for example, he has to think about how to put his arms out and he can only do so slowly. He does not automatically withdraw his hand from pain.

In control subjects coordination between limbs and body is apparent in simple tasks like raising an arm. As one raises an arm a variety of muscles in other parts of the body adjust themselves in order to keep the head and the rest of the body balanced. This is an automatic function controlled on the level of body schema. In contrast, when IW moves his arm when standing he has to think about his center of gravity and he must produce opposing movements to keep his balance. In raising his hand he does not know, without visual feedback, how far it has gone. So, in order to raise it safely he has to first assess how free and safe the space is in front of him, and how safe his body position is to allow an alteration in the center of gravity relative to raising the arm. If he wants accuracy in this movement, he requires visual perception of the arm.

In IW's case a partial but very successful motor control is instituted within the framework of a consciously maintained body image. Vision and learned motor strategies help to supplement a limited amount of information that normally serves the body schema – visual proprioception, vestibular and equilibrial information, and less so, a sense of physical effort. His body image is maintained through constant visual perception (attention to body parts or awareness of the body in the visual field) and through a series of judgments and motor strategies. Anything that might upset his perceptual or cognitive processes also affects his movement. A head cold renders IW unable to do anything and he takes to his bed. In this case his visual perception may be fairly unaffected, but the effort of concentration needed to focus conscious and attentive will, required at the beginning of all his movements, is more than he can deal with.

More generally, mental control of movement is limited in four ways. First, there are attentional limitations: IW cannot attend to all aspects of movement. Second, his rate of movement is slower than normal. The fact that movement and motor programs are consciously driven slows motility down. Third, the overall duration of motor activity is relatively short because of the mental effort or energy required. Finally, complex single movements (like walking across rough ground), and combined or compound movements (walking and carrying an egg) take more energy than simple movements.

Within this set of limitations, IW has found that a body image based primarily on visual perception can substitute for proprioception, though very poorly and inadequately. Visual feedback, for instance, involves delays that are too great to allow a normal motor activity. He has learned to make gross compensatory adjustments somewhat quickly after, or along with, the movement of a limb. Still IW has to simplify movements in order to focus his command upon them. His movements appear somewhat stiff and slow and could not be mistaken for normal. Some aspects of his movement may benefit from acquired strategies concerning the adjustment of certain muscles in particular movements. IW, however, insists that once a motor behavior has been performed it does not mean that it requires less concentration subsequently. His rehabilitation necessitated huge increases in his attentional abilities. The cognitive demands of this activity cannot be over-estimated, for other deafferented subjects have not managed such a functional recovery.

## Conclusions

The distinction between body image and body schema provides a useful conceptual framework for describing IW's case. At the same time the case tells us something about the real functional interrelations between body image and body schema.

The standard prepersonal functioning of proprioceptive information grants a certain freedom to the normal subject that is limited in IW. A normal subject can in a large measure forget about the body in the routine of the day. The body takes care of itself, and in doing so, it enables the subject to attend, with relative ease, to other practical aspects of life. The fact that IW, who lacks proprioception, is forced to think about his bodily movements and his posture all the time shows us the degree to which in normal subjects this is not the case, that is, the degree to which the body schema functions to control posture and movement nonconsciously without the intervention of a body image. This is not to deny that the body image may serve other important movement functions. Indeed, in terms of learning and developing novel movements and making them habitual one requires a certain perceptual awareness of the body.

The various limitations involved in the conscious and deliberate control of movement on the basis of a body image reinforces the idea that the body image involves an abstract and partial perception of the body. Conscious attention can be focused on only one part or area of the body at any moment. One cannot attend to all aspects of movement, and if one is forced to control movement by means of the body image, motility is slowed. The more complex the movement, the more aspects of simultaneous bodily adjustments one must be aware of, the more difficult it is to perform. The more IW can make his movements automatic through the use of learned motor strategies, and so the less attention that is required for movement, the easier and more natural it seems. In effect, movement appears relatively more coordinated and holistic to the degree that motor decisions have been made close to automatic and less attention is required. In IW, however, this degree is still far from normal, and the slightly stiff and deliberate character of his movements makes them appear less than holistically integrated.

In some circumstances, we suggested, the proper functioning of a body schema provides a higher degree of integration between body and environment, incorporating elements that are not part of the body or necessarily reflected in the body image. In one circumstance IW approaches this kind of integration. In the experience of driving it is often recounted that the car seems to be an extension of the body schema. Thus, an experienced driver doesn't need to think about or be explicitly attentive to the details of driving or the car's movements. In some instances one arrives at one's destination without a recollection of the actual details of the drive – the driving body has been on automatic pilot so to speak. To some extent this high degree of automatic control in the case of driving is facilitated by visual proprioception. Lee and Aronson (1974) point out that "the proprioceptive function of vision seems apparent enough in driving a vehicle; the driver clearly uses visual information about his and the vehicle's movement to guide the vehicle" (p. 529). IW drives and enjoys it. It seems effortless to him in comparison to walking. He reports that it is easier for him to drive 300 or 400 miles in a car than to stop and refuel. Driving actually allows him relative relaxation of attention to his bodily movement. He maintains his posture by "freezing" in place. He needs only to keep his hands within the visual field (the driving controls in his vehicle are all operated by hand), and he is assisted in a high degree by visual proprioception – the landscape rushing by – in incorporating the car into his system of motor control. IW has to think hard about walking; but not as hard about driving.

The interior of the automobile is also a much safer environment for IW than most he experiences, for his commitment to walking has led to risk. He requires a well-defined personal space surrounding him to avoid the danger of unexpected movements by others. An unexpected touch or bump can easily upset his balance. His personal boundaries are maintained visually; he constantly monitors the positions of his limbs relative to external objects.

IW's case also suggests that the body schema, and not just the body image, plays an important role in constituting a sense of body ownership. IW reports that when the neuropathy first manifested itself he felt alienated from his body. Although he still had a visual perceptual awareness of his body, and could conceptually understand that it was his own body, the fact that he could not control bodily movement may explain his sense of alienation. Stern (1985) contends that volition is the most important invariant in the sense of selfhood. Motor activity is often accompanied, if not by a conscious sense of volition, then at least by the lack of a sense of helplessness or want of control. If one loses control over motor activity, one also gains a sense of helplessness (that is, loses a sense of authorship) over one's actions.

This suggests that the control of one's body and bodily movement and the accompanying emotional value of this control play an important role in experiencing the body as owned. It seems reasonable to suggest that a subject's sense of owned embodiment is sometimes disrupted by a lack of control over the body when proprioception and the body schema fails. A normal, unalienated body image thus depends on certain body-schema processes that enable us to produce and control movement. In the first phase of the illness, IW lacked control over movement. Only after he gained back that control was he able to reconstruct the felt sense of owned embodiment. So even if the body schema functions in an anonymous way, it lends some support to a sense of owned embodiment.[10]

The conceptual distinction between body image and body schema seems to be a productive one in analyzing this case. It helps to clarify IW's motor difficulties. In turn, IW's case throws some light on normal and abnormal relations between body image and body schema. Because IW's movements are controlled more by his conscious attention than by a prepersonal body schema, they indicate extraordinary, perhaps uniquely high degrees of intentionality and personal control. They also reflect a number of limitations with regard to the holistic nature of movement and its experiential integration with the surrounding world.

## Notes

Both authors would like to thank the subject, IW, for his continued interest and help, and Anthony Marcel (Medical Research Council, Applied Psychology Unit, Cambridge, England) for his helpful comments on an earlier draft. For preparation of this paper Shaun Gallagher received support from the National Endowment for the Humanities Summer Stipend (#FT-40362-94), and as Visiting Scientist at the Medical Research Council's Applied Psychology Unit, Cambridge, England. Jonathan Cole received support from the Wessex Medical Trust and Salisbury District Hospital.

1    Thus, for example, Fisher (1972: 113) provides the following influential definition: "Body image can be considered synonymous with such terms as 'body concept' and 'body scheme.' Broadly speaking, the term pertains to how the individual perceives his own body. It does not imply that the individual's concept of his body is represented by a conscious image...Body image...represents the manner in which a person has learned to organize and integrate his body experiences." The terminological and conceptual confusion is noted by, e.g. Garner and Garfinkel, 1981; Shontz, 1974.

2    It has also been noted that "for good adaptation and responsivity to the environment the conscious perceptive field is mostly occupied by external rather than internal stimuli to which the subject tends to respond... When the subject focuses on his body, different components or images of body parts, of which the subject himself usually is unconscious, can emerge" (Ruggieri et al. 1983: 800).

3    For a discussion of developmental questions in this context, see Gallagher and Meltzoff (in press).

4    This happened in 1971 when IW was 19. The onset of the neuropathy was acute following an illness documented at the time as infectious mononucleosis. Neurophysiological tests confirm the loss of large myelinated fibers below the neck (Cole and Katifi, 1991). Also see the sensory neuronopathy described by Sternman et al. 1980.

5    The sense of effort is likely to be based on A-delta fibers, and this is very different from control subjects (see Cole and Sedgwick, 1992; Cole et al., 1995).

6    Volpe et al. (1979) have suggested that simple motor programs can proceed effectively without proprioceptive feedback. Their subjects, following cortical damage, suffered deafferentation limited to one arm. When provided tactile cues on relevant areas of the unaffected arm they could sometimes initiate motor programs that were accurate but not finely controlled. These subjects are quite different from IW in that they have lost sensation as a result of cortical damage, allowing for the possibility that their movements were guided by intact, but subcortical

motor schemas. In the case of IW visual information is the usual cue for initiating motor programs.

7   This innate cross-modal function of proprioception can be seen in studies of newborn imitation (see Gallagher and Meltzoff, in press; Meltzoff, 1990).

8   Both IW and GL lost tactile sense and proprioception, IW from the collarline down, GL from about mouth level down. IW has normal position sense for the neck, but GL has no information from her neck muscles or in the lower part of her mouth and face. Both subjects have retained vestibular information, information about head position and movement in the gravitational field. IW may be more able to focus attention on motor planning and may thus be able to construct motor images, due to the fact that he has a more stable head and neck posture than GL. One result is that IW walks; GL stays in a wheelchair. See Cole and Paillard, 1995.

9   IW's case may throw some light on the way control subjects construct motor models. For example, how do we know how to hit a golf ball first time? Feedback will not tell us. We need to launch a motor act constructed internally, based on an image. By looking at IW's capacity to do this without feedback we can begin to reflect on how we do this ourselves.

10  Oliver Sacks remarks (in the "foreword" to Cole, 1995) that the case of IW "shows how such a peripheral disorder can have the profoundest 'central' effects on what Gerald Edelman called the 'primary consciousness' of a person: his ability to experience his body as continuous, as 'owned,' as controlled, as his. We see that a disorder of touch and proprioception, itself unconscious, becomes, at the highest level, a 'disease of consciousness'" (xiii).

# References

Adame, D. D., Radell, S. A., Johnson, T. C. and Cole, S. P. (1991) "Physical fitness, body image, and locus of control in college women dancers and non-dancers." *Perceptual and Motor Skills, 72*, 91–5.

Assaiante, C., Amblard, G. and Carblanc, A. (1988) "Peripheral vision and dynamic equilibrium control in five to twelve year old children." In B. Amblard, A. Berthoz and F. Clarac (eds.), *Posture and Gait: Development, Adaptation and Modulation* (pp. 75–82). Amsterdam: Excerpta Medica.

Bernett, M. E., Cole, J. D., McLellan, D. L. and Sedgwick, E. M. (1989) "Gait analysis in a subject without proprioception below the neck." *Journal of Physiology, 417*, 102.

Brandt, T. (1988). "Sensory function and posture." In B. Amblard, A. Berthoz, and F. Clarac (eds.), *Posture and Gait: Development, Adaptation and Modulation* (pp. 127–36). Amsterdam: Excerpta Medica.

Cash, T. F. and Brown, T. A. (1987) "Body image in anorexia nervosa and bulimia nervosa: a review of the literature." *Behavior Modification, 11*, 487–521.

Cole, J. D. (1995). *Pride and a Daily Marathon*. Cambridge, Massachusetts: MIT Press.

Cole, J. D. and Katifi, H. A. (1991). "Evoked potentials in a subject with a large fibre peripheral neuropathy." *Electroencephalography and Clinical Neurophysiology, 80*, 103–7.

Cole, J. D. and Paillard, J. (1995) "Living without touch and peripheral information about body position and movement: studies upon deafferented subjects." In J. Bermúdez, A. Marcel, and N. Eilan (eds.), *The Body and the Self* (pp. 245–66). Cambridge, Mass. MIT Press.

Cole, J. D. and Sedgwick, E. M. (1992) "The perceptions of force and of movement in a man without large myelinated sensory afferents below the neck." *Journal of Physiology, 449*, 503–15.

Cole, J. D., Merton, W. L., Barrett, G., Katifi, H. A. and Treede, R. D. (1995). "Evoked potentials in a subject with a large fibre sensory neuropathy below the neck." *Canadian Journal of Physiology and Pharmacology, 73*, 234–45.

Crook, J. (1987) "The nature of conscious awareness." In C. Blakemore and S. Greenfield (eds.), *Mindwaves: Thoughts on Intelligence, Identity, and Consciousness* (pp. 383–402). Oxford: Basil Blackwell.

Denny-Brown, D., Meyer, J. S. and Horenstein, S. (1952) "The significance of perceptual rivalry resulting from parietal lesion." *Brain, 75*, 433–71.

Fisher, S. (1964) "Sex differences in body perception." *Psychological Monographs, 78*, 1–22.

Fisher, S. (1972) "Body image." In D. Sills (ed.), *International Encyclopedia of the Social Sciences*, Volume 2, New York: Collier-Macmillan.

Fisher, S. and Cleveland, S. E. (1958) *Body Image and Personality*. Princeton: D. van Nostrand.

Forget, R., and Lamarre, Y. (1995) "Postural adjustments associated with different unloadings of the forearm: effects of proprioceptive and cutaneous afferent deprivation." *Canadian Journal of Physiology and Pharmacology, 73*, 285–94.

Gallagher, S. (1986) "Body image and body schema: a conceptual clarification." *Journal of Mind and Behavior, 7*, 541–54.

Gallagher, S. (1995) "Body schema and intentionality." In J. Bermúdez, A. Marcel and N. Eilan (eds.), *The Body and the Self* (pp. 225–244). Cambridge, Mass.: MIT Press.

Gallagher, S. and Meltzoff, A. N. (in press) "The earliest sense of self and others: Merleau-Ponty and recent developmental studies." *Philosophical Psychology*.

Gardner, R. M. and Moncrieff, C. (1988) "Body image distortion in anorexics as a non-sensory phenomenon: a signal detection approach." *Journal of Clinical Psychology, 44*, 101–7.

Garner, D. M. and Garfinkel, P. E. (1981) "Body image in anorexia nervosa: measurement, theory, and clinical implications." *International Journal of Psychiatry in Medicine, 11*, 263–84.

Gibson, J. J. (1979) *The Ecological Approach to Visual Perception*. Boston: Houghton-Mifflin.

Gurfinkel, V. S. and Levick, Y. S. (1991) "Perceptual and automatic aspects of the postural body scheme." In J. Paillard (ed.), *Brain and Space* (pp. 147–62). Oxford: Oxford University Press.

Head, H. (1920) *Studies in neurology*, vol. 2. London: Oxford University Press.

Head, H. (1926) *Aphasia and Kindred Disorders of speech*, vol. 1. Cambridge: Cambridge University Press.

Head, H. and Holmes, G. (1911–12) "Sensory disturbances from cerebral lesions." *Brain, 34*, 102–245.

Jouen, F. (1988) "Visual-proprioceptive control of posture in newborn infants." In G. Amblard, A. Berthoz and F. Clarac (eds.), *Posture and Gait: Development, Adaptation, and Modulation* (pp. 13–22). Amsterdam: Excerpta Medica.

Lackner, J. R. (1988) "Some proprioceptive influences of the perceptual representation of body shape and orientation." *Brain, 3*, 281–97.

Lee, D. N. and Aronson, E. (1974) "Visual proprioceptive control of standing in human infants." *Perception and Psychophysics, 15*, 529–32.

Lee, D. N. and Lishman, J. R. (1975) "Visual proprioceptive control of stance." *Journal of Human Movement Studies, 1*, 87–95.

Melzack, R. (1989) "Phantom limbs, the self and the brain." *Canadian Psychology, 30*, 1–16.

Meltzoff, A. (1990) "Towards a developmental cognitive science: the implications of cross-modal matching and imitation for the development of representation and memory in infancy". In *The Development and Neural Bases of Higher Cognitive Functions*, vol. 608 of the *Annals of the New York Academy of Sciences* (pp. 1–37). New York: New York Academy of Sciences.

Neisser, U. (1976) *Cognition and Reality: Principles and Implications of Cognitive Psychology*. New York: W. H. Freeman.

O'Shaughnessy, B. (1995) "Proprioception and the body image." In J. Bermúdez, A. Marcel and N. Eilan (eds.), *The Body and the Self* (pp. 175–203). Cambridge, Mass.: MIT Press.

Parsons, L. M. (1990) "Body image." In M. W. Eysenck (ed.), *The Blackwell Dictionary of Cognitive Psychology* (p. 46). Oxford: Blackwell Reference.

Phillips, C. (1986) *Movements of the Hand*. Sherrington Lectures, XVII. Liverpool: Liverpool University Press.

Poeck, K. and Orgass, B. (1971) "The concept of the body schema: a critical review and some experimental results." *Cortex, 7*, 254–77.

Powers, P. S., Schulman, R. G., Gleghorn, A. and Prange, M. E. (1987) "Perceptual and cognitive abnormalities in bulimia." *American Journal of Psychiatry, 144*, 1456–60.

Roll, J. P. and Roll, R. (1988) "From eye to foot: A proprioceptive chain involved in postural control." In G. Amblard, A. Berthoz and F. Clarac (eds.), *Posture and Gait: Development, Adaptation, and Modulation* (pp. 155–64). Amsterdam: Excerpta Medica.

Roll, J. P., Roll, R. and Velay, J. L. (1991) "Proprioception as a link between body space and extrapersonal space." In J. Paillard (ed.), *Brain and Space* (pp. 112–32). Oxford: Oxford University Press.

Rothwell, J. C., Thompson, P. D., Day, B. L., Dick, J. P., Kachi, T., Cowman, J. M. A., and Marsden, C. D. (1987) "Motor cortex stimulation in man. 1. General characteristics of the EMG responses in different muscles." *Brain, 110*, 173–90.

Ruggieri, V., Milizia, M., Sabatini, N. and Tosi, M. T. (1983) "Body perception in relation to muscular tone at rest and tactile sensitivity to tickle." *Perceptual and Motor Skills, 56*, 799–806.

Saadah, E. S. M., and Melzack, R. (1994) "Phantom limb experiences in congenital limb-deficient adults." *Cortex, 30*, 479–85.

Schilder, P. (1935) *The Image and Appearance of the Human Body*. London: Kegan, Paul, Trench, Trubner and Co.

Shontz, F. C. (1974) "Body image and its disorders." *International Journal of Psychiatry in Medicine*, 5, 461–72.

Stern, D. (1985) *The Interpersonal World of the Infant*. New York: Basic Books.

Sternman, A. B., Schaumberg, H. H., and Asbury, A. K. (1980). "The acute sensory neuropathy syndrome: a distinct clinical entity." *Annals of Neurology, 7*, 354–8.

Volpe, B. T., LeDoux, J. E. and Gazzaniga, M. S. (1979) "Spatially oriented movements in the absence of proprioception." *Neurology, 29*, 1309–13.

# 8
# Natural Powers and Animate Form

## Corporeal Archetypes and Power: Preliminary Clarifications and Considerations of Sex*

### Maxine Sheets-Johnstone

*The natural body is... a discursive phenomenon.*

Ladelle McWhorter, 1989: 612

*All significant differences between men and women are thoroughly historical, social and cultural... I am indeed denying that the difference is fundamentally or significantly biological.*

Carol C. Gould, 1983: 418

*Although it is probably true that the physiological disturbances characterizing emotions... are continuous with the instinctive responses of our prehuman ancestors and also that the ontogeny of emotions to some extent recapitulates their phylogeny, mature human emotions can be seen as neither instinctive nor biologically determined.*

Alison M. Jaggar, 1989: 150

*There is nothing about being "female" that naturally binds women. There is not even such a state as "being" female. Biology is historical discourse, not the body itself.*

Donna Haraway, 1985: 72; 1989: 290

*Not only is there no causal relation between sex and gender, but more recent readers of Simone de Beauvoir have suggested that "sex" itself is a misnomer, and that the ostensibly biological reality that we designate as sex is itself an historical construct and, indeed, a political category.*

Judith Butler, 1989: 261

### Introduction

It is not uncommon to find feminist disavowals of biology. The specter of essentialism is a perennial threat to many feminists. Words uttered in a variety of politically reclamative and transformative contexts have gone some way toward mitigating the

* Maxine Sheets-Johnstone, "Corporeal archetypes and power: preliminary clarifications and considerations of sex," *Hypatia*, vol. 7 (1992), 39–76.

threat, but they have failed to cause biology to fade compliantly into the sunset. This is because however powerful the arguments they present, they cannot make evolutionary facts of corporeal life disappear. The purpose of this paper is to present such facts, demonstrate their significance, and in the process show the oppressive results when biologists themselves fail to bring these facts to the fore. Insofar as the paper goes against the current constructionist grain of much feminist thought, an introduction is called for to situate the presentation within the framework of such feminist theories and to indicate how wholesale disavowals of biology are precipitous. A brief critical look at the claims and writings of the above-cited authors will anchor the prefatory discussion.

The best place to begin is with the naive, simplistic view of the natural as a pure, unadulterated realm untainted by culture, a realm that is "clean" and even good in contrast to the realm in which repressive forces enslave us and are, one might say, bad for our health. This view of the natural is sentimentalized – or can be – in various ways, so that it appears a haven for righting all that is wrong in twentieth-century Western society. But this construal of the natural is a *mis*construal. It is well exemplified in McWhorter's attempt to correct certain misinterpreters of Foucault (they are unnamed) who, according to McWhorter, think Foucault in his writings is urging us to turn away from oppressions of the body and reclaim that natural, "clean" body which underlies all the inscriptions that subdue it (McWhorter, 1989: 612). While McWhorter is wholly right in thinking this clean body does not exist, she is wholly wrong in thinking that this body is *the natural* body. A natural body is the product of a natural history. It is in this sense a Darwinian body, a body not just shaped in morphological ways by evolution but shaped semantically – which means kinetically, gesturally, spatially, behaviorally. Because we are all natural bodies in this sense, we ourselves have a history. Our fundamental human habits and beliefs have an evolutionary past: burying our dead has an evolutionary past; so also does drawing, counting, and language. And so also does our intercorporeal semantics – as this essay will show in terms of sexual signalling behavior. When McWhorter (1989: 614) approvingly cites Nietzsche's remark about gruesome beasts grinning at us knowingly, she – like Nietzsche – fails to realize that in a substantive evolutionary sense those beasts are us. Fundamental aspects of our humanness cannot be written off as mere cultural inscriptions. They have to do with a history more ancient than we, a history in which the body is precisely not a surface on which any culture can leave its marks – arbitrarily and willy-nilly – but a three-dimensionality, a living, natural form that itself is the source of inscriptions – meanings. As I have elsewhere shown (Sheets-Johnstone, 1990), this natural form is in fact our original semantic template; it cannot be "discoursed" out of existence. In a concrete phylogenetic sense, it is a carrier of meanings, an emitter of signs, but the richness and complexity of its intrinsic, ancient inscriptions cannot be acknowledged until the conception of the body *exclusively* as a surface is recognized as the myopic cultural conception it is, that is, until the surface is seen to be the literal outer skin of a far deeper and denser body, and indeed, in a fundamental sense, to depend upon the inscriptions of that deeper, denser body.

Gould's dismissal of biology, while not resting on a postmodern foundation, can be questioned on similar grounds. In seeking to uproot Essentialism (her capitalization), she distinguishes between an abstract and a concrete universality, the latter categorization allowing, in contrast to the former, the inclusion of what distinguishes individuals within a class as well as what is common to them. On the way to setting forth arguments in support of her thesis, she notes that while "there *are* biological differences between men and women... there are infinitely many differences among individuals, any of which is logically an equal candidate for making group distinctions among humans," and adds that "in denying that the biological difference is an essential or fundamental difference, I am asserting that it becomes one only through its historical and cultural development" (Gould, 1983: 418–19). A good part of the problem is that what is being denied remains amorphous. While thinly suggested (in support of her claim of "infinitely many differences," Gould notes that a body has a certain hair color and is right-handed or left-handed), what is being denied is virtually nowhere to be found; whatever the biological difference(s) between men and women that are acknowleged, they are never specified. What is meant by "biological difference(s)" is thus by easy implication reduced to anatomy and written off before it is even identified, much less examined. Such slighting and inattentive treatments of the body demonstrate a lapse in understanding. They strongly suggest that an overzealous preoccupation with Essentialism can quickly lead one to forget evolution, which is not only the thread connecting the whole of biology from the molecular to the macroscopic, and on that account requiring careful attention, but also the thread connecting we humans to our own history – a history that must figure centrally in any just and rigorous appraisal of what it is to be human, in particular, a human body.

A similar write-off of the natural body is again apparent in Alison Jaggar's article on emotions and their place within epistemology. Jagger writes that there is nothing biological in mature human emotions. While there are biological determinants and instinctive emotional behaviors in infants and developing children, mature human emotions are thoroughly socially constituted. Apart from the implausibility of the view – that is, the unreasonableness of the claim that instincts and biology disappear, that what is in the nature of things in the beginning is *completely effaced* by culture – how in fact does one get from the one side to the other, from an instinctive, biological emotional life to one that is entirely cultural? What is the nature of *development*? Does one grow up in such a way that at a certain age, and regardless of culture, instincts are swept away? To claim that there is nothing biological in the emotions of mature human individuals can only mean that the human living body undergoes some radical transformation in the course of developing; indeed, that its affective insides molt.

One might begin weighing the soundness of this claim by considering smiling. Infants smile. In fact, Darwin ([1836–1844] 1987: 542) jotted down in one of his Notebooks, "Seeing a Baby... smile & frown, who can doubt these are instinctive – a child does not sneer." But of course children and adults also smile. Moreover when an infant, child, or adult smiles, the tendency is to smile back. If these simple observations appear to lack authority for want of experimental evidence, consider the cross-cultural studies of Irenaus Eibl-Eibesfeldt (1972), which show, for example, that surprise is consistently expressed by a widening of the eyes and a raising of the eyebrows. Consider further the cross-cultural studies of Paul Ekman (1978; 1989) and Paul Ekman et al. (1987), which show, for example, that disgust is consistently expressed by a wrinkling upward of the nose and a consequent pursing of the upper lip. From a Darwinian point of view, the findings of both Eibl-Eibesfeldt and Ekman (ethologist and psychologist, respectively) which show basic facial expressions of emotion to be universal are not surprising. Darwin ([1872] 1965) long ago identified and analyzed basic expressive human features and their links with non-human animal life. Although he did not examine situational-cultural shadings or reworkings in the manner of Eibl-Eibesfeldt and Ekman, he showed that basic human emotions exist in virtue of a common heritage, an evolutionary lineage which we hominids share with each other, and which we share in major ways with our primate relatives.

Evolutionary continuities aside, one might equally question the rectitude of Jaggar's claim on the grounds that in the throes of actual life, feelings are lived through, not just written or spoken about. Indeed, taking a cue from psychotherapist Jane Flax (1990: 218–19), one might note that there are literally de-centered individuals ("borderline" people), not just academically de-centered ones. The latter's stance from a Flaxian viewpoint might well be termed a pseudo-posture, *pseudo* because what is de-centered is not a living body reverberating with feelings that keep it in a state of perpetual imbalance, but words which may be made to appear with the scratch of a pen or the wag of a tongue. Moreover the feelings of a literally de-centered individual, while perhaps associated with present-day Western styles of living, are themselves through and through pan-human ones. Anxiety, fear, self-doubt – such feelings are not peculiar to any particular culture, any more than the human body itself is. In this context, we might ponder Susan Bordo's remark (1993) that "Whatever the effective role played by biology in human life it never exists or presents itself in 'pure' form, untouched by culture." If this statement is true, then rather than a disavowal of biology, an intensive, sustained, and unabridged examination of the body is in order precisely to elucidate those biologically invariant structures, emotional and otherwise, that vary thematically from culture to culture. We need precisely to understand "the effective role played by biology," which means we need to turn toward the body. As I have noted elsewhere, "the linguistic turn produced extraordinary insights...a corporeal turn would assuredly do no less." This is because "the corporeal turn, like the linguistic turn, requires paying attention to something long taken for granted" (Sheets-Johnstone, 1990: 19, 382).

The idea that we might successfully combine the best of two possible epistemological worlds – that of the relativist and that of the foundationalist – is put forth by Donna Haraway (1988: 579) as the problem of "how to have *simultaneously* an account of radical historical contingency...*and* a no-nonsense commitment to faithful accounts of a 'real' world." In urging a solution to the problem through "situated knowledges," Haraway begins with concerns about objectivity, which quickly become attached to concerns about an embodied or disembodied objectivity. Her point is that "we need the power of modern critical theories of how meanings and bodies get made...in order to build meanings and bodies that have a chance for life" (Haraway, 1988: 580). But the program as envisioned eludes the body in a fundamental sense; it shifts to linguistic and theoretical considerations. That this is so is clear from statements such as, "We need to learn in our bodies...how to attach the objective to our theoretical and political scanners in order to *name* where we are and are not, in dimensions of mental and physical space we hardly know how to name" (Haraway, 1988: 582). Clearly the purpose is not to understand the body but to catapult it into language. Furthermore, the term "embodiment" often covers over a schizoid metaphysics (Sheets-Johnstone, 1990: 303–4), a metaphysics that has not in fact resolved Cartesian dualism because it has not in fact taken the body and bodily experience into close and full account. The term is a lexical band-aid put on a three-century old metaphysical wound. It is not surprising, then, that the program of "embodied knowledges" (Haraway, 1988: 583) actually takes the body itself for granted in its entire epistemological enterprise; functioning as an indexical, the body is simply the place one puts one's epistemology. While it is true that "we must be hostile to easy relativisms and holisms built out of summing and subsuming parts" (Haraway, 1988: 585), we should also be wary of an "embodied objectivity" that, amid "ethnophilosophies," "heteroglossia," "deconstruction," "oppositional positioning," "local knowledges," and "webbed accounts" (Haraway, 1988: 588), in truth thoroughly distances itself from the body except as an epistemological receptacle. Unless we are wary, we will easily find ourselves distanced from the real, living body that is the very ground of our knowledge, for it lies buried at the bottom of the barrel. Yet the hope for transformative knowledge must of necessity bring that body to the surface, both because it leads to an understanding of the fundamental semantics of intercorporeal life that informs our lives and because power is interwoven in complex ways in those semantics. Certainly we can acknowledge as threatening the idea that the body is intrinsically tied to knowledge: immediately one thinks of biological sex differences, and biological sex differences lead straight to essentialism. But we must also acknowledge the possibility of the threat's blinding us, thus keeping us from examining what is actually there. Clearly, we might discover something other than what we are *assuming* is there. These unexplored assumptions might help explain why Haraway, particularly with her impressive biological background, skirts the real, living body: "Feminist embodiment . . . is not about fixed location in a reified body, female or otherwise, but about nodes in fields, inflections in orientations, and responsibility for difference in material-semiotic fields of meaning" (Haraway, 1988: 588). What do these nodes and inflections, and this responsibility have to do with breathing, pulsing, locomoting, sensing creatures? By "reified body," Haraway presumably means mere matter: the biologically given anatomical specimen splayed out like a cadaver on a laboratory table. No wonder then that she continues her description of feminist embodiment by saying that "embodiment is significant prosthesis" (Haraway, 1988: 588). What Haraway urges us to do is extend our bodies before we even understand them. A concern with objectivity and bodies should, on the contrary, translate from the very start into a concern with animate form, particularly so if the ultimate concern is with understanding and reclaiming power. As this essay will show, the animate form that is a living human body is not simply inscribed with power from without; it carries its own inscriptions.

In the context of the above critique of Haraway's program of embodied knowledges and her neglect of the actual living body in the construction of meaning, a few words should be added about Helen Longino's (1990) recent book in philosophy of science and Lorraine Code's (1991) recent book in epistemology, for each book, in a quite different way, suggests that something more is possible in the way of a body than simply "embodied" knowledges. Longino's thesis that scientific knowledge is social knowledge and her emphasis on the experiential nature of knowledge do not lead to an "unbridled relativism" (Longino, 1990: 221). On the contrary, a socially constructed science that ties knowing to experience relies on there being a basic commonality to which all appeal and may appeal when accounts of the world differ: "There is always some minimal level of description of the common world to which we can retreat when our initial descriptions of what is the same state of affairs differs" (Longino, 1990: 222). This "minimalist form of realism," as Longino terms it (1990: 222), is not that distant from the practice of phenomenology, in which one verifies by one's own experience what is described, and, if verification is not forthcoming, one goes back again (and again) "to the things themselves"[1] to see if one has missed something, if one has been sufficiently attentive to what is actually there, and so on. The procedure – to go back to the things themselves – is, of course, not unlike the way in which present-day science normally proceeds when disputes arise. But the notion that there is something basic "out there" is an epistemological claim as well as the basis of an epistemological procedure. When applied to the living body, it means not only that there is the possibility of reconciling differing viewpoints on corporeal matters of fact, but also that there are basic corporeal matters of fact to be described in the first place.[2]

Interestingly enough, Code's recognition and support of phenomenologically oriented studies which link knowing and the body – "all knowing is permeated with mood, feeling, sensibility, affectivity" – and which "ground their analyses in experience" (Code, 1991: 148) dovetail with Longino's espousal of minimal realism and its implicit vindication of the possibility of fundamental corporeal descriptions. While Code points out that "phenomenological discussions ... [are different from] the mainstream discourse in whose terms Anglo-American epistemology and philosophy of science are predominantly discussed," and adds that "purists might find it illegitimate to introduce [phenomenological discussions] into a book that engages primarily with mainstream epistemology," she goes on to affirm that "part of the project of feminist critique is to uncover the suppressions and exclusions that received ways of thinking have effected and to challenge disciplinary, methodological, and ideological boundaries" (1991: 149). Although Code's own remapping of the epistemic terrain does not incorporate the suppressed and excluded body that so often lies buried under what now appear to be traditional feminist theoretical concerns (including theory itself),[3] instances of where this excluded body could gain entrance are readily apparent for it hovers at the very threshold of the discussion. When Code (1991: 295) singles out the problem of a Foucauldian subject who is never there, for example, and points out the dangers of "discursive determinism," rather than limit herself to a defense of Foucault on theoretical grounds, she could well recall in addition her own earlier listing of convergences between her own project and that of phenomenology. The latter studies, she writes, "ground their analyses [not only] in experience" but also "in praxis and embodied existence ... [they] concentrate on *particular* experiences, specific modes of existence, from the conviction that it is in particularity and concreteness that generality – essence – can be known ... [They] do not privilege vision: perception engages all of the senses; objects are known by touch, holding, sensing their whole presence. Indeed, perception also engages a 'sixth sense' ... 'proprioception': the sense of themselves through which people 'feel [their] bodies as proper to [them] ... as [their] own' and position themselves in the world through an awareness of the shape, [and] capacities ... of their bodies" (Code, 1991: 148).[4] Clearly the Foucault-induced problem of subjectivity and agency, which as Code points out remains contested among Foucault readers, can find resolution in deeper studies of the body, which is to say in descriptive analyses of what is actually there, both corporeally and intercorporeally.

In her recent book, Judith Butler attempts to spell out how "language itself produce[s] the fictive construction of 'sex'" and how, by adopting "a performative theory of gender acts" as strategy, bodily categories – of sex, gender, sexuality, and the body itself – can be disrupted (Butler, 1990: xi, xii). In her zeal to validate the constructionist claim that with respect to sex and gender, there is "no foundation all the way down the line,"[5] she attempts to show that the body is a set of boundaries, "a surface whose permeability is politically regulated" (Butler, 1990: 139). In contrast to a Foucauldian reading of the body that requires something there – a materiality – prior to inscription, Butler wants a body with no past, with no prediscursive significance or even ontological status: "the body," she writes, "is not a 'being'" (1990: 129).[6] On these spirited-away grounds, Butler can justify a performative over expressive body. What she sacrifices, however, is a history replete with corporeal matters of fact, including expressive matters of fact.[7] Unlike a body that can be read as mere synecdoche for a social system (Butler, 1990: 132), the evolutionary body cannot be so reduced: it does not stand for, refer, or function as a trope in any way. Moreover unlike a body that has no stable identity and whose aim is to disrupt and destabilize (Butler, 1990: 140–1), the evolutionary body has an established identity that, however flukey its existence, circumstantial its form, or minuscule its lifetime, abides over time and is part of an unbroken, continuous historical process. Constructionist theories that fail to take the evolutionary body into account not only ignore the relational ties that that historical process describes and that bind us to certain corporeal acts, dispositions, and possibilities, and to a certain related intercorporeal semantics; they also put us on the edge of an unnatural history. It is as if we humans descended *deus ex machina* not just into the world but into a ready-made culture, a culture that, whatever its nature, can only be the product of an immaculate linguistic conception. Indeed, short of an accounting of the evolutionary body, we are, unlike all other living creatures, the product of grammatological creationism. It is significant that, with respect to the body, Darwinian evolutionary theory began not in speculative explanations or thoughts about the body nor with programmatic goals but with descriptive accounts of what is actually there: living, moving bodies prior to discourse.

The preceding critical remarks show that evolutionary facts of corporeal life need to be recognized and attentively examined. This essay urges just such an acknowledgment and closer examination of biology. In fact it urges a re-thinking of biology – in evolutionary terms and the intricate cultural reworkings and translations of those terms. Such a re-thinking constitutes a beginning step toward showing that there is more to biology than anatomical parts; in other words, more to the body than meets an anatomical eye – or I. There is animate form. In developing an evolutionary perspective and in considering its cultural reworkings and translations in Western society, the essay focuses on out-there-in-the-world-anyone-can-observe-them corporeal matters of fact: for example, nonhuman female primates have estrous cycles and many of them present their swollen hindquarters to males either as a sexual invitation or as a response to male sexual solicitations; human female primates do not have estrous cycles and are pan-culturally enjoined from showing their genitals. Corporeal facts such as these are points of departure for assessing our biological heritage in the form of corporeal archetypes. Persistent examination of these archetypes – as engendering certain power relations and as constituting invitational sexual signaling behaviors – culminates in an elucidation of how corporeal archetypes are used to undergird a female-denigrating "biology of human sexuality." The program of re-thinking is written in the form of a peripatetic investigation; that is, rather than writing up results, I am inviting readers to go through the process of re-thinking – to make the meditative journey themselves. In this way, not only will the import of an evolutionary beginning become apparent but the feminist perspective that informs the essay will be brought to full experience. The essay begins with an exposition of the relationship between animate form and power and goes on to examine corporeal archetypes as sex-specific and sex-neutral acts. By juxtaposing nonhuman and human animate form and sexual archetypes in the light of sexual signaling behavior, and by reckoning with the reigning Western biological paradigm of human sexuality, the essay brings to light corporeal matters of fact that subtend female oppression and the elevated sense of power that establishes and sustains that oppression.

## Animate form: the conceptual basis of power

The concept of power and concepts of how power can or might be wielded arise on the basis of *animate form*. One has only to imagine what it would be like to be another body to realize the truth of this statement. That one's concept of power derives from being the particular body one is means first of all that originally, in abstraction from any cultural overlays or constructions, whatever they might be, there is the body *simpliciter*. At the most basic level this body *simpliciter* is a human body, a crow body, an ant body, a dog body, or an orangutan body. Whatever its specification – whatever its *species*-fication – this body clearly has certain distinctive behavioral possibilities and not others: certain sensory-kinetic powers are vouchsafed to it in virtue of the animate form it is. As an *individual* instance of the animate form it is, this body may from the very beginning be blind, have a cleft palate that impedes normal articulation, have a heart defect that prevents normal exertion, have a stunted arm or one leg longer than the other such that normal range of motion or normal locomotor rhythms are precluded, have a spinal abnormality that prohibits twisting, and so on. Moreover, through some gross trick of biological fate, this body might have no ears, a big "little" to instead of a big "big" toe, or a second thumb on one hand. Furthermore, in the course of growing up, it may develop illnesses or abnormalities such as asthma, undescended testicles, deafness, scoliosis, breasts though it has a penis, or through injury, it may lose a leg. Moreover in the process of aging, its powers will necessarily change: it cannot run as far, see or hear as acutely, lift as much, dodge things as agilely as before; it may develop emphysema, be spatially amnestic, suffer Parkinson's or Alzheimer's disease. Clearly, one's concept of power and one's concepts of possible deployments of power arise on the ground of the body one is.

Translated into terms of the body *simpliciter*, the concept of power is initially generated on the basis of species-specific "I can's."[8] In the case of a human body, this means specific capabilities and possibilities such as I can stand, I can run, I can throw, I can speak, I can oppose thumb and fingers, I can climb. It naturally means at the same time certain incapabilities such as I cannot bark, I cannot brachiate through a forest canopy, I cannot fly, I cannot live either underground like a mole or in water like a fish. Many species-specific human "I can's" are shared with non-human primates – chimpanzees, for example, can also stand, throw, run, oppose thumb and fingers, and climb. Shared actions will in each case be performed in a species-specific corporeally idiosyncratic manner, but whatever the variations in performance, they do not diminish or in any way nullify the basic primate commonality. Ample and consistent evidence for this claim may be found in the primatological literature. I have shown elsewhere how a basic primate commonality is apparent in the acts of staring and of averting the eyes; in the spatial valencies that exist with reference to size, and to high and low, and front and back intercorporeal positionings; and in the performance of exaggerated body spectacles (Sheets-Johnstone, 1993).[9]

As suggested above, the body *simpliciter* is the source of individual "I can's" that qualify its species-specific "I can's." On the positive side, this might mean that a particular individual can not only threaten, but given its size, out-threaten others; that another individual can not only run, but given its superior endurance, out-run others; that still another individual in virtue of superior coordination, can not only move but move more agilely than others; and so on. In this sense, individual "I can's" qualify the basic distinctions of animate form that characterize the individual as human (chimpanzee, shark, or raven). The concept of power and concepts of possible deployments of power are thus subsumed in a repertoire of "I can's" that derive from the animate form one is both in a species-specific and an individual sense.

Sexed bodies are one aspect of animate form. The opening task of this paper is to delineate in a beginning but precise way how sexed primate bodies are linked to animate form, and to determine, again in a beginning way, whether and how, in virtue of that linkage, they are linked inescapably to certain power relations. Though a possible topic given the task, we will not be concerned with the ways in which an individual's repertoire of "I can's" might qualify its individual attractivity from the viewpoint of sexual selection theory (Darwin, [1871] 1981). In other words, that an individual has a longer and thicker penis, for example, and that those particular biological characteristics are of service in procuring a mate by enhancing display or by enhancing "internal courtship" powers (Eberhard, 1985), will not figure in the analysis that follows.[10] The concern is rather to identify and elucidate fundamental behavioral possibilities that by their very nature, their spatio-kinetic dynamics, instantiate certain power relations. In effect, by unearthing the linkage between fundamental behavioral possibilities and certain power relations, we will unearth corporeal archetypes of power.

The term *archetype* will become progressively elaborated in the course of completing the task. To be emphasized in these preliminary clarifications, however, are the common present-day practices of regarding sex and gender as exclusive (though interactive) aspects of anatomy (or biology) and culture, respectively,[11] or of making no distinction between sex and gender on the grounds that sex is as culturally determined as gender.[12] The practice fails to recognize animate form and the concrete, complex corporeal relationships that exist between animate form and power. As described above, animate form is not *mere anatomy*. Animate form is indeed *animate*; it is not the simple having of certain bodily parts and not others but more importantly, the having of certain sensory-kinetic possibilities and not others. The idea that gender is thoroughly derivative of culture, and the idea that even sex is a thoroughly historical construct, fail to recognize how basic features of animate form resonate experientially and behaviorally in sex- and ultimately gender-specific ways. Indeed, to appreciate how fine the relationship is, we must interrogate male and female bodies as specific forms of livability in the world. We must specify concrete realities of bodily life, in particular, those mundane, archetypal realities of the primate body *simpliciter*. Sexed, and ultimately gendered, human bodies can in this way be ultimately seen as fundamentally tied to certain concepts of power and to concepts of deployments of power irrespective of cultural overlays, constructions, diversifications, and so on. As suggested above, staring, averting the eyes, being higher than/lower than, facing front-end toward/facing back-end toward, making a visual spectacle of oneself are each fundamental primate behaviors that instantiate just such archetypal deployments of power; each behavior is either part of the normal repertoire of "I can's" peculiar to primates in general, or a variation peculiar to certain primates in particular. We will approach the task of delineating corporeal archetypes of power by considering *presenting*, a complex but excellent example of a certain form of livability in the world precisely because it is both a sex-specific and sex-neutral act.

## Presenting as corporeal archetype

Insofar as corporeal archetypes are behavioral forms natural to being the individual one is, they are species-specific – in the case of presenting, the form is even quasi-order-specific.[13] Moreover like the psychic archetypes which Jung (1960) describes as structurally homologous to instincts, corporeal archetypes too may be regarded homologous to instincts: they are not learned as such but are intuitively enacted and understood. Presenting is just such a form in this further sense. The basic difference between a Jungian and a corporeal archetype centers on meaning: corporeal archetypal meanings are not expressed in symbolic motifs but are themselves directly evident in the spatio-kinetic dynamics of everyday bodily behaviors. The meanings "submission" and "vulnerability" with respect to *presenting* are apt examples. The meanings are a built-in of primate bodily life. Why? Because primates generally have face-on, front-end defense systems and aggressive displays. In presenting, they face their hind-ends to a conspecific. They thus place themselves in an inferior position insofar as they cannot easily see the presented-to animal nor monitor its behavior, nor can they easily defend themselves in such a position. In addition, in presenting they frequently lower themselves toward the ground, thus giving the presented-to animal an advantage with respect to the all-pervasive biological value, *size*. The back-end presenting posture necessarily adopted by a female nonhuman primate in dorsoventral copulation thus raises a fundamental question. Viewed as a corporeal archetype, is the position one of submission for the female? Does a sexually presenting female feel vulnerable? In finer terms, do the same power relations obtain in a socio-sexual context as obtain in a socio-aggressive context?

Field observations and descriptions in the literature (e.g. Chevalier-Skolnikoff, 1975; Goodall, 1968; Sugiyama, 1969; Hall and De Vore, 1972; Enomoto, 1974) might readily incline us toward an affirmative answer. In her presenting copulatory posture, the female appears in fact dominated by the male. She is not only vulnerable – as occasional neck bites by the male might indicate – but she cannot move freely on her own. Indeed, depending on where the male rests his feet (i.e. on the ground or on the female), she may assume his entire weight. *Being on the bottom or underneath the male, and being frontally turned away from him as well*, the female clearly appears to be in an inferior position – on the nether end of power relations. In these senses, at least, she appears to submit to the male and to be vulnerable to him.

All the same, the question is difficult to answer. It may actually be the wrong one to ask, and for the following reason. While presenting behavior does not differ essentially in its two contexts – copulation on the one hand, and submission, conciliation, or deference on the other – its meaning does. Our third-person human observer classification of the behavior reflects this difference: we classify it on the one hand as a socio-sexual act, and on the other, as a socio-aggressive act. The two distinct meanings, however, derive fundamentally from the nonhuman participants themselves, the creatures actually involved in the two "contexts of utterance." Hence, we could only ask the female participants themselves for a decisive answer to the question, for only female chimpanzees themselves could testify to *a necessary affective linkage between the two contexts*. In other words, only female chimpanzees themselves could tell us whether in copulatory contexts presenting, simply in virtue of the intercorporeal postural relations it instantiates, is necessarily felt as a submissive and vulnerable posture. Given this fact, the critical and more properly informative question to ask would be whether *any* archetypal intercorporeal postures invariably carry with them certain feeling tones which, though stronger or weaker in some instances, are never muted whatever the context of utterance. Only in the answering of this broader question could we humans be relatively certain that presenting in its copulatory context is a sex-neutral and not a sex-specific archetype. Only then would we have supportive evidence for extrapolating affective meanings from one context of utterance to another.

It is worthwhile noting that by putting the question of affective linkage in the broader perspective, both the assumption (tacit or otherwise) in our very posing of the initial question and our immediate understanding of what is at stake in presenting are thrown in relief. Our immediate understanding of presenting indicates an unacknowledged common heritage of bodily understandings, that is, a heritage of understandings anchored in primate animate form. Our intuitive comprehension of certain aspects of chimpanzee presenting behavior – their "nervous and even fearful" feelings in socio-aggressive presenting, for example[14] – rests on our own personally experienced understandings of the archetypal intercorporeal meanings of front and back facings, and higher and lower positionings. With respect to the assumption that female chimpanzees feel themselves in a vulnerable or submissive position relative to males in dorsoventral mating, we extrapolate, wittingly or not, from our own sentient understandings of the archetypal intercorporeal meanings of front and back, and above and below, to the sex-specific act of another primate. Assumption and understanding alike indicate an unexamined disposition to read into sex, meanings of animate form. It should be emphasized that, from a methodological point of view, our comprehension and assumption are both rooted in *introspective* evidence: it is by consulting our own experience, whether in so many reflective acts, or in self-intuitive ways that are sedimented into our very being the body we are, that we readily come to the experiential estimations we do of "what it is like to present," that we in turn label the behavior an act of submission or an invitation to copulation, and that we readily transfer (or entertain the possibility of transferring) meaning from sex-neutral to sex-specific context of utterance. The methodological point underscores the earlier epistemological one, that an answer to the question of whether the position assumed in presenting always carries with it overtones of submission and/or vulnerability irrespective of context such that female chimpanzees consistently feel a dorsoventral mating position to be one of risk and inferiority with respect to power relations could only be had by canvassing female chimpanzees themselves.

These preliminary considerations of presenting lead to the conclusion that power relations engendered in the archetypal act of presenting are not necessarily sex-specific; they are rather more likely a function of fundamental intercorporeal postural relationships. This possibility – that submissive behavior is not a female behavior but the enactment of a certain intercorporeal spatio-kinetics (in effect, that to be a female primate is not necessarily to be submissive) – does not surface in descriptive analyses of presenting.[15] For example, Konrad Lorenz categorically states that submissive behavior is in essence female behavior, that is, it derives from, and is equated to, *female copulatory* posture: "Expression movements of social submissiveness, evolved from the female invitation to mate, are found in monkeys, particularly baboons... 'I am your woman' and 'I am your slave', are more or less synonymous" (Lorenz, 1967: 130–1). The same view, muted but still apparent, is found in assessments by primatologists: "Ritualized gestures [presenting and mounting], which reduce tension and prevent fighting, are similar to and possibly derive from the mating postures of male and female" (Napier and Napier, 1985: 75). In brief, it is not the spatio-kinetic intercorporeal relationships that are noticed but the sex of the bodies concerned. To *demonstrate* sex-specificity, however, the broader question must be addressed because *that* question is the only one humans can reasonably answer. A brief homespun example that phrases the question in terms of human intercorporeal positional valencies immediately brings this fact into close focus: in human copulation, is that body which is below another body "doomed" to an inferior status? Not only are we clearly in a position to answer that question, but the question brings to the fore a basic similarity between traditional (or traditionally pictured) human female copulatory positioning and primate female copulatory positioning in general. In fact it suggests interesting analogies, all of which would need examination.

The above preliminary considerations show that the relationship of sex to animate form raises complex issues as a result of an evolutionary viewpoint and of deepened corporeal analyses. They do not, however, tell the whole story. Indeed, we must consider that in the economy of nature generally, and in the economy of primate nature in particular, just as the same behavior may have more than one meaning, so the same behavior *may be performed by male and female alike*. Put in this perspective, the posture of female chimpanzees relative to male chimpanzees in copulation clearly does *not* have a basically or exclusively "female" meaning. The posture's fundamental archetypal meaning is sex-neutral: facing backward to, being lower than, not being in eye contact with are of the essence of a sex-neutral intercorporeality in which one individual – male or female – is in an inferior position relative to another.

This priority of a sex-neutral archetypal meaning could nevertheless be questioned. It could be claimed that by presenting in socio-aggressive encounters, the inferior individual is reduced to "behaving like a female." Rather than being seen as adopting a posture that has inherently inferior or submissive status, the individual is viewed as engaging in female behavior. But precisely insofar as *both* sexes present in non-sexual primate encounters, and to the same as well as opposite sex – just as *both sexes mount* in non-sexual primate encounters, and mount creatures of the same as well as opposite sex – the claim of an exclusive "female" meaning is not evidentially supportable. Presenting and mounting are socio-aggressive acts performed by females and males alike. It is because both sexes engage in both behaviors, and intrasexually so, that the fundamental, sex-neutral archetypal meaning of presenting is substantiated. Facing backward to, being lower than, being out of direct eye contact with – each is itself an archetypal primate behavior within the global primate archetypal behavior, presenting. The re-enacted dominance behavior of two female gelada baboons demonstrates this fact unequivocally. In a newly established gelada colony, one of the females successfully paired with the single male: she presented to him, he mounted her, and she then groomed his cape. When a second female was introduced, "[she] was eventually accepted, but only after the first, dominant female had gone through the pair-forming process with female number two, with herself in the role of the male" (Kummer, 1971: 109). (The phrase "in the role of the male," unless a simple if misleading way of identifying a different *position*, obviously assumes sex-specific archetypes – females are submissive, males are dominant – and reflects precisely the kind of biases that human observers may bring with them and that precipitously cloud over the complexity otherwise apparent in examining the relationship between animate form and sexed bodies.)

The question of whether presenting is an essentially female behavior, *and then* a socio-aggressive behavior common to all members of the species (in which case the behavior in socio-aggressive contexts has the "female" meaning it has because the behavior is proper to females) or whether presenting has an essentially sex-neutral archetypal meaning (the position being an inherently vulnerable one with no primary sexual significance) is thus at this point answerable in a straightforward way. So also is the question of whether mounting is an essentially male behavior, *and then* a socio-aggressive behavior common to all members of the species, or whether mounting has an essentially sex-neutral archetypal meaning, the position being an inherently powerful one with no primary sexual significance. In neither case does the answer controvert the possibility that power relations are a built-in of sexed bodies. The answer means only that power relations are not reducible to sexed bodies *in the case examined*. With respect to the latter, power relations are fundamentally the expression not of a sex-specific invariant but of an invariant in the spatio-kinetic semantics of animate form.

## From nonhuman primate presenting to human sitting postures

To elaborate the point, let us consider a contrapuntal, preeminently human example: sitting postures. Anthropologist Gordon Hewes's study of human postures world-wide documents male/female differences both descriptively and pictorially (Hewes, 1955). His study strongly suggests sex-specific postural archetypes. What Hewes found in surveying 480 different cultures or cultural subgroups was that certain sitting positions (or variations thereof, i.e. actual sitting, kneeling, crouching, or squatting) are typically female and certain others are typically male, irrespective of culture. For example, females seldom sit in positions in which one leg is drawn up and the other is to some degree lower and flexed. Neither do they typically stand in what is called "the Nilotic one-legged resting stance" in which an individual, holding a pole that rests against the ground and stabilizing himself with it, stands on one leg, the other leg being raised and the foot placed in some position against the standing leg. (Cattle herders in the Nilotic Sudan regularly assume this posture, hence the name.) These two postures are typically male ones. In addition to these two, males also typically sit in a position similar to a squat, but with the knees only partially flexed. Hewes notes that in our own culture this sitting or resting posture is "frequently assumed by males (and by trousered females)" (Hewes, 1955: 238). Though he does not explicitly draw attention to the fact, it is thus apparent that clothing may influence what one does with one's legs, and that rather than being a veritable sex archetype, a presumed sex-specific posture may in fact be taken up by the opposite sex and thereby become sex-neutral. But this interpretation misses an important point.

As might be indicated by his reference to "trousered females," Hewes suggests at several points that what a female does with her legs has, or may have, sexual significance. He states, for example, that "the role of taboos against female genital exposure in determination of acceptable or nonacceptable feminine postures is presumably important, but the evidence is slight" (Hewes, 1955: 238). On the other hand, he associates "one of the best cases of a feminine postural habit" – "sitting on the ground or floor with legs stretched out in the midline, sometimes with the ankles or knees crossed" – with tasks commonly performed by females:

weaving, for instance, or nursing (Hewes, 1955: 238). Labor rather than genital exposure is in effect suggested in explanation of the female posture. Yet seemingly quite similar sitting postures, in which rather than both. legs being outstretched together or crossed at some point, one leg is stretched out and the other is variously flexed at the knee "so that the foot lies above the opposite knee, beneath it, or is sat upon" (Hewes, 1955: 239), are *not* common to females. In such postures, the legs are sufficiently spread so as partially to expose genitals. It is thus possible that avoidance of genital exposure rather than labor (or other factors) is the motivation for the posture. In an instance where Hewes comments that "exposure avoidance" might explain the posture – a typically female posture in which the legs are folded to the side – he refrains from endorsing exposure-avoidance straightaway as an explanation because the posture may be the result of there being no chairs or benches to sit on, or the result of clothing restrictions. In sum, while an answer to the question of genital exposure-avoidance appears mooted for lack of clear-cut evidence, the evidence does support, and in a strong sense, sex-specific postural archetypes.

It is curious of course that no mention is made of possible *male* genital exposure or of *male* exposure-avoidance. Indeed, in another study of sitting postures, this one focused on typical Western ones (Hewes, 1957), graphics and accompanying descriptions show that males typically sit with their legs spread, females with them closed. Taken together, the graphics presented in the two studies indicate that there is indeed a difference between male and female sitting postures with respect to the spatial relationship between the legs and the degree of triangulation the relationship establishes *vis-à-vis* the genitals. Clellan Ford, an anthropologist, and Frank Beach, a psychologist whose work on sexuality is informed by an evolutionary perspective, studied "190 different societies... scattered around the world from the edge of the Arctic Circle to the southernmost tip of Australia" and observed that

> the provocative gesture of exposing the genitals has become the subject of widespread social control in every human society. There are no peoples in our sample who generally allow women to expose their genitals under any but the most restricted circumstances.                                    (Ford and Beach, 1951: 1, 94)

The question is why males are not likewise restricted. Indeed, since their genitals are far more anteriorly situated than those of females, why is it that males are not equally if not more assiduously controlled? When males sit with legs spread, their genitals are in full view. Whether they are literally or figuratively in view is in the present context of no consequence; in other words, clothes or a lack thereof are beside the point. There is clearly a double standard. But let us put the question of male genital exposure temporarily on hold and pursue the question of female genital exposure. Ford and Beach state that "although there are a few societies in which both sexes are usually nude, there are no peoples who insist upon the man covering his genitals and at the same time permit the woman to expose her genital region." They go on immediately to say that "exposure of the genitals by the receptive female seems to be an almost universal form of sexual invitation throughout the mammalian scale. Descriptions of the mating patterns characteristic of various subhuman primates... [show] the ubiquitousness of feminine exposure... The female ape or monkey characteristically invites intercourse by turning her back to the male and bending sharply forward at the hips, thus calling attention to her sexual parts" (Ford and Beach, 1951: 95).

The proscription against human females' adopting "legs-spread" sitting postures, and the correlatively unconstrained adoption of "legs-spread" sitting postures by human males, are thus linked to a sex-specific, i.e. female, evolutionary behavioral pattern. We are, in effect, led back to the act of presenting and in turn to the question, is the apparent pan-cultural proscription against human female genital exposure really a safeguard against presenting? If so, presenting might appear to be a sex-specific archetype after all in the sense of its *invitational* meaning. The earlier analysis and discussion of presenting showed only how submission and vulnerability are sex-neutral meanings of presenting; how, in other words, animate form does *not* constrain sexed bodies to certain power valencies to the exclusion of others; how, in nonhuman primate societies, both males and females present (and mount), inter-sexually and intrasexually. What was not considered earlier is how animate form *does* constrain sexed bodies. Though not analyzed in such terms, animate form in Ford and Beach's evolutionary account of *sexual invitational behavior* constrains human females to certain postural possibilities to the exclusion of others, and, from a proscriptive cultural point of view, to certain sitting postures (as documented by Hewes's studies) to the exclusion of others. This evolutionary perspective leads us necessarily to a deeper consideration of presenting as socio-sexual act, specifically, as sexual invitation and sign of "the receptive female." It leads us also, however, to consider whether animate form, with respect to sexual *invitational* behavior, does not constrain males in any analogous way to certain possibilities to the exclusion of others. That males are posturally unconstrained is in Ford and Beach's account not considered in need of explanation. Yet it should be because primate males, at least chimpanzee males, invite copulation by penile display. Indeed, Jane van Lawick Goodall, in her original report on Gombe Stream Reserve chimpanzees (Goodall, 1968: 217), notes that males took the initiative in 176 out of 213 witnessed matings, a proportion that, as I have noted elsewhere, is "already indicative of the attention properly due male sexual display" (Sheets-Johnstone, 1990: 101). A consideration of male sexual invitational behavior will bring to the fore the question of human male genital exposure. Oddly enough, initial consideration of this topic will end by shedding considerable light on presenting (leg-spreading) as sexual invitation and sign of the "receptive" female. It will in other words lead us to a first appreciation of a corporeal archetype and its cultural reworkings.

## The question of human male genital exposure

"Soliciting by the normal male [chimpanzee] is highly stylized and involves squat-ting *with knees spread wide* to display an erect penis" (Rogers, 1973: 188; italics added). Primatologist C. M. Rogers thus initially describes male chimpanzee sexual invitation. He goes on to note that "most wildborn males accompany [penile display] by slapping the ground with open palms. If a female does not present to him, he may after several seconds rise to an erect posture and execute a short dance in some respects similar to a threat display. He will then frequently alternate from one pattern to the other if not interrupted by a sexually-presenting female" (Rogers, 1973: 188).

Primatologist Franz de Waal writes that "courtship between adult chimpanzees is almost exclusively on the initiative of the male. He places himself at a little distance . . . from the oestrus female. He sits down with his back straight and *his legs wide apart* so that his erection is clearly visible" (de Waal, 1982: 159; italics added). De Waal goes on to note that the chimpanzee "sometimes . . . flicks his penis quickly up and down, a movement which makes it all the more obvious. During this show of his manhood the male supports himself with his hands behind him on the ground and thrusts his pelvis forward" (de Waal, 1982: 159).

Both accounts call attention to the position of the male's legs. Both substantiate the claim that leg-spreading focuses attention on the male's penis. Both furthermore indicate that leg-spreading is a voluntary act, at least in the sense that it is a deviation from usual positioning, that is, from the natural alignment of the legs in sitting, crouching, standing, and so on. Where purposefully enacted for sexual ends, male chimpanzee leg-spreading clearly invites copulation. In these very same ways, *bipedal* male leg-spreading – human or nonhuman – can be an invitational act. Where purposefully enacted for sexual ends, it too invites copulation. Hence, regarded simply from the viewpoint of animate form irrespective of species, leg-spreading for male and female primate alike is a way of inviting copulation. Though posturally distinctive with respect to sex – female leg-spreading is typically non-bipedal, male leg-spreading may be bipedal or not – in each case the act focuses attention on the individual's genitals and constitutes an invitational display. Where purposefully enacted for sexual ends, genital exposure equals sexual invitation.

Given the placement of primate male and human female genitalia, it is not surprising that there should be a sex difference between the two overall body postures in which leg-spreading occurs and/or is perceived as sexual invitation. A bipedal stance for a human female accomplishes nothing in the way of genital exposure; it accomplishes even less for a quadrupedal nonhuman primate female whose genitalia face posteriorly. When a human or nonhuman female primate stands up, her genitals face downward, to varying degrees depending on the species. When a human female primate is in a sitting posture, however, and specifically as her legs are spread, her genitals becomes quasi-visible and accessible. It is of interest in this context to point out that the clitoris of some New World monkeys such as the spider monkey is quite large and pendulous and that, as sexual invitation, females "abduct the thigh," i.e. *spread their legs*, to display an erect clitoris (Mitchell, 1981: 44). Animate form in this sense is clearly the constraining force that pan-culturally restricts the human female to certain postural possibilities as a safeguard against sexual invitation. Similarly – though inversely constraining and quite otherwise posturally – for a primate male. As suggested in the earlier reference to Goodall's field studies, and as explicitly shown by the above citations, penile display is a regular behavior in the repertoire of male chimpanzees (as it is also a regular behavior in the repertoire of other male primates).[16] Insofar as his penis is on the anterior surface of his body, and insofar as customary bodily facing is forward in all animals with a head-end – all such animals move forward *toward* something – a primate male can easily call attention to his penis, especially and most specifically his *erect* penis, by spreading his legs. Through the latter act, what in squatting or sitting male primates – human or nonhuman – would be partially obscured by, or figure less prominently by being visually behind, knees or legs, is put up front and made the focal point of attention; similarly, what in bipedal male primates – human or nonhuman – would normally be visible but not necessarily seen is made the focal point of attention: leg-spreading accentuates the transformation and translocation of the penis in erection. Its sex-distinct postural expressions notwithstanding, leg-spreading is thus clearly an invitational sexual act for both primate males and human primate females. Enacted for the purpose of sexual invitation, it is clearly a corporeal archetype, one whose evolutionary roots run deep, as deep as the acts of staring and averting the eyes, of making oneself higher than or lower than, of frontally facing or backing toward another, and of making an exaggerated spectacle of oneself. (The latter archetype is incidentally exemplified in Roger's description: the ground-slapping and "the short dance" – more properly called *the bipedal swagger* [Goodall, 1968: 217] – of the male chimpanzee are both spectacle behaviors, ones enacted for the purpose of gaining attention.) *All* of these acts are primate corporeal archetypes.

There may perhaps be a sensed unevenness about the above conclusion. After all, we are speaking of leg-spreading as a human corporeal archetype when human males, unlike their biological primate cousins, do not ordinarily spread their legs to invite copulation, and when human females do not, in any pan-cultural sense, invite copulation by spreading their legs. If we extend our identification of corporeal archetypes by following Ford and Beach's evolutionary lead and acknowledge female genital exposure to be the rule in mammalian sexual invitation, however, and at the same time follow the clue given by primatologists and recognize male genital exposure to be the equal rule in primate sexual invitation, we see clearly that *genital exposure is a biological archetype: leg-spreading is an invitation to copulate.* We see this all the more clearly when we consider that *exposure-avoidance* is *not* a biological rule. Exposure avoidance indeed has no place in nonhuman primate sexual relations. If we ask how there can be a corporeal archetype when its regular enactment is not in evidence, we find the rather obvious answer that cultural overlays mask the archetype; exposure-avoidance is precisely the cultural mask. Whether through the wearing of clothes, sheaths, or other ornamentation, or whether through tacit or explicit codes of conduct, genitals are consistently hidden from view. The point, of course, is that consistent hiding of the genitals not only consistently hides the genitals, but consistently hides the corporeal archetype as well. In so doing, it keeps at bay the possibility of what culture-laden humans likely envision an untempered sexuality, i.e. wild orgies typical of "the beasts."

The sexual sobriety of nudist colonists aside, it should be parenthetically noted with respect to the presumption of an untempered sexuality that if we take our cue from chimpanzees on the grounds that we are genetically closer to them than other primates, then we must literally reckon with *their* animate form and its relationship to *their* sexual practices when it comes to using what paleoanthropologists term "the comparative method," i.e. using extant chimpanzee behaviors as a standard for fleshing out ancestral hominid behaviors, and for enhancing our own self-understandings.[17] We cannot, in other words, simply assume that short of culture, our sexual behavior would mimic chimpanzee sexual behavior, nor can we with reason simply assume categorically that *their* behavior is *untempered*. On the contrary, precisely because there are uniform sexual signalling behaviors in chimpanzee societies, there are, by precisely human standards, *uniform* rather than untempered sexual behaviors. These basic considerations aside, there is furthermore no reason to assume without question that over millions of years what was practiced in our hominid beginnings did not change over time, particularly with the emergence and development of cultures. Indeed, perhaps early hominid sexual practices were more like those of extant gorillas, offspring appearing regularly but copulation being infrequent by present-day human standards. The priority of "sex," especially as it is known today in the West, was not necessarily the priority of yesteryear, especially a yesteryear reaching into the millions. It is of interest to note in this context the observation of one primatologist *vis-à-vis* chimpanzee, hamadryas baboon, and Guinea baboon male behavior: "The maturing male in all these groups seems to be concerned more with status, control, and courtship than with copulation, an activity he would have perfected in early adolescence" (Hanby, 1976: 37). It is well to keep in mind too that where primates do not have to forage for themselves – that is, where food procurement is not an everyday, time- and effort-consuming activity – sexual behavior and preoccupations are heightened. The priority of "sex" in the United States today appears related to just such leisure. The relationship is born out by those "kept" situations where chimpanzees, as in de Waal's study (de Waal, 1982), live in a natural environment but feed wholly unnaturally, i.e. on food apportioned by human caretakers: their sexual – and political – interactions are intensified. With their food needs cared for, the chimpanzees, after all, have not much else to do but interact with each other. Can something similar be said of present-day Western humans?

In sum, while humans, like other creatures, are constrained by animate form to certain sexual invitational possibilities to the exclusion of others – possibilities that originally, no doubt, served in positive ways to perpetuate the species – they are also reversely constrained by culture. Their repertoire of invitational "I can's" is in consequence a complex conjunction of evolutionary and cultural factors. The complexity of the conjunction is substantively apparent in the act of leg-spreading – its archetypal primate heritage, and its cultural restrictions and freedoms. By describing in finer terms how, with respect to animate form, the advent of consistent bipedality radically changed the nature of primate sexual invitational behavior, we can come to a deeper understanding of primate sexual signaling behavior and the present-day pan-cultural proscription against human female leg-spreading. We can, in short, come to a deeper understanding of a radical shift in sexual signaling powers.[18] We can in turn begin to elucidate the formidable socio-political implications of present-day biological explanations of human sexuality by way of "the receptive female."

## Sexual signaling behavior and the reigning Western biological explanation of human sexuality

With the advent of consistent bipedality, female genitalia were no longer permanently on display; male genitalia were. Moreover while extant nonhuman primate penes are normally hidden and extruded only upon arousal – and presumably, ancestral nonhuman primate penes were similarly hidden and extruded only upon arousal – a human's penis is permanently exposed – and presumably an ancestral hominid's penis was similarly permanently exposed.[19] Furthermore the anatomical placement of female genitalia changed; the placement of male genitalia did not change. While penes were still anteriorly located on the primate body, vaginas became more anteriorly located. In brief, the standard primate morphological/visual relationship that heretofore obtained with respect to male genitalia and to female genitalia was radically altered by consistent bipedality: what was normally hidden in quadrupedal male primates became exposed in bipedal male primates; what was normally exposed in quadrupedal female primates became hidden in bipedal female primates.[20] This radically changed relationship necessarily meant a radical change in sexual signaling behavior, behavior that is an essential part of normal mating for any species whose members must come in direct contact with one another in order to mate. From the perspective of animate form what was before accomplished through both penile display and presenting – what might basically if figuratively be described as invitation by mutual "leg-spreading" (taking *presenting* in Ford and Beach's sense of "genital exposure"), and basically if idealistically described as a situation of mutually recognized readiness and potency – was now accomplished only through penile display. Exclusive reliance on penile display is axiomatic given hominid animate form: only what is exposed, visibly apparent, can minimally count as a sexual signal, and then, through enhancement of some kind, become a display.[21]

Biologist Adolf Portmann calls attention precisely to such basic visual signaling when he shows in detail how visual patternings on animate forms signal "genital-end" and "head-end," for example, and in turn form the basis of behavioral displays (Portmann, 1967). Evidence of just such a basic visibility and subsequent enhancement through display is apparent in the present context: a human male does not first have to spread his legs to call attention to his penis; being an upright creature, his penis is already there, exposed, in full visible sight.[22] What leg-spreading does is enhance or intensify exposure – as Western guitar-playing, rock-singing males might readily testify. In biological terms, they are enacting a human male sexual display, a sexual *display* in precisely the sense defined: by their actions they accentuate *an already present signal*. Indeed, in conjunction with the advent of consistent bipedality one might speak with reason both of *an intensification of male sexuality with respect to signalling readiness and potency through penile display, and correlatively, of a loss of natural sexual signaling in females*. With the advent of consistent bipedality and the anterior shift in female genitalia, not only was presenting per se no longer an anatomically possible way of inviting sexual relations or of demonstrating sexual readiness and potency, but a female who no longer had estrous cycles would no longer have anything to display to begin with in the way of periodic swellings and coloration changes. The question is, what did hominid females do to invite copulation in the absence of presenting?

The only minimally sure way of answering the question is by appeal to leg-spreading: primate sexual invitation is by genital exposure. The question has never been answered on these grounds because the question has never been asked to begin with; and it has never been asked to begin with because the terms of the discourse have been changed. The question has been swallowed up in the fundamental Western biological characterization of human, that is, hominid, sexuality as "year-round receptivity." With the central concentration on females being receptive "year-round" – hominid females are not constrained to estrous cycles like other primates – a familiar biological picture of human sexuality emerges: hominid males are conceived as being always ready for any sexual adventure and hominid females are conceived as being always available – even if not always willing. There are multiple issues involved in this viewpoint.[23] Our exclusive concern here is to show how the shift in discourse – from sexual invitational signaling behavior to sexual "receptivity" – by trading basically in physiology rather than in corporeal archetypes and their cultural proscriptions, undercuts female sexuality at the same time that it propels it to evolutionary prominence.

Conceived simply as being receptive "year-round," human female primates are conceived as lacking any natural sign of sexual readiness and potency, certainly not any natural sign on the order of vulval swellings and changes in coloration, or on the order of penile erection with its visible upward movement and its changes in size, texture, and shape. Conceived as lacking any natural sign of readiness and potency, human female primates are in turn conceived as lacking natural powers of sexual expression. This means that on the one hand, there is no bodily organ to be consulted to determine a female's true sexual disposition, and on the other, that there is no bodily organ by which a female can express her sexual yearnings. She is simply open and available "year-round." From this current Western, essentially male point of view, a human female invites copulation simply by being there. She herself is an invitation. Hence, wherever human sexual readiness and potency exist, there is a human male – and a female to be found to satisfy it. Sociobiological anthropologist Donald Symons affirms this human state of affairs unequivocally in his text *The Evolution of Human Sexuality* when he states that "women inspire male sexual desire simply by existing" (Symons, 1979: 284). Insofar as his book is used as a textbook and is considered a major formulation of human sexuality, it will warrant consistent attention in the continuing critical analysis of female "year-round receptivity." His account of female sexuality may indeed be treated as a paradigm of the prevailing Western biological view and as such is an excellent prism through which to show the intricate cultural translations and reworkings of leg-spreading as corporeal archetype of primate sexual invitational behavior.

Not unexpectedly, "year-round receptivity" reduces human female sexuality not only to male readiness and potency but to male fantasies. Symons affirms this reduction as well when he writes that "pornotopia is and always has been a male fantasy realm; easy, anonymous, impersonal, unencumbered sex with an endless succession of lustful, beautiful, orgasmic women reflects basic male wishes" (Symons, 1979: 177). The basic theorem is unmistakable: human males are sexually insatiable; females are receptive "year-round." By neglecting serious study of the body itself,[24] and instead fastening on pornography and on cultural studies of sex practices to locate "human universals" (Symons's term), such putatively biological accounts cannot hope to come to grips with the origin and evolution of human sexuality. Not only do they mistake current practices for originary/evolutionary ones,[25] but they ignore from the very beginning both the radical shift in primate animate form that defines consistent bipedality and the related questions it raises about hominid sexual signalling behavior.[26] It is quite easy to see how, through such formulations of the origin and evolution of human sexuality, the notion of females as sex objects is strengthened at the same time that it is steadfastly maintained. Not only this, but it is easy to see how females themselves become transformed into two opposing cultural psychic archetypes: the witch/temptress and the goddess/mother, a man's she devil or the figure who gives him birth. As Jung points out, the real woman dissolves in such primitive images. She dissolves because her individuality gives way to "infantile dominants," that is, to archaic visions tied on the one hand to fear and on the other to worship (Jung, 1976: 236).

A natural sign is unequivocal – "where there's smoke, there's fire." A female conceived simply as receptive "year-round" can give no such definitive invitational signal. Her true sexual dispositions of the moment are never visibly apparent. Certainly she can spread her legs, but she cannot spread them without going against cultural proscriptions, thus going against what is deemed "moral." To reclaim her natural sexuality would mean in effect to be wanton, corrupt, degenerate, even wicked. More than this, it would put her at severe risk. By adding leg-spreading to simply being there, she doubles sexual invitation and runs a double risk. As if this were not enough, in taking the double risk she not only emphatically shows herself open and available to the male to whom she addresses her display, but she may well be considered showing herself open and available to any and all males who might witness or hear of her leg-spreading. Exposure-avoidance in this sense guarantees both her reputation and her safety. At the same time, however, her "year-round receptivity" puts and keeps her in a perpetual double bind: from a male point of view, she is "damned if she does and damned if she doesn't." The double bind is reflected in the notion that females are capricious; they do not know what they want. They will flirt, they will hold your hand, they will kiss you, but they will not "go all the way"; or, they will "go all the way," but they are either loose women to begin with or sorry and unsatisfied women in the end. Once more it is easy to see how females are transformed into a cultural psychic archetype of destruction. Capricious temptresses, they are incarnations of the devil.

As briefly indicated earlier, there is another remarkable side to the implications of "year-round receptivity." Human females are regarded as being without desire. Since they no longer signal naturally like most other female primates – since they have no organ proper to sexual desire – they cannot possibly have sexual desires. Since they are without sexual desire, they spread their legs not as a genuinely felt invitation or response to an invitation but as an allowance. Symons's characterization of copulation as a "female service" indicates precisely this conception of females (Symons, 1979: ch. 8). Females can *always* spread their legs; it is merely a matter of their choosing to do so. The principle of female choice – the principle first described at length by Darwin whereby females select certain males over others in light of their superior qualities, e.g. more ornamented, better armed, more vigorous, and so on (Darwin, [1871] 1981: 262) – is egregiously weakened, even negated, by the conception. Conceived as rendering a service to males, females do not actually choose males in a Darwinian sense; they choose only to accommodate a male. The warpedness of this emaciated version of female choice is particularly well highlighted by recent, highly detailed accounts of female choice that focus on female discrimination of male genitalia on the basis of their "internal courtship" powers (Eberhard, 1985). The significance of this latter research is best appreciated in the context of internal fertilization since much of Darwin's original evidence for female choice came from studies of birds, creatures who do not actually copulate. Accordingly, the recent studies of female choice alluded to are concerned with features of male genitalia precisely because male genitalia contact female genitalia directly in sexual reproduction by internal fertilization, because male genitalia vary more than female genitalia, because males compete for females, because specialized structures in male genitalia tend to evolve rapidly through female choice, and because male genitalia in turn are taxonomically significant with respect to speciation. It is understandable why in *this* context, female choice – in the strong, original Darwinian sense – is of central concern. In those creatures who reproduce by internal fertilization, females choose one male over another in terms of his ability to stimulate her more fully "by squeezing her harder, touching her over a wider area, rubbing her more often, and so on" (Eberhard, 1985: 71). Reduced simply to "year-around receptivity," a human female is far removed from such discriminations. She is simply open and available "year-round"; even her capacity for orgasm – if she has orgasms or had them – being, in Symons's sociobiological account, "a byproduct of selection for male orgasm" (Symons, 1979: 94).

Now if a human female has no sexual desire, she can hardly be motivated even for the sheer pleasure of "internal courtship" to choose one male over another for his greater stimulatory powers. She can merely *allow herself to be copulated*. The locution is the natural extension of the phrase some scientists have used to describe female sexuality: "continuously copulable."[27] The phrase gives ample testimony to the conception of female sexuality as a sexuality both without desire and without choice in any discriminating and autonomous sense of the word. In fact, female choice in Symons's work cryptically passes over into male hands; it is actually defined in terms of *male power*. Symons writes that "Darwin identified two types of sexual selection: intersexual selection, based on female choice of males (*'the power to charm the females'*), and intrasexual selection, based on male-male competition ('the power to conquer other males in battle')" (Symons, 1979: 22; italics added). As is apparent, in Symons's account sexual selection is synonymous with male power in *both* intersexual and intrasexual selection. His use of the term "intersexual *selection*" notwithstanding, there is not the slightest hint of *female choice*. But then the parenthetical definition that Symons gives of intersexual selection is actually one of his own making; though attributed to Darwin, the definition is not Darwin's. Both of Symons's definitional quotations are in fact taken from a passage in which Darwin is describing not sexual selection per se, but advantageous modifications in male animate form that result from sexual selection. The modifications are advantageous, Darwin explains, in sofar as they "make one male victorious over another, either in fighting or in charming the female" (Darwin, [1871] 1981: 278). In the specifically relevant passage, Darwin, after commenting on how sexual selection can confer advantages beyond those of natural selection, goes on to say that "we shall further see ... that the power to charm the female has been in some few instances more important than the power to conquer other males in battle" (Darwin, [1871] 1981: 279). In this context of *advantageous modifications*, Darwin is indeed speaking of, and in fact contrasting, two male powers; *he is not in this passage defining the two types of sexual selection* – intersexual and intrasexual. In Darwin's account, as in the accounts of evolutionary biologists generally, there is no question but that the former type of selection proceeds by female choice, the latter by male–male competition. The former is hence not a power of males but of females. To deny that the power exists is one thing. To transform it surreptitiously into a male power is quite another.

As if the usurpation were not sufficient, Symons in fact completely and explicitly devalues female choice as a factor in the evolution of humans, affirming in its place *intrasexual* selection: "Although copulation is, and presumably always has been, in some sense a female service or favor, hominid females evolved in a milieu in which physical and political power was wielded by adult males" (Symons, 1979: 203). His judgment is peculiar given both the substantiated evolutionary importance of female choice (it is the major factor creating "runaway selection" of certain male traits, for example)[28] and the quintessential linkage of female choice to male–male competition: males compete with one another in a variety of ways to win females, but they do not win females automatically with the winning of the competition. As Darwin originally noted, "males which conquer other males ... do not obtain possession of the females ... independently of choice on the part of the latter" (Darwin, [1871] 1981: 262). The above-mentioned studies of male genitalia are of considerable interest in this context. Were we to take seriously Symons's definition of intersexual selection, we would have to ask in what "the power to charm the females" consists. Since he nowhere spells it out, we could genuinely wonder in what specific capability this male power would have rested in terms of the evolution of human sexuality – and in what it might rest today. As noted above, for creatures who reproduce by internal fertilization, internal courtship powers can be of singular importance in the successful pursuit of a mate. The genitalia of hominid males would in this fundamental sense be no different from the genitalia of males of other species which reproduce by internal fertilization. The stimulatory powers bequeathed by animate form in both a species-specific and individual sense would have to figure in any account of "the power [of hominid males] to charm the females." Indeed, in a properly exemplified view of hominid intersexual selection,

hominid penile display – particularly the display of an erect penis – would have to
be taken into account since it would have visually indicated to females the internal
courtship powers of the displaying male.[29] On *this* view of the evolution of human
sexuality, the power of male genitalia is not simply the power to deliver sperm. It is
the power to give pleasure, and it would thereby understandably have been a power
subject to sexual selection by females. (The power to give pleasure obviously figures
in the relationship among desire, pleasure, and sexual act, a relationship of central
concern to both Sartre [1956] and Foucault [1980; 1986; 1988], and warrants study
in its own right.)

Spelled out succinctly in the terms of the critical analysis thus far, "year-round
receptivity" reduces female choice to two logically related facts: a human/ancestral
hominid female has/had no sexual desire, and therefore she cannot have/have had
any motivation for choosing one male rather than another or even any motivation for
choosing sheer sexual pleasure; lacking any motivation for choosing one male rather
than another or for choosing sheer sexual pleasure, she is/was simply choosing to
spread her legs or not. From this summary perspective, it is once more readily clear
how the received Western biological account of human sexuality gives way on the
one hand to the notion of females as sex objects – founts of orgasmic pleasure for
men – and on the other hand to the transformation of the female herself into a
cultural psychic archetype. On the former reading, female invitation – leg-spreading
– is a mere allowance; on the latter reading, it is a trap: the female body is an
insidious lure that tempts but does not allow, or if it allows, is evil. Klaus Theweleit,
in his thoroughgoing analysis of Nazi sexual politics, practices, propaganda, dic-
tums, images, metaphors, and more, gives perhaps the ultimate picture of the female
body as the archetype of evil (Theweleit, 1987). Whether allowance or trap, sexual
invitation has no felt significance for the female. What is spreading or not spreading
its legs is not a subject but an object.

Clearly the negation of choice is the negation of power. Autonomy disappears. To
say as above that a female is "*choosing* to spread her legs or not" is true only in the
abstract. That this is so becomes immediately apparent when we consider *allowance*
concretely in the given paradigmatic context of "continuous copulability" or "year-
round receptivity." When a female *allows* herself to be copulated, she is *allowing* at
some point along the continuum, or at the extreme, of two possible senses of
allowing, neither of which engages her as an authentic subject. She can allow
copulation in the sense of letting it happen as a "service or favor," in which case
it is difficult to imagine her in any vigorous or involved way caught up in the act, or
she can allow it in the sense of submitting physically to male sexual power. In
essence, these two senses reduce to the possibility that a female can spread her legs
voluntarily or they can be spread for her by force. Given the two possible senses, it
is not surprising that with the conception of females as receptive "year-round," and
with the denial of female choice, rape becomes a distinctive and most obvious male
possibility. Neither is it surprising that rape figures as a prime factor in Symons's
explanation of "copulation as a female service." And neither, finally, is it surprising
that in that explanation, Symons finds rapists' actions justly explicable. "Many
feminists," he writes, "call attention to male anger as a motive in some rapes but
fail to note what is obvious in many interviews with rapists, that the anger is partly
sexual, aimed at women because women incite ungratifiable sexual desire" (Symons,
1979: 284). It is in this context – a single sentence later – that he remarks "women
inspire male sexual desire simply by existing." We are, in effect, back to what is
perhaps the first cultural reworking of the primate corporeal archetype of exposure

as sexual invitation, the notion that females invite copulation simply by being there. Appended to this notion, however, is the seemingly added consequence that if their existence puts them under perpetual risk of sexual attack, that is *their* problem. Though not a "facultative adaptation," rape is an act natural to males: "the evidence [from rapists] does appear to support the views . . . that human males tend to desire no–cost, impersonal copulations . . . hence that there is a possibility of rape wherever rape entails little or no risk."[30] The section of the book in which Symons discusses rape is titled "Forcible rape." (Is there actually another kind? Is a person less a person in an ethical sense if mentally retarded, asleep, or unconscious?)

One last aspect of the reigning Western biological explanation of human sexuality vis-à-vis sexual signaling behavior warrants special comment. As discussed earlier, when human sexuality is characterized as "loss of estrus" – i.e. a human female is receptive "year-round" – it is virtually a foregone conclusion that a human female cannot possibly have any sexual desire. She has nothing to have it *with*. There is a further scientific dimension to this deficiency that should be pointed out. All functions need an *organ*. In Western thinking as evidenced by Western medicine, there is no function without a structure. A vagina is a mere passageway, an opening.[31] A clitoris is obviously a structure, but it is not an *organ of desire*, the stuff of which sexual yearnings are made visibly present in one's own experience and in the experience of others. As a belatedly (in the West) discovered feature of female anatomy, a clitoris is regarded only as an organ of sexual pleasure. The contrast with a penis is manifestly remarkable: a penis is *both* an organ of desire and an organ of pleasure. There is no mistaking male sexual desire and pleasure – no equivocation, no ambiguity. Male sexual desire and pleasure are indeed commonly conceived as wrapped up in one. The visible disequilibrium in animate form between human male and human female in effect reinforces the Western biological explanation of human sexuality as "year-round receptivity." It reinforces the notion of women as *always* capable of spreading their legs, of *allowing* something sexual to transpire, of being in Freudian terms "the passive sex," so passive in fact that, being under no periodic pressure to copulate, being simply receptive "year-round," the human female is under no pressure to copulate all. Only her desire to have a child – presuming, of course, she knows of the connection between copulation and pregnancy – impels her "naturally" to copulate. Sexual desire is thus conclusively for the female a desire *manqué*; what she experiences is only reproductive desire.

## Year-round receptivity and penile display: uncovering the hidden relationship

The foregoing critical analysis of "year-round receptivity" can be extended to reveal a further socio-political dimension of the cultural reworking and translation of genital exposure as corporeal archetype. That evolutionary scientists concerned with the evolution of human sexuality have failed to remark on the obvious – on penile display – and that some of them have either reinterpreted Darwin's fundamental principle of female choice in sexual selection or forgotten it altogether in invoking the principle of "year-round female receptivity" show just how clearly the question of animate form and of sexual signaling behavior has been overlooked. How an ancestral male or female hominid would have invited sexual union is a question nowhere raised; in turn, the question of genital exposure within the evolution of human sexuality – from ancestral to present-day times – is nowhere raised. Over-

sight of the obvious is particularly queer in light of the enormous literature on, and
concern with, sexual signaling behavior in nonhuman primates. It is all the more
queer in light of the fact that, as indicated earlier, nonhuman primate behavior is
regularly used as an analogical standard to infer ancestral hominid behaviors. How
could the sexual impact of consistent bipedality be missed? How in turn could penile
display be missed? It is important to emphasize the oversight, the focus instead on
"year-round receptivity," and the enormous primatological literature because present-day Western cultural attitudes are so heavily influenced by science. We are
indeed the inheritors *and practitioners* of precisely the *scientia sexualis* Foucault
(1980) describes. By failing to see the obvious and reckon with its archetypal
significance, and by using data on nonhuman primate sexual behavior only to
contrast estrous cycles with "year-round receptivity," evolutionary scientists, perhaps justifying their own personal predilections, have skewed the picture of human
sexuality and sizably influenced present-day Western cultural attitudes in the
following way.

The characterization of hominid sexuality as "year-round receptivity" can itself
be characterized as the replacement of periodic leg-spreading (presenting as per
estrous cycles) by continual leg-spreading. It is difficult not to judge this view of
hominid sexuality as a shallow male account, male because it focuses *all* attention on
the female and fails to investigate male genitalia and sexual signalling behavior,
shallow because it similarly fails to investigate consistent bipedality and animate
form, and gives no reference to penile display. It avoids the question of male genital
exposure entirely. In a broad sense, the view coincides with Western cultural
practice generally; that is, a male's body is not anatomized nor is it ever made an
object of study in the same way as female bodies. The net result is that the penis is
never made public, never put on the measuring line in the same way that female
sexual body parts are put on the measuring line. On the contrary, a penis remains
shrouded in mystery. It is protected, hidden from sight. What is normally no more
than a swag of flesh in this way gains unassailable stature and power. To call
attention to it by actually exposing it, let alone actually displaying it by leg-spreading, is in consequence readily regarded not as an invitation, but as a threat.[32] As an
object perpetually protected from public view and popular scientific investigation, it
is conceived not as the swag of flesh it normally is in all the humdrum acts and
routines of everyday life but as a Phallus, an organ of unconditioned power. Indeed,
a new corporeal archetype is born, the archetype of power par excellence. This
archetype is a cultural translation of penile display. The translation deviates considerably from the evolutionary original in that the archetype is not *of* the body itself
but a *symbol* of the body, a corporeal archetype once removed, so to speak. We know
this because however much and in whatever ways we are seduced or intimidated by
the symbol and myth of the Phallus, we know that the real everyday thing pales in
comparison; it is no match for perpetual engorgement. Nonetheless, the archetype
prevails: it is as if Western human males were in a steady state of tumescence.
Ironically, of course, male exposure-avoidance protects this image by not giving it
the lie. But the cultural masking is not what basically sustains the archetype. What
basically sustains the archetype is "year-round receptivity." *The male correlate of
"year-round receptivity" is perpetual erection.* The two go hand in hand. Our eyes
focused wholly on "year-round receptivity," the myth of a perpetually erect penis is
kept alive: males are *always* ready for any sexual adventure. Our attention caught up
wholly in "loss of estrus," penile display, its male signaling correlate, remains
invisible and thereby forever present as possibility if not actuality: females can

always provide a service; they can always be threatened. In these circumstances, it is no wonder that the Phallus remains indomitable, retaining its sovereign hold on the Western sexual psyche, and that sexual power is conceived to be a solely male prerogative. The overarching power of the Phallus derives from an imaginary repertoire of "I can's" peculiar to human males – males like those who pin their research and their dreams on "year-round receptivity," and who are thereby always ready and potent, never uncontrollably flaccid or sexually spent – for all that "easy, anonymous, impersonal, unencumbered sex with an endless succession of lustful, beautiful, orgasmic women."

## Notes

1  This phrase – "to the things themselves" (*zu den Sachen selbst*) – is a well-known Husserlian dictum. Husserl used it to plead the need for, and the way to, a sound and consummate epistemology.

2  In her earlier discussion of human evolution, Longino accepts without question standard fragmentary practice in evolutionary biology. She writes that "the main questions addressed in the search for human origins are standardly grouped into two categories: anatomical evolution and social evolution," and goes on to note that "there are some changes central to human development that are captured by neither of these categories...like locomotion" (Longino, 1990: 104). That something as fundamental as locomotion fits into neither basic category should give pause enough for questioning them. Clearly the dichotomy as well as the categories themselves obliterate the possibility of examining animate form. Accordingly, a retreat to a common level of experience depends on prior clarification of what is being described. If one starts with a sundered specimen – or with synecdochic renditions of the body – one can hardly arrive at understandings of animate form.

3  An overemphasis by many feminists on theory, especially to the exclusion of practice, is viewed by other feminists as deleterious. Barbara Christian, for example, writes that "when Theory is not rooted in practice, it becomes prescriptive, exclusive, elitist," and she goes on to voice strong concerns about the way in which "Theory" can become "*authoritative discourse*" (Christian, 1989: 231, 233).

4  Re proprioception: Code's quote is from Oliver Sack's *The Man Who Mistook His Wife for a Hat.*

5  This phrase comes from William Saroyan's play *The Time of Your Life*. The words are uttered several times over in the course of the play by an otherwise near-mute character. The phrase, of course, could be uttered with equal conviction by a foundationalist to a relativist or by a relativist to a foundationalist. It might be noted that the rhetoric of the relativist's anti-foundationalist claims can at times exceed the bounds of truth, as when Judith Butler (1990: 12) includes Husserl in her list of philosophers who are part of the dualistic philosophical tradition "that supports relations of political and psychic subordination and hierarchy." The inclusion is clearly without foundation, as any familiarity with Husserl's *Ideas II* (1989) and his consistent concern with the fundamental significance of what he calls "I can's" and "kin-estheses" attests.

6  Arleen Dallery (1989) makes a not dissimilar claim on behalf of *écriture féminine*. However she contradicts her own onto–essentialist denials when she insists that "a 'real' body prior to discourse is meaningless" (1989: 59) and that "there is no fixed, univocal, ahistorical woman's body as the referent of this [*écriture féminine*] discourse" (1989: 63) at the same time that she celebrates "woman's erotic embodiment" (1989: 56) complete with, e.g. labia (1989: 59) and speaks of "feminine structures of erotic embodiment where self and other are continuous, in pregnancy, childbirth, and nursing" (1989: 54). Unless the stuff of erotic "embodiment" and the designated feminine "structures" exist only on paper, or unless we grant philosophic license along with poetic, it is difficult to know how to reconcile an actual living body – a moving, resonating, species-specific form (and, in fact, in terms of pregnancy, childbirth, and nursing, a *sex*-specific animate form) – with something that has no meaning outside of language and that, even as languaged, has no historically invariant identity.

7 I am referring to Charles Darwin's *The Expression of the Emotions in Man and Animals* ([1872] 1965) as well as to *The Origin of Species* ([1859] 1968) and *The Descent of Man and Selection in Relation to Sex* ([1871] 1981).

8 The phrase is sometimes erroneously attributed to Merleau-Ponty. It in fact comes from the somatic studies of Edmund Husserl, in particular his insightful and seminal descriptive analyses of "the kinestheses." See especially Husserl (1989); but see also, for example, Husserl (1970: 106–8, 161, 217, 331–2), Husserl (1973: 97), and Husserl (1980: 106–12).

9 In addition to their detailed description and cross-species comparative analyses in *The Roots of Power: Animate Form and Gendered Bodies* (Sheets-Johnstone, forthcoming 1993), several of these basic primate commonalities figured centrally in a paper titled "Corporeal archetypes and postmodern theory" presented by Sheets-Johnstone at the American Philosophical Association Pacific Division meeting in March 1992 at a symposium titled Philosophy of Body-mind.

10 For a discussion of these aspects of animate form, see Sheets-Johnstone (1990), particularly ch. 7, "Hominid bipedality and sexual selection theory."

11 See Hubbard (1990), Fausto-Sterling (1985), Harding (1987) Keller (1987), and Lowe (1982).

12 See Butler (1989; 1990), Poovey (1988), and Dallery (1989).

13 Humans belong to the biological order called Primates, to the biological family called Hominidae (which includes the great apes), and to the genus *Homo*.

14 "Presenting, which is usually a gesture of submission, is often accompanied by nervous, even fearful, behavior on the part of the presenting animal, whereas mounting, conversely, in baboons is usually an indicator of relative dominance" (Hall and DeVore, 1972: 174).

15 It is notable that a woman primatologist, Mireille Bertrand, who did her studies and fieldwork in the 1960s in India, France, and Thailand, is an exception. In her book-length monograph on stumptail macaques, she writes: "Social presenting has generally been assumed to originate from the sexual one: a monkey may avoid the aggression of a superior by taking the posture of the receptive female, which is supposed to be both submissive and sexually arousing" (1969: 185–6). She goes on to say that "This interpretation involves certain difficulties," and, after itemizing them, concludes, "Thus it is possible that social presenting does not derive from sexual presenting" but is rather connected with perineal grooming: "Perineal presenting may have acquired a submissive connotation because the performer stands still and waits, does not take the initiative of the next move, and shows its rump and back, that is, what it would show if it were fleeing" (Bertrand, 1969: 186). It is furthermore of interest to note Bertrand's initial remarks on sex and genital displays: "The importance of sex among monkeys and apes is in general grossly overestimated by the layman, as it was by some of the first primatologists." She writes that the misconception may be explained by two reasons: first, "infra-human primates use genitalia in a variety of social signals outside a sexual context, and these are interpreted as sexual by human observers"; and second, "in captivity, sex and genital displays may be exaggerated when animals are confined, kept in artificial, sexually imbalanced groupings" (Bertrand, 1969: 178). Bertrand's analysis says as much about human primates, and obviously male human primates in terms of the history of primatology and zoology, as it does about nonhuman primates.

16 See, for example, Hall (1960), Wickler (1969), and Ploog et al. (1963). For detailed discussions of this behavior and its import, see Sheets-Johnstone (1990, ch. 4, 7).

17 For a justification of this methodological practice, see Washburn (1950) and Lancaster (1975).

18 The shift may, of course, be related in deep and poignant ways to many feminists' felt lack of, and present-day search for, "a desire of their own." See in particular Benjamin (1986).

19 Insofar as male genitalia are regularly utilized as a taxonomic standard, the assumption of similarity is in each case a reasonable one.

20 For a full discussion of the radical shift and its evolutionary significance, see Sheets-Johnstone (1990, ch. 7).

21 The difference between signal and display is succinctly defined by primatologist Claud Bramblett: "Some signals have been affected by natural selection, i.e., *ritualized*, so that the signal is exaggerated and incorporates several elements that make it more complex. We call such a signal a *display* (Bramblett, 1976: 47). Female primate "sexual swellings," as vulval changes are called, and presenting aptly exemplify the basic difference: the signal is exaggerated by the act.

22  Linda Lopez McAlister (personal communication 1991) reminded me that "in some centuries [males] have taken to stuffing their cod-pieces," and she drew my attention to the fact that "cosmetic surgeons . . . now do penile-enhancement surgery."

23  Certainly a prime issue revolves about the notion of biology as an objective science untainted by cultural biases. Within this issue lies also the question of the way in which, and the degree to which, biologists play into an already established cultural *eidos* and the degree to which they help create it. (Discussion of the issue addressed in this paper emphasizes the latter dimension but is not meant to suggest that the former dimension is nonexistent.) Another prime issue involves a synecdochic rendition of *female*. For a detailed discussion of this rendition and a critical analysis of Sartre's characterization of females as "being-in-the-form-of-a-hole," see Sheets-Johnstone (forthcoming 1993, ch. 5: "Corporeal archetypes and Sartre's 'psychoanalytic of things'").

24  It is of considerable interest to note that in Symons's book, there is no entry in the index for *genitals*, for *penis*, or for *vagina*. For a book on the evolution of human sexuality, this would seem to be an extremely serious omission.

25  See Gould and Lewontin (1979). See also Symons's optimistic view that "if humans exhibit relatively uniform dispositions under a wide range of environmental conditions, these dispositions probably were uniformly adaptive among our Pleistocene ancestors and hence develop in a relatively stereotyped manner" (1979: 71). Symons casually links present-day sexual behavior with sexual behavior originating three million and more years ago, and this without any reference to the body itself.

26  In this context, perhaps the foremost positive value of the doctrine of cultural relativism is to caution us about where we look for human universals. Cultural practices are no match for corporeal archetypes.

27  The phrase, which Symons uses (1979: 106), comes originally from Frank A. Beach (1974: 357).

28  In addition to Eberhard's work (1985), see Ronald A. Fisher's original formulation of runaway selection (Fisher, 1958: 150–3).

29  Lest it be thought that such discrimination is farfetched, it might be helpful to point out that field and experimental evidence show that female bowerbirds, for instance, "show a strong preference for particular males," and this on the basis of the bowers the males build. The females discriminate with fine attention the number of decorations on the bower platform, the color of the decorations, the "well-built[ness]" of the bower, and the "overall quality" of the bower (Borgia, 1986: 92, 100, 99).

30  Symons (1979: 284). Symons actually goes on to gloss this appraisal with the statement that, "these impulses [of males to rape females] are part of human nature because they proved adaptive over millions of years." Not only does he claim that rape is a *hominid male genetic endowment*, but he goes on to say that any change in the arrangement "might well entail a cure worse than the disease": "Where males can win females' hearts through tears rather than spears, through a show of vulnerability rather than strut and swagger, many will do so, but the desires persist and the game remains essentially the same. Given sufficient control over rearing conditions, no doubt males could be produced who would want only the kinds of sexual interactions that women want; but such rearing conditions might well entail a cure worse than the disease" (Symons, 1979: 285).

31  The conception of female sexuality as an anatomical passageway or opening recalls Sartre's famous statement "sex is a hole" (Sartre, 1956: 614). For critical assessments of Sartre's psychological ontology of sex, see Collins and Pierce (1973–4), Pierce (1975), and Sheets-Johnstone (forthcoming 1993, ch. 5). It is of interest to note in this context that Sartre's psychological ontology of sex appears actually to contradict his earlier phenomenological ontology of sex as desire. In his phenomenological analysis of desire as *the* mode of being by which we realize sex, i.e. come to know ourselves and others as sexed beings, Sartre is at pains, one might say, to emphasize, on the one hand, the distinctions between desire and pleasure and between desire and sexual act, and, on the other hand, the goal of desire as *reciprocal* incarnation. Desire has clearly nothing to do with *holes*. See Sartre (1956: 382–98).

32  The literature on exhibitionism is of interest to review in this context. See, for example, Stoller (1976: 202–3) and Jones and Frei (1979: 63–70). The literature on penile display as threat display is of equal interest to review. See, for example, Wickler (1969: 164–7), Eibl-Eibesfeldt (1975: 428–31), and Sheets-Johnstone (1990: 189–91).

# References

Beach, Frank A. (1974) "Human sexuality and evolution." In *Reproductive Behavior*, ed. William Montagna and William A. Sadler. New York: Plenum Press.

Benjamin, Jessica (1986) "A desire of one's own: psychoanalytic feminism and intersubjective space." In *Feminist Studies/Critical Studies*, ed. Teresa de Lauretis. Bloomington: Indiana University Press.

Bertrand, Mireille. (1969) *The Behavioral Repertoire of the Stumptail Macaque*. Basel (Switzrland): Karger. Published simultaneously as *Bibliotheca Primatologica* 11.

Bigwood, Carol. (1991) "Renaturalizing the body (with the help of Merleau-Ponty)." *Hypatia* 6(3): 54–73.

Bordo, Susan (1993). *Unbearable Weight: Feminism Western Culture, and the Body*. Berkeley: University of California Press.

Borgia, Gerald. (1986) "Sexual selection in bowerbirds." *Scientific American* 254: 92–100.

Bramblett, Claud. (1976.) *Patterns of Primate Behavior*. Palo Alto: Mayfield.

Butler, Judith. (1989) "Gendering the body: Beauvoir's philosophical contribution." In *Women, Knowledge, and Reality: Explorations in Feminist Philosophy*, ed. Ann Garry and Marilyn Pearsall. Boston: Unwin Hyman.

Butler, Judith (1990) *Gender Trouble*. New York: Routledge.

Chevalier-Skolnikoff, Suzanne (1975) "Heterosexual copulatory patterns in stumptail macaques (*Macaca arctoides*) and in other macaque species." *Archives of Sexual Behavior* 4(2): 199–220.

Christian, Barbara (1989) "The race for theory." In *Gender and Theory*, ed. Linda Kauffmann. New York: Basil Blackwell.

Code, Lorraine. 1991. *What can she Know?* Ithaca: Cornell University Press.

Collins, Margery and Christine Pierce (1973–74) "Holes and slime: sexism in Sartre's psychoanalysis." *Philosophical Forum* 1(2): 112–27.

Dallery, Arleen (1989) "The politics of writing (the) body: *écriture féminine*". In *Gender/Body/Knowledge*, ed. Alison M. Jaggar and Susan R. Bordo. New Brunswick: Rutgers University Press.

Darwin, Charles ([1836–1844] 1987). *Charles Darwin's Notebooks: 1836–1844*, ed. David Kohn and Paul H. Barrett. Ithaca: Cornell University Press.

Darwin Charles ([1859] 1968) *The Origin of Species*. Middlesex (England): Penguin.

Darwin, Charles ([1871] 1981) *The Descent of Man and Selection in Relation to Sex*. Princeton: Princeton University Press.

Darwin, Charles ([1872] 1965) *The Expression of the Emotions in Man and Animals*. Chicago: University of Chicago Press.

de Waal, Franz (1982) *Chimpanzee Politics: Power and Sex among the Apes*. New York: Harper Colophon Books.

Eberhard, William G. (1985) *Sexual Selection and Animal Genitalia*. Cambridge: Harvard University Press.

Eibl-Eibesfeldt, Irenaus (1972) "Similarities and differences between cultures in expressive movements." In *Non-verbal communication*, ed. R. A. Hinde. New York: Cambridge University Press.

Eibl-Eibesfeldt, Irenaus (1975) *Ethology*, 2d edn. New York: Holt, Rinehart and Winston.

Ekman, Paul (1978) "Facial expression." In *Nonverbal Behavior and Communication*, ed. Aron W. Siegman and Stanley Feldstein. Hillsdale, NJ: Lawrence Erlbaum.

Ekman, Paul (1989) "The argument and evidence about universals in facial expressions of emotion." In *Handbook of Social Psychophysiology*, ed. H. Wagner and A. Manstead. New York: John Wiley and Sons.

Ekman, Paul, W. V. Friesen, M. O'Sullivan, A. Chan, I. Diacoyanni-Tarlatzis, K. Heider, R. Krause, W. A. Le Compte, T. Pitcairn, P. E. Ricci-Bitti, K. R. Scherer, M. Tomita and A. Tzavaras (1987) "Universals and cultural differences in the judgements of facial expressions of emotion." *Journal of Personality and Social Psychology* 53: 712–17.

Enomoto, Tomas (1974). "The sexual behavior of Japanese monkeys." *Journal of Human Evolution* 3: 351–72.

Fausto-Sterling, Anne (1985), *Myths of Gender*. New York: Basic Books.

Fisher, Ronald A. (1958) *The Genetical Theory of Natural Selection*, 2d edn. New York: Dover.

Flax, Jane (1990). *Thinking Fragments*. Berkeley: University of California Press.

Ford, Clellan S. and Frank A. Beach (1951) *Patterns of Sexual Behavior*. New York: Harper Torchbooks.

Foucault, Michel (1980) *The History of Sexuality*, trans. Robert Hurley. New York: Vintage Books.

Foucault, Michel (1986). *The Use of Pleasure*, trans. Robert Hurley. New York: Vintage Books.

Foucault, Michel (1988) *The Care of the Self*, trans. Robert Hurley. New York: Vintage Books.

Goodall, Jane van Lawick. (1968) "The behaviour of free-living chimpanzees in the Gombe Stream Reserve." *Animal Behaviour Monographs* 1/3.

Gould, Carol C. (1983) "The woman question: philosophy of liberation and the liberation of philosophy." In *Philosophy of Woman*, ed. Mary B. Mahowald. Indianapolis: Hackett Publishing.

Gould, Stephen Jay and Richard Lewontin (1979) "The spandrels of San Marco and the Panglossian paradigm: a critique of the adaptationist programme." *Proceedings of the Royal Society of London*, Series B, Biological Science 205: 581–98.

Hall, K. R. L. (1960). "Social vigilance behaviour of the Chacma baboon (*Papio ursinus*)." *Behavior* 16: 261–94.

Hall, K. R. L. and Irven De Vore (1972). "Baboon social behavior." In *Primate patterns*, ed. Phyllis Dolhinow. New York: Holt, Rinehart and Winston.

Hanby, J. (1976) "Sociosexual development in primates." In *Perspectives* in *Ethology*, vol. 2, ed. P. P. G. Bateson and Peter H. Klopfer. New York: Plenum Press.

Haraway, Donna. (1985) "A manifesto for cyborgs: science, technology, and socialist feminism in the 1980s." *Socialist Review* 15(2): 65–107.

Haraway, Donna. (1988) "Situated knowledges: the science question in feminism and the privilege of partial perspective." *Feminist Studies* 14(3): 575–99.

Haraway, Donna. (1989) *Primate Visions*. New York: Routledge.

Harding, Sandra (1987) "The instability of the analytical categories." In *Sex and Scientific Inquiry*, ed. Sandra Harding and Jean F. O'Barr. Chicago: University of Chicago Press.

Hewes, Gordon W. (1955) "World distribution of certain postural habits." *American Anthropologist* (n.s.) 57(2): 231–44.

Hewes, Gordon W. (1957) "The anthropology of posture." *Scientific American* 196: 123–32.

Hubbard, Ruth (1990) *The Politics of Women's Biology*. New Brunswick: Rutgers University Press.

Husserl, Edmund (1970) *The Crisis of European Sciences and Transcendental Phenomenology*, trans. David Carr. Evanston: Northwestern University Press.

Husserl, Edmund (1973) *Cartesian Meditations*, trans. Dorion Cairns. The Hague: Nijhoff.

Husserl, Edmund (1980) *Ideas Pertaining to a Pure Phenomenology and to a Phenomenological Philosophy*. Third Book: *Phenomenology and the Foundations of the Sciences* (commonly known as *Ideas III*), trans. T. E. Klein and W. E. Pohl. Boston: Nijhoff.

Husserl, Edmund (1989) *Ideas Pertaining to a Pure Phenomenology and to a Phenomenological Philosophy*. Second Book: *Studies in the Phenomenology of Constitution* (commonly known as *Ideas II*), trans. R. Rojcewicz and A. Schuwer. Boston: Kluwer.

Jaggar, Alison M (1989) "Love and knowledge: emotion in feminist epistemology." In *Gender/Body/Knowledge*, ed. Alison M. Jaggar and Susan R. Bordo. New Brunswick: Rutgers University Press.

Jones, Ivor H. and Dorothy Frei (1979) "Exhibitionism: a biological hypothesis". *British Journal of Medical Psychology* 52: 63–70.

Jung, Carl G. (1960) *On the Nature of the Psyche*, trans. R. F. C. Hull. Bollingen Series 20. Princeton: Princeton University Press.

Jung, Carl G. (1976) *Psychological Types*, trans. R. F. C. Hull. Bollingen Series 20. Princeton: Princeton University Press.

Keller, Evelyn Fox (1987) "The gender/science system; or, Is sex to gender as nature is to science?" *Hypatia* 2(3): 37–49.

Kummer, Hans (1971) *Primate Societies*. Chicago: Aldine.

Lancaster, Jane B. (1975) *Primate Behavior and the Emergence of Human Culture*. New York: Holt, Rinehart and Winston.

Longino, Helen E. (1990). *Science as Social Knowledge*. Princeton: Princeton University Press.

Lorenz, Konrad. (1967) *On Aggression*, trans. Marjorie K, Wilson. New York: Bantam.

Lowe, Marion (1982) "Social bodies: the interaction of culture and women's biology." In *Biological Woman – the Convenient Myth*, ed. Ruth Hubbard, Mary Sue Henifer and Barbara Fried. Cambridge, MA: Schenkman.

McWhorter, Ladelle. (1989) "Culture or nature? The function of the term 'body' in the work of Michel Foucault." *Journal of Philosophy* 86(11): 608–14.

Mitchell, G. (1981) *Human Sex Differences: a Primatologist's Perspective*. New York: Van Nostrand Reinhold.

Napier, J. R. and P. H. Napier. (1985) *The Natural History of the Primates*. London: British Museum (Natural History).

Pierce, Christine (1975) "Philosophy (review essay)". *Signs* 1 (2): 487–503.

Ploog, D. W., J. Blitz, and F. Ploog (1963) "Studies on social and sexual behavior of the squirrel monkey (*Saimiri sciureus*)." *Folia primatologica* 1: 29–66.

Poovey, Mary (1988) "Feminism and deconstruction." *Feminist Studies* 14(1): 51–65.

Portmann, Adolf (1967.) *Animal Forms and Patterns*, trans. Hella Czech. New York: Schocken Books.

Rogers, C. M. (1973) "Implications of primate early rearing experiment for the concept of culture." In *Precultural Primate Behavior*, ed. Emil Menzel. Basel: Karger.

Sartre, Jean-Paul (1956.) *Being and Nothingness*, trans. Hazel Barnes. New York: Philosophical Library.

Sheets-Johnstone, Maxine (1990) *The Roots of Thinking*. Philadelphia: Temple University Press.

Sheets-Johnstone, Maxine (1993). *The Roots of Power: Animate Form and Gendered Bodies*. State University of New York Press.

Stoller, Robert J. (1976) "Sexual deviations." In *Human Sexuality in Four Perspectives*, ed. Frank A. Beach. Baltimore: Johns Hopkins University Press.

Sugiyama, Yukimaru. (1969) "Social behavior of chimpanzees in the Budongo Forest, Uganda." *Primates* 10: 197–225.

Symons, Donald (1979) *The Evolution of Human Sexuality*. Oxford: Oxford University Press.

Theweleit, Klaus (1987) *Male Fantasies*. Minneapolis: University of Minnesota Press.

Washburn, Sherwood L. (1950) "The analysis of primate evolution with particular reference to the origin of man." *Cold Spring Harbor Symposia on Quantitative Biology* 15: 57–78.

Wickler, Wolfgang (1969) "Sociosexual signals and their intra-specific imitation among primates." In *Primate Ethology*, ed. Desmond Morris. Garden City, NY: Anchor Books.

# 9

# Affectivity and Eros

## Affectivity, Eros and the Body*

### *Donn Welton*

*I realized today in an impressive though confused way that the reality of bodies is and only can be a reality of interposition; bodies are mutually interposed or interpose themselves. The function of the body is at one and the same time to bind together and to separate.*

Gabriel Marcel, May 14, 1916[1]

If the importance of Husserl's theory of mental acts and intentionality, the richest find of his earlier writings through *Ideas I* (1913),[2] was immediately recognized and mined by his contemporaries,[3] it is no less true that his notion of the body, which almost takes shape behind his back in the manuscripts we now call *Ideas II* (first draft, 1912–15),[4] is one whose potential we have only begun to explore.[5] Merleau–Ponty was the first who knew what to do with it.[6] So masterful was his appropriation of the notion that philosophers working after him found only slag, considered the quarry exhausted, and turned it over to the psychologists, who, of course, knew better than to believe the philosopher. Even here, though, it was those phenomenological psychologists who were oriented to descriptive, experimental results who found the notion most useful, especially in their theories of perception; the psychoanalysts, captivated by Heidegger's 1928 analysis of *Dasein*,[7] were anxious to guard their domain from biological intrusions and kept even Paul Schilder's 1923 attempt[8] to integrate body and ego analysis at arm's length. But the movement of thought, in particular the search for an appropriate notion of embodiment by feminist thinkers, has sent both philosophers and psychologists scurrying back to that same mine. Now we realize that the rich vein Merleau-Ponty worked leads to yet another, one that we did not see – perhaps, could not see – simply because we kept digging along the original seam. And now we suspect that this vein is not one but two, involving a structural difference between masculine and feminine embodiment.

In this paper I will be concerned with the relationship between affectivity and the body in general only to the extent that it sheds light on the question of eros and the body in particular. But we have a question, at the outset, of whether it is even appropriate to tether the notion of eros to that of the body. I will approach this by examining whether the first formulations of the notion of lived-body, designed to

* A first draft of this paper was included as a conference paper in *Phenomenology: Past and Future*, The Thirteenth Annual Symposium of the Simon Silverman Phenomenology Center (Pittsburg: The Simon Silverman Phenomenology Center, Duquesne University, 1996), pp. 55–98.

provide a notion of embodiment supporting cognition, can be applied to the question of affects and feelings.

The first section of this paper will take its bearing from Husserl's concept of the lived-body but, in order to save space, will not go into its analysis here.[9] I will assume that the essays by Drew Leder, Shaun Gallagher, and Jonathan Cole in this volume have provided the reader with an introduction to this important notion, as I then go on and make a point about a limitation of the concept in Husserl and, to some extent, Merleau-Ponty. I will suggest that the fundamental defect in the early phenomenological concept of the body is that while it does provide a bridge between the morphology of the body and the domain of feeling, it fails to cross over and recast its notion of the body in terms of its desires. It has what might be called a "perceptual" body but not a "pathetic" body.

As a gateway to an account of affections in relation to the body, the second section looks at Freud's attempt to relate eros, the body and the ego, chiding him for mixing a biological with a quasi-phenomenological description of the body, for treating the need for affection (love) as a biologically configured, instinctual drive (his version of eros), and for severing the quality of affects and the body, thus reducing the body to a set of zones, a site, in which the struggle between blind libidinal wishes and the rule of the Father takes place. I also raise the question of whether inscription theories of gender difference rely on a notion of the body identical to Freud's.

A basic flaw in Freud's account that we must be careful not to carry into our own is his confusion between drives, affects and emotions. In the third section I will attempt to sketch the difference between needs, desires and emotions, and then suggest that in early infancy the child lacks emotions, i.e. its feelings have not yet developed into emotions. Since emotions, I will suggest, are clearly intentional or have a necessary relationship to intentional acts, feelings can be construed as preintentional. I will then probe the notions of need and desire. This then allows us to return to the notion of the body and further explore its role in the differentiation of need and the desire for affection.

Since I am interested in looking at the tie between the lived-body, affectivity and affection and then in seeing the connection between affection and gender identity, I turn to a version of object-relations theory that is both phenomenological and interpretative in its approach, to the ground-breaking work of Nancy Chodorow. The powerful insight controlling her theory is the idea that the young child's sense of its gender (either masculine or feminine) is neither biologically determined nor a cultural idea learned at the level of symbolic interaction, a socially defined concept that it "internalizes." Rather gender identity and difference is developed at the level of "feeling" and involves "the quality of affect in a relationship";[10] it arises by age two or three within a triangulated field of involvement between child, mother, and father. Or if we still insist on speaking of internalizations, we must say that "the earliest internalizations are preverbal and experienced in a largely somatic manner."[11] It is an affective construction, one at play in the deepest psychosomatic dimensions of family interactions "before" what we usually call social learning comes into play for the child. The fourth section will be interested, then, in seeing how the body and affects are understood by her theory. Is she able to connect desire and the body internally? Does she take us beyond the ambivalent stance Freud takes to the body? Or is this a place where her own theory needs to be supplemented by a theory of the body? We will conclude by asking if there are any implications of our approach for the issue of gender identity.

This paper also has a secondary motif, one that lingers about its margins. It will not be directly discussed but frames the logic of our analysis. With the 1900 publication of Freud's *Interpretation of Dreams*,[12] psychology became firmly divided between an experimental or empirical method and a more interpretative or psycho-analytic mode of psychological investigation. Even in the phenomenological reinter-pretations of psychology, this tension persists. I am convinced that an investigation of this tension would find its conceptual and perhaps its historical roots in the difference between Husserl's notion of intentionality and Heidegger's category of *Dasein*, and the way that one or the other was taken as foundational by different investigators. While neither the experimental nor the interpretative approach used a naive theory of the body, and while both were informed by Scheler's, Husserl's, and Heidegger's understanding of it as lived-body, they both tended to start with consciousness or being-in-the-world and approach the body "from the top down." In this paper I am taking the opposite tack by reconsidering what is meant by the body and then using it as our point of entry to the concept of the mind or the psyche. Perhaps understanding the movement from body-image to flesh and inte-grating the notion of affectivity into that of the lived-body might display a possible way of reconciling or at least rectifying a descriptive with an interpretative account within the domain that belongs to a phenomenology of the body.[13]

## The body and affectivity

Apprehending the "manifestation," the "expression" of conscious acts and episodes is already mediated by the apprehension of the lived-body as lived-body.

(Husserl, 1913)[14]

Clearly the body possesses a physicality that it shares with the rest of the material world. We can poke and prod it at will, measure its weight and meter its fluids, lift and whirl it about. It seems to be as much an object as anything else we can take in hand or perceive by our senses. At the same time, bodies are not merely buffeted about by the winds and drenched in waters, but move on their own and are "animated." Should that body we are experiencing be *mine*, should that body be the one whose movements are *my* movements, whose injury I know as *my* pain, then the body seems to belong much more to the category of the subject than the object, or, even more unsettling, to be suspended precariously between them both. We sense this of our own body but also of bodies that approach us and, on dark nights, threaten us. They, too, seem to stand apart from other physical things.

Descartes was convinced that one could make a distinction between a dead and a living body but for him this was due only to the presence of yet another physical element, motion, which the corpse does not have:

And let us recognize that the difference between the body of a living man and that of a dead man is just like the difference between, on the one hand, a watch or other automation (that is, a self-moving machine) when it is wound up and contains in itself the corporeal principle of the movements for which it is designed, together with everything else required for its operation; and, on the other hand, the same watch or machine when it is broken and the principle of its movement ceases to be active.[15]

But phenomenology would place this type of movement, which Descartes under-stands in physical and causal terms, within his neurophysiological account of the body and thus situate both at a level different from the one in which we "live" our body. The body as we are directly acquainted with it, as it forms the center and the source of our actions, factors in our experience in a way very different from a self-moving machine. In an effort to capture this difference Husserl introduces his celebrated distinction between *Körper* and *Leib*, between physical body and lived-body, between the body under an objectifying scientific description and the body under an experiential description.

This difference immediately renders problematic what philosophy and psychology took to be the self-evident term in their attempts to unravel the relationship between body and mind, between affectivity and personhood. Introducing it requires us to rethink the very notion of the body itself "before" we turn our attention to the psyche. In so doing it places the issue on new ground and challenges our standard approaches to the question of the person.

The genius of the phenomenological notion of the lived-body is that it generates the notion of the body from the *experiencing* body. Its morphology arises not just because the infant becomes acquainted with the "image" of its body (seeing/seen/seeing) but, even more basic, with its felt surfaces (touching/touched/touching). With the lived-body phenomenology discovers a hidden ground, an unsynthesizable field of significance, that accounts for the *incarnation* of thought; it shows how cognition finds its roots in that which cannot be enclosed within the circle of its own reflections.

But such a great gain came at a cost. While this would have to be qualified in any number of ways, the primary deficiency of the phenomenological notion of the body is that it was not able to do justice to the elusive domain of feelings, to the passions, to what Freud during this same time would put forth as the problem of eros. The account of affectivity centered about a dispute as to the nature of a transcendental esthetic, and thus was circumscribed by the concerns of epistemology. We do have the body in an experiential register. But it has not yet been caught up in the conflict of desires, not yet burdened by its own passions. I will call this the question of affectivity.

We are attempting to press further. Since there is an interplay of surfaces before there is a body-ego and before there is any distinction between its "own" body and the mother's breast, we can suggest that touch roots the irreducible *presencing* of the body to itself in the *relation* of the body to that of the mother.[16] Furthermore, recognizing that this initial connection is established by touch means that it is not "cognitive" but "affective." But how can we go from here to a full and rich account of affectivity? How can we draw the desire for love into this analysis?

These questions provide our handling of the body with focus, for in this paper my interest is to show the relevance of the concept of the lived-body neither to an understanding of the processes of cognition,[17] nor to an account of lived-space,[18] nor to an understanding of the structure of feminine intentionality nested in women's actions and movements in space,[19] but to envision how the lived-body functions in what can be broadly construed as a phenomenological psychoanalytic account of affection, one of the most underdeveloped areas of study today. If I am correct, this issue can be approached only through an analysis that internally connects the morphology of the body with the deployment of affects. In other words, we must develop a notion of the body that attends not only to its shapes and surfaces, its schemes of ingression and egression, but also to its rhythms, vapors, and fluids, to the play of active and reactive forces, and then to its role in the configuration of affects in general and affection in particular. In short, we need to deepen our characterization of the lived-body by a notion of the *flesh*.

## Eros and body-ego

The problem of the quality of instinctual impulses and of its persistence throughout their various vicissitudes is still very obscure and has hardly been attacked up to the present.                                                          (Sigmund Freud, 1923)[20]

Attempting to connect the notion of the lived-body with that of eros sends us back to the work of Freud. But in order to situate his theory of affection we must begin with a pair of concepts, the notions of "basic trust" and "basic fault," that are central to object relations theory. These notions characterize the underlying, *global* emotional sense a child and then an adult has of itself. As such they enframe the way *particular* stages of development and different interactive scenes will run their course.

Basic trust or fault originates in the earliest stages of a child's development, even before it differentiates itself from its mother. It produces an underlying, general manner of framing experiences "whose influence extends widely, probably over the whole psycho-biological structure of the individual, involving in varying degrees both his mind and his body."[21] It arises from the felt or lived quality of the care given the small child by its caregiver. With the absence of overwhelming anxiety and the presence of continuity, the child develops basic trust, which comes to constitute "reflexively a core beginning of self or identity."[22] When there is some major discrepancy in the early phases between needs and both physical and psychological care, the child develops basic fault, "an all-pervasive sense, sustained by enormous anxiety, that something is not right, is lacking in her or him."[23] While all of this originates in a "preverbal period before the infant is self-consciously social,"[24] it is still the actions of the caregiver and the quality of her/his involvement with the child that "condition the growth of the self and the infant's basic emotional self-image (sense of goodness or badness, all-rightness or wrong-ness),"[25] and that exert, in the words of Anna Freud, "a selective growth of some, and hold back, or fail to stimulate and libidinalize, the growth of other potential-ities."[26] This determines "certain basic trends" in the development of the child, affecting even its motility.

### *The reduction to eros*

But how is one to characterize the most basic of desires whose satisfaction produces a sense of basic trust? What is this elusive need that is consolidated as it is satisfied by the caring parent? Freud called it eros, which he first attempted to characterize as a distinct type of biological, instinctual drive, sexual in nature (*Geschlechtstrieb*), governed by the pleasure principle, by the need to resolve felt tension; and then, in the face of difficulties surrounding what is meant by pleasure, described it as a level of erotic desire that is articulated by the interplay of its bodily zones, objects, and aims. This shift, I will suggest, introduced a change in his characterization of the body and of its relationship to psychic life, and realigns its role in our understanding of eros.

We are immediately struck with the difficulties Freud encountered when he attempts to specify the nature of eros in his famous 1905 *Three Essays on the Theory of Sexuality*. On the one hand, hunger is viewed as the prototype of the need for affection and, perhaps, its satisfaction as what generates the first site of erotic pleasure:

The child's lips, in our view, behave like an erotogenic zone, and no doubt stimulation
by the warm flow of milk is the cause of the pleasurable sensation. The satisfaction of
the erotogenic zone is associated, in the first instance, with the satisfaction of the need
for nourishment...No one who has seen a baby sinking back satiated from the breast
and falling asleep with flushed cheeks and a blissful smile can escape the reflection that
this picture persists as a prototype [*maßgebend bleibt*] of the expression of sexual
satisfaction in later life.[27]

At the same time, Freud recognizes that there is a sensual thumb sucking whose
purpose, obviously, is not connected to taking in nourishment. It leads to sleep or
"to a motor reaction in the nature of an organism."[28] And it is this, he claims, that is
the prototype (*Muster*) of infantile sexual expression. The separation of sensual
sucking from nutritional sucking sends Freud looking for different principles to
explain its motives. While the need for nourishment or self-preservation is what
governs nutritional sucking, the independence of sensuous sucking is due to the fact
that it becomes dominated by the pursuit of pleasure alone. More accurately, one of
the component elements of nutritional sucking, the pleasure that accompanies and
produces satiation, separates itself from others, reorganizes the activity of sucking
under it, and seems simultaneously to create a psychological need or desire for it.
The fact that satisfaction comes largely from the subject's own body[29] leads Freud to
speak of it as autoerotic.

But Freud quickly recognizes that the notion of pleasure alone, understood as a
resolution of bio-physical tension, is not restrictive enough to allow him to characterize this underlying need or drive as sexual, the cornerstone of his theory. He
struggles in the *Three Essays* to find a principle of differentiation and attempts to
locate it in the nature of the stimuli themselves. An erotogenic zone, he claims, is a
part of the body in which "stimuli of a certain sort evoke a sensation of pleasure of a
determinate quality."[30] The stimuli producing the pleasure, he adds, are governed
by "special conditions," but he admits to not knowing what they are. And this is
followed by yet a more serious doubt:

it seems less certain whether the character of the pleasurable sensation evoked by the
stimulus should be described as a "specific" one – a specific quality in which the sexual
moment would be contained precisely.[31]

The effort to find a qualitative differentiation within the notion of pleasure, one that
would allow us to set erotic off from other types of sensations, then, fails. But this is
more than a minor inconsistency in Freud's account. It means that the notion of
pleasure, controlled, as it was, in the case of ingestion by yet other features of the
experience and a biological mandate, cannot be directly transferred to the notion of
basic infantile needs, which is what Freud must have if he is to call it erotic.

What Freud was attempting in the *Three Essays* was to move from a certain
qualitative property located in the sensations themselves to an understanding of
erotogenic zones or parts of the body. While Freud held that certain zones are
disposed or "predestined"[32] in this way – to the point where the pattern of zones
(oral, anal, genital) is universal – the zones seem to be no more than sites, giving eros
its particular developmental form but contributing nothing to the quality of the
sensations: "any other part of the skin or mucous membrane can take over the
functions of an erotogenic zone," he tells us.[33] It is only the cathexis of a certain
part or surface of the body by this class of sensations, sexual in themselves, that
eroticizes it:

> The erotogenic property can be attached to individual places on the body in a particularly marked way ... The quality of the stimulus has more to do with producing the pleasurable feeling than has the nature of the place on the body.[34]

Since the quality of eros is independent of its "locations" (*Stellen*) on the body, and since the body is understood only as a physical organism consisting of places or zones possessing a "susceptibility to stimulation" (*Reizbarkeit*),[35] it is not surprising, then, to see Freud's description of eros using quantitative notions, such as "energy," "force," and "flow," and neuro-biological images, such as "drive," "impulse," and "intensity." Even though he clearly distinguishes, say, between nutritional sucking and sensuous sucking, initially the latter is "attached to" the former, only becoming distinguished later. Since erotic drives are "anaclitic,"[36] their force reduces to a certain qualification of needs and drives biological in nature.

Given these parameters, Freud has no choice but to identify the need for affection (*Zärtlichkeit*), as it factors into the notion of basic trust, with sexual love. And this produces a very specific characterization of affection:

1  Affection is treated as a "drive." Analogous to the way hunger is a drive whose object is food and whose aim is eating or sucking, so affection can be thought of only as a need whose object is the mouth and whose aim is its stimulation and, thereby, the satisfaction of the drive (to stay with the oral stage). Since this maps directly onto adult life, Freud feels justified in positing an "identity" between affection and sexual love.[37]

2  He treats affection as what can submit to direct excitation. Neurophysical tension is what produces our awareness of the need. Its resolution involves a pattern of stimulation that is applied directly to the body. As a result it is the release of neurophysical tension that comes with satiation that "remains the measure" of how we are to conceptualize eros proper.[38] By a "reflection that cannot be escaped" (*der wird sich sagen müssen*), but actually by a questionable transference of signified back to its signifier, of the type back to the prototype, that first desire of the child is also specified as sexual.

3  He undervalues the relational dimension of affection by turning object into aim, by assuming that the object to which affection is related is controlled by the aim of stimulating one's own body. This yields a particular result: whatever we mean by affection must fit the pattern of what is autoerotic. This, in fact, is what gives Freud his notion of primary narcissism. The initial stage of primary narcissism is where a difference between the process of experiencing and the object experienced emerges, having been fused to that point, but it is organized in such a way that the one experiencing and the one experienced are the same: the zones of the body, which are the sites giving rise to desire, are also the objects whose stimulation and satisfaction produce the reduction of tension. This level of primary need can be understood only as what is capable of being met by self-stimulation, by playing with oneself, in short, by masturbation.

4  The level of "global" needs, which generally frame and motivate particular needs, are restricted to biological mandates. Hunger is a drive based in self-preservation. Affection, given this restriction, can only be related to the need to procreate. Affection becomes eros due to the teleological organization of it by instinct.

This leads us to ask, then, whether the identification of affection and eros, this most basic of all of Freud's discoveries, is a methodologically induced extrapolation, one resulting from the fact that psychoanalysis transposes an account of drives into a characterization of desires, excitations into affection, autoeroticism into love. We are doing more than engaging in yet another form of "infantile amnesia"[39] to question it.

Freud's first account leaves us, then, with a contrast between the level of physical-biological need and the level of psychological need. But his identification of the need for affection with eros means that he understands the level of psychological as "anaclitic" and thus as derived from the biological. His corresponding notion of the body, which is treated only as a physical organism, cannot be used to correct the account or to mediate the two levels of description.[40]

While it is not easy to locate this shift in one place, Freud seems to move away from this earlier model and, in its place, introduce a notion of erotic desire characterized not by the quality of sensation but by the interplay of zones, objects, and aims. Or to turn this another way, it is the deployment of desire across the surfaces of the body that constitutes the quality of eros. And the result of this, I want to suggest now, is to push his account toward a second notion of the body and, at the same time, to discover its internal tie to the notion of the (development of) ego. To get at this we must see how Freud's later work connects his notion of the ego to that of the body, and then handles the idea of eros.

One could construe this shift as a natural consequence of searching for the erotogenic property or quality of desire. Simply introducing the pleasure principle will not do, for we find pleasure in countless ways that have nothing to do with eros. Even for Freud, not all pleasure is erotic, and, as he came to recognize quite early, not all eros is pleasurable. The pleasure principle, used as a way of specifying a single set of sensations, could never be sufficient to explain the quality of eros. Freud moves, as he entitled one of his books, beyond the pleasure principle.[41]

## *The body-ego*

*The Ego and the Id*, one of Freud's last theoretical works published almost two decades (1923) after the *Three Essays*, breaks with his earlier characterization of the ego as that system in the psyche that is descriptively conscious and dynamically repressing, which Freud then set in opposition to the unconscious system of the psyche housing what is dynamically repressed. The ego, he realizes, includes both what is conscious – perceptions, control of movement, overseeing its own processes – and what is unconscious – repressions of certain trends from the mind, resistance to approaching repressed materials, self-criticism, and certain ego-instincts (self-preservation in particular). "A part of the ego, too, . . . may be *Ucs.*, undoubtedly is *Ucs.*"[42] Since the ego includes both what is conscious as well as what is unconscious, we can no longer identify it with the conscious. We are forced to rethink its organization as a system. Indeed, we now have to rethink what is meant by the very notion of consciousness itself.

Freud, returning to an approach first tried in his *Interpretation of Dreams*,[43] decides to use external and internal perceptions as his point of entry to what he means by consciousness and, thereby, the ego:

> What consciousness yields consists essentially of perceptions of excitations coming from the external world and of feelings of pleasure and unpleasure which can only arise from within the mental apparatus.[44]

Consciousness is best understood, he now suggests, not as an agent but as a descriptive quality of mental states. By setting it in contrast to what is (descriptively) preconscious – which is marginal or latent at the moment but open to being attended to – and what is (descriptively) unconscious – which, for a variety of reasons, lies beyond what we can recall or attend to – Freud can distinguish between percepts, thoughts and feelings, and use this to move to a characterization of the mind in terms of different systems (ego, superego, and id).

Percepts are simply presentations of external objects or events and we are aware of them directly. It makes no sense, Freud believes, to speak of unconscious perceptions, though to the extent that memory is a part of perception, what is preconscious must also be in play. By contrast, ideas or thoughts are, in themselves, unconscious. Only when they are wedded to a "word-presentation" can they be part of the same system (which is conscious but can also include the preconscious). This means, in effect, that "apart from feelings" any thought arising from within becomes conscious much like an external perception, i.e. by the interposition of signs "internal thought-processes are made into perceptions."[45] This leads to the crucial difference between thoughts and feelings or sensations of pleasure and pain: feelings, like thoughts, can be unconscious but they do not require the intervention of signs to enter into the preconscious or to become conscious. Where we do become "directly" aware of them, it results largely from them crossing certain quantitative thresholds, usually in a situation where resistance has been overcome.[46]

This allows Freud to move into a new theory of the systems of the psyche in general, and of the ego in particular. Perceptual consciousness and the preconscious form the nucleus of the ego as a system.[47] As a partially enveloping cortex, somewhat like the painted top of an egg, it rests upon and even "extends" into "unconscious feelings" and desires, which now form a system of its own, which Freud labels the "id."[48]

Since it is the notion of conscious awareness across a variety of perceptual experiences relating us to the world that provides the point of entry to what Freud means by the ego, Freud is immediately led to think of it in terms of its spatiality. If the ego registers stimuli coming from "without," it must be possible to assign to it "a position in space."[49] He describes it as "a system which is spatially the first one reached from the external world."[50] Consciousness, he argues, must be the *surface* of the id[51] or, better, the surface of "the mental apparatus."[52] It has, therefore, an "extension of surface differentiation" and lies "on the borderline between outside and inside."[53] At first he identifies this surface as the cerebral cortex, and even flirts with the notion of the "cortical homunculus"[54] – an image of the body projected upon the brain according to the distribution of affected brain regions – to explain the sense in which the ego is extended. But he also presses beyond this and roots this spatialized ego in the surface of the body itself:

> The ego is ultimately derived from bodily sensations, chiefly from those springing from the surface of the body. It may thus be regarded as a mental projection of the surface of the body; besides ... representing the superficies of the mental apparatus.[55]

This description of the body (which the ego, at this level, *is*) is different from his earlier treatment and we find him employing a notion much closer to the lived-body. He even argues that the perceptual modality that gives me access to its special character is not sight but touch: "[A person's own body] is *seen* like any other object, but to the *touch* it yields two kinds of sensations, one of which may be equivalent to an internal perception."[56] The doubling of sensation, of a touched that is also touching, as well as the experience of bodily, pain is what gives the body its "special position among the other objects in the world of perception"[57] and, at this level, gives us access to the "surface" of the ego. "The ego is first and foremost a bodily ego; it is not merely a surface entity, but is itself the projection of a surface."[58] Since perceptual consciousness is what is deployed across the body and since perceptual consciousness first specifies what is meant by the ego, Freud understands this body as the system forming the "nucleus" of the ego.[59]

Before we press further and turn to the issue of affectivity proper, we must pause to note an important outcome of this notion of the body-ego. The development of a theory of the ego (and its character) in Freud's later theory produces a much deeper sensitivity to object-relational issues in the development of personality. Melancholia, for example, results from replacing a lost (love) object, cathected by erotic desires stemming from the id, by an "identification" in which what has been lost is set up inside the ego.[60] Significantly, Freud recognizes that in the first stage of development, the oral, object-cathexis and identification are "indistinguishable from each other."[61] Experientially there is no contrast between inside and outside, between the autoerotic and the aleoerotic production of pleasure, and, finally, between the deployment of erotic desires coming from within and the excitation of the surfaces of the body coming from without. Only as the result of ongoing experience does the ego come to distinguish itself simultaneously from the id – with desires that it, reins in hand, must ride – and from the body – which it must now direct along courses of action – and from the ego of the other – that ambivalent source of both love and law.

With a much more developed notion of the ego, Freud is better able to account for the formation of a particular personality. A person's character is a "precipitate" of abandoned object-cathexes that it conserves through identification, and it "contains the history of those object-choices."[62] This opens upon Chodorow's thesis that in the first stage of primary identification, where there is no perceived difference between self and other, the quality of the relationship to others establishes a framework in which a child's character is developed. As Freud puts it, the first relationship to the parents is a "direct and immediate identification" that takes place "earlier than any object-cathexis."[63]

All of this points not only to a second notion of the body in Freud, one that helps ground his later concern with the ego and its development, but also suggests a key to what potentially could be a different concept of eros for Freud. The dynamics of touching and touch, distributed across not only the body's touching of itself but also its being touched by another, and then the "projection" of the ego that arises from the interplay of the surfaces of the body with the environment in which it is situated, gives us a way of accounting for a form of (self) consciousness before there is a self. It provides a level of constitution that is pre-egological at the same time that it promises to yield an internal connection between the body, our first relationship to a caregiver, and the development of the ego; now the quality of the relationship to the other, as it is both configured by and distributed across the perceptual systems and surfaces of the body, becomes the field from which the ego arises. In short, it allows Freud to finally make a distinction between primary and secondary narcissism. Apart from our concern to separate the need for affection from eros, this second notion of the body also holds out possibilities for his characterization of eros. Rather than viewing eros as a certain set of sensations, internally organized by an erotic quality, that attach themselves to yet other (biological) drives and become associated with different zones of the body, it promises a much more relational notion of eros, one that, in fact, may break it apart as a single instinct.[64] Perhaps its quality is not a feature of isolatable sensations but is internally tied to the intertwining of zones, objects, and aims and to the way in which their organization articulates the relation we have to others at the level of desire.

Freud, ultimately, did not take this path. Rather his later work, increasingly speculative, only deepened his reliance on the notion of instinct, diversifying his one basic instinct into two, eros and thanatos, and even escalating them into a cosmology.[65] Freud's late theory does connect ego and body as well as character (understood as the precipitate of history of object-choices) and the "style" of bodily action (habitual body). And this would mean that to the extent that a particular desire is the product of the interplay between lived-body, object-choices, identifications and basic needs, he can account for it. But what he cannot connect is the configuration of basic needs or what he calls instincts and the body or, for that matter, the ego. And this means that he cannot tie the quality of eros as a distinct affect to the body, to the flesh. The body is only the field in which eros plays out its war with culture, i.e. the ego, like the body at this level, "behaves essentially passively in life," and "we are 'lived' by unknown and uncontrollable forces."[66] In fact, his efforts to understand eros in terms of its "energy" drive him further from that connection, for it argues that the libido put at the disposal of the ego (and which presumably fuels its systems) is a "desexualized eros."

The consequence of this for Freud is that he effectively eliminates the body (the body-ego), the lived-body, from the production of gender, i.e. it is only as its features and zones become imbued with a meaning that arises in the conflict between instinct and the law of the father that it becomes integrated into the construction of gender. Gender identity, as it involves the body, can be understood only as the question of how we move from a masculine or feminine instinctual *predisposition* located in the id to the development of the masculine or feminine sexual *disposition* of the ego (and thus to its schematization in the body). The outcome of the oedipal complex, Freud says, "may be taken to be the forming of a precipitate in the ego, consisting of these two identifications in some way united with each other."[67] But this means that whatever gender differences it comes to exhibit are the result of inscription. In itself it is little more than a site, a blank tablet, which is to say that it is not productive, does not possess a morphology of its own that in some way controls the constitution of gender identity.

## Needs, desires and the body

Joy and sadness are not in the heart like blood is in the heart, sensations of touch are not in the skin like bits of its organic tissue. . . .                    Husserl (1910/11)[68]

Our discussion of Freud has made all the more urgent a phenomenology of affection that connects it to the notion of the body that we have developed thus far, and then to a plausible description of psychological development. We will not attempt to sketch a comprehensive theory of affects but only introduce those related notions needed to unfold the structure of affection. Given the scope of this paper, I can only hope to construct "adductively" a plausible model. The task of securing my speculations would need much more than I can provide here.

## *Needs, demands and the body*

Hunger and thirst, we can readily agree, are felt as needs. Given their importance for our survival, we can even characterize them as basic needs. However, Harlow's famous experiment in which hungry, infant monkeys chose a terry cloth puppet without a bottle over a wire mesh puppet with a bottle,[69] as well as the presence in breast-feeding behavior of a sensuous sucking that goes on well after the nutritional needs of the infant are met, allow us to suggest that there are inborn needs that cannot be reduced to bio-physical ones. Not only human infants but other animals as well exhibit patterns of behavior that are independent of the need for food and that are interactive in nature. Bowlby has argued for a "primary object clinging" theory:

> There is in infants an in-built propensity to be in touch with and to cling to a human being. In this sense there is a "need" for an object independent of food which is as primary as the "need" for food and warmth.[70]

While Freud takes infantile sexuality as modeled on the need for nourishment, this experimental work begins to point to yet another cluster of desires, to the need for *affection*, and to what is, perhaps, more global and suffusive than what Freud called eros. In addition to Freud's physiologically based drives that operate according to the pleasure principle, drawn beyond the infant's own body to the mother's breast only because of the physical need for food (ego's self-preservation instinct), we may have basic demands that cluster around what is a need for enveloping warmth and care. If so, this secures a social relationality to affectivity as a feature of its structure. The problem with Freud positing libido or sexual drive as primary is that he confused one component of infantile lived-body life with the whole, or, to put it more accurately, he assumed that this one drive is primary and the basis of all the others. To use his own term, perhaps it is eros that is anaclitic on affection and not simply identical with it.

Saying that the relationship of affection to the caregiver is the prototype of all later adult sexuality is not to thereby characterize affection as eros. We refuse to identify them at the outset and without further justification. And this allows us to approach the question of childhood sexuality in a new light: perhaps the eroticiza-tion of the need for affection by small children is itself a product of broken relations, of the chill of neglect, and, in the worst cases, of abuse. Or even if we take eros as a component of infantile affectivity (and not the one drive or the basis of all the others), then it would prevail or become the most important largely as the result of a disruption of stable and healthy parent–child relations. Perhaps the loss of "basic trust" and the sense of "basic fault" is what swells its river beds and causes eros to dominate in the development of a child. When Freud, in rejecting his own earlier theory, decided that scenes of seduction, reported in memory and discovered through the interpretation of dreams, are not real but the product of imagination, he lost that connection to the quality of relationships that might have eventually forced him to see infantile eros as produced, as a qualitative transformation of affection rather than its substance.

We must, I am suggesting, speak of a plurality of basic needs and should not assume that one is more primitive, with others deriving their force by virtue of being attached to it. Particularly important for our purposes, the bio-physical need for heat and nutrition must not be confused with the need for warmth and affection, nor must we assume, as did Freud, that the latter can be directly identified with eros.

But where do we "place" basic needs, whether they be hunger or affection? Freud himself views them as physical, bodily drives, ultimately related to biological instincts, which simultaneously belong to the primary processes of consciousness. But perhaps the need for affection, first of all, is a complex belonging to a different order, to the lived-body with which we are directly and experientially acquainted.[71] No doubt, such needs are sensed but this does not entail that they are mental episodes, if that means locating them in a stream of consciousness distinct from the body and disassociating their structure from systems of bodily exchanges and actions. No doubt, basic needs are the result of complex biological and neurological processes, but that does not make them identical to those processes per se. Neurotransmitters producing the sense of hunger are not themselves hungry; the regions of the cortex associated with affection are not themselves in love. The connection between the lived-body and the biological, physiological, and neurological systems of the organic body can be understood causally provided that we treat needs as "macro" features produced by complex neurophysiological "micro" processes and states of the physical body, and then add the further claim that such macro features forming the lived-body are realized only in the organic body, thus avoiding a dualism of lived- and organic body.[72] This model suggests that the relationship between them is more puzzling than between flying and the material and causal properties of an airplane.

Connecting needs and the body, on this model, should not be understood as filling Descartes's corpse with motion, for it involves a system of organization that is different from that of the physical body. This is the basis of my suggestion that basic needs are not physical impulses, then registered by consciousness, but rather that basic needs are complex affective structures that are deployed across the surfaces and actions of the lived-body. At the same time they are also different from what we usually mean by mental acts. Notice that hunger can exist just as a need, without being hunger *for* a particular substance or for a particular type of food. The need for affection, as well, can be sensed without it being structured as affection-for, even less as consciousness-of. Still, they are not simply "reactive" states of the body, such as the feelings of relaxation or boredom. They are "proactive" and send us looking beyond the body, even if we do not know for what. Needs create *demands*.

In very young infants demands are simply cries with neither a subject from which they are emanating nor an object to which they are addressed. Only when they are satisfied in a certain way do they return to structure needs, which for their part take on increasing specificity to certain types of fulfillment. At the same time satisfaction seems to enlarge needs beyond their initial boundaries. The warmth of the terry cloth puppet does serve to specify the need for affection but then it becomes increasingly uninteresting to the baby monkey. Something more is required.

## Desires and the body

In the ongoing cycles of need, demand, and satisfaction, demands are only partially met, sometimes going unfulfilled. Often they encounter frustrations and delays. As a result, a gap develops in which substitutions and deferred objects begin to play a role. The pacifier makes its appearance or the child turns to surrogates, even images, to which it can relate. With this change, for reasons we will explore in a moment, need is (re)configured as desire.[73]

We must pause to foreclose a possible misunderstanding. Desires – and, even less so, needs and demands – should not be identified with emotions, at least not in the

sense in which we apply that term to adults. While they are clearly a part of the
process in which emotions arise, desires and their vicissitudes function as "setting
conditions" for the configuring and development of emotions.[74] If we speak of
emotions – such as anger, curiosity, fear, and even wanting – as intentional in the
sense that they are directed to or, at least, related to an object or specifiable complex,
then desires, by contrast, are "preintentional" in that they configure the background
against which such objects take on their affective valences and values.

Desires, we have seen, arise in the gap between needs and demands more or less
satisfied. In this gap, which we now want to examine, substitutions and deferred
objects begin to play a role. But how are we to understand these dynamics?

One could argue that metonymy enters, and with it the first difference between
signifier and signified. One item comes to stand for another and thus becomes a
sign. The introduction of signs and signification at the level of the imaginary could
then explain the structure of desire. Since the signs are themselves produced by the
culture and thus embody relations of power, we can understand the way in which
desire is constructed socially and the way in which the level of bodily organization is
a social product. In Nietzsche's words, "our body is but a social structure composed
of many souls."[75] In principle this approach is embraced by strong social inscription
theories. But is this how desire is configured? Do we already have language with
encoded social relations in play at this level?

There is, first of all, a problem in the way the analysis is set up. Freud views early
childhood experiences as largely conflictual, as full of tension and frustration. While
psychologists spend a good part of their waking life dealing with people for whom
this is quite true, and while the currents of our times may be sweeping us ever
further in this direction, there is no essential reason why this is the case. In fact,
early childhood experience is often the opposite, or, at least, ranges between times of
harmony and frustration. Initially desire is configured not so much by the difference
from the mother but by merging with her. Indeed, we know of countless situations
in which it is precisely the lack of a gap that prevails, where it is not absence but
suffocating presence, not difference but fusion that becomes the problem. Object-
relations theory understands this point far better than Freud.

But, second, even if we think only in terms of a gap, of a lack of satisfaction, I do
not think that we should immediately characterize this difference semiotically.
Associations and substitutions need not be construed as significations, at least not
at this early stage of development, not in attempting to understand that level of
desire that enters into basic trust and fault. For in the case of the young infant the
field of desire is deployed across the body.[76] At this level desire is not representational though it is clearly protentional, is not referential though it is clearly relational, is not an act as much as it is an action. Where there is a gap, it is filled not by
a sign but an (imaginary) profile of the desired mother, whose absence is only
another form of her givenness, another form of contact, body to body, with the
infant. That profile does not "signify" or "stand in" for her but, in the early phase
of development, just is the way she is present. The mistake is to assume that the
absent mother is not present, that this absence is not just a hollow in the heart of
presence, that the interplay of absence and presence itself requires something
present which represents absence. While the *difference* between profile and whole,
between partial mother and the impossible complete mother, is what allows desire to
be configured, the movement from one to the other does not carry the infant
through the symbolic. The desire of the infant reaches for the mother not by a
movement of signification, an act of interpretation, but on the basis of syntheses of

identity and difference, of sameness and contrast that are themselves controlled by the affective valences in play. To side with Husserl and Merleau-Ponty, we do not have meaning but sense configuring desire; but then to go beyond them, we do not have sense but affective *values* at work. Desire-for cannot be reduced in structure to consciousness-of, and consciousness-of cannot be reduced to signification.

Yet, third, there is no doubt that this sets the stage for the introduction of signification proper. The gap between profile and object allows the name to enter and, with it, the reconfiguration of schemata of differences into oppositions coded semiotically. In addition the mother has had her desires developed into emotions through linguistically mediated modes of regulating her relation to the child. But the next step we must take with caution. It might seem that as soon as we understand affection as relational and as a bond of "primary identification" with no distinction for the infant between mother and itself, and as soon as we have linguistically mediated codes that regulate the desires of the mother, then there could not be "prelinguistically" structured desires. Desires would necessarily be social constructions. But the constitution of desire cannot be reduced to its regulation, even for the mother. She not only has a range of emotions, running from mute, blind passions that know no name to highly, articulated feelings that took a lifetime of reading to develop, but even in the case of the latter there is always a "surplus" of affects that constantly throws us beyond our ability to organize them. And if we return to the small child and if we want to keep signification in any way tethered to the learning of language, then we cannot treat those desires that bond the small child with its mother as dependent upon signifiers. Kristeva insists on this same point in her own terms when she speaks of "the instinctual semiotics, preceding meaning and signification."[77] Rather than desire being at the mercy of language, perhaps it is language that is at the mercy of desire.

In rejecting the thesis that signification constitutes desires at the stage of primary identification, we keep the first deployment of desires connected to the body, to both its morphology and its schemata, its rhythms and its fluids. In the mother–child relation we have a bipolar field, even if one of the poles experiences no difference between itself and the other. Given the rhythms of demands and adequate satisfaction, desire becomes merged delight, the infant's participation in what Kristeva might call *jouissance*.[78] But given the gap between demand and supply, primary identification contains the seeds of its own dissolution.

## Affectivity, the flesh, and the body

> At birth, the infant is not only totally dependent but does not differentiate itself cognitively from its environment. It does not differentiate between subject/self and object/other. This means that it does not differentiate the gratification of its needs and wants. The infant experiences itself as merged or continuous with the world generally, and with its mother or caretakers in particular.
>
> (Chodorow, 1978)[79]

Having briefly touched upon a limit to earlier phenomenological notion of the lived-body in the first section, having then connected this notion to that of the ego in our critique of Freud, and having just sketched in the previous section a notion of affects that does not confuse eros and affection and that corrects or supplements the notion of lived-body, I now turn to a discussion that explores the relational structure of affectivity and shows how Chodorow's own analysis of affectivity needs to be grounded in a concept of the body. Having used affectivity to supplement the phenomenological notion of the body, I am now using the lived-body to supplement her object-relational account of affectivity, a move I deem necessary to carry it outside the orbit of Freud's theory of eros. The result of this move will be to bind the dynamics of affectivity in general and affection in particular to the morphology of the lived-body. I will then conclude by suggesting, but not developing, one strategic implication for our understanding of gender analysis.

What Chodorow inaugurates, but has some difficulty stabilizing, is a distinction between the Freudian notion of eros and what we are calling affection. On the one hand, there are times where she seems only to add a relational dimension to Freud's eros. On the other hand, eros is freed from Freud's hydraulic metaphors, which are replaced by the dynamics of affective interchange. The notions of basic trust and basic fault, we suggested, work at the level of affection as a relational complex with "pathetic" values. Affection is to be mapped onto an interactive grid that involves exchanges at the level of feeling, not onto an "economics of nervous forces," as Freud first attempted in his abandoned 1895 project.[80]

Chodorow is quite correct, then, in resisting the reductionism of a "quantitative line of approach."[81] Affectivity in general and the desire for affection in particular cannot be construed as an element of the body under a biological description. As we suggested in the last section, there are undoubtedly any number of biological, hormonal, and neurological "micro" processes that are causally connected, but a particular affect is a "macro" feature or whole and it functions at a different level. While it comes by "the intermission of the nerves," as Descartes might put it,[82] affection is not a property of the nerves. The neurons and synapses supporting it do not themselves feel, do not themselves want.

Does the desire for affection, then, belong to the "mind?" We will use the ambiguous stance that Chodorow takes toward the involvement of the body in the early stages of development as a point of entry to this question. I will suggest that she depends upon and uses a notion of the lived-body, even expanding it by the notion of affectivity, at critical junctures in her analysis, but that ultimately it cannot be integrated into her theory because she buys into the same bifurcation of the human person as Freud, accepting only the level of psychological systems, states, and relations in opposition to the material or biological level, which in principle cannot be factored into a theory using interpretative strategies.

## The relational structure of affectivity

Chodorow describes very early development in terms of an initial stage of primary identification (birth to the fourth month) and a second symbiotic stage (four or five months through the first year). During the first stage the infant lacks precisely those oppositional structures that are essential to mental life proper, lacks that sense of alterity that is basic to the generation of self-identity. There is no differentiation between inside and outside, between I and not-I, and, as a consequence, between subject and object. It undergoes experience, though we should hesitate to call it that, in such a way that active and reactive, source and goal, touching and touched form an undifferentiated affective complex.

Freud, following Ellis, introduces the term "autoerotic" in an effort to capture the affective dynamics of these first stages,[83] which he draws together into one, calling it the oral stage.[84] For if we distinguish between the *object*, as the object toward which erotic desire is drawn, and the *aim*, as the act, governed by the pleasure principle, toward which the instinct tends, then at this level the object just is the aim, i.e. the arousal of pleasure comes through the stimulation of one's own body.[85] But this should give us pause: can autoeroticism, and the corollary notion of primary narcissism, be the best explanation if the young infant has neither a sense of its body as an object nor, by contrast, a sense of the source of its experiences? Granted that lack of difference, how can we argue that eros is reflexively directed? If we want to argue that in these early stages the infant does cathect an object, then it seems much more plausible that this object is the mother, keeping in mind that this is a "cathexis of someone it does not yet differentiate from its self."[86] And this seems all the more plausible when we realize that this caregiver is the one providing gratification and affection.

Understanding the way in which even this stage is developed only in relation to the mother yields a crucial difference from Freud on the issue of how affection is structured. For Freud eros is specifiable in terms of the maturational unfolding of the different erotogenic zones (oral, anal, phallic) with the relation to the mother or father being *external* to the configuration of desire. Since eros is configured autoerotically the caregiver serves only to frustrate or gratify the need, only to intensify or extinguish it. But object-relations theory insists upon the "fundamental sociality" of the infant and its needs.[87] And even in this first stage, where there is no direct awareness of the difference between inside and outside, between self and parent, its desires are relationally structured: "the infant can be emotionally related to an object, even as its self and object representations are merged."[88] As the infant is touched, held, carried, and nourished, its need for warmth and enclosure is met with consistency and care and, as a result, its need configured into the desire for affection.

Even in the second stage, from the fourth or fifth month through the first year, the child does not yet have a delimited sense of self and there is oscillation between knowing the mother as separate and not separate. Chodorow speaks of a vague "cognitive" recognition of separateness, while emotionally the child "experiences itself as within a common boundary and fused, physically and psychologically, with its mother."[89] This leads to two interrelated concepts, essential to any psychoanalytic account.

On the one hand, since the gratification of its most elementary desires are "emotionally related to an object," they develop into a bond of primary love. This emerges as the infant's cathexis of its environment "becomes focused on those primary people, or that person, who have been particularly salient in providing gratification and a holding relationship."[90] What we have, then, is a "primary need for human contact for itself," what I am calling the need for affection, not what Freud calls eros, for it is the opposite of autoeroticism, that movement of desire that "concentrates all its libido on its self."[91]

On the other hand, the young child does not experience gratification and protection as coming from the mother. It is caught up in an "archaic, egoistic way of loving" not because eros is directed inward but because there is a "complete lack of reality sense in regard to the interests of the love-object."[92] Primary narcissism is best understood not by the notion of self-affection, of autoeroticism, as Freud would have it, for the simple reason that the tie to the mother's breast is more fundamental than "self" pleasure, i.e. self-pleasure is itself supported by this tie, even if the infant does not yet clearly distinguish subject (self) and object. And this allows object-relations theorists to place primary narcissism within a broader structure: it involves a relation to the Other but one in which the Other is so "within" that he or she cannot be experienced as "without." It is "an unintended consequence of the infant's lack of reality sense and perception of its mother as separate."[93] The oscillation here arises because the infant, while not able to distinguish its feelings from that of the caregiver, is still cathecting the mother, and thus is dependent on her.

## From affectivity to the body

Chodorow wants to distance herself from those theories that account for gender identity and mothering by recourse to biology. Not only has she opened a field of analysis, the life of the psyche, that is very different from the one covered in biology, she also employs an interpretative, phenomenological method quite different from its causal, explanatory accounts. In thinking about their relationship, we do find some setting conditions for psychological trends, she recognizes. There are important hormonal differences between male and females that seem related to behavior. And she concedes that the "hormones associated with pregnancy, childbirth and lactation may contribute to a 'readiness' to care for a young infant on the part of the woman who has just given birth."[94] But studies also show that just the exposure to a newborn, the contact with the baby after birth, is also a major factor in developing carekeeping behavior. "Whatever the hormonal input to human maternal behavior, it is clear that such hormones are neither necessary nor sufficient for it."[95] Even if one grants a physiological component to mothering it lasts only a few months at most.[96]

In dispensing with a necessary and sufficient causal tie between biology and mothering, however, Chodorow tends to dispense with any account of the body as a feature of psychoanalytic explanation. At the same time her relational description of primary love requires the introduction of something like a field on the basis of which mental life and the ego arise. This latter requirement, I want to suggest, frees up a very different account of the body for Chodorow's analysis, one that makes contact with the notion of the lived-body we have developed in this paper.

If the small child has neither an egological or egocentric consciousness, nor an experiential difference between inner and outer, nor a felt opposition between subject (self) and object, then one cannot rely on a notion of consciousness, as it is structured by these contrasts, to account for their origins. The place to turn is to the notion of the lived-body, not as an object experienced but as a relational field and interactional nexus that undergirds what will eventually becomes acts of consciousness and a sense of the self. At one point Chodorow does introduce a characterization of the body that functions at this level, even speaking of "a personal body scheme."[97] But while she treats the body in terms of its experiences she, following Winnicott, views the body not as the field from or out of which the ego develops but only as one of the two factors contributing to the origin of the self.[98] On the one hand, we have an "inner" physical experience of body integrity which, over time, provides us with a personal body scheme. This produces a sense of the permanence of physical separateness and of the predictable boundedness of the body. On the other hand, there is a "more internal 'core' of the self," which she understands as a "central crystallization point" of the feeling of self. It is produced through "inner" sensations and emotions and results in ego boundaries and a personal psychic reality. As they both become demarcated from the "object world," a person's self or identity develops.

Even in Chodorow's own terms, there are several problems with this analysis:

1  It relies on an opposition between "inner" and "outer" precisely in order to then
   account for the difference between inner and outer. But if the infant does not
   experience its affects as "inner," as she has argued, then sensations associated
   with feelings cannot become an "internal" core of the self.
2  It depends upon a contrast between "physical" and "psychic" domains of
   experience, which she has argued cannot be experienced as such by the small
   child, in order to then differentiate bodily and psychic reality.
3  She seems to back into something like the old doctrine of specific nerve energies
   since she assumes that "inner" sensations themselves will split between those
   that give us an inner experience of the body (thought to be the product of
   proprioceptors in earlier neurological theory) and those that give us inner
   feelings and emotions (often associated with interoceptors).
4  Rather than integrating the notion of the ego with that of the body she seems to
   treat them as *parallel* sources of the self and we are left wondering if or how they
   intersect. Though she understands them both relationally we are left in the
   quagmire of a duality, if not dualism, of body and ego.

But there clearly is another path open for an object-relations account, one that I
think will lead to solid ground: let the ego emerge from the body.

The story might run something like this. The starting point is a merged body in
which there is no difference between inner and outer. The body, at first, is only a
surface without depth, an unbounded field with clusters of sensorial episodes some
of which awash it in cravings, other of which are simply lived through. They are
affective with only their distribution providing them with location and their felt
qualities providing them with valences. Through the repeated cycles of needs and
satisfaction, first for nutrition and then for affection, the field begins to take on
organization at the same time that the surface begins to take on depth.[99]

With the movement of parts of the body and then of the whole body itself, a sense
of the difference between "here" and "there" is acquired. The body runs up against
what it cannot move or cross. It senses forces pushing against it and, in the face of
their stubborn presence, begins to develop an awareness of itself as both different
and bounded. Or it finds its cravings for food or its yearning for warmth go
unfulfilled and frustration ensues. With desires the body becomes flesh. It comes
to sense the mother as "here" and then "gone," and thereby itself as both counter-
positioned and limited. Through its movements and their restraint, through the
awareness of its own limits, the infant acquires a sense of a bounded body, of "body
integrity."[100] Since this sense comes before anything like "a personal psychic
reality," its boundaries should not be immediately identified with "ego boundaries"
or "a sense of personal psychological division from the rest of the world."[101]

This sets the condition for moving from a merged body to a separate ego. Over
time hands reach out to things and with that comes a gradual polarization of the
field of experience into actions and what is acted upon, into consciousness-of-
something, and eventually into subject and object. It is only with the development
of this structure that we can really speak of the crystallization of a "feeling of self"
and then of a "sense of identity."[102]

Chodorow, it seems, reaches for something like a notion of the lived-body
and begins to integrate it into her account. At the same time her theory is committed to the opposition between physical body and psyche without a clear sense of

the contrast between physical and lived body. When she relies on certain experiential features of the body (which clearly do not belong to a strict physical characterization of it) she leaves them dangling without support or immediately assumes that we are already at the level of psyche. What I am suggesting is that the lived-body allows one to account for primary love and thus a primary bond between body and world out of which "personal psychic reality" and "ego boundaries" arise.

## From the body to affectivity

I want to conclude with one surprising result of our deliberations. Given the way in which Chodorow is often read, perhaps even the way she reads herself, we are surprised to see her at one point incorporating the sexual difference between male and female into her analysis and moving from there to our sense of gender. In context she is arguing for a certain reversal of Freud's approach: it is not the oedipal crisis that accounts for gender identity but quite the reverse. That crisis is a product of our knowledge about gender.[103] With "rare exception" gender identity is "firmly and irreversibly established" for both sexes by the time a child turns three.[104] And this leads to a significant reconstruction of the development of eros in her account. While for Freud the need for affection was reduced to eros, a specific drive qualitatively distinct from others and only localized, not determined, by the maturational unfolding of different erotogenic zones (oral, anal, phallic), for Chodorow the zones themselves are internal to the quality of affection. This is because eros is essentially relational and because the zones are understood in object-relations theory as vehicles for personal contact.[105] As a result the configuration of the body cannot be severed, as in Freud, from the "substance" of affection. Affects, at this level, exist only as distributed across a bodily field. This is why Chodorow recognizes that physical experience and a child's perception of its own genitals are also necessary to create "a gendered body-ego."[106] "Most girls early establish an unequivocally female gender identity with realistic perception of their own genital organs."[107] While these perceptions are always circumscribed not only by a system of signifiers but also by various forms of interaction, basic morphological differences between the sexes and an experience of them which runs deeper than the way they are interpreted socially must also be in play. And this entails that there is a deep connection between the bodily difference between male and female and a root sense of oneself as masculine or feminine. This hint cries out for deeper analysis,[108] but even if time allowed we should not attempt it here because we have only the first step in an account of the body before us.

I find that a recent book by Elizabeth Grosz[109] is also ambivalent in its approach to the lived-body. Though much more sensitive to the "organic" dimensions of the body-image than most theorists, she tends to jump directly from the relationality of bodily constitution (which must be in play at the "organic" level) to "social meaning in Western, patriarchal cultures,"[110] from the body's "relations with others" to "shared socio-cultural conceptions of bodies."[111] No doubt there is a social, cultural conception of the body and no doubt it is "etched into and lived as part of the body image"[112] that we come to have. Social meanings provide the body image with an organization that reflects larger cultural constructions. But she also recognizes a fundamental *relationality* to the body at the *organic* level and it is this which stands between the "double sensations" giving us the material body, on the one hand, and "cultural construction," on the other.

In recognizing the difference between the organic and socio-psychical components of the body-image, Grosz opens a door that she is reluctant to enter. I certainly agree that "the body image does not map a biological body onto a psycho-social domain, providing a kind of translation of material into conceptual terms" and that there is a "mutual dependence of the psychical and the biological."[113] But if not only each "psychological" but each physiological change in the body "has concomitant effects on changes in the body image,"[114] then gender must be connected to sex and cannot be construed only as the *result* of social construction. And this seems to be where she lands in her concluding statement that "there is an intimate connection between the question of sexual specificity (biological sexual differences) and psychical identity"[115] in the construction of the body image. This means not only that the organic is located in a web of cultural significances but, at the same time, that the organic cannot be dissolved into the cultural, and, ultimately, that there is a nonreductive yet internal relationship between sex and gender.[116]

In this paper I have attempted to catch the desire for love and its internal connection to the body at its very inception. This account, I should emphasize, is only the beginning of the story. Even here I have not done justice to the impact of language, which at this level communicates much more by tones and feelings than by cognitive content. From here we would have to provide an account of the thick and multiple dimensions of bodily constitution and move to the body of spatially delimited movements and actions, then to acquired skills and what Mauss calls bodily technique,[117] and even further to the development of collective taste and what Bourdieu describes as a *habitus*.[118] But our attending to affectivity and the body apart from the way it is caught up in these dimensions and our discovery of a rich interplay between the body and affectivity means that the body cannot be construed as only a blank *tablet* "onto which a culture's fantasies of sexual difference are etched," only as an empty *screen* "onto which the mother's – and culture's – desires, [and] wishes – are projected."[119] Nor is it merely docile, a victim bound or a patient dissected by the hands of epistemic practices that determine its material features. Rather the body is an *actional* yet *relational* nexus of constitution with a certain morphology and with certain pathetic intensities and values at play that is not reducible to the field of socially constructed meanings and significance.

The flesh, wild and active, makes its own demands.

## Notes

1   Entry on May 14, 1916, *Metaphysical Journal*, trans. by Bernard Wall (Chicago: Henry Regnery Co., 1952), p. 132.

2   Edmund Husserl, *Ideen zu einer reinen Phänomenologie und phänomenologischen Philosophie*, vol. 1: *Allgemeine Einführung in die reine Phänomenologie*, in *Jahrbuch für Philosophie und phänomenologische Forschung* (Halle a.d.S.: Niemeyer, 1913), pp. 1–323; reprinted as Edmund Husserl, *Ideen zu einer reinen Phänomenologie und phänomenlogischen Philosophien*, vol. 1: *Allgemeine Einführung in die reine Phänomenologie*, vol. II: *Ergänzende Texte (1912–1929)*, ed. by Karl Schuhmann (The Hague: Martinus Nijhoff, 1976); Edmund Husserl, *Ideas Pertaining to a Pure Phenomenology and to a Phenomenological Philosophy*, vol. 1: *General Introduction to a Pure Phenomenology*, trans. by F. Kersten (The Hague: Martinus Nijhoff, 1983).

3   Note the enthusiasm of Max Scheler in his "The idols of self-knowledge," *Selected Papers*, trans. by David Lachterman (Evanston, Illinois: Northwestern University Press, 1973), p. 41, for example.

4   Edmund Husserl, *Ideen zu einer reinen Phänomenologie und phänomenologischen Philosophie*, vol. 2: *Phänomenologische Untersuchungen zur Konstitution*, ed. by Marly Biemel (The Hague:

Martinus Nijhoff, 1952); Edmund Husserl, *Ideas Pertaining to a Pure Phenomenology and to a Phenomenological Philosophy*, vol. 2: *Studies in the Phenomenology of Constitution*, trans. by R. Rojcewicz and Andre Schuwer (Boston: Kluwer Academic Publishers, 1989).

5  Though they were working on the idea at the same time, Scheler's work on the difference between physical and lived-body was published well before Husserl's became available even in manuscript form, yet it did not capture the imagination of philosophers and psychologists. We find passing references to it in his "Die Idole der Selbsterkenntnis [1911]," collected in *Abhandlungen und Aufsätze* (Leipzig: Verlag der Weissen Bücher, 1915); "The idols of self-knowledge," *Selected Philosophical Essays*. But the bulk of the theory is buried in a few sections (part II, section VI, A, e and f) of his massive *Der Formalismus in der Ethik und die materiale Werthethik*, ed. by Maria Scheler (Bern: Francke, 1966 [first edition: 1913, 1916; second edition: 1921; third edition: 1927]); *Formalism in Ethics and Nonformal Ethics of Values*, trans. by Manfred Frings and Roger Funk (Evanston, Illinois: Northwestern University Press, 1973).

6  Though Merleau-Ponty had access to the manuscripts in the Husserl Archives in Louvain and studied them as he was writing his *Phenomenology of Perception*, published in 1945, Husserl's theory of the lived-body did not become generally available until *Ideen II* was published in 1952. Cf. Maurice Merleau-Ponty, *Phénoménologie de la perception* (Paris: Gallimard, 1945); *Phenomenology of Perception*, trans. by Colin Smith (New York: Routledge and Kegan Paul, 1962).

7  Martin Heidegger, *Sein und Zeit* (Tübingen: Niemeyer, 1967); *Being and Time*, trans. by J. Macquarrie and E. Robinson (New York: Harper and Row, 1962).

8  Paul Schilder, *Das Körperschema* (Berlin, Springer Verlag, 1923); *The Image and Appearance of the Human Body: Studies in the Constructive Energies of the Psyche* (New York: International Universities Press, 1978). For an discussion of his work see Elizabeth Grosz, *Volatile Bodies: Toward a Corporeal Feminism* (Bloomington, Indiana: Indiana University Press, 1994), pp. 67–83.

9  See Donn Welton, "Soft, smooth hands: Husserl's phenomenology of the body," *Continental Theories of the Body*, ed. by Donn Welton (Blackwell, forthcoming), for an account of Husserl's theory of the body.

10 Nancy Chodorow, *The Reproduction of Mothering: Psychoanalysis and the Sociology of Gender* (Berkeley, California: University of California Press, 1978), p. 50.

11 *The Reproduction of Mothering*, p. 50.

12 Sigmund Freud, *Die Traumdeutung. Studienausgabe*, vol. II (Frankfurt am Main: Fischer Verlag, 1972); *The Interpretation of Dreams*, trans. by James Strachey (New York: Avon Books, 1965).

13 I would argue, however, that there are characterizations of the body that exceed the resources of a structural phenomenological account, especially those involving concrete ethical and religious dimensions, and that must turn to hermeneutics in order to bring them to analysis. On this issue see my essay in this collection, "Biblical bodies." The point I am making now has to do with the relationship between a straightforward descriptive and an interpretative account only as it operates within phenomenological eidetics.

14 Edmund Husserl, *Zur Phänomenologie der Intersubjektivität. Erster Teil: 1905–1920*, ed. by Iso Kern, *Husserliana*, vol. 13 (The Hague: Martinus Nijhoff, 1973), p. 70.

15 René Descartes, *The Passions of the Soul*, in *The Philosophical Writings of Descartes*, trans. by J. Cottingham, R. Stoothoff, Dugald Murdoch (Cambridge: Cambridge University Press, 1985), I, 331–2.

16 In this paper I will describe the relationship between infant and parent as a relationship between infant and mother not for sociological reasons (biological mothers are the primary caregiver) but for structural reasons (biological mothers have a bodily connection, as a result of both their prenatal and postnatal ties to the infant, that fathers do not). It may turn out, of course, that males do step into the relation of mothering. On this issue of the mother see most recently "Save the mother," ch. 6 of Kelly Oliver, *Womanizing Nietzsche: Philosophy's Relation to the "Feminine"* (New York: Routledge, 1995).

17 See the suggestive attempt in this direction found in Hubert Dreyfus, "The role of intelligent behaviour," ch. 7 of *What Computers Still Can't Do* (Cambridge, Mass.: The MIT Press, 1992).

18  See Elmar Holenstein's essay "The zero-point of orientation," trans. *Continental Theories of the Body*, ed. Donn Welton (Blackwell, forthcoming).

19  See Iris Young's ground breaking essay "Throwing like a girl" in this collection.

20  *The Ego and the Id*, trans. Joan Riviere (New York: Norton, 1960), p. 34.

21  Michael Balint, *The Basic Fault: Therapeutic Aspects of Regression* (London: Tavistock Publications, 1968), p. 22 as cited in Chodorow, *The Reproduction of Mothering*, p. 59.

22  Chodorow, *The Reproduction of Mothering*, p. 59.

23  Ibid.

24  Ibid.

25  Ibid.

26  Anna Freud, "Contribution to discussion, 'The theory of the parent–infant relationship'," *International Journal of Psycho-Analysis*, vol. 43, p. 241 as cited in Chodorow, *The Reproduction of Mothering*, p. 58.

27  *Drei Abhandlungen zur Sexualtheorie* [1905], *Studienausgabe* (Frankfurt am Main: Fischer Verlag, 1972), pp. 88–9; *Three Essays on the Theory of Sexuality*, trans. by James Strachey (New York: Basic Books, 1962), pp. 47–8. Unless otherwise noted always cited after *Three Essays*.

28  *Drei Abhandlungen*, p. 87; *Three Essays*, p. 110.

29  *Drei Abhandlungen*, p. 88; *Three Essays*, p. 48.

30  *Drei Abhandlungen*, p. 90; *Three Essays*, p. 49.

31  Ibid. modified.

32  Ibid.

33  Ibid.

34  Ibid.

35  Ibid.

36  Cf. *The Ego and the Id*, p. 21.

37  Cf. *Drei Abhandlungen*, p. 126; *Three Essays*, p. 89.

38  *Drei Abhandlungen*, p. 89; *Three Essays*, p. 48.

39  "I believe, then, that infantile amnesia, which turns everyone's childhood into something like a prehistoric epoch and conceals from him the beginnings of his own sexual life, is responsible for the fact that in general no importance is attached to childhood in the development of sexual life ... As long ago as in the year 1896 I insisted on the significance of the years of childhood in the origin of certain important phenomena connected with sexual life, and since then I have never ceased to emphasize the part played in sexuality by the infantile factor." *Drei Abhandlungen*, pp. 83–4; *Three Essays*, p. 42.

40  To indicate where this is going, since it will take us a while to get there, I am looking for a richer picture in which the identity of affection and erotic love is rejected, the notion of basic trust operates at the level of the need for affection, and the relation to the other becomes integrated into our understanding of basic needs. This approach would reserve the notion of eros proper for puberty and beyond. Yet we still would speak of the protoerotic, which comes via autoaffection and is zone specific, and of the possibility of its channels being prematurely flooded, in the case of abuse and certain neuroses.

41  *Beyond the Pleasure Principle*, trans. by James Strachey (New York: Norton, 1961).

42  *The Ego and the Id*, p. 8.

43  See ch. 7.

44  *Beyond the Pleasure Principle*, p. 18.

45  *The Ego and the Id*, p. 13.

46  Cf. ibid., p. 12.

47  Ibid., p. 13.

48  Ibid.

49  *Beyond the Pleasure Principle*, p. 18.

50  *The Ego and the Id*, p. 9.

51  Ibid., p. 14.

52  Ibid., p. 9.

53  *Beyond the Pleasure Principle*, p. 18.

54  *The Ego and the Id*, p. 16.

55  A footnote added to the English translation of *The Ego and the Id* (1927), p. 16.

56  *The Ego and the Id*, p. 15.

57  Ibid.

58  Ibid., p. 16.

59  Ibid., p. 18.

60  Ibid., pp. 18–19.

61  Ibid., p. 19.

62  Ibid.

63  Ibid., p. 21.

64  Cf. *Drei Abhandlungen*, p. 80; *Three Essays*, p. 39 for Freud's emphatic emphasis that the "sexual instinct" that we find in puberty – whose aim is copulation, leading to "a release of the sexual tension" and to "a temporary extinguishing of the sexual drive" (p. 60; p. 15) – is in play in early childhood, modified only by the lack of physical development.

65  *Beyond the Pleasure Principle*, pp. 32–4.

66  *The Ego and the Id*, p. 13.

67  Ibid., p. 24.

68  *Intersubjektivität*, I, 115.

69  H. Harlow and M. Zimmerman, "Affectional responses in the infant monkey," *Science*, vol. 130 (1959), 421–32.

70  John Bowlby, *Attachment*, vol. 1 of *Attachment and Loss* (London: Penguin Books, 1971), p. 222, as cited in Chodorow, *The Reproduction of Mothering*, p. 65.

71  I think we can describe these without having to claim they are "instinctual," i.e. it seems to me that "instinctual," if we are to use the notion at all, applies best to patterns of behavior and not to states of (certain) feelings.

72  Cf. John Searle, *Minds, Brains and Science* (Cambridge, Mass.: Harvard University Press, 1984).

73  The terms *need, demand,* and *desire* echo Lacan but the analysis is rather different due to my hesitation to amalgamate desire and eros. See Jacques Lacan, *The Four Fundamental Concepts of Psycho-Analysis*, trans. by Alan Sheridan (New York: Norton, 1978), pp. 154–6. We must be careful to avoid equivocating with the term "desire." We are applying this notion to children before they have "thoughts" or even intentional acts. It is manifest by reaching or moving out, by trying to get, and thus is found in *all* the actions of the infant. This must be set in contrast to desire which is necessarily intentional in structure and which is ordinarily in play for adults. Not only is desiring there a desiring-of-X but its tie to action need not be direct: we often do things we do not want to or, because of a conflict of desires, undertake no action at all. Desire in the latter sense is identical to an act of wanting.

74  Our every day talk of desires usually refers to desires that have undergone a process of development and maturation. They fall under the category of what I am calling emotions in this paper.

75  Friedrich Nietzsche, *Beyond Good and Evil*, trans. by Walter Kaufmann (New York: Random House, 1966), section 19.

76  We purposely set aside the question of dreams in order to focus on the primary interactions between infant and mother.

77  Julia Kristeva, *Revolution in Poetic Language*, trans. by Margaret Waller (New York: Columbia University Press, 1984), p. 49.

78  *Revolution*, passim.

79  *The Reproduction of Mothering*, p. 61.

80  Letter to Wilhelm Fliess, May 29, 1895, *Standard Edition of the Complete Psychological Works of Sigmund Freud* (London: Hogarth Press, 1971), I, 283. The "project for a scientific psychology" is found in *Standard Edition*, I, 280–397.

81  Freud, Letter to Fliess, May 25, 1895, *Standard Edition*, I, 283.

82  Descartes, *The Passion of the Soul*, part I, article XXII, cited according to *The Philosophical Works of Descartes*, trans. by E. Haldane and G. Ross (Cambridge: Cambridge University Press, 1968), I, 342.

83  *Three Essays*, p. 47.

84  Ibid., pp. 16–18, 45–7.

85  Ibid., pp. 1, 49–51.

86  *Reproduction of Mothering*, p. 61.

87   Ibid., p. 63.
88   Ibid., p. 62.
89   Ibid., p. 62.
90   Ibid., p. 64.
91   Ibid., p. 63.
92   Ibid., p. 62.
93   Ibid., p. 62.
94   Ibid., p. 27.
95   Ibid., p. 28.
96   Ibid., p. 29.
97   Ibid., p. 68.
98   In what follows I am reproducing her analysis in *The Reproduction of Mothering*, pp. 67–8 but only putting the terms I want to emphasize in quotation marks.
99   This is where its sense of basic trust (or basic fault) comes into play.
100  Cf. *The Reproduction of Mothering*, p. 67.
101  Ibid., p. 68.
102  Ibid., p. 67.
103  Ibid., p. 151.
104  Ibid., p. 150.
105  Ibid., p. 48.
106  Ibid., p. 150.
107  Ibid., p. 150.
108  Again, what cuts short any development of this hint is Chodorow's tendency to collapse an account of the body into a discussion of the biological body. This tendency has only been exacerbated in a more recent collection of her essays. She grants that "we clearly live an embodied life; we live with those genital and reproductive organs and capacities, those hormones and chromosomes, that locate us physiologically as male or female." *Feminism and Psychoanalytic Theory* (New Haven, Conn.: Yale University Press, 1989), p. 101. But she does not attempt to sort out just what this involves and quickly moves to yet a second level of constitution which "represents," "shapes," and "chooses" its own interpretation of the first. Or she gives us a straw man argument, turning an interest into this question into the trivial thesis that sex "determines" gender: "Bodies would be bodies (we do not want to deny people their bodily experience). But particular bodily attributes would not necessarily be so determining [?] of who we are, what we do, how we are perceived, and who are our sexual partners", *Feminism and Psychoanalysis*, p. 102. Her account there of core gender identity, which is now established not in the first three but the first two years, eliminates any account of the experience of the body scheme. The only reference is to "an early, non-verbal, unconscious, almost somatic sense of primary oneness with the mother", *Feminism and Psychoanalysis*, p. 109. The analysis, then, dispenses with any experience of genital difference and revolves about differential enforcement of gender role expectations by the parents. We do not have an interesting discussion of the body even in her own terms, though *The Reproduction of Mothering* makes it an essential element of her account.
109  Elizabeth Grosz *Volatile Bodies: Toward a Corporeal Feminism* (Bloomington, Ind.: Indiana University Press, 1994).
110  Ibid., p. 82.
111  Ibid., p. 84.
112  Ibid., p. 82.
113  Ibid., p. 85.
114  Ibid., p. 84.
115  Ibid., p. 85.
116  A fuller analysis of this issue would have to look at the question of whether a significantly different social and political order could change the *relationship* (itself) between the "organic" and the body as constructed through socially shared meanings. For example, it might be that slaves are reduced socially to the organic, to bodies as sources of work-power, while masters, in giving over material labor to slaves, subordinate the organic to the social, to "dress." But this is a very different thing from saying that we can dissolve the structure of the organic into its cultural or socio-political significance. And if we think there are necessarily and dangerous

political implications that follow from this we simply have failed to heed Iris Young's caution not to identify too quickly the issue of gender identity with that of male domination. See her "Is male gender identity the cause of male domination?" *Throwing Like a Girl*, pp. 36–61.

117   Marcel Mauss, "Les technique du corps," *Journal de Psychologie*, vol. 32 (1936); reprinted in Marcel Mauss, *Sociologie et anthropologie* (Paris: Presses Universitaires de France, 1968).

118   Pierre Bourdieu, *Distinction: A Social Critique of the Judgment of Taste*, trans by R. Nice (Cambridge, Mass. Harvard University Press, 1984). See the paper by Ed Casey in this collection.

119   Grosz, *Volatile Bodies*, p. 75 uses these terms in characterizing Freud's and Schilder's notion of the body.

# 10
## Habitualities

## The Ghost of Embodiment:
## on Bodily Habitudes and Schemata

### Edward Casey

*There is not a word, not a form of behavior which does not owe something to purely biological being – and which at the same time does not elude the simplicity of animal life, and cause forms of vital behavior to deviate from their pre-ordained direction, through a sort of leakage and through a genius for ambiguity which might serve to define human beings.*

Maurice Merleau-Ponty, *Phenomenology of Perception*

*Then, like Hegel's cunning of Reason, the wisdom of the cultural process would consist in putting to the service of its own intentions natural systems which have their own reasons.*

Marshall Sahlins, "Colors and cultures"

## I

Human embodiment was among the first victims of the Cartesian revolution in philosophy. This embodiment – the lived fact of experiencing the world from and in and with just this body, my body – was exorcized or, perhaps more exactly, volatilized. Given the forced choice between *res extensa* and *res cogitans*, the lived body (for which the Germans have invented a separate word: *Leib*) had no place to go: still worse, no place of its own. But like any good ghost, it has returned to haunt its exorcizors. Albeit an unwanted guest ("ghost" and "guest" are cognates), such a body – everybody's body – stayed on without warrant, spooking self-assured philosophical and scientific discourse about "body" (which is to say, again in German, *Körper*, "body-as-object"). Unwelcome as it has been, embodiment acts as the covert basis of human experience and of coherent connection among human beings: a basis and connection that occur not only in time but in space (and more particularly in place).

"The ghost of embodiment" refers to this factor of lastingness – of lingering across space and place and time and history. For embodiment lingers in periods of philosophical neglect (such as the Cartesian era from which we are only now beginning to emerge) just as it also endures in the face of massive cultural vicissitudes. I shall not dwell on the first form of remaining[1] as I am much more interested in exploring how the lived body subsists through the cultural inlays and overlays that have, in contemporary parlance, "written it."

Not only subsists, but carries culture and brings it to bear by performing it outright.

In the current climate of cultural constructionism – when an overdue recognition has been accorded to the importance of accumulated history and acquired language, and of ethnic and gender differences that are not given but constituted (and constituted not merely by individuals but by whole groups of human beings) – it is timely to ponder the fate of things that are too often considered to be imponderable. One of these "things" is the human body as it is lived by human persons. This body has been of central concern for phenomenologists such as Husserl and Merleau-Ponty in earlier parts of this century, and more recently for feminist theorists such as Irigaray and Butler. Where phenomenologists focus on *anyone's* lived body in its sensory and orientational powers, feminists have discerned the different ways this same body is lived by men and women. Butler, in particular, attempts to show how something as seemingly extra-discursive as the lived body remains a posit, if not an effect, of discourse about this body.[2] Its materiality may not be created by discourse (to hold this amounts to discursive idealism), but it is what it is for us because of the ways we talk and write about it. Butler's emphasis on the performative aspects of gender identity strikes a clarion chord in a miasma of confusion and prejudice. She is surely right to bring into the light of day the manifold learned behaviors of gender: to show how much of gender is *enacted* mimetically rather than being merely the supposedly "natural" "expression" of existing bodily structures, however anatomical or "innate" they are presumed to be. Butler has begun to spell out, in *Gender Trouble* and *Bodies that Matter*, the many ways that (to reverse the infamous Napoleonic-Freudian formula) "anatomy is *not* destiny": for example, by showing that "tacit normative criteria [in]form the [very] matter of bodies"[3] This is important and valuable work – a work of reclamation as it were. Where Freud had declared that "where id was, there ego shall be,"[4] Butler would say that where the opaque matter of unexamined presupposition is, there the illuminable body of cultural practice and social prohibition can be seen for what it is.

In the very face of Butler's convincing constructionism, I nevertheless want to ask whether there are modes of embodiment that resist being reclaimed so quickly or so well – that are not the ghostly creatures of "the prior delimitation of the extra-discursive,"[5] much less the residua of certain texts. Are there not aspects of bodily being that, if not undecipherable or uninscribable, are still not the mere positings of discursive or textual practices? One such aspect is found in the primate origins of human bodily behavior, especially as discussed by Maxine Sheets-Johnstone in *The Roots of Power*. Another is revealed in the assessment of the natural environment as it impinges on bodily conduct – as explored by ecologically sensitive contemporaries such as Gary Snyder or Wendell Berry. But I prefer to follow another path into the darkness – one that does not pit *ecos* or *bios* against *socius*, and thus prefers to avoid mere antagonism or reactionism. Could it be, I find myself wondering (and invite you to wonder with me), that the body's ghostly essence lies in its very capacity to be at once thoroughly natural and thoroughly cultural – not unlike the Spinozan infinite attributes of Extension and Thought, which together characterize all things all the way through, despite their intrinsic differences? And I ask you to ponder, too, whether it is precisely because the body is such a dense matrix of nature and culture that it presents itself to us – indeed, *must* present itself – as obscure, as having a "genius for ambiguity" in Merleau-Ponty's altogether apt phrase.

## II

Only if body were obdurate matter on the one hand or an epiphenomenon of spirit on the other, could we usefully apply the designations "nature" or "culture" to it in some exclusive way. But body is no such matter and no such epiphany of spirit. It is its own unique realm or type of being, one that lends itself to both natural and cultural modulations. And always to both at once, in varying combinations and connections. Never a physical or metaphysical monolith (despite continual efforts to depict it as such), body, the human body, is metamorphic in its being – even if it tends to be sedimentary in its habits and igneous in its moods.

All too often, however, we fall prey to thinking of the body in extreme terms, sometimes regarding it as simply and solely "natural" – i.e. biological, genetic, racial, somatotypic (i.e. "ectomorphic," "mesomorphic") – and sometimes considering it as a purely cultural creation: as the mere composite of certain gestures or movements that are socially conditioned, or as the expression of certain interests and ideologies. I say that "we" fall prey to these extreme conceptions without referring to the further fact that this we is itself an amalgam of nature and culture, their conjoint creation. This is shown by the sheer fact that the same "we" tend to think of the relation between nature and culture as involving a forced choice between them, putting them into opposed and mutually exclusive positions to start with. But the choice and the opposition are themselves shaped by antecedent choices and oppositions that make this particular choice and opposition possible: consider only the way the folk psychology of a people deeply affects such matters. Furthermore, any such cultural precedents themselves reflect certain physical and physiological constraints such as the character of the human brain, limits of bodily strength, the structure of the hand, etc. And the very ideas of "character," "limit," and "structure" are in turn culturally constituted.

What, then, are we to make of this conceptual regress, in which we keep spiralling back in criss-crossing causal series, without any certainty that we can determine which series is the most formative? (Even the idea of "most formative" is culturally contingent.) Does the swirling vortex of natural and cultural forces mean that we should give up the very effort to sort out nature from culture, or even body from mind? Here we are tempted to claim that the very distinction of nature vs. culture, or that of body vs. mind, is itself a cultural artefact, a factitious invention of modernity.[6] Yet this claim begs an important question: just what induces a given modern thinker to make such distinctions in the first place? Might it not be the recognition of a discrepancy or otherness which that thinker could not fully contain in accustomed cultural categories and was therefore tempted to attribute to "nature" or "body," which become names for a recalcitrant otherness that resists cultural assimilation – on the very admission of culture itself? Either that admission is to be respected or, if it is not, the burden of proof falls on the skeptic who holds that even the culturally unassimilable is cultural in character.

One could also argue that the natural and the cultural are always already so completely assimilated with each other – so deeply co-implicated – that it would be futile to tease them apart: otherness is already sameness in some sufficiently generous sense.[7] Merleau-Ponty puts it this way:

> Everything is cultural in us (our *Lebenswelt* is "subjective") (our perception is cultural-historical) and everything is natural in us (even the cultural rests on the polymorphism of wild being).[8]

Yet it is one thing to hold that the natural and the cultural are thoroughly inter-twined and quite another to maintain that, because of this interpenetration, there is no point in trying to distinguish them at all. In the interest of distinction and in the effort to retrieve the body from its ghostly exile, let us consider some quite particular instances of embodiment with respect to what is contributed by natural forces and as to which cultural conditions operate and how they do so. We shall proceed in three stages, each increasingly complex and elusive. First, by an analysis of the learning (or relearning) of bodily skills; then, by a look at the acquisition and sedimentation of taste; finally, by a consideration of hysterical symptoms.

## III

The year 1936 marked the appearance of Marcel Mauss's article, "Les techniques du corps." It was also the year in which Lacan first presented his ideas on the mirror phase; and the same year saw, by curious convergence, the publication of Anna Freud's *The Ego and the Mechanisms of Defence* and Sartre's *Transcendence of the Ego*. All four events went virtually unnoticed at the time, yet each can be said to be of capital importance for considering the status of the body in contemporary thought. For there is an intimate link between the formation of the ego and the body of the subject. Freud had said (twice!) in *The Ego and the Id* that the ego "is first and foremost a body-ego."[9] This is not to say that body and conscious ego form one continuous entity; in the same text of 1923 Freud proposed that large parts of the ego, those that are the products of repression, are unconscious. But it *is* to suggest that the imbrication between soma and psyche is very close indeed.[10] Lacan and Anna Freud went on to spell out the procedures by which the ego of the individual, the core of the psychic self, is formed. Both of them insisted on the importance of identification, in Anna Freud's case "identification with the aggressor" – which includes imitation of the aggressor's bodily gestures – while Lacan emphasized identification with the image of oneself in the mirror, that is, with one's already existing body as it perceives itself before itself.[11] Sartre added that the ego has exactly the same status as the body of the subject: both are constituted, transcendent *objects* of pure consciousness.

Mauss, for his part, insisted on the utter specificity of bodily techniques. Remark-ing on his inability to give up his entrenched practice of swallowing water and spitting it out as he swam – a common practice of swimmers of his generation – the French sociologist made this remark:

> It was stupid, but I still make this gesture [of swallowing-and-spitting]: I cannot free myself of my technique. Here is thus a specific bodily technique, a gymnastic art perfected in our time. Yet *such specificity is the character of all [bodily] techniques.*[12]

Freud, Lacan, Sartre, and Anna Freud would all agree with Mauss that those bodily practices that have to do with personal (and more particularly with egological) identity are all specific in character. But what does it mean to say this? Is there no *general* technique of the body? And what does the specificity in question tell us about the incursion of culture into bodily practices?

Let us stay for a moment with Mauss's own preferred example of swimming. Recently, I have been swimming a fair amount – or, more exactly, relearning how to swim. I have had no instructor, but have been trying to get back into the sport on the basis of a small set of dimly grasped body memories, a few unformulated thoughts as to how I might swim more efficiently, as well as furtive and envious glances at fellow and sister swimmers who stream past me in the fast lane of my local pool. Buoying me up in the water, then, has been a loose assemblage of memories, thoughts, and perceptions.

But what is actually happening when I relearn a basic bodily skill such as swimming? I am reviving, and also reshaping, a tacit corporeal schema – where "schema" implies not just form or pattern but something much more dynamic: a basic way of doing something, a manner of proceeding, a mode of acting. A schema for bodily action, such as that for doing the crawl stroke, is intermediary between image and rule, thus between the specific and the general: between the condensed specificity of an image (which gives me just *one* version of how to do the stroke) and the generality of the rule (which remains abstract and normative: how anyone, anywhere, could in principle do this stroke). Nevertheless, as I make my flailing way, floundering if not yet foundering, I catch myself summoning up demi-images of "the right form" ("every technique, properly speaking, has its form,"[13] says Mauss) as well as a sense of the right rule (as in the Kantian schematism for causality, it is a matter of "objective succession": first this arm goes out of the water and over the head, then the immersed head turns to the side to catch a breath, then the other arm swings over, with the legs kicking all the while). Thanks to the corpreal schema I possess, I effect a spontaneous alliance with image and rule alike: the image (however dim and merely recollective it may be) affords detail and, as it were, leads the way into the stroke itself, as if it were an initiatory amulet; the rule reassures me that this is the socially sanctioned "right way" to swim the crawl stroke, even if it is not the *ideal* way to do it. (I here leave aside a host of further questions: can the ideal form of swimming a given stroke ever be realized by *any* individual swimmer? Is there only one such ideal form for each stroke? Is this ideal sensuous or quasi-sensuous – as Kant proposes – or is it strictly abstract in a Platonic mode? Is not the body *as body* foredoomed to fall short of any such ideal; is this not why the body needs the guidance of rules, which it can at least "follow" in Wittgenstein's ample sense, even if it cannot embody the ideal stroke *überhaupt?*)

One thing is clear: neither the image nor the rule needs to be stated in so many words, that is, in anything like a text. I might, of course, consult a treatise on swimming the crawl stroke, one which includes both images and words. Helpful as such a treatise might be, however, I do not require it in relearning to swim – nor do I even need it in learning how to swim in the first place. Indeed, the insertion of a text or text-like entity into the circumstance would be distinctly counter-performative, making me only more self-conscious of what I am trying deliberately if not desperately to do. Ultimately, the water I place myself in and the body placed there teach me more than any set of words I read or hear. For they induce the schema by the actual means of which I swim. The fact that this schema presents itself to me in an informal amalgamation of memories, perceptions, and thoughts, far from being a problem, represents a perfectly adequate instance of the kind of open-ended hybridization that is appropriate to the occasion. The schema is in this respect *general enough to be specific*.

The crawl stroke schema itself, that which I embody as I swim this particular stroke, is socially transmitted – and thus socially determined. Mauss tells us that it was from observing the variety of swimming techniques across different generations in France that he first began to ponder the question of "bodily practices."[14] My own simple schematic pictorial rule of the crawl stroke is inherited from a certain, admittedly fragmentary history of learning this same stroke. The stroke is, in Mauss's striking formulations, "an efficacious traditional act," "the work (*l'ouvrage*) of collective practical reason."[15] But to be the *work* of a socialized reason, even a traditionalized reason, is not necessarily to be the *text* of such a reason. It is only to be its deliverance or outcome – its "accomplishment," as *l'ouvrage* can also be translated. From this collectively constituted source comes my individuated bodily practice, which *realizes* (and re-realizes) the source in so many motions; the schema of this practice transmits the general form of the stroke from the social mass of more or less competent swimmers to the given imperfect swimmer who, like myself, is learning or relearning the stroke in his or her own way. Just as my body is between me and you – it *is the mediatrix of every social scene* – so the schema at stake in learning and relearning bodily skills exists between the generality of others and the specificity of myself, instigating in *me* the form which *they* have instituted, "e-ducating" me.[16] And I lead the form back out into publicity and visibility by per-forming it, forming it *through* my bodily practice.

Educators or instructors, whether actually or only implicitly present, convey to the learner the schema that represents the condensation, the gist, the gesture of the technique. Indeed, it is precisely because the teacher is not able to be continually present that the schema plays such a critical role; it stands in for the absent teacher, much as a text stands in for its absent or dead author; but, unlike a text, the bodily schema is intrinsically indeterminate, oscillating as it does between image and rule. It is indeterminate because the body as lived and experienced is itself indeterminate: the body is "our general medium for having a world,"[17] and as such is easily overlooked – becoming a spectral presence, a wraith of my life. Not surprisingly, then, corporeal schemata have no final or definitive formulation. It is sufficient to assimilate, literally to incorporate, the bodily movements of an instructor (or, lacking this mentor, an exemplary image of myself as once performing the stroke) in order to learn, or to re-learn, the technique in question.[18] These movements become my movements (or mine again), but only thanks to the intermediacy of the schema that allows the perceived or remembered performativity of the instructor to be deposited in the customary body of the fledgling performer.

The foregoing analysis allows us to infer that the indisputable social determination of conduct is not something starkly superimposed from without, since the social moment (here, the moment of learning or relearning a basic skill possessed primarily by others) operates from within by way of identification with the exemplary other and with the tradition which this other embodies so instructively. This identification is found in my body and nowhere else, and it stays in my body thanks to the schema in which it is embedded. By the same token, we cannot say that the biological basis of an action such as swimming is simply supplied from below, as if this basis were an unformed and unproblematic substratum, a brute given. The formation of skillful bodily actions, their in-formation, is part of these actions from the beginning. Even the "dog paddle" is a form of swimming, a consistent and particular way of keeping one's head above water; it, too, is learned and internalized, even if it is never taught as an exemplary way to swim (hence, doubtless, its attribution to another species).[19]

It follows that in the intermediate realm constituted by the corporeal schemata of skilled actions, the natural and the cultural are always already conjoined. Nothing here is entirely natural,[20] nor is anything entirely cultural either. Or rather, everything is both at once, albeit differentially so. I swim with my biological body but as I am taught by others. I swim by or through the body that connects self and other as surely as its schemata link image and rule, the specific and the general, and also past and present. I swim rather than sink by virtue of the schema that, more or less successfully executed, keeps me afloat.


# IV

It is certainly not adequate to think of my lived body as a mere instrument, yet we must, by the same token, be able to think of the body in terms that allow for the learning of skills and other habitudes. Just as works of art may be conceived as "quasi-subjects" (in Dufrenne's term), so skilled bodies as culturally in-formed can be considered "quasi-technical." In other words, the body can be considered as if it were an organ for the acquisition and sedimentation of skillful actions. And I say "technical" rather than "mechanical," since it is a matter of *technique* in the Maussian sense, which requires a body that is at once: (1) able to learn particular skilled responses on the basis of certain minimal sensori-motor capacities and basic bodily motions (ultimately dependent on the central nervous system, the brain, and appropriate musculature); (2) socially absorptive and responsive, that is, sensitive to occasions of possible instruction as they arise in the immediate life of the learner; (3) "docile" enough (in Foucault's sense) to submit to the rigors of learning new skills in given institutional settings.

To endorse the body's quasi-technicality does not mean capitulating to the temptation to consider the lived body as an objective body. We can respect Merleau-Ponty's fierce resistance to this temptation, while remaining open to such less than completely objectifying designations as "apparatus" (Freud, Lyotard), "régime" (Foucault), "habitus" (Bourdieu), "cyborg" (Haraway), etc. Each of these epithets is exemplary of the body in its quasi-technicality. Not entirely unlike the Aristotelian notion of soul (*psychē*) as the "first actuality" of the body, its most formative *form*, each serves to normalize the lived body's biological propensities and involuntary actions. We are thus brought back to the intermediacy of the body as what Bergson calls a "place of meeting and transfer"[21] *between* biology and culture, the physical and the social. Precisely as such an inter-place, the lived body lends itself to cultural enactments of the most varied sorts, all of which are themselves dependent on particular corporeal techniques for their own realization.

Pierre Bourdieu's book *Distinction: A Social Critique of the Judgment of Taste*, published in 1979 and inspired by Mauss's essay of 1936, delineates the social arrangements that bodily techniques afford and support in matters of taste. Bourdieu analyzes, for example, class and gender differences in eating practices of the French working class, finding (among other things) that

> Fish tends to be regarded as an unsuitable food for [working class] men, not only because it is a light food, insufficiently "filling," which would only be cooked for health reasons, i.e. for invalids and children, but also because, like fruit (except bananas) it is one of the "fiddly" things which a man's hands cannot cope with and which make him childlike...but, above all, it is because fish has to be eaten in a way which totally contradicts the masculine way of eating, that is, [fish has to be eaten] with restraint, in small mouthfuls, chewed gently, with the front of the mouth, on the tips of the teeth (because of the bones). The whole masculine identity – what is called virility – is at stake in these two ways of eating, nibbling and picking, as befits a woman, or [eating with] with whole-hearted male gulps and mouthfuls...[22]

From this analysis – and others like it – Bourdieu concludes that "taste, a class culture turned into nature, that is, *embodied*, helps to shape the class body...the body is the most indisputable materialization of class taste."[23] He tellingly invokes what he calls "the whole body schema." Such a schema, operating on and with existing "biological differences," is put into practice by "differences in bearing, [i.e.] differences in gesture, posture and behavior which express a whole relationship to the social world."[24]

Bodily schemata of taste are specifications in turn of the *habitus* that is the hinge between nature and culture. Bourdieu defines *habitus* as "an acquired system of generative schemata" that enable it to be "the product of the work of inculcation and appropriation necessary in order for products of collective history, [that is], objective structures such as those of language, economy, etc., to succeed in reproducing themselves more or less completely, in the form of durable dispositions, in [human] organisms..."[25] As a *system* of schemata, the *habitus* is what enables comparatively enduring bodily "dispositions" and continually changing surrounding "situations" to be drawn together in the inculcation of taste.[26]

Thanks to this clue from Bourdieu, we can begin to appreciate the deep commonalities between skill and taste. Both involve an essential reference to an exemplary type (e.g. the model crawl stroke, the right way to eat as a French working-class man) as well as an image of this type (whether perceptual, memorial, or imaginative). But both also invoke a rule by which the image is rendered operative (a "correct," if not ideal, sequence of coordinated movements, whether those of swimming the crawl or masticating meat). Taken together, the image and rule facilitate in the lived body a set of practices that represent the performance, the realization, of the skill or taste in question. Further, both skill and taste require bodily schemata as the means by which images and rules are knit together. Without bodily schemata, the images would be merely static condensations and the rules abstract formulae. With them, images and rules configurate in a lived body that incarnates culture even as it transmutes nature.[27]

## V

It is surely striking that we have now been led twice to the notion of schema: first in relation to the learning of a basic bodily *skill* such as swimming, then in regard to the question of *taste* as exhibited in eating practices. It is the lived body in its quasi-technicality that possesses and exercises schemata, those of basic skills as well as those of the subtleties of taste. In neither case do we have to do with the laying down of cultural constructions on pre-existing bodily givens but, rather, with a circumstance in which the (biologically) given and the (culturally) constructed conjoin and become (literally) complicated in the crucible of the body. Of course, material conditions and cultural formations meet in many places: buildings, works of art, technology. But only in the meeting-place of the living-moving body do they undergo such dynamic interaction. The dynamism, I have been suggesting, is due to the schema, which is at once self-same and yet alterable. It is self-same as involving a *habitus* that guarantees continuity of action, and it is alterable insofar as habitudes (unlike mere routines) are open to innovation: as Dewey, Merleau-Ponty, and Bourdieu all insist.[28]

I do not mean to imply that bodily skills are on precisely the same plane as matters of taste. The latter presuppose the former and appropriate them for their own purposes. Taste is more encompassing than skill insofar as on its basis an entire "life-style" may be generated.[29] Moreover, taste, unlike skill, *always* reflects class and gender differences, incorporating and reinforcing them (though also, at times, transforming them). Taste transmutes physical things (e.g. items of food and clothing) into signs and, still more importantly, makes social necessities into individually felt virtues. I come to "like" (and even to crave) that which, nevertheless, is a quite limited range of things made available to me as a member of a certain social class or as having a determinate sexual identity: again, fish if I am French and female.[30] Indeed, there are no effective limits to the extent to which taste may shape our bodily practices. It is so pervasive of the person that it may influence the very choice of which basic skills are to be learned in the first place: I may decide to learn how to swim not for purposes of sheer survival or just for pleasure but because my peers have encouraged me to do so – and to do so in a very particular, not to say peculiar, way: like swallowing and spitting while swimming.

# VI

Nature and culture meet, then, in the lived body. They meet, for example, in the insistent but subtle way that right-and left-handedness infiltrate and influence an entire metaphoricity and symbology of a given culture.[31] They meet as well in the manner in which basic color terms, at once remarkably congruent and yet discretely variant across different cultures, reflect both the physiological optics of vision and the peculiarities of naming in diverse natural languages. As Marshall Sahlins has put it: "it is not, then, that color terms have their meanings imposed by the constraints of human and physical nature; it is that they take on such constraints insofar as they are meaningful."[32] Only those constraints are "taken on" (i.e. assumed, assimilated, made use of) that bear significance or can be made to bear it. *Bodily* constraints in particular – the ways our sheer physicality delimits and determines us – are massively and not exceptionally meaning-bearing. It follows that such culturally specific phenomena as ritual and style represent ways of taking corporeal pre-givens – e.g. certain modular motions and shapes – and giving them a local habitation and a name: a place (and time) of enactment and a particular designatable role in the practices of that culture. The list of culturally specified ways of carrying corporeal constraints farther into the realm of meaning – carrying them, I would insist, on the backs of habitually structured schemata of the body – could continue indefinitely.

If I have been stressing skill and taste, this is above all because, taken together, they reveal the range of the human body's capacity for exhibiting and enacting what Merleau-Ponty calls "incarnate meaning."[33] Skills inhabit one end of this spectrum, representing the circumstances when bodily capabilities and proclivities lend themselves to manipulation and training: when, as Foucault would say, the "intelligible body" becomes the "useful body."[34] What counts for the useful body (which is not even the whole of the quasi-technical body!) is learning and performance, the start and finish of one continuous process. Taste occupies the other end of the spectrum, the situation where bodily determination as useful and skillful is submerged in matters of preference and value – matters so pervasive that, in the final analysis, nothing in a given culture is not, directly or indirectly, a matter of taste, including style and ritual as these eventuate in such concrete practices as dress, table manners, or blowing one's nose![35] What counts in taste is the slow and often non-reflective process of inculcation and staying within the rules. The inculcation implies whole scopes or types of action taken as showing sensible or sensitive taste; and the rule-bound behavior need not seek finesse (indeed, finesse in taste risks being considered merely precious, whereas finesse in a skill is altogether fitting).[36]

Taken to the limit, skill tends toward sheer repetition of the sort that is resistant to change of any sort: Mauss found that, despite his best intentions, he could not give up his early habit of swallowing a mouthful of water and spitting it out with each successive swimming stroke. The skillful body may get locked into a particular practice that, whatever its initial utility, becomes anachronistic and counter-productive or that can come to seem simply embarrassing. The same body is also conscriptable by a dominant state institution into the obedient postures of an all too docile body, that is, the body all too easily bent to the service of that institution, especially in characteristic modern forms of extensive supervenient control.[37] Taste in turn is easily conscripted by the preferences of the dominant class – dominant economically and politically as well as culturally – so as to become "correct" taste, i.e. the decorum of a "civilized" elite who alone are held to have not just "good" or "acceptable" but "fine" taste.[38] The very genius of taste to operate in the midst of virtually any constraint and to make something socially commensurable and con-genial out of what is deeply conflictual is here put into abeyance. Further, taste all too often entails a notion of normalization that in principle excludes the eccentric and literally ab-normal. In this case, taste becomes "proper taste," i.e. what one *ought to do* in a given situation.[39]

Short of these extremes and despite their manifest differences, bodily enacted skills and tastes land one in a middle realm that, on the one hand, is only quasi-technical and not rigidly stylized and that, on the other, is a matter of receptive and spontaneous consensus and not of elitist exclusions. It is precisely this intermediate corporeal domain that is most fully enlivened and structured by habitudes and schemata – those mediating factors *par excellence* that, by their very action and interaction, constitute nature and culture as covalent, if not always equal, partners in the common enterprise of creating a genuinely incarnate meaning.[40]

# VII

Disparate as they are in so many ways, skill and taste both exhibit a certain voluntarism: I can choose to acquire new skills or re-acquire old ones, and I can decide to change my taste – though this change may prove to be arduous indeed. But if the acquiring of skills is deliberate, that of taste is often semi-deliberate; I tend to pick up tasteful behaviors merely by commingling with the apposite social milieu. On the other hand, there are some bodily practices that are strictly non-deliberate, i.e. involuntary, insofar as they are not only not initially chosen (this much is true of most practices of taste) but decidedly recalcitrant to subsequent modification. I have in mind psychopathological symptoms of the sort that dominate the lives of those who suffer from them – that literally control their movements beyond any conscious choice in the matter. The automatism of these movements remains, however, schematic and habitual, and they deserve discussion along with skill and taste as a third class of phenomena in which nature and culture are inextricably embroiled, yet with revealing differences from the cases previously considered.

Such a discussion is all the more called for inasmuch as my analysis thus far has involved an implicit double limitation: the self-restrictedness of skillful action, on the one hand, and the restrictedness by others of taste on the other. I myself decide as to how pervasive in my life a skill such as swimming will be, whereas others typically take the lead in taste: they literally "show the way." But in the case of psychopathology it is not at all clear whether self or other is determinative of practical actions: indeed, it is not certain that this very distinction remains pertinent, given that the very meaning of "self" and "other" is in question in the more extreme forms of such suffering.[41]

I shall restrict myself here to an examination of hysteria, in which there is no such thing as explicit learning (though there is a certain kind of mimetic performance) and no such thing as gradual inculcation or playing by accepted rules (though there is a complex connivance with such rules). Hysterical symptoms are neither self-limited (they are notable precisely for their exuberant unpredictability) nor the mere internalization of the norms of a society or its elite. They are as seemingly unskilled as they are ostensibly in dubious taste. Yet they remain valid instances of taking on bodily constraints and making them into something still more, indeed much more, meaningful than vagrant bodily motions. Freud says of Dora, for instance, that meaning was "lent to, soldered as it were" to her symptoms in such a way as to become inseparable from them.[42] Despite the soldering, such symptoms were enigmatic both to Dora and to her immediate social milieu. Unlike skill and taste, which incorporate and display cultural and social interests and norms more or less transparently, hysterical symptoms are initially opaque even if ultimately quite significant, that is to say, *telling*.[43] They are "ghosts" of an embodiment unknown to itself in terms of first origin and final sense: shadows cast by this origin or sense that have fallen upon the hysteric's body and on the body politic with which this body is covertly continuous.

Hysterical symptoms make of this body a memory machine, a mnemonic (and demonic) device.[44] Hysterics, as Breuer and Freud already noted in their "Preliminary communication" of 1893, "suffer mainly from reminiscences"[45] – memories in and on their bodies, which thereby serve *as bearers of unconsciously retained memories*. Hysterical symptoms are to be considered "mnemic symbols,"[46] and as such they are ghostly traces in the body, *remnants* of unabreacted experiences.

This story is well known and has itself become an integral part of late modern Western culture. I want to single out just two aspects that are especially pertinent to the problematic of this paper: the suppressed social significance of hysteria and the apparatus of conversion and somatic compliance. As to the social significance, we need only notice that, despite Freud's emphasis on the highly individuated trajectories of the neurosis and on its "idiopathic products,"[47] this emphasis in no way precludes the massive presence of social determinants in its actual constitution. Nor does the density of the body,[48] its sheer biological heft, in any way bar such presence. On the contrary: just because the body is such a compact entity – as thick physically as it is opaque psychologically – it is a propitious scene for the transmutation of social structures into concrete symptoms. To be dense is to be capable of harboring diverse, covertly situated types of meaning, including those with cryptic social significance. In its very density, the hysteric's body is, as it were, an *idiosyncratic habitus*. It is a *habitus* as a set of predispositions to act in certain ways, yet is idiosyncratic in that the style of action is peculiar to a given hysteric's body and is not merely imitative of more general, normative practices. The same body, nevertheless, represents a schematization of social structures, since hysterical symptoms internalize such structures (and *their* pathologies) by inversion, denial, projection, and other forms of repression. The idiopathy is a sociopathy.

Indeed, at *both* extremes of their history, hysterical symptoms are social in status on the Breuer–Freud model. At the beginning: in the form of specific prohibitions that prevent the abreaction or catharsis that would put to rest the wayward affect which is the energetic basis of the eventual symptom. At the end: in the specifically "symbolic" character of the symptoms themselves. Mnemic symbols of a hysterical sort are not natural givens; like dream images, they are formed by primary processes of condensation and displacement which themselves are designed to evade the censorship of the socialized self.[49] Hence, both in the (aborted) first reaction to a trauma and in the (eventual) symptomatic expression of it, sociality is powerfully determinative. For this very reason, hysterical symptoms are at once protests against the reigning social order and yet also collusions with it.[50]

This ambivalent relation to sociality – at once resistant and conniving – is itself made possible by the human body's "genius for ambiguity," its never being quite entirely what it gives itself out to be. And this ambiguity in turn is founded on the body's capacity for conversion and for compliance which are centrally at stake in hysteria. "Conversion" is the main mechanism of hysterical symptom formation:

> In hysteria, the incompatible idea is rendered innocuous by its sum of excitation being *transformed into something somatic*. For this I should like to propose the name of *conversion*.[51]

The affect aroused by the initial trauma, then, is converted into a corporeal state such as paralysis or anesthesia. But this state – in short, the symptom – requires a body part in which to be lodged. The liability of this part to be chosen and used in such a way as this reflects its "somatic compliance," a term first employed prominently by Freud in the case of Dora. Such compliance means that a region of the body – e.g. Dora's throat in the instance of her hysterical coughing – offers itself as "a privileged medium [or locus] for the symbolic expression of unconscious conflict."[52] For the compliant zone has a "capacity for conversion," indeed "a psychophysical aptitude for transposing very large sums of excitation [i.e. affects] into somatic innervation."[53] (Hysterical somatic compliance thus differs from the compliance of taste, in which the pertinent *habitus* openly – and not secretly – colludes with prevailing social norms, and from that of skill, in which a more or less dextrous body submits itself willingly to the discipline of learning the skill in order to attain consciously chosen goals.)

The closely related ideas of psychophysical conversion and somatic compliance – the latter is the organic condition of possibility for the former – suggest that the body is never taken over entirely by the social basis of its own symptoms. Undeniable and powerful as this social basis is, it requires a foothold (or handhold, or throathold, etc.) in the body if it is to be fully effective. To be determined, even overdetermined, by social structures is still to need somatic constraints against which to lean and upon which to rely. For the hysteric's symptoms to "enter into the conversation"[54] – as Freud puts it revealingly – they must find leverage in the patient's own body: indeed, they must find a home-place there. From that place they speak, re-entering the social nexus from which they first arose (and from which they have become so deeply alienated).

Freud conceives such a body-place in two striking metaphors: on the one hand, it is "like the grain of sand around which an oyster forms its pearl," while, on the other, it is to be understood as "a pre-existing structure of organic connections, much as festoons of flowers are twined around a wire."[55] Notice that common to both metaphorical phrases is the adverb "around," not "upon" or "over." Just as symptoms twine around a somatically compliant part of the body, so we can say more generally that the cultural arises around the natural, the social around the somatic instead of upon or over it – as in too many models of strict stratification.[56] As with symptoms that become one with the patient's very flesh, so a society is tightly bound round (and doubtless in) the bodies of its subjects: so tightly as to be inseparable from these bodies (*socius*, the Latin root of "society," means "companion").

The body remains in the center. Throughout, it is the congenial or compliant other side of the social subject, its intimate inside as it were. The bodily and the social are inseparable in practice even if they are distinguishable upon analysis – both psychoanalysis and socioanalysis – with the result that we cannot claim that one is finally dissolved into, much less becomes, the other. It is a question not of this vs. that but of this in that.[57]

This logic of co-implication comes close to what Freud himself concludes in discussing the question as to whether the symptoms of hysteria are of psychical or somatic origin:

> Like so many other questions to which we find investigators returning again and again without success, this question is not adequately framed. The alternatives stated in it do not cover the real essence of the matter. As far as I can see, every hysterical symptom involves the participation of *both* sides.[58]

The "both" is finally both body and mind, body and society, nature and culture. It is a matter of a mutual (but not necessarily symmetrical) participation in which each of the paired partners retains an undiminished and indissoluble force of its own.

The same is true of normalized, non-neurotic practices of skill and taste. In all three cases, nature and culture require each other in their very difference: culture calling for body (as a narrow place and thick entity in which to express, and sometimes to repress, its aims and demands), body calling for culture (as the indispensable scene of acknowledgment, whether in emotional abreaction, articulation in words, or other socially specific ways). Each is a limit for the other; yet each invades and pervades the other. *Les extrêmes se touchent.* They come into each other's presence in the massive, yet elusive, fact of their co-implication. Rather than being pristine opposites incapable of contamination, each exists to be con-taminated by the other.[59]

It becomes evident that it was wrong – wrong because artificial and factitious – to have posited nature and culture as separate poles to begin with: a bad nineteenth-century habit, for which there were equally bad nineteenth-century solutions. Yet the problem of how the natural and the cultural (including the "social") relate to each other is still with us in the latter part of the twentieth century. My suggestion has been that they are not *re*joined from positions of initial separation but instead are always already *con*joined, never not intertwined to some discernible degree. They are coeval epicenters in the common field of habitual-schematic interaction, immersed and immanent in this field instead of standing out from it as exclusive poles. Even (and precisely) as extremes, nature and culture come to be what they are only from within the highly schematized, habitual middle realm co-inhabited by bodily skills, by collective tastes, and (however unstably) by idiosyncratic symptoms.

I have suggested as well that the body is the agent, the pivot, the crux, of this same middle realm. In the body and through it – by its unique signature – culture coalesces and comes to term. It comes into its own there. Without embodiment, culture would be schematic in the perjorative sense of empty or sketchy. It would be a ghost of itself. By the same token, the body, were it not to bear and express culture, to implicate and explicate it, would be itself a ghost: a reduced residue, an exsanguinated shadow, of its fully encultured liveliness.

The body was bled out and abandoned by Descartes not just because he did not recognize its status as "lived," i.e. diversely experiential and self-reflexive, but also (and perhaps more critically) because he did not concern himself with its cultural and social dimensions. But this does not mean that we should reduce the lived body in turn to an object or product, an effect or posit, of discourse, as has been an increasing temptation in poststructuralist thought. This, too, renders the body a specter of itself, a paper-thin textual entity: it is to refuse to recognize the body as at once insinuating and insinuated, permeating and permeated, when it comes to culture and the social.

It is time to return to the body both as a lived presence and as a cultural and social force in its own right. Only then can the ghost of embodiment, which has haunted so much of modern philosophical thought, be exorcized and embodiment itself restored. The body that will then come forth is not just a grain of sand or a stretch of wire: Freud's images intimate something far too settled, far too much like a merely physical thing. The body alive, or re-enlivened, is part and parcel of the cultural and social nexus that not only surrounds it but, finally, *is it*. Yet it, in turn, *is this nexus*. Or we could say that each element twists around the other, not unlike a double helix. But I am running out of metaphors, and so I shall let matters stand just here, at this appropriately indeterminate ending-point – where the inconclusiveness of bodily being contests any account purporting to provide the last word on this delicate matter.

## Notes

1   The remaining is already evident in Descartes himself. He admits to Queen Elizabeth that "everyone feels that he is a single person with both body and thought so related by nature that the thought can move the body and feel the things which happen to it" (letter of June 28, 1643 as translated by A. Kenny, *Descartes: Philosophical Letters* [Oxford: Clarendon Press, 1970], p. 142). Drew Leder has demonstrated how Descartes's body mind dualism "reifies the absences and divergences that always haunt our embodied being" (Drew Leder, *The Absent Body* [Chicago: University of Chicago Press, 1989], p. 108).

2   "To claim that discourse is formative is not to claim that it originates, causes, or exhaustively composes that which it concedes; rather, it is to claim that there is no reference to a pure body which is not at the same time a further formation of that body" (Judith Butler, *Bodies That Matter: On the Discursive Limits of "Sex"* [New York: Routledge, 1993], p. 10).

3   Ibid., p. 54. This strong claim, which makes the very constitution of bodily matter dependent on prior metaphysical and epistemological criteria, is in my view much more controversial than a claim also made (and embedded in a question) in the same paragraph in which this claim appears: "a bodily schema is not simply an imposition on already formed bodies, but part of the formation of bodies" (ibid.). This latter statement comes close to the position I shall advocate in this essay.

4   Sigmund Freud, *The Ego and the Id*, tr. J. Strachey, *Standard Edition of the Complete Psychological Works of Sigmund Freud* (London: Hogarth Press, 1971), XIX, 53.

5   *Bodies that Matter*, p. 11. I owe this reference and that on p. 10 to Kelly Oliver, in her unpublished paper, "Save the mother: psychoanalysis and ethics."

6   Merleau-Ponty attributes to "the Cartesian tradition" a "reflective attitude" that "simultaneously purifies the common notions of body and soul by defining the body as the sum of its

parts with no interior, and the soul as a being wholly present to itself without distance" (*Phenomenology of Perception*, tr. C. Smith [New York: Humanities Press, 1962], p. 198).

7   I am distinguishing "sameness" from "identity," where the latter excludes difference altogether: as in "identity" theories of mind-as-(nothing but)-matter – notably in certain current neurological models of mind – or (in a more nineteenth-century mode) of matter-as-(nothing but)-mind.

8   M. Merleau-Ponty, *The Visible and the Invisible*, tr. A. Lingis (Evanston: Northwestern University Press, 1968), p. 253.

9   Sigmund Freud, *The Ego and the Id*, p. 27. This statement is said to apply to the "conscious ego" (ibid.). For Freud, the body-ego is an ego defined in terms of body surfaces.

10  I say "psyche" in order to capture more adequately than does "mind" Freud's preferred term *Seele*, which is capacious enough to include unconscious as well as conscious aspects. See my paper, "Unconscious mind and pre-reflective body," forthcoming in J. Morley and D. Olkowski, *Merleau-Ponty: Desires and Imaginings* (New York: Humanities Press, 1996).

11  In this way Lacan detailed the hitherto unknown "specific action" postulated (but not specified) by Freud in his essay "On narcissism": an action by which the ego is first formed. For Anna Freud's discussion of identification with the aggressor – which often includes specific bodily actions of imitation – see *The Ego and the Mechanisms of Defense* (London: Hogarth, 1968), pp. 109–21.

12  Marcel Mauss, "Les techniques du corps," *Journal de Psychologie* (1936), vol. 32; reprinted in M. Mauss, *Sociologie et anthropolgie* (Paris: Presses Universitaires de France, 1968), p. 367. My italics.

13  Ibid., p. 367.

14  Ibid., pp. 366–7, p. 382.

15  Ibid., p. 371 and p. 369 respectively. The full phrase of the second citation is "l'ouvrage de la raison pratique collective et individuelle." Mauss adds "et individuelle" because what is learned socially must be *enacted* by individuals. On the social determination of basic categories and forms of intuition, see Emile Durkheim, *The Elementary Forms of the Religious Life*, tr. J. W. Swain (London: Allen & Unwin, 1915), pp. 21–5.

16  I hyphenate "educate" and put it in parentheses so as to indicate that it is a question of something more than imitation. As Mauss remarks, "in all the elements of the art of employing the human body the facts of *education* dominate. The notion of education can be superimposed on that of imitation" (Mauss, "Les techniques du corps," p. 369; his italics).

17  Merleau-Ponty, *Phenomenology of Perception*, p. 146.

18  It is, once more, a question of identification, not now with my own mirror image or my aggressive rival but with the educative movements of the teacher or his or her surrogate. As Mauss says, "The individual borrows the series of movements of which he is composed from the act executed before him or with him by others" (p. 369).

19  Although it may not be the object of any particular instruction, the dog paddle is not part of a pre-constituted bodily repertoire – in the manner, say, of breathing or of one's diastolic and systolic heart movements. Mere flailing as it may appear to be, the dog paddle is nevertheless in-formed with the sagacity of swimming, albeit a sagacity in this case shared with members of another species.

20  "In sum, there does not perhaps exist a 'natural manner' with the adult" (Mauss, p. 370).

21  Henri Bergson, *Matter and Memory*, tr. N. M. Paul and W. S. Palmer (New York: Anchor, 1959), p. 168.

22  Pierre Bourdieu, *Distinction: A Social Critique of the Judgment of Taste*, tr. R. Nice (Cambridge: Harvard University Press, 1984), pp. 190–1. I have substituted "at stake" for "involved." Bourdieu adds: "the practical philosophy of the male body [entailing] a sort of power, big and strong, with enormous, imperative, brutal needs, which is asserted in every male posture, especially when eating, is also the principle of the division of foods between the sexes, a division which both sexes recognize in their practices and their language" (p. 192).

23  Ibid., p. 190. His italics. Bourdieu adds that taste is "an incorporated principle of classification which governs all forms of incorporation, choosing and modifying everything that the body ingests and digests and assimilates, physiologically and psychologically" (ibid.).

24  Ibid., p. 192. But Bourdieu also concludes, much less plausibly, that "the body [is] a social product which is the only tangible manifestation of the 'person'" (p. 192). This last step goes

one step too far. It is one thing to hold (as Bourdieu also says) that "bodily properties are perceived *through* social systems of classification" (ibid., p. 193; my italics) and quite another to maintain that these systems – more precisely, the signs emitted by such systems – act to *constitute* the perceived body, which only "seem[s] grounded in nature" (ibid.). Only "seems grounded"? Why not *actually* so grounded: which is not incompatible with a social over-determination by class and gender distinctions that nevertheless stop short of complete constitution. Or, more exactly, these distinctions do constitute the major ways in which the body is a signifying entity, a set of somatic signs, but *not* the body as presignifying – i.e. as material (biological and physical) and even as expressive (assuming that expressivity does not require a separate set of discrete signs for its conveyance). Thus I find the following statement of Bourdieu's at once redundant and problematic: "There are no merely 'physical' facial signs; the colour and thickness of lipstick, or expressions, as well as the shape of the face or the mouth are immediately read as indices of a 'moral' physiognomy, socially characterized, i.e. of a 'vulgar' or 'distinguished' mind, naturally 'natural' or naturally 'cultivated'" (ibid., pp. 192–3). This is redundant insofar as the purely physical is not yet semiotic, and it is problematic insofar as the expressivity of a physiognomy need not be taken as an indicative sign, an index, of something else.

25   The first phrase cited in this sentence is from Pierre Bourdieu, *Outline of a Theory of Practice*, tr. R. Nice (Cambridge: Cambridge University Press, 1977), p. 95; the second citation is from p. 85. (I have changed "schemes" to "schemata"; and slightly altered the translation of the second quotation.) On p. 82, Bourdieu defines *habitus* as "a system of lasting, transposable dispositions which, integrating past experiences, functions at every moment as a *matrix of perceptions, appreciations, and actions* and makes possible the achievement of infinitely diversified tasks, thanks to analogical transfers of schemes permitting the solution of similarly shaped problems" (his italics). "Appreciations" clearly refers to taste.

26   "The dispositions and the situations which combine synchronically to constitute a determinate conjuncture are never wholly independent" (ibid., p. 83).

27   This is not to say that skill and taste are altogether alike. There are at least three critical differences. (1) In learning or relearning a skill, I need not be joining (or rejoining) a given group: when I decided to learn how to swim again, it was no part of my intention to become a member of a swimming team, or even of the casual group of swimmers who gather on Wednesday nights at the Stony Brook gym: I would be just as content if I were able to swim in a private pool all by myself. The deliberate choice of relearning swimming is matched by the choice of whether I will make swimming a social activity. In contrast, the enactment of taste is forcibly social: there are no solo performances of taste. Even when done literally alone, the French working man perforce rejoins other members of his class of common fellow masticators. Where there can be strictly privatized swimming, there can be no fully idiosyncratic eating. (2) In enacting a skill I not only undertake an agile action but in so doing I enter into something quite material, indeed elemental: e.g. water in the case of swimming, wood in that of carpentry. A skillful action thus entails its own characteristic material medium. In exhibiting taste, on the other hand, I do not undergo such elemental immersion alone; I also enter into an entire social nexus that is neither material nor elemental – even if this has its own concreteness and density on its own terms. (3) A skill certainly requires habits qua settled routines: that is to say, specific corporeal bases for knowing how to perform a certain action with comparative facility. But habits do not *habitus* make: the latter (as the English equivalent "habitude" insinuates) entails elements of slow sedimentation over time, resulting in durable dispositions to act in particular prescribed ways (I can learn certain skills in a matter of minutes; I inculcate taste over periods of indefinite duration); of agreement by convention rather than agreement out of a concern for efficiency; of immanent style (the relation between taste and style is very close: both are deeply ingredient in the total life-form of their practitioners); and of knowledge that is more than know-how – a knowledge that is not so much learned as *absorbed* from the appropriate social milieu, "taken in" rather than merely "taken up," as with so many skills.

28   Cf. John Dewey, *Human Nature and Conduct* (New York: Henry Holt, 1922), pp. 66 ff. and Maurice Merleau-Ponty, *Phenomenology of Perception*, tr. C. Smith (New York: Humanities Press, 1962), pp. 145–6.

29   "Taste, the propensity and capacity to appropriate (materially or symbolically) a given class of classified, classifying objects or practices, is the generative formula of life-style" (*Distinction*, p.

173). Cf. also ibid., p. 174: "taste is the basis of the mutual adjustment of all the features associated with a person."

30    "Taste is the practical operator of the transmutation of things into distinct and distinctive signs... It continuously transforms necessities into strategies, constraints into preferences, and, without any mechanical determination, it generates the set of 'choices' constituting life-styles... It is a virtue made of necessity which continuously transforms necessity into virtue by inducing 'choices' which correspond to the condition of which it is the product" (ibid., pp. 174–5).

31    On right vs. left-handedness in human culture, see Robert Hertz's classical essay, "The pre-eminence of the right hand," in R. Needham (ed.), *Right and Left: Essays on Dual Symbolic Classification* (Chicago: University of Chicago Press, 1973), pp. 3 ff.

32    Marshall Sahlins, "Colors and cultures," in J.L. Dolgin, D. S. Kemnitzer, and D. M. Schneider (eds.), *Symbolic Anthropology: A Reader in the Study of Symbols and Meanings* (New York: Columbia University Press, 1977), p. 167; in italics in the original.

33    "Incarnate meaning is the central phenomenon of which body and mind, sign and sense are abstract moments" (*Phenomenology of Perception*, p. 166).

34    Michel Foucault, *Discipline and Punish: The Birth of the Prison*, tr. A. Sheridan (New York: Pantheon, 1979), p. 136.

35    On rituals of the table, and blowing one's nose, see Norbert Elias, *The Civilizing Process: The History of Manners*, tr. E. Jephcott (New York: Urizen, 1978), ch. 2, sections IV and VI.

36    Concerning the comparative latitude (and yet outer limits) of social rules, e.g. for table manners, see the variant texts translated by Elias, *The Civilizing Process*, pp. 84–99.

37    On the docile body, see Foucault, *Discipline and Punish*, part 3, ch. 1.

38    On the evolution of the idea of "civilized" (vs. "cultural"), see Elias, *The Civilizing Process*, ch. 1, part 1.

39    If one does not act in proper taste – and this means *do it bodily* – one acts not so much in bad taste as without taste, tastelessly, inducing all the cultural opprobrium such aberrant action brings with it. Bourdieu remarks astutely that "nothing seems more ineffable, more incom-municable, more inimitable, and, therefore, more precious, than the values given body, *made* body by the transubstantiation achieved by the hidden persuasion of an implicit pedagogy, capable of instilling a whole cosmology, an ethic, a metaphysic, a political philosophy, through injunctions as insignificant as 'stand up straight' or 'don't hold your knife in your left hand'" (*Outline of a Theory of Practice*, p. 94; his italics).

40    "Incarnate meaning is the central phenomenon of which body and mind, sign and sense are abstract moments" (*Phenomenology of Perception*, p. 166).

41    This is not to suggest, however, that the neurotic engages in *anonymous* actions. On the contrary: they are highly personalized. It is *habitus* that is properly anonymous in status. See Christina Schües, "The anonymous powers of the habitus," in *The Newsletter of the Study Project in Phenomenology of the Body* (1994), vol. 7, no. 1, pp. 12–25 as well as Elizabeth A. Behnke, "A readers' guide and commentary" to the same essay by Schüess in ibid., pp. 25–37.

42    S. Freud, "*Fragment of an Analysis of a Case of Hysteria,*" in *Standard Edition*, VII, 41. (I shall refer to this henceforth as "the Dora case.)

43    Jennifer Church of Vassar College points out that skills respect bodily anatomy in ways that hysterical symptoms do not. But I disagree with her observation tha "hysteria uses the body for a task that is essentially non-bodily – i.e. to say what would be 'better' said to language" (e-mail communication of April 21, 1995). The hysteric's body, on my view, *already says* in corporeal terms what is meant to be communicated – and it does so both eloquently and efficiently, so long as it can come to be adequately interpreted (e.g. by psychoanalysis or more expressly by somato-analysis).

44    As Bourdieu observes in treating "the dialectic of objectification and embodiment": "If all societies and, significantly, all the 'totalitarian institutions', in Goffman's phrase, that seek to produce a new man through a process of 'deculturation' and 'reculturation' set such store on the seemingly most insignificant details of dress, bearing, physical and verbal manners, the reason is that, treating the body as a memory, they entrust to it in abbreviated and practical, i.e. mnemonic, form the fundamental principles of the arbitrary content of the culture. The principles em–bodied in this way are placed beyond the grasp of consciousness, and hence cannot be touched by voluntary, deliberate transformation, [and] cannot even be made

explicit" (*Outline of the Theory of Practice*, p. 94; Bourdieu underlines "dress," "bearing," and "manners").

45  J. Breuer and S. Freud, *Studies on Hysteria*, in Standard Edition II, 7. In italics in the original.

46  On mnemic symbols, see *Five Lectures on Psychoanalysis*, in Standard Edition, XI, 16–17, and *Studies on Hysteria*, in Standard Edition, II, 297.

47  *Studies on Hysteria*, in Standard Edition, II, 4: "our experiences have shown us, however, that the most various symptoms, which are ostensibly spontaneous and, as one might say, idio-pathic products of hysteria, are just as strictly related to the precipitating trauma as the phenomena to which we have just alluded and which exhibit the connection quite clearly" (in italics in original).

48  The density is *not* that of consciousness. Freud's first use of "defile" is in reference to consciousness as a place of restricted movement of repressed memories: cf. *Studies on Hysteria*, *in Standard Edition*, II, 291. He uses the phrase "narrow defile" at the beginning of chapter 3 of *The Interpretation of Dreams* to signify the moment of passing through the analysis of a specimen dream and then discovering the prospect of its meaning as a form of wish fulfill-ment.

49  The connection between the psychic trauma and the symptom consists in "what might be called a 'symbolic' relation between the precipitating cause and the pathological phenomenon – a relation such as healthy people form in dreams" (*Studies on Hysteria*, p. 39). Freud makes it clear in chapters 4 to 6 of *The Interpretation of Dreams* that both condensation and displace-ment (especially the latter) aim at producing a "distorted" manifest dream that evades the censorship of the official ego.

50  Concerning this point, Susan Bordo cites Catherine Clément – "the hysterics are pointing; they are pointing" – and then remarks that "the pathologies of female protest function, paradoxically, as if in collusion with the cultural conditions that produce them, reproducing rather than transforming precisely that which is being protested ... Female pathology reveals itself here as an extremely interesting social formation, through which one source of potential for resistance and rebellion is pressed into the service of maintaining the established order" (Susan R. Bordo, "The body and the reproduction of feminity: a feminist appropriation of Foucault," in A. M. Jaggar and Bordo (eds), *Gender/ Body/ Knowledge: Feminist Reconstructions of Being and Knowing* (New Brunswick: Rutgers University Press, 1989), p. 22; the citation from Clément's *The Newly Born Woman* is from ibid., p. 20.)

51  "The neuro-psychoses of defense," in Standard Edition, III, 49; his italics ("sum of excita-tion" are also italicized). Freud adds: "the conversion may be either total or partial. It proceeds along the line of the motor or sensory innervation which is related – whether intimately or more loosely – to the traumatic experience. By this means the ego succeeds in freeing itself from the contradiction [i.e. the incompatible idea]; but instead, it has burdened itself with a mnemic symbol, which finds a lodgment in consciousness, like a sort of parasite" (ibid.).

52  This is the definition of "somatic compliance" in J. Laplanche and J.-B. Pontalis, *The Language of Psychoanalysis*, tr. D. Nicholson-Smith (New York: Norton, 1973), p. 423.

53  "The neuro-psychoses of defense," p. 50.

54  For the idea of symptoms as "entering into the conversation," see *Studies on Hysteria*, in Standard Edition, II, 148, 296.

55  Dora case, p. 113.

56  Not that Freud is immune to the lure of stratificational models: in the Dora case as well, he says that "in *the lowest stratum* we must assume the presence of a real and organically determined irritation of the throat" (ibid., pp. 97–8; my italics). Compare here Merleau-Ponty's view: "it is impossible to superimpose on man a lower layer of behavior which one chooses to call 'natural', followed by a manufactured cultural or spiritual world. Everything is both manufactured and natural in man" (*Phenomenology of Perception*, p. 189). This statement presages the later passage from the working notes of *The Visible and the Invisible* which I have cited in the text above (cf. note 8).

57  As Derrida is wont to put it, it is a matter of "neither/nor, that is, *simultaneously* either *or*" (Jacques Derrida, *Positions*, tr. A. Bass [Chicago: University of Chicago Press, 1981], p. 43; his italics).

58  Dora case, p. 40; his italics. Freud continues: the symptom "cannot occur without the presence of a certain degree of *somatic compliance* offered by some normal or pathological process in or connected with one of the bodily organs. And it cannot occur more than once – and the capacity for repeating itself is one of the characteristics of a hysterical symptom – unless it has a psychical significance, a *meaning*" (ibid.; his italics).

59  Each exists, we might say, to leak into the other, to be "a being by promiscuity": "It is in the universal structure 'world' – encroachment of everything upon everything, *a being by promiscuity* – that is found the reservoir whence proceeds this new absolute life" (Merleau-Ponty, *The Visible and the Invisible*, working note of January, 1960; p. 234; my italics).

# PART III
## The Flesh of Culture

# 11
## Biblical Roots

## Biblical Bodies
### *Donn Welton*

Biblical bodies? How could we as philosophers approach such a notion? Even more pressing, why would we bother? Have we not purged the discourse of the body of mythic images and finally seen it under the cool, blue light of analysis alone? Are we not finally done with that bad denigration that has worked its way through countless years of Christian philosophy, from Augustine onward? And is not this concept the primary source of a dualistic concept of the person which fuels the Cartesian view of our existence as fragmented, as split into antagonistic substances, a view that has wreaked havoc in the theory of mind as well as the theory of the person?[1]

It would be easy for philosophers, if not theologians, to leave these texts behind were it not for the fact that the very movement of current thought has carried us back into their orbit, for they place the body at the intersection of good and evil, life and death, addressing issues that we are only beginning to formulate. Recent developments over the past few decades[2] have pressed us to understand the body first in terms of modalities of existence or levels of constitution, but then in terms of "genetic"[3] or "genealogical" categories that look to various material, psychological, and social matrices to account for its concrete historical specificity, and, finally, in terms of ethical issues that connect the body to questions of human virtue and emancipation. Crudely put, we find this trajectory at work in:

- the phenomenological difference between the physical body and lived-body, introduced by Husserl and extended by Merleau-Ponty;
- the development of the notion of incarnation in an ontological register in the later Merleau-Ponty;
- a recognition of the intertwining of being and symbol, of existence and narrative in Ricœur, and an attempt to move beyond the resources of a structural phenomenology of personhood into a hermeneutics of human existence in the context of our struggle with good and evil;
- the juxtaposition of the issue of power, normalizing practices, and bodily constitution in Foucault, which attempts to understand the way the gestures and even the structures of the body articulate the practices, values, and habits of a culture;
- the attention devoted to the constitution of the body in feminist writers, such as Chodorow, Kristeva, and Irigaray, which places it at the intersection of material existence, psychological dynamics, cultural inscription, and ethical life.

For our purposes I would place special stress on Foucault and Ricœur. Building upon seminal but underdeveloped insights in Nietzsche, Foucault understands that the notion of the body must be brought together with the question of power, in particular with systems of powers that inscribe their relations on the very organization and dynamics of the body. The body is caught up in normalizing practices in such a way that its form is articulated by such systems, even as it exhibits them, contrary to Husserl's images of a self-originating and self-organizing center of its own actions. The surface of the body itself becomes constituted through the play of forces, and we come to understand the extent to which "our body is but a social structure composed of many souls," as Nietzsche put it.[4]

Ricœur, whose ideas lend support to the approach I am taking in this essay, pushes us beyond a genealogical account. The question of "sources" cannot finally displace an analysis of "grounds," as I will argue in the final section. For he treats our existence as suspended between the finite and the infinite but also reinterprets the Heideggerian notion of fallenness, returning it to the concrete ethical and religious struggles in which we find ourselves. Only by understanding the symbols and narratives that articulate those struggles will we gain access to this dimension, which has been pushed to the margins of what can be uncovered through a reflective phenomenological analysis in the style of Heidegger's *Being and Time*.

If we ask where we might look for the first appearance in the history of Western thought for notions of the body and then of the flesh that places them at the intersection of a rich heritage of ethical, social, and political practices and that speaks of dimensions of constitution that go beyond the circumscription of the notion of the body by that of materiality (Plato, Aristotle), mechanism (Hobbes, Descartes, empiricism), or sensibility (Kant, Hegel), we might be surprised to discover that it is found in Hebrew biblical and New Testament texts. The very notions that the body is thick with desires and actions, that it is configured not so much by "causes" as by motivational matrices not of its own making, that the organization of its own powers can be returned to it in ways that enslave it, that it is bound up with the trajectory of our ethical and religious life, are all found in these texts. As recent theories advance toward richer accounts of the multidimensional constitution of bodily life, paying special attention to ethical struggles and moral issues, they increasingly move into the same orbit in which we find the biblical notion. At the same time, we should not miss the critical edge that biblical texts might bring to current discussions: the challenge they pose is whether we can restrict the sources and dynamics of bodily constitution to psycho-social and socio-political registers, themselves articulated in terms of epistemic practices. Must we not look through and, perhaps, beyond them to ethical and religious dimensions as well?

My assumption here is that these texts, whatever their limitations, place the body at the intersection of the finite and the fallible, the flesh and virtue, and then of materiality and life, and articulate the body in a way that is profoundly different from the Greeks and, as a consequence, from Christian philosophy. These texts, for the most part, are not shaped by Greek thinking and categories, though they do insist, as did the Greeks, on raising the question of the body in a metaphysical register. They have been marginalized by modern philosophy from Descartes on, and even more so by postmodern thought, because of the mistaken assumption that Jewish and Christian philosophers have translated and then exhausted the philosophically relevant content of these texts. Postmodern thinkers tend to place them within an onto-theological framework, shared with Western philosophy, that has been superceded or, at least, dismantled. Even though most thinkers would agree that in that old battle between Athenian and Christian thought, the first took the second captive,[5] philosophers still have not looked hard at biblical texts to see whether the concept of the body at work there is different from, say, Augustine's or Aquinas's appropriation of it and, perhaps, is suggestive for current thinking about the issue. Given this neglect, this essay will spend more time on simply recovering the content of those texts than it would like.

To establish this assumption I would have to argue that biblical texts come from sources that are independent of Greek thought, which is no small task. While the radical difference between the Greek philosophical schools and the conceptual roots of the scriptures has never been seriously doubted for the Hebrew biblical texts, recent developments in biblical scholarship have also argued this for New Testament texts as well, reversing an approach that has prevailed from the days of Bultmann.[6] The result of this has been not only to discover a deeper continuity between the Hebrew Bible and the New Testament than previously thought, but also to attune us to the very different dimension of existence on which these texts focus and the different frame of reference that controls their analysis. To find a counterpart in the Greek world we have to look beyond its philosophers to either the Sophists or the playwrights. However, this assumption about the independence of sources calls for at least an essay or two in its own right that would involve an extensive discussion of the relevant historical research. In the course of this piece I can hope to show only something analogous to this at the conceptual level. I will attempt to do so by placing these texts in the context of a phenomenology or philosophy of the body in the first section, and then set up the contrast between that phenomenology and their special problematics, and allow them to speak in their own terms. Finally, I will raise only one methodological issue in conclusion: whether this approach is plausible in the context of a genealogical account in the style of Nietzsche.

We can turn this point another way. The Heideggerian and deconstructive project of moving "behind" the onto-theological framework of the Western tradition, first established by Plato, left us with precious little by way of texts – only a handful of pre-Socratic fragments. Given its richness, it is surprising that philosophers have paid virtually no attention to what was, for the most part, a parallel yet radically different world of writing and reflection.[7] It may be the case that in its very effort to set itself in opposition to Greek thought, which began in earnest with the early apologists of the second century, Christendom gradually employed its terms of discussion and subverted much of its distinct content, a development that reached its first full synthesis in Augustine. Perhaps it is time for a recovery of that earlier vision.

The second reason why philosophers might return to the biblical notion of the body is because of its importance in understanding the richness and diversity of the different streams that flow into our current conception(s) of the self. It is easy to overlook the fact that Christianity underwent periodic revolutions in which it attempted to shake free of itself and recover the clarity and rich dynamic of its original beliefs. This was especially true during the Reformation, with its leveling of the vocational difference between clergy and laity through its valorization of the full range of human activities as sacred. In some ways the Reformation was an effort to extricate the kernel of the Christian message from its illegitimate involvement with the Greek tradition. Perhaps nothing sets it in contrast to medieval Christendom more than the Reformation's rejection of its denigration of the body. Within certain moral boundaries the powers of the body were fully celebrated. Once again the old texts were allowed to sing. "I will give thanks to Thee, for I am fearfully and wonderfully made," as says the Psalmist, who continues, "Wonderful are thy works" (Psalm 139: 14). This was especially true of sex. The Song of Solomon is full of delight in sensuous involvement: "My beloved is to me a pouch of myrrh which lies all night between my breasts" (Song 1: 13). "Your lips, [my] bride, drip honey; honey and milk are under your tongue (Song 4: 11). "I am my beloved's and my beloved is mine" (Song 6: 3). Even Paul's somewhat dour advice to married couples (1 Cor. 7) has the effect of confirming sexual intimacy as normal and healthy. Culturally speaking, a unique blending of erotic and moral life was encouraged by these texts, and it became one of the prevailing sources for our notion of the self.

The work of Charles Taylor[8] and his excavation of the Puritan tradition has argued that these ideas flowed historically into England and North America in particular, and that they shape our philosophical understanding of the self. The affirmation of ordinary life, so alien to the Platonic tradition, was the bedrock on which its understanding of the body was developed. In leveling the difference between washing dishes and preaching the Scriptures, William Perkins emphasizes the source from which actions are done:

> So contrariwise he is spiritual which is renewed in Christ, and all his workes which spring from faith seeme they ever so grosse . . . yea deedes of matrimonie [i.e. sex] are pure and spirituall . . . and whatsoever is done within the lawes of God though it be wrought by the body, as the wipings of shoes and such like, however grosse they appeare outwardly, yete are they sanctified.[9]

Benjamin Wadsworth, an American Puritan, said that spouses "should endeavour to have their affections really, cordially and closely knit, to each other." Not to do so runs contrary to God's design, for "the indisputable Authority, the plain Command of the Great God, requires Husbands and Wives, to have and manifest very great affection, love and kindness to one another."[10] The essentially human and liberating quality of sex is, finally, affirmed by Jeremy Taylor when he declares that "the marital love is a thing pure as light, sacred as a temple, lasting as the world."[11] As Taylor argues, this idea contributes to a central feature of our culture, the ideal of "companionate marriage," which first began to grow in the seventeenth century in England and America and which underlies our whole contemporary understanding of marriage.[12] In our zeal to dismiss "Puritanical" views of sex we fail to realize that for the English speaking world they led the way in setting it, along with the material and practical dimension of our all too human existence, free from the strictures of a hellenized Christianity.

My goal in this essay is not to defend or critique the biblical notion of the body but to gain purchase on it. Perhaps the biggest barrier in the way of sympathetically understanding it is the fact that we cannot *place* it conceptually. Even after we break free of the reduction of the body to its physical existence by introducing and developing the concept of lived-body (as do several essays in this collection), and enrich this provisional notion by moving to a typology of various matrices of bodily constitution (as we will do in the next section), we still have not located the field in which its descriptions make sense, be they true or false. As a result the notions that surround it seem like a mixture of biology and psychology or, perhaps, pathology and sociology. Even those who view them sympathetically tend to move to the argument that we are dealing only with metaphors that point to psychological dynamics, since efforts to apply their import to the corporeal leave us bewildered. One of our main tasks, then, will be to situate the biblical notion. We will do so by paying particular attention to the distance to be traversed from a strictly philosophical analysis of the body to the account of the body as found in the biblical texts.

My working hypothesis in this essay is that the signs and narratives surrounding the signifiers "body" and "flesh" function to carry us to a certain depth beyond what can be discovered by a straightforward eidetics of the body, such as we find in Husserl and the early Merleau-Ponty, or by an ontology of the flesh implicit in Heidegger and explicit in the later Merleau-Ponty, or even by a genealogy of body and power as traced in the important writings of Foucault. As I will suggest, taking an invaluable hint from Ricœur,[13] we gain access to this depth only through the mediation of a religious dimension to existence that comes to expression in these texts. To oversimplify, by recourse to them we move beyond the resources of a structural ("static") and a developmental ("genetic") phenomenology of the various "levels" of bodily constitution, and then beyond a phenomenological ontology, which places the concrete life of the body in the context of our finitude and fallibility, to a study of the body's implication in our "fallen" and then "redeemed" existence.[14] We discover here not the sense in which the body is bound by its own essential structures but infected with a certain weakness or, perhaps, infected with a hideous strength that is its weakness, and then the sense in which it is cleansed and transformed with a certain strength or, perhaps, transformed by a certain weakness that is its strength. Here we find the body in its dissonance within the trajectories of an ethical life and then, through a certain reversal, as it is caught up in dynamics that place our incarnate existence in relation to a larger process of redemption and transformation. These texts create the clearing in which we can see the body in this light. In what follows, then, we must not only avoid a certain reduction of their content to other modes of analysis, however valid they be and also however essential they are to a full, systematic account of the body. In so doing we must also suspend a certain theoretical interest that closes down the scope of the body to what can be "objectified" by theory alone, allowing for the possibility of its articulation in ethical and religious languages whose grammar is different from theoretical discourse.

This last point has direct implications for the hermeneutics that we will employ when we finally turn to the biblical texts; I should say a preliminary word here. Our analysis must be rather different from a piece of inductive exegesis in which one attempts to lift the literal content of a concept from what can be understood only as its metaphorical and mythical setting. If we think of our task as one of extracting from the welter of symbols and dynamic descriptions a few direct descriptive propositions that refer to the body or codify the "theory" of the body there – a task that must assume a prior acquaintance with the body that we are looking for and what will count as its standard description – we will miss what is most suggestive about those texts. This language generally functions at a level that comes before a division into literal and metaphorical. If one insists on using that contrast, rather then being "metaphorical" descriptions of what we could otherwise apprehend or understand, these signs are more like "literal" descriptions of what cannot be envisioned without them. By establishing the level at which biblical language does its work, I hope to set it free.

## The body and the dialectics of finitude

Phenomenology provisionally "neutralizes" the symbols and narratives that are used to articulate the concrete deployment of our lives in an effort to get at transcendental structures.

Husserl himself came to realize that this was at work from the outset in his own phenomenology but misunderstood its consequences. In an important text penned just before *Formal and Transcendental Logic*[15] he expressly contrasts "scientific statements," which will form the discourse of the natural and human sciences, with the "descriptive statements of everyday life." The latter are "occasional" or "situational" statements and "are related to the concrete situation in which the ego, in the course of its life, has its experiential evidence . . . in terms of its practical intentions."[16] Husserl is clear that phenomenology suspends the question of the validity of the *content* of *both* sets of statements in order to get at an account of their production, of their "constitution." At the same time, the *type* of discourse that phenomenology itself was to employ, now in a transcendental register, was the first. It was to consist of a set of "objective" terms in strict propositional strings. Such expressions and propositions are not productive, do not exercise intentional functions of their own: their sole function is to reflect, to mirror, to represent. Everyday discourse, laden as it is with folk theory, was excluded. Husserl understands "occasional" discourse as that type of language which is not "objective." Meaning and reference mutually condition each other, for meaning is specified in terms of the actual objects or situations to which signs refer, while the referents are configured only in a concrete situation in which the actual intentions and beliefs of the speaker are understood. If used in a transcendental register, it would have been *constituting*, producing the very conditions or structures to which it refers and which it would attempt to articulate. As this would have drawn the whole world into that sphere from which it was expelled, threatening to undo the fundamental difference between transcendental conditions and the beings so conditioned, between the constituting and the constituted, Husserl had no choice but to exclude it. But with this the task of hermeneutics is also suspended.

An important consequence attends this exclusion: when consistent with that principle constitutive of its undertaking, phenomenology as a reflective, eidetic discipline cannot disclose the actual course of our choices, of our use and abuse of freedom, of our moral struggles, of our slow dance in the face of tragedy, or, to come to the point, of our body as the site of such actions and struggles. If the Bible contains a number of prescriptions that relate to the body, and if it uses certain bodily images (defilement, stain, stopped ears, blind eyes, etc.) that fall outside the scope of what the rigorous descriptions of phenomenology can employ but that are essential to its disclosure of the human condition, that is always because it understands the flesh above all else as a site of contestation. But Husserl leaves us with the question: can we connect the two? How can one internally connect an eidetics of the body with that field of experience where something like a "body of sin" or a "body redeemed" could be in play?

In this section I will attempt to find the bridge through a sketch of various facets of the body that do lend themselves to a structural phenomenological analysis. Let us begin where it does, with the perceptual body, and then place it in relation to yet two other matrices of constitution, what I will call the "pathetic" body and the "praxical" body, seeing, finally, how all three make up the "dispositional" body. I want to attempt to read the three notions of receptive, pathetic, and praxical body from the perspective of finitude or, better, to catch its emergence as we move from the first to the third. This account will be much too brief and, even at that, necessarily one-sided as I will not deal with yet other structural dimensions of the person different from the body. I can justify this omission only with the claim that however they are sorted out, the body will anchor the notion of finitude.

## *The perceptual body*

An eidetics of the body begins by connecting the perspectival nature of perception to the body.

Things are always given from one side, through one of multiple *profiles*. Profiles are views, adumbrations, *perspectives*. If we take the ideal of an object given according to all its perspectives as our definition of adequate givenness, then perception must be understood as essentially inadequate. Yet objects are given not only inadequately but also in limited fashion: the extent of our cognition of things is controlled by what is practically required or possible.

The fact that objects are always given in profiles means that they are always presented from a certain *point of view*. A point of view mediates the views or "looks" of the object. A point of view entails a *standpoint* from which the object is viewed. It leads us back to the *body*. Since the body consists of more than a "stationary eye" and is the body of free movement, we can say that its progressive explorations of an object are such that in moving from one point of view to another we move from one standpoint to another. Still, my point of view is always from somewhere, from a Here, and is not everywhere, from nowhere. The There can exist only in virtue of a Here; the Here can be defined only in terms of a There. As a result, not only the objects of my gaze but I myself am *situated*.

My body provides me not just with my point of access to objects in the world but, more basically, with my opening to the world itself. In fact, the notion of perspective is but a narrowing down of this more basic openness.[17] The world can never be encompassed in a single gaze, never be exhausted in a single sound; correlatively, I am bound to it in such a way that it can only be approached by me, that each act of perception is partial and calls forth yet other acts. As situated, then, I am *finite*. Finitude means more than the idea that our acts of cognition have no resting place, that they cascade into an open future without an end; it also means that each new point of view displaces others, setting them in the shadows, that each act of uncovering also involves covering.

But as it stands this account is incomplete. Our relation to things is such that we are "beyond" what is directly given in at least a twofold sense. First, each side or profile given indicates a whole which exceeds what is directly given, a whole whose presence can be understood only by recourse to that movement of indication that forms the core of perceptual intentionality, by recourse to what, strictly speaking, "transgresses" the side perceived as we apperceive the whole. We have only the front side directly; yet we see the object as a whole with its backside. The first seven notes of Beethoven's Ninth may be ringing in our ears yet it is the symphony that we are listening to. There is a certain "surplus" in our acts of perception without which the whole object would lack its concrete presence for us. But this means that all perception involves a crucial "protentional" dimension whose expectations are then confirmed or canceled or sometimes just placed in suspension. Whether it be a "passive" expectation in which our gaze is guided only by the present course of perception or an "active" anticipation in which we are deliberately looking for something, we can be mistaken not only about what is coming but, as new experience retroactively reframes our past and present cognitions, also about what we already know. This is not an accidental but an essential part of embodied experience. As finite we are also *fallible*. Without the capacity to err we would lack the capacity to perceive.

Second, there is a deepening of our openness to the world which comes into play when the *determinations* of things are themselves enriched by possible lines of *articulation*. Speech multiplies the possible significance of things and even brings into play a stance of affirmation or denial that itself exhibits, as it rests upon, the powers of the will.[18] The excess of the spoken over what is referred to, then of speaking over the spoken, and, finally, of the powers of freedom over those of intellect creates that gap in which something like both the beauty and the misery of our existence can dwell. The possibility of misspeaking dwells in this situated excess, even when our talk consists of no more than straightforward descriptions of the perceptual world. As this excess is essential to speech, it is necessarily fallible. Without the capacity to misspeak we would lack the capacity to speak. Rooted in the body, speech extends the body beyond itself.

## Pathetic body

The whole realm of affects, of feelings, of *pathos*, and then of emotions is notoriously difficult to categorize. We recall that Descartes expelled the passions from the mind without a clear sense of where to place them. In his *Treatise of Man*[19] he proposes a reductive account that strictly identifies them with the humors of the body and the mechanical action of vaporized blood as it passes through the fibrils of the nerves and is registered in the brain; the *Passions of the Soul*,[20] by contrast, locate them in the soul. The very different notion of the body just introduced might cut a way beyond this unstable account. But how?

The object serving as transcendental clue for the analysis above was bare, stripped down to its presence for a body that, for its part, came into view only in terms of its involvement in cognition. By rescinding the abstraction which makes that account possible, we turn to the object with its range of "pathetic" and, in the next subsection, pragmatic qualities. Objects are not just colored and textured, they are also shocking, repulsive, even hideous, enticing, desired, even craved. They not only have weight but are heavy or light, they not only have shape but also are handy or perhaps broken. The body, in turn, not only touches but caresses, not only sees but beholds, not only hears but listens. It consists not only of eyes and ears but also hands and feet.

In short, the sensible must be reinserted into the sensuous. We tend to gather the sensuous under the notion of feeling but I suspect that feelings are only part, perhaps the underbelly, of what is at play here. If we take πάθος in the broad sense, stressing not so much the notion of suffering as passion or, better, desire as it arises in the intentional circuit running between the body and its objects, then we can view the sensuous body as the "pathetic body." But here we must also provisionally employ an idea that can be established only at the outcome of the analysis: if we no longer think of the body as "part" of the subject but conceive of it as a dimension of the person, then we will not hesitate to use the structure of intentional life as our point of approach to it. In the first moment above we read from the intentional structure of perception to the place and function of the perceptual body. With this second moment we now move from the structure of *desire* to the place and function of the "pathetic" body.

It is tempting to treat objects belonging to the order of desire (whether wanted or detested) as the product of an interpretation of pre-given, perceptual objects by mental acts that add affective qualities to them. This mistaken approach, common among the empiricists from Locke onward, is inevitable if we assume that bare perceptual objects are first not only in the order of knowing but also the order of being. From the perspective of a genetic phenomenology of experience, however, bare perceptual objects are an abstraction, second in order to desired objects or practical objects. Generally we are initially engaged with an object as something we want, even as something we want to use, before we are engaged by its sheer physical properties, even though a later reflection might be able to abstract out the latter as one of the motives for that engagement. If this is so, then it is not the perceptual whole object/profile structure but the affective or practical quality of the whole that is primary.

Wholes belonging to the order of desire, especially those that are only anticipated, function primarily to draw or, perhaps, repel me but do so in such a way that we are occupied only with the object as desired. A desired object, even if just projected, does exhibit profiles but it is precisely its quality as desirable that allows certain aspects to stand forth and invite my interest. Accordingly, objects of desire have perspectives controlled by affective valences.

An object can appear at the level of desire only if it calls to us, solicits our attention. The trajectory runs from the real or imagined object toward us. That which senses its alluring or repelling force is the flesh.

As flesh, the body is motivated by the absent object drawing or repulsing it and moves toward or away from the object. In this way the object places the body, not the reverse. The particular opening here is established by the object as it invites us to enter a *situation* that it has founded. I am distant or There in relation to its Here. In moving toward the object I am being drawn into the circuit of its valences. This movement of the flesh leads not only to enhanced presentations of the object and the generation of richer senses of the object, which become the source of new acts of perception, but also to a fuller deployment of desire and the generation of inclinations, which eventually become the motivating force for acts of the will.[21]

We can take this analysis yet another step. There is a further change in dynamics that enters when that object desired by the flesh is yet itself flesh. Whether it be the breasts of the mother or that of a lover, desire is reconfigured by the rhythms of need, reaching toward, contact, satisfaction, and melding. Given time and development, what begins as an infant's basic need to maintain its place inside the flesh of those who provide for it becomes transformed into eros, that form of desire that is sustained by the gap or distance between our flesh and that of the other. The act of touching another, in which what is touched is sensed only as itself touching, establishes a circuit of exchanges in which two become one flesh and each becomes part of the other. Because this reaches into dimensions of our being that only an occasional poet or singers have been able to articulate, we should not think of this exchange as a form of communication so much as a form of *communion*.

Desires bring us not only before an object but before a situation in which we are engaged with the longed-for object. In its presence I am no longer an invisible center, a "null point" in terms of which the rest of the world is organized but thick with desire. As being drawn, we find ourselves "hurling" toward things, yet as still approaching we are "hindered" by the world. We sense not only the desired object but the desiring flesh. In extending its hands, in reaching for what is desired, the flesh senses itself directly but still as only limited and delimited. As a result, the flesh is never transparent to itself as it knows itself only through the situations that call it forth. In this double movement of being *drawn* toward a desired object as one *approaches* it, there is a yet a third moment, reflexive in nature, in which we are brought before our flesh as *finite*.

Feelings are not only tied to affective objects but can be even more general in nature and related to the whole of our being. In so doing they tend to become moods (e.g. depression, ecstatic joy, anguish). In fact, one could argue, taking a clue from Heidegger, that all specific affects are situated in moods that themselves disclose our being situated as a whole. Moods have the effect of enclosing and delimiting the flesh "from below." It is no longer lost in the object of its desire, but thick and opaque, turned to things only as it is turned toward itself. Brought before itself as it is brought to the world, the body senses itself only in its difference from yet other bodies, be they physical or lived. They become Other. Difference yields to distancing and, as a result, "the center for which all things are and from which all things appear is no longer merely the zero origin of looking but is rather self-attachment,"[22] an idea imperfectly captured by Freud's thesis that the first feelings we have are autoerotic. As self-attachment is deployed though desire, it becomes imbued with self-preference. "It is here that egoism, as well as vice, finds its opportunity: out of difference or otherness it makes a preference."[23] The finitude of the flesh open up its *fallibility*, the possibility that it will become its own greatest object of desire. To the extent that our flesh is tied to that of another, as we find in communion, fallibility introduces a special element not found in our relationship with things, that of *vulnerability*.

## *Praxical body*

The body is not only a perceiving but also an engaged, not only an affective but an effective body. We not only move around the thing we perceive, not only are moved by the things we desire but we also move them, act upon and incorporate them into our projects. Our account must move from the "docile" to the "dexterous" body. At the same time, this raises the question of power. Our task, then, is to trace the finitude and the fallibility of the flesh in the context of power as it is first experienced.

In practical contexts the qualities of the given are determined by their relationship to the body-in-action and the environment making that possible, be it that of the farm, the factory, the furniture shop. This means that we must rescind yet a second abstraction that allowed us to isolate objects of desire, for even they are normally bound up with our actions with and upon them. The body has *powers* that are articulated as they are deployed in our involvement with practical matters. Be it a doorstop we have made or the saw used to cut it, the whole object has features that are generated by its tie to the body-in-action. In general, we can say that objects of action have perspectives controlled by *schemes* of action and that these schemes give us their significance. What is a doorstop if not something "ready-to-hand" that can be placed by me in front of or under the door? And what is the saw if not something that can be taken in hand and used to exercise as it extends its powers?

At the same time that schemes of action account for the determinations of concrete objects, our actions are bound to the contexts in which they take place. If something breaks or is ill suited to achieve a certain task, we are turned to other tools that could do the task, to the shop in which we are working and to the available resources. The horizon at play in our labor becomes thematic and we glimpse not only other tools that could be used but also the powers of the body that could be engaged. Tools are situated by questions of suitability to a task; the actions of the body are situated by issues of skill, such as whether the body possesses the powers and the ability to carry out the project.

The question of the powers of the body brings us face to face with the sense in which they are circumscribed. This is built into the very notion of "trying," that feature of all actions that comes to the fore in the face of resistance. Tasks involve effort, often toil, as we meet stubborn opposition with each log we lift, each nail we drive, or as we encounter the powers of other bodies that resist ours. We also discipline the body in the hope of acquiring greater skill, yet its very structure and native endowment constantly sets limit to what can be actually achieved. The resistance that always attends work and the limited powers of our body makes us aware of the *finitude* of the actional body.

The fact that the powers of the body are limited means that it can fail at the task at hand. We try but without success. Lack of sleep or food or the presence of disease often lead to a diminution of its powers. Or we grow old or grow weak and our strength wanes. Through all of this we are brought before the *fallibility* of the praxical body.

## Dispositional body

These three overlapping and interacting types of bodily constitution give rise to, as they flow from, what we can call the dispositional body. We should understand them not as levels with the second developing from the first and the third from them both but as *matrices* each of which is engaged in varying degrees according to the particular way we are involved in situations. If priority or a "grounding" function goes to one, then this is a function of one modality being the appropriate way of assimilating or engaging the situation. But taken together in terms of their interaction, we can speak of the dispositional body, of a body thick with its own history of habitual inclinations that supports each of our actions with a fixed system of motivations. The body develops its own singular character, its own proclivities, its own thick style, its own propensities that characterize our own particular way of being open to the world. The dispositional body results from the sedimentation of its ways of perceiving and feeling, and then from its skills and tendencies, forming a certain whole, a character, a personal body.

The notion of the habitual body carries what we mean by the flesh, that side of our character most related to the palpable context or environment in which we find ourselves. We always approach that environment with a body bearing the sediment of past experience. It has corporeal memory and thus brings anticipations of its own rooted in its habitual style of assimilating things. Rather than this being yet another matrix, the habitual body is that site where the perceptual, affective, and praxical matrices congeal into that body that we know as our own and that each action "inherits." The crucial difference is that now are looking at the body in the context of its temporal development. Only now can we speak of it as a dimension of the person.

The notion of dispositional body is what roots the idea of our finitude as a whole. The dispositional body is what is always already there in each action we carry out. From the perspective of that action, it is the body that I have received, that I have "inherited." At the same time, it solidifies the flesh that I am and thus congeals my perspective into an inescapable standpoint, a place in which I am and from which I cannot move.

## The flesh and the problematics of fallenness

We are not simply living but *engaged* beings. We do not simply understand our existence, as if detached from all places, located in what is noplace, but *walk* a path that thought would never find sufficient reasons to trod. We not only use language but we *speak*; we not only criticize but we also *affirm*; we not only consider but we also *confess*. It is these excesses of concrete existence that philosophy has always had so much difficulty snaring in its nets. Yet without tracking the concrete movement of that existence, we will miss what is most perplexing about it.

If our relationship to ourselves is internally connected, as Levinas has suggested,[24] to encountering the Other face-to-face, then we quickly discover our existence as laden with issues of value, with the ethical, with a special responsibility for others, with the question of the sacred, on the one hand, but then, on the other, with conflict, with a struggle against vice, against violence, against the idolatry of unbridled consumerism, made all the more intense because these things also flow from our lusts, from our prejudices, from our blindness, from our resentments. It seems that our existence is fertile ground but cursed with both good and bad seed. This inescapable mixture is what we can understand by the "fallenness" of our existence.

How are we to do justice to this new field of concern? While we will concentrate on biblical texts, the various terms that are used to describe the body across a number of cultures describe not only the structures of fallibility but also a corporeal existence that is "already" fallen. They articulate the body from the perspective of an ethics, which always presupposes that we have in some sense missed the mark, and then of a metaphysics, which places the body within the larger conflict between life and death. As Ricœur has argued, there is a decisive difference between an "abstract" account of the body considered as a dimension of personhood and a "concrete" analysis of the body as caught up in ethical and psychological conflicts produced by the affirmations and commitments we as persons make. This entails a shift in method, a move from a phenomenology of the body that deals with the body in terms of its possibilities to a hermeneutics of the signs, symbols, and narratives that place the body in the context of our struggles against vice and, finally, our affirmations of life over death.[25] This shift allows us to capture our fallenness in a way that does not turn it back into an issue of finitude. The approach I am pursuing here, then, rejects the thesis that finitude and its experiential counterpart in fragility constitutes the fallenness of our body in particular and our existence in general. Finitude creates the *possibility* of fallenness, not its necessity. As a result it is crucial to distinguish those structural features of the flesh that place it as an essential dimension of our being human from the specific configuration and deployment of the flesh in its concrete living.

For now let us concentrate on the transition from fallibility to fallenness by marking the difference between them and then by looking at fallenness as it emerges in each of the categories of the finite body. In so doing we are following the notion of the flesh as it becomes *extended* beyond an account of finitude into one of fallenness. This brief analysis is designed to show that each dimension of the body and then the body as a whole can become willfully directed in a multiplicity of ways. It will fall to the next three sections to set in motion the appropriate terms and dynamics surrounding the body as fallen.

1 Perceptual body.

As the center of a space that it throws up around it, the body is situated as a Here in opposition to a There. The difference between "my" body and "the other" body arises from this primitive opposition. This contrast organizes the normal activities of *assimilating* what is other to what is mine – for every perception involves this – and of *appropriating* what is There and carrying it Here, so necessary for the preservation of the life of the body. But these schemes create a space in which something like *subsuming* what is other under what is mine and then *misappropriating* what is There by making it Here can arise. *Preferences* necessary to sustain the body can become *self-preferences* designed to enhance the flesh and turn it into our sole source of pleasure.

2 Pathetic body.

Affects bring us under the sway of the world and then other bodies. Acts of desire are enclosed by their intentional object. Our pathetic relationship to things is under the sway of the affective *valences* that give desired objects their particular thickness; such valences can themselves become chosen for their own sake, can becomes *values*, which has the result of turning the object into a *means* for the satisfaction of desire. In the case of eros, where the object is itself another body, the *communion* of desires that runs between them can be broken and one become *subordinated* to the other. The "closure" of two becoming one is torn apart by one becoming two and then one becoming subservient to the other. Sex becomes "open," an urge with an endless horizon. When Sartre describes eros as caught in the inescapable alternative of sadism and masochism, he describes a real possibility of love, but it is one under the regimen of open eros. Finally, as affects become extended into moods, as we already mentioned, they enclose the subject and we find only distance between ourselves and other. *Self-attachment* can enter and with it *egoism*, that peculiar desire that places the self at the center of our affections. Here we often find the splitting of the manifest body from the self-body, with the former protecting the latter.

3 Praxical body.

The *powers* possessed by the body are necessary for our actions upon the things we use. In learning to build things we also learn to master our own powers, turning them into productive labor. Our powers can be exercised in a way that respects the integrity of what is used. When labor is productive and responsive to the integrity of things, we have a relationship of *stewardship*. But our powers can also *overpower* things and treat them only as raw stuff upon which we exercise our will. In turn, our labor can turn upon the labor of others and we can exercise its powers over them, bring their laboring bodies under our control. With this, stewardship degenerates into *domination*. The practical necessity of exercising power over what is other degenerates into an economic and political domination of the alien.

4 Habitual body.

The "sedimentation" of these three matrices with their own fallen tendencies and individual styles into a body that is also finite is what creates the *bondage* of the body. Its directions, its affects, its powers lead it away from itself. Body as habitual becomes the body as the residual effect of perverse finitude. As habitual, it is a body that we always and already have, that we bring to each situation as something established and settled. As habitual, it is our *original* body. As habitual, the body bears our fallenness, a point that will be emphasized in the texts to which we will turn shortly.

To set up and give a certain context to the discussion that follows, let me extend our discussion thus far in the following ways. These next ideas follow from what we just introduced but would require a fuller account of the person to develop and then secure.

Since the finitude of our existence is not itself the source of our fallenness, we must connect it not to what we are structurally, but to the exercise of the capabilities that we have. This involves several dimensions of our being, but among them, central in the texts that we will look at, is the will. The notion of the flesh becomes extended yet a second time, taking on a wider meaning than we gave it above, one that situates it in the larger context of our thinking and the deliberate choices that we make. Still, referring to this as "flesh" brings home the fact that thought and choice are articulated through the actions we perform. As such it can be used to characterize the trajectory of existence as a whole. To live "according to the flesh," which now crosses the categories of "body" and "soul," is to live under the governance of pleasure. We must be precise here. Pleasure itself is not evil. Indeed, it is "joy" and a surprising peace even in the midst of adversity that is the portion of the upright person. Pleasure, in yet a deeper sense, is one of the concomitant features of a freed life. But rather it is pleasure as *telos*, as *a way of life*, that is problematic. Seeing its maximization as a way of life entails that we choose, that we come to prefer it to everything else.[26] Fallenness, in the final analysis, follows from finitude only in the context of intentional actions or, by extension, the "inner" root of action, the inclination of the heart built up by countless choices. "Evil requires a specific act of preference,"[27] Ricœur reminds us.

Secondly, the body opens up the possibility of fallenness but it does not exhaust its scope or range. The approach I am taking already sets a limit to the outcome of this analysis: to the extent that the fallenness "infects" the body, it will always take the form of a transformation of its finitude. Yet even here I am not giving a genealogy of the fallen body nor could I with what we have discussed thus far. Accounting for the body involves other dimensions of the person, especially the confluence of intentions and feelings, of acts of the will and preferences, not to mention an analysis of its psychological "reproduction" and its social "dissemination." Each of the matrices we described above would have to be reinterpreted or further described in the context of that which bears the transcendence of the person, that which opens the realm of possibility, and that which sets not only the fallenness of the body in relation to its liberation but also the finitude of the person in relation to the infinite. A fuller account would carry us beyond an account of the body of flesh into one of persons of flesh, a task that must await another occasion. Perhaps you might consider this only as a first installment in that larger project. The "fall" comes into focus here only as what haunts the present. Nor are we giving a full typology of types of evil. Rather we are tracing only those aspects of fallenness that intersect with the body and that provide a specific articulation or schematization of possibilities already built into the very nature of a finite body.

Thirdly, it is good to be reminded that "the Bible never speaks of sin except in the perspective of the salvation that delivers from sin," as Ricœur puts it.[28] We can transpose this principle, so crucial to any understanding of the import of the biblical texts, to read: it never speaks of fallen flesh except in the perspective of the liberation of the bondage of the flesh. The diagnostics, as it were, is always a precursor to treatment. I will attempt to capture one as it moves into the other, for without this we have less than half the story.

Finally, the shift from a structural account, which, like all theoretical discourse, always involves a necessary objectification of the phenomena under consideration, to a mode of analysis that captures the body as it factors into our "confessions" of failure and our "celebrations" of victory means that we must turn to the *discourse* of those confessions and celebrations. In what follows we will concentrate on the body as it is found in the texts of the Bible. We move from phenomenology to hermeneutics, for without this shift we cannot do justice to the concrete deployment of bodily existence. We are capturing the body from the perspective of the conflict experienced by those who affirm, who live by a faith, whose sensibilities, paradoxically, initially serve to heighten the conflict between the flesh and the rules of righteous conduct, between an evil that has somehow taken root in us and the high expectations of a virtuous life, between death-bound subjectivity and the liberating potential of the "Spirit of Life." This body is situated in the "history of salvation" and thus its analysis requires us to understand the narratives that bring that history to expression.

## The emergence of the concept of the flesh in the Hebrew Bible

The Hebrew term *bâsâr*, which we render with our English word *flesh*, is the most comprehensive name used to denote the external, fleshly aspect of human nature.[29] We are said to be "clothed" with "skin" and "flesh" and "knit together" with "bones and sinews" (Job 10: 11). It is used to denote our material, finite, and often frail existence. By contrast, our term *body* is rendered by a cluster of Hebrew terms, including *bâsâr*, as if there is not direct equivalent.[30] In any case it takes up a secondary position to the concept of the flesh, which dominates the account.

The Hebrew Bible always moves to the question of the flesh from the perspective of its efforts to understand human persons in the context of the economy of redemption and salvation. That economy requires a preface that describes the creation of all things; the notion of the flesh is retrospectively situated in that context. According to the book of Genesis, God produced a single humanity dyadically structured. This is described by the story of God reaching into the side of Adam, removing that one part connected to his breath or soul, fashioning or, literally, "building" it into a woman, and then returning her to him as one of the same substance, of the same flesh, yet as Other, as fundamentally different (Gen. 2: 21–3). As complementary, they *are* one flesh (Gen. 1: 23) and, in the subsequent context of the history of the fall and redemption, are presented with the task of *becoming* one flesh (Gen. 2: 24). The notion of the flesh here could not be further from that which turns it into a synonym of sinful nature. The two-one as flesh is characterized as "good" (Gen. 1: 31), even the pinnacle of a well-ordered creation. As flesh they are the product of God's direct creative activity and represent the fruit of that labor (Gen. 1: 27). Nothing could be further from the Greek conception of materiality and finitude as itself the source of evil.

The eating of the tree of the knowledge of good and evil and then the moral and spiritual decline up to the days of Noah, unfolded in dramatic fashion, is designed to bring home the idea that the cumulative actions and choices that humankind made in its independence from God produced a change in the "way" of the flesh: "And God looked on the earth, and behold, it was corrupt; for all flesh had corrupted their way upon the earth" (Gen. 6: 12).[31] The flesh becomes caught up in communal choices and actions: social "violence" causes God to turn his back on "all flesh"

(Gen. 6: 13). The story of the Ark, we might suggest, is about a second beginning, one that takes over the first but this time we commence where the first account ends. Echoing Genesis 2, what enters the ark is the "male and female of all flesh" (Gen. 7: 16). Just as there was one thing forbidden in the garden, so there is one prohibition instituted after the flood: "Every moving thing that is alive shall be food for you; I give all to you, as [I gave] the green plant. Only you shall not eat flesh with its life, [that is,] its blood." (Gen. 9: 3,4). In place of a prohibition against the tree of the knowledge of good and evil there is a ban on eating the life of what is flesh. This seems to involve two different features: (1) what has fleshly life cannot be the source from which we live; and (2) the separation of the blood (its life) from the flesh of the animal is necessary to set it apart and render it suitable for food, for sustaining and nourishing our flesh.

With this comes the crucial interplay of flesh, life, and blood, a cluster of images that will be mixed in various ways and control the entire account of body and flesh to follow. We see them intertwined next in the covenant made with Abraham: "And you [Abraham] shall be circumcised in the flesh of your foreskin; and it shall be the sign of the covenant between Me and you" (Gen. 17: 11). It returns when Israel slays lambs and eats "flesh" the night of the exodus as they escape from the land of bondage with its "pots of flesh" (Exod. 12: 8; 16: 3). As the sacrificial system becomes established, flesh is required for many of the sacrifices, all involving sin, such as the burnt and the sin-offering. There is a cleaning, a freeing of the one sacrificing from the stain and defilement of sin, the immediate result of actions that transgress the law. Yet the priests also eat the flesh of the sin-offerings (Exod. 29: 32; Lev. 6: 25), as that which releases from sin also becomes the nourishment making possible a living that is a serving.

Notice also that during this period Israel is reminded of the prohibition against eating the blood:

> For [as for the] life of all flesh, its blood is [identified] with its life. Therefore I said to the sons of Israel, "You are not to eat the blood of any flesh, for the life of all flesh is its blood; whoever eats it shall be cut off."                    (Lev. 17: 14)

> Only be sure not to eat the blood, for the blood is the life, and you shall not eat the life with the flesh. You shall not eat it; you shall pour it out on the ground like water. You shall not eat it, in order that it may be well with you and your sons after you, for you will be doing what is right in the sight of the Lord.                    (Deut. 12: 23–25)

In dramatic contrast, the words of judgment issued by the prophet Ezekiel speak of the Lord God preparing a sacrifice of "mighty men" and "princes of the earth" for the birds and beast of the field in which they will both "eat flesh and drink blood" (Ezek. 39: 17), not only utterly destroying their bodies but extinguishing their very life forever.

These texts never single out the flesh per se as the primary source from which moral corruption stems. Lust, for example, comes from the soul (Deut. 12: 15, 20, 41; 14: 26) or the heart (Psalm 81: 12; Prov. 6: 25; cf. Ezek 33: 31), not the flesh. At the same time immoral actions "defile" or "stain" our fleshly existence (cf. Gen. 34: 5; Isa. 59: 1) rendering it and even its clothing in need of washing (Psalm 51: 2; Isa. 1: 16).

If I am correct, the issue of life – its preservation and its enlargement in a context that recognizes its fragility and fallenness – is at the center of the different uses of the notion of the body and then the various regulations surrounding it. In Genesis the body is referred to only in relation to procreation and childbirth (Gen. 15: 4; 25: 23). But in Leviticus the body comes under ceremonial rules that fall into roughly five categories:

1  medical regulations having to do with leprosy, boils and burns that are found in or on the body;
2  seminal emissions and sex, bringing in ceremonial uncleanness but only temporally "until evening" (Lev. 15: 18);
3  menstruation renders the woman and any that might touch her unclean: she for seven days, they until evening (Lev. 15: 19). Interestingly, the shedding of blood and issues of blood affect the standing of the body ceremonially more than does semen and sex. "And if a man actually lies with her, so that her menstrual impurity is on him, he shall be unclean seven days, and every bed on which he lies shall be unclean" (Lev. 15: 24). In addition the loss of blood brings the woman into a state that requires not only bathing but a cleansing touching upon the economy of atonement; she is to offer a sacrifice of two turtledoves or pigeons (Lev. 15: 29);
4  the handling of sacrifices and other related services of the priest involving blood or death often requires the washing of the body (Lev. 16: 24–8);
5  Finally, any involvement with death, be it an animal found dead or another human, brings with it the need for cleansing (Lev. 17: 15). Related to this is a prohibition against marking the body, either by incisions or by writing (Lev. 19: 28). The writing that this body bears is to be by the invisible hand of the Living One.

In these texts there are two conditions of the flesh that are especially disclosive of how our corporeal existence is caught in an order that exceeds the sphere of moral choices. They push the account of the flesh beyond a psychology of stain and guilt into an ontology in which it is caught in the battle between life and death. The first is the disease of leprosy, dealt with extensively in Leviticus 13 and 14. It becomes emblematic of the fallen flesh, of the flesh caught in a condition not of its own making yet capable of being cured. The connection to a fallen creation is found in the fact that for the one cured a unique sacrifice is involved that points to the termination of the condition and then the liberation of the diseased person: two birds were used, one slain, the other dipped in its blood (which is also sprinkled on the cured leper) and then allowed to fly free. Interestingly, these texts go out of their way to indicate that leprosy infects the Gentiles' world as well, as we see in the story of Naaman and his famous cure:

> So he went down and dipped [himself] seven times in the Jordan, according to the word of the man of God; and his flesh was restored like the flesh of a little child, and he was clean."                                                                                          (II Kings 5: 14)

The second is the affliction of Job, a "righteous man" overtaken not only by disease but by calamity. Evil is poured out on him. He loses his possessions, his family. His fate is not brought on by moral transgression, by hidden actions that break the law, though his three friends intimate that this must be the case. Rather he is caught in a struggle between God and Satan, one that overwhelms him as it is played out across his flesh: "My flesh is clothed with worms and a crust of dirt; my skin hardens and runs," he tells us (Job 7: 5). There is no ceremony to be performed, no sacrifice to be made, no action that can change his situation. In its place, though, there is a hope that also revolves around the flesh, perhaps the only place in the Hebrew Bible where we find such: "Even after my skin is destroyed, yet from my flesh I shall see God" (Job 19: 26).

These two portraits, one of the leper and the other of unmerited affliction, place the body in relation to a fallen creation that snares it in unexpected ways and places it in opposition to us. Job's soul knows bitterness and would gladly "choose suffocation, death rather than my pains" (Job 7: 15). There is a splitting, special to disease and suffering, which isolates the person and effects a reduction of their existence to their afflicted flesh, even beyond to their "bone" (Job 2: 5) This is the state in which the soul becomes lost in a body that threatens to devour it.

All of these situations, both the various ceremonies surrounding the body as well as disease and suffering, have the effect of singling out the body, of turning it into an object of attention, of allowing us to distinguish between it and the soul. The contrast seems to be a function of these extraordinary situations. Outside these limiting conditions, however, we see that the language of the body and that of the soul coalesce and even allow for a mixture of elements. It is surprising how easily one flows into the other in the passages that follow. The body is more than an analogy of the soul; it is the soul transposed into its visceral presence.

> A tranquil heart is life to the body, but passion is rottenness to the bones. (Prov. 14: 30)

> The words of a whisperer are like dainty morsels, And they go down into the innermost parts of the body. 					(Prov. 18: 8)

> When I kept silent {about my sin}, my body wasted away Through my groaning all day long. 					(Psalm 32: 3)

> For our soul has sunk down into the dust; our body cleaves to the earth. (Psalm 44: 25)

This is especially true of that most transformed of bodies in the Hebrew Bible:

> Immediately the word concerning Nebuchadnezzar was fulfilled; and he was driven away from mankind and began eating grass like cattle, and his body was drenched with the dew of heaven, until his hair had grown like eagles' [feathers] and his nails like birds' [claws]. 					(Dan. 4: 33)

Hunger and thirst are especially descriptive of the desires of the heart:

> O GOD, Thou art my God; I shall seek Thee earnestly; My soul thirsts for Thee, my flesh yearns for Thee, In a dry and weary land where there is no water. (Psalm 63: 1)

The singing of the heart is the singing of the flesh, while the fear of the soul is the trembling of the flesh:

> My soul longed and even yearned for the courts of the LORD; My heart and my flesh sing for joy to the living God. 					(Psalm 84: 2)

> My flesh trembles for fear of Thee, And I am afraid of Thy judgments.
> 					(Psalm 119: 120)

Sometimes what is "inner" is also described with terms that belong to the "outer."
Even when the heart of stone is replaced by another, it is called the heart of flesh:

> Moreover, I will give you a new heart and put a new spirit within you; and I will
> remove the heart of stone from your flesh and give you a heart of flesh. (Ezek. 36: 26)

The words of wisdom that find lodging in the heart also have a transformative
effect upon the body:

> My son, give attention to my words; Incline your ear to my sayings. Do not let them
> depart from your sight; Keep them in the midst of your heart. For they are life to those
> who find them, And health to all their whole body.                    (Prov. 4: 20–22)

In similar fashion the text containing God's word is something taken into the body,
as when Ezekiel is told to eat what has been written:

> And He said to me, "Son of man, feed your stomach, and fill your body with this scroll
> which I am giving you." Then I ate it, and it was sweet as honey in my mouth.
> (Ezek. 3: 3)

The free movement from the language of the body to the language of the soul and
of the heart, does not arise because one, the body, offers a literal base from which we
can interpret metaphors applied to the other, the soul. Rather we have a discourse of
the body and the soul that does not assume that one is more accessible than the
other. It functions prior to the difference between literal and metaphorical discourse.
And this is a result of the fact that the notion of the body coming to articulation in
these texts precedes its objectified version portrayed in the neutralized language of
phenomenology.

As we look at the texts of the Hebrew Bible, we are struck with how the body is
caught up into the account of persons standing in relationship to God. In these texts
the whole person is constantly in view and the difference between body and soul is
treated like *two variations on a single theme*. The dyadic structure of "inner" and
"outer" or of "within" and "without," constantly at play in their descriptions of the
person, is never pushed into a dichotomy of two substances looking for a point
where they can "intermingle":

> It is impossible to miss the distinction intended in these passages, and yet we are not to
> think of it as a dualism of soul and body in the Platonic sense. Rather, *basar* and *nephesh*
> are to be understood as different aspects of man's existence as a twofold entity. It is
> precisely this emphatic anthropological wholeness that is decisive for the twofold
> nature of the human being.[32]

As a consequence of this, the primary focus is on actions and their motivations, not
on consciousness or subjectivity or any of the other thick versions of interiority that
have haunted modern philosophy since Descartes. Soul and body are inward and
outward variations on the person, two ways of playing the melody of a life lived
before a personal God.

Only after certain thresholds are crossed, only in situations where there is a
breakdown in the rhythms of everyday life and worship do these texts call attention
to the body. After sexual intercourse, menstruation, or handling a person with the
disease of leprosy, there is the need for a special washing, which has the effect of

turning the body into an object of special concern. What unifies these regulations is that they all have to do with *life*, with its generation and preservation, or its degeneration and disease. On the whole we could say that these regulations are not an arbitrary set of rules but were designed as part of what is involved in preserving a life, both individual and corporate, in *relationship* with a living God, one who is loving but also righteous and holy. Without seeing this the regulations directed to the flesh and the body appear random and, except for obvious medical cases, peculiar.

But there is also a deeper, darker account of the flesh. Disease and then tragedy can strike. These codes were designed to prevent or, failing this, to address this. The flesh is understood not just ethically but metaphysically. Death, too, has its regimen; it, too, can bring our finitude under its dominion.

## Body and soul in the synoptic Gospels

The concept of the body (σωμα) in the synoptic Gospels (Matthew, Mark, and Luke), not surprisingly, is identical to the concept of the body we found in the Hebrew Bible.[33] They, too, understand the body through the concept of action; its parts and dynamics exhibit the life of the whole person. This notion is behind a number of the hyperboles and images used in the Sermon on the Mount:

> The lamp of the body is the eye; if therefore your eye is clear, your whole body will be full of light. But if your eye is bad, your whole body will be full of darkness. If therefore the light that is in you is darkness, how great is the darkness!
>
> (Matt. 6: 22, 23)

These texts, however, also describe cases where this is not the case, where our actions lose their integrity and thus are given "honest names" that only allow one to "do with impunity whatever one wishes."[34] In an effort to interpret the true import of the Hebrew Bible, the heart is understood as the source of many of the actions we perform and, in this sense, distinct from the body. This is prominent in the many attacks upon hypocrisy. Hypocrisy is the opposite of integrated actions, the cases in which, as they create this difference, the actions we undertake have nothing to do with the inner motives and, in fact, function mainly to mask or conceal them:

> Woe to you, scribes and Pharisees, hypocrites! For you are like whitewashed tombs which on the outside appear beautiful, but inside they are full of dead men's bones and all uncleanness. Even so you too outwardly appear righteous to men, but inwardly you are full of hypocrisy and lawlessness.                        (Matt. 23: 27–8)

> Do you not understand that everything that goes into the mouth passes into the stomach, and is eliminated? But the things that proceed out of the mouth come from the heart, and those defile the man. For out of the heart come evil thoughts, murders, adulteries, fornications, thefts, false witness, slanders. These are the things which defile the man; but to eat with unwashed hands does not defile the man.   (Matt. 15: 17–20)

But even here this difference is sometimes captured by a distinction between two parts of the body:

> When therefore you give alms, do not sound a trumpet before you, as the hypocrites do in the synagogues and in the streets, that they may be honored by men. Truly I say to

you, they have their reward in full. But when you give alms, do not let your left hand know what your right hand is doing that your alms may be in secret . . .

(Matt. 6: 2–4)

As in the Hebrew Bible, we have a continuum ranging from an identity of the whole person with the body (or the soul) to a situation where the heart or the soul stands in conflict with the body (its actions, its demands). Rather than an integration we have a splitting or dividing of the person, which is produced by a certain false emphasis upon the external aspects of religious and ethical practices. Here Jesus comes to speak of the body's possible divergence from the heart. In particular, it is the use of a set of practices to simultaneously fulfill religious duties and requirements and yet to leave the person's attitudes, wants, and motivations masked, that uncovers an "inner" space in which we can find, in their difference from the actions, the person's heart or soul-life.

In the Gospels the person, I want to stress, is understood primarily in terms of the category of life, *modulated* into inner and outer. Perhaps it is more accurate to say that the Gospels do not have concepts of the body and soul as much as they have concepts of body-life and soul-life. This might explain why they are not identical, often being set in contrast, yet they also blend one into the other. In some verses we can see the term *soul* (ψυχὴν) being used as equivalent to life:

Arise and take the Child and His mother, and go into the land of Israel; for those who sought the Child's life [ψυχὴν] are dead.                                    (Matt. 2: 20)

And He said to them, "Is it lawful on the Sabbath to do good or to do harm, to save a life [ψυχὴν] or to kill?" But they kept silent.                                    (Mark 3: 4)

Notice how the body modulates ψυχὴν in these verses:

And He said to His disciples, "For this reason I say to you, do not be anxious for [your] life [ψυχὴν], [as to] what you shall eat; nor for your body, [as to] what you shall put on. For life [ψυχην] is more than food, and the body than clothing.

(Luke 12: 22–23. Cf. Matt 6: 25)

In yet other verses it is used to refer to the whole inner life of the person with its natural preferences and habits:

Then Jesus said to His disciples, "If anyone wishes to come after Me, let him deny himself, and take up his cross, and follow Me. For whoever wishes to save his soul-life [ψυχὴν] shall lose it; but whoever loses his soul-life [ψυχὴν] for My sake shall find it.

(Matt. 16: 24–25, translation altered)

The synoptic texts do have the difference between inner and outer, between what is manifest and what is not, but as in the Hebrew Bible this is very much like the difference between two variations on a theme, not between two types of substances.

While the term *body* prevails in the synoptic Gospels the term *flesh* (σὰρξ) dominates the Gospel of John. It is found only four times in the synoptics (Matt. 16: 17; 26: 41; Mark 14: 38; Luke 24: 39) when not citing a text from the Hebrew Bible, in contrast to five occurrences in the Gospel of John alone (1: 14; 3: 6; 6: 51, 55, 63). In both Luke and John it refers to the natural body, emphasizing its being material and concrete, and then being limited and restricted:

> See My hands and My feet, that it is I Myself; touch Me and see, for a spirit does not
> have flesh and bones as you see that I have.                          (Luke 24: 39)

> And the Word became flesh, and dwelt among us...                          (John 1: 14)

It also covers the limited resources of our natural life and learning:

> And Jesus answered and said to him, "Blessed are you, Simon Barjona, because flesh
> and blood did not reveal [this] to you, but My Father who is in heaven.
>                                                         (Matt. 16: 17)

> ...that which is born of the flesh is flesh...                          (John 3: 5)

> It is the Spirit who gives life; the flesh profits nothing; the words that I have spoken to
> you are spirit and are life.                          (John 6: 63)

In addition, there is an extension of the notion of both body and flesh that goes far
beyond the Hebrew Bible. In the Gospel of John they are also used to refer to the
mystical body of Christ after resurrection, which the believer can experience and
thereby be nourished.

> He who eats My flesh and drinks My blood has eternal life, and I will raise him up on
> the last day. For My flesh is true food, and My blood is true drink...
>                                                         (John 6: 54–5)

It, no doubt, came as a shock to those working within the framework of Greek
thought that what Jesus offered was not his mind or soul but his "flesh" or body,
symbolized in the element of the bread:

> And while they were eating, Jesus took [some] bread, and after a blessing, He broke [it]
> and gave [it] to the disciples, and said, "Take, eat; this is My body."
>                                                         (Matt. 26: 26)

In fact, the interplay we found in the Hebrew Bible is repeated in the symbolism of
the Lord's Supper: the very same elements, the blood and the body, are offered.
What is supplied to the believer, then, is something broader and more basic than the
soul: it is the *life* of the incarnate Logos. One does not receive something like
"Jesus's consciousness" but something different in scope and more basic in being.
One is supplied with His Life, with all of its integration of inner and outer, of heart
and actions, that can nourish our life and effect its transformation. This is why, in
the last analysis, the believer is understood as part of the body of Christ and why his
or her union with Christ is best understood in terms of an "organic" connection to
the body of Christ (cf. 1 Cor. 10: 16).

## Dimensions of the body in the Letter to the Romans

The fullest treatment of the body and the flesh in the biblical texts, however, is
found in Paul's letter to the Romans, chapters 6 to 8 in particular. I will concentrate
on this very difficult text in the remainder of this essay, attending to the way in
which both the notions of fallenness and salvation are played out across the body and

then to the method of analysis. I will be much briefer than I should but even at that this account will have a number of twists and turns. Let me assume that the reader has recently read the text or will take a few moments to do so now. And let me assume that he or she finds it deeply puzzling, perhaps perplexing.

I want to suggest that in Romans 6 to 8 Paul moves form a *structural* to a *dynamic* account of the body first in terms of the *ethical* contrast between righteous and unrighteous actions and character, and then in terms of the *metaphysical* difference between life and death. The first is found in Romans 6 to 7, the second in Romans 7 and 8. The shift is marked by a difference in the characterization of the body: it is referred to not just as a "body of sin" (Rom. 6: 6) but also as a "body of death" (Rom. 7: 24). Paul does not stop at a morally based notion of the flesh but moves on to an existential analysis of the flesh, though both are articulated in the context of a vertical relationship to God and of a process of emancipation involving the Spirit. This means that it is only by treating the dynamics surrounding the flesh that one understands what it is. The profoundly temporal character of the analysis in the Hebrew Bible and the New Testament places our understanding of the being of the flesh in the context of its becoming.

## A structural account of ethical liberation

Paul's first account of the body views it *positionally* as situated first in a fallen and then a "new" creation. He puts it this way:

> Therefore we have been buried with Him through baptism into death, in order that as Christ was raised from the dead through the glory of the Father, so we too might walk in newness of life. For if we have become united with [Him] in the likeness of His death, certainly we shall be also [in the likeness] of His resurrection, knowing this, that our old self [literally, man or humanity] was crucified with [Him,] that our body of sin might be done away with, that we should no longer be slaves to sin; for he who has died is freed from sin.                                                  (Rom. 6: 4–7)

Given the development of the book of Romans we should understand this passage as concerned not with how a relationship with God is first established by the believer but with the issue of the change in standing that comes with that relationship. This is not a matter of a new birth but of a changed "walk in newness of life." By contrast, Paul views the body itself and, more broadly, our inherited humanity as caught up in a fallen creation that places us under a certain type of bondage. It is not that we are slaves to the body but rather that the body is a slave to "sin," is a "body of sin" (Rom 6: 6). This phrase should be treated as a subjective genitive, i.e. not the body that is sin but sin's body. Sin, too, operates by a principle of incarnation. The body loses itself by becoming an instrument. This is why Paul in this context speaks of "sin reign[ing] in your mortal body that you should obey its lusts" (Rom. 6: 12). Or even more radically, "So now, no longer am I the one doing it, but sin which indwells me" (Rom. 7: 17). These locutions are motivated by the fact that for Paul it is not the materiality of the body that is the source of evil and yet what is evil can come to take up its reign in that very body. This diagnosis is intertwined with a remedy: Christ's death here functions to terminate the reign of sin and death; his resurrection to initiate the new order of life. In becoming identified or "united" with Him the believer is placed in that same position in a twofold sense: he or she becomes "dead" to and thereby "freed" from the demands of sin and death; and he or she becomes "raised from the dead" and thereby inducted into "the newness of life." Just as death is "no longer is master over Him" (Rom. 6: 9) so we are to "consider yourselves to be dead to sin, but alive to God in Christ Jesus" (Rom 6: 11). This first introduction, structural in nature, is not concerned with how this liberation is worked out experientially over time. This lack calls forth another step in the analysis.

### A dynamic account of ethical liberation

The question of how this change in position translates into experience is addressed in this way:

> Therefore do not let sin reign in your mortal body that you should obey its lusts, and do not go on presenting the members of your body to sin [as] instruments of unright-eousness; but present yourselves to God as those alive from the dead, and your members [as] instruments of righteousness to God. For sin shall not be master over you, for you are not under law, but under grace.                    (Rom. 6: 12–14)

Using the structural differences as his guiding thread, Paul introduces a dynamic analysis of the body's involvement in the order of sin and death and then of its release from that order. The body becomes "sin's body" as a result of our "pre-senting the members" of our body as "instruments of unrighteousness" (Rom. 6: 13). Actions give flesh to moral qualities and, as a result, implicate a moral universe. Actions whose intentional component consciously violates what is right, as well as those that further what is good, produce a change that belongs to the order of the body, of the habitual, of our tendencies and inclinations. In this context, Paul encourages the believer, having been placed in a new order, to let the members of the body becomes "instruments of righteousness." In so doing the body itself becomes part of a larger process of "sanctification" (Rom 6: 19). The change in position thereby becomes a change in disposition. The challenge this presents to contemporary theory could not be clearer: one cannot conceptualize the body without thinking of it in the context of a moral universe.

At the same time, Paul introduces a subtle but profound difference as to how this operates for those who belong to the new creation. He turns to the question of how experientially we can escape from the dominance of improper actions. Is this a matter of understanding what is right and then bringing our actions into conformity with it? This approach is foundational to all systems that reduce the religious to the ethical and that view the understanding of moral laws as the motivating source of moral actions. But Paul sets his approach in opposition to this in a single line: "For you are not under law, but under grace" (Rom. 6: 14). Or even stronger, we died not just to the reign of sin through the body of Christ but also to the natural efforts to correct this by appeal to ethical rules: "You also were made to die to the Law through the body of Christ" (Rom. 7: 4). He points to a different source, grace, and speaks of being joined "to another, to Him who was raised from the dead, that we might bear fruit for God" (Rom 7: 4). By becoming joined to the life of Christ, the believer draws from a very different source. Moral action is understood as a result of the growth of this life, as "fruit." The law, by contrast, functions only to *expose*, not overcome, the weakness of the flesh and even to *incite* the flesh to willful misdeeds, "for apart from the Law sin [is] dead," i.e. dormant (Rom. 7: 8). To put it actively: "when the commandment came, sin became alive, and I died" (Rom 7: 9). Paul connects the body to this process: "For while we were in the flesh, the sinful passions, which were [aroused] by the Law, were at work in the members of our body to bear fruit for death" (Rom. 7: 5). The crucial point is that the law is ineffectual, is powerless to truly break the bondage of those vices that have taken on flesh. But this problem also pushes the analysis to the next level, for Paul's emphasis upon "presenting" depends upon a notion of the will. Is not this precisely part of the problem: "for the wishing is present in me, but the doing of the good [is] not" (Rom 7: 18)?

## Structural analysis and existential liberation

The treatment of immoral or unrighteous actions as "fruit for death" or, by contrast, of moral actions and a virtuous character as "fruit for God" transposes Paul's analysis and places it in the broader context of the existential opposition between life and death. Paul moves into this by tracking a conflict experienced by those who rely only on the moral laws and attempt to live a life in conformity to it:

> For I joyfully concur with the law of God in the inner man, but I see a different law in the members of my body, waging war against the law of my mind, and making me a prisoner of the law of sin which is in my members. Wretched man that I am! Who will set me free from the body of this death? (Rom. 7: 22–24)

To catch the import of this we should attend to a contrast that is already in play in the passages cited above. There is a crucial distinction to be made between sins and sin, between sins understood as produced by wrong choices and attitudes and sin understood as part of the human condition. One is an ethical notion that applies to actions that violate the moral order. The other is ultimately an existential notion in which sin catches one up in its throes and which, as part of a dispositional heritage not of our own making, is related to our deep tendency toward egotism, selfishness and fear of the other. It is existential because Paul related it to being "dead" (cf. Eph. 2: 1). What makes the analysis of the body in Romans 6 to 8 unique is that it places the body in relation to both. The body is the body of moral actions; it is also the bearer of this dispositional heritage; as played out across its surfaces, as welling from its sources, as deployed in its actions, it becomes a "body of death." This is what a knowledge of the law is incapable of changing. Still, the phrase "body of this death" does not refer to the mortal or finite flesh but rather the body given over to passions "at work in the members of our body" that then "bear fruit for death" (Rom 7: 5).

Conflict arises because two different principles or "laws" interact experientially. On the one hand, I know the moral law, "the law of God," with the "mind" (the leading aspect of the soul-life). On the other hand, I find a different principle at work in the "flesh," which Paul calls "the law of sin and death" (Rom. 8: 2). This gives us the parameters of the conflict: while I "delight" in the ideals of virtue contained in the law of God,

> I see a different law in the members of my body, waging war against the law of my mind, and making me a prisoner of the law of sin which is in my members.
> (Rom. 7: 23)

The law, which I know and even agree with, is impotent in the face of entrenched habits that are contrary to that law. This leads Paul to speak of the body not just as the site in which sin but also (spiritual) death comes to take up its residence: "Wretched man that I am! Who will set me free from the body of this death?" (Rom. 7: 24).

Paul's solution to this dilemma comes by introducing another "law" that points to yet another source for our actions. He speaks of this as "the law of the Spirit of life," which sets us free from the law of sin and death (Rom 8: 2). It does this, on the one hand, by releasing one from past failures: "There is therefore now no condemnation for those who are in Christ Jesus" (Rom. 8: 1). On the other hand, it provides one with a different source from which one can live: one can now "walk" not "according to the flesh, but according to the Spirit" (Rom. 8: 4).

## Dynamic analysis and existential liberation

This account of the law of the Spirit of life is immediately amplified by a dynamic account of how we come to experience its efficacy. The Spirit that Paul envisions here is directly connected to the issue of life. He even thinks of the Spirit under this description as that which Christ became through the process of death and resurrection: "The first man, Adam, became a living soul, the last Adam [became] a life-giving spirit" (1 Cor. 15: 45). He then encourages us to realize that the liberating force of the Spirit becomes effective when the mind is directed to or set not on the flesh or even on the law but on the Spirit (Rom 8: 5). "For the mind set on the flesh is death, but the mind set on the Spirit is life and peace" (Rom. 8: 6). The Spirit is what gives us life (cf. II Cor 3: 6), i.e. supplies us with the type of nourishment that transforms one in ways that attempting to follow moral rules cannot do. This is what Paul elsewhere calls "sowing" the Spirit and "reaping" life whose quality is "eternal" (Gal 6: 8). While the body is mortal and its full "redemption" is only something that one can "await" (Rom 8: 23), this process of transformation, Paul is convinced, extends to the body today, if in a limited way:

> But if the Spirit of Him who raised Jesus from the dead dwells in you, He who raised Christ Jesus from the dead will also give life to your mortal bodies through His Spirit who indwells you.                                                      (Rom. 8: 11)

Let me suggest figure 1 as a way of summarizing the various dimensions of this analysis.

|                        | Structural analysis                                                                      | Dynamic analysis                                                                          |
|------------------------|------------------------------------------------------------------------------------------|-------------------------------------------------------------------------------------------|
| Morality and the flesh | Ethical opposition between righteous and unrighteous Focus: virtuous actions and character | Negative: bondage to sin, under the law Positive: freed from sin, under grace              |
| Metaphysics and the flesh | Ontological opposition between life and death Focus: redemption of the body            | Negative: faulted existence bearing "fruit unto death" Positive: dynamics of emancipation |

*Figure 1*

The starting point of the account of Romans 6 to 8, one that Paul has attempted to secure by the arguments of the earlier chapters, is that we are persons of flesh caught up in a struggle with sin and death as it has come to reside in us. He thinks of the believer as engaged in a battle for life in which the first foes are internal. These chapters outline a conflict dividing the person and pitting not just different principles or powers but also, as a consequence, different "parts" of the person against one another. Initially, the flesh is the body seen under the aspect of its bondage to sin and death. Thus the term *flesh* generally carries the notion of the body as caught in the throes of a fallen creation. The primary antagonists are the "flesh" and the "mind," which, left to themselves, generate a splitting between the body and the soul. Locked in this dynamic, the body remains captured in the circuit of life and death in which death "reigns" (Rom. 5: 17, 21) and our body remains our other. It is only when a third element, the "Spirit of Life," enters (Rom. 8) that the body becomes part of the "new creation." For Paul the redemption of the person necessarily involves a "positional" redemption of the body, both present and future. But this is a placeholder for the idea that the body in general and the flesh in particular can undergo a "dispositional" transformation. The process of emancipation introduces an unshackling of the body from its bondage to what destroys it and a recovery and integration of its full powers into the "new person."

The body for Paul is not reducible to a material object or bio-physical entity, for it belongs to the moral and spiritual universe as much as it belongs to the physical world. As such it is flesh. In the final analysis the New Testament does not argue for a rejection of the body but for its redemption and its transformation into a site of moral and spiritual disclosure. This sketch alone should indicate how far we are from the theory of the body found in Platonism.

## Beyond good and evil

These ideas give rise to thought, to yet another level of philosophical analysis. I can pursue only a single line of reflection, one that I hope will further clarify the method at play in this essay.

I have not given an account of the genesis of finite and then faulted existence but only its structure and dynamics. These pages do not attempt to frame a "genealogical" account but what can be called an "originary" account, an analysis of finitude and fallenness as it endlessly occurs. Let me use a brief comparison with Nietzsche as a way of showing how this type of analysis might stand on its own and the sense in which it attempts to move "beyond good and evil." As the notion of fallenness is clearly the more problematic of the two I will concentrate on it.

Nietzsche understands the substance of Christianity as essentially a morality whose content is entirely natural and can be accounted for genealogically. The notion of virtue in general is understood as rooted initially in "force," in the violence necessary to integrate individuals into a group, and then in the gradual acceptance of its codes as customs and, eventually, as freely affirmed rules.[35] This feeds into the Freudian picture of the law functioning as superego restricting and redirecting an untamed libido that stands in opposition to it. For Nietzsche and Freud the law is derived from the culture, and conscience is the product of the internalization or "inscription" of its codes, while for biblical texts ethical ideals and principles have a legitimacy that is not reducible to matters of custom or convention, as they are grounded in the nature of God. Of course, without the rules we do not have the notion of deviation and thus fallenness.

Nietzsche and Freud give us a naturalistic accounts of the *source* of moral rules, of the difference between good and evil. Their content is completely accounted for through a genealogical account, which simultaneously adds to this an analysis of how destructive conventional morality is. What neither seem to realize is that a certain critique not just of immorality but of the "weakness" of a moral style of life is very much a part of the New Testament texts. The difference is not that it places its own moral code in opposition to yet others, though we can find this too, but that it turns upon its own moral code as impossible and, worse, enslaving should it be taken as an end in itself, should it be understood simply as a rule book to be understood and followed. Not only does it recognize that there is a morality that arises from natural sources (and may be a perversion of genuine morality) but that on its own morality is ineffectual. The recurrent attack upon religion in the Biblical texts usually has this in focus.

Still, the deeper challenge of these texts is that they require us to move beyond a consideration of *sources* alone and also to give an account of its *ground*. The nature of virtues is grounded in the nature of God metaphysically, while its realization in the life of the believer is understood as the result or the "fruit" of an ongoing, growing relationship with that God. Nietzsche's account assumes that recourse to sources eliminates the need for recourse to grounds, as if they are mutually exclusive. But an "altogether human" account of how moral codes or rules develop or of how moral rules are learned from one's parents or the culture does not exclude a consideration of whether or not those rules are themselves legitimate or whether those rules cannot be understood in the context of certain recurrent or invariant structures essential to what we are. A theory that accounts for all moral rules through learning does not eliminate yet another level of consideration where we ask about the quality of such rules, about their possible destructive or emancipatory import.

Nietzsche, of course, anticipates this difference and attempts to block this move by the introduction of a metaphysical hypothesis that eliminates any recourse to grounds. His idea that God is dead and then his notion of the Eternal Return is designed to undercut any appeal to vertical in contrast to horizontal accounts of existence, be it the Judeo-Christian notion of God, Mencius's concept of the Tao, or Plato's theory of the Good. But this is done inconsistently, for the image of the Eternal Return, while perhaps not itself a cosmological doctrine, certainly functions as a trope designed to repel one from this axis of analysis. In doing so, it plays in a transcendental register and cannot itself be derived from a genealogical account. In its efforts to reduce grounds to sources it functions as ground. It, too, can be understood genealogically only at the risk of a crude psychologism or biologism.

If I have understood these texts correctly, fallenness as "original" must be defined as a recurrent *mixture* of motives attending moral actions that produce a splitting of the person into "flesh" and "spirit." Ironically, Romans 7 views this situation as one that is exacerbated by the "law of God," not cured by it. It portrays a person who has fallen into the temptation of taking the substance of Christianity as morality and then attempting to live in accordance with its ethical teachings. This involves reflecting upon the intuitive difference between right and wrong or the Christian code of conduct (the standard having been greatly escalated as a result of Jesus's teaching) and then positing the attainment of Christian virtue as the basic principle and governing goal of one's life. This leads to grief, to failure, because there are always areas in which we are "weak," i.e. where the "flesh" is "stronger" than even our desire to do what is right. This is the conflict that anyone who has a moral code might experience but it is heightened not only because the biblical notion of virtue is high, going beyond behavior to motives and attitudes, even touching upon one's disposition, but also because the usual recipes for remedy circle back to the will and we are left with little more than Plato's notion of a certain "high spirited" part of the soul coming to its assistance with courage and fortitude or Heidegger's recommendation of resoluteness. To collapse the religious into the moral, to replace the "Spirit of life" with the "law of God," is only to rescore the quiet songs of fallen existence for full orchestra. The path of morality leads to a dividing of the person. As Nietzsche understood all too well, "in morality man treats himself not as an '*individuum*' but as a '*dividuum*'."[36] Fallenness is precisely this splitting. In reducing the Christian life to the moral life, one has not escaped fallenness but only created another variation on it. The opposition at play here is not between the tree of good and the tree of evil, but between the tree of life and the tree of the knowledge of good and evil. In the final analysis this is the opposition situating the discourse of the flesh for the New Testament.

## Notes

Special thanks to Charles Drew, Leo Lipis, and Talia Welch for their assistance with this essay.
1  See Gilbert Ryle, *The Concept of the Mind* (New York: Barnes and Noble, 1949); Maurice Merleau-Ponty, *Phenomenology of Perception*, trans. by Colin Smith (New York: Routledge and Kegan Paul, 1962); Susan Bordo, *The Flight to Objectivity* (Albany: State University of New York Press, 1987), only to mention a few.
2  For these and other developments see *Continental Theories of the Bodies*, ed. by Donn Welton (forthcoming), as well as other essays in this volume.
3  Throughout this essay the term "genetic" is used to refer to that side of phenomenological method that Husserl set in contrast to "static" analysis, not as we find it currently in biology.
4  Friedrich Nietzsche, *Beyond Good and Evil*, trans. by Walter Kaufmann (New York: Random House, 1966), section 19.
5  The story is actually much more complex.
6  For one of the best examples of this direction see Craig Evans, *Word and Glory: On the Exegetical and Theological Background of John's Prologue, Journal for the Study of the New Testament, Supplemental Series*, vol. 89 (Sheffield: Sheffield Academic Press, 1993). Also cf. Martin Hengel, *Die Johanneische Frage* (Tübingen: Siebeck, 1993).
7  No doubt, Bultmann's treatment of these texts probably influenced Heidegger, which may be one of the reasons that Heidegger does not devote any attention to them. At the same time Heidegger's ontology of existence as outlined in *Being and Time* certainly gave Bultmann the frame of reference and basic existential categories that facilitated his program of demythologization. They were colleagues at Marburg from 1923 to 1928. Heidegger attended his seminars and considered him the only interesting light in that "foggy hole." As cited in Hugo Ott, *Martin Heidegger*, trans. by Allan Blunden (London: Fontana Press, 1994), p. 125.
8  See Charles Taylor, *Sources of the Self: The Making of the Modern Identity* (Cambridge, Mass.: Harvard University Press, 1989), especially part III.
9  As quoted in Taylor, *Sources of the Self*, p. 224.
10  Ibid., p. 226.
11  Ibid.
12  Ibid., p. 227.
13  The only philosopher who has attended to this difference is Paul Ricœur. One will hear echoes of his account throughout this essay as the difference between fallibility and fallenness is one that organizes his approach. See his *Fallible Man: Philosophy of the Will*, trans. by Charles Kelbley (Chicago: Henry Regnery, 1965), *The Symbolism of Evil*, trans. by Emerson Buchanan

(Boston: Beacon Press, 1967) and, most recently, *Oneself as Another*, trans. by Kathleen Blamey (Chicago: University of Chicago Press, 1992).

14 Here I am following the turn that Paul Ricœur takes as he moves from *Fallible Man* to *Symbolism of Evil*.

15 In Edmund Husserl *Formale und transzendentale Logik. Versuch einer Kritik der logischen Vernunft*, ed. by P. Janssen, *Husserliana*, vol. 17 (The Hague: Martinus Nijhoff, 1974), pp. 437–46. Written between 1922 and 1926.

16 Ibid., 440.

17 Ricœur, *Fallible Man*, p. 62.

18 Ibid., pp. 52–3.

19 René Descartes, *Treatise on Man*, trans. by Thomas Hall (Cambridge: Harvard University Press, 1972).

20 René Descartes, *The Passions of the Soul*, in *The Philosophical Writings of Descartes*, trans. by John Cottingham, Robert, Stoothalf, Dugald Murdock (Cambridge: Cambridge University Press, 1985), pp. 325–404.

21 See Ricœur, *Fallible Man*, pp. 78–9 on this point.

22 Ibid., p. 85.

23 Ibid.

24 Emmanuel Lévinas, *Totality and Infinity: An Essay on Exteriority*, trans. by A. Linguis (Pittsburgh: Duquesne University Press, 1969), passim.

25 The distinction between phenomenology and hermeneutics here is oversimplified as there is a question as to the relationship between a descriptive and interpretative approach *within* the domain of phenomenological analysis itself. For a study of how this is sorted out in a theory of affectivity, see my essay "Affectivity, eros and the body" in this volume.

26 Cf. Ricœur, *Fallible Man*, p. 143.

27 Ibid.

28 *Symbolism of Evil*, p. 274.

29 See the entry under *bâsâr* in the *Theological Dictionary of the Old Testament*, ed. by G. J. Botterwech and H. Ringgren, trans. by J. Willis (Grand Rapids, Michigan: Eerdmans, 1975), II, 325.

30 *Bâsâr*, which occurs over 270 times in the Hebrew Bible, can be translated "flesh," "body," by extension "person," also fading into "kin," "nakedness," even "self." The English notion of the flesh is uniformly rendered by *bâsâr*, with the term *she,êr* being use only on a few occasions. Often affects or feelings are said to come from either flesh or soul. Compare how *bâsâr* functions in Psalm 63: 21 with how *nephesh* is used in Deut. 12: 20 and II Sam. 3: 21; Prov. 21: 20. Still, on some occasions *bâsâr* is set in contrast to *nephesh* (soul) as in Isa. 10: 18.

By contrast we have different terms for our concept of the body. The dead body of a man is referred to using the term *nephesh* (e.g. Num. 9: 6–16), a term that in other contexts should be rendered "soul" or "person" (e.g. Num. 15: 27–31). The term *beten* also means "belly" or "womb" (e.g. Deut. 28: 11, 18) and, by extension, the deepest recesses of the person or the seat of desire (cf. Job 15: 35; 20: 20; Prov. 18: 8, 20). The word *gevîyyâh* (I Sam. 31: 10, 12) means body, dead or alive, while *gûwphâh*, itself derived from the word "to hollow" and, figuratively, "to close or shut" (*gûwph*, Neh. 7: 3), is used only of a corpse (I Chr. 10: 12, only occurrence). Flesh and body, however, are never used in opposition to each other. (In Prov. 5: 11, which refers to "your flesh and your body" being consumed, the term for body is *she,êr*, which can be rendered body, flesh, even kinsman or kinswoman (Lev. 18: 12, 13), and thus is just another way of restating *bâsâr*). On these terms see *Theological Dictionary of the Old Testament*, and *Theological Wordbook of the Old Testament*, ed. by R. L. Harris (Chicago: Moody Press, 1980).

31 All quotations from the Bible come from *The New American Standard Bible* (Nashville, Tennessee: Broadman and Holman Publishers, 1960).

32 N. P. Bratsiotis, "*bâsâr*," *Theological Dictionary of the Old Testament*, II, 326.

33 Σῶμα is found some thirty times in the synoptic Gospels.

34 François de La Rochefoucault as cited in Friedrich Nietzsche, *Human, All Too Human*, trans. by Marion Faber (Lincoln, Nebraska: University of Nebraska Press, 1984), section 36.

35 Cf. Nietzsche, *Human, All Too Human*, section 99.

36 Nietzsche, *Human, All Too Human*, section 57.

# 12

# Situated Bodies

## Throwing Like a Girl*

### *Iris Young*

In discussing the fundamental significance of lateral space, which is one of the unique spatial dimensions generated by the human upright posture, Erwin Straus pauses at "the remarkable difference in the manner of throwing of the two sexes"[1] (p. 157). Citing a study and photographs of young boys and girls, he describes the difference as follows:

> The girl of five does not make any use of lateral space. She does not stretch her arm sideward; she does not twist her trunk; she does not move her legs, which remain side by side. All she does in preparation for throwing is to lift her right arm forward to the horizontal and to bend the forearm backward in a pronate position. . . . The ball is released without force, speed, or accurate aim. . . . A boy of the same age, when preparing to throw, stretches his right arm sideward and backward; supinates the forearm; twists, turns and bends his trunk; and moves his right foot backward. From this stance, he can support his throwing almost with the full strength of his total motorium . . . The ball leaves the hand with considerable acceleration; it moves toward its goal in a long flat curve. (pp. 157–60)[2]

Though he does not stop to trouble himself with the problem for long, Straus makes a few remarks in the attempt to explain this "remarkable difference." Since the difference is observed at such an early age, he says, it seems to be "the manifestation of a biological, not an acquired, difference" (p. 157). He is somewhat at a loss, however, to specify the source of the difference. Since the feminine style of throwing is observed in young children, it cannot result from the development of the breast. Straus provides further evidence against the breast by pointing out that "it seems certain" that the Amazons, who cut off their right breasts, "threw a ball just like our Betty's, Mary's and Susan's" (p. 158). Having thus dismissed the breast, Straus considers the weaker muscle power of the girl as an explanation of the difference, but concludes that the girl should be expected to compensate for such relative weakness with the added preparation of reaching around and back. Straus explains the difference in style of throwing by referring to a "feminine attitude" in relation to the world and to space. The difference for him is biologically based, but he denies that it is specifically anatomical. Girls throw in a way different from boys because girls are "feminine."

* Iris Young, "Throwing like a girl," *Throwing Like a Girl* (Bloomington, Indiana: Indiana University Press, 1990), pp. 141–59.

What is even more amazing than this "explanation" is the fact that a perspective that takes body comportment and movement as definitive for the structure and meaning of human lived experience devotes no more than an incidental page to such a "remarkable difference" between masculine and feminine body comportment and style of movement, for throwing is by no means the only activity in which such a difference can be observed. If there are indeed typically "feminine" styles of body comportment and movement, this should generate for the existential phenomenologist a concern to specify such a differentiation of the modalities of the lived body. Yet Straus is by no means alone in his failure to describe the modalities, meaning, and implications of the difference between "masculine" and "feminine" body comportment and movement.

A virtue of Straus's account of the typical difference of the sexes in throwing is that he does not explain this difference on the basis of physical attributes. Straus is convinced, however, that the early age at which the difference appears shows that it is not an acquired difference, and thus he is forced back onto a mysterious "feminine essence" in order to explain it. The feminist denial that the real differences in behavior and psychology between men and woman can be attributed to some natural and eternal feminine essence is perhaps most thoroughly and systematically expressed by Beauvoir. Every human existence is defined by its *situation*; the particular existence of the female person is no less defined by the historical, cultural, social, and economic limits of her situation. We reduce women's condition simply to unintelligibility if we "explain" it by appeal to some natural and ahistorical feminine essence. In denying such a femine essence, however, we should not fall into that "nominalism" that denies the real differences in the behavior and experiences of men and women. Even though there is no eternal feminine essence, there is "a common basis which underlies every individual female existence in the present state of education and custom."[3] The situation of women within a given sociohistorical set of circumstances, despite the individual variation in each woman's experience, opportunities, and possibilities, has a unity that can be described and made intelligible. It should be emphasized, however, that this unity is specific to a particular social formation during a particular epoch.

Beauvoir proceeds to give such an account of the situation of women with remarkable depth, clarity, and ingenuity. Yet she also, to a large extent, fails to give a place to the status and orientation of the woman's body as relating to its surroundings in living action. When Beauvoir does talk about the woman's bodily being and her physical relation to her surroundings, she tends to focus on the more evident facts of a woman's physiology. She discusses how women experience the body as a burden, how the hormonal and physiological changes the body undergoes at puberty, during menstruation and pregnancy, are felt to be fearful and mysterious, and claims that these phenomena weigh down the woman's existence by tying her to nature, immanence, and the requirements of the species at the expense of her own individuality.[4] By largely ignoring the situatedness of the woman's actual bodily movement and orientation to its surroundings and its world, Beauvoir tends to create the impression that it is woman's anatomy and physiology *as such* that at least in part determine her unfree status.[5]

This essay seeks to begin to fill a gap that thus exists both in existential phenomenology and feminist theory. It traces in a provisional way some of the basic modalities of feminine body comportment, manner of moving, and relation in space. It brings intelligibility and significance to certain observable and rather ordinary ways in which women in our society typically comport themselves and move differently from the ways that men do. In accordance with the existentialist concern with the situatedness of human experience, I make no claim to the universality of this typicality of the bodily comportment of women and the phenomenological description based on it. The account developed here claims only to describe the modalities of feminine bodily existence for women situated in contemporary advanced industrial, urban, and commercial society. Elements of the account developed here may or may not apply to the situation of woman in other societies and other epochs, but it is not the concern of this essay to determine to which, if any, other social circumstances this account applies.

The scope of bodily existence and movement with which I am concerned here is also limited. I concentrate primarily on those sorts of bodily activities that relate to the comportment or orientation of the body as a whole, that entail gross movement, or that require the enlistment of strength and the confrontation of the body's capacities and possibilities with the resistance and malleability of things. The kind of movement I am primarily concerned with is movement in which the body aims to accomplish of a definite purpose or task. There are thus many aspects of feminine bodily existence that I leave out of this account. Most notable of these is the body in its sexual being. Another aspect of bodily existence, among others, that I leave unconsidered is structured body movement that does not have a particular aim – for example, dancing. Besides reasons of space, this limitation of subject is based on the conviction, derived primarily from Merleau-Ponty, that it is the ordinary purposive orientation of the body as a whole toward things and its environment that initially defines the relation of a subject to its world. Thus a focus upon ways in which the feminine body frequently or typically conducts itself in such comportment or movement may be particularly revelatory of the structures of feminine existence.[6]

Before entering the analysis, I should clarify what I mean here by "feminine" existence. In accordance with Beauvoir's understanding, I take "femininity" to designate not a mysterious quality or essence that all women have by virtue of their being biologically female. It is, rather, a set of structures and conditions that delimit the typical *situation* of being a woman in a particular society, as well as the typical way in which this situation is lived by the women themselves. Defined as such, it is not necessary that *any* women be "feminine" – that is, it is not necessary that there be distinctive structures and behavior typical of the situation of women.[7] This understanding of "feminine" existence makes it possible to say that some women escape or transcend the typical situation and definition of women in various degrees and respects. I mention this primarily to indicate that the account offered here of the modalities of feminine bodily existence is not to be falsified by refering to some individual women to whom aspects of the account do not apply, or even to some individual men to whom they do.

The account developed here combines the insights of the theory of the lived body as expressed by Merleau-Ponty and the theory of the situation of women as developed by Beauvoir. I assume that at the most basic descriptive level, Merleau-Ponty's account of the relation of the lived body to its world, as developed in the *Phenomenology of Perception*, applies to any human existence in a general way. At a more specific level, however, there is a particular style of bodily comportment that is typical of feminine existence, and this style consists of particular *modalities* of the structures and conditions of the body's existence in the world.[8]

As a framework for developing these modalities, I rely on Beauvoir's account of woman's existence in patriarchal society as defined by a basic tension between immanence and transcendence.[9] The culture and society in which the female person dwells defines woman as Other, as the inessential correlate to man, as mere object and immanence. Woman is thereby both culturally and socially denied by the subjectivity, autonomy, and creativity that are definitive of being human and that in patriarchal society are accorded the man. At the same time, however, because she is a human existence, the female person necessarily is a subjectivity and transcendence, and she knows herself to be. The female person who enacts the existence of women in patriarchal society must therefore live a contradiction: as human she is a free subject who participates in transcendence, but her situation as a woman denies her that subjectivity and transcendence. My suggestion is that the modalities of feminine bodily comportment, motility, and spatiality exhibit this same tension between transcendence and immanence, between subjectivity and being a mere object.

Section I offers some specific observations about bodily comportment, physical engagement with things, ways of using the body in performing tasks, and bodily self-image, which I find typical of feminine existence. Section II gives a general phenomenological account of the modalities of feminine bodily comportment and motility. Section III develops these modalities further in terms of the spatiality generated by them. Finally, in section IV, I draw out some of the implications of this account for an understanding of the oppression of women, as well as raise some further questions about feminine being in the world that require further investigation.

# I

The basic difference that Straus observes between the way boys and girls throw is that girls do not bring their whole bodies into the motion as much as the boys do. They do not reach back, twist, move backward, step, and lean forward. Rather, the girls tend to remain relatively immobile except for their arms, and even the arms are not extended as far as they could be. Throwing is not the only movement in which there is a typical difference in the way men and women use their bodies. Reflection on feminine comportment and body movement in other physical activities reveals that these also are frequently characterized, much as in the throwing case, by a failure to make full use of the body's spatial and lateral potentialities.

Even in the most simple body orientations of men and women as they sit, stand, and walk, one can observe a typical difference in body style and extension. Women generally are not as open with their bodies as are men in their gait and stride. Typically, the masculine stride is longer proportional to a man's body than is the feminine stride to a woman's. The man typically swings his arms in a more open and loose fashion than does a woman and typically has more up and down rhythm in his step. Though we now wear pants more than we used to and consequently do not have to restrict our sitting postures because of dress, women still tend to sit with their legs relatively close together and their arms across their bodies. When simply standing or leaning, men tend to keep their feet farther apart than do women, and we also tend more to keep our hands and arms touching or shielding our bodies. A final indicative difference is the way each carries books or parcels; girls and women most often carry books embraced to their chests, while boys and men swing them along their sides.

The approach that people of each sex take to the performance of physical tasks that require force, strength, and muscular coordination is frequently different.

There are indeed real physical differences between men and women in the kind and limit of their physical strength. Many of the observed differences between men and women in the performance of tasks requiring coordinated strength, however, are due not so much to brute muscular strength as to the way each sex *uses* the body in approaching tasks. Women often do not perceive themselves as capable of lifting and carrying heavy things, pushing and shoving with significant force, pulling, squeezing, grasping, or twisting with force. When we attempt such tasks, we frequently fail to summon the full possibilities of our muscular coordination, position, poise, and bearing. Women tend not to put their whole bodies into engagement in a physical task with the same ease and naturalness as men. For example, in attempting to lift something, women more often than men fail to plant themselves firmly and make their thighs bear the greatest proportion of the weight. Instead, we tend to concentrate our effort on those parts of the body most immediately connected to the task – the arms and shoulders – rarely bringing the power of the legs to the task at all. When turning or twisting something, to take another example, we frequently concentrate effort in the hand and wrist, not bringing to the task the power of the shoulder, which is necessary for its efficient performance.[10]

The previously cited throwing example can be extended to a great deal of athletic activity. Now, most men are by no means superior athletes, and their sporting efforts more often display bravado than genuine skill and coordination. The relatively untrained man nevertheless engages in sport generally with more free motion and open reach than does his female counterpart. Not only is there a typical style of throwing like a girl, but there is a more or less typical style of running like a girl, climbing like a girl, swinging like a girl, hitting like a girl. They have in common first that the whole body is not put into fluid and directed motion, but rather, in swinging and hitting, for example, the motion is concentrated in one body part; and second that the woman's motion tends not to reach, extend, lean, stretch, and follow through in the direction of her intention.

For many women as they move in sport, a space surrounds us in imagination that we are not free to move beyond; the space available to our movement is a constricted space. Thus, for example, in softball or volleyball women tend to remain in one place more often than men do, neither jumping to reach nor running to approach the ball. Men more often move out toward a ball in flight and confront it with their own countermotion. Women tend to wait for and then *react* to its approach, rather than going forth to meet it. We frequently respond to the motion of a ball coming toward us as though it were coming *at* us, and our immediate bodily impulse is to flee, duck, or otherwise protect ourselves from its flight. Less often than men, moreover, do women give self-conscious direction and placement to their motion in sport. Rather than aiming at a certain place where we wish to hit a ball, for example, we tend to hit it in a "general" direction.

Women often approach a physical engagement with things with timidity, uncertainty, and hesitancy. Typically, we lack an entire trust in our bodies to carry us to our aims. There is, I suggest, a double hesitation here. On the one hand, we often lack confidence that we have the capacity to do what must be done. Many times I have slowed a hiking party in which the men bounded across a harmless stream while I stood on the other side warily testing my footing on various stones, holding on to overhanging branches. Though the others crossed with ease, I do not believe it is easy for *me*, even though once I take a committed step I am across in a flash. The other side of this tentativeness is, I suggest, a fear of getting hurt, which is greater in women than in men. Our attention is often divided between the aim to be realized in motion and the body that must accomplish it, while at the same time saving itself from harm. We often experience our bodies as a fragile encumbrance, rather than the media for the enactment of our aims. We feel as though we must have our attention directed upon our bodies to make sure they are doing what we wish them to do, rather than paying attention to what we want to do *through* our bodies.

All the above factors operate to produce in many women a greater or lesser feeling of incapacity, frustration, and self-consciousness. We have more of a tendency than men do to greatly underestimate our bodily capacity.[11] We decide beforehand – usually mistakenly – that the task is beyond us, and thus give it less than our full effort. At such a halfhearted level, of course, we cannot perform the tasks, become frustrated, and fulfill our own prophecy. In entering a task we frequently are self-conscious about appearing awkward and at the same time do not wish to appear too strong. Both worries contribute to our awkwardness and frustration. If we should finally release ourselves from this spiral and really give a physical task our best effort, we are greatly surprised indeed at what our bodies can accomplish. It has been found that women more often than men underestimate the level of achievement they have reached.[12]

None of the observations that have been made thus far about the way women typically move and comport their bodies applies to all women all of the time. Nor do those women who manifest some aspect of this typicality do so in the same degree. There is no inherent, mysterious connection between these sorts of typical comportments and being a female person. Many of them result, as will be developed later, from lack of practice in using the body and performing tasks. Even given these qualifications, one can nevertheless sensibly speak of a general feminine style of body comportment and movement. The next section will develop a specific categorical description of the modalities of the comportment and movement.

## II

The three modalities of feminine motility are that feminine movement exhibits an *ambiguous transcendence*, an *inhibited intentionality*, and a *discontinuous unity* with its surroundings. A source of these contradictory modalities is the bodily self-reference of feminine comportment, which derives from the woman's experience of her body as a *thing* at the same time that she experiences it as a capacity.

1. In his *Phenomenology of Perception*,[13] Merleau-Ponty takes as his task the articulation of the primordial structures of existence, which are prior to and the ground of all reflective relation to the world. In asking how there can be a world for a subject, Merleau-Ponty reorients the entire tradition of that questioning by locating subjectivity not in mind or consciousness, but in the *body*. Merleau-Ponty gives to the lived body the ontological status that Sartre, as well as "intellectualist" thinkers before him, attribute to consciousness alone: the status of transcendence as being for itself. It is the body in its orientation toward and action upon and within its surroundings that constitutes the initial meaning-giving act (p. 121, pp. 146–7). The body is the first locus of intentionality, as pure presence to the world and openness upon its possibilities. The most primordial intentional act is the motion of the body orienting itself with respect to and moving within its surroundings. There is a world for a subject just insofar as the body has capacities by which it can approach, grasp, and appropriate its surroundings in the direction of its intentions.

While feminine bodily existence is a transcendence and openness to the world, it is an *ambiguous transcendence*, a transcendence that is at the same time laden with immanence. Now, once we take the locus of subjectivity and transcendence to be the lived body rather than pure consciousness, all transcendence is ambiguous because the body as natural and material is immanence. But it is not the ever-present possibility of any lived body to be passive, to be touched as well as touching, to be grasped as well as grasping, which I am referring to here as the ambiguity of the transcendence of the feminine lived body. The transcendence of the lived body that Merleau-Ponty describes is a transcendence that moves out from the body in its immanence in an open and unbroken directedness upon the world in action. The lived body as transcendence is pure fluid action, the continuous calling-forth of capacities that are applied to the world. Rather than simply beginning in immanence, feminine bodily existence remains in immanence or, better, is *overlaid* with immanence, even as it moves out toward the world in motions of grasping, manipulating, and so on.

In the previous section, I observed that a woman typically refrains from throwing her whole body into a motion, and rather concentrates motion in one part of the body alone, while the rest of the body remains relatively immobile. Only part of the body, that is, moves out toward a task, while the rest remains rooted in immanence. I also observed earlier that a woman frequently does not trust the capacity of her body to engage itself in physical relation to things. Consequently, she often lives her body as a burden, which must be dragged and produced along and at the same time protected.

2. Merleau-Ponty locates intentionality in motility (pp. 110–12); the possibilities that are opened up in the world depend on the modes and limits of the bodily "I can" (pp. 137, 148). Feminine existence, however, often does not enter bodily relation to possibilities by its own comportment toward its surroundings in an unambiguous and confident "I can." For example, as noted earlier, women frequently tend to posit a task that would be accomplished relatively easily once attempted as beyond their capacities before they begin it. Typically, the feminine body underuses its real capacity, both as the potentiality of its physical size and strength and as the real skills and coordination that are available to it. Feminine bodily existence is an *inhibited intentionality*, which simultaneously reaches toward a projected end with an "I can" and withholds its full bodily commitment to that end in a self-imposed "I cannot."[14]

An uninhibited intentionality projects the aim to be accomplished and connects the body's motion toward that end in an unbroken directedness that organizes and unifies the body's activity. The body's capacity and motion structure its surroundings and project meaningful possibilities of movement and action, which in turn call the body's motion forth to enact them: "To understand is to experience the harmony between what we aim at and what is given, between the intention and the performance" (p. 144; see also pp. 101, 131, and 132). Feminine motion often severs this mutually conditioning relation between aim and enactment. In those motions that when properly performed require the coordination and directedness of the whole body upon some definite end, women frequently move in a contradictory way. Their bodies project an aim to be enacted but at the same time stiffen against the performance of the task. In performing a physical task the woman's body does carry her toward the intended aim, often not easily and directly, but rather circuitously, with the wasted motion resulting from the effort of testing and reorientation, which is a frequent consequence of feminine hesitancy.

For any lived body, the world appears as the system of possibilities that are correlative to its intentions (p. 131). For any lived body, moreover, the world also appears to be populated with opacities and resistances correlative to its own limits and frustrations. For any bodily existence, that is, an "I cannot" may appear to set limits to the "I can." To the extent that feminine bodily existence is an inhibited intentionality, however, the same set of possibilities that appears to be correlative to its intentions also appears to be a system of frustrations correlative to its hesitancies. By repressing or withholding its own motile energy, feminine bodily existence frequently projects an "I can" and an "I cannot" with respect to the very same end. When the woman enters a task with inhibited intentionality, she projects the possibilities of that task – thus projects an "I *can*" – but projects them merely as the possibilities of "someone," and not truly *her* possibilities – and thus projects an "*I* cannot."

3. Merleau-Ponty gives to the body the unifying and synthesizing function that Kant locates in transcendental subjectivity. By projecting an aim toward which it moves, the body brings unity to and unites itself with its surroundings; through the vectors of its projected possibilities it sets things in relation to one another and to itself. The body's movement and orientation organizes the surrounding space as a continuous extension of its own being (p. 143). Within the same act in which the body synthesizes its surroundings, moreover, it synthesizes itself. The body synthesis is immediate and primordial. "I do not bring together one by one the parts of my body; this translation and this unification are performed once and for all within me: they are my body itself" (p. 150).

The third modality of feminine bodily existence is that it stands in *discontinuous unity* with both itself and its surroundings. I remarked earlier that in many motions that require the active engagement and coordination of the body as a whole in order to be performed properly, women tend to locate their motion in part of the body only, leaving the rest of the body relatively immobile. Motion such as this is discontinuous with itself. The part of the body that is transcending toward an aim is in relative disunity from those that remain immobile. The undirected and wasted motion that is often an aspect of feminine engagement in a task also manifests this lack of body unity. The character of the inhibited intentionality whereby feminine motion severs the connection between aim and enactment, between possibility in the world and capacity in the body, itself produces this discontinuous unity.

According to Merleau-Ponty, for the body to exist as a transcendent presence to the world and the immediate enactment of intentions, it cannot exist as an *object* (p. 123). As subject, the body is referred not onto itself, but onto the world's possibilities. "In order that we may be able to move our body towards an object, the object must first exist for it, our body must not belong to the realm of the 'in-itself'" (p. 139). The three contradictory modalities of feminine bodily existence – ambiguous transcendence, inhibited intentionality, and discontinuous unity – have their root, however, in the fact that for feminine existence the body frequently is both subject and object for itself at the same time and in reference to the same act. Feminine bodily existence is frequently not a pure presence to the world because it is referred onto *itself* as well as onto possibilities in the world.[15]

Several of the observations of the previous section illustrate this self-reference. It was observed, for example, that women have a tendency to take up the motion of an object coming *toward* them as coming *at* them. I also observed that women tend to have a latent and sometimes conscious fear of getting hurt, which we bring to a motion. That is, feminine bodily existence is self-referred in that the woman takes herself to be the *object* of the motion rather than its originator. Feminine bodily existence is also self-referred to the extent that a woman is uncertain of her body's capacities and does not feel that its motions are entirely under her control. She must divide her attention between the task to be performed and the body that must be coaxed and manipulated into performing it. Finally, feminine bodily existence is self-referred to the extent that the feminine subject posits her motion as the motion that is *looked at*. In section IV, we will explore the implications of the basic fact of the woman's social existence as the object of the gaze of another, which is a major source of her bodily self-reference.

In summary, the modalities of feminine bodily existence have their root in the fact that feminine existence experiences the body as a mere thing – a fragile thing, which must be picked up and coaxed into movement, a thing that exists as *looked at and acted upon*. To be sure, any lived body exists as a material thing as well as a transcending subject. For feminine bodily existence, however, the body is often lived as a thing that is other than it, a thing like other things in the world. To the extent that a woman lives her body as a thing, she remains rooted in immanence, is inhibited, and retains a distance from her body as transcending movement and from engagement in the world's possibilities.

# III

For Merleau-Ponty there is a distinction between lived space, or phenomenal space, and objective space, the uniform space of geometry and science in which all positions are external to one another and interchangeable. Phenomenal space arises out of motility, and lived relations of space are generated by the capacities of the body's motion and the intentional relations that that motion constitutes. "It is clearly in action that the spatiality of our body is brought into being and an analysis of one's own movement should enable us to arrive at a better understanding" (p. 102, cf. pp. 148, 149, 249). In this account, if there are particular modalities of feminine bodily comportment and motility, it must follow that there are also particular modalities of feminine spatiality. Feminine existence lives space as *enclosed* or confining, as having a *dual* structure, and the woman experiences herself as *positioned* in space.

1. There is a famous study that Erik Erikson performed several years ago in which he asked several male and female pre-adolescents to construct a scene for an imagined movie out of some toys. He found that girls typically depicted indoor settings, with high walls and enclosures, while boys typically constructed outdoor scenes. He concluded that females tend to emphasize what he calls "inner space," or enclosed space, while males tend to emphasize what he calls "outer space," or a spatial orientation that is open and outwardly directed. Erikson's interpretation of these observations is psychoanalytical: girls depict "inner space" as the projection of the enclosed space of their wombs and vaginas; boys depict "outer space" as a projection of the phallus.[16] I find such an explanation wholly unconvincing. If girls do tend to project an enclosed space and boys to project an open and outwardly directed space, it is far more plausible to regard this as a reflection of the way members of each sex live and move their bodies in space.

In the first section, I observed that women tend not to open their bodies in their everyday movements, but tend to sit, stand, and walk with their limbs close to or closed around them. I also observed that women tend not to reach, stretch, bend, lean, or stride to the full limits of their physical capacities, even when doing so would better accomplish a task or motion. The space, that is, that is *physically* available to the feminine body is frequently of greater radius than the space that she uses and inhabits. Feminine existence appears to posit an existential enclosure between herself and the space surrounding her, in such a way that the space that belongs to her and is available to her grasp and manipulation is constricted and the space beyond is not available to her movement.[17] A further illustration of this confinement of feminine lived space is the observation already noted that in sport, for example, women tend not to move out and meet the motion of a ball, but rather tend to stay in one place and react to the ball's motion only when it has arrived within the space where she is. The timidity, immobility, and uncertainty that frequently characterize feminine movement project a limited space for the feminine "I can."

2. In Merleau-Ponty's account, the body unity of transcending performance creates an immediate link between the body and the outlying space. "Each instant of the movement embraces its whole space, and particularly the first which, by being active and initiative, institutes the link between a here and a yonder" (p. 140). In feminine existence, however, the projection of an enclosed space severs the continuity between a "here" and a "yonder." In feminine existence there is a *double spatiality*, as the space of the "here" is distinct from the space of the "yonder." A distinction between space that is "yonder" and not linked with my own body possibilities and the enclosed space that is "here," which I inhabit with my bodily possibilities, is an expression of the discontinuity between aim and capacity to realize the aim that I have articulated as the meaning of the tentativeness and uncertainty characterizing the inhibited intentionality of feminine motility. The space of the "yonder" is a space in which feminine existence projects possibilities in the sense of understanding that "someone" could move within it, but not I. Thus the space of the "yonder" exists for feminine existence, but only as that which she is looking into, rather than moving in.

3. The third modality of feminine spatiality is that feminine existence experiences itself as *positioned in* space. For Merleau-Ponty, the body is the original subject that constitutes space; there would be no space without the body (pp. 102, 142). As the origin and subject of spatial relations, the body does not occupy a position coequal and interchangeable with the positions occupied by other things (p. 143, pp. 247–9). Because the body as lived is not an *object*, it cannot be said to exist *in* space as water is *in* the glass (pp. 139–40). "The word 'here' applied to my body does not refer to a determinate position in relation to other positions or to external coordinates, but the laying down of the first coordinates, the anchoring of the active body in an object, the situation of the body in the face of its tasks" (p. 100).

Feminine spatiality is contradictory insofar as feminine bodily existence is both spatially constituted and a constituting spatial subject. Insofar as feminine existence lives the body as transcendence and intentionality, the feminine body actively constitutes space and is the original coordinate that unifies the spatial field and projects spatial relations and positions in accord with its intentions. But to the extent that feminine motility is laden with immanence and inhibited, the body's space is lived as constituted. To the extent, that is, that feminine bodily existence is self-referred and thus lives itself as an *object*, the feminine body does exist *in* space. In section I, I observed that women frequently react to motions, even our own motions, as though we are the object of a motion that issues from an alien intention, rather than taking ourselves as the subject of motion. In its immanence and inhibition, feminine spatial existence is *positioned* by a system of coordinates that does not have its origin in her own intentional capacities. The tendency for the feminine body to remain partly immobile in the performance of a task that requires the movement of the whole body illustrates this characteristic of feminine bodily existence as rooted *in place*. Likewise does the tendency of women to wait for an object to come within their immediate bodily field, rather than move out toward it.

Merleau-Ponty devotes a great deal of attention to arguing that the diverse senses and activities of the lived body are synthetically related in such a way that each stands in a mutually conditioning relation with all the others. In particular, visual perception and motility stand in a relation of reversibility; an impairment in the functioning of one, for example, leads to an impairment in the functioning of the other (pp. 133–7). If we assume that reversability of visual perception and motility, the previous account of the modalities of feminine motility and the spatiality that arises from them suggests that visual space will have its own modalities as well.

Numerous psychological studies have reported differences between the sexes in the character of spatial perception. One of the most frequently discussed of these conclusions is that females are more often "field-dependent." That is, it has been claimed that males have a greater capacity for lifting a figure out of its spatial surroundings and viewing relations in space as fluid and interchangeable, whereas females have a greater tendency to regard figures as embedded within and fixed by their surroundings.[18] The above account of feminine motility and spatiality gives some theoretical intelligibility to these findings. If feminine body spatiality is such that the woman experiences herself as rooted and enclosed, on the reversibility assumption it would follow that visual space for feminine existence also has its closures of immobility and fixity. The objects in visual space do not stand in a fluid system of potentially alterable and interchangeable relations correlative to the body's various intentions and projected capacities. Rather, they too have their own *places* and are anchored in their immanence.

## IV

The modalities of feminine bodily comportment, motility, and spatiality that I have described here are, I claim, common to the existence of women in contemporary society to one degree or another. They have their source, however, in neither anatomy nor physiology, and certainly not in a mysterious feminine essence. Rather, they have their source in the particular *situation* of women as conditioned by their sexist oppression in contemporary society.

Women in sexist society are physically handicapped. Insofar as we learn to live out our existence in accordance with the definition that patriarchal culture assigns to us, we are physically inhibited, confined, positioned, and objectified. As lived bodies we are not open and unambiguous transcendences that move out to master a world that belongs to us, a world constituted by our own intentions and projections. To be sure, there are actual women in contemporary society to whom all or part of the above description does not apply. Where these modalities are not manifest in or determinative of the existence of a particular woman, however, they are definitive in a negative mode – as that which she has escaped, through accident or good fortune, or, more often, as that which she has had to overcome.

One of the sources of the modalities of feminine bodily existence is too obvious to dwell upon at length. For the most part, girls and women are not given the opportunity to use their full bodily capacities in free and open engagement with the world, nor are they encouraged as much as boys are to develop specific bodily skills.[19] Girls' play is often more sedentary and enclosing than the play of boys. In school and after-school activities girls are not encouraged to engage in sport, in the controlled use of their bodies in achieving well-defined goals. Girls, moreover, get little practice at "tinkering" with things and thus at developing spatial skill. Finally, girls are not often asked to perform tasks demanding physical effort and strength, while as the boys grow older they are asked to do so more and more.[20]

The modalities of feminine bodily existence are not merely privative, however, and thus their source is not merely in lack of practice, though this is certainly an important element. There is a specific positive style of feminine body comportment and movement, which is learned as the girl comes to understand that she is a girl. The young girl acquires many subtle habits of feminine body comportment – walking like a girl, tilting her head like a girl, standing and sitting like a girl, gesturing like a girl, and so on. The girl learns actively to hamper her movements. She is told that she must be careful not to get hurt, not to get dirty, not to tear her clothes, that the things she desires to do are dangerous for her. Thus she develops a bodily timidity that increases with age. In assuming herself to be a girl, she takes herself to be fragile. Studies have found that young children of both sexes categorically assert that girls are more likely to get hurt than boys are,[21] and that girls ought to remain close to home, while boys can roam and explore.[22] The more a girl assumes her status as feminine, the more she takes herself to be fragile and immobile and the more she actively enacts her own body inhibition. When I was about thirteen, I spent hours practicing a "feminine" walk, which was stiff and closed, and rotated from side to side.

Studies that record observations of sex differences in spatial perception, spatial problem-solving, and motor skills have also found that these differences tend to increase with age. While very young children show virtually no differences in motor skills, movement, spatial perception, etc., differences seem to appear in elementary school and increase with adolescence. If these findings are accurate, they would seem to support the conclusion that it is in the process of growing up as a girl that the modalities of feminine bodily comportment, motility, and spatiality make their appearance.[23]

There is, however, a further source of the modalities of feminine bodily existence that is perhaps even more profound than these. At the root of those modalities, I have stated in the previous section, is the fact that the woman lives her body as *object* as well as subject. The source of this is that patriarchal society defines woman as object, as a mere body, and that in sexist society women are in fact frequently regarded by others as objects and mere bodies. An essential part of the situation of being a woman is that of living the ever-present possibility that one will be gazed upon as a mere body, as shape and flesh that presents itself as the potential object of another subject's intentions and manipulations, rather than as a living manifestation of action and intention.[24] The source of this objectified bodily existence is in the attitude of others regarding her, but the woman herself often actively takes up her body as a mere thing. She gazes at it in the mirror, worries about how it looks to others, prunes it, shapes it, molds and decorates it.

This objectified bodily existence accounts for the self-consciousness of the feminine relation to her body and resulting distance she takes from her body. As human, she is a transcendence and subjectivity, and cannot live herself as mere bodily object. Thus, to the degree that she does live herself as mere body, she cannot be in unity with herself, but must take a distance from and exist in discontinuity with her body.

The objectifying regard that "keeps her in her place" can also account for the spatial modality of being positioned and for why women frequently tend not to move openly, keeping their limbs closed around themselves. To open her body in free, active, open extension and bold outward-directedness is for a woman to invite objectification.

The threat of being seen is, however, not the only threat of objectification that the woman lives. She also lives the threat of invasion of her body space. The most extreme form of such spatial and bodily invasion is the threat of rape. But we daily are subject to the possibility of bodily invasion in many far more subtle ways as well. It is acceptable, for example, for women to be touched in ways and under circumstances that it is not acceptable for men to be touched, and by persons – i.e. men – whom it is not acceptable for them to touch.[25] I would suggest that the enclosed space that has been described as a modality of feminine spatiality is in part a defense against such invasion. Women tend to project an existential barrier closed around them and discontinuous with the "over there" in order to keep the other at a distance. The woman lives her space as confined and closed around her, at least in part as projecting some small area in which she can exist as a free subject.

This essay is a prolegomenon to the study of aspects of women's experience and situation that have not received the treatment they warrant. I would like to close with some questions that require further thought and research. This essay has concentrated its attention upon the sorts of physical tasks and body orientation that involve the whole body in gross movement. Further investigation into woman's bodily existence would require looking at activities that do not involve the whole body and finer movement. If we are going to develop an account of the woman's body experience in situation, moreover, we must reflect on the modalities of a woman's experience of her body in its sexual being, as well as upon less task-oriented body activities, such as dancing. Another question that arises is whether the description given here would apply equally well to any sort of physical task. Might the kind of task, and specifically whether it is a task or movement that is sex-typed, have some effect on the modalities of feminine bodily existence? A further question is to what degree we can develop a theoretical account of the connection between the modalities of the bodily existence of women and other aspects of our existence and experience. For example, I have an intuition that the general lack of confidence that we frequently have about our cognitive or leadership abilities is traceable in part to an original doubt of our body's capacity. None of these questions can be dealt with properly, however, without first performing the kind of guided observation and data collection that my reading has concluded, to a large degree, is yet to be performed.

## Notes

This essay was first presented at a meeting of the Mid-West Division of the Society for Women in Philosophy (SWIP) in October 1977. Versions of the essay were subsequently presented at a session sponsored by SWIP at the Western Division meetings of the American Philosophical Association, April 1978; and at the third annual Merleau-Ponty Circle meeting, Duquesne University, September 1978. Many people in discussions at those meetings contributed gratifying and helpful responses. I am particularly grateful to Professors Sandra Bartky, Claudia Card, Margaret Simons, J. Davidson Alexander, and William McBride for their criticisms and suggestions. Final revisions of the essay were completed while I was a fellow in the National Endowment for the Humanities Fellowship in Residence for College Teachers program at the University of Chicago.

1   Erwin W. Straus, "The upright posture," *Phenomenological Psychology* (New York: Basic Books, 1966), pp. 137–65. References to particular pages are indicated in the text.

2   Studies continue to be performed that arrive at similar observations. See, for example, Lolas E. Kalverson, Mary Ann Robertson, M. Joanne Safrit and Thomas W. Roberts, "Effect of guided practice on overhand throw ball velocities of kindergarten children," *Research Quarterly* (American Alliance for Health, Physical Education and Recreation) 48 (May 1977), pp. 311–18. The study found that boys achieved significantly greater velocities than girls did. See also F. J. J. Buytendijk's remarks in *Woman: A Contemporary View* (New York: Newman Press, 1968), pp. 144–5. In raising the example of throwing, Buytendijk is concerned to stress, as am I in this essay, that the important thing to investigate is not the strictly physical phenomenon, but rather the manner in which each sex projects her or his Being-in-the-world through movement.

3   Simone de Beauvoir, *The Second Sex* (New York: Vintage Books, 1974), p. xxxv. See also Buytendijk, p. 175–6.

4   See Beauvoir, *The Second Sex*, chapter 1, "The data of biology."

5   Firestone claims that Beauvoir's account served as the basis of her own thesis that the oppression of women is rooted in nature and thus requires the transcendence of nature itself to be overcome. See *The Dialectic of Sex* (New York: Bantam Books, 1970). Beauvoir would claim that Firestone is guilty of de-situating woman's situation by pinning a source on nature as such. That Firestone would find inspiration for her thesis in Beauvoir, however, indicates that perhaps de Beauvoir has not steered away from causes in "nature" as much as is desirable.

6   In his discussion of the "dynamics of feminine existence," Buytendijk focuses precisely on those sorts of motions that are aimless. He claims that it is through these kinds of expressive movements – e.g. walking for the sake of walking – and not through action aimed at the accomplishment of particular purposes that the pure image of masculine or feminine existence is manifest (*Woman: A Contemporary View*, p. 278–9). Such an approach, however, contradicts the basic existentialist assumption that Being-in-the-world consists in projecting purposes and goals that structure one's situatedness. While there is certainly something to be learned from reflecting upon feminine movement in noninstrumental activity, given that accomplishing tasks is basic to the structure of human existence, it serves as a better starting point for investigation of feminine motility. As I point out at the end of this essay, a full phenomenology of feminine existence must take account of this noninstrumental movement.

7   It is not impossible, moreover, for men to be "feminine" in at least some respects, according to the above definition.

8   On this level of specificity there also exist particular modalities of masculine motility, inasmuch as there is a particular style of movement more or less typical of men. I will not, however, be concerned with those in this essay.

9   See Beauvoir, *The Second Sex*, chapter 21, "Woman's situation and character."

10  It should be noted that this is probably typical only of women in advanced industrial societies, where the model of the bourgeois woman has been extended to most women. It would not apply to those societies, for example, where most people, including women, do heavy physical work. Nor does this particular observation, of course, hold true in our own society for women who do heavy physical work.

11  See A. M. Gross, "Estimated versus actual physical strength in three ethnic groups," *Child Development* 39 (1968), pp. 283–90. In a test of children at several different ages, at all but the youngest age level, girls rated themselves lower than boys rated themselves on self-estimates of strength, and as the girls grow older, their self-estimates of strength become even lower.

12  See Marguerite A. Cifton and Hope M. Smith, "Comparison of expressed self-concept of highly skilled males and females concerning motor performance," *Perceptual and Motor Skills* 16 (1963), pp. 199–201. Women consistently underestimated their level of achievement in skills such as running and jumping far more often than men did.

13  Maurice Merleau-Ponty, *The Phenomenology of Perception*, trans. Colin Smith (New York: Humanities Press, 1962). All references to this work are noted in parentheses in the text.

14  Much of the work of Seymour Fisher on various aspects of sex differences in body image correlates suggestively with the phenomenological description developed here. It is difficult to use his conclusions as confirmation of that description, however, because there is something of a speculative aspect to his reasoning. Nevertheless, I shall refer to some of these findings with that qualification in mind.

    One of Fisher's findings is that women have a greater anxiety about their legs than men do, and he cites earlier studies with the same results. Fisher interprets such leg anxiety as being anxiety about motility itself, because in body conception and body image the legs are the body parts most associated with motility. See Fisher, *Body Experience in Fantasy and Behavior* (New York: Appleton-Century Crofts, 1970), p. 537. If his findings and his interpretation are accurate, this tends to correlate with the sort of inhibition and timidity about movement that I am claiming is an aspect of feminine body comportment.

15    Fisher finds that the most striking difference between men and women in their general body image is that women have a significantly higher degree of what he calls "body prominence," awareness of and attention to the body. He cites a number of different studies that have the same results. The explanation Fisher gives for this finding is that women are socialized to pay attention to their bodies, to prune and dress them, and to worry about how they look to others. Fisher, pp. 524–5. See also Fisher, "Sex differences in body perception," *Psychological Monographs* 78 (1964) no. 14.

16    Erik H. Erikson, "Inner and outer space: reflections on womanhood," *Daedelus* 3 (1964), pp. 582–606. Erikson's interpretation of his findings is also sexist. Having in his opinion discovered a particular significance that "inner space," which he takes to be space *within* the body, holds for girls, he goes on to discuss the womanly "nature" as womb and potential mother, which must be made compatible with anything else the woman does.

17    Another of Fisher's findings is that women experience themselves as having more clearly articulated body *boundaries* than men do. More clearly than men do, they distinguish themselves from their spatial surroundings and take a distance from them. See Fisher, *Body Experience in Fantasy and Behavior*, p. 528.

18    The number of studies with these results in enormous. See Eleanor E. Maccoby and Carol N. Jacklin, *The Psychology of Sex Differences* (Palo Alto, Calif.: Stanford University Press, 1974), pp. 91–8. For a number of years psychologists used the results from tests of spatial ability to generalize about field independence in general, and from that to general "analytic" ability. Thus it was concluded that women have less analytical ability than men do. More recently, however, such generalizations have been seriously called into question. See, for example, Julia A. Sherman, "Problems of sex differences in space perception and aspects of intellectual functioning," *Psychological Review* 74 (1967), pp. 290–9. She notes that while women are consistently found to be more field-dependent in spatial tasks than men are, on nonspatial tests measuring field independence, women generally perform as well as men do.

19    Nor are girls provided with examples of girls and women being physically active. See Mary E. Duquin, "Differential sex role socialization toward amplitude appropriation," *Research Quarterly* (American Alliance for Health, Physical Education and Recreation) 48 (1977), pp. 188–92. A survey of textbooks for young children revealed that children are thirteen times more likely to see a vigorously active man than a vigorously active woman and three times more likely to see a relatively active man than a relatively active woman.

20    Sherman (see note 18) argues that it is the differential socialization of boys and girls in being encouraged to "tinker," explore, etc., that acounts for the difference between the two in spatial ability.

21    See L. Kolberg, "A cognitive-developmental analysis of children's sex-role concepts and attitudes," in E. E. Maccoby (ed.), *The Development of Sex Differences* (Palo Alto, Calif.: Stanford University Press, 1966), p. 101.

22    Lenore J. Weitzman, "Sex role socialization," in Jo Freeman, (ed.), *Woman: A Feminist Perspective* (Palo Alto, Calif.: Mayfield Publishing Co., 1975), pp. 111–12.

23    Maccoby and Jacklin, *The Psychology of Sex Differences*, pp. 93–4.

24    The manner in which women are objectified by the gaze of the Other is not the same phenomenon as the objectification by the Other that is a condition of self-consciousness in Sartre's account. See *Being and Nothingness*, trans. Hazel E. Barnes (New York: Philosophical Library, 1956), part III. While the basic ontological category of being for others is an objectified for itself, the objectification that women are subject to is being regarded as a mere in itself. On the particular dynamic of sexual objectification, see Sandra Bartky, "Psychological oppression," in Sharon Bishop and Marjories Weinzweig, (ed.), *Philosophy and Women* (Belmont, Calif.: Wadsworth Publishing Co., 1979), pp. 33–41.

25    See Nancy Henley and Jo Freeman, "The sexual politics of interpersonal behavior," in Freeman (ed.), *Woman: A Feminist Perspective*, pp. 391–401.

# Pregnant Embodiment

## *Iris Young\**

The library card catalog contains dozens of entries under the heading "pregnancy": clinical treatises detailing signs of morbidity; volumes cataloging studies of fetal development, with elaborate drawings; or popular manuals in which physicians and others give advice on diet and exercise for the pregnant woman. Pregnancy does not belong to the woman herself. It is a state of the developing fetus, for which the woman is a container; or it is an objective, observable process coming under scientific scrutiny; or it becomes objectified by the woman herself as a "condition" in which she must "take care of herself." Except, perhaps, for one insignificant diary, no card appears listing a work that, as Kristeva puts it, is "concerned with the subject, the mother as the site of her proceedings."[1]

We should not be surprised to learn that discourse on pregnancy omits subjectivity, for the specific experience of women has been absent from most of our culture's discourse about human experience and history. This essay considers some of the experiences of pregnancy from the pregnant subject's viewpoint. Through reference to diaries and literature, as well as phenomenological reflection on the pregnant experience, I seek to let women speak in their own voices.

Section I describes some aspects of bodily existence unique to pregnancy. The pregnant subject, I suggest, is decentered, split, or doubled in several ways. She experiences her body as herself and not herself. Its inner movements belong to another being, yet they are not other, because her body boundaries shift and because her bodily self-location is focused on her trunk in addition to her head. This split subject appears in the eroticism of pregnancy, in which the woman can experience an innocent narcissism fed by recollection of her repressed experience of her own mother's body. Pregnant existence entails, finally, a unique temporality of process and growth in which the woman can experience herself as split between past and future.

This description of the lived pregnant body both develops and partially criticizes the phenomenology of bodily existence found in the writings of Straus, Merleau-Ponty, and several other existential phenomenologists. It continues the radical undermining of Cartesianism that these thinkers inaugurated, but it also challenges their implicit assumptions of a unified subject and sharp distinction between transcendence and immanence. Pregnancy, I argue, reveals a paradigm of bodily experience in which the transparent unity of self dissolves and the body attends positively to itself at the same time that it enacts its projects.

Section II reflects on the encounter of the pregnant subject with the institutions and practices of medicine. I argue that within the present organization of these institutions and practices, women usually find such an encounter alienating in several respects. Medicine's self-identification as the curing profession encourages others as well as the woman to think of her pregnancy as a condition that deviates from normal health. The control over knowledge about the pregnancy and birth process that the physician has through instruments, moreover, devalues the privileged relation she has to the fetus and her pregnant body. The fact that in the

* Iris Young, "Pregnant embodiment," *Throwing Like a Girl* (Bloomington, Indiana: Indiana University Press, 1990), pp. 160–74.

contemporary context the obstetrician is usually a man reduces the likelihood of bodily empathy between physician and patient. Within the context of authority and dependence that currently structures the doctor-patient relation, moreover, coupled with the use of instruments and drugs in the birthing process, the pregnant and birthing woman often lacks autonomy within these experiences.

Before proceeding, it is important to note that this essay restricts its analysis to the specific experience of women in technologically sophisticated Western societies. The analysis presupposes that pregnancy can be experienced for its own sake, noticed, and savored. This entails that the pregnancy be chosen by the woman, either as an explicit decision to become pregnant or at least as choosing to be identified with and positively accepting of it. Most women in human history have not chosen their pregnancies in this sense. For the vast majority of women in the world today, and even for many women in this privileged and liberal society, pregnancy is not an experience they choose. So I speak in large measure for an experience that must be instituted and for those pregnant women who have been able to take up their situation as their own.

I

The unique contribution of Straus, along with Merleau-Ponty and certain other existential phenomenologists, to the Western philosophical tradition has consisted in locating consciousness and subjectivity in the body itself. This move to situate subjectivity in the lived body jeopardizes dualistic metaphysics altogether. There remains no basis for preserving the mutual exclusivity of the categories subject and object, inner and outer, I and world. Straus puts it this way:

> The meaning of "mine" is determined in relation to, in contraposition to, the world, the Allon, to which I am nevertheless a party. The meaning of "mine" is not comprehensible in the unmediated antithesis of I and not-I, own and strange, subject and object, constituting I and constituted world. Everything points to the fact that separateness and union originate in the same ground.[2]

As Sarano has pointed out, however, antidualist philosophers still tend to operate with a dualist language, this time distinguishing two forms of experiencing the body itself, as subject and as object, both transcending freedom and mere facticity.[3] Reflection on the experience of pregnancy, I shall show, provides a radical challenge even to this dualism that is tacitly at work in the philosophers of the body.

To the extent that these existential phenomenologists preserve a distinction between subject and object, they do so at least partly because they assume the subject as a unity. In the *Phenomenology of Perception*, for example, Merleau-Ponty locates the "intentional arc" that unifies experience in the body, rather than in an abstract constituting consciousness. He does not, however, abandon the idea of a unified self as a condition of experience.

> There must be, then, corresponding to this open unity of the world, an open and indefinite unity of subjectivity. Like the world's unity, that of the *I* is invoked rather than experienced each time I perform an act of perception, each time I reach a self-evident truth, and the universal *I* is the background against which these effulgent forms stand out: it is through one present thought that I achieve the unity of all my thoughts.[4]

Merleau-Ponty's later work, as well as more recent French philosophy, however, suggests that this transcendental faith in a unified subject as a condition of experience may be little more than ideology.[5] The work of Lacan, Derrida, and Kristeva suggests that the unity of the self is itself a project, a project sometimes successfully enacted by a moving and often contradictory subjectivity. I take Kristeva's remarks about pregnancy as a starting point:

> Pregnancy seems to be experienced as the radical ordeal of the splitting of the subject: redoubling up of the body, separation and coexistence of the self and an other, of nature and consciousness, of physiology and speech.[6]

We can confirm this notion of pregnancy as split subjectivity even outside the psychoanalytic framework that Kristeva uses. Reflection on the experience of pregnancy reveals a body subjectivity that is decentered, myself in the mode of not being myself.

As my pregnancy begins, I experience it as a change in my body; I become different from what I have been. My nipples become reddened and tender; my belly swells into a pear. I feel this elastic around my waist, itching, this round, hard middle replacing the doughy belly with which I still identify. Then I feel a little tickle, a little gurgle in my belly. It is my feeling, my insides, and it feels somewhat like a gas bubble, but it is not; it is different, in another place, belonging to another, another that is nevertheless my body.

The first movements of the fetus produce this sense of the splitting subject; the fetus's movements are wholly mine, completely within me, conditioning my experience and space. Only I have access to these movements from their origin, as it were. For months only I can witness this life within me, and it is only under my direction of where to put their hands that others can feel these movements. I have a privileged relation to this other life, not unlike that which I have to my dreams and thoughts, which I can tell someone but which cannot be an object for both of us in the same way. Adrienne Rich reports this sense of the movements within me as mine, even though they are another's.

> In early pregnancy, the stirring of the fetus felt like ghostly tremors of my own body, later like the movements of a being imprisoned within me; but both sensations were *my* sensations, contributing to my own sense of physical and psychic space.[7]

Pregnancy challenges the integration of my body experience by rendering fluid the boundary between what is within, myself, and what is outside, separate. I experience my insides as the space of another, yet my own body.

> Nor in pregnancy did I experience the embryo as decisively internal in Freud's terms, but rather, as something inside and of me, yet becoming hourly and daily more separate, on its way to becoming separate from me and of itself....
> 
> Far from existing in the mode of "inner space," women are powerfully and vulnerably attuned both to "inner" and "outer" because for us the two are continuous, not polar.[8]

The birthing process entails the most extreme suspension of the bodily distinction between inner and outer. As the months and weeks progress, increasingly I feel my insides, strained and pressed, and increasingly feel the movement of a body inside me. Through pain and blood and water this inside thing emerges between my legs, for a short while both inside and outside me. Later I look with wonder at my mushy middle and at my child, amazed that this yowling, flailing thing, so completely different from me, was there inside, part of me.

The integrity of my body is undermined in pregnancy not only by this externality of the inside, but also by the fact that the boundaries of my body are themselves in flux. In pregnancy I literally do not have a firm sense of where my body ends and the world begins. My automatic body habits become dislodged; the continuity between my customary body and my body at this moment is broken.[9] In pregnancy my prepregnant body image does not entirely leave my movements and expectations, yet it is with the pregnant body that I must move. This is another instance of the doubling of the pregnant subject.

I move as if I could squeeze around chairs and through crowds as I could seven months before, only to find my way blocked by my own body sticking out in front of me – but yet not me, since I did not expect it to block my passage. As I lean over in my chair to tie my shoe, I am surprised by the graze of this hard belly on my thigh. I do not anticipate my body touching itself, for my habits retain the old sense of my boundaries. In the ambiguity of bodily touch, I feel myself being touched and touching simultaneously, both on my knee and my belly.[10] The belly is other, since I did not expect it there, but since I feel the touch upon it, it is me.[11]

Existential phenomenologists of the body usually assume a distinction between transcendence and immanence as two modes of bodily being. They assume that insofar as I adopt an active relation to the world, I am not aware of my body for its own sake. In the successful enactment of my aims and projects, my body is a transparent medium.[12] For several of these thinkers, awareness of my body as weighted material, as physical, occurs only or primarily when my instrumental relation to the world breaks down, in fatigue or illness.

> The transformation into the bodily as physical always means discomfort and malaise. The character of husk, which our live bodiness here increasingly assumes, shows itself in its onerousness, bringing heaviness, burden, weight.[13]

Being brought to awareness of my body for its own sake, these thinkers assume, entails estrangement and objectification.

> If, suddenly, I am no longer indifferent to my body, and if I suddenly give my attention to its functions and processes, then my body as a whole is objectified, becomes to me an other, a part of the outside world. And though I may also be able to feel its inner processes, I am myself excluded.[14]

Thus the dichotomy of subject and object appears anew in the conceptualization of the body itself. These thinkers tend to assume that awareness of my body in its weight, massiveness, and balance is always an alienated objectification of my body, in which I am not my body and my body imprisons me. They also tend to assume that such awareness of my body must cut me off from the enactment of my projects; I cannot be attending to the physicality of my body and using it as the means to the accomplishment of my aims.

Certainly there are occasions when I experience my body only as a resistance, only as a painful otherness preventing me from accomplishing my goals. It is inappropriate, however, to tie such a negative meaning to all experience of being brought to awareness of the body in its weight and materiality. Sally Gadow has argued that in addition to experiencing the body as a transparent mediator for our projects or an objectified and alienated resistance or pain, we also at times experience our bodily being in an esthetic mode. That is, we can become aware of ourselves as body and take an interest in its sensations and limitations for their own sake, experiencing them as a fullness rather than a lack.[15] While Gadow suggests that both illness and aging can be experiences of the body in such an esthetic mode, pregnancy is most paradigmatic of such experience of being thrown into awareness of one's body. Contrary to the mutually exclusive categorization between transcendence and immanence that underlies some theories, the awareness of my body in its bulk and weight does not impede the accomplishing of my aims.

This belly touching my knee, this extra part of me that gives me a joyful surprise when I move through a tight place, calls me back to the matter of my body even as I move about accomplishing my aims. Pregnant consciousness is animated by a double intentionality: my subjectivity splits between awareness of myself as body and awareness of my aims and projects. To be sure, even in pregnancy there are times when I am so absorbed in my activity that I do not feel myself as body, but when I move or feel the look of another I am likely to be recalled to the thickness of my body.

I walk through the library stacks searching for the *Critique of Dialectical Reason*; I feel the painless pull of false contractions in my back. I put my hand on my belly to notice its hardening, while my eyes continue their scanning. As I sit with friends listening to jazz in a darkened bar, I feel within me the kicking of the fetus, as if it follows the rhythm of the music. In attending to my pregnant body in such circumstances, I do not feel myself alienated from it, as in illness. I merely notice its borders and rumblings with interest, sometimes with pleasure, and this esthetic interest does not divert me from my business.

This splitting focus both on my body and my projects has its counterpart in the dual location I give to myself on my body. Straus suggests that in everyday instrumental actions of getting about our business, comprehending, observing, willing, and acting, the "I" is located phenomenologically in our head. There are certain activities, however, of which dancing is paradigmatic, where the "I" shifts from the eyes to the region of the trunk. In this orientation that Straus calls "pathic" we experience ourselves in greater sensory continuity with the surroundings.[16]

The pregnant subject experiences herself as located in the eyes and trunk simultaneously, I suggest. She often experiences her ordinary walking, turning, sitting as a kind of dance, movement that not only gets her where she is going, but also in which she glides through space in an immediate openness. She is surprised sometimes that this weighted solidity that she feels herself becoming can still move with ease.

Pregnancy roots me to the earth, makes me conscious of the physicality of my body not as an object, but as the material weight that I am in movement. The notion of the body as a pure medium of my projects is the illusion of a philosophy that has not quite shed the Western philosophical legacy of humanity as spirit.[17] Movement always entails awareness of effort and the feeling of resistance. In pregnancy this fact of existence never leaves me. I am an actor transcending through each moment to further projects, but the solid inertia and demands of my body call me to my limits not as an obstacle to action, but only as a fleshy relation to the earth.[18] As the months proceed, the most ordinary efforts of human existence, such as sitting, bending, and walking, which I formerly took for granted, become apparent as the projects they themselves are. Getting up, for example, increasingly becomes a task that requires my attention.[19]

In the experience of the pregnant woman, this weight and materiality often produce a sense of power, solidity, and validity. Thus, whereas our society often devalues and trivializes women, regards women as weak and dainty, the pregnant woman can gain a certain sense of self-respect.

> This bulk slows my walking and makes my gestures and my mind more stately. I suppose if I schooled myself to walk massively the rest of my life, I might always have massive thoughts.[20]

There was a time when the pregnant woman stood as a symbol of stately and sexual beauty.[21] While pregnancy remains an object of fascination, our own culture harshly separates pregnancy from sexuality. The dominant culture defines feminine beauty as slim and shapely. The pregnant woman is often not looked upon as sexually active or desirable, even though her own desires and sensitivity may have increased. Her male partner, if she has one, may decline to share in her sexuality, and her physician may advise her to restrict her sexual activity. To the degree that a woman derives a sense of self-worth from looking "sexy" in the manner promoted by dominant cultural images, she may experience her pregnant body as being ugly and alien.

Though the pregnant woman may find herself desexualized by others, at the same time she may find herself with a heightened sense of her own sexuality. Kristeva suggests that the pregnant and birthing woman renews connection to the repressed, preconscious, presymbolic aspect of existence. Instead of being a unified ego, the subject of the paternal symbolic order, the pregnant subject straddles the spheres of language and instinct. In this splitting of the subject, the pregnant woman recollects a primordial sexual continuity with the maternal body, which Kristeva calls "jouissance."[22]

The pregnant woman's relation to her body can be an innocent narcissism. As I undress in the morning and evening, I gaze in the mirror for long minutes, without stealth or vanity. I do not appraise myself, ask whether I look good enough for others, but like a child take pleasure in discovering new things in my body. I turn to the side and stroke the taut flesh that protrudes under my breasts.

Perhaps the dominant culture's desexualization of the pregnant body helps make possible such self-love when it happens. The culture's separation of pregnancy and sexuality can liberate her from the sexually objectifying gaze that alienates and instrumentalizes her when in her nonpregnant state. The leer of sexual objectification regards the woman in pieces, as the possible object of a man's desire and touch.[23] In pregnancy the woman may experience some release from this alienating gaze. The look focusing on her belly is not one of desire, but of recognition. Some may be repelled by her, find her body ridiculous, but the look that follows her in pregnancy does not alienate her, does not instrumentalize her with respect to another's desire. Indeed, in this society, which still often narrows women's possibilities to motherhood, the pregnant woman often finds herself looked at with approval.

> As soon as I was visibly and clearly pregnant, I felt, for the first time in my adolescent and adult life, not-guilty. The atmosphere of approval in which I was bathed – even by strangers in the street, it seemed – was like an aura I carried with

me, in which doubts, fears, misgivings, met with absolute denial. This is what women have always done.[24]

In classical art this "aura" surrounding motherhood depicts repose. The dominant culture projects pregnancy as a time of quiet waiting. We refer to the woman as "expecting," as though this new life were flying in from another planet and she sat in her rocking chair by the window, occasionally moving the curtain aside to see whether the ship is coming. The image of uneventful waiting associated with pregnancy reveals clearly how much the discourse of pregnancy leaves out the subjectivity of the woman. From the point of view of others pregnancy is primarily a time of waiting and watching, when nothing happens.

For the pregnant subject, on the other hand, pregnancy has a temporality of movement, growth, and change. The pregnant subject is not simply a splitting in which the two halves lie open and still, but a dialectic. The pregnant woman experiences herself as a source and participant in a creative process. Though she does not plan and direct it, neither does it merely wash over her; rather, she *is* this process, this change. Time stretches out, moments and days take on a depth because she experiences more changes in herself, her body. Each day, each week, she looks at herself for signs of transformation.

> Were I to lose consciousness for a month, I could still tell that an appreciable time had passed by the increased size of the fetus within me. There is a constant sense of growth, of progress, of time, which, while it may be wasted for you personally, is still being used, so that even if you were to do nothing at all during those nine months, something would nevertheless be accomplished and a climax reached.[25]

For others the birth of an infant may be only a beginning, but for the birthing woman it is a conclusion as well. It signals the close of a process she has been undergoing for nine months, the leaving of this unique body she has moved through, always surprising her a bit in its boundary changes and inner kicks. Especially if this is her first child she experiences the birth as a transition to a new self that she may both desire and fear. She fears a loss of identity, as though on the other side of the birth she herself became a transformed person, such that she would "never be the same again."

Finally her "time" comes, as is commonly said. During labor, however, there is no sense of growth and change, but the cessation of time. There is no intention, no activity, only a will to endure. I only know that I have been lying in this pain, concentrating on staying above it, for a long time because the hands of the clock say so or the sun on the wall has moved to the other side of the room.

> Time is absolutely still. I have been here forever. Time no longer exists. Always, Time holds steady for birth. There is only this rocketing, this labor.[26]

## II

Feminist writers often use the concept of alienation to describe female existence in a male dominated society and culture.[27] In this section I argue that the pregnant subject's encounter with obstetrical medicine in the United States often alienates her from her pregnant and birthing experience. Alienation here means the objectification or appropriation by one subject of another subject's body, action, or product of action, such that she or he does not recognize that objectification as having its origins in her or his experience. A subject's experience or action is alienated when it is defined or controlled by a subject who does not share one's assumptions or goals. I will argue that a woman's experience in pregnancy and birthing is often alienated because her condition tends to be defined as a disorder, because medical instruments objectify internal processes in such a way that they devalue a woman's experience of those processes, and because the social relations and instrumentation of the medical setting reduce her control over her experience.

Through most of the history of medicine its theoreticians and practitioners did not include the reproductive processes of women within its domain. Once women's reproductive processes came within the domain of medicine, they were defined as diseases. Indeed, by the mid-nineteenth century, at least in Victorian England and America, being female itself was symptomatic of disease. Medical writers considered women to be inherently weak and psychologically unstable, and the ovaries and uterus to be the cause of a great number of diseases and disorders, both physical and psychological.[28]

Contemporary obstetricians and gynecologists usually take pains to assert that menstruation, pregnancy, childbirth, and menopause are normal body functions that occasionally have a disorder. The legacy that defined pregnancy and other reproductive functions as conditions requiring medical therapy, however, has not been entirely abandoned.

Rothman points out that even medical writers who explicitly deny that pregnancy is a disease view normal changes associated with pregnancy, such as lowered hemoglobin, water retention, and weight gain, as "symptoms" requiring "treatment" as part of the normal process of prenatal care.[29] Though 75 percent to 88 percent of pregnant women experience some nausea in the early months, some obstetrical textbooks refer to this physiological process as a neurosis that "may indicate resentment, ambivalence and inadequacy in women ill-prepared for motherhood."[30] Obstetrical teaching films entitled *Normal Delivery* depict the use of various drugs and instruments, as well as the use of paracervical block and the performance of episiotomy.[31]

A continued tendency on the part of medicine to treat pregnancy and childbirth as dysfunctional conditions derives first from the way medicine defines its purpose. Though medicine has extended its domain to include many bodily and psychological processes that ought not to be conceptualized as illness or disease – such as child development, sexuality, and aging, as well as women's reproductive functions – medicine continues to define itself as the practice that seeks cure for disease. Pellegrino and Thomasma, for example, define the goal of medicine as "the relief of perceived lived body disruption" and "organic restoration to a former or better state of perceived health or well-being."

> When a patient consults a physician, he or she does so with one specific purpose in mind: to be healed, to be restored and made whole, i.e., to be relieved of some noxious element in physical or emotional life which the patient defines as disease – a distortion of the accustomed perception of what is a satisfactory life.[32]

These are often not the motives that prompt pregnant women to seek the office of the obstetrician. Yet because medicine continues to define itself as the curing profession, it can tend implicitly to conceptualize women's reproductive processes as disease or infirmity.

A second conceptual ground for the tendency within gynecological and obstetrical practice to approach menstruation, pregnancy, and menopause as "conditions" with "symptoms" that require "treatment" lies in the implicit male bias in medicine's conception of health. The dominant model of health assumes that the normal, healthy body is unchanging. Health is associated with stability, equilibrium, a steady state. Only a minority of persons, however, namely adult men who are not yet old, experience their health as a state in which there is no regular or noticeable change in body condition. For them a noticeable change in their bodily state usually does signal a disruption or dysfunction. Regular, noticeable, sometimes extreme change in bodily condition, on the other hand, is an aspect of the normal bodily functioning of adult women. Change is also a central aspect of the bodily existence of healthy children and healthy old people, as well as some of the so-called disabled. Yet medical conceptualization implicitly uses this unchanging adult male body as the standard of all health.

This tendency of medical conceptualization to treat pregnancy as disease can produce alienation for the pregnant woman. She often has a sense of bodily well-being during her pregnancy and often has increased immunity to common diseases such as colds, flu, etc. As we saw in the previous section, moreover, she often has a bodily self-image of strength and solidity. Thus, while her body may signal one set of impressions, her entrance into the definitions of medicine may lead her to the opposite understanding. Even though certain discomforts associated with pregnancy, such as nausea, flatulence, and shortness of breath, can happen in the healthiest of women, her internalization of various discussions of the fragility of pregnancy may lead her to define such experience as signs of weakness.

Numerous criticisms of the use of instruments, drugs, surgery, and other methods of intervention in obstetrical practice have been voiced in recent years.[33] I do not wish to reiterate them here, nor do I wish to argue that the use of instruments and drugs in pregnancy and childbirth is usually inappropriate or dangerous. The instrumental and intervention orientation that predominates in contemporary obstetrics, however, can contribute to a woman's sense of alienation in at least two ways.

First, the normal procedures of the American hospital birthing setting render the woman considerably more passive than she need be. Most hospitals, for example, do not allow the woman to walk around even during early stages of labor, despite the fact that there is evidence that moving around can lessen pain and speed the birthing process. Routine breaking of the amniotic sack enforces this bed confinement. Women usually labor and deliver in a horizontal or near-horizontal position, reducing the influence of gravity and reducing the woman's ability to push. The use of intravenous equipment, monitors, and pain-relieving drugs all inhibit a woman's capacity to move during labor.

Second, the use of instruments provides a means of objectifying the pregnancy and birth that alienates a woman because it negates or devalues her own experience of those processes. As the previous section described, at a phenomenological level the pregnant woman has a unique knowledge of her body processes and the life of the fetus. She feels the movements of the fetus, the contractions of her uterus, with an immediacy and certainty that no one can share. Recently invented machines tend to devalue this knowledge. The fetal-heart sensor projects the heartbeat of the six-week-old fetus into the room so that all can hear it in the same way. The sonogram is receiving increasing use to follow the course of fetal development. The fetal monitor attached during labor records the intensity and duration of each contraction on white paper; the woman's reports are no longer necessary for charting the progress of her labor. Such instruments transfer some control over the means of observing the pregnancy and birth process from the woman to the medical personnel. The woman's experience of these processes is reduced in value, replaced by more objective means of observation.

Alienation within the context of contemporary obstetrics can be further produced for the pregnant woman by the fact that the physician attending her is usually a man. Humanistic writers about medicine often suggest that a basic condition of good medical practice is that the physician and patient share the lived-body experience.[34] If the description of the lived-body experience of pregnancy in the previous section is valid, however, pregnancy and childbirth entail a unique body subjectivity that is difficult to empathize with unless one is or has been pregnant. Since the vast majority of obstetricians are men, then, this basic condition of therapeutic practice usually cannot be met in obstetrics. Physicians and pregnant women are thereby distanced in their relationship, perhaps more than others in the doctor-patient relation. The sexual asymmetry between physician and patient also produces a distance because it must be desexualized. Prenatal checkups follow the same procedure as gynecological examinations, requiring an aloof matter-of-factness in order to preclude attaching sexual meaning to them.[35]

There is a final alienation the woman experiences in the medical setting, which derives from the relations of authority and subordination that usually structure the doctor-patient relation in contemporary medical practice. Many writers have noted that medicine has increasingly become an institution with broad social authority on a par with the legal system or even organized religion.[36] The relationship between doctor and patient is usually structured as superior to subordinate. Physicians often project an air of fatherly infallibility and resist having their opinions challenged; the authoritarianism of the doctor-patient relations increases as the social distance between them increases.[37]

This authority that the physician has over any patient is amplified in gynecology and obstetrics by the dynamic of gender hierarchy. In a culture that still generally regards men as being more important than women and gives men authority and power over women in many institutions, the power the doctor has over the knowledge and objectification of her body processes, as well as his power to direct the performance of her office visits and her birthing, are often experienced by her as another form of male power over women.[38]

Philosophers of medicine have pointed out that the concept of health is much less a scientific concept than a normative concept referring to human well-being and the good life.[39] I have argued that there exists a male bias in medicine's concept of health insofar as the healthy body is understood to be the body in a steady state. This argument suggests that medical culture requires a more self-consciously differentiated understanding of health and disease.[40] Contemporary culture has gone to a certain extent in the direction of developing distinct norms of health and disease for the aged, the physically impaired, children, and hormonally active women. Such developments should be encouraged, and medical theorists and practitioners should be vigilant about tendencies to judge physical difference as deviance.

Moreover, to overcome the potentialities for alienation that I have argued exist in obstetrical practices, as well as other medical practices, medicine must shed its self-definition as primarily concerned with curing. Given that nearly all aspects of human bodily life and change have come within the domain of medical institutions and practices, such a definition is no longer appropriate. There are numerous life states and physical conditions in which a person needs help or care, rather than medical or surgical efforts to alter, repress, or speed a body process. The birthing woman certainly needs help in her own actions, being held, talked to, coached, dabbed with water, and having someone manipulate the emergence of the infant. Children, old people, and the physically impaired often need help and care though they are not diseased. Within current medical and related institutions there exist professionals who perform these caring functions. They are usually women, usually poorly paid, and their activities are usually seen as complementing and subordinate to the direction of activities such as diagnostic tests, drug therapies, and surgical therapies performed by the physicians, usually men. The alienation experienced by the pregnant and birthing woman would probably be lessened if caring were distinguished from curing and took on a practical value that did not subordinate it to curing.

## Notes

1  Julia Kristeva, "Motherhood according to Giovanni Bellini," in *Desire in Language* (New York: Columbia University Press, 1980), p. 237.
2  Erwin Straus, *Psychiatry and Philosophy* (New York: Springer Verlag, 1969), p. 29.
3  J. Sarano, *The Meaning of the Body*, James H. Farley, trans. (Philadelphia: Westminster Press, 1966), pp. 62–3.
4  Maurice Merleau-Ponty, *The Phenomenology of Perception*, Colin Smith, trans. (New York: Humanities Press, 1962), p. 406.
5  See Rosalind Coward and John Ellis, *Language and Materialism* (London: Routledge and Kegan Paul, 1977).
6  Julia Kristeva, "Women's time," Jardin and Blake, trans., *Signs*, vol. 7 (1981), p. 31; cf. Kristeva, "Motherhood according to Giovanni Bellini," p. 238.
7  Adrienne Rich, *Of Woman Born* (New York: W. W. Norton, 1976; Bantam paperback edition, p. 47).
8  Rich, pp. 47–8.
9  See Merleau-Ponty, *Phenomenology of Perception*, p. 82.
10  On the ambiguity of touch, see Merleau-Ponty, p. 93; see also Erwin Straus, *Psychiatry and Philosophy*, p. 46.
11  Straus discusses an intentional shift between the body as "other" and as self; see *The Primary World of the Senses* (London: The Free Press, 1963), p. 370.
12  Merleau-Ponty, pp. 138–9.
13  Hans Plügge, "Man and his body," in Spicker (ed.), *The Philosophy of the Body* (Chicago: Quadrangle Books, 1970), p. 298.
14  Straus, *Primary World of the Senses*, p. 245.
15  Sally Gadow, "Body and self: a dialectic," *Journal of Medicine and Philosophy*, vol. 5 (1980), pp. 172–85.
16  See Straus, "Forms of spatiality," in *Phenomenological Psychology* (New York: Basic Books), especially pp. 11–12.
17  Elizabeth V. Spelman, "Woman as body: ancient and contemporary views," *Feminist Studies*, vol. 8 (1982), pp. 109–23.
18  On the relation of body to ground, see R. M. Griffith, "Anthropology: man-a-foot," in *Philosophy of the Body*, pp. 273–92; see also Stuart Spicker, "*Terra Firma* and infirma species: from medical philosophical anthropology to philosophy of medicine," *Journal of Medicine and Philosophy*, vol. 1 (1976), pp. 104–35.
19  Straus's essay "The upright posture" well expresses the centrality of getting up and standing up to being a person; in *Phenomenological Psychology*, pp. 137–65.
20  Ann Lewis, *An Interesting Condition* (Garden City, NY: Doubleday, 1950), p. 83. When I began reading for this essay I was shocked at how few texts I found of women speaking about their pregnancies; this book is a rare gem in that regard.

21 Rich discusses some of the history of views of pregnancy and motherhood; see op. cit., *Of Woman Born*, chapter IV.

22 Kristeva, "Motherhood according to Giovanni Bellini," op. cit., p. 242; Marianne Hirsch makes a useful commentary in "Mothers and daughters," *Signs*, vol. 7 (1981), pp. 200–22.

23 Sandra Bartky, "On psychological oppression," in Bishop and Weinzweig (ed.), *Philosophy and Women* (Belmont, Calif.: Wadsworth Publishing Co., 1979), pp. 330–41.

24 Rich, p. 6.

25 Lewis, op. cit., p. 78.

26 Phyllis Chesler, *With Child: A Diary of Motherhood* (New York: Thomas Y. Crowell, 1979), p. 116.

27 Ann Foreman, *Femininity As Alienation* (London: Pluto Press, 1977); Sandra Bartky, "Narcissism, femininity and alienation," *Social Theory and Practice*, vol. 8 (1982), pp. 127–43.

28 Barbara Erenreich and Deirdre English, *For Her Own Good* (Garden City, NY: Doubleday, 1978), chapters 2 and 3.

29 Barbara Katz Rothman, "Women, health and medicine," in Jo Freeman (ed.), *Women: A Feminist Perspective* (Palo Alto, Calif.: Mayfield Publishing Co., 1979), pp. 27–40.

30 Quoted in Gena Corea, *The Hidden Malpractice: How American Medicine Treats Women as Patients and Professionals* (New York: William Morrow, 1977), p. 76.

31 Rothman, op. cit., p. 36.

32 E. D. Pellegrino and D. C. Thomasma, *A Philosophical Basis of Medical Practice* (New York: Oxford University Press, 1981), p. 122; earlier quotes from p. 76 and p. 72, respectively.

33 Suzanne Arms, *Immaculate Deception: A New Look at Women and Childbirth in America* (Boston: Houghton Mifflin, 1975); D. Haire, "The cultural warping of childbirth," *Environmental Child Health*, vol. 19 (1973), pp. 171–91; and Adele Laslie, "Ethical issues in childbirth," *Journal of Medicine and Philosophy*, vol. 7 (1982), pp. 179–96.

34 Pellegrino and Thomasma, op. cit., p. 114.

35 J. Emerson, "Behavior in private places: sustaining definitions of reality in gynecological examinations," in H. Dreitzen (ed.), *Recent Sociology*, no. 2 (London: Macmillan, 1970), pp. 74–97.

36 See E. Friedson, *The Profession of Medicine* (New York: Dodd and Mead Co., 1970); Irving K. Zola, "Medicine as an institution of social control," *The Sociological Review*, vol. 2 (1972), pp. 487–504; and Janice Raymond, "Medicine as patriarchal religion," *Journal of Medicine and Philosophy*, vol. 7 (1982), pp. 197–216.

37 See G. Ehrenreich and J. Ehrenreich, "Medicine and social control," in John Ehrenreich (ed.), *The Cultural Crisis of Modern Medicine* (New York: Monthly Review Press, 1979), pp. 1–28.

38 See B. Kaiser and K. Kaiser, "The challenge of the women's movement to American gynecology," *American Journal of Obstetrics and Gynecology*, vol. 120 (1974), pp. 652–61.

39 Pellegrino and Thomasma, op. cit, pp. 74–6; see also Tristam Engelhardt, "Human well-being and medicine: some basic value judgments in the biomedical sciences," in Engelhardt and Callahan, ed., *Science, Ethics and Medicine* (Hastingson-Hudson, NY: Ethics and the Life Sciences, 1976), pp. 120–39; and Caroline Whitbeck, "A theory of health" in Caplan, Engelhardt, and McCartney (eds.), *Concepts of Health and Disease: Interdisciplinary Perspectives* (Reading, Mass.: Addison-Wesley, 1981), pp. 611–26.

40 Arlene Dallery, "Illness and health: alternatives to medicine," in E. Schrag and W. L. McBride (ed.), *Phenomenology in a Pluralistic Context: Selected Studies in Phenomenology and Existentialism* (Albany: State University of New York Press, 1983), pp. 167–76.

# "Throwing Like a Girl": Twenty Years Later

## *Iris Young*

Two years before my eighteen-year-old daughter was born, I began writing the essay, "Throwing like a girl," first published in *Human Studies* in 1980. In this early effort to use the tools and texts of existential phenomenology for feminist philosophy, I reflected on my own experience as a girl and woman in mid-twentieth-century white working-class urban America. Though I was an athletic child, organized sports were not available to me, and I was inhibited in my movements by the obligation to wear skirts most of the time. As an adolescent I put away childish running and punch ball, and with my friends practiced sexy mincing walks. As a young adult I wanted to be desirable, but I felt frozen and frightened by whistles and obscene remarks sometimes hurled at me as I walked through city streets. "Throwing like a girl" aimed to theorize the effects of feminine socialization and sexual objectification on a woman's world-making movements, describing us as unable to be free in movement.

A look at my daughter's growing up and young adulthood shows me that a great deal has changed. Jeans have been her normal daily wear since she could walk, with dresses reserved only for special parties or piano recitals. It seems to me that she and her friends move and carry themselves with more openness, more reach, more active confidence, than many of my generation did. She has been able to take athletic opportunities for granted. There is at least as much danger of sexual assault for her as there was for me, but acceptable norms of male street behavior seem to have altered such that she endures fewer vocalized objectifications than she might have twenty years ago.

The changes in the social context in which girls and women move are significant enough that I would have guessed that "Throwing like a girl" might seem antiquated to young women today. Some people have reported to me, however, that it continues to resonate with college age women. In the remainder of this essay, however, I will not speculate further on the degree to which the social environment for women's movement has changed. Instead, I will discuss some philosophical limitations I see in that essay after twenty years of feminist theory. I conclude, however, that some of the limitations I identify also account for the continuing force of the essay.

## Femininity as contradiction

"Throwing like a girl" brings Maurice Merleau-Ponty's phenomenology of spatiality to bear on women's gendered experience. It makes no direct criticism of Merleau-Ponty for not attending to gender, even though it would be appropriate to criticize a philosophy that locates subjectivity in the body for not asking whether sexed and gendered bodies express differing subjectivities. Instead, the essay accepts the existential humanism Merleau-Ponty assumes, that is, that phenomenology uncovers and describes basic structures of universal human experience. Following the lead of Simone de Beauvoir and many other humanist feminists before and after her, "Throwing like a girl" implicitly constructs the project of feminist criticism as showing how women in patriarchal society are excluded and inhibited from full expression of that universal humanity.

The essay assumes the account of body comportment, motility, and spatiality which Merleau-Ponty lays out in the *Phenomenology of Perception* as the proper account of subjectivity at a level that abstracts from gender. It seeks to concretize that account by specifying what the essay calls gendered *modalities* of the general categories of body experience and spatiality Merleau-Ponty theorizes. It assumes that there is a general level of theorizing where gender (or class or cultural) difference does not appear in a phenomenological ontology, and then more specific, less abstract accounts where they do.

To construct its account of the specific modalities of feminine body comportment and motility, the essay superimposes Simone de Beauvoir's framework for describing women's existence in male-dominated society on Merleau-Ponty's framework for describing the lived body. Beauvoir describes women's situation in male-dominated society as that of being forced to live out a contradiction. Masculine culture and male desire position her as the Other, an objectified projection of masculine dreams and fears. Much about her life is in this way confined to making herself into an object, an in-itself; in Beauvoir's language, feminine existence is confined to immanence. Women are, however, even under the oppressions of patriarchy, active subjects, full of wit and wile, with active projects of their own. For Beauvoir, then, women's condition in male-dominated society is fundamentally contradictory: she must try to be a for-itself-in-itself. Beauvoir relies on a dichotomy between transcendence and immanence to fashion her account. Human subjects instantiate transcendence inasmuch as we are conscious, creative, and formulate projects. As such, women instantiate transcendence. Male-dominated institutions, however, assign women roles that thwart this transcendence, and aim to confine women to the immanence of natural objects and species being.

Within this Beauvoirian framework, the strategy "Throwing like a girl" follows is to articulate a set of contradictory modalities of feminine body comportment, motility, and spatiality: inhibited intentionality, ambiguous transcendence, and discontinuous unity. The description of each shows women in male-dominated society struggling to live out free transcendent subjectivity within the requirements of immanence and objectification. The continuing resonance of the essay may bespeak the fruitfulness of the strategy.

## Doubts about transcendence and immanence

Many feminist philosophers, including myself in later writings, have criticized Beauvoir's dichotomy of transcendence and immanence. Beauvoir accepts a dichotomy between culture and nature, and criticizes the society that identifies men with culture and women with nature. As with many metaphysical dichotomies, it is easy to show how this one privileges one term as the full and the good and locates the other as the negative supplement. This particular dichotomy denigrates embodiment and nurturing activity, and celebrates abstraction and fabrication.

One of the purposes of the next paper on female body experience I wrote, "Pregnant embodiment," is to confront this very dichotomy, not only in Beauvoir, but in the entire framework of existential phenomenology. That paper describes phenomenologically the subjectivity of pregnancy as split, plural and thus a dialectical subject in process that need not choose between self-reference and transcendence. That paper also questions the assumption of the unity of subjectivity that "Throwing like a girl" also assumes with the phenomenological tradition as normative for consciousness. Since the lived body experience of pregnancy cannot be aptly described under such an assumption, I suggest that this throws the framework itself into question. "Pregnant embodiment," finally, questions the subject–object dichotomy implicit in much phenomenology of the body, according to which awareness of the body's thingness distracts from active transcendence through the body. That essay takes seriously the weightiness and biological process of the body as themselves indicators of purposiveness and temporality.[1]

In a more recent paper I challenge Beauvoir's relegation of women's traditional domestic work to the category of immanence. While some domestic work is mere life maintenance, vitally important but sub-historical, home-making also consists in the meaningful arrangement of things in dwelling space. I argue that domestic work has a specifically temporal and historical dimension, as the preservation of meaningful things. This account questions the primacy that the transcendence–immanence distinction gives to futurity.[2]

## Universal as masculine

"Throwing like a girl" contains an implicit tension between its humanism and its effort to specify the modalities of that human universal. On the one hand, it accepts uncritically the assumption that there are standards and values of free human life as such, and that in male-dominated society men are enabled to realize those standards and values to a greater extent than women. The values of universal humanity, that is, are largely coincidental with the masculine role in this male-dominated society, and the goal is to de-gender them and extend them to everyone.

On the other hand, "Throwing like a girl" implicitly questions a notion of universal humanity by aiming to specify the concrete modalities of feminine body experience. That effort leads naturally to the question, are there not comparably specific masculine modalities, and if so what are they? (To this day I am not aware than any philosopher of the body has addressed this question in a sustained and systematic way.) While the essay gestures toward this question, it also blocks the way to answering it. If in male-dominated society the humanly universal standards of freedom and creativity tend to be expressed by masculine norms and behavior, then how can there also be specifically masculine modalities?

Reflection on another unexamined assumption of the essay reveals some possible areas of masculine specificity. The essay assumes a rather instrumentalist account of the motility and spatiality of the lived body. Its body as subject is a purposive actor, with specific objectives it moves out into the world to accomplish. This body is more or less free insofar as it is enabled or inhibited from achieving its objectives. Sport, labor, and travel are its paradigms of bodily activity, all with clear instrumentalist structures. I believe that I derived this instrumentalist bias from the Merleau-Ponty of *The Phenomenology of Perception*, and more generally from the existential phenomenological tradition which originates with Heidegger's *Being and Time*. I could be persuaded, however, that the Merleau-Ponty of the *Phenomenology* also expresses several less instrumentalist interpretations of the body than does "Throwing like a girl," and in the later Merleau-Ponty such instrumentalism recedes.

If we make explicit this unexamined construction of the lived body as instrumentally oriented, we can notice the construction as based on a masculine, and not gender neutral, model of action. The instrumentalist-purposive model of action privileges plan, intention, and control. These are attributes of action most typical of masculine-coded comportment and activities. Modern Western culture may have elevated such a model of action to the paradigm of creative action, but clearly such a model does not cover the full scope of modes of action. Jürgen Habermas distinguishes communicative action from instrumental action, for example, and it could be fruitful to ask about the modalities of the lived body enabling communicative action.

The model of action "Throwing like a girl" takes as paradigmatic, that is, may harbor masculinist bias that values typically masculine activities more than the typically feminine. This bias may account for another potential weakness of the essay, namely, that it constructs an account of women's body comportment only as oppressed. In the world of this essay, women are inhibited, hesitant, constrained, gazed at, and positioned. Women appear primarily as the victims of a patriarchal culture that refuses to admit us to full humanity. It continues to be too true that women suffer damage and disadvantage in male dominated society. Against some post-feminist complaints that such claims themselves amount to belittling or disempowering women, I would insist that a primary feminist task must continue to be exposing and criticizing the violence, overwork, and sexual exploitation that many women suffer as women. Nevertheless, a description of women's body comportment and motility might also look for specifically valuable aspects of women's experience. My more recent essays on female body experience aim to be more many-sided in this way, describing both social harms to women and specific, if unrecognized, values in some aspects of femininely gendered experience.

## Could it be done differently?

"Throwing like a girl" accepts too uncritically, I have suggested, the opposition between transcendence and immanence, the necessary unity of the acting subject, and an instrumentalist model of action as universal and fundamental. It implicitly defines the feminist project only as that of exposing how male-dominated society excludes women from highly valued male activities, rather than also looking for how it devalues female activities. One could imagine a less limited, more self-conscious project of philosophically describing feminine body comportment, motility and spatiality. Such a project might, for example, interrogate more the adequacy of Merleau-Ponty's theory in the *Phenomenology of Perception*, even as it sought to apply that theory.

This project might look for specifically feminine forms of movement that cannot easily be brought under the unifying instrumentalist model but are nevertheless about work or accomplishing goals. An amazing passage from one of Tillie Olsen's short stories, for example, describes a kitchen dance in which a farm woman cans her tomatoes while mindful of the colicky baby she holds between her arm and her hip. The movement is plural and engaged, to and fro, here and yonder, rather than unified and singly directed. What might a phenomenology of action look like which started from the mundane fact that many of us, especially women, often do several things at once?

Though in these few pages of reflection I have signaled some possible limitations of the essay "Throwing like a girl," still I must say that I could not write it differently even today. If the essay continues to reveal aspects of women's situations and human possibilities, then I think this is partly due to its structure and assumptions. It is very useful to combine the frameworks of great thinkers and stretch them to descriptions of worldly experience on which they themselves have little reflected. Direct interrogation of those frameworks themselves often distracts us from the theorizing that uses them to see the world in revealing ways.

The essay's theoretical and rhetorical power, moreover, owes much to its manner of constructing the modalities of women's body comportment and spatiality as contradictory. Without the assumption of dichotomous categorizations like sub-ject–object, transcendent–immanent, unity–plurality, however, such a description of experience as contradictory would not be possible. I conclude, then, that "Throwing like a girl," remains a useful and viable work in its own terms, terms whose truthfulness may at the same time obscure and exaggerate. Such limitations are inevitable. They have no antidote in trying to be comprehensively true without obscuring or exaggerating. Instead of curing the partiality of accounts, the proper response is to accept that partiality, and hope that other essays voice other questions and other aspects of experience.

## Notes

1  "Pregnant embodiment: subjectivity and alienation," in *Throwing Like a Girl and Other Essays in Feminist Philosophy and Social Theory* (Bloomington: Indiana University Press, 1990).
2  "House and home: feminist variations on a theme," forthcoming in I. M. Young, *Intersecting Voices: Dilemmas of Gender, Political Philosophy, and Policy* (Princeton: Princeton University Press, 1997).

# 13
## Slender Bodies

# Reading the Slender Body*

## *Susan Bordo*

In the late Victorian era, arguably for the first time in the West, those who could afford to eat well began systematically to deny themselves food in pursuit of an esthetic ideal.[1] Certainly, other cultures had dieted. Aristocratic Greek culture made a science of the regulation of food intake, as a road to self-mastery and the practice of moderation in all things.[2] Fasting, aimed at spiritual purification and domination of the flesh, was an important part of the repertoire of Christian practice in the Middle Ages.[3] These forms of diet can clearly be viewed as instruments for the development of a "self" – whether an "inner" self, for the Christians, or a public self, for the Greeks – constructed as an arena in which the deepest possibilities for human excellence may be realized. Rituals of fasting and asceticism were therefore reserved for the select few, aristocratic or priestly, who were deemed capable of achieving such excellence of spirit. In the late nineteenth century, by contrast, the practices of body management begin to be middle-class preoccupations, and concern with diet becomes attached to the pursuit of an idealized physical weight or shape; it becomes a project in service of body rather than soul. Fat, not appetite or desire, became the declared enemy, and people began to measure their dietary achievements by the numbers on the scale rather than by the level of their mastery of impulse and excess. The bourgeois "tyranny of slenderness" (as Kim Chernin has called it)[4] had begun its ascendancy (particularly over women), and with it the development of numerous technologies – diet, exercise, and, later on, chemicals and surgery – aimed at a purely physical transformation.

Today, we have become acutely aware of the massive and multifaceted nature of such technologies and the industries built around them. To the degree that a popular critical consciousness exists, however, it has been focused largely (and not surprisingly) on what has been viewed as pathological or extreme – on the unfortunate minority who become "obsessed" or go "too far." Television talk shows feature tales of disasters caused by stomach stapling, gastric bubbles, gastrointestinal bypass operations, liquid diets, compulsive exercising. Magazines warn of the dangers of fat-reduction surgery and liposuction. Books and articles about bulimia and anorexia nervosa proliferate. The portrayal of eating disorders by the popular media is often lurid; audiences gasp at pictures of skeletal bodies or at item-by-item descriptions of the mounds of food eaten during an average binge. Such presentations create a "side show" relationship between the ("normal") audience and those on view ("the

* Susan Bordo, "Reading the slender body," *Unbearable Weight: Feminism, Western Culture, and the Body* (Berkeley: University of California Press, 1993), pp. 185–212.

freaks"). To the degree that the audience may nonetheless recognize themselves in the behavior or reported experiences of those on stage, they confront themselves as "pathological" or outside the norm.

Of course, many of these behaviors *are* outside the norm, if only because of the financial resources they require. But preoccupation with fat, diet, and slenderness are not abnormal.[5] Indeed, such preoccupations may function as one of the most powerful normalizing mechanisms of our century, insuring the production of self-monitoring and self-disciplining "docile bodies" sensitive to any departure from social norms and habituated to self-improvement and self-transformation in the service of those norms. Seen in this light, the focus on "pathology," disorder, accident, unexpected disaster, and bizarre behavior obscures the normalizing function of the technologies of diet and body management. For women, who are subject to such controls more profoundly and, historically, more ubiquitously than men, the focus on "pathology" (unless embedded in a political analysis) diverts recognition from a central means of the reproduction of gender.

In this essay I examine the normalizing role of diet and exercise by analyzing popular representations through which their cultural meaning is crystallized, metaphorically encoded, and transmitted. More specifically, I pursue here Mary Douglas's insight that images of the "microcosm" – the physical body – may symbolically reproduce central vulnerabilities and anxieties of the "macrocosm" – the social body.[6] I will explore this insight by reading, as the text or surface on which culture is symbolically written, some dominant meanings that are connected, in our time, to the imagery of slenderness.[7]

The first step in my argument is a decoding of the contemporary slenderness ideal so as to reveal the psychic anxieties and moral valuations contained within it – valuations concerning correct and incorrect management of impulse and desire. In the process I describe a key contrast between two different symbolic functions of body shape and size: (1) the designation of social position, such as class status or gender role; and (2) the outer indication of the spiritual, moral, or emotional state of the individual. Next, aided by the significant work of Robert Crawford, I turn to the social body of consumer culture in order to demonstrate how the "correct" management of desire in that culture, requiring as it does a contradictory double-bind construction of personality, inevitably produces an unstable bulimic personality-type as its norm, along with the contrasting extremes of obesity and self-starvation.[8] These symbolize, I will argue, the contradictions of the social body – contradictions that make self-management a continual and virtually impossible task in our culture. Finally, I introduce gender into this symbolic framework, showing how additional resonances (concerning the cultural management of female desire, on the one hand, and female flight from a purely reproductive destiny, on the other) have over-determined slenderness as the current ideal for women.

## Contemporary anxiety and the enemy flab

In the magazine show "20/20," several ten-year-old boys were shown some photos of fashion models. The models were pencil-thin. Yet the pose was such that a small bulge of hip was forced, through the action of the body, into protuberance – as is natural, unavoidable on any but the most skeletal or the most tautly developed bodies. We bend over, we sit down, and the flesh coalesces in spots. These young boys, pointing to the hips, disgustedly pronounced the models to be "fat." Watching the show, I was appalled at the boys' reaction. Yet I could not deny that I had also been surprised at my own current perceptions while re-viewing female bodies in movies from the 1970s; what once appeared slender and fit now seemed loose and flabby. *Weight* was not the key element in these changed perceptions – my standards had not come to favor *thinner* bodies – rather, I had come to expect a tighter, smoother, more contained body profile.

The self-criticisms of the anorectic, too, are usually focused on particular soft, proturberant areas of the body (most often the stomach) rather than on the body as a whole. Karen, in Ira Sacker and Marc Zimmer's *Dying to Be Thin*, tries to dispel what she sees as the myth that the anorectic misperceives her whole body as fat:

> I hope I'm expressing myself properly here, because this is important. You have to understand. I don't see my whole body as fat. When I look in the mirror I don't really see a fat person there. I see certain things about me that are really thin. Like my arms and legs. But I can tell the minute I eat certain things that my stomach blows up like a pig's. I know it gets distended. And it's disgusting. That's what I keep to myself – hug to myself.[9]

Or Barbara, from Dalma Heyn's article on "Body vision":

> Sometimes my body looks so bloated, I don't want to get dressed. I like the way it looks for exactly two days each month: usually, the eighth and ninth days after my period. Every other day, my breasts, my stomach – they're just awful lumps, bumps, bulges. My body can turn on me at any moment; it is an out-of-control mass of flesh.[10]

Much has been made of such descriptions, from both psychoanalytic and feminist perspectives. But for now I wish to pursue these images of unwanted bulges and erupting stomachs in another direction than that of gender symbolism. I want to consider them as a metaphor for anxiety about internal processes out of control – uncontained desire, unrestrained hunger, uncontrolled impulse. Images of bodily eruption frequently function symbolically in this way in contemporary horror movies and werewolf films (*The Howling, A Teen-Age Werewolf in London*) and in David Cronenberg's remake of *The Fly*. The original *Fly* imagined a mechanical joining of fly parts and person parts, a variation on the standard "half-man, half-beast" image. In Cronenberg's *Fly*, as in the werewolf genre, a new, alien, libidinous, and uncontrollable self literally bursts through the seams of the victims' old flesh. (A related, frequently copied image occurs in *Alien*, where a parasite erupts from the chest of the human host.) In advertisements, the construction of the body as an alien attacker, threatening to erupt in an unsightly display of bulging flesh, is a ubiquitous cultural image.

Until the 1980s, excess weight was the target of most ads for diet products; today, one is much more likely to find the enemy constructed as bulge, fat, or flab. "Now," a typical ad runs, "get rid of those embarrassing bumps, bulges, large stomach, flabby breasts and buttocks. Feel younger, and help prevent cellulite build-up . . . Have a nice shape with no tummy." To achieve such results (often envisioned as the absolute eradication of body, as in "no tummy") a violent assault on the enemy is usually required; bulges must be "attacked" and "destroyed," fat "burned," and stomachs (or, more disgustedly, "guts") must be "busted" and "eliminated." The increasing popularity of liposuction, a far from totally safe technique developed specifically to suck out the unwanted bulges of people of normal weight (it is not recommended for the obese), suggests how far our disgust with bodily bulges has gone. The ideal here is of a body that is absolutely tight, contained, "bolted down," firm: in other words, a body that is protected against eruption from within, whose internal processes are under control. Areas that are soft, loose, or "wiggly" are unacceptable, even on extremely thin bodies. Cellulite management, like liposuction, has nothing to do with weight loss, and everything to do with the quest for firm bodily margins.

This perspective helps illuminate an important continuity of meaning in our culture between compulsive dieting and body-building, and it reveals why it has been so easy for contemporary images of female attractiveness to oscillate between a spare, "minimalist" look and a solid, muscular, athletic look. The coexistence of these seemingly disparate images does not indicate that a postmodern universe of empty, endlessly differentiating images now reigns. Rather, the two ideals, though superficially very different, are united in battle against a common enemy: the soft, the loose; unsolid, excess flesh. It is perfectly permissible in our culture (even for women) to have substantial weight and bulk – so long as it is tightly managed. Simply to be slim is not enough – the flesh must not "wiggle." Here we arrive at one source of insight into why it is that the image of ideal slenderness has grown thinner and thinner throughout the 1980s and early 1990s, and why women with extremely slender bodies often still see themselves as fat. Unless one takes to muscle-building, to achieve a flab-free, excess-free body one must trim very near the bone.

## Slenderness and the inner state of the self

The moral – and, as we shall see, economic – coding of the fat/slender body in terms of its capacity for self-containment and the control of impulse and desire represents the culmination of a developing historical change in the social symbolism of body weight and size. Until the late nineteenth century, the central discriminations marked were those of class, race, and gender; the body indicated social identity and "place." So, for example, the bulging stomachs of successful mid-nineteenth-century businessmen and politicians were a symbol of bourgeois success, an outward manifestation of their accumulated wealth.[11] By contrast, the gracefully slender body announced aristocratic status; disdainful of the bourgeois need to display wealth and power ostentatiously, it commanded social space invisibly rather than aggressively, seemingly above the commerce in appetite or the need to eat. Subsequently, this ideal began to be appropriated by the status-seeking middle class, as slender wives became the showpieces of their husbands' success.[12]

Corpulence went out of middle-class vogue at the end of the century (even William Howard Taft, who had weighed over three hundred pounds while in office, went on a reducing diet). Social power had come to be less dependent on the sheer accumulation of material wealth and more connected to the ability to control and manage the labor and resources of others. At the same time, excess body weight came to be seen as reflecting moral or personal inadequacy, or lack of will.[13] These associations are possible only in a culture of overabundance – that is, in a society in which those who control the production of "culture" have more than enough to eat. The moral requirement to diet depends on the material preconditions that make the *choice* to diet an option and the possibility of personal "excess" a reality. Although slenderness continues to retain some of its traditional class associations ("a woman can never be too rich or too thin"), the importance of this equation has eroded considerably since the 1970s. Increasingly, the size and shape of the body have come to operate as a market of personal, internal order (or disorder) – as a symbol for the emotional, moral, or spiritual state of the individual.

Consider one particularly clear example, that of changes in the meaning of the muscled body. Muscularity has had a variety of cultural meanings that have prevented the well-developed body from playing a major role in middle-class conceptions of attractiveness. Of course, muscles have chiefly symbolized and continue to symbolize masculine power as physical strength, frequently operating as a means of coding the "naturalness" of sexual difference. But at the same time, they have been associated with manual labor and proletarian status, and they have often been suffused with racial meaning as well (as in numerous film representations of sweating, glistening bodies belonging to black slaves and prizefighters). Under the racial and class biases of our culture, muscles thus have been associated with the insensitive, unintelligent, and animalistic (recall the well-developed Marlon Brando as the emotionally primitive, physically abusive Stanley Kowalski in *A Streetcar Named Desire*). Moreover, as the body itself is dominantly imagined within the West as belonging to the "nature" side of a nature/culture duality, the *more* body one has had, the more uncultured and uncivilized one has been expected to be.

Today, however, the well-muscled body has become a cultural icon; "working out" is a glamorized and sexualized yuppie activity. No longer signifying inferior status (except when developed to extremes, at which point the old association of muscles with brute, unconscious materiality surfaces once more), the firm, developed body has become a symbol of correct *attitude*; it means that one "cares" about oneself and how one appears to others, suggesting willpower, energy, control over infantile impulse, the ability to "shape your life." "You exercise, you diet," says Heather Locklear, promoting Bally Matrix Fitness Centre on television, "and you can do anything you want." Muscles express sexuality, but controlled, managed sexuality that is not about to erupt in unwanted and embarrassing display.[14]

To the degree that the question of class still operates in all this, it relates to the category of social mobility (or lack of it) rather than class *location*. So, for example, when associations of fat and lower-class status exist, they are usually mediated by moral qualities – fat being perceived as indicative of laziness, lack of discipline, unwillingness to conform, and absence of all those "managerial" abilities that, according to the dominant ideology, confer upward mobility. Correspondingly, in popular teen movies such as *Flashdance* and *Vision Quest*, the ability of the (working-class) heroine and hero to pare, prune, tighten, and master the body operates as a clear symbol of successful upward aspiration, of the penetrability of class boundaries to those who have "the right stuff." These movies (as one title makes explicit) are contemporary "quest myths"; like their prototype, *Rocky*, they follow the struggle of an individual to attain a personal grail, against all odds and through numerous trials. But unlike the film quests of a previous era (which sent Mr Smith to Washington and Mr Deeds to town to battle the respective social evils of corrupt government and big business), *Flashdance* and *Vision Quest* render the hero's and heroine's commitment, will and spiritual integrity through the metaphors of weight loss, exercise, and tolerance of and ability to conquer physical pain and exhaustion. (In *Vision Quest*, for example, the audience is encouraged to admire the young wrestler's perseverance when he ignores the fainting spells and nosebleeds caused by his rigorous training and dieting.)

Not surprisingly, young people with eating disorders often thematize their own experience in similar terms, as in the following excerpt from an interview with a young woman runner:

Well, I had the willpower, I could train for competition, and I could turn down food any time. I remember feeling like I was on a constant high. And the pain? Sure, there was pain. It was incredible. Between the hunger and the muscle pain from the constant workouts? I can't tell you how much I hurt.

You may think I was crazy to put myself through constant, intense pain. But you have to remember, I was fighting a battle. And when you get hurt in a battle, you're proud of it. Sure, you may scream inside, but if you're brave and really good, then you take it quietly, because you know it's the price you pay for winning. And I needed to win. I really felt that if I didn't win, I would die . . . all these enemy troops were coming at me, and I had to outsmart them. If I could discipline myself enough – if I could keep myself lean and strong – then I could win. The pain was just a natural thing I had to deal with.[15]

As in *Vision Quest*, the external context is training for an athletic event. But here, too, that goal becomes subordinated to an internal one. The real battle, ultimately, is with the self. At this point, the limitations of the brief history presented in the opening paragraph of this essay are revealed. In that paragraph, the contemporary preoccupation with diet is contrasted to historical projects of body management that were suffused with moral meaning. In this section, however, I have suggested that examination of even the most shallow representations (teen movies) discloses a moral ideology – one, in fact, seemingly close to the aristocratic Greek ideal described by Foucault in *The Use of Pleasure*. The central element of that ideal, as Foucault describes it, is "an agonistic relation with the self" – aimed, not at the extirpation of desire and hunger in the interests of "purity" (as in the Christian strain of dualism), but at a "virile" mastery of desire through constant "spiritual combat."[16]

For the Greeks, however, the "virile" mastery of desire took place in a culture that valorized moderation. The culture of contemporary body-management, struggling to manage desire in a system dedicated to the proliferation of desirable commodities, is very different. In cultural fantasies such as *Vision Quest* and *Flashdance*, self-mastery is presented as an attainable and stable state; but, as I argue in the next section of this essay, the reality of the contemporary agonism of the self is another matter entirely.

## Slenderness and the social body

Mary Douglas, looking on the body as a system of "natural symbols" that reproduce social categories and concerns, has argued that anxiety about the maintenance of rigid bodily boundaries (manifested, for example, in rituals and prohibitions concerning excreta, saliva, and the strict delineation of "inside" and "outside") is most evident and intense in societies whose external boundaries are under attack.[17] Let me hypothesize, similarly, that preoccupation with the "internal" management of the body (that is, management of its desires) is produced by instabilities in what could be called the macro-regulation of desire within the system of the social body.

In advanced consumer capitalism, as Robert Crawford has elegantly argued, an unstable, agonistic construction of personality is produced by the contradictory structure of economic life.[18] On the one hand, as producers of goods and services we must sublimate, delay, repress desires for immediate gratification; we must cultivate the work ethic. On the other hand, as consumers we must display a boundless capacity to capitulate to desire and indulge in impulse; we must hunger for constant and immediate satisfaction. The regulation of desire thus becomes an ongoing problem, as we find ourselves continually besieged by temptation, while socially condemned for overindulgence. (Of course, those who cannot afford to indulge their desires as consumers, teased and frustrated by the culture, face a much harsher dilemma.)

Food and diet are central arenas for the expression of these contradictions. On television and in popular magazines, with a flip of the page or barely a pause between commercials, images of luscious foods and the rhetoric of craving and desire are replaced by advertisements for grapefruit diets, low-calorie recipes, and exercise equipment. Even more disquieting than these manifest oppositions, however, are the constant attempts by advertisers to mystify them, suggesting that the contradiction doesn't really exist, that one can "have it all." Diets and exercise programs are accordingly presented with the imagery of instant gratification ("From fat to fabulous in 21 days," "Size 22 to size 10 in no time flat," "Six minutes to an Olympic-class stomach") and effortlessness ("3,000 sit-ups without moving an inch . . . 10 miles of jogging lying flat on your back," "85 pounds without dieting," and even, shamelessly, "Exercise without exercise"). In reality, however, the opposition is not so easily reconciled. Rather, it presents a classic double bind, in which the self is torn in two mutually incompatible directions. The contradiction is not an abstract one but stems from the specific historical construction of a "consuming passion" from which all inclinations toward balance, moderation, rationality, and foresight have been excluded.

Conditioned to lose control at the mere sight of desirable products, we can master our desires only by creating rigid defenses against them. The slender body codes the tantalizing ideal of a well-managed self in which all is kept in order despite the contradictions of consumer culture. Thus, whether or not the struggle is played out in terms of food and diet, many of us may find our lives vacillating between a daytime rigidly ruled by the "performance principle" and nights and weekends that capitulate to unconscious "letting go" (food, shopping, liquor, television, and other addictive drugs). In this way, the central contradiction of the system inscribes itself on our bodies, and bulimia emerges as a characteristic modern personality construction. For bulimia precisely and explicitly expresses the extreme development of the hunger for unrestrained consumption (exhibited in the bulimic's uncontrollable food binges) existing in unstable tension alongside the requirement that we sober up, "clean up our act," get back in firm control on Monday morning (the necessity for purge – exhibited in the bulimic's vomiting, compulsive exercising, and laxative purges).

The same structural contradiction is inscribed in what has been termed (incorrectly) the "paradox" that we have an "epidemic" of anorexia nervosa in this country "despite the fact that we have an overweight majority."[19] Far from paradoxical, the coexistence of anorexia and obesity reveals the instability of the contemporary personality construction, the difficulty of finding homeostasis between the producer and the consumer sides of the self. Bulimia embodies the unstable double bind of consumer capitalism, while anorexia and obesity embody an attempted resolution of that double bind. Anorexia could thus be seen as an extreme development of the capacity for self-denial and repression of desire (the work ethic in absolute control); obesity, as an extreme capacity to capitulate to desire (consumerism in control). Both are rooted in the same consumer-culture construction of desire as overwhelming and over-taking the self. Given that construction, we can only respond either with total submission or rigid defense.

Neither anorexia nor obesity is accepted by the culture as an appropriate response. The absolute conquest of hunger and desire (even in symbolic form) can never be tolerated by a consumer system – even if the Christian dualism of our culture also predisposes us to be dazzled by the anorectic's ability seemingly to transcend the flesh. Anorectics are proud of this ability, but, as the disorder progresses, they usually feel the need to hide their skeletal bodies from those around them. If cultural attitudes toward the anorectic are ambivalent, however, reactions to the obese are not. As Marcia Millman documents in *Such a Pretty Face*, the obese elicit blinding rage and disgust in our culture and are often viewed in terms that suggest an infant sucking hungrily, unconsciously at its mother's breast: greedy, self-absorbed, lazy, without self-control or willpower.[20] People avoid sitting next to the obese (even when the space they take up is not intrusive); comics feel no need to restrain their cruelty; socially, they are considered unacceptable at public functions (one man wrote to "Dear Abby," saying that he was planning to replace his brother and sister-in-law as honor attendants at his wedding, because "they are both quite overweight"). Significantly, the part of the obese anatomy most often targeted for vicious attack, and most despised by the obese themselves, is the stomach, symbol of consumption (in the case of the obese, unrestrained consumption taking over the organism; one of Marcia Millman's interviewees recalls how the husband of a friend called hers "an awful, cancerous-looking growth").[21]

## Slenderness, self-management, and normalization

Self-management in consumer culture, I have been arguing, becomes more elusive as it becomes more pressing. The attainment of an acceptable body is extremely difficult for those who do not come by it "naturally" (whether aided by genetics, metabolism, or high activity-level) and as the ideal becomes firmer and tauter it begins to exclude more and more people. Constant watchfulness over appetite and strenuous work on the body itself are required to conform to this ideal, while the most popular means of "correction" – dieting – often insures its own failure, as the experience of deprivation leads to compensatory binging, with its attendant feelings of defeat, worthlessness, and loss of hope. Between the media images of self-containment and self-mastery and the reality of constant, everyday stress and anxiety about one's appearance lies the chasm that produces bodies habituated to self-monitoring and self-normalization.

Ultimately, the body (besides being evaluated for its success or failure at getting itself in order) is seen as demonstrating correct or incorrect attitudes toward the demands of normalization itself. The obese and anorectic are therefore disturbing partly because they embody resistance to cultural norms. Bulimics, by contrast, typically strive for the conventionally attractive body shape dictated by their more "normative" pattern of managing desire. In the case of the obese, in particular, what is perceived as their defiant rebellion against normalization appears to be a source of the hostility they inspire. The anorectic at least pays homage to dominant cultural values, outdoing them in their own terms:

> I wanted people to look at me and see something special. I wanted to look in the face of a stranger and see admiration, so that I would know that I accomplished something that was just about impossible for most people, especially in our society . . . From what I've seen, more people fail at losing weight than at any other single goal. I found out how to

do what everyone else couldn't: I could lose as much or as little weight as I wanted.
And that meant I was better than everyone else.[22]

The anorectic thus strives to stand above the crowd by excelling at its own rules; in so doing, however, she exposes the hidden penalties. But the obese – particularly those who claim to be happy although overweight – are perceived as not playing by the rules at all. If the rest of us are struggling to be acceptable and "normal," we cannot allow them to get away with it; they must be put in their place, be humiliated and defeated.

A number of talk shows have made this abundantly clear. On one, much of the audience reaction was given over to disbelief and to the attempt to prove to one obese woman that she was *not* happy: "I can't believe you don't want to be slim and beautiful, I just can't believe it." "I heard you talk a lot about how you feel good about yourself and you like yourself, but I really think you're kidding yourself." "It's hard for me to believe that Mary Jane is really happy...you don't fit into chairs, it's hard to get through the doorway. My God, on the subway, forget it." When Mary Jane persisted in her assertion that she was happy, she was warned, in a viciously self-righteous tone, that it would not last: "Mary Jane, to be the way you are today, you had better start going on a diet soon, because if you don't you're going to get bigger and bigger and bigger. It's true."[23] On another show, in an effort to subdue an increasingly hostile and offensive audience one of the doctor-guests kept trying to reassure them that the "fat and happy" target of their attacks did not *really* mean that she didn't *want* to lose weight; rather, she was simply tired of trying and failing. This construction allows people to give their sympathy to the obese, assuming as it does the obese person's acknowledgment that to be "normal" is the most desired goal, elusive only because of personal inadequacy. Those who are willing to present themselves as pitiable, in pain, and conscious of their own unattractiveness – often demonstrated, on these shows, by self-admissions about intimate physical difficulties, orgies of self-hate, or descriptions of gross consumption of food, win the sympathy and concern of the audience.

## Slenderness and gender

It has been amply documented that women in our culture are more tyrannized by the contemporary slenderness ideal than men are, as they typically have been by beauty ideals in general. It is far more important to men than to women that their partner be slim.[24] Women are much more prone than men to perceive themselves as too fat.[25] And, as is by now well known, girls and women are more likely to engage in crash dieting, laxative abuse, and compulsive exercising and are far more vulnerable to eating disorders than males. But eating disorders are not only "about" slenderness, any more than (as I have been arguing) slenderness is only – or even chiefly – about being physically thin. My aim in this section, therefore, is not to "explain" facts about which so much has now been written from historical, psychological, and sociological points of view. Rather, I want to remain with the image of the slender body, confronting it now both as a gendered body (the slender body as female body – the usual form in which the image is displayed) and as a body whose gender meaning is never neutral. This layer of gender-coded signification, suffusing other meanings, overdetermines slenderness as a contemporary ideal of specifically *female* attractiveness.

The exploration of contemporary slenderness as a metaphor for the correct management of desire must take into account the fact that throughout dominant Western religious and philosophical traditions, the capacity for self-management is decisively coded as male. By contrast, all those bodily spontaneities – hunger, sexuality, the emotions – seen as needful of containment and control have been culturally constructed and coded as female.[26] The management of specifically female desire, therefore, is in phallocentric cultures a doubly freighted problem. Women's desires are by their very nature excessive, irrational, threatening to erupt and challenge the patriarchal order.

Some writers have argued that female hunger (as a code for female desire) is especially problematized during periods of disruption and change in established gender-relations and in the position of women. In such periods (of which our own is arguably one), nightmare images of what Bram Dijkstra has called "the consuming woman" theme proliferate in art and literature (images representing female desire unleashed), while dominant constructions of the female body become more sylphlike – unlike the body of a fully developed woman, more like that of an adolescent or boy (images that might be called female desire unborn). Dijkstra argues such a case concerning the late nineteenth century, pointing to the devouring sphinxes and bloodsucking vampires of *fin-de-siècle* art, and the accompanying vogue for elongated, "sublimely emaciated" female bodies.[27] A commentator of the time vividly describes the emergence of a new body-style, not very unlike our own:

> Women can change the cut of their clothes at will, but how can they change the cut of their anatomies? And yet, they have done just this thing. Their shoulders have become narrow and slightly sloping, their throats more slender, their hips smaller and their arms and legs elongated to an extent that suggest that bed, upon which the robber, Procrustes, used to stretch his victims.[28]

The fact that our own era has witnessed a comparable shift (from the hourglass figure of the fifties to the androgynous, increasingly elongated, slender look that has developed over the past decade) cries out for interpretation. This shift, however, needs to be interpreted not only from the standpoint of male anxiety over women's desires (Dijkstra's analysis, while crucial, is only half the story) but also from the standpoint of the women who embrace the "new look." For them it may have a very different meaning; it may symbolize, not so much the containment of female desire, as its liberation from a domestic, reproductive destiny. The fact that the slender female body can carry both these seemingly contradictory meanings is one reason, I would suggest, for its compelling attraction in periods of gender change.[29]

To elaborate this argument in more detail: earlier, I presented some quotations from interviews with eating-disordered women in which they describe their revulsion to breasts, stomachs, and all other bodily bulges. At that point I subjected these quotations to a gender-neutral reading. While not rescinding that interpretation, I want to overlay it now with another reading, which I present in "Anorexia nervosa: psychopathology as the crystallization of culture." There, I suggest that the characteristic anorexic revulsion toward hips, stomach, and breasts (often accompanied by disgust at menstruation and relief at amenorrhoea) might be viewed as expressing rebellion against maternal, domestic femininity – a femininity that represents both the suffocating control the anorectic experiences her own mother as having had over her, *and* the mother's actual lack of position and authority outside the domestic arena. (A Nike ad embodies both these elements, as the "strength" of the mother is depicted in the containing arm that encircles her small daughter, while young women reading the ad are reassured that they can exercise *their* strength in other, non-maternal ways.) Here we encounter another reason for anxiety over soft, protuberant body-parts. They evoke helpless infancy and symbolize maternal femininity as it has been constructed over the past hundred years in the West. That femininity, as Dorothy Dinnerstein has argued, is perceived as both frighteningly powerful and, as the child comes increasingly to recognize the hierarchical nature of the sexual division of labor, utterly powerless.[30]

The most literal symbolic form of maternal femininity is represented by the nineteenth-century hourglass figure, emphasizing breasts and hips – the markers of reproductive femaleness – against a fragile wasp waist.[31] It is not until the post-World War II period, with its relocation of middle-class women from factory to home and its coercive bourgeois dualism of the happy homemaker-mother and the responsible, provider-father, that such clear bodily demarcation of "male" and "female" spheres surfaces again. The era of the cinch belt, the pushup bra, and Marilyn Monroe could be viewed, for the body, as an era of "resurgent Victorianism."[32] It was also the last coercively normalizing body-ideal to reign before boyish slenderness began its ascendancy in the mid-1960s.

From this perspective, one might speculate that the boys who reacted with disgust or anxiety to fleshy female parts were reacting to evocations of maternal power, newly threatening in an age when women are making their way into arenas traditionally reserved for men: law, business, higher education, politics, and so forth.[33] The buxom Sophia Loren was a sex goddess in an era when women were encouraged to define their deepest desires in terms of service to home, husband, and family. Today, it is required of female desire, loose in the male world, to be normalized according to the professional (and male) standards of that world; female bodies, accordingly, must be stripped of all psychic resonances with maternal power. From the standpoint of male anxiety, the lean body of the career businesswoman today may symbolize such a neutralization. With her body and her dress she declares symbolic allegiance to the professional, white, male world along with her lack of intention to subvert that arena with alternative "female values." At the same time, insofar as she is clearly "dressing up," *playing* male (almost always with a "softening" fashion touch to establish traditional feminine decorativeness, and continually cautioned against the dire consequences of allotting success higher priority than her looks), she represents no serious competition (symbolically, that is) to the real men of the workplace.

For many women, however, disidentification with the maternal body, far from symbolizing reduced power, may symbolize (as it did in the 1890s and 1920s) freedom from a reproductive destiny and a construction of femininity seen as constraining and suffocating. Correspondingly, taking on the accoutrements of the white, male world may be experienced as empowerment by women themselves, and as their chance to embody qualities – detachment, self-containment, self-mastery, control – that are highly valued in our culture. The slender body, as I have argued earlier, symbolizes such qualities. "It was about power," says Kim Morgan, speaking in the documentary *The Waist Land* of the obsession with slenderness that led to her anorexia, "that was the big thing...something I could throw in people's faces, and they would look at me and I'd only weigh this much, but I was strong and in control, and hey *you're* sloppy."[34] The taking on of "male" power as self-mastery is another locus where, for all their surface dissimilarities, the shedding of weight and the development of muscles intersect. Appropriately, the new "Joy of cooking" takes place in the gym, in one advertisement that shamelessly exploits the associations of female body-building with liberation from a traditional, domestic destiny.

In the intersection of these gender issues and more general cultural dilemmas concerning the management of desire, we see how the tightly managed body – whether demonstrated through sleek, minimalist lines or firmly developed muscles – has been overdetermined as a contemporary ideal of specifically female attractiveness. The axis of consumption/production is gender-overlaid, as I have argued, by the hierarchical dualism that constructs a dangerous, appetitive, bodily "female principle" in opposition to a masterful "male" will. We would thus expect that when the regulation of desire becomes especially problematic (as it is in advanced consumer cultures), women and their bodies will pay the greatest symbolic and material toll. When such a situation is compounded by anxiety about *women's* desires in periods when traditional forms of gender organization are being challenged, this toll is multiplied. It would be wrong to suppose, however, that it is exacted through the simple *repression* of female hunger. Rather, here as elsewhere, power works also "from below," as women associate slenderness with self-management, by way of the experience of newfound freedom (from a domestic destiny) and empowerment in the public arena. In this connection we might note the difference between contemporary ideals of slenderness, coded in terms of self-mastery and expressed through traditionally "male" body symbolism, and mid-Victorian ideals of female slenderness, which symbolically emphasized reproductive femininity corseted under tight "external" constraints. But whether externally bound or internally managed, no body can escape either the imprint of culture or its gendered meanings.

## Notes

This piece originally appeared in Mary Jacobus, Evelyn Fox Keller, and Sally Shuttleworth, eds., *Body/Politics: Women and the Discourses of Science* (New York: Routledge, 1989). I wish to thank Mary Jacobus, Sally Shuttleworth, and Mario Moussa for comments and editorial suggestions on the original version.

1  See Keith Walden, "The road to Fat City: an interpretation of the development of weight consciousness in Western society," *Historical Reflections* 12, no. 3 (1985): 331–73.

2  See Michel Foucault, *The Use of Pleasure* (New York: Random House, 1986).

3  See Rudolph Bell, *Holy Anorexia* (Chicago: University of Chicago Press, 1985); and Caroline Walker Bynum, *Holy Feast and Holy Fast: The Religious Significance of Food to Medieval Women* (Berkeley: University of California Press, 1987), pp. 31–48.

4  See Kim Chernin, *The Obsession: Reflections on the Tyranny of Slenderness* (New York: Harper and Row, 1981).

5  See Thomas Cash, Barbara Winstead, and Louis Janda, "The great American shape-up," *Psychology Today* (April 1986); and "Dieting: the losing game," *Time* (Jan. 20, 1986), among numerous other general reports. Concerning women's preoccupation in particular, see note 24 below.

6  See Mary Douglas, *Natural Symbols* (New York: Pantheon, 1982); and her *Purity and Danger* (London: Routledge and Kegan Paul, 1966).

7  This approach presupposes, of course, that popular cultural images *have* meaning and are not merely arbitrary formations spawned by the whimsy of fashion, the vicissitudes of Madison Avenue, or the logic of post-industrial capitalism, within which (as has been argued, by Fredric Jameson and others) the attraction of a product or image derives solely from pure differentiation, from its cultural positioning, its suggestion of the novel or new. Within such a postmodern logic, Gail Faurschou argues, "Fashion has become the commodity 'par excellence.' It is fed by all of capitalism's incessant, frantic, reproductive passion and power. Fashion *is* the logic of planned obsolescence – not just the necessity for market survival, but

the cycle of desire itself, the endless process through which the body is decoded and recoded, in order to define and inhabit the newest territorialized spaces of capital's expansion." ("Fashion and the cultural logic of postmodernity," *Canadian Journal of Political and Social Theory* 11, no. 1–2 [1987]: 72.) While I don't disagree with Faurschou's general characterization of fashion here, the heralding of an absolute historical break, after which images have become completely empty of history, substance, and symbolic determination, seems itself an embodiment, rather than a demystifier, of the compulsively innovative logic of postmodernity. More important to the argument of this piece, a postmodern logic cannot explain the cultural hold of the slenderness ideal, long after its novelty has worn off. Many times, in fact, the principle of the new has made tentative, but ultimately nominal, gestures toward the end of the reign of thinness, announcing a "softer," "curvier" look, and so forth. How many women have picked up magazines whose covers declared such a turn, only to find that the images within remained essentially continuous with prevailing norms? Large breasts may be making a comeback, but they are attached to extremely thin, often athletic bodies. Here, I would suggest, there are constraints on the pure logic of postmodernity – constraints that this essay tries to explore.

8   See Robert Crawford, "A cultural account of 'health': self-control, release, and the social body," in John McKinlay (ed.), *Issues in the Political Economy of Health Care* (New York: Methuen, 1985), pp. 60–103.

9   Ira Sacker and Marc Zimmer, *Dying to Be Thin* (New York: Warner, 1987), p. 57.

10  Dalma Heyn, "Body vision?" *Mademoiselle* (April 1987): 213.

11  See Lois Banner, *American Beauty* (Chicago: University of Chicago Press, 1983), p. 232.

12  Banner, *American Beauty*, pp. 53–5.

13  See Walden, "Road to Fat City," pp. 334–5, 353.

14  I thank Mario Moussa for this point, and for the Heather Locklear quotation.

15  Sacker and Zimmer, *Dying to Be Thin*, pp. 149–50.

16  Foucault, *The Use of Pleasure*, pp. 64–70.

17  See Douglas, *Purity and Danger*, pp. 114–28.

18  See Crawford, "A cultural account of 'health.'"

19  John Farquhar, Stanford University Medical Center, quoted in "Dieting: the losing game," *Time* (February 20, 1986): 57.

20  See Marcia Millman, *Such a Pretty Face: Being Fat in America* (New York: Norton, 1980), esp. pp. 65–79.

21  Millman, *Such a Pretty Face*, p. 77.

22  Sacker and Zimmer, *Dying to Be Thin*, p. 32.

23  These quotations are taken from transcripts of the *Donahue* show, provided by Multimedia Entertainment, Cincinnati, Ohio.

24  The discrepancy emerges very early. "We don't expect boys to be that handsome," says a nine-year-old girl in the California study cited above. "But boys expect girls to be perfect and beautiful. And skinny." A male classmate agrees: "Fat girls aren't like regular girls," he says. Many of my female students have described in their journals the pressure their boyfriends put on them to stay or get slim. These men have plenty of social support for such demands. Sylvester Stallone told Cornelia Guest that he liked his woman "anorexic"; she immediately lost twenty-four pounds (*Time* [April 18, 1988]: 89). But few men want their women to go that far. Actress Valerie Bertinelli reports (*Syracuse Post-Standard*) how her husband, Eddie Van Halen, "helps keep her in shape": "When I get too heavy, he says, 'Honey, lose weight.' Then when I get too thin, he says, 'I don't like making love with you, you've got to gain some weight.'"

25  The most famous of such studies, by now replicated many times, appeared in *Glamour* (Febuary 1984): a poll of 33,000 women revealed that 75 percent considered themselves "too fat," while only 25 percent of them were above Metropolitan Life Insurance standards, and 30 percent were *below* ("Feeling fat in a thin society," p. 198). See also Kevin Thompson, "Larger than life," *Psychology Today* (April 1986); Dalma Heyn, "Why we're never satisfied with our bodies," *McCall's* (May 1982); Daniel Goleman, "Dislike of own body found common among women," *New York Times*, March 19, 1985.

26  On cultural associations of male with mind and female with matter, see, for instance, Dorothy Dinnerstein, *The Mermaid and the Minotaur: Sexual Arrangements and Human Malaise* (New

York: Harper and Row, 1976); Genevieve Lloyd, *The Man of Reason* (Minneapolis: University of Minnesota Press, 1984); and Luce Irigaray, *Speculum of the Other Woman* (Ithaca: Cornell University Press, 1985).

27  Bram Dijkstra, *Idols of Perversity* (New York: Oxford University Press, 1986), p. 29.

28  "Mutable beauty," *Saturday Night* (February 1, 1892): 9.

29  Mary Jacobus and Sally Shuttleworth (personal communication), pointing to the sometimes boyish figure of the "new woman" of late Victorian literature, have suggested to me the appropriateness of this interpretation for the late Victorian era; I have, however, chosen to argue the point only with respect to the current context.

30  Dinnerstein, *The Mermaid and the Minotaur*, pp. 28–34. See Chernin, *The Obsession*, for an exploration of the connection between early infant experience and attitudes toward the fleshy female body.

31  Historian LeeAnn Whites has pointed out to me how perverse this body symbolism seems when we remember what a pregnant and nursing body is actually like. The hourglass figure is really more correctly a symbolic advertisement to men of the woman's reproductive, domestic *sphere* than a representation of her reproductive *body*.

32  See Banner, *American Beauty*, pp. 283–5.

33  It is no accident, I believe, that Dolly Parton, now down to one hundred pounds and truly looking as though she might snap in two in a strong wind, opened her new show with a statement of its implicitly anti-feminist premise: "I'll bust my butt to please you!" (Surely she already has?) Her television presence is now recessive, beseeching, desiring only to serve; clearly, her packagers are exploiting the cultural resonances of her diminished physicality. Parton, of course, is no androgynous body-type. Rather, like Vanna White of *Wheel of Fortune* (who also lost a great deal of weight at one point in her career and is obsessive about staying thin), she has tremendous appeal to those longing for a more traditional femininity in an era when women's public presence and power have greatly increased. Parton's and White's large breasts evoke a nurturing, maternal sexuality. But after weight-reduction regimens set to anorexic standards, those breasts now adorn bodies that are vulnerably thin, with fragile, spindly arms and legs like those of young colts. Parton and White suggest the pleasures of nurturant female sexuality without any encounter with its powers and dangers.

34  *The Waist Land: Eating Disorders in America*, 1985, Gannett Corporation, MTI Teleprograms. The analysis presented here becomes more complicated with bulimia, in which the hungering "female" self refuses to be annihilated, and feminine ideals are typically not rejected but embraced.

# 14
# Regimented Bodies

## Male Bodies and the "White Terror"*
### Klaus Theweleit

### Sexuality and the drill

#### The body reconstructed in the military academy

By what means is a young boy made a soldier? How does he become what
Canetti terms a "stereometric figure"?[1] How does body armor attain its final
form, what are its functions, how does the "whole" man who wears it function –
and above all – what is the nature of his ego, what is its site (which I believe must be
identifiable)? And finally, what is the nature of the soldier's sexuality? What
processes in the act of killing give him the pleasure he can apparently no longer
find elsewhere?

As a rule, it was in the military academy – *the* German officer school – that the
German officer acquired his finished form. One account of the changes undergone
by the soldier body is given by Salomon.[2] The following precise reconstruction of
his description should serve to highlight some of the differences between the
language these men use in confrontation with what is alien (a language of reality
destruction) and the language in which they describe their own bodily exterior – or,
more specifically, the workings of their own musculature. Salomon at times waxes
positively lyrical; apparently his musculature is not the site of his anxieties.

He describes the military academy as an "institution" (*Anstalt*), a place where the
cadet lives behind prison bars. He has no right of exit from the prison; it is granted
only in reward for strict adherence to its governing laws.

Relationships between the inmates are, without exception, hierarchical. When the
cadet enters the academy, his position in the hierarchy is initially determined by his
age; he has to earn any subsequent position. All the cadets have a place within a
direct order of rank. Each knows exactly which cadets are "above" him and which
"below." Each has the power to command and punish those below and the duty to
obey those above. The occupant of the lowest position in the hierarchy must find
another whom even he can dominate or he is finished.

If a cadet fails to exercise his rights over his inferiors, he is despised or demoted.
Thus the situation never arises. Privilege is universally exercised. There are no gaps
in the cadet's daily round of duties. Only those who have sufficiently mastered the
art of demand fulfillment can squeeze a few seconds for other activities.

* Klaus Theweleit, "Male bodies and the 'White Terror'," *Male Fantasies* (Minneapolis, Minnesota: Minneapolis Press, 1989), vol. II, pp. 143–76.

Everything is planned and everything is public. Withdrawal is impossible, since there is no place to retreat to. Toilet doors leave the head and feet of the seated occupant exposed. Trousers have no pockets.

When the cadet receives a letter, he has to open it and present the signature for inspection. Letters signed by women are read by the officer distributing the mail and (usually) torn up. Only letters from mothers are handed on.

None of the cadets lives in private. The dormitories have open doors. Talking from bed to bed is forbidden. The dormitory is kept under surveillance through a window in a wooden partition, behind which an officer sits and keeps watch.[3]

The beds are narrow, hard, and damp. Any boy found hiding his head under the pillows is labeled a "sissy" (*Schlappschwanz*). "Sissies" are put on "report." There are reports for every infringement; but the only way a boy can carry out the extra duties they impose is by neglecting his existing duties. If his negligence is noticed, he is put on report again. One crime punishable by report is a failure to keep equipment in order – which is unavoidable, since the regulations are too numerous to follow them all to the letter. Therefore after the first report, others are bound to follow.

Boys who want to go to the toilet at night have to wake the duty officer. In this case too, punishment invariably follows. Unusual behavior of any kind is punished by forfeit; the boy is deprived of food, leave, or the opportunities for relaxation that are in any case minimal, no more than momentary easings of pressure.

In cadets who wish to remain such, all this very soon produces a "quite extra-ordinarily thick skin."[4] The "thick skin" should not be understood metaphorically.

On his second day in the academy, Salomon had already sensed "that here, for the first time in his life, he was not subject to arbitrary conditions, but to a single law."[5] He experiences this as good fortune. He resolves to bear every punishment meted out to him, gives himself the necessary "internal wrench," and stands stiffly erect. Everything up to now has been "arbitrary" – and school continues to be so. School is an activity performed by teachers, powerless wielders of power – ridiculous. The boy enters the institution at the age of twelve. It is at the beginning of puberty and under the "pressure" of its "water" (Freud),[6] that he experiences the good fortune of subjection to a law. Freud saw puberty as a phase of transition to fully formed sexual organization, the completion of which manifests itself in the capacity for heterosexual object-choice.[7] But the military academy transforms this "unusually intense wave of the libido"[8] into something other than "object-relationships."

The cadet never receives instructions; he recognizes his mistakes only in the moment of transgression from the reactions of others who already know the score. With slight variations according to his cleverness, each newcomer thus necessarily repeats the mistakes of his predecessors, who in turn recognize and welcome the apparent opportunity to treat their successors as they themselves have previously been treated. Justice works on the principle of equal torment for all. The principle is strictly adhered to; there are no grounds on which a mistake might be considered excusable.

The punishments meted out to fellow cadets are oriented exclusively to the body. For a minor transgression on his very first day, Salomon is made to balance a tray of knick-knacks on his outstretched hands (and woe betide him should any of them fall). He is then made to crouch with an open pair of compasses wedged between his heels and buttocks. If he moves even infinitesimally upward or downward, the compasses will either stab him in the buttocks or drop on the floor. But if he succeeds in staying still, the reward, as always, will be immediate advancement. He will no longer be the lowest in the hierarchy of "sacks" (*Säcke*) – "sack" being the name for all newcomers who are treated accordingly, emptied out, punched into shape, and refilled.

Younger boys courageous enough to defend themselves gain respect. But even if they win the occasional fist-fight with older boys, punishment always remains the prerogative of their elders.

A further first day experience reported by Salomon: he recalls a talk by an officer on the importance of learning how to die.

Night, cold bed, cold blankets, the morning wash in cold water. The boy who hesitates, even momentarily, is immersed and showered by others. Breakfast by hierarchy. The boy who grabs a roll before his turn gets nothing. For the last in the pecking order, there remains the smallest portion, a crumb. To be last is impermissible.

Physical exercise, even before breakfast:

> If I failed to pull myself up far enough for my nose to pass the bar, or to keep my knees straight while pulling my legs upward, the dormitory leader would give generous assistance by punching the tensed muscles of my upper arm with his clenched fist. This did indeed make it possible to identify the ultimate limits of my strength.[9]

Every exercise reaches the "ultimate limits," the point where pain shifts to pleasure:

> The climbing apparatus was ten meters high; it had a ladder, various perches, and smooth wooden walls. We climbed up and jumped down, hesitating for one tense moment at the top, leaping blind, tasting the full weight of the drop, slamming into the ground with a force that sent a terrible shock reverberating from the heels through the lower back, then into the rest of the body.[10]

If the cadet has any kind of choice, it is one between different punishments. He is offered the alternative of a caning on the behind, or forfeiting leave – he chooses the beating. The body swallows attack after attack until it becomes addicted. Every exertion becomes a "means of enhancing an already intoxicated consciousness, of adding strength to strength."

The boy who fails to transform rituals of bodily pain into "intoxicated conscious-ness"[11] (the mental intoxication of a head that crowns a powerful body) is cast out, as was the spy from the ritual speech or the unwilling participant from block parade-formations.

One passage in Salomon's book describes a certain cadet named Ulzig standing rigid with terror. He is the only nonswimmer to have failed to jump from a three-meter board. Many have already had to be pulled from the water to save them from drowning. But they continue to jump, half-blind, their limbs aching, until they can swim. Salomon learns to swim on the third day; but Ulzig leaves the institution – he is fetched away by his father, a "mountain of a father," a major. The cadets would have liked to give him a good beating, but were stopped by the officer in charge of swimming (a leper is not for beating).

> I had gradually adapted. The service no longer appeared to me as a machine racing along mysteriously, its actions unexpected and apparently unmotivated. Instead, the few figures with whom I had any kind of relationship were now clearly and concretely emerging from the confusion. I was as determined as ever to defend myself when

necessary, but my resolve was now less often broken by perplexity. Slowly, I began to lift my head higher.[12]

As Salomon himself becomes a component in the machine, he no longer perceives it as racing on its way somewhere above him. Once the machine is no longer external to him and he himself no longer its victim, it begins to protect him:

> In the end, I found myself living a life of absolute solitude. At times, I surrendered with a zeal born of desperation and unhappiness to this most painful of feelings. The only common feature in all my unrelated perceptions was...the exceptional and universal ruthlessness that underlay them. This was the only indication of any purpose behind the whole machinery of the Academy. It was the basis on which it was constructed and imbued with life. My merciless subjection to the bitter reality of absolute isolation had originally seemed incongruous in a place where no one even momentarily escaped observation or control. But even the warmest comradeship remained far removed from simple friendship and from the brotherly stream that flows from hand to hand and heart to heart.[13]

At this point in the book, Salomon has been only partially assimilated. While he considers "exceptional ruthlessness" an acceptable goal for the workings of the machinery, he himself remains half outside it, a lonely young man in search of "the brotherly stream." He then gradually comes to realize that the stream can be found only on the outside as a stream of pain. At this point, he integrates himself entirely.

> It was, I believed, my own inadequacy that erected an iron barrier between myself and my comrades. I tried repeatedly to break it down; but even the most forceful expression of my lost yearning for human warmth and clumsy intimacy would have been useless. Even outside the academy, an air of sordidness surrounded such gestures; inside, they were still more likely to offend sensibilities. My pitiful efforts to struggle free of my cocoon rebounded against rubber walls; yet I continued to search for some escape. The futility of my efforts was made bitterly clear to me; yet at the same time, doors were opened as wide, at least, as they were able.[14]

The opportunity to escape from the "cocoon" is presented on one occasion by a different kind of emission: a fart. In a rare conversation with the cadets, an officer suddenly becomes human as he remarks, in a not unfriendly tone, "What a stench! Somebody open a window!" Salomon's desire for "human warmth" grasps at this welcome evidence of a human interior, a smell that has broken the "iron barrier"; he murmurs as in a trance: "He who smelt it, dealt it"[15] – the moment the words slip from him, he realizes they have made his isolation total...

The officer orders Salomon to come to his room and grills him until he reveals the name of the boy who taught him the saying. Having "ratted" on a fellow–cadet, Salomon is "put in the shithouse" (*in Verschiss getan*) – the expression denotes the breaking off of all communication. Having spoken of something that no longer forms, or is permitted to form, part of the cadet's existence, he himself is treated as nonexistent, foul as the foulest air. "Even my own brother was now inclined to give credence to my theory that I was a foundling. 'No brother of mine' he said, 'could do anything like this.' "[16]

In the end, the culprit is released from the shithouse; the effect of this particular form of punishment seems insufficiently external. The penalty takes a new form as an assault on his bodily periphery. Payment is made in the only valid currency, which is pain:

The cadets stood around me in a semicircle. Each one held a knout in his hand, long leather thongs attached to a wooden stick that was used for beating the dirt out of clothes. Glasmacher stepped forward, took me by the arm, and led me over to the table. I climbed up, not without difficulty, and lay down on my stomach. Glasmacher took my head in his hands, pressed my eyes shut, and forced my skull hard against the surface of the table. I gritted my teeth and tensed my whole body. The first blow whistled. I jerked upward, but Glasmacher held me tight; the blows rained down on my back, shoulders, legs, a frenzied fire of hard, smacking blows. My hands were tightly gripped around the edge of the table, I beat out a rhythm with my knees, shins, and toes in an attempt to expel the excruciating pain. Now all the torment seemed to move through my body and implant itself in the table; again and again my hips and loins slammed against the wood and made it shudder with me; every blow recharged the bundle of muscles and skin, blood and bones and sinews, with slingshot force, till my whole body stretched under tension and threatened to burst in its lower regions. I gave my head over entirely to Glasmacher's hands, wrenched myself shut, and finally lay still and moaning. "Stop!" Corporal First-Class Glöcklen commanded, and the assembled company jumped back instantly. I slid slowly from the table. Glasmacher stepped up to proffer his hand, and said, "Peace! The affair is closed."[17]

More than this, he has been accepted. He has experienced the sensations that indicate other men's affection; he now numbers among their beloved.

The only site at which feelings have legitimate existence is the body as a "bundle of muscles and skin, blood and bones and sinews." This is the message hammered out by the drill; each new exercise is structured around it, as is every punishment detail. No feeling or desire remains unclarified, all are transformed into clear perception: the desire for bodily warmth into a perception of the heart of bodily pain; the desire for contact into a perception of the whiplash.

And little by little the body accepts these painful interventions along its periphery as responses to its longing for pleasure. It receives them as experiences of satisfaction. The body is estranged from the pleasure principle, drilled and reorganized into a body ruled by the "pain principle": what is nice is what hurts . . .

And, finally, the "sack" is given his equatorial baptism[18] – a form of torture that appears in German navy tales, unsurprisingly, as one of the high points in the life of a sailor:

There was an official ceremony to mark the end of one's days as a sack. On the appointed day, to the great joy of their older comrades, the sacks were individually summoned to the company room, where a dentist from the city would be busy with his instruments. Every sack then had to sit on a small stool, while the tooth-flicker (Zahnfips), as the comrades called him, messed around for a while in the poor offender's wide-open mouth with a long pair of pliers; he would then take a firm grip on all his remaining baby teeth and pull them one after the other. As I stood bent over the bucket, spitting blood beneath the wicked smile of the tooth-flicker, Glasmacher consoled me by saying that it had formerly been customary to take the sacks to the dispensary and fill them with the appropriate dose of castor oil to ensure they were purged both internally and externally.[19]

As his last baby teeth swim away in a bucket of blood, so too do the residues of his anchorage in mother-ocean and a rock stretches its head from the collar of his uniform.

I began to notice my body stiffening, my posture gaining in confidence. When I thought back to childhood games at home, I was filled with bitter shame. It had become quite impossible to move with anything other than dignity. On the rare occasions when a senseless desire for freedom surfaced, it invariably shattered against a new determination and will. My new-found capacity to follow orders to the letter was double compensation for losing the joys of roving unrestrained.[20]

Then the first visit home:

A deep chasm divided me from the habits and customs of my so-called parental home, a chasm I felt neither the desire nor the compulsion to bridge. I found any kind of solicitous care quite intolerable, and the broad stream of my mother's empathy only made me wish to breathe the harsher air of the corps again.[21]

In becoming *capable* of following orders to the letter – he is by this point no longer forced to do so – Salomon liberates himself from the family unit. His function is now to operate within a different formation – although the "stream of his mother's empathy" is still able to reach him.

Does this stream have anything to do with the flow in the new machine of which Salomon has become a happily functioning component?

The machine's flow is continuous, a totality that maintains every component in appropriate and uninterrupted motion. It has no cut-off points, it never pauses: if the machinery of the military academy ever stops running, it is done for. To turn it off is impossible.

This machinery is the antithesis of the desiring-machine, whose principle – "the joys of roving unrestrained" – Salomon explicitly renounces. The "and now? ... so that was that" gives way to the pleasure of existing as a component within a whole machine, a macromachine, a power machine in which the component does not invest his own pleasure, but produces that of the powerful. The man pleasurably invests his self only as a thoroughly reliable part of the machine. His line from this point on: the machine must run, the faster the better; it breaks down, it won't be my fault ...

Remarkably enough: the component itself, in becoming a component, becomes whole – a whole that is simultaneously subordinate and dominant. It has precisely determined functions and very specific couplings to other parts; it no longer possesses its former functional multiplicity. There must have been some problem with multiplicity; its potential must have been threatening – for the component gladly accepts the wholeness it finds in the totality machine.

The machinery – and I think this is very important – transforms functions such as "thinking," "feeling," "seeing" (potential multiplicity functions with the power to develop myriad couplings) into movement, movements of the body. Salomon's new thinking follows a very specific tempo:

Here even the most improbable actions were redolent with significance. The simplest salute became a symbol of submission to an authority that bound both parties in mutually fruitful association. The slow march, tempo one hundred fourteen, became the physical and spiritual expression of discipline to the brink of death.[22]

## The troop as totality-machine

Canetti's description of the soldier as a "stereometric figure" restricts attention to the individual soldier, to his body armor and the supporting armor surrounding it: the barrack walls, the block formations of the troop, etc. Since he neglects to

consider the *function* of the soldier as machine component, he falls short of describing the construction of the machine *in toto*.[23]

> The colonel raised his hand to his helmet. The regiment began marking time, four
> thousand legs rising in unison and descending to stamp the ground; up and away, the
> first company pitched its legs high as if pulled by a single cord, then set them down on
> grass and soil, eighty centimeters between them, foot to foot – the flag approaches...
>
> A single sword hurled itself upward, flashed, and dropped deep to the ground; the
> earth turned to dust under hundreds of marching feet; the earth rumbled and groaned;
> two hundred fifty men were passing, touching close one after another, two hundred
> fifty rifles on their shoulders, a line sequence straight as an arrow above a line of
> helmets, shoulders, knapsacks straight as an arrow; two hundred fifty hands hissing
> back and forth; two hundred fifty legs tearing bodies onward in cruel, relentless
> rhythm.[24]

The impression of a machine being set in motion as the "finished" cadets march
off to war is created quite intentionally by Salomon, as is the sense that the machine
is both one of war and of sexuality ("bodies...in cruel, relentless rhythm").
Salomon's description of bodies as "tearing...onward," emphasizes the machine's
violent nature.

Two aspects of its construction are stressed: the uniformity of its contours ("as if
pulled by a single cord"; "a line sequence straight as an arrow") and the large
number of its functionally equivalent components ("four thousand legs rising in
unison"; "two hundred fifty hands hissing"; "two hundred fifty legs tearing").

The soldier's limbs are described as if severed from their bodies; they are fused
together to form new totalities. The leg of the individual has a closer functional
connection to the leg of his neighbor than to his own torso. In the machine, then,
new body-totalities are formed: bodies no longer identical with the bodies of
individual human beings.

> The brigade was a single body, destined to be bound in solidarity.[25]
>                     (H. Plaas, describing the Ehrhardt Naval Brigade.)

Each individual totality-component moves in precise unison with every other: "One
troop, one man and one rhythm" (Plaas).[26]

The principal goal of the machine seems to be to keep itself moving. It is entirely
closed to the external world. Only in combination with another machine absolutely
like itself can it join together to create some larger formation.

What then *produces* the machine?

> The second company, the third, the fourth. Endlessly, it rolled onward, a broad front
> advancing, never wavering, wall after wall, the whole regiment a machine with rows
> ranged deep, implacable, precise, four thousand human beings and one regiment,
> whipped by the hymn of martial music. Who could oppose it? Who would set himself
> against this power, youth, and discipline, this eager thousand formed in a single will?
> The forest border seemed to tremble and retreat; the earth shook and reared, clatter of
> weapons and crunch of leather, dark eyes under brims of helmets. The 109th Regi-
> mental Grenadiers: guards' piping, white wings, a four hundred year tradition. Formed
> and steeled through long years, sworn to the flag, practiced in the art of death, plucked
> from the loins of a people and sent into war. And so the regiment marched, tempo one
> hundred fourteen, twelve companies, warstrong, prepared for death, ninety rounds in
> the cartridge case of every man, hard biscuits and ammunition in his rucksack, coat

rolled and boots new. Muscles like ropes, broad-chested, tough-jointed, wall of bodies
born of discipline; this was the front, the frontier, the assault, the element of storm and
resistance; and behind it stood Germany, nourishing the army with men and bread and
ammunition.[27]

In the first instance, what the troop-machine produces is itself – itself as a totality
that places the individual soldier in a new set of relations to other bodies; itself as a
combination of innumerable identically polished components.

The troop also produces an expression: of determination, strength, precision; of
the strict order of straight lines and rectangles; an expression of battle, and of a
specific masculinity. Or to put it another way, the surplus value produced by the
troop is a code that consolidates other totality formations between men, such as the
"nation."

As Salomon's text also shows with striking clarity, the troop-machine produces
the front *before reaching it*: it *is* the front. As the troop sets itself in motion, the
border itself is displaced. Even in peacetime, front and border are part of the troop.
War is the condition of its being. It always has a border to defend, a front to advance
(its own). The only thing that changes if war is declared is that the same process
becomes easier and more satisfying. War offers an opportunity for discharge, for the
front to be released from internal pressure. In peacetime, the front presses inward
toward its own interior, compressing the individual components of the machine. It
produces internal tensions of high intensity that press for discharge.

The crucial impulse behind the regeneration of the machine seems to be its desire
for release – and release is achieved when the totality-machine and its components
explode in battle. A strange productive principle: the machine produces its own new
boundaries by transgressing the boundaries it erects around itself.

The troop machine is not independent; it has no autonomous existence. It is
connected to Germany by an umbilical cord that feeds it with bread, spare parts, and
munitions. Its energy-machine is "Germany."

As long as the energy circuit symbiosis with "Germany" continues to function,
the machine marching to war can be presented as the supreme totality, the universal
sum total. What Neruda says of the ocean ("And you lack nothing"), is realized for
Jünger in the battle-machine: lack is transcended.

> ... there are times when we feel light and free in our heavy armor, sensing, despite the
> weight, the impetus and the power which drive us forward.
>    We move most easily in battle-formation; for the power and will of the blood speaks
> most directly from the battle-machine. We are stirred as human beings are seldom
> stirred by (troops) marching by ... for they represent the will of a people to greatness
> and dominance, shaped in its most effective form, as steely hard implements. They
> contain all we have, all we think, all we are; modern man marching to battle is modern
> man in his most characteristic form ... He is a whole, not one part only.[28]

The same utopian impulse was recognized by Foucault as part of a whole
tradition of representations of the military machine.

> Historians of ideas usually attribute the dream of a perfect society to the philosophers
> and jurists of the eighteenth century; its fundamental reference was not to the state of
> nature, but to the meticulously subordinated cogs of a machine, not to the primal social
> contract, but to permanent coercions, not to fundamental rights, but to indefinitely
> progressive forms of training, not to the general will but to automatic docility.[29]

## *The totality-component: figure of steel*

Once in battle, the formation dissolves. The macromachine separates out into its components. Each component in the soldierly totality-body has been made functional by the drill; battle gives it the opportunity to prove that its own function conforms to the functioning principle of the machine itself. Each totality-components becomes a miniature of the machine.

> This was a whole new race, energy incarnate, charged with supreme energy. Supple bodies, lean and sinewy, striking features, stone eyes petrified in a thousand terrors beneath their helmets. These were conquerors, men of steel tuned to the most grisly battle. Sweeping across a splintered landscape, they heralded the final triumph of all imagined horror. Unimaginable energies were released as these brave troops broke out to regain lost outposts where pale figures gaped at them with madness in their eyes. Jugglers of death, masters of explosive and flame, glorious predators, they sprang easily through the trenches. In the moment of encounter, they encapsulated the spirit of battle as no other human beings could. Theirs was the keenest assembly of bodies, intelligence, will, and sensation.[30]

Jünger's imaginary man is portrayed as a physical type devoid of drives and of psyche; he has no need of either since all his instinctual energies have been smoothly and frictionlessly transformed into functions of his steel body. This passage seems to me to crystallize a tendency that is evident throughout Jünger's writing: a tendency toward the utopia of the body machine.

In the body-machine the interior of the man is dominated and transformed in the same way as are the components of the macromachine of the troop. For Jünger, then, the fascination of the machine apparently lies in its capacity to show how a man might "live" (move, kill, give expression) without emotion. Each and every feeling is tightly locked in steel armor.

The "new man"[31] sired in the drill (the drill as organized battle of the old men against himself) owes allegiance only to the machine that bore him. He is a true child of the drill-machine, created without the help of a woman, parentless. His associations and relationships bind him instead to other specimens of the new man, with whom he allows himself to be united to form the macromachine troop. All others belong only "under" him – never alongside, behind, or in front.

The most urgent task of the man of steel is to pursue, to dam in, and to subdue any force that threatens to transform him back into the horribly disorganized jumble of flesh, hair, skin, bones, intestines, and feelings that calls itself human – the human being of old:

> These are the figures of steel whose eagle eyes dart between whirling propellers to pierce the cloud; who dare the hellish crossing through fields of roaring craters, gripped in the chaos of tank engines; who squat for days on end behind blazing machine-guns, who crouched against banks ranged high with corpses, surrounded, half-parched, only one step ahead of certain death. These are the best of the modern battlefield, men relentlessly saturated with the spirit of battle, men whose urgent wanting discharges itself in a single concentrated and determined release of energy.
>
> As I watch them noiselessly slicing alleyways into barbed wire, digging steps to storm outward, synchronizing luminous watches, finding the North by the stars, the recognition flashes: this is the new man. The pioneers of storm, the elect of central Europe. A whole new race, intelligent, strong, men of will. Tomorrow, the

phenomenon now manifesting itself in battle will be the axis around which life whirls ever faster. A thousand sweeping deeds will arch across their great cities as they stride down asphalt streets, supple predators straining with energy. They will be architects building on the ruined foundations of the world.[32]

The new man is a man whose physique has been machinized, his psyche eliminated – or in part displaced into his body armor, his "predatory" suppleness. We are presented with a robot that can tell the time, find the North, stand his ground over a red-hot machine-gun, or cut wire without a sound. In the moment of action, he is as devoid of fear as of any other emotion. His knowledge of being able to do what he does is his only consciousness of self.

This, I believe, is the ideal man of the conservative utopia: a man with machine-like periphery, whose interior has lost its meaning (the technocrat is his contemporary manifestation).

This is not a utopia from the technologization of the means of production; it has nothing to do with the development of machine technology. That development is simply used to express a quality specific to the bodies of these men. The mechanized body as conservative utopia derives instead from men's compulsion to subjugate and repulse what is specifically human within them – the id, the productive force of the unconscious. The soldier male responds to the successful damming in and chaoticizing of his desiring-production from the the moment of his birth (if not earlier) by fantasizing himself as a figure of steel: a man of the new race.[33]

The armor of the soldier male may transform his incarcerated interior into the fuel that speeds him forward; or it may send it spinning outward. As something external to him, it can then be combatted; and it assails him constantly, as if it wished him back: it is a deluge, an invasion from Mars, the proletariat, contagious Jewish lust, sensuous woman.

The conservative utopia of the mechanized body, the body made machine in its totality, does not, then, derive from the development of the industrial means of production, but from the obstruction and transformation of human productive forces.

### Preliminary comments on the agency of the ego

If we now review the various functions, both of the totality armor of the "figure of steel" and of the periphery of the troop as totality, then what emerges as their most striking common feature is their function as external boundaries of the person as front: they are organs of reality-control, of control and defense against the drives. The functions of defense, both against threatening feelings and against thinking, seem to be performed by the body armor, the musculature of the individual totality component, or by the bodily form of the troop – the totality machine into which the component inserts itself.

Freud's second topographical schema of the psychic apparatus represents all these functions as fulfilled by the psychic agency of the "ego."[34] But by the end of the first chapter in volume 1, it had become clear that the soldier males were incapable of possessing an "ego" in the Freudian sense. The ego is formed through processes of identification during the phase of the dissolution of the Oedipus complex, a "stage" that these men never reach. The question thus posed in volume 1 was that of the origin of their "reality-competence"; why did these men not atrophy in "autistic" psychoses?

One possible response to that question now emerges. Since the "ego" of these men cannot form from the inside out, through libidinal cathexis of the body's periphery and identification, they must acquire an enveloping "ego" from the outside. My suspicion is that cathexis occurs as a result of coercion; it is forced upon them by the pain they experience in the onslaught of external agencies. The punishments of parents, teachers, masters, the punishment hierarchies of young boys and of the military, remind them constantly of the existence of their periphery (showing them their boundaries), until they "grow" a functioning and controlling body armor, and a body capable of seamless fusion into larger formations with armorlike peripheries. If my assumptions are correct, the armor of these men may be seen as constituting their ego.

A Freud distanced from the pleasure principle was able to write that

> the way in which we gain new knowledge of our organs during painful illnesses is perhaps a model of the way by which in general we arrive at the idea of our body.[35]

In a society that replaces the experience of pleasure in the body with its experience of pain this is irrefutably a statement of positivist truth. Drill and torture, it seems, are to be seen as the extremes of more general forms of bodily perception. (Now, in the process of being whipped, I know what my ass is capable of feeling and where exactly it's located. Now, as they kick me between the legs, I have my very first sense of my prick's enormous sensitivity . . .)

I feel pain, therefore I am. Where pain is, there "I" shall be – the psychic agency of the I as ego.

In a section entitled "The ego and the maintenance mechanisms" I shall be investigating the significance of this form of the "I" for the white terror and its agents more closely. First, however, I want to examine some of the further features of the drill and the battle situation.

### Blackouts

Ernst Röhm writes of his training for officer rank:

> From the very beginning, we ensigns were treated with the utmost severity. Many was the time we stumbled back to barracks thoroughly beaten down at the end of a day on duty. Once, we were all consigned to the dispensary, having fainted during exercises; we only gradually recovered.[36]

Fainting, or any related state, was no accident; it appears to have been a planned element within training. In *Sittengeschichte des Weltkrieges* (*Moral History of the World War*), edited by Hirschfeld, the situation is described as follows:

> The phenomena that have come to be known as "twilight states" (*Dämmerzustände*) can probably be interpreted as acute psychotic reactions to the miseries of the soldier's existence. They involve drowsiness, accompanied by spatial and temporal disorientation and loss of memory.[37]

In common soldiers, these states often culminated in angry tirades against men in uniform. This was not the case for ensigns and cadets, since they themselves hoped to become officers. What, then, happened to them during and after blackouts? Salomon as a cadet:

And I learned to stand to "Attention!" Legs shaking, palms sweating slightly – and still, "Stand to attention!" Stomach walls straining, shoulders aching, a red wave slowly appearing before me, swelling and circling ponderously, then disappearing again; tiny dreams approaching from a distance, growing, filling out, grasping at my heart, my eyes, then suffocating; fleeting thoughts sweeping softly onward, tangling together, rolling to a ball in a brain that was heavy, rolling, springing away in knots together. I learned to "Stand to attention!"[38]

Killinger gives his all in the presence of the Kaiser, in a boat race between the crews of various navy vessels. His team wins. Then (he calls himself "Peter" in the text)

there was a glass of champagne waiting in the cadet's mess, a treat from the officer in charge of naval cadets. Suddenly Peter's world turned black and started spinning, blood spurted from his nose; he remembered nothing from that moment. He awoke in the military hospital. The cadet officer and the staff physician were standing beside his cot. "Well, how do you feel now? You overtaxed yourself a little. But you'll get over it soon enough – with a constitution like yours."

"Damn and blast," thought Peter, "I've let the side down." The cadet officer guessed his thoughts. "Don't worry about it. If the others had pushed themselves hard enough to collapse as you did we might have won by three lengths."[39]

Strangely enough, Peter is expressly praised for his collapse. Why? He has pushed himself beyond his own limits – but his very capacity to do so can be taken as evidence of enormous physical strength. An undrilled body would be unlikely to be able to reach "saturation point," as his does.

But this is not all. The moment at which the man enters a state of apparent blackout, or loses consciousness entirely following excessive physical exertion, seems in some way comparable to the moment of tension-and-release in orgasm.

The crucial difference between orgasm and the soldier's blackout is the absence of any intrinsic limit to the kind of physical exertion in which the soldier (or indeed the sportsman) engages. Unless exercise is voluntarily contained, or interrupted, it inevitably stretches the man beyond his limits; unlike orgasm, it does not produce bodily equilibrium, but disrupts it. Even the "ease" that Salomon experiences after "standing to attention" is the antithesis of the ease following orgasm. Standing at ease demands absolute tensing of the muscles; again, the only available form of release is loss of consciousness.

The blackout does appear momentarily to unite two normally antagonistic elements within the soldier; his body armor, as "masculine" repressor, merges with the repressed – his incarcerated "feminine" interior. Full consciousness – all the man; perceptual functions – is flooded and submerged precisely because the flow cannot be allowed to escape further. There is a clearly discernible dynamic of flow and release, yet it remains internal: a red wave approaching and disappearing; "tiny dreams" that "suffocate" in the heart; and thoughts that "spring away in knots together." The flow transforms itself and seeps away internally. The process appears intensified in the case of Killinger, whose nose spurts blood as he loses consciousness – as if his whole body had become an ejaculating phallus.

In the cases cited above, the body armor does indeed appear to become the displaced site of orgiastic potency; in the moment of blackout, at the climax of tension, the body armor surrenders to the wave that is inundating consciousness. Orgasm is not so much experienced as suffered. And, in contrast again to orgasm between lovers, the blackout threshold is raised on each new occasion. The more highly drilled the body armor, the more it must strain to reach its limits. The drill produces a heightened capacity, not for release but for tension. It digs out a new demand for the stream of the libido. The stream no longer flows as ejaculation and release of bodily tension, but pours across the sensory perception of the man and extinguishes it. The process is comparable to the man blowing a fuse in some internal short circuit; his current flows, but touches nothing external. The circuit is ingrained into the man himself, and he knows his potential; he learns to draw on it and play with it – for the point of blackout does not have to be reached in every instance.

There is also a second relationship in play here: the man's relationship to the commanding officer, or to the person for whose sake he makes physical effort – in Killinger's case, the Kaiser. The prize for the victors of the boat race is an audience with the Kaiser ("My congratulations. You have done well. May you continue to gain honor by your work on the *Stein*").[40] A second goal of physical exertion is, then, to see contentment in the face of the commanding officer, to be praised by a man in a superior position. And, as the man loses consciousness through overexertion, his superior does indeed appear satisfied – as if he too is reaching orgasm.

Could it be, then, that hallucinatory union with the superior (even with the Kaiser himself) occurs in the state of blackout? That the forbidden loving penetration of man into man takes place imaginarily in this blackness? (The voice and gaze of the superior have certainly always been a penetrating presence.)

Ferenczi in his genital theory draws distinctions between what he sees as three stages of unification in the sexual act. Union is achieved in "hallucinatory" form by the organism as a whole, in partial form by the penis, and in absolute form by the secretion.[41]

The "union" achieved by the soldier (with himself/his superior) is clearly limited to the hallucinatory form. In the preceding chapter, I noted the association between key situations of satisfaction (all of which were preceded by hallucinatory object-substitution) and two central perceptions: the "bloody miasma" and the "empty space." A third perception can now be added: the blackness of unconsciousness in blackout, produced when the man oversteps the limits of his strength. One of the three perceptions is dominant in every action of the White Terror; their significance will be discussed later in this chapter.

I have indicated that the bodies of the cadets were quite intentionally driven beyond their limits. But there was more; in some cases their lives were consciously endangered. Lieutenant Ehrhardt, on his year as a naval cadet:

> They saw the blazing heat as a useful means of teaching a poor naval cadet a lesson. So, for example, our crew squad was once put on punishment detail in the boat between one and two in the afternoon, at the very time when blissful sunshine turned to blistering heat.
>
> Hard labor, coupled in my case with the particular injustice of being punished when I had broken no regulations, triggered an eruption of boyish defiance: I purposely let my oar fall overboard. The NCO, who had been watching me, ordered the cutter to row back immediately and reported me to the guard officer. As punishment, I was forced to run up and down the topmast ten times – an excessive demand under any circumstances, but an act of almost horrible cruelty in the tropical heat of Brazil. Toward the end, I was already half unconscious as I groped and felt my way down along the shrouds; but I said nothing, clenched my teeth, and somehow made it to the

lavatory below deck. Once there, I dropped to the cool stone tiles, gasped for breath a few more times, then lay unconscious.Such tricks were often played on naval cadets. They had to be strong as horses, or they withdrew from the service. In the end, we were all agile as cats and tough as elephants' hides.[42]

The squirming resistance of the narrator's body is dismissed here as "boyish." Even for the properly functionalized body, terror is "almost horrible cruelty" – but only "almost." The boy withstands it. Had he fallen from the mast – and this did happen on occasion – he would have been considered not to have trained himself adequately for his position as machine component; it would have been necessary to discard him. Holding out was proof of his reliability: he could be trusted inside the machine. Von Selchow:

> It was a damned hard year that lay behind us, that first year as cadets on the HMS *Stein*. With a ruthlessness hard to match, cadet officer Lieutenant Nordmann had driven us back and forth between theoretical and practical duties. We were never permitted a free moment. He had us doing every kind of filthy, heavy duty, always longer than the sailors, always rougher than the stokers. In those twelve months, each of us had resolved at least twelve times to turn his back on this drudgery when we returned home.
>   But as cadet officer, he knew how to take young men in hand; he knew our aim was one day to become leaders of men.[43]

One day, during an inspection of the ship, Selchow faints while hanging from the yards. He feels dizzy and knows he has time to climb down, but he refuses to do so and tries instead to hang on. He fails and is caught (though he could also have smashed himself to pieces on the deck). Massive uproar, accusations of drunkenness! But a number of the others are similarly overcome, and the inspection is called off. The culprit is finally identified: contaminated liver sausage. Still, better to fall than voluntarily vacate the yards and succumb to dizziness in the presence of the Kaiser.[44]

Selchow suffers a particularly violent blackout at the end of his training year at sea. He returns to Kiel only weeks before the final theoretical exam that is to make him an officer, only to be struck by some unidentified illness. He loses consciousness and lies comatose in a military hospital for several weeks while his doctors search in vain for the cause. As if through a mist, he hears the doctors say that he is likely to die. But he has the "will to live"... and as always, he pulls through.[45]

The drill brings the man to the very edge of dissolution. In the coma, a new structure, a new body grows onto him. When he awakes from this process of transformation, he has become physically and psychically another, a new man.

### The absorption of sexual desire

The most obvious consequence of the drill was its suppression of any "desire for women" (to the extent that such desire existed in the first place). The fact was an open secret; as Salomon writes, "any kind of pubescent urge was amply absorbed in the exercise of duties."[46] In response to a rumor that his food had been laced with anaphrodisiacs, Schauwecker remarks:

> But physical exertion was a far better antidote to erotic feeling than any drug could ever be. Eroticism was simply out of the question; it was a luxury of the everyday complacency of peacetime.[47] We had no time for such ridiculousness.[48]

Or if they did, it was immediately expunged. The staff sergeant in one of Vogel's stories bellows: "Toe the line, it's good for you – might stop you wanting to have a wank tonight."[49]

To most of the men, this lack of any relationship with a woman seemed in any case quite normal. That this was true for all of them made it a pleasurable position to be in.

The open obscenity of the idiom in the barracks may well have served to obscure a far more crucial transformation occurring in the soldier: the transformation of eros. By including "heterosexual" references in their repertoire of obscenities, the soldiers' language could obscure the fact that "women" and any kind of "love relationship" were no longer significant issues to the soldier. He was more likely to be interested in the following:

> A rifle in the hands of a noncommissioned officer from the Treptow school was a work of art. Whatever we grasped and twirled – rifles, beer glasses, girls – we were unbeatable. Even by the guards.[50]

What fascinates the soldier in drill is the activity of grasping, its synchronicity, its exactitude – and not *what* is grasped. "The very feeling of holding a rifle was rejuvenating".[51]

All these texts return repeatedly to the idea of the soldier as a work of art and of his movements as "beautiful." Never an emotion, all is expression.

> Perfection: this was the crucial issue. Penetrating to the very limits of human ability, shaping our world to its most polished form. From the standpoint of the front only one kind of man could be seen to have achieved perfection: the professional soldier (*Landsknecht*).[52]

The "polisher" referred to here is a man familiar to us as the creator of the polished precision component within the total fascist artwork of the army: the drill instructor.

The drill instructor sees himself unambiguously as a molder of men; a young god at work.

> It was really the most pleasant, rewarding work, turning those young recruits, awkward and unpolished (they generally arrived from the country), into soldiers, serviceable people... Mistakes made in their training could never have been remedied. The issue that the young officer in charge of recruits was called upon to settle was crucial both to people and fatherland: it was the question of whether an enthusiastic, indifferent, or even slightly cowed civilian would become a lifelong soldier.[53]

As General Maercker continues, the prewar army was generally successful in crafting "lifelong soldiers"; the "cowed civilian" did indeed become a thing of the past:

> the peacetime army had schooled the German people in physical discipline, obedience, order, and loyalty. Their work was to become a source of strength for a whole army of workers in our industries, and of strict order and manly restraint in our German labor unions.[54]

Such praise even pleased the occasional Wilhelminian union leader.[55] In the eyes of the soldier male, only the army was capable of creating what Röhm called "serviceable human beings": men bearing the stamp of military quality. To him, only the drill could serve as the birthplace of what he saw unquestionably as the only true human beings. The drill was a giant machine of transformation and rebirth,[56] created not only to serve the military, but society in general.

### "Prussian socialism"

> I have often wondered why this kind of education suited my taste so much better than the far easier and less disciplined life I would have had at school. My conclusion is that it was because as naval cadets we all wanted to be what our teachers and superiors had already become. As officers, they served as models for us. We assumed everything we did on their orders to be necessary. We appreciated why it had to be done.[57]
>
> (Lieutenant Ehrhardt)

Salomon, describing the teaching staff at the cadet academy:

> Instructors of officer rank were the only teachers who confounded the efforts of even the most fertile imaginations to find nicknames for them – quite simply because these men were in no way ridiculous.[58]

Ernst Röhm, on his training as infantry officer:

> an ensign was required to perform every duty to perfection. However painful this might have seemed, it was of course quite proper. Our education was founded on the guiding principle that an officer had not only to have subjected his own body to the physical demands he now made of his men; he had also to have outshone his subordinates in fulfilling them. I have often looked back gratefully to the lessons I learned in my wartime schooling.[59]

Less crucial here, it seems to me, than the drilled cadet's wish to follow in the footsteps of his training officer, is the reality of the possibility that he would eventually do so (this was the essential distinction between officers and rank-and-file training). Within a matter of years, the cadet, or ensign, had real prospects of attaining whatever position would give him his desired status as torturer. This was why, unlike the common soldier, he had no need to hate the torturer as a matter of principle. (He was more likely to feel envious or jealous.)

In Röhm's description, the superior also functions as an actual physical model; he has outstripped his subordinates in subjecting his own body to the physical demands he now makes of them. Having achieved the goal of training – which is to acquire a new and better body – he now represents it to others. His new body fulfills his desire for a guarantee that he can be "in no way ridiculous." By demonstrating himself to be physically the better man, the officer can be perceived as the better lover in the martial encounters he desires between man and man.

In Freud's *Mass Psychology and Ego Analysis*, the military officer is equated with the father; but the equation is a false one.[60] Paternal authority derives its special terror precisely from the fact that its validity never needs to be demonstrated. A father never has to show that he can do what he demands of his son, nor is it even necessary for him to be capable of doing so – he always remains his son's better. His power is tyrannical, capricious; established by laws, axiomatic. It is unjust. The power of the training officer, by contrast, is made to appear legitimate by his capacity, and willingness, to do what he demands of others. As a son in the process of advancement, the training officer is in principle the equal of the cadet he drills – moreover the cadet is capable of one day becoming the better of his instructor.

The father commands his son: "Thou shalt become like thy father; but thou shalt never do as thy father does." In officer training this paternal double-bind is replaced by a utopian vision of justice. If the cadet overcomes the obstacles presented to him, the promise of promotion will actually be fulfilled; it is *possible* to become general. In the family in which the man has been a son, he can by contrast never become the father – not if he "eclipses" his father a million times over.

This relationship between officer and cadet is central to the "Prussian socialism" (or "socialism of the front") whose spirit pervades the writings of the soldier males. They see the military as the consummate form of socialism; for it assigns to each man his rightful place in the hierarchy.[61]

In rank-and-file training, by contrast, the notion of Prussian socialism had no material content. It was almost inconceivable that recruits would one day be superior in rank to their instructor. He would always remain superior, his seniority always perceived as bludgeoning coercion.

Even for common soldiers, the instructor never corresponded to Freud's construct of the beloved *Führer*-figure, a "father" whom the soldier identified with his "ego ideal." On the contrary, the martinet instructor was often seen as an ignoramus whose only skill lay in exploiting his borrowed power to order around grown men, men who, outside the barracks (or even on the battlefield), were in every respect his superiors.

## Notes

1  Canetti, Elias. *Crowds and Power*, trans. by Carol Stewart, Harmondsworth: Penguin, 1973.
2  Salomon, Ernst von (ed.), *Die Kadetten*. Berlin, 1933. The following references are taken from the first part of the book, which describes how Salomon settles into the academy (up to 70). Further details are given for direct quotes only.
3  For an account of how from the eighteenth century onward the construction of prisons came to serve as the model for types of social supervision, see Michel Foucault, *Discipline and Punish: The Birth of the Prison*, trans. Alan Sheridan (New York: Vintage, 1979), 195 ff., particularly plates 3 and 4: panopticon and discipline.
4  Salomon, *Die Kadetten*, 44.
5  Ibid., 48.
6  Freud, *Analysis Terminable and Interminable*, in Standard Edition (SE), vol. XXIII, 226. See also *Introductory Lectures on Psychoanalysis*, SE, vol. XVI, 312.
7  Freud, *An Outline of Psycho-Analysis*, SE, vol. XXIII, 155; see also *Psycho-Analytic Notes on an Autobiographical Account of a Case of Paranoia*, SE, vol. XII, 60–1.
8  As elsewhere, Freud calls such an urge: *Psycho-Analytic Notes*, SE, vol. XII, 63. On the puberty of German boys of the time, see Erikson, "The legend of Hitler's childhood," 307 ff.
9  Salomon, *Die Kadetten*, 42.
10  Ibid., 68.
11  Ibid., 49.
12  Ibid., 55–6.
13  Ibid., 56.
14  Ibid., 57.
15  Ibid., 58.
16  Ibid., 61.
17  Ibid., 62–3.
18  The term refers to the custom of throwing a sailor into the ocean the first time he crosses the equator (Tr.).

19 Salomon, *Die Kadetten*, 63–4.

20 Ibid., 64.

21 Ibid., 69.

22 Ibid., 65.

23 "Walls…in the end become part of him," Canetti emphasizes (*Crowds and Power*, 362). By contrast, his account of the command is very precise (349–50).

24 Salomon, *Die Kadetten*, 114.

25 Plaas, Hartmut. 'Das Kapp-Unternehmer. Aus dem Tagebuch eines Sturmsoldaten,' *Das Buch vom Deutschen Freikorpskämpfer*. Salomon, Ernst von, ed. Berlin, 1935, 344 ff.

26 Ibid., 178. In Voick, Herbert. *Rebellen um Ehre. Mein Kampf und die nationale Erhebung.* Gütersloh, 1932, we find the "troop with a soul of steel" (66).

27 Salomon, *Die Kadetten*, 115.

28 Jünger, Ernst. *Feuer und Blut*. Berlin, 1929.

29 Foucault, *Discipline and Punish*, 169, describes how from the eighteenth century onward the human body was disciplined in relation to the construction of social institutions, which were meant to serve as models for the body. His description pays less attention to the body's actual physical changes. See 135–70.

30 Jünger, *Kampf als inneres Erlebnis*, 32–33; see also 55.

31 The German is "Der neue Mensch" which could also be translated "the new human being" since Theweleit's point is however precisely that the species being created is *masculine*, "men" has been used here as a general term for human beings (Tr.).

32 Ibid., 74. Also Buschbecker, Karl Matthias. *Wie unser Gesetz es befahl*, Berlin, 1936, 132, 181; Volck, *Rebellen um Ehre*, 104, 144.

33 Manfred Nagl's *Science Fiction in Deutschland* (Tübingen, 1972), a survey based on extremely interesting material, shows that the attempt to create a superman in the image of the machine, by excluding women in favor of machines, is not an invention of the futurists. It is a core element of "pre-fascist" 19th century literature, which, to a large extent, has been dismissed as "trivial" by literary history (see e.g., 125 ff.).

34 See volume 1, chapter 1, section 24, "Preliminary Findings," note 13.

35 Freud, *The Ego and the Id*, SE, vol. XIX, 25–6.

36 Röhm, *Die Geschichte eines Hochverräters*, Munich, 1928; fourth edition, 1934, 16.

37 Hirschfeld, Magnus, ed. *Sittengeschichte des Weltkriegs*, 2 vols. Leipzig, 1930, vol. 2, 180.

38 Salomon, *Die Kadetten*, 30.

39 Killinger, Manfred von. *Der Klabautermann, Eine Lebensgeschichte.* Munich, 1936, 106.

40 Ibid., 105.

41 Ferenczi, "Versuch einer Genitaltheorie," in *Schriften zur Psycho analyse*, 2 vols. Frankfurt, 1970–71, vol. II, 333.

42 Freksa, Friedrich. *Kapität Ehrhardt, Abenteuer und Schicksal*. Berlin, 1927, 33–4.

43 Selchow, Bogislav von. *Hundert Tage aus meinem Leben*. Leipzig, 1936, 38.

44 Ibid., 41–2.

45 Ibid., 66–7.

46 Salomon, *Die Kadetten*, 89 and 77–8.

47 Schauwecker, Franz. *Aufbruch der Nation*. Berlin, 1929, 91–2.

48 Von Killinger, *Der Klabautermann*, 48.

49 Bruno Vogel, *Es lebe der Krieg*, cited in Hirschfeld, *Sittengeschichte des Weltkriegs*, vol. 2, 163.

50 Schauwecker, *Aufbruch der Nation*, 63. See also Goote, Thor, *Wir fahren den Tod*, Berlin, 1930, 182; Eggers, Kurt. *Der Berg der Rebellen*. Leipzig, 1937, 34–5. On the absorption of sexuality via drill/war, see also Freska, *Kapitän Ehrhardt*, 29–30; Jünger, *Feuer und Blut*, 33; Bronnen, Arnolt, *Rossbach*. Berlin, 1930, 145; Schauwecker, *Aufbruch der Nation*, 315; Zöberlein, Hans, *Der Befehl des Gewissens*. Munich, 1937, 670.

51 Salomon, *Die Kadetten*, 66.

52 Jünger, *Feuer und Blut*, 55. (The term *Landsknecht* refers historically to soldiers recruited from within the German empire [Tr.].)

53 Röhm, *Die Geschichte eines Hochverräters*, 22.

54 Maercker, Ludwig Rolf Georg. *Vom Kaiserherr zur Reichswehr*. Leipzig, 1921, 307. See also the section on "Ausbildung, Erziehung und inneres Leben der Truppe," 306–22.

55   See also the position on war taken by the trade union leaders Husemann and Sachse in Heinrich Tauber, *Die Sozialisierung des Ruhrberghaus* (Frankfurt, 1973), 14 ff.

56   Schramm speaks of "higher rebirth in formation" in Schramm, Wilhelm von. "Schöpferische Kritik des Kriegers," *Krieg und Krieger*, ed. by Ernst Jünger. Berlin, 1930. pp. 31–50, 41.

57   Freska, *Kapitän Ehrhardt*, 34.

58   Salomon, *Die Kadetten*, 89.

59   Röhm, *Die Geschichte eines Hochverräters*, 17–18.

60   For Freud to study army organization would have been well and good, if the type of army he described had really existed. He usually proceeded by developing theories from case studies, not the reverse. With the army, by contrast, he considered it unneccessary to start with its concrete structure, or the psychic structure of its soldiers. He contented himself with reading Le Bon's book on mass psychology, then applying its theoretical findings, together with his own from an earlier period, to the army and other hierarchical non-masses. He then drew up a whole model of the functions of an absolutely nonexistent Oedipal army—all for the stated purpose of criticizing Wilhelminian militarism (his starting point was the high suicide rate in the German army) and arguing for further improvements. He pulled a Freudian wish-fulfillment army out of a hat—an army such as Ebert himself might have wished for. The work was published in 1921, a date that clearly demonstrates how efficiently the insulating system of the father of psychoanalysis could function to exclude the actual limits of history (Freud, *Group Psychology and the Analysis of the Ego, in SE*, vol. 18).

61   "At that time, those of us who had been in the most complete socialist organization, the Prussian army, returned home qualified to join a movement which, founded as it was on self-discipline and obedience, endeavored to anchor the purpose of labor not in acquisition but in service, and which strove to create the kind of socialism which Spengler was shortly afterward to describe as the completion of Prussianism." Günther, "Hamburg," in JKR, 40, referring to O. Spengler, *Preussentum und Sozialismus* (Munich, 1924). See also Heinz, Friedrich W. *Die Nation grieft an. Geschichte und Kritik des soldatischen Nationalismus.* Berlin, 1932, 14; Heinz, Friedrich W. *Sprengstoff.* Berlin, 1930, 27–8; Jünger, *Feuer und Blut*, 217; Dwingler, Edwin. *Auf halbem Wege.* Jena, 1939, 272–3; Gengler, Ludwig F. *Rudolf Berthold. Sieger in 44 Luftschlachten. Erschlagen in Bruderkampf für Deutschlands Freiheit.* Berlin, 1934, 103–4. It is often said that the basis of "Prussian socialism" in the *Freikorps* was the affinities that service created between officers and men. Many officers served in the ranks. See in particular Schricker, Rudolf. *Rotmord über München.* Berlin, 1934, 190; W. von Schramm, *Schöpferische Kritik des Krieges*, complained that war was being waged "devoid of the style of natural democracy befitting its essence." (42) "Natural democracy" = the best man wins. Otto Strasser uses the term "German socialism." His intention here is to undermine the socialism of the labor movement. He wants to "make economically independent existence equally as widespread as the number of our national comrades who desire such independence." He concludes: "Anyone who recognizes the racial dangers posed by our urban conglomerations will also regard as an obligatory national duty the goal of systematically *reversing urbanization*. Reversing urbanization is a consequence of the need for autarchy and the introduction of the hereditary fief in agricultural property law. For the natural and desired outcome of both these goals is the *re-agrarianization of Germany*" (Otto Strasser, *Aufbau des Sozialismus* [Leipzig, 1932] 39).

# 15
## Sculpted Bodies

# Women and the Knife:
# Cosmetic Surgery and the Colonization
# of Women's Bodies*

*Kathryn Pauly Morgan*

## Introduction

Consider the following passages:

> If you want to wear a Maidenform Viking Queen bra like Madonna, be warned: A body like this doesn't just happen ... Madonna's kind of fitness training takes time. The rock star *whose muscled body was recently on tour* spends a minimum of three hours a day working out.  ("Madonna passionate about fitness" 1990; italics added)

> A lot of the contestants [in the Miss America Pageant] do not owe their beauty to their Maker but to their Re-Maker. Miss Florida's nose came courtesy of her surgeon. So did Miss Alaska's. And Miss Oregon's breasts came from the manufacturers of silicone.  (Goodman, 1989)

> Jacobs [a plastic surgeon in Manhattan] constantly answers the call for cleavage. "Women need it for their holiday ball gowns."  ("Cosmetic surgery for the holidays," 1985)

> We hadn't seen or heard from each other for 28 years ... Then he suggested it would be nice if we could meet. I was very nervous about it. How much had I changed? I wanted a facelift, tummy tuck and liposuction, all in one week.
> (A woman, age forty-nine, being interviewed for an article on "older couples" falling in love; "Falling in love again" 1990)

> It's hard to say why one person will have cosmetic surgery done and another won't consider it, but generally I think people who go for surgery are more aggressive, they are the doers of the world. It's like makeup. You see some women who might be greatly improved by wearing make-up, but they're, I don't know, granola-heads or something, and they just refuse.
> (Dr Ronald Levine, director of plastic surgery education at the University of Toronto and vice-chairman of the plastic surgery section of the Ontario Medical Association; "The quest to be a perfect 10," 1990)

* Kathryn Pauly Morgan, "Women and the knife: cosmetic surgery and the colonization of women's bodies," *Hypatia*, vol. 6, no. 3 (1991), 25–53.

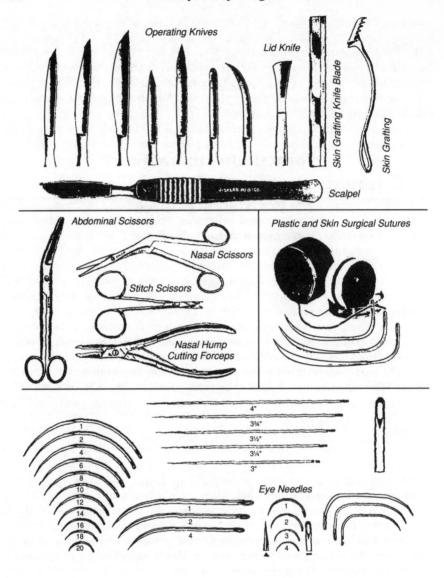

*Figure 1*

Another comparable limitation [of the women's liberation movement] is a tendency to reject certain good things only in order to punish men...There is no reason why a women's liberation activist should not try to look pretty and attractive.

(Markovic, 1976)

Now look at the needles and at the knives. Look at them carefully. Look at them for a long time. *Imagine them cutting into your skin.* Imagine that you have been given this surgery as a gift from your loved one who read a persuasive and engaging press release from Drs John and Jim Williams that ends by saying "The next morning the limo will chauffeur your loved one back home again, with a gift of beauty that will last a lifetime" (Williams, 1990). Imagine the beauty that you have been promised...

This paper is about women and about the knives that "sculpt" our bodies to make us beautiful forever. I want to explore this topic for five reasons. First, I am interested in the project of developing a feminist hermeneutics that tries to understand the words and choices of women situated in an interface position with various so-called experts in Western culture.

Second, I experience genuine epistemic and political bewilderment when I, as a feminist woman, think about contemporary practices and individual choices in the area of elective cosmetic surgery.[1] Is this a setting of liberation or oppression – or both?

Third, I have come to realize that this is a "silent" (if not silenced) topic both in mainstream bioethics and in recent ground-breaking discussions in feminist medical ethics.[2] Apart from some tangential references, there is virtually no discussion, feminist or otherwise, of the normative and political issues that might be raised in relation to women and elective cosmetic surgery. I believe we need a feminist framework and critique to understand why *breast augmentation*, until recently, was the most frequently performed kind of cosmetic surgery in North America ("New bodies for sale") and why, according to *Longevity* magazine, 1 in every 225 adult Americans had *elective* cosmetic surgery in 1989. We need a feminist analysis to understand why actual, live women are reduced and reduce themselves to "potential women" and choose to participate in anatomizing and fetishizing their bodies as they buy "contoured bodies," "restored youth," and "permanent beauty." In the face of a growing market and demand for surgical interventions in women's bodies that can and do result in infection, bleeding, embolisms, pulmonary edema, facial nerve injury, unfavorable scar formation, skin loss, blindness, crippling, and death, our silence becomes a culpable one.

Fourth, I situate this topic in the larger framework of the contemporary existential technologizing of women's bodies in Western culture. We are witnessing a *normalization* of elective cosmetic surgery. As the author of an article targeted to homemakers remarks, "For many women, it's no longer a question of *whether* to undergo cosmetic surgery – but what, when, by whom and how much" (McCabe, 1990). Not only is elective cosmetic surgery moving out of the domain of the sleazy, the suspicious, the secretively deviant, or the pathologically narcissistic, *it is becoming the norm*. This shift is leading to a predictable inversion of the domains of the deviant and the pathological, so that women who contemplate *not using* cosmetic surgery will increasingly be stigmatized and seen as deviant. I believe it is crucial that we understand these normative inversions that are catalyzed by the technologizing of women's bodies.

Finally, I am intrigued by the deeper epistemological and metaphysical dynamics of the field of cosmetic surgery. For example, a recent hospital-sponsored *health* conference advertised a special session on "facial regeneration" by asking, "Are you looking in the mirror and, seeing the old you, wishing you could be seeing the you that you used to be?" and then promising that this previous, youthful "you" could be regenerated. As a philosopher, I am shocked at the extent to which patients and cosmetic surgeons participate in committing one of the deepest of original philosophical sins, the choice of the apparent over the real. Cosmetic surgery entails the ultimate envelopment of the lived temporal *reality* of the human subject by technologically created appearances that are then regarded as "the real." Youthful appearance triumphs over aged reality.

## "Just the facts in America, ma'am"

As of 1990, the most frequently performed kind of cosmetic surgery is liposuction, which involves sucking fat cells out from underneath our skin with a vacuum device. This is viewed as the most suitable procedure for removing specific bulges around the hips, thighs, belly, buttocks, or chin. It is most appropriately done on thin people who want to get rid of certain bulges, and surgeons guarantee that even if there is weight gain, the bulges won't reappear since the fat cells have been permanently removed. At least twelve deaths are known to have resulted from complications such as hemorrhages and embolisms. "All we know is there was a complication and that complication was death," said the partner of Toni Sullivan, age forty-three ("hardworking mother of two teenage children" says the press; "Woman, 43, dies after cosmetic surgery," 1989). Cost: $1,000–$7,500.

The second most frequently performed kind of cosmetic surgery is breast augmentation, which involves an implant, usually of silicone. Often the silicone implant hardens over time and must be removed surgically. Over one million women in the United States are known to have had breast augmentation surgery. Two recent studies have shown that breast implants block X-rays and cast a shadow on surrounding tissue, making mammograms difficult to interpret, and that there appears to be a much higher incidence of cancerous lumps in "augmented women" ("Implants hide tumors in breasts, study says" 1988). Cost: $1,500–$3,000.

"Facelift" is a kind of umbrella term that covers several sorts of procedures. In a recent Toronto case, Dale Curtis "decided to get a facelift for her fortieth birthday... Bederman used liposuction on the jowls and neck, removed the skin and fat from her upper and lower lids and tightened up the muscles in the neck and cheeks... 'She was supposed to get a forehead lift but she chickened out,' Bederman says" ("Changing faces," 1989). Clients are now being advised to begin their face-lifts in their early forties and are also told that they will need subsequent facelifts every five to fifteen years. Cost: $2,500–$10,500.

"Nips" and "tucks" are cute, camouflaging labels used to refer to surgical reduction performed on any of the following areas of the body: hips, buttocks, thighs, belly, and breasts. They involve cutting out wedges of skin and fat and sewing up the two sides. These are major surgical procedures that cannot be performed in out-patient clinics because of the need for anesthesia and the severity of possible post-operative complications. Hence, they require access to costly operating rooms and services in hospitals or clinics. Cost: $3,000–$7,000.

The number of "rhinoplasties" or nose jobs, has risen by 34 percent since 1981. Some clients are coming in for second and third nose jobs. Nose jobs involve either the inserting of a piece of bone taken from elsewhere in the body or the whittling down of the nose. Various styles of noses go in and out of fashion, and various cosmetic surgeons describe the noses they create in terms of their own surnames, such as "the Diamond nose" or "the Goldman nose" ("Cosmetic surgery for the holidays," 1985). Cost: $2,000–$3,000.

More recent types of cosmetic surgery, such as the use of skin-expanders and suction lipectomy, involve inserting tools, probes, and balloons *under* the skin either for purposes of expansion or reduction (Hirshson, 1987).

Lest one think that women (who represent between 60 and 70 percent of all cosmetic surgery patients) choose only one of these procedures, heed the words of Dr Michael Jon Bederman of the Centre for Cosmetic Surgery in Toronto:

We see working girls, dental technicians, middle-class women who are unhappy with their looks or are aging prematurely. And we see executives – both male and female . . . Where before someone would have a tummy tuck and not have anything else done for a year, frequently we will do liposuction and tummy tuck and then the next day a facelift, upper and lower lids, rhinoplasty *and other things*. The recovery time is the same whether a person has one procedure or *the works*, generally about two weeks.

("Changing faces," 1989; italics added)

In principle, there is no area of the body that is not accessible to the interventions and metamorphoses performed by cosmetic surgeons intent on creating twentieth century versions of "femina perfecta."[3]


## From artifice to artifact: the creation of robo woman?

In his article "Toward a philosophy of technology," Hans Jonas (1979) distinguishes between premodern and modern technology. Part of what is especially characteristic of modern technology, he suggests, is that the relationship of means and ends is no longer unilinear but circular, so that "new technologies may suggest, create, even impose new ends, never before conceived, simply by offering their feasibility . . . Technology thus adds to the very objectives of human desires, including objectives for technology itself" (Jonas, 1979: 35). In 1979, Jonas only speculates about the final stage of technological creation: "Are we, perhaps, on the verge of a technology, based on biological knowledge and wielding an engineering art which, this time, has man [*sic*] himself for its object? This has become a theoretical possibility . . . and it has been rendered morally possible by the metaphysical neutralizing of man" (Jonas, 1979: 41). We now know that the answer to Jonas's question is yes. We have arrived at the stage of regarding ourselves as both technological subject and object, transformable and literally creatable through biological engineering. The era of biotechnology is clearly upon us and is invading even the most private and formerly sequestered domains of human life, including women's wombs. I interpret the spectacular rise of the technology of cosmetic surgery as a form of biotechnology that fits this dialectical picture of modern technology.

The domain of technology is often set up in oppositional relation to a domain that is designated "the natural." The role assigned to technology is often that of transcendence, transformation, control, exploitation, or destruction, and the technologized object or process is conceptualized as inferior or primitive, in need of perfecting transformation or exploitation through technology in the name of some "higher" purpose or end, or deserving of eradication because it is harmful or evil.

Although there continue to be substantive theoretical challenges to its dominant metaphors, Western scientific medicine views the human body essentially as a machine.[4] The machine model carries with it certain implications, among which is the reduction of spirit, affect, and value to mechanistic processes in the human body. This perspective also facilitates viewing and treating the body in atomistic and mechanical fashion, so that, for example, the increasing mechanization of the body in terms of artificial hearts, kidneys, joints, limbs, and computerized implants is seen as an ordinary progression within the dominant model. Correlative with the rise of the modeling of the human brain as an information-processing machine, we are witnessing the development of genetic engineering; transsexual surgery; the technological transformation of all aspects of human conception, maternity, and birthing; and the artificial prolongation of human life.

What is designated "the natural" functions primarily as a frontier rather than as a barrier. While genetics, human sexuality, reproductive outcome, and death were previously regarded as open to variation primarily in evolutionary terms, they are now seen by biotechnologists as domains of creation and control. Cosmetic surgeons claim a role here too. For them, human bodies are the locus of challenge. As one plastic surgeon remarks:

> Patients sometimes misunderstand the nature of cosmetic surgery. It's not a shortcut for diet or exercise. *It's a way to override the genetic code.*
>                    ("Retouching nature's way," 1990; italics added)

The beauty culture is coming to be dominated by a variety of experts, and consumers of youth and beauty are likely to find themselves dependent not only on cosmetic surgeons but on anesthetists, nurses, estheticians, nail technicians, manicurists, dietitians, hairstylists, cosmetologists, masseuses, aroma therapists, trainers, pedicurists, electrolysists, pharmacologists, and dermatologists. All these experts provide services that can be bought; all these experts are perceived as administering and transforming the human body into an increasingly artificial and ever more perfect object. Think of the contestants in the Miss America pageant who undergo cosmetic surgery in preparation for participation. Reflect on the headline of the article in *Newsweek* (May 27, 1985) on cosmetic surgery: "New bodies for sale."

How do these general remarks concerning technology and the body apply to women – and to which women – and why? For virtually all women as women, success is defined in terms of interlocking patterns of compulsion: compulsory attractiveness, compulsory motherhood, and compulsory heterosexuality, patterns that determine the legitimate limits of attraction and motherhood.[5] Rather than aspiring to self-determined and woman-centered ideals of health or integrity, women's attractiveness is defined as attractive-to-men; women's eroticism is defined as either nonexistent, pathological, or peripheral when it is not directed to phallic goals; and motherhood is defined in terms of legally sanctioned and constrained reproductive service to particular men and to institutions such as the nation, the race, the owner, and the class – institutions that are, more often than not, male-dominated. Biotechnology is now making beauty, fertility, the appearance of heterosexuality through surgery, and the appearance of youthfulness accessible to virtually all women who can afford that technology – and growing numbers of women are making other sacrifices in their lives in order to buy access to the technical expertise.

In Western industrialized societies, women have also become increasingly socialized into an acceptance of technical knives. We know about knives that can heal: the knife that saves the life of a baby in distress, the knife that cuts out the cancerous growths in our breasts, the knife that straightens our spines, the knife that liberates our arthritic fingers so that we may once again gesture, once again touch, once again hold. But we also know about other knives: the knife that cuts off our toes so that our feet will fit into elegant shoes, the knife that cuts out ribs to fit our bodies into corsets, the knife that slices through our labia in episiotomies and other forms of genital multilation, the knife that cuts into our abdomens to remove our ovaries to cure our "deviant tendencies" (Barker–Benfield, 1976), the knife that removes our breasts in prophylactic or unnecessary radical mastectomies, the knife that cuts our "useless bag" (the womb) if we're the wrong color and poor or if we've "outlived our fertility," the knife that makes the "bikini cut" across our pregnant bellies to facilitate the cesarean section that will allow the obstetrician to go on holiday. We know these knives well.

And now we are coming to know the knives and needles of the cosmetic surgeons – the knives that promise to sculpt our bodies, to restore our youth, to create beauty out of what was ugly and ordinary. What kind of knives are these? Magic knives. Magic knives in a patriarchal context. Magic knives in a Eurocentric context. Magic knives in a white supremacist context. What do they mean? I am afraid of these knives.

## Listening to the women

In order to give a feminist reading of any ethical situation we must listen to the women's own reasons for their actions (Sherwin, 1984–85 and 1989). It is only once we have listened to the voices of women who have elected to undergo cosmetic surgery that we can try to assess the extent to which the conditions for genuine choice have been met, and look at the consequences of these choices for the position of women. Here are some of those voices:

*Voice 1* (a woman looking forward to attending a prestigious charity ball): "There will be a lot of new faces at the Brazilian Ball."
("Changing faces" 1989) [Class/status symbol]

*Voice 2*: "You can keep yourself trim...But you have no control over the way you wrinkle, or the fat on your hips, or the skin of your lower abdomen. If you are *hereditarily predestined* to stretch out or wrinkle in your face, you will. If your parents had puffy eyelids and saggy jowls, you're going to have puffy eyelids and saggy jowls."
("Changing faces," 1989) [Regaining a sense of control; liberation from parents; transcending hereditary predestination]

*Voice 3*: "Now we want a nose that makes a statement, with tip definition and a strong bridge line."                         ("Changing faces," 1989) [Domination; strength]

*Voice 4*: "I decided to get a facelift for my fortieth birthday after ten years of living and working in the tropics had taken its toll."
("Changing Faces," 1989) [Gift to the self; erasure of a decade of hard work and exposure]

*Voice 5*: "I've gotten my breasts augmented. I can use it as a tax write-off."
("Changing Faces," 1989) [Professional advancement; economic benefits]

*Voice 6*: "I'm a teacher and kids let schoolteachers know how we look and they aren't nice about it. A teacher who looks like an old bat or has a big nose will get a nickname."
("Retouching nature's way: is cosmetic surgery worth it?" 1990)
[Avoidance of cruelty; avoidance of ageist bias]

*Voice 7*: "I'll admit to a boob job."
(Susan Akin, Miss America of 1986 quoted in Goodman, 1986) [Prestige; status; competitive accomplishments in beauty contest]

*Voice 8* (forty-five year old grandmother and proprietor of a business): "In my business, the customers expect you to look as good as they do."
   (Hirschson, 1987) [Business asset; economic gain; possible denial of grandmother status]

*Voice 9*: "People in business see something like this as showing an overall aggressive-ness and go-forwardness. *The trend is to, you know, be all that you can be.*"
   ("Cosmetic surgery for the holidays," 1985) [Success; personal fulfillment]

*Voice 10* (paraphrase): "I do it to fight holiday depression."
   ("Cosmetic surgery for the holidays," 1985) [Emotional control; happiness]

*Voice 11*: "I came to see Dr X for the holiday season. I have important business parties, and the man I'm trying to get to marry me is coming in from Paris."
   ("Cosmetic surgery for the holidays," 1985) [Economic gain; heterosexual affiliation]

Women have traditionally regarded (and been taught to regard) their bodies, particularly if they are young, beautiful, and fertile, *as a locus of power* to be enhanced through artifice and, now, through artifact. In 1792, in *A Vindication of the Rights of Woman*, Mary Wollstonecraft remarked: "Taught from infancy that beauty is woman's scepter, the mind shapes itself to the body and roaming round its gilt cage, only seeks to adorn its prison." How ironic that the mother of the creator of *Frankenstein* should be the source of that quote. We need to ask ourselves whether today, involved as we are in the modern inversion of "our bodies shaping themselves to our minds," we are creating a new species of woman-monster with new artifactual bodies that function as prisons or whether cosmetic surgery for women does represent a potentially liberating field of choice.[6]

When Snow White's stepmother asks the mirror "Who is fairest of all?" she is not asking simply an empirical question. In wanting to continue to be "the fairest of all," she is striving, in a clearly competitive context, for a prize, for a position, for power. The affirmation of her beauty brings with it privileged heterosexual affili-ation, privileged access to forms of power unavailable to the plain, the ugly, the aged, and the barren.

The Voices are seductive – they speak the language of gaining access to trans-cendence, achievement, liberation, and power. And they speak to a kind of reality. First, electing to undergo the surgery necessary to create youth and beauty artifi-cially not only appears to but often actually does give a woman a sense of identity that, to some extent, she has chosen herself. Second, it offers her the potential to raise her status both socially and economically by increasing her opportunities for heterosexual affiliation (especially with white men). Third, by committing herself to the pursuit of beauty, a woman integrates her life with a consistent set of values and choices that bring her wide-spread approval and a resulting sense of increased self-esteem. Fourth, the pursuit of beauty often gives a woman access to a range of individuals who administer to her body in a caring way, an experience often sadly lacking in the day-to-day lives of many women. As a result, a woman's pursuit of beauty through transformation is often associated with lived experiences of self-creation, self-fulfillment, self-transcendence, and being cared for. The power of these experiences must not be underestimated.[7]

While I acknowledge that these choices can confer a kind of integrity on a woman's life, I also believe that they are likely to embroil her in a set of interrelated contradictions. I refer to these as "Paradoxes of choice."

## Three paradoxes of choice

In exploring these paradoxes, I appropriate Foucault's analysis of the diffusion of power in order to understand forms of power that are potentially more personally invasive than are more obvious, publicly identifiable aspects of power. In the chapter "Docile bodies" in *Discipline and Punish*, Foucault (1979: 136–7) highlights three features of what he calls disciplinary power:

1  The *scale* of the control. In disciplinary power the body is treated individually and in a coercive way because the body itself is the *active* and hence apparently free body that is being controlled through movements, gestures, attitudes, and degrees of rapidity;
2  the *object* of the control, which involves meticulous control over the efficiency of movements and forces;
3  the *modality* of the control, which involves constant, uninterrupted coercion.

Foucault argues that the outcome of disciplinary power is the docile body, a body "that may be subjected, used, transformed, and improved" (Foucault 1979: 136). Foucault is discussing this model of power in the context of prisons and armies, but we can adapt the central insights of this notion to see how women's bodies are entering "a machinery of power that explores it, breaks it down, and rearranges it" through a recognizably political metamorphosis of embodiment (Foucault 1979: 138).[8] What is important about this notion in relation to cosmetic surgery is the extent to which it makes it possible to speak about the diffusion of power throughout Western industrialized cultures that are increasingly committed to a technological beauty imperative. It also makes it possible to refer to a set of experts – cosmetic surgeons – whose explicit power mandate is to explore, break down, and rearrange women's bodies.

### Paradox 1: the choice of conformity – understanding the number 10

While the technology of cosmetic surgery could clearly be used to create and celebrate idiosyncrasy, eccentricity, and uniqueness, it is obvious that this is not how it is presently being used. Cosmetic surgeons report that legions of women appear in their offices demanding "Bo Derek" breasts ("Cosmetic surgery for the holidays," 1985). Jewish women demand reductions of their noses so as to be able to "pass" as one of their Aryan sisters who form the dominant ethnic group (Lakoff and Scherr, 1984). Adolescent Asian girls who bring in pictures of Elizabeth Taylor and of Japanese movie actresses (whose faces have already been reconstructed) demand the "Westernizing" of their own eyes and the creation of higher noses in hopes of better job and marital prospects ("New bodies for sale," 1985). Black women buy toxic bleaching agents in hopes of attaining lighter skin. What is being created in all of these instances is not simply beautiful bodies and faces but white, Western, Anglo-Saxon bodies in a racist, anti-Semitic context.

More often than not, what appear at first glance to be instances of choice turn out to be instances of conformity. The women who undergo cosmetic surgery in order to compete in various beauty pageants are clearly choosing to conform. So is the woman who wanted to undergo a facelift, tummy tuck, and liposuction all in one week, in order to win heterosexual approval *from a man she had not seen in twenty-eight years* and whose individual preferences she could not possibly know. In some ways, it does not matter who the particular judges are. Actual men – brothers, fathers, male lovers, male beauty "experts" – and hypothetical men live in the esthetic imaginations of women. Whether they are male employers, prospective male spouses, male judges in the beauty pageants, or male-identified women, these modern day Parises are generic and live sometimes ghostly but powerful lives in the reflective awareness of women (Berger, 1972). A woman's makeup, dress, gestures, voice, degree of cleanliness, degree of muscularity, odors, degree of hirsuteness, vocabulary, hands, feet, skin, hair, and vulva can all be evaluated, regulated, and disciplined in the light of the hypothetical often-white male viewer and the male viewer present in the assessing gaze of other women (Haug, 1987). Men's appreciation and approval of achieved femininity becomes all the more invasive when it resides in the incisions, stitches, staples, and scar tissue of women's bodies as women choose to conform. And, as various theorists have pointed out, women's public conformity to the norms of beauty often signals a deeper conformity to the norms of compulsory heterosexuality along with an awareness of the violence that can result from violating those norms.[9] Hence the first paradox: that what looks like an optimal situation of reflection, deliberation, and self-creating choice often signals conformity at a deeper level.

### Paradox 2: liberation into colonization

As argued above, a woman's desire to create a permanently beautiful and youthful appearance that is not vulnerable to the threats of externally applied cosmetic artifice or to the natural aging process of the body must be understood as a deeply significant existential project. It deliberately involves the exploitation and trans-formation of the most intimately experienced domain of immanence, the body, in the name of transcendence: transcendence of hereditary predestination, of lived time, of one's given "limitations." What I see as particularly alarming in this project is that what comes to have primary significance is not the real given existing woman but her body viewed as a "primitive entity" that is seen only as potential, as a kind of raw material to be exploited in terms of appearance, eroticism, nurturance, and fertility as defined by the colonizing culture.[10]

But for whom is this exploitation and transformation taking place? Who exercises the power here? Sometimes the power is explicit. It is exercised by brothers, fathers, male lovers, male engineering students who taunt and harass their female counter-parts, and by male cosmetic surgeons who offer "free advice" in social gatherings to women whose "deformities" and "severe problems" can all be cured through their healing needles and knives.[11] And the colonizing power is transmitted through and by those women whose own bodies and disciplinary practices demonstrate the efficacy of "taking care of herself" in these culturally defined feminine ways.

Sometimes, however, the power may be so diffused as to dominate the conscious-ness of a given woman with no other subject needing to be present. As Bartky notes, such diffused power also signals the presence of the colonizer:

> Normative femininity is coming more and more to be centered on woman's body...
> Images of normative femininity...have replaced the religious oriented tracts of the
> past. The woman who checks her makeup half a dozen times a day to see if her
> foundation has caked or her mascara has run, who worries that the wind or the rain
> may spoil her hairdo, who looks frequently to see if her stockings have bagged at the

ankle, or who, feeling fat, monitors everything she eats, *has become, just as surely as the inmate of the Panopticon, a self-policing subject, a self committed to a relentless self-surveillance. This self-surveillance is a form of obedience to patriarchy.*

(Bartky, 1988: 81; italics added)

As Foucault and others have noted, practices of coercion and domination are often camouflaged by practical rhetoric and supporting theories that appear to be benevolent, therapeutic, and voluntaristic. Previously, for example, colonizing was often done in the name of bringing "civilization" through culture and morals to "primitive, barbaric people," but contemporary colonizers mask their exploitation of "raw materials and human labor" in the name of "development." Murphy (1984), Piercy (1980), and I (Morgan, 1989) have all claimed that similar rhetorical camouflage of colonization takes place in the areas of women's reproductive decision-making and women's right to bodily self-determination. In all of these instances of colonization the ideological manipulation of technology can be identified, and, I would argue, in all of these cases this technology has often been used to the particular disadvantage and destruction of some aspect of women's integrity.[12]

In electing to undergo cosmetic surgery, women appear to be protesting against the constraints of the "given" in their embodied lives and seeking liberation from those constraints. But I believe they are in danger of retreating and becoming more vulnerable, at that very level of embodiment, to those colonizing forms of power that may have motivated the protest in the first place. Moreover, in seeking independence, they can become even more dependent on male assessment and on the services of all those experts they initially bought to render them independent.

Here we see a second paradox bound up with choice: that the rhetoric is that of liberation and care, of "making the most of yourself," but the reality is often the transformation of oneself as a woman for the eye, the hand, and the approval of the Other – the lover, the taunting students, the customers, the employers, the social peers. And the Other is almost always affected by the dominant culture, which is male-supremacist, racist, ageist, heterosexist, anti-Semitic, ableist and class-biased.[13]

## *Paradox 3: coerced voluntariness and the technological imperative*

Where is the coercion? At first glance, women who choose to undergo cosmetic surgery often seem to represent a paradigm case of the rational chooser. Drawn increasingly from wider and wider economic groups, these women clearly make a choice, often at significant economic cost to the rest of their life, to pay the large sums of money demanded by cosmetic surgeons (since American health insurance plans do not cover this elective cosmetic surgery).

Furthermore, they are often highly critical consumers of these services, demanding extensive consultation, information regarding the risks and benefits of various surgical procedures, and professional guarantees of expertise. Generally they are relatively young and in good health. Thus, in some important sense, they epitomize relatively invulnerable free agents making a decision under virtually optimal conditions.

Moreover, on the surface, women who undergo cosmetic surgery choose a set of procedures that are, by definition, "elective." This term is used, quite straightforwardly, to distinguish cosmetic surgery from surgical intervention for reconstructive or health-related reasons (e.g. following massive burns, cancer-related forms of mutilation, etc.). The term also appears to distinguish cosmetic surgery from apparently involuntary and more pathologically transforming forms of intervention in the bodies of young girls in the form of, for example, foot-binding or extensive genital mutilation.[14] But I believe that this does not exhaust the meaning of the term "elective" and that the term performs a seductive role in facilitating the ideological camouflage of the *absence of choice*. Similarly, I believe that the word "cosmetic" serves an ideological function in hiding the fact that the changes are *noncosmetic*: they involve lengthy periods of pain, are permanent, and result in irreversibly alienating metamorphoses such as the appearance of youth on an aging body.

In order to illuminate the paradox of choice involved here, I wish to draw an analogy from the literature on reproductive technology. In the case of reproductive self-determination, technology has been hailed as increasing the range of women's choices in an absolute kind of way. It cannot be denied that due to the advances in various reproductive technologies, especially IVF and embryo freezing, along with various advances in fetology and fetal surgery, there are now women with healthy children who previously would not have had children. Nevertheless, there are two important ideological, choice-diminishing dynamics at work that affect women's choices in the area of the new reproductive technologies. These dynamics are also at work in the area of cosmetic surgery.

The first of these is the *pressure to achieve perfection through technology*, signaled by the rise of new forms of eugenicist thinking. More profoundly than ever before, contemporary eugenicists stigmatize potential and existing disabled babies, children, and adults. More and more frequently, benevolently phrased eugenicist pressures are forcing women to choose to submit to a battery of prenatal diagnostic tests and extensive fetal monitoring in the name of producing "perfect (white) babies." As more and more reproductive technologies and tests are invented (and "perfected" in and on the bodies of fertile women), partners, parents, family, obstetricians, and other experts on fertility pressure women to submit to this technology in the name of "maximized choice" and "responsible motherhood." As Achilles (1988), Beck-Gernsheim (1989), Rothman (1984), Morgan (1989) and others have argued, women are being subjected to increasingly intense forms of coercion, a fact that is signaled by the intensifying *lack of freedom* felt by women to refuse to use the technology if they are pregnant and the technology is available.

The second important ideological dynamic is *the double-pathologizing of women's bodies*. The history of Western science and Western medical practice is not altogether a positive one for women. As voluminous documentation has shown, cell biologists, endocrinologists, anatomists, sociobiologists, gynecologists, obstetricians, psychiatrists, surgeons, and other scientists have assumed, hypothesized, or "demonstrated" that women's bodies are generally inferior, deformed, imperfect, and/or infantile. Medical practitioners have often treated women accordingly. Until the rise of the new reproductive technologies, however, women's reproductive capacities and processes were regarded as definitional of normal womanhood and normal human reproduction. No longer is that the case. As Corea (1985) and others have so amply demonstrated, profoundly misogynist beliefs and attitudes are a central part of the ideological motivation for the technical development of devices for completely extrauterine fetal development. Women's wombs are coming to be seen as "dark prisons." Women are viewed as threatening irresponsible agents who live in a necessarily antagonistic relationship with the fetus. And women's bodies in general are coming to be viewed as high-risk milieus since fetal development cannot be continuously monitored and controlled in order to guarantee the best possible "fetal outcome" (particularly where middle- and upper-class white babies are concerned).

Increasingly, "fully responsible motherhood" is coming to be defined in techno-logy-dependent terms and, in a larger cultural context of selective obligatory maternity, more and more women are "choosing to act" in accord with technological imperatives prior to conception, through conception, through maternity, and through birthing itself. Whether this is, then, a situation of increased choice is at the very least highly contestable. Moreover, in a larger ideological context of obligatory and "controlled" motherhood, I am reluctant simply to accept the reports of the technologists and fertility experts that their patients "want access" to the technology as a sufficient condition for demonstrating purely voluntary choice.[15]

A similar argument can be made regarding the significance of the pressure to be beautiful in relation to the allegedly voluntary nature of "electing" to undergo cosmetic surgery. It is clear that pressure to use this technology is on the increase. Cosmetic surgeons report on the wide range of clients who buy their services, pitch their advertising to a large audience through the use of the media, and encourage women to think, metaphorically, in terms of the seemingly trivial "nips" and "tucks" that will transform their lives. As cosmetic surgery becomes increasingly normalized through the concept of the female "make-over" that is translated into columns and articles in the print media or made into nationwide television shows directed at female viewers, as the "success stories" are invited on to talk shows along with their "makers," and as surgically transformed women win the Miss America pageants, women who refuse to submit to the knives and to the needles, to the anesthetics and the bandages, will come to be seen as deviant in one way or another. Women who refuse to use these technologies are already becoming stigmatized as "unliberated," "not caring about their appearance" (a sign of disturbed gender identity and low self-esteem according to various health-care professionals), as "refusing to be all that they could be" or as "granola-heads."

And as more and more success comes to those who do "care about themselves" in this technological fashion, more coercive dimensions enter the scene. In the past, only those women who were perceived to be *naturally* beautiful (or rendered beautiful through relatively conservative superficial artifice) had access to forms of power and economic social mobility closed off to women regarded as plain or ugly or old. But now womanly beauty is becoming technologically achievable, a commodity for which each and every woman can, in principle, sacrifice if she is to survive and succeed in the world, particularly in industrialized Western countries. Now tech-nology is making obligatory the appearance of youth and the reality of "beauty" for every woman who can afford it. Natural destiny is being supplanted by technologic-ally grounded coercion, and the coercion is camouflaged by the language of choice, fulfillment, and liberation.

Similarly, we find the dynamic of the double-pathologizing of the normal and of the ordinary at work here. In the technical and popular literature on cosmetic surgery, what have previously been described as *normal* variations of female bodily shapes or described in the relatively innocuous language of "problem areas," are increasingly being described as "deformities," "ugly protrusions," "inadequate breasts," and "unsightly concentrations of fat cells" – a litany of descriptions designed to intensify feelings of disgust, shame, and relief at the possibility of recourse for these "deformities." Cosmetic surgery promises virtually all women the creation of beautiful, youthful-appearing bodies. As a consequence, more and more women will be labeled "ugly" and "old" in relation to this more select population of surgically created beautiful faces and bodies that have been contoured and augmented, lifted and tucked into a state of achieved feminine excellence. I suspect that the naturally "given," so to speak, will increasingly come to be seen as the technologically "primitive"; the "ordinary" will come to be perceived and evaluated as the "ugly." Here, then, is the *third paradox*: that the technological beauty imperative and the pathological inversion of the normal are coercing more and more women to "choose" cosmetic surgery.

## Are there any politically correct feminist responses to cosmetic surgery?

Attempting to answer this question is rather like venturing forth into political quicksand. Nevertheless, I will discuss two very different sorts of responses that strike me as having certain plausibility: the response of refusal and the response of appropriation.[16] I regard both of these as utopian in nature.

### The response of refusal

In her witty and subversive parable, *The Life and Loves of a She-Devil*, Fay Weldon puts the following thoughts into the mind of the cosmetic surgeon whose services have been bought by the protagonist, "Miss Hunter," for her own plans for revenge:

> He was her Pygmalion, but she would not depend upon him, or admire him, or be grateful. He was accustomed to being loved by the women of his own construction. A soft sigh of adoration would follow him down the corridors as he paced them, visiting here, blessing there, promising a future, regretting a past: cushioning his footfall, and his image of himself. But no soft breathings came from Miss Hunter. [He adds, ominously,]...he would bring her to it.                    (Weldon, 1983: 215–16)

But Miss Hunter continues to refuse, and so will many feminist women. The response of refusal can be recognizably feminist at both an individual and a collective level. It results from understanding the nature of the risks involved – those having to do with the surgical procedures and those related to a potential loss of embodied personal integrity in a patriarchal context. And it results from understanding the conceptual shifts involved in the political technologizing of women's bodies and contextualizing them so that their oppressive consequences are evident precisely as they open up more "choices" to women. "Understanding" and "contextualizing" here mean seeing clearly the ideological biases that frame the material and cultural world in which cosmetic surgeons practice, a world that contains racist, anti-Semitic, eugenicist, and ageist dimensions of oppression, forms of oppression to which current practices in cosmetic surgery often contribute.

The response of refusal also speaks to the collective power of women as consumers to affect market conditions. If refusal is practiced on a large scale, cosmetic surgeons who are busy producing new faces for the "holiday season" and new bellies for the "winter trips to the Caribbean" will find few buyers of their services. Cosmetic surgeons who consider themselves body designers and regard women's skin as a kind of magical fabric to be draped, cut, layered, and designer-labeled, may have to forgo the esthetician's ambitions that occasion the remark that "the sculpting of human flesh can never be an exact art" (Silver, 1989). They may, instead, (re)turn their expertise to the victims in the intensive care burn unit and to the crippled limbs and joints of arthritic women. This might well have the consequence of (re)converting those surgeons into healers.

Although it may be relatively easy for some individual women to refuse cosmetic surgery even when they have access to the means, one deep, morally significant facet of the response of refusal is to try to understand and to care about individual women who do choose to undergo cosmetic surgery. It may well be that one explanation for why a woman is willing to subject herself to surgical procedures, anesthetics, post-operative drugs, predicted and lengthy pain, and possible "side-effects" that might include her own death is that her access to other forms of power and empowerment are or appear to be so limited that cosmetic surgery is the primary domain in which she can experience some semblance of self-determination. Lakoff and Scherr comment on this:

> No responsible doctor would advise a drug, or a procedure, whose clearly demonstrated benefits do not considerably out-weigh its risks, so that a health-threatening drug is not prescribed responsibly except to remedy a life-threatening condition. But equally noxious drugs and procedures are medically sanctioned merely to "cure" moderate overweight or flatchestedness – hardly life-threatening ailments... The only way to understand the situation is to agree that those conditions *are*, in fact, perceived as life-threatening, so dangerous that seriously damaging interventions are justified, any risk worth taking, to alleviate them.                    (Lakoff and Scherr, 1984: 165–6)

Choosing an artificial and technologically designed creation of youthful beauty may not only be necessary to an individual woman's material, economic, and social survival. It may also be the way that she is able to choose, to elect a kind of subjective transcendence against a backdrop of constraint, limitation, and imman-ence (in Beauvoir's sense of this term).

As a feminist response, individual and collective refusal may not be easy. As Bartky, I, and others have tried to argue, it is crucial to understand the central role that socially sanctioned and socially constructed femininity plays in a male supremacist, heterosexist society. And it is essential not to underestimate the gender-constituting and identity-confirming role that femininity plays in bringing woman-as-subject into existence while simultaneously creating her as patriarchally defined object (Bartky, 1988; Morgan, 1986). In these circumstances, refusal may be akin to a kind of death, to a kind of renunciation of the only kind of life-conferring choices and competencies to which a woman may have access. And, under those circumstances, it may not be possible for her to register her resistance in the form of refusal. The best one can hope for is a heightened sense of the nature of the multiple double-binds and compromises that permeate the lives of virtually all women and are accentuated by the cosmetic surgery culture.

As a final comment, it is worth remarking that although the response of refusal has a kind of purity to recommend it, it is unlikely to have much impact in the current ideological and cultural climate. In just one year, the number of breast augmentations has risen 32 percent; eye tucks have increased 31 percent; nose jobs have increased 30 percent; face lifts have increased 39 percent; and liposuction and other forms of "body contouring" have become the most popular form of cosmetic surgery ("New bodies for sale," 1985). Cosmetic surgeons are deluged with demands, and research in the field is increasing at such a rapid pace that every area of the human body is seen as open to metamorphosis. Clearly the knives, the needles, the cannulas, and the drugs are exercising a greater and greater allure.

Nevertheless, the political significance of the response of refusal should not be underestimated in the lives of individual women since achieved obligatory femininity is a burden borne by virtually all women. And this response is one way of eliminating many of the attendant harms while simultaneously identifying the ways that the technological beauty imperative increasingly pervades our lives.

## The response of appropriation

In their insightful essay, "The feminine body and feminist politics," Brown and Adams remark that "since the body is seen as the site of *action*, its investigation appears to combine what are otherwise characterized as discrete sites, the theoretical and the political, in an original unity" (Brown and Adams, 1979: 35). Rather than viewing the womanly/technologized body as a site of political refusal, the response of appropriation views it as the site for feminist action through transformation, appropriation, parody, and protest. This response grows out of that historical and often radical feminist tradition that regards deliberate mimicry, alternative valorization, hyperbolic appropriation, street theater, counterguerrilla tactics, destabilization, and redeployment as legitimate feminist politics. Here I am proposing a version of what Judith Butler regards as "Femininity politics" and what she calls "Gender performatives." The contemporary feminist guerrilla theater group Ladies Against Women demonstrates the power of this kind of response. In addition to expressing outrage and moral revulsion at the biased dimensions of contemporary cosmetic surgery, the response of appropriation targets them for moral and political purposes.

However, instead of mourning the temporal and carnal alienation resulting from the shame and guilt experienced prior to surgery and from the experience of loss of identity following surgery, the feminist theorist using the response of appropriation points out (like postmodernists) that these emotional experiences simply demonstrate the ubiquitous instability of consciousness itself, that this is simply a more vivid lived instance of the deeper instability that is characteristic of *all* human subjectivity. Along with feeling apprehension about the appropriation of organic processes and bodies by technology, what this feminist theorist might well say is that the technologies are simply revealing what is true for *all* embodied subjects living in cultures, namely, that *all* human bodies are, and always have been, dialectically created artifacts (Lowe, 1982; Haraway, 1978, 1989). What the technologies are revealing is that women's bodies, in particular, can be and are read as especially saturated cultural artifacts and signifiers by phenomenologically oriented anthropologists and forensic archeologists (even if they have never heard about Derrida or postmodernism). Finally, present practices in cosmetic surgery also provide an extremely public and quantified reckoning of the cost of "beauty," thereby demonstrating how both the processes and the final product are part of a larger nexus of women's commodification. Since such lessons are not always taught so easily or in such transparent form, this feminist theorist may well celebrate the critical feminist ideological potential of cosmetic surgery.

Rather than agreeing that participation in cosmetic surgery and its ruling ideology will necessarily result in further colonization and victimization of women, this feminist strategy advocates appropriating the expertise and technology for feminist ends. One advantage of the response of appropriation is that it does not recommend involvement in forms of technology that clearly have disabling and dire outcomes for the deeper feminist project of engaging "in the historical, political, and theoretical process of constituting ourselves as subjects as well as objects of history" (Hartsock,

1990: 170).[17] Women who are increasingly immobilized bodily through physical weakness, passivity, withdrawal, and domestic sequestration in situations of hysteria, agoraphobia, and anorexia cannot possibly engage in radical gender performatives of an active public sort or in other acts by which the feminist subject is robustly constituted. In contrast, healthy women who have a feminist understanding of cosmetic surgery are in a situation to deploy cosmetic surgery in the name of its feminist potential for parody and protest.

Working within the creative matrix of ideas provided by Foucault, Kristeva (1982), and Douglas (1966), Judith Butler notes:

> The construction of stable bodily contours relies upon fixed sites of corporeal permeability and impermeability...The deregulation of such (heterosexual) exchanges accordingly disrupts the very boundaries that determine what it is to be a body at all.
>
> (1990: 132–3)

As Butler correctly observes, parody "by itself is not subversive" (139) since it always runs the risk of becoming "domesticated and recirculated as instruments of cultural hegemony." She then goes on to ask, in relation to gender identity and sexuality, what words or performances would

> compel a reconsideration of the *place* and stability of the masculine and the feminine? And what kind of gender performance will enact and reveal the performativity of gender itself in a way that destabilizes the naturalized categories of identity and desire?
>
> (Butler, 1990: 139)

We might, in parallel fashion, ask what sorts of performances would sufficiently destabilize the norms of femininity, what sorts of performances will sufficiently expose the truth of the slogan "Beauty is always made, not born." In response I suggest two performance-oriented forms of revolt.

The first form of revolt involves revalorizing the domain of the "ugly" and all that is associated with it. Although one might argue that the notion of the "ugly" is parasitic on that of "beauty," this is not entirely true since the ugly is also contrasted with the plain and the ordinary, so that we are not even at the outset constrained by binary oppositions. The ugly, even in a beauty-oriented culture, has always held its own fascination, its own particular kind of splendor. Feminists can use that and explore it in ways that might be integrated with a revalorization of being old, thus simultaneously attacking the ageist dimension of the reigning ideology. Rather than being the "culturally enmired subjects" of Butler's analysis, women might constitute themselves as culturally liberated subjects through public participation in Ms Ugly Canada/America/Universe/Cosmos pageants *and use the technology of cosmetic surgery to do so*.

Contemplating this form of revolt as a kind of imaginary model of political action is one thing; actually altering our bodies is another matter altogether. And the reader may well share the sentiments of one reviewer of this paper who asked: "Having oneself surgically mutilated in order to prove a point? Isn't this going too far?" I don't know the answer to that question. If we cringe from contemplating this alternative, this may, in fact, testify (so to speak) to the hold that the beauty imperative has on our imagination and our bodies. If we recoil from *this* lived alteration of the contours of our bodies and regard it as "mutilation," then so, too, ought we to shirk from contemplation of the cosmetic surgeons who de-skin and alter the contours of women's bodies so that we become more and more like athletic or emaciated (depending on what's in vogue) mannequins with large breasts in the shop windows of modern patriarchal culture. In what sense are these not equivalent mutilations?

What this feminist performative would require would be not only genuine celebration of but *actual* participation in the fleshly mutations needed to produce what the culture constitutes as "ugly" so as to destabilize the "beautiful" and expose its technologically and culturally constitutive origin and its political consequences. Bleaching one's hair white and applying wrinkle-inducing "wrinkle creams," having one's face and breasts surgically pulled down (rather than lifted), and having wrinkles sewn and carved into one's skin might also be seen as destabilizing actions with respect to aging. And analogous actions might be taken to undermine the "lighter is better" aspect of racist norms of feminine appearance as they affect women of color.

A second performative form of revolt could involve exploring the commodification aspect of cosmetic surgery. One might, for example, envision a set of "Beautiful Body Boutique" franchises, responsive to the particular "needs" of a given community. Here one could advertise and sell a whole range of bodily contours; a variety of metric containers of freeze-dried fat cells for fat implantation and transplant; "body configuration" software for computers; sewing kits of needles, knives, and painkillers; and "skin-Velcro" that could be matched to fit and drape the consumer's body; variously-sized sets of magnetically attachable breasts complete with discrete nipple pumps; and other inflation devices carefully modulated according to bodily aroma and state of arousal. Parallel to the current marketing strategies for cosmetic breast surgeries,[18] commercial protest booths, complete with "before and after" surgical make-over displays for penises, entitled "The penis you were always meant to have" could be set up at various medical conventions and health fairs; demonstrations could take place outside the clinics, hotels, and spas of particularly eminent cosmetic surgeons – the possibilities here are endless. Again, if this ghoulish array offends, angers, or shocks the reader, this may well be an indication of the extent to which the ideology of compulsory beauty has anesthetized our sensibility in the reverse direction, resulting in the domesticating of the procedures and products of the cosmetic surgery industry.

In appropriating these forms of revolt, women might well accomplish the following: acquire expertise (either in fact or in symbolic form) of cosmetic surgery to challenge the coercive norms of youth and beauty, undermine the power dynamic built into the dependence on surgical experts who define themselves as estheticians of women's bodies, demonstrate the radical malleability of the cultural commodification of women's bodies, and make publicly explicit the political role that technology can play in the construction of the feminine in women's flesh.

## Conclusion

I have characterized both these feminist forms of response as utopian in nature. What I mean by "utopian" is that these responses are unlikely to occur on a large scale even though they may have a kind of ideal desirability. In any culture that defines femininity in terms of submission to men, that makes the achievement of femininity (however culturally specific) in appearance, gesture, movement, voice, bodily contours, aspirations, values, and political behavior obligatory of any woman who will be allowed to be loved or hired or promoted or elected or simply allowed to live, and in any culture that increasingly requires women to purchase femininity through submission to cosmetic surgeons and their magic knives, refusal and revolt exact a high price. I live in such a culture.

## Notes

Many thanks to the members of the Canadian Society for Women in Philosophy for their critical feedback, especially my commentator, Karen Weisbaum, who pointed out how strongly visualist the cosmetic surgery culture is. I am particularly grateful to Sarah Lucia Hoagland, keynote speaker at the 1990 C-SWIP conference, who remarked at my session, "I think this is all wrong." Her comment sent me back to the text to rethink it in a serious way. Thanks also to the two anonymous *Hypatia* reviewers for their frank, helpful, and supportive response to an earlier version of this paper.

1  This paper addresses only the issues generated out of *elective* cosmetic surgery which is sharply distinguished by practitioners, patients, and insurance plans from reconstructive cosmetic surgery which is usually performed in relation to some trauma or is viewed as necessary in relation to some pressing health care concern. This is not to say that the distinction is always clear in practice.

2  I regard the *Hastings Center Report* and *Philosophy and Medicine* as the discipline-establishing journals in mainstream bioethics. The feminist literature to which I am referring includes the double special issue of *Hypatia*, 1989 (vol. 4, nos. 2 and 3), the anthology *Healing Technology* (Ratcliff, 1989), and the entire journal series *Women and Health* and *Women and Therapy* through 1990. With the exception of a paper by Kathy Davis on this topic which has just appeared (1991) the only discussions that *do* exist discuss the case of Quasimodo, the Hunchback of Notre Dame!

3  For a thorough account of how anatomical science has conceptualized and depicted the ideal female skeleton and morphology, see Russett's *Sexual Science: The Victorian Construction of Womanhood* (1989) and Schiebinger's *The Mind Has No Sex? Women in the Origins of Modern Science* (1989), especially the chapter titled "More than skin deep: the scientific search for sexual difference."

4  Although the particular kind of machine selected as paradigmatic of the human body has shifted from clocks to hydraulics to thermodynamics and now to information-processing models, the Cartesian machine-modeling of the body continues to dominate and is, obviously, the one most congenial to the correlative technologizing of the human body, which literally metamorphoses the body into a machine.

5  I say "virtually all women" because there is now a nascent literature on the subject of fat oppression and body image as it affects lesbians. For a perceptive article on this subject, see Dworkin (1989). I am, of course, not suggesting that compulsory heterosexuality and obligatory maternity affect all women equally. Clearly women who are regarded as "deviant" in some respect or other – because they are lesbian or women with disabilities or "too old" or poor or of the "wrong race" – are under enormous pressure from the dominant culture *not* to bear children, but this, too, is an aspect of patriarchal pronatalism.

6  The desire to subordinate our bodies to some ideal that involves bringing the body under control is deeply felt by many contemporary women (apart from any religious legacy of asceticism). As Bartky (1988) and Bordo (1985; 1989a; 1989b) have noted, this is an aspect of the disembodying desires of anorexic women and women who "pump iron." In the area of cosmetic surgery, this control is mediated by the technology and expertise of the surgeons, but the theme is continually articulated.

7  A similar point regarding femininity is made by Sandra Bartky (1988) in her discussion of "feminine discipline." She remarks that women will resist the dismantling of the disciplines of femininity because, at a very deep level, it would involve a radical alteration of what she calls our "informal social ontology":

> To have a body felt to be "feminine" – a body socially constructed through the appropriate practices – is in most cases crucial to a woman's sense of herself as female

and, since persons currently can *be* only as male or female, to her sense of herself as an existing individual.... The radical feminist critique of femininity, then, may pose a threat not only to a woman's sense of her own identity and desirability but to the very structure of her social universe.                                           (Bartky, 1988, 78)

8   I view this as a recognizably *political* metamorphosis because forensic cosmetic surgeons and social archaeologists will be needed to determine the actual age and earlier appearance of women in cases where identification is called for on the basic of existing carnal data. See Griffin's (1978) poignant description in "The anatomy lesson" for a reconstruction of the life and circumstances of a dead mother from just such carnal evidence. As we more and more profoundly artifactualize our own bodies, we become more sophisticated archaeological repositories and records that both signify and symbolize our culture.

9   For both documentation and analysis of this claim, see Bartky (1988), Bordo (1985; 1989a; 1989b), and Rich (1980).

10  I intend to use "given" here in a relative and political sense. I don't believe that the notion that biology is somehow "given" and culture is just "added on" is a tenable one. I believe that we are intimately and inextricably encultured and embodied, so that a reductionist move in either direction is doomed to failure. For a persuasive analysis of this thesis, see Lowe (1982) and Haraway (1978; 1989). For a variety of political analyses of the "given" as primitive, see Marge Piercy's poem "Right to life" (1980), Morgan (1989), and Murphy (1984).

11  Although I am cognizant of the fact that many women are entering medical school, the available literature is preponderantly authored by men most of whom, I would infer, are white, given the general demographics of specializations in medical school. I also stress the whiteness here to emphasize the extent to which white norms of beauty dominate the field. I think of these surgeons as akin to "fairy godfathers" to underscore the role they are asked to play to "correct," "improve," or "render beautiful" what girls and women have inherited from their mothers, who can only make recommendations at the level of artifice, not artifact.

12  Space does not permit development of this theme on an international scale but it is important to note the extent to which pharmaceutical "dumping" is taking place in the so-called "developing countries" under the ideological camouflage of "population control and family planning." See Hartman (1987) for a thorough and persuasive analysis of the exploitative nature of this practice.

13  The extent to which ableist bias is at work in this area was brought home to me by two quotations cited by a woman with a disability. She discusses two guests on a television show. One was "a poised, intelligent young woman who'd been rejected as a contestant for the Miss Toronto title. She is a paraplegic. The organizers' lame excuse for disqualifying her: 'We couldn't fit the choreography around you.' Another guest was a former executive of the Miss Universe contest. He declared, 'Her participation in a beauty contest would be like having a blind man compete in a shooting match'" (Matthews 1985).

14  It is important here to guard against facile and ethnocentric assumptions about beauty rituals and mutilation. See Lakoff and Scherr (1984) for an analysis of the relativity of these labels and for important insights about the fact that use of the term "mutilation" almost always signals a distancing from and reinforcement of a sense of cultural superiority in the speaker who uses it to denounce what other cultures do in contrast to "our culture."

15  For the most sustained and theoretically sophisticated analysis of pronatalism operating in the context of industrialized capitalism, see Gimenez (1984). Gimenez restricts her discussion to working-class women but, unfortunately, doesn't develop a more differentiated grid of pro-natalist and antinatalist pressures within that economic and social group. For example, in Quebec there are strong pressures on Francophone working class women to reproduce, while there is selective pressure against Anglophone and immigrant working women bearing children. Nevertheless, Gimenez's account demonstrates the systemic importance of pronatalism in many women's lives.

16  One possible feminist response (that, thankfully, appears to go in *and* out of vogue) is that of feminist fascism, which insists on a certain particular and quite narrow range of embodiment and appearance as the only range that is politically correct for a feminist. Often feminist fascism sanctions the use of informal but very powerful feminist "embodiment police," who feel entitled to identify and denounce various deviations from this normative range. I find this

feminist political stance incompatible with any movement I would regard as liberatory for women and here I admit that I side with feminist liberals who say that "the presumption must be on the side of freedom" (Warren, 1985) and see that as the lesser of two evils.

17  In recommending various forms of appropriation of the practices and dominant ideology surrounding cosmetic surgery, I think it important to distinguish this set of disciplinary practices from those forms of simultaneous Retreat-and-Protest that Susan Bordo (1989a: 20) so insightfully discusses in "The body and the reproduction of femininity": hysteria, agoraphobia, and anorexia. What cosmetic surgery shares with these gestures is what Bordo remarks upon, namely, the fact that they may be "viewed as a surface on which conventional constructions of femininity are exposed starkly to view, through their inscription in extreme or hyperliteral form." What is different, I suggest, is that although submitting to the procedures of cosmetic surgery involves pain, risks, undesirable side effects, and living with a heightened form of patriarchal anxiety, it is also fairly clear that, most of the time, the pain and risks are relatively short-term. Furthermore, the outcome often appears to be one that generally enhances women's confidence, confers a sense of well-being, contributes to a greater comfort-ableness in the public domain, and affirms the individual woman as a self-determining and risk-taking individual. All these outcomes are significantly different from what Bordo describes as the "languages of horrible suffering" (Bordo 1989a: 20) expressed by women experiencing hysteria, agoraphobia, and anorexia.

18  A booth of this sort was set up in a prominent location at a large "Today's Woman Fair" at the National Exhibition grounds in Toronto in the summer of 1990. It showed "before" and "after" pictures of women's breasts and advertised itself as "The breasts you were always meant to have." One special feature of the display was a set of photographs showing a woman whose breasts had been "deformed" by nursing but who had finally attained through cosmetic surgery the breasts "she was meant to have had." I am grateful to my colleague June Larkin for the suggestion of the analogous booth.

# References

Achilles, Rona (1988) "What's new about the new reproductive technologies?" Discussion paper: Ontario Advisory Council on the Status of Women. Toronto: Government of Ontario.

Barker-Benfield, G. J. (1976) *The Horrors of the Half-known Life*. New York: Harper and Row.

Bartky, Sandra Lee (1988) "Foucault, femininity, and the modernization of patriarchal power." In *Femininity and Foucault: Reflections of Resistance*. Irene Diamond and Lee Quinby, eds. Boston: Northeastern University Press.

Beck-Gernsheim, Elisabeth (1989) "From the pill to test-tube babies: new options, new pressures in reproductive behavior." In *Healing Technology: Feminist Perspectives*. Kathryn Strother Ratcliff, ed. Ann Arbor: University of Michigan Press.

Berger, John (1972) *Ways of Seeing*. New York: Penguin Books.

Bordo, Susan R. (1985) "Anorexia nervosa: psychopathology as the crystallization of culture." *The Philosophical Forum* 2 (Winter): 73–103.

Bordo, Susan R. (1989a) "The body and the reproduction of femininity: a feminist appropriation of Foucault." In *Gender/Body/Knowledge: Feminist Reconstructions of Being and Knowing*. Alison Jaggar and Susan Bordo, eds. New Brunswick, NJ: Rutgers University Press.

Bordo, Susan R. (1989b) "Reading the slender body." In *Women, Science and the Body Politic: Discourses and Representations*. Mary Jacobus, Evelyn Fox Keller and Sally Shuttleworth, eds. New York: Methuen.

Brown, Beverley and Parveen Adams (1979) "The feminine body and feminist politics." *M/F* 3: 35–50.

Brownmiller, Susan (1984) *Femininity*. New York: Simon and Schuster.

Burk, J., S. L. Zelen and E. O. Terena (1985) "More than skin deep: a self-consistency approach to the psychology of cosmetic surgery." *Plastic and Reconstructive Surgery* 6(2): 270–80.

Butler, Judith (1990) *Gender Trouble: Feminism and the Subversion of Identity*. New York: Routledge.

"Changing faces" (1989) *Toronto Star*. May 25.

"Computer used to pick hairstyles" (1989) *Globe and Mail*.

Corea, Gena (1985) *The Mother Machine*. New York: Harper and Row.

"Cosmetic surgery for the holidays" (1985) *Sheboygan Press*. New York Times News Service.

Davis, Kathy (1991) "Remaking the she-devil: a critical look at feminist approaches to beauty." *Hypatia* 6(2): 21–43.

Diamond, Irene and Lee Quinby, eds. (1988) *Feminism and Foucault: Reflections on Resistance*. Boston: Northeastern University Press.

Douglas, Mary (1966) *Purity and Danger*. London: Routledge and Kegan Paul; New York: Praeger.

Dworkin, Sari (1989) "Not in man's image: lesbians and the cultural oppression of body image." *Women and Therapy* 8(1, 2): 27–39.

Easlea, Brian (1981) *Science and Sexual Oppression: Patriarchy's Confrontation with Woman and Nature*. London: Weidenfeld and Nicolson.

"Facial regeneration" (1990) *Health: A Community Education Service of the Froedtert Memorial Lutheran Hospital*. Supplement to *Milwaukee Journal*, August 26.

"Falling in love again" (1990) *Toronto Star*. July 23.

Foucault, Michel (1979) *Discipline and Punish: The Birth of the Prison*. Alan Sheridan, trans. New York: Pantheon.

Foucault, Michel (1988) "Technologies of the self: the political technology of the individual." In *The Technologies of the Self*. Luther H. Martin, Huck Gutman and Patrick Hutton, eds. Amherst: University of Massachusetts Press.

Fraser, Nancy (1989) *Unruly Practices: Power, Discourse, and Gender in Contemporary Social Theory*. Minneapolis: University of Minnesota Press.

Gimenez, Martha (1984) "Feminism, pronatalism, and motherhood." In *Mothering: Essays in Feminist Theory*. Joyce Trebilcot, ed. Totowa, NJ: Rowman and Allenheld.

Goodman, Ellen (1989) "A plastic pageant." *Boston Globe*. September 19.

Griffin, Susan (1978) "The anatomy lesson." In *Woman and Nature: The Roaring Inside her*. New York: Harper and Row.

Haraway, Donna (1978) "Animal sociology and a natural economy of the body politic," Parts I, II. *Signs: Journal of Women in Culture and Society* 4(1): 21–60.

Haraway, Donna (1989) *Primate Visions*. New York: Routledge.

Hartman, Betsy (1987) *Reproductive Rights and Wrongs: The Global Politics of Population Control and Contraceptive Choice*. New York: Harper and Row.

Hartsock, Nancy (1990) "Foucault on power: A theory for women?" In *Feminism/Postmodernism*. Linda Nicholson, ed. New York: Routledge.

Haug, Frigga, ed. (1987) *Female Sexualization: A Collective Work of Memory*. Erica Carter, trans. London: Verso.

Hirshson, Paul (1987) "New wrinkles in plastic surgery: an update on the search for perfection." *Boston Globe Sunday Magazine*. May 24.

Holmes, Helen Bequaert and Laura Purdy, eds. (1989) *Hypatia* Special Issues on Feminist Ethics and Medicine 4(2, 3).

"Implants hide tumors in breasts, study says" (1988) *Toronto Star*. July 29. Summarized from article in *Journal of the American Medical Association* July 8, 1988.

Jaggar, Alison and Susan R. Bordo, eds. (1989) *Gender/Body/Knowledge: Feminist Reconstructions of Being and Knowing*. New Brunswick, NJ: Rutgers University Press.

Jonas, Hans (1979) "Toward a philosophy of technology." *Hastings Center Report* 9, 1 (February): 34–43.

Kristeva, Julia (1982) *The Powers of Horror: An Essay on Abjection*. Leon Roudiez, trans. New York: Columbia University Press.

Lakoff, Robin Tolmach and Raquel Scherr (1984) *Face Value: The Politics of Beauty*. Boston: Routledge and Kegan Paul.

"Long, strong, perfect nails usually not nature's own" (1988) *Toronto Star*. August 18.

"Looking for Mr Beautiful" (1990) *Boston Globe*. May 7.

Lowe, Marion (1982) "The dialectic of biology and culture." In *Biological Woman: The Convenient Myth*. Ruth Hubbard, Mary Sue Henifin, and Barbara Fried, eds. Cambridge, MA: Schenkman.

Luria, Gina and Virginia Tiger (1976) *Everywoman*. New York: Random House.

McCabe, Nora (1990) "Cosmetic solutions." *Homemaker Magazine* (September): 38–46.

"Madonna passionate about fitness" (1990) *Toronto Star*. August 16.

Markovic, Mihailo (1976) "Women's liberation and human emancipation." In *Women and Philosophy: Toward a Theory of Liberation*. Carol Gould and Marx Wartofsky, eds. New York: Capricorn Books.

Matthews, Gwyneth Ferguson (1985) "Mirror, mirror: self-image and disabled women." *Women and Disability: Resources for Feminist Research* 14(1): 47–50.

Mies, Maria (1988) "From the individual to the dividual: in the supermarket of 'reproductive alternatives.'" *Reproductive and Genetic Engineering* 1(3): 225–37.

Morgan, Kathryn Pauly (1986) "Romantic love, altruism, and self-respect: an analysis of Simone De Beauvoir." *Hypatia* 1(1): 117–48.

Morgan, Kathyn Pauly (1987) "Women and moral madness." In *Science, Morality and Feminist Theory*. Marsha Hanen and Kai Nielsen, eds. Special issue of the *Canadian Journal of Philosophy* supplementary volume 13: 201–226.

Morgan, Kathryn Pauly (1989). "Of woman born: how old-fashioned! New reproductive technologies and women's oppression." In *The Future of Human Reproduction*. Christine Overall, ed. Toronto: The Women's Press.

Murphy, Julie [Julien S] (1984) "Egg farming and women's future." In *Test-tube Women: What Future for Motherhood?* Rita Arditti, Renate Duelli-Klein, and Shelley Minden, eds. Boston: Pandora Press.

"New bodies for sale" (1985) *Newsweek* May 27.

"New profile took 3 years" (1989) *Toronto Star*. May 25.

Osherson, Samuel, and Lorna Amara Singhham (1981) "The machine metaphor in medicine." In *Social Contexts of Health, Illness and Patient Care*. E. Mishler, ed. New York: Cambridge University Press.

Piercy, Marge (1980) "Right to life." In *The Moon is Always Female*. New York: A. Knopf.

"The quest to be a perfect 10" (1990) *Toronto Star*. February 1.

Ratcliff, Hathryn Strother, ed. (1989) *Healing Technology: Feminist Perspectives*. Ann Arbon University of Michigan Press.

Raymond, Janice (1987) Preface to *Man-made Woman*. Gena Corea et al., eds. Bloomington: Indiana University Press.

"Retouching nature's way: is cosmetic surgery worth it?" (1990) *Toronto Star*. February 1.

Rich, Adrienne (1980) "Compulsory heterosexuality and lesbian existence." *Signs: Journal of Women in Culture and Society* 5(4): 631–660.

Rothman, Barbara Katz (1984). "The meanings of choice in reproductive technology." In *Test-tube Women: What Future for Motherhood?*. Rita Arditti, Renate Duelli-Klein, and Shelley Minden, eds. Boston: Pandora Press.

Russett, Cynthia Eagle (1989) *Sexual Science: The Victorian Construction of Womanhood*. Cambridge: Harvard University Press.

Schiebinger, Londa (1989) *The Mind has no Sex? Women in the Origins of Modern Science*. Cambridge: Harvard University Press.

Schoenfielder, Lisa, and Barb Wieser, eds. (1983) *Shadow on a Tightrope: Writings by Women on Fat Oppression*. Iowa City: Aunt Lute Press.

Sherwin, Susan (1984–85) "A feminist approach to ethics." *Dalhousie Review*. 64(4): 704–713.

Sherwin, Susan (1987) "Feminist ethics and in vitro fertilization." In *Science, Morality, and Feminist Theory*. Marcia Hanen and Kai Nielsen, eds. Special issue of *Canadian Journal of Philosophy* Supplementary Volume 13: 265–284.

Sherwin, Susan (1989) "Feminist and medical ethics: two different approaches to contextual ethics." *Hypatia* 4(2): 57–72.

Silver, Harold (1989) "Liposuction isn't for everybody." *Toronto Star*. October 20.

Warren, Mary Anne (1985) *Gendercide: The Implications of Sex Selection*. Totowa, NJ: Rowman and Allenheld.

Warren, Virginia (1989) "Feminist directions in medical ethics." *Hypatia* 4(2): 73–87.

Weldon, Fay (1983) *The Life and Loves of a She-Devil*. London: Coronet Books; New York: Pantheon Books.

Williams, John, M. D. and Jim Williams (1990) "Say it with liposuction." From a press release; reported in *Harper's* (August).

"Woman, 43, dies after cosmetic surgery" (1989) *Toronto Star*. July 7.

# 16
## Virtual Bodies

# Bodies, Virtual Bodies and Technology
## *Don Ihde*

Late twentieth-century "technospeak" includes talk about "VR" [virtual reality] and "RL" [real life] within which there is much speculation about virtual bodies. In what should be recognized by now as a familiar speculative projection, the question is posed as to whether VR will supplant or replace RL. Such techno-worries are not new: in the fifties the question of "artificial intelligence" replacing human intelligence was a publicized popular theme; much earlier Luddite-era worries were about machines replacing humans in the productive process – here, were the AI analog to be retroprojected, one might rephrase the issue as machine muscle replacing human muscle. And I even remember a worry during the early days of Masters and Johnson's sexuality investigations when a colleague of mine wondered whether the male member might not be replaced by sophisticated vibrators.

I cite these techno-worries because, not only do they reoccur with each new advance, but because the success or failure of the pattern projected often remains ambiguous. For the most part, male members have not been replaced, although the increasingly sophisticated techniques of artificial insemination, stem sperm cell interspecies implantation, do widen the gap between sex-procreation possibilities and other non-reproductive sexual activity. And the machine-muscle replacement of much labor has occurred in many areas of production, so long that is, as the process is one designed within a closed system (robotics); whereas AI seems reduced to indirect applications, again within closed game situations (such as chess playing), rather than open context, lifeworld situations. Neither muscle or mind has reached out into the open world except in human-technology symbiotic forms. In the cases of human-technology symbiotics, both mind and muscle have transformed our worlds. But the worry over VR "replacing" RL also fits into this history of techno-worries, and it begins with the standard form of replacement worry.

In this essay, I wish to address the themes of virtual bodies in relation to 'lived' bodies (in the phenomenological and Merleau-Pontean senses) and the roles which are played by the technologies which relate to virtual and lived bodies. By way of setting a context, however, I want to begin with several phenomenological excercises in non-technological examples.

## Non-technological virtuality

In the process of teaching phenomenology, I have always employed thought experiments utilizing "imaginative variations," clearly a Husserlian tactic. One such device which I used for many years was to ask the class (upper division under-graduates) to imagine doing something which they had not in fact done, but would like to do, and then begin a critical phenomenological description of this imagined action.

What emerged as a pattern over many classes and years was that the action frequently, even dominantly, chosen was some variant upon flying, with examples often taken from a parachute jump. When asked to undertake the description, a second set of patterns emerged: the classes usually divided between what I call (after R. D. Laing), an "embodied" and a "disembodied" mode of the parachute jump. The embodied parachutist described take-off, attaining altitude, the leap from the open door to experience the rush of wind in the face, the sense of vertigo felt in the stomach, and the sights of the earth rushing towards one as one fell. The disembod-ied describer sees an airplane take-off, climb, and sees someone (identified with himself or herself) jump from the door and speed towards the earth. Obviously, in these two cases, where one's body is located in the self-identification is a major issue.

A second step in the analysis calls for varying between the two "perspectives." One feature which a phenomenological analysis shows is a variation between what could be called full or multidimensioned experience and a visual objectification of presumed body experience. So, when asked, where does one feel the wind? Or the vertigo in the stomach? Can it be felt "out there" in the disembodied perspective? The answers quickly show a partial primacy to the embodied perspective. One does not feel the wind in the face "out there" or the stomach phenomenon "out there"; indeed, upon being pushed it is interesting to note that disembodied observers admit (usually) that they don't see their own faces in the quasi-other who is identified as themselves. The full, multidimensioned, experience gestalts in the here-body of the embodied perspective, whereas the visual objectification out-there is spectacle-like.

While both perspectives are possible – and I shall show shortly how deeply embedded both perspectives are in our cultural actions – there is a dialectic which can be shown which gives a quasi-primacy to the here-body with respect to full sensory embodiment experience, compared to the quasi-otherness of the disembod-ied perspective which nevertheless is a possible perspective which has its own advantages. But the dialectic is weighted with sensory richness given to and within the here-body perspective – I shall associate this perspective with the "RL body." The partially disembodied or body as quasi-other perspective is already a kind of "virtual body" in a non-technological projection. This form of virtuality is an image-body.

Let us switch for a moment to another popular form of non-technologized virtual body experience. I refer to the much publicized forms of "out-of-body" experiences. Here the describer, perhaps recalling a situation in an emergency room, claims to have left his or her body, looks down upon this previous body from some floating perspective, and describes the activities going on. The floating perspective is usually temporary (how many permanently leave the body can't be known!), and the "out-of-body" experience returns to a later waking up experience "in" one's own body. Phenomenologically, however, this form of experience is parallel to the previously described embodied/disembodied parachute variation, although the popular liter-ature does not recognize this.

In the out-of-body case, the now visually objectified body – the one down there on the operating table as image body – is "identified" with "my body", but under the perspective of not being the "now me" which is implicitly identified with the floating perspective. However, the floating perspective is the "now-me" and the "here-body" which is embodied in the new position. I suspect that an interogator could again note that the multisensory sense of the here-body would locate this in the floating location. The very me/not-me of the body on the table is an indicator of the "virtuality" of the me-as-other-body in this experience.

## The incredible lightness of being (seated/lying)

Let us push the here-body, fully sensory body experience a little more. It is precisely the imaginative situation (the students are seated, not unlike the philosopher's standard position) and the already only quasi-conscious (lying down) positions which make the move to "floating" positions more likely. These are, in other words, already only quasi-active situations. And although the subjects in our two variations are not as pathologically impaired as Merleau-Ponty's Schneider, who cannot "be" his active body, they are far from what some of us call the "sports body" or active body implied as the secret norm of the lived body implicit in *The Phenomenology of Perception*.[1] It is the here-body in action which provides the centered norm of myself-as-body. This is the RL body in contrast to the more inactive or marginal "VR" bodies which make the shift to the quasi-disembodied perspectives possible.

If I am right about the secret norm of a here-body in action, it should also be noted that such a body experience is one which is not simply co-extensive with a body outline or one's "skin." The intentionality of bodily action goes beyond one's bodily limits – but only within a regional, limited range. A good example may be taken from martial arts experience wherein one can "feel" the aimed blows even from behind, and one aims one's own activity beyond any simple now-point. One's "skin" is at best polymorphically ambiguous and, even without material extension, the sense of the here-body exceeds its physical bounds.

A second ambiguity should also be preliminarily noted, as phenomenological literature has long shown: one can simultaneously both experience one's here-body from its inner core, while also having a partial, but only partial, "external" perception. I can see my hands, feet, part of my frontal visible body from the focal point of my vision.

Combining these multistable ambiguities, one can begin to appreciate how complex the issues of virtuality may become. The opening to a sliding perspective from the multidimensioned experience of my here-body towards the image-body perspectives lie within these ambiguities.

## Extending the here-body

Heretofore, my examples have differentiated a here-body from a virtual or image-body as a disembodied "over-there" body. The bistability of these two perspectives may be expanded and made complex in many social and cultural activities. For example, in previous work I have shown how a reading perspective which makes a god's eye view possible, gets worked out within European culture in activities as seemingly distant from bodies in navigational practice. Europeans locate where they are from a disembodied, overhead perspective. Contrarily, the here-body is made central in South Pacific navigational practice which makes all motion and direction relativistically referential to the navigator's here-body ("Tahiti is approaching us as the ocean passes our bow.") But, also, in all these cases I have not included nor attended to any technologies as such. *Technologies can radically transform the situation, including one's sense of one's body.*

This transformation has been descriptively analyzed within classical phenomenology. Heidegger's tool analysis[2] noted that objects, such as hammers, are taken into the ways in which humans project themselves into work practices. In using hammers, the hammer "withdraws" as a separate object and is taken into the action being performed. But, in terms of the language of embodiment, it was Merleau-Ponty who took account of the way in which technologies may be embodied, as in the blind man's cane or the woman's feathered hat. In the first instance, the cane/roadway touch is what the walker experiences – his body is extended through the cane which becomes part of his here-body experience. In the more radical sense of the hat feather, the sense of her here-body – even without a touch – is extended beyond the outline of the wearer's body. In all three of these examples, one's sense of embodiment changes, although in a reduced and focused way – it is a quasi-extension entailing the here-body. The very materiality of the technology allows this extendability. The tactility which may be had through hammers, canes, and feathers is "real" but also less than "naked" in its perceptibility. The hardness – but not the coldness – of the nail is experienced through the hammer; the multidimensional "click" of the sidewalk cement and its textured resistance is felt through the cane – but not its grayness; the very draft of wind in a near miss may be felt through the feather – but the extent of the doorway opening remains opaque in its extent. Each of the missing elements can be filled in only by the full bodily sensory awareness which is part of the ordinary experience of the artifact-user's world.

## Degrees of virtuality

It is in the attempt to overcome these reductions that the newer forms of virtuality take shape. Ultimately, virtual embodiment has as its inner trajectory, to become the perfect simulacrum of full, multisensory bodily action. Once this is discerned, one can easily see how far the technologization of virtual reality has to go.

A brief look at imaging media is instructive here. Early technologies, such as the telephone and the phonograph, or such as still photography followed by motion pictures, were "monosensory" as either audio or visual media. Phenomenologically, however, the experiencer constantly experiences multidimensionally; thus the monosensory quality of these media easily reveal the technological reductions which are simultaneous with the more dramatic amplifications and magnifications which occur within the auditory or visual media. One could not see the caller, nor could one hear the speaker in the silent movie. An early response to this reductive limitation was to make the monosensory dimension richer – silent movies called for more mime, more gestural significations, thus producing a kind of visual exaggeration, while the singer on the phonograph also could exaggerate vocal gesture.

However, a richer technological trajectory for media did not long follow only monosensory beginnings – within a few decades movies (1889) became "talkies" (1927) and the medium became audio-visual. Bidimensional audio-visual media are effectively now the "norm" of many communicative media (cinema, television, camcorders, most multi-media presentations including computers, etc.) The audio-visual has become deeply sedimented in our seeing/hearing and thus is culturally taken-for-granted in our experience. But also this audio-visual plateau has been the norm now for nearly half a century.

Far less success, although again noted from the times of very early media developments, has been attained with respect to tactility, kinesthetic, gustatory, or olfactory dimensions which were noted as possibilities for media. Theaters with shaking floors, "smellovision," have been attempted, but far more dominant are projected synesthetic attempts to induce the multidimensional experience – synesthetic vertigo in cinerama or maxi-theatres, auditory overkill with dolby or sensurround sounds, are the equivalents to early mime and gestural compensations which remain within the possibilities of the audio–visual.

I take account of this recent history (which actually begins at the very end of the nineteenth century, accelerating only in the twentieth) because it relates intimately to technologized attempts at virtual embodiment. Within this history the ambiguity of the embodied/disembodied or here-body/image-body continues. If, for example, we begin with the here-body variant, then one can quickly see that media employ the same perceptual referencing which I noted in Pacific navigation. The "viewer" is actually seated in the theater in a fixed position, but the imaged "world" is then set in motion and referentially aims at the "viewer." The tracks of the roller-coaster slide, as it were, under the viewer's seat, until the apogee is reached, then tilting to show a downwards, vertiginous acceleration, the synesthetic "fall" begins. Here the imaged version of "Tahiti comes to me" is the roller-coaster descent which rushes towards me in screened quasi-realism. In contrast, were one to see a shot of a roller-coaster from "out there" so that one sees the screaming riders, the synesthestic effect either disappears or is muted (occurring if at all in the here-body position). It is the other who is seen to have the vertigo. The virtual "realism" is enhanced when the imaged environment refers back to the seated viewer.

All these effects presuppose the privilege of the mostly motionless (seated) viewer. They are the technological equivalents to the assembly line or other relatively closed system within which the technologies may perform the limited actions which are the machine worlds we know. For the viewer to become an actor – one must move into the equivalent of the screen-theatre environment. This becomes a possible trajectory for an (embodied) virtual body.

Earlier attempts to inject more interactivity may be noted in the range of simulators which originated with military technologies. During the early days of World War II, it was noted that if fighter pilots could somehow survive the first five air battles, their chances of long-term survival became much higher. If, therefore, one could simulate what needed to be known before actual battle, the chances for survival might improve. It was this plan which resulted in the first Link Trainers which allowed dogfight practice to occur inside an early virtual reality situation. The trainer had a projected scene on the cockpit window, the entire trainer moved with the control stick, sounds and as much realism as possible were injected. Today these effects are made highly sophisticated in contemporary military and industrial simulators which are used to train pilots, tank personnel, or drivers. Roadways, runways, unexpected critical situations, all rush towards the participant, (the seated) viewer, with as much realism as the imaging process can summon. Here, though, the situation is much more interactive in that simulation controls call for actual bodily action which itself enhances the synesthetic effect and adds at least restricted tactile-kinesthetic aspects to the experience.

Commercial entertainment applications followed – the video games in parlors or homes, with mostly boys and their dads plugged into projected scenarios of aliens, realistic "Russians" or other enemies which fill virtual reality entertainment tech-nologies. (My son and I both play Flight Simulator, with some interesting differ-ences – we both prefer the Lear Jet as the airplane of choice due to its high maneuverability and capacities which are built into the program [compared to the Cessna or the WWI biplane]. But our attitudes are different – I had a quasi-sweat when I got lost over an Iowa cornfield and ended in a crash. Mark seems to enjoy deliberately smashing into Chicago's tall buildings on take-off, and then repeating, with the disembodied perspective, the scenes of the crash from the quasi-distance of that perspective as the plane parts fall to earth. "Lives," after all, are infinitely repeatable in virtual reality. I wonder if Nietzsche thought of this possibility in his theory of repeatable infinite choices? Or, is the doctrine of eternal recurrence simply an anticipation of video-game culture?)

Yet, phenomenologically, this admittedly more actional technological space is but a small step from previous more passive audio-visual situations. The flyer remains seated and the screen-world backprojects the framed action to the viewer. Action remains minimal in the movement and synesthetic amplification of the body through the "joy stick." It betokens only a small movement into bodily action with minimal kinesthetic and tactile components now enhancing the audio-visual. It's all hand–eye coordination, enhanced in the context of hypergraphics, sound effects, and synesthestic amplification. (We remain far from "virtual food," and as early smello-vision showed, the compressed time-frames of theatres are not enough to remove and add smells in sequence as in the more durational spans of ordinary life.)

In terms of present virtual simulations, we have but one more step to go – the step to the technologically "wired" body cages which include "face sucker" goggles, gloves, and perhaps even strapped-in motion cages as shown in the recent film *Lawnmower Man*. These developments display a slightly different tactic with regard to the here-body referencing previously noted. One of the shortcomings of other simulation forms has to do with the "framing," which has always differentiated the artificiality of the technologically imaged from the wider world. The video-game, even with a very large screen, remains "framed" by the screen. And, while the screen may even surround the viewer in maximal settings, the quasi-depth of the screen remains a detectable film-artifact. Everything is "in front of" the participant. In the tactics of the technological cage, one follows a direction developed earlier in sensory deprivation experiments. One "surrounds" the participant with the tech-nological cocoon which is equivalent to making one's "world" much closer and more encompassing. The mini-TVs up close to the eyes, the body suit, the wired gloves, all enclose the participant in the up–close environment of the technologically encased envelope from the RL world. This enclosure, however, is not neutral nor "trans-parent" – its vestigial presence may produce both a sense of irreality and disorienta-tion, of a kind of claustrophobia which is known to produce nausea in some participants. Again, the effects are similar to those of sensory deprivation experi-ments in the seventies. But whereas the deprivation experiments damped out the body/world differences, the VR version makes the world a hyper-world.

Once again, phenomenologically, the VR cage remains but a degree of virtuality of the open, but framed version in the video-game. It does – so far primitively – introduce tactility and kinesthetic effect into the medium, and thus is a step beyond the merely audio-visual, seated context. But even with this greater degree of actional possibility, most VR programs – except for the most expensive and sophisticated – lack the feedback found in full bodily engagement. Actions taken usually lack the sense of "contact." And the price remains that of closing to a greater degree, the openness of the RL world in order to attain its effect. VR vertigo remains an insulating vertigo. It remains VR "theater." It is, however, a very special kind of theater. Its audience is individual (although there are also settings in which multiple players engage), its world programmed with the usual logic trees of choices (none of which provides the ambiguities or openness of RL) which while complex, do not adapt to learning novel possibilities.

Here we reach one horizon from which the original techno-worry fed. Could VR replace RL? Only if theater could replace actual life. Yet, only the bumpkin rushes to the stage to rescue the maiden from the villain. The late twentieth century is apparently filled with willing bumpkins! Like theater, however, VR developments contain devices which "enhance" and distract from RL contexts.

## Imaging the technologically polymorphic possibilities

Morphing things in the VR "world" and the use of hypergraphic techniques which use bright colors and lighting effects are part of the theatricality of current VR. (It is interesting to note in passing that the contemporary version of the long-standing "automaton worry" of Cartesian philosophy has been changed. The older Cartesian worry was about whether or not we could be deceived by a cleverly contrived robot, a look-alike. The new worry is about whether hyper-reality is such that "reality isn't enough anymore," as my undergraduates say.) Movie versions of VR and other simulations are indicative here: in the film *Lawnmower Man* the eponymous character has a VR sexual encounter with his other, in the movie both he and she are "morphed" into fantastic shapes and interactions – projected in this case as image-bodies in the second perspective for the movie viewers – ending with an imaged Georgia O'Keefe-like "orgasm" climax. In the end, however, how different is this from other movie techniques which add romantic music, off-center shots, and suggestive body-parts? The difference is simply one of non-human morphed shapes and the suggestion that the technologies make hyper-sex different. VR is a latecomer theatrical development which forefronts techno–imaging.

Imaging, now technologically embodied, makes polymorphy – particularly of visual shaping – a forefront phenomenon. I have already noted the morphing of human body shapes in *Lawnmower Man*, but there is a continuum of variations, all of which do different degrees of morphing with respect to the VR/RL portrayal of bodies. *Roger Rabbit* refined older cartoon/human interaction by making the "toon" have a three-dimensional, and thus presumably more "life-like" characteristic for the fictive being. Here the toon/human (image) world is a hybrid. Farther to the "right" and into a kind of presumed "realism", are the newer computer effects which make presumed real entities hyper-real. *Jurassic Park* computer-generates some very life-like dinosaurs, and more recently, *Twister* magnifies tornados into hyperwinds. To the left are the already irreal morphings which either show "realistic" looking oddities such as the parasitic alien animals in *Aliens*, or abstract, evaporative (spiritual?) forms, such as the high speed travel morphing in science fiction – *Stargate*, warp speed in *Star Trek*, etc.

In one sense, "morphing" is more a revival than an innovation. It is a return to pre-modernity in the sets of cultural beliefs that things actually could transmute or "morph." For devils to inhabit human bodies, for human witches to take on animal shapes, for the possibilities of monsters, prodigies, and freaks, all were pre-modern "morphs." Imaging, particularly techno-sophisticated visual imaging, re-invents this polymorphism of bodily possibilities. Its culture is a bricolage, where boundaries and distinctions are blurred, parts interchanged, hybrids produced.

In this context, the body, bodies, are but one target. Morphing, rapid exchange of the embodied and disembodied perspectives, on to the horizons of gender blurring (these are enhanced in the more reductive and still mostly monosensory internet contexts where linguistic morphing is the norm), are all part of the same cultural movement. In one respect all this could be harmless, simply a new variant of ancient fascination with the bizzare and with curiosities. It echoes the earliest history of pre-cinema *camera obscura* theater wherein paying customers would come to see the magic lantern back-projected images of devils and ghosts upon the screen, or perhaps, it even goes so far back as to reach to Plato's pre-cinema cave wherein images of images were the only "realities" for the dwellers prior to Platonic sun therapy.

In each case, however, the illusions are harmless only so long as the experiencer knows the difference between theater and daily life, so long as one living RL does not become bumpkin-like, and take VR as the "real." This would be the Platonic solution. For Plato it was the liberation from the cave and the emergence into sunlight which taught the difference. But in a broader, more phenomenological sense, both RL and VR are part of the Lifeworld and VR is thus both "real" as a positive presence and "part" of RL.

## Virtual bodies as techno-fantasy

I want to conclude this foray into virtual bodies with something of an epistemological moral: VR is a phenomenon which fits neatly into our existential involvements with technologies. Here the question is a deeper one involving our desires and fantasies which get projected into our technologies.

Concerning the existentiality of our technologies, particularly those which implicate embodiment, I have earlier made this point:

> The direction of desire opened by embodied technologies also has its positive and negative thrusts. Instrumentation in the knowledge activities, notably science, is the gradual extension of perception into new realms. The desire is to see, but seeing is seeing through instrumentation. Negatively, the desire for pure transparency is the wish to escape the limitations of the material technology. It is a platonism returned in a new form, the desire to escape the newly extended body of technological engagement. In the wish there remains the contradiction: the user both wants and does not want the technology. The user wants what the technology gives but does not want the limits, the transformations that a technologically extended body implies. There is a fundamental ambivalence toward the very human creation of our own earthly tools.[3]

This contrary desire applies with particular pathos and poignancy to desires and fantasies of body. And whereas the VR/RL distinction gets blurred, seemingly crossed, or fantasized about, there is another aspect of technology/bodies which is more than play, more than theater and ordinary life. That is, of course, the way in which we increasingly literally incorporate (pun is deliberate) technologies.

Prostheses, from the simple tooth crown to an artificial limb, are base level examples. Techno-fantasies romanticize prosthetic amplifications as "bionic" which theatrically are precisely the actualization of the existential contradictions concerning technologies. *Robocop*, *Bionic Man*, *Terminator* all have more powerful than human prostheses, which in fantasy nevertheless function as freely and spontaneously as one's lived body. But actual users of prosthetic devices know better – prostheses are "better" than going without (the tooth, the limb, the hand), but none have the degree of transparent, total "withdrawal" of a tool totally embodied. All remain simply more permanently attached ready-to-hand tools.

Yet, when one's body fails, or is irreparably injured, or parts of it are removed, the prosthesis becomes a viable and helpful compromise. It's just that we apparently can't have both the technological empowerment and the perfect transparency at the same time.

But the more extreme the situation, the stronger the fantasy may become – I close with an actual incident. Some years ago I had a number of discussions with a person I have never met face to face about the fantasized desire on the part of some people who wish to be actually and permanently "wired" to their computers. The closest I came to a full conversation (e-mail was the initial medium), was by telephone, and in the last conversation I wondered why anyone could actually wish for such wiring. My conversant then revealed that he was a severe rheumatoid arthritic – and I understood precisely, because my own mother had had the same disease. Her body had become so sclerotized that she was confined to a wheelchair; to eat someone had to place a spoon into the fixed fingers of her hand; talking, of course, was possible, but had she been able to use a computer she would have had to hunt and peck with a pencil, a letter at a time. The fantasy of bypassing an arthritic body, of becoming embodied anew, even through a computer, was understandable. But it is understandable precisely on the condition that the free-flowing, active "sports body" which remains the secret norm of Merleau-Pontean bodily intentionality, is no longer the living possibility of my opening to the world.

VR 'bodies' are thin and never attain the thickness of flesh. The fantasy which says we can simultaneously have the powers and capacities of the technologizing medium, without its ambiguous limitations and so thoroughly incorporate it into ourselves that it becomes living body is a fantasy of desire. And when we emerge from the shadows, effects, and hyper-realities of the theater into the sunlight in the street, it is not Plato's heaven we find, but the mundane world in which we can walk, and converse, and even find a place in which to eat.

## Notes

1  Maurice Merleau-Ponty, *Phenomenology of Perception*, trans. Colin Smith (London: Routledge and Kegan Paul, 1962).
2  Martin Heidegger, *Being and Time*, trans. John Macquarrie and Edward Robinson (New York: Harper and Row, 1962), sections 15 and 16, pp. 95–107.
3  Don Ihde, *Technology and the Lifeworld* (Bloomington: Indiana University Press, 1990), pp. 75–6.

# INDEX